WINDOW
TREATMENTS

WINDOW
TREATMENTS

KARLA J. NIELSON

JOHN WILEY & SONS, INC.

New York   Chichester   Weinheim   Brisbane   Singapore   Toronto

*To those who struggle with the challenges and
celebrate the successes of planning and treating
windows*

Designed by Keano Design Studio

This book is printed on acid-free paper. ☺

Copyright © 1990 by John Wiley & Sons, Inc. All rights reserved.

Published simultaneously in Canada.

This publication is designed to provide accurate and authoritative information in regard to the
subject matter covered. It is sold with the understanding that the publisher is not engaged in
rendering professional services. If professional advice or other expert assistance is required, the
services of a competent professional person should be sought.

Library of Congress Cataloging-in-Publication Data:

Nielson, Karla J.
    Window treatments / Karla J. Nielson.
        p.   cm.
    Bibliography: p.
    Includes index.
    ISBN 0-471-28946-9
    1. Drapery in interior decoration.   2. Windows in interior
decoration.   I. Title.
NK2115.5.D73N54   1989
747'.3—dc19   88-5395

Printed in the United States of America

10 9 8 7

Contents

Foreword

The entity known as the American window-covering industry is relatively new. Only in the last few years has a specific identity evolved from the collective focus of practicing professionals who specialize in manufacturing, distributing, and retailing products to cover and decorate windows. Until now no comprehensive resource existed that encompassed the history, application, and practice that defines this evolving profession. And yet the window-covering industry is one of the few remaining bastions where consumers still rely heavily on the sales consultant, decorator, or designer to guide them to a fashionable, yet functional, solution to their window-covering needs.

This book will benefit all professionals associated with this business. It serves as a useful source of information to veteran decorators that will enhance their credibility as knowledgeable consultants. And novice aspirants will find that it contains literally hundreds of useful facts, ideas, and applications that will save them years of trial and error as well as help guide them in developing a productive career.

This work will help solve many of today's window treatment challenges and will prove to be a very worthwhile investment in the career development of all window treatment professionals.

JOHN A. CLARK
President
Draperies & Window Coverings Magazine

Acknowledgments

The efforts of many go into the making of a book, and I have been fortunate in the writing of this text to be the recipient of the services of a number of fine people.

First and most important I must thank my husband, children, parents, and other family members for their continual encouragement. I also appreciate the support of my colleagues in the Department of Design at Brigham Young University. Their enthusiasm was a great moral booster over the years in which this book was in preparation.

Thanks to Dr. Steven Walker for the initial editing, and to typists Lorraine Johnson, Jannette Sanford, and Gayle Nielson. Thanks also to architect Stanley R. Covington for his contribution of authentic Japanese shoji screen designs, and Ardy Greening, Paul Kern, and Mark Bayless for contemporary art-glass designs.

Artists who worked on the inkline illustrations include Jim Park, Ken Lindquist, Gordon Smart, Caryn Pulsipher, Curtis Asplund, and Greg Thomas. Diane Headman contributed information on folk painting. The period interiors in chapter 1 were masterfully rendered by architectural artist Patricia "Tol" Clawson, principal of Clawson Associates Architectural Rendering.

Final editing was done by Susan Gies. I am most grateful to all these professionals and to the staff at Van Nostrand Reinhold for turning the vision of this book into reality.

Introduction

For millennia, windows have been a source of light, ventilation, and inspiration to all cultures. Originally mere cutouts in the wall, no more than holes covered with mats, skins, or oiled cloths, they have become a focal point of modern architecture. Clearly technology has been a boon to the contemporary window, offering a wide selection of types, shapes, and colors of glass. Yet nothing can be quite so architecturally charming and worthy of preservation as traditionally styled windows glazed with antique glass.

Natural light, or sunshine, is welcome and warming to us, and we often plan and cover windows so that we may work and live in harmony with the seasons. Further, appropriately selected treatments that are well planned and proportioned give comfort, security, and privacy to the occupants of a home, public space, or work space. These are valuable criteria when making window treatment choices.

Yet perhaps the most important choice of all is that of the most suitable windows and loveliest, most appropriate coverings to produce an aesthetic effect that will be deeply pleasing for years to come. This is the window treatment challenge to the designer or decorator and, when achieved, can produce not only beautiful and practical window treatments but a great deal of satisfaction in a job well done.

Traditionally, interior design students have received little academic training in window treatments and are expected to learn about the subject on their own after they have entered the profession. Wherever the reader's starting point lies, this book forms the basis for a study of window treatments from both a philosophical and a pragmatic viewpoint and encompasses a gamut of interior design considerations. In the first chapter the history and contemporary use of glass is discussed, and window treatment needs are evaluated in terms of aesthetics, solar gain, and energy efficiency. Chapter 2 details the reasons for covering windows and the many factors that the designer must balance when making the right choice for a window covering. Chapter 3 illustrates popular styles of windows often seen by the designer and suggests both appropriate treatments and ways to achieve proper measurements. Chapter 4 takes a romantic look at the history behind the period stylings that are lovingly re-created and adapted for today's lifestyles. Chapter 5 presents guidelines for selecting window treatment fabrics, as well as illustrating the range of styles in draperies, curtains, shades, and other soft treatments. It also presents the process of constructing soft treatments and suggests ways to properly care and clean fabric used at the window. Chapter 6 contains information on figuring costs and yardages and specifying soft window coverings, and chapter 7 covers the wide selection of hard window treatments. Combining hard and soft treatments is the topic of chapter 8, and the final chapter presents important information about dealing with clients and manufacturers in both residential and nonresidential window treatments.

The names and addresses of hundreds of companies are listed in appendices 1 through 11, which are intended to inform the professional of many of the sources for window treatment components that are on the market today. Appendices 12 and 13 contain technical information on fabric fibers, textures, construction, coloring, and finishing, to supplement the discussion of fabric in chapter 5. In addition, three glossaries define window treatment, fabric, and business-related terminology. Finally, an extensive bibliography refers the interior designer or decorator to sources of specialized information.

Window Treatments is the result of many years of practical experience derived from selling window treatments, researching for a master's degree, teaching a university interior-design textiles course, actively participating in the World of Window Coverings trade show and seminars, and writing several series of articles published in *Draperies and Window Coverings* magazine. The topic has been well worth pursuing because the business of window coverings has risen out of relative obscurity into a multibillion-dollar industry that has a high profile in today's interior design marketplace. New, innovative products are introduced each season, and competitive pricing structures as well as stock window-covering merchandise make window treatments more affordable than ever. Yet the demand for fine custom design and decoration has also risen, and it exacts a price. Quality draperies, curtains, shades, and top treatments, along with the classic hard treatments—blinds, shutters, and screens—are used individually and in combination as a significant part of interior design. Certainly every interior designer and decorator, as well as all those who deal, specify, or select window treatments for residential or nonresidential use, can benefit from an increased understanding of the criteria that contribute to effective window-covering choices. This book, then, is intended to augment the neophyte's or veteran's knowledge of an important, profitable, and, above all fascinating field.

Chapter 1 USING THE WINDOW TO THE BEST ADVANTAGE

The task of selecting an appropriate window treatment for a particular window in a particular setting can be at once challenging and enjoyable—challenging because of the many factors to be considered (interior window requirements such as light, view, ventilation, safety, wall space, furniture arrangement, solar gain, and energy conservation may play an equal bill to site factors such as climate, orientation, prevailing breezes, architectural style, and setting or location); enjoyable because, when most or all of these factors and requirements are met, the window can truly be used to the best advantage, and the result can produce great satisfaction.

Understanding the client's needs and demands for today's windows is crucial for the interior designer. An understanding of the history and evolution of the window also will give depth and perspective to the way we treat our windows and to what we expect from them.

THE EVOLUTION OF THE WINDOW

The word *window* is derived from the Old Norse word for wind, *vindr*, combined with the word for eye, *auga*, to make *vindauga*. Literally translated this meant an "eye" of the house through which wind entered. And indeed one of the most vital functions of windows is ventilation. For centuries windows were mere cutouts in ceilings or walls that provided ventilation for open fires. Only the occasional window was introduced to permit a little light or a glimpse of the outside world. Historically windows were small in order to increase protection against intruders and inclement weather.

When Angles, Saxons, and Jutes settled in England (c. 425 A.D.) and the Germanic dialects mingled, *vindauga* evolved into the Old English words *wind* and *eage* (eye). In Middle English the term changed further into *windowe*. It then found its way into contemporary American English usage as *window*.

For years the word *window* described only an opening in the wall. The nomenclature for the material used to cover these openings, or *fenestrations,* evolved separately. The word *pane,* used to designate the glass in contemporary fenestrations, was derived from the Latin *pannus,* a cloth or rag, and certainly window treatments were of the utmost simplicity. For most of human history, the majority of window openings were draped with animal skins or cloth. The ancient Egyptians, for example, simply hung mats at their windows. Even our Pilgrim and pioneer forebears covered their windows with shutters and oiled cloth, skins, or rags in inclement weather.

Glass windows as an architectural commonplace are a recent development. Indeed, only in the past few centuries has glass been used for glazing windows. *Glazing* is derived from the Middle English word for glass, *glasen,* and it was during the Middle Ages that glass began to be set in place (hence the origin of *glazier,* one who cuts glass and sets it in windows). During the Dark Ages, or medieval era, clear and colored, or stained, glass was used in cathedrals and public buildings in complex and astonishingly beautiful patterns. This inspired the titled nobility of Europe to begin using glass in their castles. Yet even as late as the sixteenth century, glass was such a precious commodity that when a king, duke, or lord moved his residence, the glass was removed and reglazed into the new castle. When the nobleman died the glass went not with the castle but to the executors of the will, for the castle was considered perfect without glass.

It was not until the late nineteenth century that factories succeeded in supplying domestic glass in ample quantities to the American homebuilder. In the past hundred years, glass technology has advanced at a phenomenal pace. It is easy now to take for granted the variety of laminated, bronzed, reflective, filtering, or multilayered insulated glass readily available to those who wish to incorporate transparency and beauty in their homes and places of work.

THE SPECTRUM OF GLASS

When the designer works on an older building, the glass may not be completely clear and flawless. Today's float glass is the result of centuries of research by trial and error to produce the perfect sheet of glass. It may very well be necessary, in commercial or residential restoration work, in adaptive reuse, or in remodeling work, that "old" glass be retained because of the character, interest, or authenticity it brings to both the exterior and the interior. The designer may even be called on to have historic glass reproduced to match existing pieces or replace broken ones.

There are basically five types of glass that the designer should know: crown glass, broad glass or cylinder glass, plate glass, sheet glass, and float glass.

Crown Glass

Crown glass (fig. 1–1) is a type of clear, brilliant glass that used to be made by dipping the end of a *pontil rod,* or blowing stick, in molten glass, blowing a large bubble, then spinning the rod in the opening of an oven; the centrifugal force caused the bubble to "flash" open in a way similar to the sudden opening of a wet umbrella. The glass was then a flat disc, roughly a meter in diameter. Surfaces were never parallel; the glass was thinner at the edges than in the center of the disc, called the crown, bullion, or bull's-eye. Bull's-eye segments, often of slightly greenish tint, are seen in many historic settings. The small pieces that could be cut from the disc were fire polished and brilliant and are preferred even today for art glass.

a

b

1-1 Crown glass.

a The making of clear, brilliant crown glass in the eighteenth century.

b The crown, bullion, or bull's-eye of crown glass set in small panes. The bull's-eye is translucent because it was connected to the pontil, or blowing rod.

Broad Glass

Broad glass was made by blowing a long, tubular bubble, then extending it by swinging the rod above the head. The cylinder was heated in a furnace until the end blew out from pressure, or both ends were cut off to create a "muff." One side was slit open, and the glass was laid on a smooth slab and reheated. As it softened it opened out and flattened from its own weight and then was ironed with a wooden hoe (fig 1–2a). This glass can be easily identified because it is curiously wavy, as if seen through rippled water. It is not as clear or as brilliant as crown glass because it was worked as it cooled.

A refinement of broad glass, called *cylinder glass* (fig. 1–2b), was reheated in a *lear* (flattening oven). This glass was used extensively during the Victorian era. In fact nearly a million square feet of cylinder glass were produced for the Crystal Palace in England in 1851.

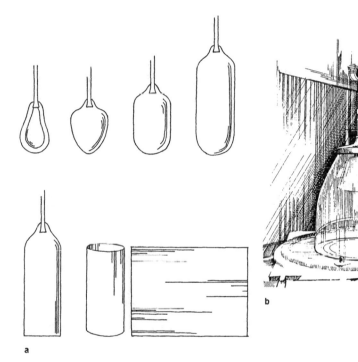

1-2 Cylinder glass.

a The stages of broad, or blown cylinder, glass. The glassmaker blew a long bubble, shaped it into a cylinder, sliced it into a muff, and then cut it open and reheated the glass, ironing it on a slab until it was flat. This glass was wavy and translucent.

b Drawn (vertically extruded) cylinder glass was a mechanically produced version of broad glass in use until 1903. Drawn cylinder glass was wavy or wrinkled because the inside area was smaller than the outside. This glass is seen in many older buildings.

Plate Glass

Plate glass (fig. 1–3) was made by pouring molten glass onto a *casting table* (as a result, this material later became known as *cast glass*) and rolling it out with a heavy iron roller before it annealed. (A crude glass made this way, dating up to 79 A.D., was found in the buildings of Pompeii when the city was excavated in 1754, much to the surprise of the Western world.) Annealing is the slow cooling of flat glass, which strengthens and tempers it and prevents brittleness. This glass found extensive favor in Europe and was used to glaze the famous Hall of Mirrors at Versailles near Paris, France. Plate glass was costly and duller than crown glass, but it was available in large sizes.

Sheet Glass

Sheet glass has been produced by a variety of methods, including drawing, or guiding the molten glass through different rollers. The rollers, which guide the viscose glass as it is extruded upward, leave characteristic "draw

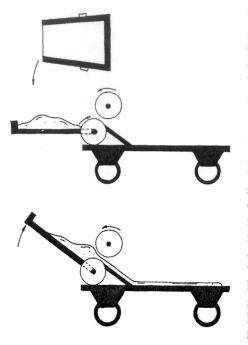

1-3 One method of making plate, or cast, glass. The molten glass was poured and then fed or guided through rollers onto the casting table, and ground and polished to achieve transparency.

lines," or "music lines." These lines will help the designer identify sheet glass in buildings dating from 1900 through the 1970s, when float glass came onto the market. Sheet glass also is made by casting and grinding or polishing glass. Drawn sheet glass invariably has parallel marks from the rollers or slightly wider thickness at one end of the sheet caused by gravity pulling down the glass as it anneals.

Float Glass

Float glass is the process by which most of modern glass is made. A continuous ribbon of molten glass moves out of the melting furnace along the surface of completely flat molten metal, causing the glass to be flat, too (fig. 1–4). Because the glass does not touch any hard surface, the natural forces of surface tension and gravity bring it to a perfectly uniform thickness. Today's float glass is brilliant, transparent, and nearly free of flaws and distortions. The electrofloat process passes an electric current through the metal and displaces ions that are exchanged with those of the glass to leave a layer of copper or other "reflecting" metal on the surface. Float glass can be produced in virtually any thickness and can be made to be low-E, or low emission, screening out harmful ultraviolet rays. Glass of the future promises to be stronger, more insulative of temperature and sound, and offered in an even wider variety of colors and surface textures than we know today.

Other Types of Glass

Also frequently used are glass block and art glass. Art glass includes such a vast spectrum of colored "stained" glass that an examination of the types is beyond the scope of this book. Beveled glass is hand-ground or molded to have mitered or angled (beveled) edges, and textured glass is formed by casting or drawing. Glass also is available with wire reinforcement. Popular too is Plexiglas, which is not glass but a clear, hard, strong plastic that is less vulnerable to breakage, although it scratches and mars more easily than glass.

Glass Today

Glass is made of about 70 percent silica sand, 13 percent lime, 12 percent soda, plus small amounts of other materials, such as metal. This mixture is heated to a high point, where it melts together into a transformed viscose liquid; as it cools it becomes hard. Glass is inherently a rigid liquid, not a solid material, which explains why cracks spread. There are no internal bonds in plain glass to stop the crack or to prevent glass from shattering. This makes it susceptible to stress.

Tempered glass is much stronger than plain glass. It will not crack, shatter, or break easily, and it is required by code for low-set or low-angled

1-4 The float glass process. Molten metal holds the glass solution perfectly flat until it cools and hardens. The result is uniform and flawless. The molten metal chambers also may exchange ions to coat the glass with a bronzed or reflective surface. The glass proceeds directly to the annealing (slowly cooling) oven, and then is cut into sheets.

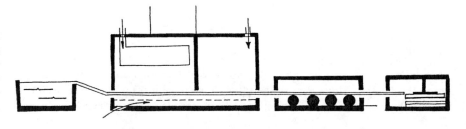

windows where safety is a concern. Tempered or strengthened glass is produced by the following methods:

- Adding other materials to the molten glass.

- Laminating (titanizing) the glass with a reinforcing skin of another material.

- Thermal toughening, or heating the glass above its transformation point and then quickly cooling it. (This process can be conducted chemically, using ion exchanges for similar results. The interior contracts so that it is permanently compressed, preventing a crack from spreading.)

The impact strength of toughened glass is four to ten times greater than untempered glass.

Laminated glass consists of two or more glass panes with a layer of tough transparent vinyl sandwiched between. The three layers are subjected to heat and pressure, which bond them into a single construction.

Any type of glass listed above can be mounted in two layers (double glazing) or three layers (triple glazing) to create insulative "thermal pane" windows.

THE IMPORTANCE OF WINDOWS

Today's window provides four vital functions: light, air (ventilation), protection, and visual expanse/beauty. Windows contribute to many of the comforts of the contemporary interior because they let in what users want in and keep out what they want out. For example, windows can help heat the interior in winter, magnifying the diminished rays of the low-set sun. Opened in springtime windows invite fresh air and fragrance into homes and work spaces. Closed in late summer, windows keep us dry and secure from thunderstorms; they protect us from cold and snow in winter, and from wind any time it blows.

It is true that ventilation and light admission may be effectively handled through electrical devices, and today many high-rise buildings are "sealed environments" (with fixed, nonoperable glass) or "windowless interiors," so that temperature, light, and air quality may be perfectly controlled. However, there is debate as to the potential health hazards of sealed environments, since fresh air and full-spectrum light (sunshine) are essential to the health and well-being of humans. Fresh air and sunshine are two reasons why windows are desirable in contemporary architecture. One aspect that cannot be duplicated in windowless environments is the beauty, interest, and even drama of nature, which one can enjoy without being directly exposed to the discomforts of seasonal change and inclement weather. Large picture windows or glass walls make the exterior a visual extension of the interior. Even small windows in work areas are considered preferable to windowless offices.

WHICH WINDOWS AND WHERE

Several factors are carefully evaluated before an architect decides not only *which* windows to install in a new home or building but also *where* they are to be used. Designers and knowledgeable clients can influence or even specify the type and placement of windows in new construction. In remodeling and in adaptive reuse projects, the interior designer or interior architect (one who is qualified to specify structural, spatial, and system planning) can be particularly influential. He or she can select and plan windows in tandem with the architectural team or construction company, with a perspective on their interior use that architects or builders may not always consider. This is because the interior designer or interior architect has the responsibility to make the windows livable, functional, and beautiful to the occupants of the proposed space.

Placement of windows is worth careful scrutiny and is largely the subject of this chapter. (Types of windows are discussed in chapter 2.) The primary factors on which window decisions are based fall into two categories:

1. The evaluation of the site where the building is located or will be constructed.

2. The evaluation of the interior window requirements.

THE EXTERIOR EVALUATION

The factors that make up the exterior evaluation part of the "program" (the list of requirements) for new construction or remodeled buildings include the following: climate, orientation, prevailing breezes, architectural style, and setting or location.

Climate

Climate is an important factor when planning and selecting windows. From a practical point of view, the more extreme (colder or hotter) the climate or the seasons of the year, the fewer windows should be included. This is because glass is an excellent conductor of cold and heat. (See "Solar Gain and Energy Conservation" and "Energy-Efficient Window Treatments" at the end of this chapter.)

Particularly for cold temperature extremes the use of double or triple glazing or thermal panes (two or three layers of glass) can become important. Although extra glazing costs more initially, these additional layers pay for themselves in reduced heating and cooling costs and result in a more comfortable living environment. When windows cannot be replaced, exterior or interior storm windows will make the interior less vulnerable to extremes in temperature.

The choice of window frames for cold weather also is a variable. Wooden frames are better natural insulators than metal frames, but wood is costly and requires greater upkeep. Wood-framed windows are available with exterior frames that are sheathed, or "clad" with a thin sheet of enameled metal or vinyl; some types are even color keyed to suit building materials. Enameled metal or vinyl surfaces provide ease of maintenance. Metal (usually aluminum) frames are specified more often than wood, largely due to the more modest cost breakdown. Quality metal window frames should include a *thermal break* (an extrusion between the inner and outer frames that prevents heat and cold conduction). Poorly made metal window frames not only will conduct heat and cold but also may not be "tight," leaking large amounts of hot or cold air into the interior, so quality is of utmost importance. Metal frames are widely available in silver, bronze, or white. They require little or no upkeep.

For warm climates and in the summer, layering and thermal breaking are less crucial than the matter of keeping the sunshine *off* the glass. One can protect windows from the direct rays of the sun by means of exterior and interior shading devices, such as awnings, overhangs, porches, and landscaping (trellises, hedges, trees, and so on). Summer storm windows are tinted glass or plastic panels that can be mounted on the inside or outside of the window. Sunscreens (similar to insect screens) that are mounted on the outside reflect up to 80 percent of the sunshine, thereby largely keeping the sun off the glass.

See also "Energy Efficiency" in this chapter for additional suggestions for treating windows against the extremes of climate and seasonal temperature change.

Orientation

The direction windows face is a prime concern when making the most of natural light. Orientation has direct bearing on the size, type, and placement of windows and their subsequent treatment.

Windows on the north side of a building bring in cold air through infiltration and conduction. Fewer north windows make interiors in cold climates easier to bear. However, north windows admit clear, constant, even light and also may be desirable for exterior style, ventilation, or view. For these reasons they are preferred by artists. North windows rarely need glare control and may be left "untreated" in the day. (Glare on the north side will be from reflected surfaces such as glass, asphalt, and concrete.) When nighttime privacy is the primary concern, a treatment that opens fully during the day and closes completely at night may be a good choice. Virtually any of the treatments listed in chapters 5 and 7 will work well on north windows if the climate or season is not too cold.

If the climate is cold, then energy conservation should be a priority. Treatments that keep out cold include metallized pleated shades (to an extent), insulated fabric shades and shutters, and lined or insulated draperies, coupled with cornices or other insulative top treatments. The disadvantage of these treatments is that (except for metallized translucent pleated shades), when they are closed, the light and view are largely removed.

Morning light from the east is bright and cheerful. It often brings clear, warm light into the building. The clarity of east light is due to the fact that airborne impurities of the previous day have settled during the coolness of the night. This means that east light may cause severe brightness; the clarity of the light can expose dust, spots, and fingerprints on furniture, walls, and cabinetry. Bright sunlight is damaging to wood furniture and can fade and destroy textiles. For these reasons a light-diffusing treatment may be required. Examples include sheers, semisheers, and casements (knit or woven fabrics) and pleated shades, blinds, and shutters that are meant to stay closed during the day, admitting light but filtering its brightness.

Another possible problem of east orientation is "solar gain." This means that bright, clear light can heat up an interior too quickly in warm climates or seasons (although it is welcome in colder climates or seasons). This is due in part to the difficulty in protecting the window against the low, straight early morning sunlight. An exterior awning or solar screen (sunscreen) will keep the heat off the window. Effective interior treatments include metallized pleated shades, vinyl pull shades, some vertical louvers, and, to an extent, miniblinds. Opaque fabrics, particularly thermal-backed or -lined, will be effective in controlling the eastern morning light. Once the sun is high in the sky, heat gain from the eastern exposure will be diminished, and the treatment can be opened fully. Keep in mind that many treatments, such as sheers, casements, shutters, or blinds, will control this heat gain to an extent, which may be all that is necessary given individual circumstances.

The west exposure is the hottest. West-facing window glass magnifies the lingering rays of the afternoon sun, which in the summer can make domestic or office life nearly intolerable. Sunlight from the west also compounds deterioration; colored fabrics fade quickly and wood furniture becomes damaged. The afternoon light is hazy because the impurities of traffic, smog, and so on have accumulated during the day and are suspended in the atmosphere. Because of this, west light, although hot and intense, may be somewhat pleasant and dreamy. Awnings and sunscreens will prevent the heat from hitting the glass; other buildings, as well as trellises, hedges, and foliage, can help control the sunlight at its lowest point. Interior treatments that are best for the west orientation include all the diffusing window coverings: vertical and horizontal blinds; pleated shades; shutters; sheers; casements; or thin, lightweight fabrics.

The south exposure (fig. 1–5) should contain most of the windows. Distant rays of winter sun can heat the interior through large expanses of glass, significantly reducing heating bills through the cold months. (A greenhouse or solar panel collectors must always be oriented toward the south—the only exposure where sunlight is guaranteed year-round.) Since south-facing windows amplify direct sunlight that shines into the interior in winter, fabrics and wall and floor coverings must be selected with durability in mind. The durability of the textile will depend on the quality and type of the fiber and on the strength of the construction. (For more information on fibers that are sensitive to sunlight deterioration, see appendix 12.) Because the sun stays in the south from morning to evening in winter, there also is high risk of sun damage to wood furniture. If the furniture cannot be rearranged, then the window must be protected from brightness or direct sunlight.

A properly placed overhang prevents the high summer sun from sending hot rays into the southern side of a building, filling the interior with pleasant "indirect" sunlight instead. Awnings, trellises, or deciduous (summer leaf-bearing, winter leaf-barren) trees accomplish the same effect: the tree or vine loses its leaves in winter to permit the rays to reach the interior through the bare branches. An overhang or projection should be calculated to extend to the point needed for protection against the sun during warm seasons and should allow the winter sun to enter the room (see fig. 1–5). In summer deciduous leaves and foliage prevent sunshine from penetrating, and trees produce cooler temperatures through evaporation.

Southern exposures may need light/glare control with any of the diffusing treatments previously discussed. Also, a heavy, opaque treatment may be required to seal or fully cover the glass at night. When solar gain is obtained during the winter, the glass will lose that heat back to the outside after the sun goes down. This is because heat always gravitates toward cold (see "Solar Gain and Energy Conservation" later in this chapter). In-

1-5 Orientation.

a   South window orientation in the winter takes advantage of the rays of the low-set sun. Sunshine on the south is the most consistent.

b   In the summer an architectural overhang or deciduous trees keeps steep-angled rays from penetrating the building.

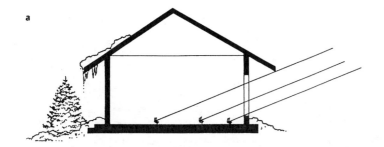

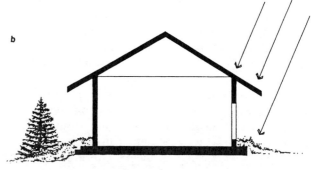

sulative shades that stack out of the glass area would be a good choice, as would heavy drapery (perhaps lined and interlined) that can close completely when the sun sets.

For each orientation where heat/light gain is a problem, there is one more consideration. Note the exterior ground cover. If there is cement, asphalt, stone, rocks, brick, or bare dirt, the heat will be intensified, and the reflective light will increase. Lawn (sod), foliage ground cover, trees, and shrubs will decrease reflected light and will lower temperatures. Consider suggesting to the client that these factors be altered to protect the window or enhance the benefits of the orientation (see fig. 1–5). Landscape architects and registered nursery workers could step in at this point upon your recommendation.

Prevailing Breezes

The architect or designer who is able to specify the exterior location of windows will be concerned with prevailing breezes for one of two reasons: to take advantage of them or to avoid them.

The architect will evaluate the breezes according to the time of year as well. In most geographic locations breezes flow steadily from certain directions in particular seasons, and these breeze patterns may have been a prime consideration when the building was designed. Obstacles in natural air-current lanes may diffuse a too-strong breeze or divert a desired breeze. Figure 1–6a illustrates obstacles in the breeze pattern that deter ventilation; figure 1–6b shows the contrast of breezes that can be utilized where the path of prevailing breezes is not deterred. In winter cold air should be drained away from the building or house rather than being trapped around the building with fences or vegetation. This also may be accomplished with proper landscaping (fig. 1–7).

1-6 Breeze patterns.

a Obstacles in the breeze pattern deter ventilation.

b A clear path of prevailing breezes allows for desired ventilation.

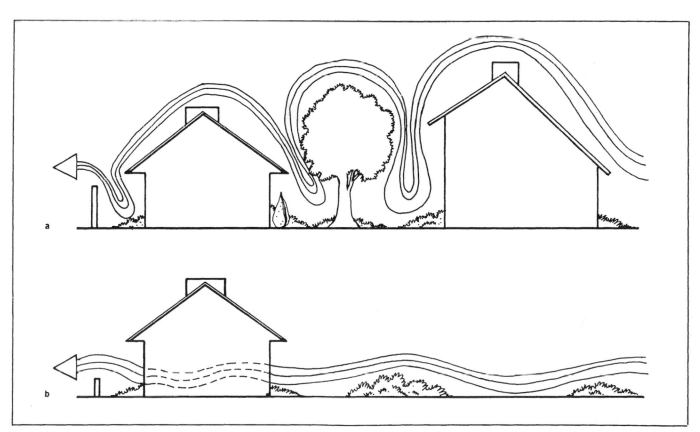

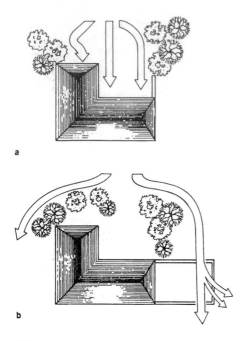

1-7 Breeze patterns.

a Prevailing breeze trapped and directed into the building by vegetation and fence—a serious problem in cold seasons or climates but an asset for ventilation in warm climates.

b Vegetation and fence deflecting and draining cold air away from the building.

Architectural Style

The style of the building may be the prime determining factor of window placement as well as selection. For example, historic architecture is accurate primarily because of proportion, building materials, color, and detail. The detail includes the correct style and type of window: for instance, sash or casement windows or stained or beveled glass. The detail, further, must be placed properly to be historically accurate. Windows in traditional architecture are not placed at whim but to achieve an ordered, balanced, and proper facade. These windows may be necessary regardless of climate, orientation, or prevailing breezes. Stylistic authenticity is a key factor when establishing the character of the architecture. Window companies are making authenticity convenient and maintenance free. Metal or wood dividers are available from many manufacturers to form muntin-and-mullion bars for rectangular single- or double-hung English windows and French casement windows and for the more medieval diamond-shaped mullions used extensively today in contemporary "traditional" architecture. Such dividers may be ordered between the panes of double glazing to produce a flat piece of glass inside and outside that is easy to clean and maintain. Snap-in grids of metal or wood also are available at reasonable prices. These may be removed for easy window washing or for painting. Since many architectural styles require special windows to reproduce a look of authenticity—the ranch-strip window or the plate-glass window, for example—window manufacturers can custom-make nearly any style and dimension of window or window arrangement specified for new construction or remodeling work.

In contemporary architecture the same rules apply, only in a different sense. The balance may be less formal and rigid but still crucial to the success of the style.

Handsome windows do much to build character and beauty into the architecture. Once interior requirements are met, slight adjustments may be necessary to create a pleasing exterior relationship between glass and wall (see the sections "Light," "View," and "Ventilation" below). Groupings of windows of similar size, architectural style, and functional type, for example, usually are more attractive than irregularly placed windows of various sizes.

Setting or Location

A cliché among architects and designers is that the value and desirability of a home or building depends on three things: location, location, and location. Where a building is located—in the city, suburbs, or country; in an exclusive, middle-income, or poor area; or on a large, medium-size, or small lot—will determine the value of that property and its architecture. The loveliest of buildings need compatible surroundings, and this factor often determines the style of new construction. For example, when a building is erected in an area of strictly modern and progressive architecture, the windows of that building can render it compatibly modern as well. In historic settings the windows are one of the prime determinants of authenticity.

Since location also implies the image or prestige level of the architecture (and the status and wealth of its occupants), this will have a bearing on the type and quantity of windows and window coverings. In contemporary architecture the miniblind or vertical louver may suffice; wooden shutters or blinds accomplish the same look but with greater richness. In traditional architecture miniblinds or verticals may be quite out of place, unless the feeling is one of adaptation rather than authenticity. Then a layered look may be the best window treatment specification (see chapter 8). The look of window coverings from the exterior of the building should ideally be compatible with (but not necessarily the same as) nearby architecture.

THE INTERIOR EVALUATION

Factors to be evaluated from the interior standpoint when one selects and places windows include the following: light, view, ventilation, safety, cleaning, and solar gain and energy conservation. Ideally the interior designer who understands these essential factors would play a key role in the actual selection of window type and placement. Where this is not the case, the designer is responsible for making the most of what is there. Whether dealing with residential or nonresidential work, the interior designer needs to focus on the functions required of the window in the individual room and then analyze how, through a good choice of window treatments, optimum use of each window can be obtained.

Light

Illumination is perhaps the primary function of today's window. Light is crucial for the well-being of humans, and natural light has proven to be the most healthful because it contains all the types of rays in a balanced full spectrum. The only type of ray within sunlight that is not healthful is ultraviolet light, which may be screened out with low-E, or low-emission, glass. Too much sunlight, which causes heat and glare, also can be tempered with bronzed or tinted glass and with the addition of solar screens or sunscreens.

Natural light enables the occupant to enjoy the range of daily and seasonal variations, and this variety is in itself quite healthful and can be uplifting. Although the amount of light needed may vary from room to room, a general rule of thumb is that window square footage should equal at least 10 percent of floor space. For individual rooms an interview of the users may be necessary to determine the optimal amount of light. Evaluate what tasks or functions will be performed in the room, then scrutinize the level of natural lighting for the best performance of these tasks.

As discussed under "Orientation," a different kind of light is obtained from each direction. The quantity and quality of light from each direction will further depend on several factors:

- How large the glass area is.

- Whether there are windows in more than one wall.

- What is found in outside landscaping. (Shading from trees, trellises, and shrubbery will darken or limit the light, whereas shading from asphalt, concrete, and water will increase the amount and intensity of light.)

- The color and texture of the walls and interior furnishings. (Light values and smooth textures will cause natural light to appear brighter and clearer; dark colors and rough textures will deepen and soften light.)

- The color and quantity (number of layers, for example) of existing window treatments.

- The existence of awnings or architectural projections or overhangs.

- Surrounding buildings or "cityscape," which may cast shadows on the window, and their construction materials and colors (clear versus bronzed glass; light versus dark exterior finish materials).

- The climate or season (bright, clear skies versus dark, overcast, or smoggy atmosphere).

- The shape of the windows. (Short, wide windows give a broad, shallow distribution of light; tall, thin windows give a slender, deep light penetration.)

- The placement of the window. (The higher the window, the deeper the light penetration.)

- The arrangement. (Groupings of windows give a more even distribution of light than separated windows, and windows on two or more walls also give a more even distribution and better balance of light.)

Remember that windows that do provide natural light may not be a constant source of light. As the sun moves, the window treatment may need to be adjusted to a closed, partly open, or fully open position in order to block out or screen light or to unobstruct natural light.

Window treatments that block out most or all light include draperies with blackout linings, solidly interlaced woven woods, opaque vinyl roller shades, blackout-lined or insulated fabric shades, opaque vertical louvers, and fully closed horizontal blinds.

Window coverings that screen light include knit and woven casement draperies and curtains; lace, sheer, and semisheer fabrics; and lightweight, thin fabrics. Horizontal and vertical blinds partially opened will filter light, as will shutters and many woven woods. Shoji or fusuma (pierced/carved) screens, bamboo "matchstick" shades, pleated fabric shades, and roller shades of translucent material all soften and shade bright light.

Treatments that do not obstruct light include sheer fabrics; fully opened horizontal and vertical blinds; and any treatment, including draperies, shades, shutters, and screens, that will stack off the glass completely.

View

One need only thumb through architecture and interior design books to see that often the most beautiful or impressive architecture seems to possess the best view. The mansion or building overlooking the bay, the city, the lake, the meadow, the prairie, or the ski resort leaves many of us wondering why we work in a cramped office or live in an apartment or condo looking at the heart of the city, or why we live on a small suburban lot hemmed in by neighboring yards and fences. Those who are fortunate to work or live where the location does offer a pleasant view often enjoy expansive windows that frame that view. Large expanses of glass extend indoor space outward, making outdoor living areas a visual part of the house.

However, a panorama is not the only view to be appreciated through glass windows. The sight of clouds, sunshine, rain, snow, or a tranquil blue or blustery gray sky can be exhilarating and therapeutic. An opportunity to view the changing seasons in our own yards or even windowboxes is very important to many of us. This is particularly true for clients who garden as a pastime and thrill to see the fruits (and flowers) of their labors.

The designer must not encumber a fenestration that is literally a "window on the world" (however limited the view of the world may be). Select a treatment that can stack off the glass completely and then close for privacy and security when needed.

Although a no-view window may require a treatment that *is* the focal point, treatments at a view window should be simplified so that the view will be unencumbered. Draperies should be hung wide enough to clear the glass completely when opened; they should be structural enough so that they do not compete with the view decoratively (fig. 1–8). Shades, shutters, blinds, and other treatments should be specified and installed with this same principle in mind. Sun-glare disruption of an east or west vista may be avoided by blocking the sun's low rays with fences, shrubbery, awnings, trellises, or overhangs.

When a beautiful view may be captured, the placement of horizontal "divisions" (strips of wall or muntin divider bars) is not recommended. Horizontal bars placed between 4 feet 8 inches and 6 feet from the floor interfere with the view of average-height people who are standing. Bars placed between 3 feet 8 inches and 4 feet 2 inches impede the visual perspective of people in a seated position, as, for example, those who do deskwork. For average-height people in a relaxed position, bars should not be placed between 3 feet 2 inches and 3 feet 6 inches.

Sunscreens or insect screens, too, should be located out of those horizontal division ranges. To keep a view clear, screen only areas with absolutely necessary operations and specify sliding or removable screens for the seasons when windows are not opened.

Tinted glass aids a view window where glare is a problem. When the glare is discovered after the architecture is complete, tinted glass panels may be installed over the glass on the inside. Extra glazing also provides additional insulation. There are options for screening glare with window treatments that do not eliminate the view. Roller shades and adhesive window film of clear, tinted plastic are available. Metallized pleated shades can be obtained in translucent (nearly transparent) fabrics. Sheer draperies will allow the occupant to enjoy the view in the daytime without restriction. Horizontal and vertical louvered blinds and large-scale shutters can be adjusted to position where the glare is deflected and the view is still visible. Each of these treatments, except the window film (which is adhered to the glass), can be stacked off at night for the enjoyment of a dramatic nighttime panorama.

When there is *no* view, then the window may call for a more visually demanding and decorative treatment. Ways to enhance the window itself and take the emphasis off the view include layered treatments (see chapter 8) with undertreatments such as blinds or shutters; sheer, semisheer, casement, or lace fabrics; or pleated or custom decorative fabric shades. Overdraperies may be of rich or exquisite fabric or of fabric with interesting patterns and colors. Tiebacks are more demanding of attention than straight draperies; fabrics puddled onto the floor look richer than to-the-floor treatments. Curtains may be short and frilly, ruffled, or busy, to attract attention. Valances and top treatments, particularly those with patterns, curves, or trimmings, also demand the viewer to acknowledge the window's presence.

Ventilation

Even if you are dealing with a reliable heating and cooling system, there will be days and evenings in all seasons when a breeze is desired. Remember that the optimal amount of ventilation may depend on prevailing

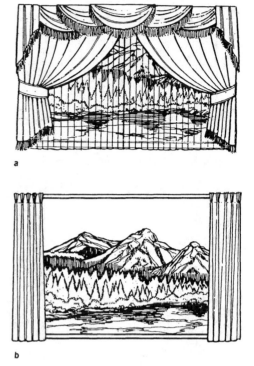

1-8 View.

a A beautiful view is obstructed by an excessively elaborate treatment.

b A simple treatment pulled off the glass gives emphasis to the lovely view.

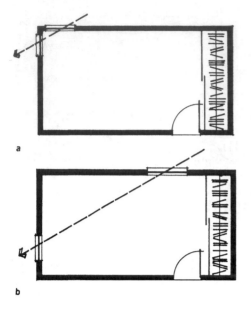

1-9 Window placement.

a   Poor window placement provides inadequate cross-ventilation.

b   Good cross-ventilation achieved through thoughtful window placement.

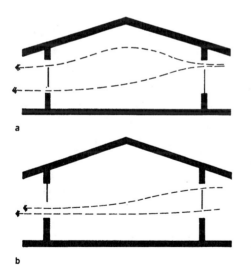

1-10 (*above*) Window placement.

a   Lateral window openings are too high in the wall for good ventilation.

b   Lateral window placement draws ventilation and desirable breezes lower into the interior, where they are needed.

1-11 (*right*) Deterring or enhancing ventilation at the window.

a   Window covering inhibits ventilation and flaps in the breeze.

b   Window treatment pulled off the glass allows unobstructed ventilation.

breezes. The operation load of central air conditioning can be significantly reduced through proper ventilation. In many locations opening windows at night can bring in sufficient cool air to keep the interior cool during most or all of the next day. Hinged and casement windows allow for the most ventilation, as they can be opened to expose all the window area; top-hinged awning windows can even be left open when it rains. Sliding-glass windows (horizontal or vertical) open to expose one-half the total glass area. The designer also may advise the client that ventilating air will be cooler when the window is shaded, and shade from foliage (trees, vines and so on) is cooler because of the evaporative process than shade from architecture. Further, ventilating air is cooler when the ground area is lawn or ground cover rather than dirt, concrete, asphalt, or other reflective surfaces.

Natural air can clean and freshen an interior in a way that no man-made device or cleaning preparation can. There are times when we feel that our interiors are simply in need of an "airing out" and that this can be satisfactorily accomplished only by throwing open the windows.

The position of the window in the wall is crucial to good ventilation. Air should be free to circulate through the main body of the room, not cutting through only a corner but moving from one side of the room to the other, as seen in figure 1–9. This is known as proper cross-ventilation and is the most effective and healthful window arrangement.

Another aspect to proper cross-ventilation is the lateral placement of operable windows. Ideally air should not only move at floor or ceiling levels but also circulate through the middle of the room where the occupants are. Figure 1–10a shows an arrangement where the window openings are too high, and figure 1–10b illustrates a lateral window placement that draws ventilation and desirable breezes lower into the interior, where they are needed.

Unfortunately the designer may not have any control over the placement of the windows in the wall. However, the window treatment selection can do much to deter or to encourage prevailing breezes to ventilate an interior. The treatment should not make it cumbersome to reach the mechanisms for opening the window and, most important, should not deter the breeze, as illustrated in figure 1–11. While it is possible that a strong breeze will enter even if the treatment is in the way, it also is true that flapping curtains, blinds, shades, and so on can be damaged by the force of the breeze and can be irritatingly noisy.

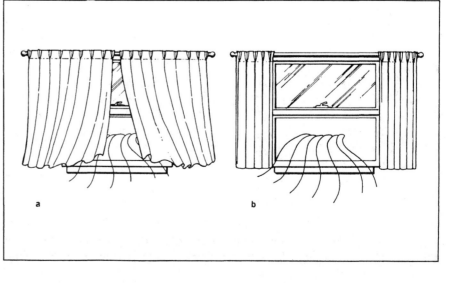

Safety

There are two main aspects of safety in windows: personal safety against accidents and safety against burglary and assault.

Windows that are operable should be equipped with safety devices such as bars that prevent awning or hopper windows from opening so far that someone could fall out, and with mechanisms such as cranks, levers, and locking devices that are sturdy and durable. It is important that the designer check these things and make recommendations to the client about repair before new window treatments are installed.

Sliding glass patio doors sometimes are so clear that they tempt people to "walk through" the glass, causing mild to severe injury. Design window treatments that make it obvious that glass is present, or consider adding decals, stickers, or suspended art glass in front of the door at eye level. Those most likely to be hurt by walking into sliding glass are young children and older people. It is good to advise the client of this danger.

Large windows may be an open invitation to burglary and vandalism. A common burglary tactic is to cut openings in the middle of large panes of glass for entrance and exit. Access to large windows should be difficult, and the windows should be well lighted from the outside, if possible. Sliding windows and doors are relatively easy to open even when the lock is securely in place. A rod or wooden dowel placed in the track can serve as an extra security measure.

Many fine security systems are on the market, and the client may do well to research out the feasibility of installing such a system. It is the responsibility of the designer to advise the client on all aspects of window safety. This concern is becoming increasingly serious; it is not uncommon for litigation to be instigated against designers who have not been conscientious in seeing to the safety and welfare of their clients through interior furnishings. The designer should always specify a treatment that will close and be opaque at night to prevent anyone from seeing in. This will lessen the temptation to burglarize by protecting the interior and its occupants against visibility.

Cleaning

Cleaning windows is a major concern for some people. It is good for the designer to make the following recommendations:

- When cleaning, the client should remove or secure the window treatment as far out of the way as possible to avoid damage to the fabric or to other material from cleaning solutions.

- The client should consider the purchase of professional cleaning equipment, such as squeegees, sponges, and extension (telescoping) handles, and should consult professional cleaning-supply companies as to the best product for cleaning glass, such as ammonia.

- The client should take advantage of professional window-cleaning services. Advise him or her to shop around and call two or more services for an estimate.

SOLAR GAIN AND ENERGY CONSERVATION

Heat gain, solar-heat gain, or *solar gain* all refer to heat that is absorbed into the interior through glass windows or through passive or active solar

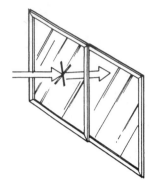

a

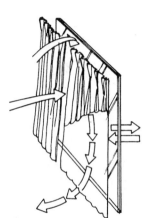

b

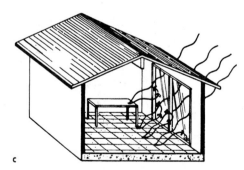

c

1–12 Heat loss and gain.

a Heat may be lost or gained at the window via conduction, or direct heat transfer through a material such as glass or metal.

b Convection or infiltration is the exchange of warm air for cool air (or cool air for warm air), creating a reverse chimney effect in winter.

c Solar-heat gain through radiation. Reradiated or refracted rays become shorter and weaker, creating the "greenhouse effect."

collectors. A greenhouse space also is considered a solar collector. Solar gain is desirable whenever mechanical heating systems are in operation. When a "solar" building is planned, much of the heating needs can be filled with the proper placement of glass windows. Although a complete discussion of solar heating is beyond the scope of this book, it is well worth the effort for the interior designer to find out more about it. Presented here is a brief overview.

Heat gain usually is obtained on the south of the home during the daytime hours. When the sun goes down, the windows that were *collectors* of heat become *releasers* of heat, and as much heat can be lost back through the windows as was gained during the day. In windows that do not provide daytime solar heat gain, up to 40 percent of the building's heat can be lost through untreated, single-glazed windows. Therefore the term *movable insulation* has come into play; this refers to exterior or interior window coverings that can be moved into place to prevent excess heat loss or unwanted heat gain in windows.

Clients and interior designers alike have become increasingly aware that windows should be treated to conserve energy. They understand that steps should be taken to keep needed energy (heated or cooled air) from escaping the interior and unwanted temperature exchanges from taking place at the window. In other words *energy conservation* means keeping out the heat in summer and the cold in winter, keeping air-conditioned air inside in the hot months and heated air inside in the cold months.

In general, people have become interested in energy conservation for two reasons: (1) to control the rising cost of heating and cooling a home or building (many energy-efficient treatments will pay for themselves over a two- to five-year period), and (2) to add comfort to the interior by treating the window so that excess heat gain and heat loss is eliminated—no more hot or cold window areas. The desire to conserve energy for the sake of conserving nonrenewable resources is, unfortunately, felt by only a small percentage of the public.

Energy conservation is an area where clients want designers to be knowledgeable. The client rarely wants energy-efficient treatments at the expense of beauty. Rather, he or she wants window treatments that are beautiful *and* efficient. In order to possess this knowledge, the designer needs to understand how heat/cold transfer takes place and what is necessary to prevent this transfer.

Deterring Window Energy Loss

Windows lose and gain heat through three different processes—conduction, convection, and radiation. *Conduction* is the transfer of heat through objects (fig. 1–12a). Glass is an excellent conductor of heat and cold, as are metal window frames that do not have a *thermal break extrusion* (nonconductive rubber) between the inner and outer frame. Wood, on the other hand, does not conduct heat or cold but rather insulates against it, as does fiberglass.

Convection is the movement of heat toward cold through air (fig. 1–12b). The human body loses and gains heat from the air, so that if warm air is migrating toward a cold window, we are losing some of our own body heat in the process. This causes us to feel a cold draft in a room.

Radiation is the transfer of heat from the sun to the room, and the bouncing back, or reradiation, from objects to the glass (figure 1–12c). Reradiation wavelengths are shorter and weaker and are not able to repenetrate the glass. Radiation trapped in the interior causes the "greenhouse effect" of solar gain.

Conduction, convection, and radiation can make windows energy villains, unless steps are taken to deter losses. There are many ways that the window itself can be altered to become tighter. These include caulking, weatherstripping, adding storm windows, or replacing decayed window frames with new ones, perhaps double or thermal pane, or even triple glazing. Beyond double and triple glazing, new types of glass can be bronzed or tinted various shades of brown, blue, or green and coated with metallized surfaces to reflect the sun's heat (reflected heat may intensify solar gain into neighboring buildings, however). High-rise buildings encased in reflective glass reportedly require less air conditioning.

Almost as effective as summer storm panels (tinted glass) is the application of tinted adhesive cellophane film to windows. This film is available through most glass companies in various brown, green, and blue hues. A problem with this film is that after a few seasons it may begin to crack and peel, becoming unsightly, so that it has to be scraped off before a new layer can be applied. Improvements in the film may make it more durable in the future. It is more or less a permanent installation and cannot be removed during the winter, as can tinted summer storm windows.

ENERGY-EFFICIENT WINDOW TREATMENTS

New products are continually appearing on the market that attempt to solve the problem of winter heat loss and summer heat gain at the window. The number of choices may be confusing, especially since many vary in their energy-conserving effectiveness. Variables such as the materials used, the type and quality of the installation, the size and location of the treatment, and whether there is an edge-sealing system render any treatment more or less efficient. There usually are several good alternative treatments for any given window, each with its advantages and disadvantages.

It is good to remember that there may be *no* single treatment that is the only perfect energy *and* aesthetic answer. For example, the treatment that is the most energy conserving also may eliminate natural light, ventilation, and/or view, and an either/or choice may cause the occupant to reject the entire notion of saving energy at the window in favor of light or view. Often the challenge in making window treatments energy-efficient also lies in making them aesthetically attractive. Specify handsome fabrics and materials that will stand the test of time and not attract undue attention in a way that could become trite or tiresome. Make the material comforting and visually pleasing as well.

Energy-saving window treatments can be categorized according to two functions: (1) insulation against winter heat loss and (2) shading and protection against summer heat gain. Some treatments can do both efficiently, since the objective is to keep the interior insulated against temperature extreme. However, some treatments may be more effective at one than at the other. The interior designer will do well to consult with manufacturers of energy-efficient products when a challenging window-covering situation arises. Manufacturers and distributors are eager to help solve energy-loss and -gain problems.

Insulation Against Winter Heat Loss

The objective of any winter insulation treatment is to prevent heat loss through convection or conduction. The homeowner should ensure that the window itself will not allow heat transfer, by weather stripping and repairing existing windows, replacing leaky ones, installing storm panels for double or triple glazing, or adding exterior insulating shutters. Window insulation results from a stationary barrier of air. That is why double and triple glazing is far better at keeping out cold than single glazing. The wider the space between the layers of glass, the greater the insulative value of the air barrier.

In addition the interior of the window can be covered with an energy-efficient material. The effectiveness of an insulative treatment often depends on its ability to create a trapped, dead-air space between the room and the glass. Fiberglass insulation is excellent not only because it does not conduct energy but also because it has air spaces within the fiber mass. Its insulative value may be further enhanced with a moisture barrier (a nonbreathable layer of plastic, for example) and with an edge-sealing system (discussed below).

When selecting an energy-efficient window treatment, primary importance should be given to its *R-value* (resistance to heat loss.) Table 1–1 gives general ratings to types of glazing and window coverings. The higher the rating, the better the resistance against heat loss.

The R-value of any treatment may be enhanced through *edge sealing* the treatment to stop the exchange of heated air for cold air at the glass. An edge-sealing system (the treatment is attached to the window frame via a track, magnets, snaps, fasteners, weights, or a frame) is important when the window itself leaks energy and allows air currents to move too freely, which can destroy the effectiveness of the window treatment insulation. In new construction where glass is tight and frames are insulative, edge seals are less important. This is even more true for large expanses of glass because the total perimeter of the edge compared in ratio to the glass area decreases as the window size increases.

Table 1-1 Comparative R-values

Typical Exterior Walls	R-values
Typical exterior wall with 3 ½ inches insulation	14.00
"Superinsulated" walls with 8–12 inches insulation plus plastic moisture barrier	40.00

Windows Without Any Treatment	R-values
Single glazing (one layer of glass)	0.88–0.89
Double glazing (two layers of glass)	1.72–1.81
Triple glazing	2.70–2.80

Energy-Efficient Window Treatments	R-values	With Double Glazing at R = 1.81
Pleated fabric shades, nonmetallized	1.03	2.84
Venetian blinds, miniblinds, micro-miniblinds	1.20	3.01
Vertical blinds	1.40	3.21
Translucent polypropylene interior storm windows	1.51	3.32
Lined drapery, sealed (attached to wall, covered at top, leading edges secured)	1.54	3.35
Heavy single-layer roller shades, unsealed	1.57	3.38
Louvered shutters	1.59	3.40
Unlined woven-wood Roman shades	1.59	3.40
Heavy single-layer roller shades, of reflective fabric, unsealed	1.99	3.80
Aluminized thermal drapery lining with drapery	3.19	4.00
Opaque, metallized pleated shades	3.19	4.00
Lined woven-wood Roman shades	3.19	4.00
Heavy single-layer roller shades of reflective fabric, sealed	2.44	4.25
Insulated Roman shades, sealed	3.19–3.39	4.00– 5.20
Exterior/interior insulating shutters	7.29–9.10	9.10–10.91

Edge seals also help prevent condensation caused when warm, moist air hits a cold glass surface. A *moisture barrier,* or nonpenetrable vinyl or plastic layer coupled with an edge-sealing system, will allay condensation.

For winter energy conservation the most insulative treatments are those that are heavy and opaque, thus stopping the flow of heat transferred by conduction and convection. Solar gain in the winter via radiation needs to be trapped in the interior at night. One of the most effective and commonly used of the soft window treatments is the fabric shade (Roman, balloon, or flat roller shade or panel). Another energy-conserving treatment is the insulative shutter, which may be mounted on the interior or the exterior of the building.

Window treatment insulators, or movable insulation, that conserve heat loss are more effective if they are heavy and opaque—the thicker the better. Those placed close to the glass will stop air movement and those placed a few inches away will create a more insulative pocket of dead air. A good way to achieve this is with insulative fabric (Roman or balloon) shades, which consist of five main parts. The combination of these layers gives the fabric shade an R-value of about 4.0 when it is used with double-glazed glass (see table 1–1). Figure 1–13 illustrates these five parts:

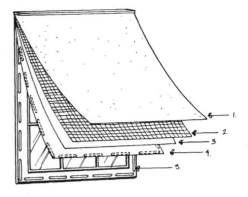

1-13 The five basic components of an energy-efficient interior fabric window shade: (1) decorative outer fabric; (2) insulating fiber batt; (3) vapor barrier, such as plastic; (4) lining material; and (5) edge seals.

1. Outer covering (closest to the room). Should be a sturdy, aesthetically pleasing fabric, a wood panel, or a fabric-covered cardboard.

2. Insulating material such as polyester fiberfill (quilt batting), plastic bubble film, or an air space. A blanket of trapped air is a superior insulator.

3. Vapor barrier—a plastic film or translucent or transparent plastic, vinyl, or polypropylene sheeting. The vapor barrier will prevent moisture condensation and transfer of warm air to the glass by convection.

4. Lining material (closest to the glass). Should be resistant to sunlight deterioration, shrinkage, and moisture damage. A light color is best aesthetically. An aluminized fabric facing in keeps heat in the room during the winter. Facing out in the summer, it reflects solar heat. There are many types of linings:

   - Reflective foil fabrics are aluminized so that the shiny side can face into the room in winter to retain heat and face outside in summer to reflect heat.
   - Suede fabrics with air pockets act as a thermal barrier.
   - Foam-backed fabrics are good insulators but may deteriorate after a prolonged period of sunlight exposure.
   - Vinyl fabrics are impervious to air and moisture.

5. Edge seals increase the effectiveness of window insulation, as discussed above.

Insulative fabric shades are a custom-made or factory-made treatment. Some workrooms specialize in them, perhaps even with a franchise. Prices are fairly high, yet they can actually save money in the long run by lowering heating and cooling costs.

Increasing the R-value of Window Treatments

There are ways to effectively increase the R-value of existing or selected treatments. The following suggestions are categorized according to treatment: draperies and curtains, shades, shutters and panels, blinds, exterior treatments, and layered treatments.

Increasing drapery and curtain R-values may be accomplished as follows:

- Attach sides to wall with ook-and-loop fasteners, magnetic "tape" or strips, or snap strips. You can also use carpet or upholstery tacks or staples (be careful not to damage the fabric), or wood molding, which requires fewer tacks and can be removed for cleaning.

- Specify ceiling-to-floor and wall-to-wall draperies whenever possible.

- Cover an area larger than the window size, forcing heated air to take a longer course to get to the glass.

- Make the overlap (where drapery headings meet and overlap at the top) as deep and generous as possible (2 inches on each side is standard). This can secure an additional 10 percent energy conservation.

- Add a closed fabric valance, wooden/upholstered cornice, or wooden shelf to prevent air from escaping to the glass over the top of the drapery (fig. 1–14a). Wood is a superior insulator, so a wooden treatment will be more energy-efficient.

- Install a lambrequin or cantonniere to seal tops and sides. A four-sided lambrequin, or window box, will seal the entire perimeter of the drapery treatment.

- Specify that extra weights be sewn into the drapery. Gravity will then pull the drapery even closer to the floor.

- "Seal" the bottom by pushing the drapery hem to the wall with snaps, tape, hook-and-loop fasteners, or magnetic tape.

- The bottom hem may be tucked securely behind a curtain rod, sturdy elastic tape, or wooden dowel attached to the wall at the bottom of the treatment. (This may cause the draperies to wrinkle.)

- Use a *draft dodger,* a fabric tube filled with sand and placed in front of the bottom hem (or used to push the hem against the wall). This technique has been used for centuries in the form of rags, rugs, paper, or wood pushed up against doors to stop floor drafts.

- Install heat deflectors of clear plastic or custom made of wood at floor heat registers to channel forced warm air or radiant heat into the room instead of up the window treatment shaft.

- Add automatic light- or temperature-sensing devices that will open the treatment during daylight and close it at night.

Increasing shade R-values may be accomplished as follows:

- Vertical tracks on each side of the window allow the fabric of vinyl shades to slide up and down within the track. These can be made by a carpenter and painted or stained to match the wall paint or color of the shade.

- Magnetic strips glued to the window frame and sewn into the fabric sides and bottom of Roman and balloon shades seal the sides as the shade is lowered.

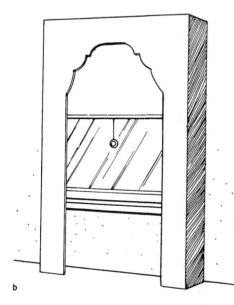

1-14 An upholstered cornice or pelmet, or a lambrequin or cantonniere that extends to the floor, can help deter convection leading to heat loss around:

a   Draperies.
b   Shades.

- Snap strips or hook-and-loop fasteners can be used in place of magnetic strips, although they are more awkward to handle and require manipulating the shade by hand.

- Fasten the shade to the window sill or wall with hook-and-eye or hook-and-loop fasteners, snaps, or magnetic strips.

- Wooden side clamps with spring-loaded hinges can be clamped down on the lowered shade, sealing the edges.

- Install a top-closed cornice, valance, lambrequin, or even a shadow-box frame around the window to deter heat loss or heat gain through convection (fig. 1–14b).

- Add flexible weather stripping.

- Compound the shade itself with layers of insulative fabrics.

- Install a drapery over the shade that can close at night and in cold weather.

- Program automatic window treatment controls to close during certain times of the day or in response to high temperatures.

Increasing shutter and panel R-values may be accomplished as follows:

- Specify insulative shutters. These largely consist of four layers: an outer covering, front and back (wood or fabric-covered wood), a frame, and an inner layer of rigid insulative material. Figure 1–15 illustrates fabric covered and wooden insulating shutters.

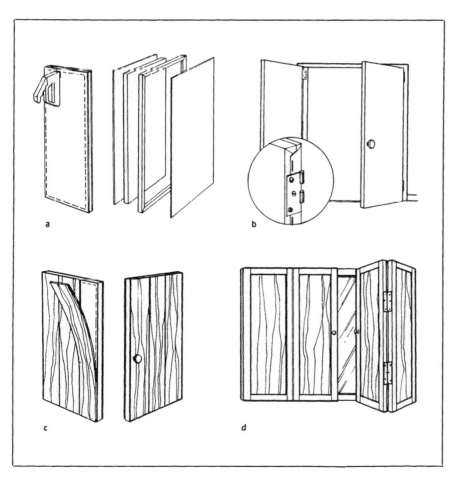

1-15 Insulative shutters.

  a Exploded view showing the four layers. These consist of: two outer layers of wood, a frame, and a layer of rigid insulation.

  b Insulative shutters hinged in casement fashion at the window.

  c Strips of wood applied as a finish material.

  d Wood-finished insulative shutters set as bifolds at the window.

• Order or construct pop-in panels. These are simple to make as an addition to an existing window treatment and can be removed and stored nearby when not in place at the window. Figure 1–16a shows a view of pop-in panels being constructed. The panel consists of solid insulation board to which fabric is stapled or glued. Wooden lath makes a frame around the panel, and flexible weather-stripping tape is used to make a tight seal at the window. Figures 1–16 b–c show pop-in panels in place at the window.

• Weather strip around edges of existing shutters or panels to prevent air leakage.

• Hinges should be recessed into the frame, and wooden strips should be rabbeted (given an L-shaped overlapping edge). This is something that quality shutter manufacturers will offer as standard.

• An overlapping wooden frame could be constructed for sliding or stationary panels or shutters (do not construct a frame that will interfere with the operation of the shutters).

• Overlapping edges on the back side of sliding panels can be weather stripped.

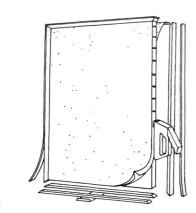

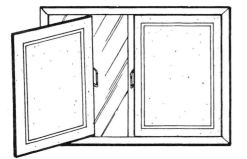

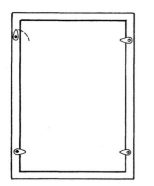

1-16 Pop-in insulative panels.

a Pop-in panels made from covered rigid insulation with a wood or plastic frame and weather stripping. The front fabric is decorative; the back is reflective (aluminum or coated) fabric or white lining fabric.

b Decorative pop-in panels set in the window frame.

c Window clips hold this pop-in panel in place.

Venetian blinds, miniblinds, micro-miniblinds, and vertical-louver blinds are not energy-efficient winter treatments (although they are relatively effective as summertime reflective treatments). The louvers or slats cannot close tightly to form a solid barrier between room and glass. Therefore the best way to increase the R-value of blinds is to layer them with another treatment. These are some suggestions:

• Over the top of the blinds, install draperies of a heavy, opaque fabric that can be drawn off the glass when desired and closed tightly when the weather is very cold outside. Better still, hang the draperies from ceiling to floor and/or cover them with a top-closed cornice or valance.

• Place pop-in panels (see fig. 1–16) or heavy vinyl roller shades next to the glass, behind the blind.

• Add an insulating shade over the top of the blind that would seal at the edges (see section on shades above).

• Add storm windows.

There are a few exterior treatments that have been proven very effective at increasing the resistance to heat loss. These include exterior insulating shutters (see fig. 1–15) and rolling shutters (see fig. 1–21). Exterior treatments may be desirable when the interior design calls for a stark "untreated" window or where there is lack of stacking space for draperies or fabric shades. Exterior treatments will be more desirable when there is operational or remote control from the inside of the building. Exterior treatments such as insulating shutters and rolling shutters also may increase protection against breaking and entering.

Layered treatments are one of the best means of increasing the resistance to heat flow. Draperies, curtains, and top treatments may be used for aesthetic softening and decoration in a room, while the real energy efficiency may take the form of an undertreatment such as an insulative shade, solid shutter, or even pop-in panels (see figs. 1–13, 1–15, and 1–16). Or, blinds or shutters may be layered with draperies and topped with a valance or cornice to create a partial dead-air space and prevent air from traversing the glass. Layered treatments also may bring greater beauty or aesthetic appeal to the room (see also chapter 8).

Shading and Protection Against Summer Heat Gain

The most effective method to reduce summer heat gain is to prevent the sun's rays from striking the glass. Once the glass is warm, some heat will transfer into the building through radiation and conduction. (Heat gain from convection can be controlled by closing doors and windows.) Ironically the radiation transfer that is most desirable in winter is the biggest problem in summer.

Shading is the key to keeping temperatures low at the window. Solar-heat gain can be reduced by as much as 80 percent if a window is shaded totally, with air circulation possible between the glass and the shading device. The other 20 percent heat gain is due mainly to convection and conduction.

A large, densely foliaged tree is the best shading device. It can transpire up to a hundred gallons of water each day, equal to several room-size air conditioners. This moisture-cooling effect can drop the temperature in the shade as many as 20 degrees cooler than in the sunshine. Other vegetation, such as vines on trellises and shrubbery, can reduce heat and glare by cutting reflection. Air temperature usually is 10 degrees cooler over lawn or ground cover than over bare soil, and far cooler than over cement.

Architectural overhangs such as extended eaves, porches, patio covers, or carports also are effective shading devices, although they usually will not shade roofs and cannot cool through evaporation. A calculated overhang can allow for winter sun penetration and still shade when the summer sun is high (see fig. 1–5). Architectural overhangs might be constructed on the advice of the design professional. Bear in mind, however, that these are fairly expensive.

Exterior shutters also can block sunlight for an 80 percent reduction in solar heat gain. Light-colored shutters reflect sunlight, hindering heat and brightness from penetrating the glass. Disadvantages include the cost and the need to adjust the louvers from the outside. Shutters can be side-mounted or awning-mounted (fig. 1–17). Side-hinged shutters should have movable louvers to encourage ventilation. Awning shutters work well as solid shutters, although unrelenting sunshine is damaging to wood, causing it to warp and split.

Awnings are canvas fabric or metal units that shade windows like umbrellas yet permit air circulation and ventilation (fig. 1–18). Solar-heat gain can be reduced with awnings by as much as 65 percent on windows facing south and 77 percent on those facing east or west. The effectiveness of awnings depends on whether the fabric or metal is light enough in color to reflect the sunlight and opaque enough to exclude direct and indirect sunlight. Any heat absorbed by the awning will be transferred indoors through conduction and convection, so hot, trapped air must have an escape route, such as a narrow gap. Some awnings can be electronically retracted or rolled up from inside the building. Awnings are costly treatments and may restrict light and view if they cannot be retracted. Select light colors that will be less likely to fade and look old.

Solar screens or sunscreens are tightly meshed insect screens available in black, metallized (reflective), or colored plastic or metal. Solar screens can block 50 to 60 percent of the sunlight striking the screen (fig. 1–19). One advantage is that they can be used with windows open, encouraging ventilation. Another advantage is that they can "breathe" so

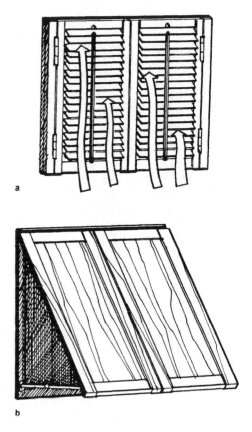

1-17 Exterior shutters.

a Exterior shutters with movable louvers can block light and still allow some ventilation.

b Awning shutters are alternatives for shading glass.

1-18 Fabric and metal awnings may be retracted when solar gain is not a problem.

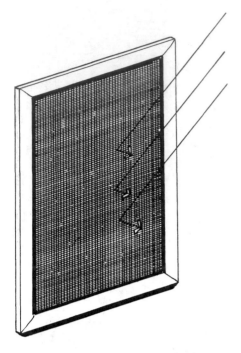

1-19 Solar screens reflect up to 60 percent of sunlight off tight metal or plastic mesh surfaces. Such exterior shading treatments also allow the window to "breathe" so that the glass does not expand and crack from intense heat.

that there is no heat buildup between the screen and the glass. Solar screens are modestly priced. In winter they can be replaced with storm windows. Solar screens may restrict the view slightly.

Exterior roller shades consist of horizontal slats of bamboo or plastic woven with cotton or nylon cord (fig. 1–20). These shades are raised by pulling the cord by hand and wrapping the cord around a cleat so that the shade can be secured at any level. The least expensive of exterior treatments, they are available in stock sizes at department, home-improvement, and import stores. Roller shades leave air free to circulate between the shade and the glass. They can provide adequate shading during the day, then be rolled up at night so as not to obstruct ventilation. Disadvantages include the necessity of hand operation and the removal and storage of the shade for winter. There also can be aesthetic problems: plastic roller shades are sometimes manufactured in objectionable colors and bamboo shades disintegrate after prolonged exposure to the sun.

Automated exterior rolling shutter/shades are exterior shading devices made of connected metal slats (fig. 1–21). Rolling shutters work like rolling shades, may be operated from the inside, and block up to 80 percent of solar-heat gain. Rolling shutters or shades are custom-made to the dimension of the window and add a certain amount of exterior security. They also let in some light through the slat connectors so that the room is not totally darkened because of the shade.

Interior treatments that protect against excessive solar gain are those that reflect sunlight back out the window, thereby reducing the need to run air-conditioning units as often or as long. The most effective treatments are those that screen the entire area where the sunlight hits glass. Those that are opaque and solid are the most effective in reducing solar-heat gain, but they also eliminate light and view. Thus it is possible that the client will pass up a treatment that is highly effective as a solar-heat reducer in favor of one that allows some light and visual expanse.

Another potential problem of heavily insulative interior treatments is that, if they trap too much sunlight between the glass and the treatment, the temperatures can climb up to 300 degrees Fahrenheit. This can cause several problems, the most serious of which is deterioration of the window treatment fabric and the expansion of the glass, which was not designed to withstand intense temperatures and can crack as a result. A good approach may be to couple interior treatments with exterior treatments such as awnings or sunscreens. In this way the interior treatment may be used to screen light and glare but may not need to completely cut off all light and view.

Another sound approach is the use of automated louvered shutters that are programmed to tilt according to the sun's angle, thus continually shading the interior. The slats allow air to circulate, preventing excessive heat buildup.

Table 1–2 lists the most commonly used interior treatments that are effective in reducing solar-heat gain. To the right of the treatments is an indication of how each treatment will likely perform in reducing the heat that has already come through the window. This translates into the opposite figure (subtracted from 100) called a *shading coefficient*, which is the amount of shading that takes place. The coefficient numbers that are lowest indicate the best shading treatments.

New shading treatments are continually being developed and marketed. A good window treatment distributorship will keep the designer up to date on innovative products and supply information on request on shading percentages and/or shading coefficients.

1-20 Bamboo shades and plastic shades are inexpensive, hand-operated devices. They also may be used as an interior shading or light-screening treatment.

1-21 Automated exterior roller shades, or rolling shutters, are effective sunlight blockers that may be operated from inside the building.

Table 1-2 Interior Shading Devices

Interior Window Treatment	Heat Reduction Percentage	Shading Coefficient
Aluminized fabric or shade material (reflects heat/light)	80–95	.20–.05
Insulated Roman/balloon shade (vapor barrier, fiberfill, lining, and outer fabric)	80–95	.20–.05
Pleated fabric shade with aluminum backing	54–61	.46–.39
Vertical louvers with vinyl slats	50–60	.50–.40
White opaque roller shade	50	.50
Drapery with white lining	45–50	.55–.50
Shutters	40–50	.60–.50
White translucent roller shade	44	.56
Unmetallized white pleated-fabric shade	43	.57
Semi-open-weave drapery fabric	39–42	.61–.58
Miniblinds, closed	30–40	.70–.60
Miniblinds, open 45 degrees	20–30	.80–.70

Chapter 2 WHY COVER THE WINDOW?

When the glass window has so much going for it, why cover it? That is a question many architects and designers have repeatedly asked. Indeed, in many instances the best treatment is no treatment. With the inception of *curtain-wall construction* (a skeleton of wood or metal sheathed with entire walls of glass) came an awareness of the advantages of leaving windows bare:

- The window provides a visual expanse, making the outdoors seem like an extension of the indoors. This can be particularly desirable if the outside is lovely or if the room itself is small, too crowded, or visually busy.

- A bare window allows the frank expression and appreciation of the glass itself for its inherent beauty. This can be an appropriate adjunct to many different room themes, particularly contemporary ones.

- There is no maintenance of treatments necessary, such as the need for sending draperies to the cleaners, dusting or sonic cleaning of miniblinds and vertical louvers, vacuuming of pleated fabric shades, and so on.

- There is an unencumbered view of sunshine, the many moods of rain, the majestic falling of snow, tumbling leaves, blooming flowers, and the silent, stark beauty of winter. These are the themes of nature that make bare windows so attractive.

Many homes or buildings—especially those surrounded by hundred-acre woods or breathtaking seascapes—can pull off this naked feat successfully. However, in the United States over 90 percent of the population lives on less than 2 percent of the land, which in and of itself would seem to indicate a need to cover the window. But privacy is, of course, only one issue. Glare control, sound absorption, energy conservation, safety, aesthetics, and just plain comfort are concerns that are often collectively or individually important enough for us to cover our windows.

THE BENEFITS OF COVERING

Privacy

It is a simple law of nature that we look toward a light source. What this means is that the lovely view we gaze out on during the day can be someone else's equally clear view gazing in at night. Transparent and translucent diaphanous sheers and some lightweight casement cloths will give enough privacy in the day when it is lighter outside, but this same type of fabric will assure no privacy at night when indoor lights are on. Even some hardline treatments, such as bamboo shades, require opaque under- or overdrapery, or a shade or blind that will close completely for nighttime privacy. The designer should carefully interview the client to assess the needs for privacy and to see that those needs are fulfilled.

Safety

Safety is an increasingly important consideration at a time when crime rates across the country are climbing alarmingly. Valuable art, furniture, or electronic equipment seen through a window are potential targets for theft, and it is frequently an undraped or inadequately covered window that invites personal assault. Even a "pinhole" in a window covering can be enough to tell potential intruders what they want to know.

This factor becomes more significant when the designer considers the rapid rise in designer liability and litigation. It is not too farfetched to imagine a client instigating a law suit or litigation against the designer who overlooked the protection of the client and property by specifying insufficient window coverings. Even if a window itself is a glorious architectural feature with a view that is stunning, the wise designer will still provide means for nighttime privacy and safety. This can be as simple as an opaque vinyl pull shade, blind, or vertical louver that can be stacked discretely out of the way in the daylight hours and closed securely at night.

The designer should never assume that a treatment will provide complete visual privacy and safety until a sample has been installed or tried out *in situ* (at the site) in the very window where it is to be installed. A length of the fabric, for example, should be tacked up and the lights turned up for a tryout. A thorough designer will find that the attention to these types of details will save frustration and even anguish later on for all concerned. The American Society of Interior Designers, the Institute of Business Designers, the Interior Design Educator's Council, and the National Council for Interior Design Qualifications each maintains in its definition of interior designing that it is the professional responsibility of the designer to "enhance the quality of life and protect the health, safety, and welfare of the public."

Glare Control

The advent of curtain-wall construction in modern architecture has resulted in such dramatic contributions as panoramic views, expansive light sources, and passive solar heating. However, direct sun shining on these large panes on eastern, southern, and western exposures may result in glare—directional light that is so steady and bright as to cause irritation.

Glare is often, but not always, accompanied by a buildup of heat, which is the case where large picture windows and plate-glass installations are used. However, glare is not always accompanied by heat. In fact, glare is not always the result of too much light. Glare can result from a situation in which one directional light source causes areas of light contrasted by deep shadows where natural light is lacking. Then the glare-versus-dark-spots will cause eye strain, fatigue, and irritation. Glare of this type can occur at any orientation, even at a northern exposure, and particularly if surfaces outside will reflect greater light than is desired in the interior. The designer should evaluate surfaces such as concrete drives, walks, patios, blacktop streets, parking lots, and even water. Glare may be intensified by reflection off another building, particularly when there are many reflective surfaces, such as glass, steel, or concrete.

Window coverings that control glare yet still allow adequate natural light include transparent and translucent sheer draperies or curtains and lightweight casement cloths. Hardline treatments such as shutters, horizontal and vertical blinds, and transparent tinted pull or fabric pleated shades also effectively reduce glare. The designer should make adjustments for the effects of direct sun shining on these materials so that the cost effectiveness in relation to expected years of service may be properly evaluated.

Sound Absorption

Fabric treatments muffle outside noise, especially when lined and interlined or hung in successive layers. Fabrics also can absorb indoor noises from appliances, stereos, televisions, loud conversations, and even the click-clicking of heels on hard-surface floors. Even a simple treatment, such as a draw drapery, curtain, or soft top treatment, can be effective in absorbing sound. Certain of the hardline treatments, such as factory-made pleated shades, also will absorb sound, and vertical louvers may even be specified in fabric, or with fabric inserts.

Fabric used anywhere else in the interior will be effective in reducing noise, too. Fabric on walls, at the bed, as upholstery, as textile on the floor, or even on the ceiling can augment the muffling effect.

Comfort

A textile at the window in a friendly color and pattern will go a long way toward establishing a warm and comforting interior. A draped window, like a draped bed, can provide a feeling of security. The designer should recognize that the most charming view by day will turn into a foreboding void at night. Many people feel isolated and insecure looking at a black vastness, and even more nervous at the possibility that someone is staring back at them out of that darkness.

Comfort given by fabric should not be overlooked in nonresidential settings. Often offices, banks, retail businesses, and medical facilities benefit their personnel and clientele with the comfortable feeling that fabric gives to an interior. Hotels and resorts, establishments in which the main criterion is the comfort of the patron, use generous amounts of patterned fabric.

Energy Conservation

Window coverings can and do increase energy efficiency. For example, fabric absorbs heat ten times more effectively than does bare glass. The cost of running a building can be significantly reduced in terms of heating and air-conditioning costs when there has been a careful evaluation of the need to conserve energy at the window. Another important factor is the lack of physical comfort that an improperly treated window can cause. A window that is treated for energy efficiency will benefit the user in more than one way. Insulated Roman or pouf shades specially constructed to fit the window size can yield dramatic results in energy conservation and room comfort. Pleated fabric and vinyl shades, miniblinds, vertical louvers, and shutters also are effective at reducing heating and cooling losses. (See chapter 1 for more information on energy efficiency in window treatments.)

Aesthetics

It is quite possible that the view looking out is not a beautiful one. In many commercial districts unsightly factories may constitute the view. In residential situations the view may be a neighbor's matching window, another building or alleyway, or even a brick wall. Camouflaging these undesirable views can be accomplished with window coverings. The warmth of wood shutters; the clean, sleek lines of blinds and pleated shades; and the pattern, texture, and color of fabrics that complement the interior are all ways to increase the aesthetics of the interior. Window treatments can add character, charm, and interest indoors.

SUITING THE WINDOW: MEETING THE NEED

The needs of windows vary. Every window assuredly will not have the same requirements. So the question to be answered is: Which treatment is best for a particular window, in a particular room, in a particular home or building, at a particular time, and for a particular client? The first consideration when selecting a window covering should be: What needs must be met? A careful evaluation and filling of needs often will fill the wants of the client. The client who desires a beautiful treatment should realize that as pretty to look at as a certain window treatment may be, it can become a sizable and continual frustration if it is not practical for the given circumstances. With window coverings the adage applies, pretty is as pretty does.

For example, an aging single-glazed window frame that leaks profuse amounts of hot or cold air will require a heavy, tightly fitting insulative shade or other energy-efficient treatment. Although it may be lovely to look at, a scanty covering on such a window would make the window unbearable to be near. On the other hand a large triple-glazed window may not require heavy covering but rather glare control; a small window may demand a treatment that leaves the glass area completely unobstructed for maximum light availability. Fundamentally important is that the treatment allow the window to operate the way it was intended to, swinging in or out or sliding vertically or horizontally. The often-used hardware must be accessible.

It is important for the client to recognize that needs vary from window to window. It is quite acceptable to use different treatments in the same room provided that they are compatible in style. For example, an east window and a north window in the same room have different needs. The east window may need glare control, while the north window may not. The addition of a retractable louvered blind on the east window, perhaps layered with a drapery that matches the north covering, would be a good selection. Another example might be windows of different sizes and locations in an interior. A room that has a pair of small windows on each side of a fireplace, as well as two picture windows on opposite walls, will require different treatments. The large picture windows may be draped, perhaps even formally, and the small windows might be treated with shutters or shades in the same color as the drapes.

Surveying the Requirements

It is helpful to compile a list of requirements for covering a certain window or set of windows. The designer should go over the list with the clients so that they may be certain that the selection of treatments will be best for the given circumstances. The following checklist suggests that practical considerations are equally as important as aesthetic ones.

- Is the architecture surrounding the window beautiful or aesthetically intriguing, or is it an eyesore or one that lacks architectural interest?

- Is the window itself attractive, or does it need aesthetic help? What about the proportion of the window? Is it too tall, too wide, too squatty, or awkwardly placed in the wall? Are the panes appropriate for the style of the room? Are they nicely proportioned and well fitted?

- Do the actual dimensions of the window need to be visually altered? Should the window appear longer, taller, or wider to achieve pleasing proportions? Is there a pair, a trio, or a series of windows that need to be visually or aesthetically united? Are there windows of varying sizes that can appear the same if draped with similar dimensions?

- Are the muntins and mullions (dividing bars) in good shape or are they splitting apart? Is the paint in poor condition?

- How much light is needed or desired from the window? If optimum light is desired, then the covering will need to stack off the glass entirely when opened. The less light that is needed, the more glass may remain covered when the draperies are open.

- Is there room for a window covering to stack off on one side, both sides, or above or below the frame? Will stackback area be restricted by light switches, outlets, heat registers, built-in architecture or cabinetry, or furniture?

- Are there specific needs for privacy? Is there an activity taking place after dark (work, leisure, and so on) that would dictate opaque coverage of the window?

- What safety factors need to be taken into consideration? In residential situations people who live alone may want to feel that the window gives safety and security. Valuable possessions may need to be protected against the temptation to burglarize. In nonresidential situations users may need security against potential intruders; equipment may need to be screened from the public eye.

- Is glare a problem? Excessive directional light that builds up heat in the interior and irritates and fatigues the user may occur at any time of day on the south exposure; in the morning on the east; in the afternoon on the west; and seldom on the north unless from reflection off shiny surfaces.

- Is there excessive heat gain? If so the window may need reflective or light-colored coverings that still allow some light to penetrate. Heat gain accompanied by too much light will require a room-darkening or energy-conserving treatment.

- Is there excessive heat loss? Since they receive no direct sunlight, north windows are coldest and need more insulative covering than windows with other exposures. Regardless of orientation any window not properly insulated loses heat in cold-climate winters. Tightly fitting heavy fabrics or ceiling-to-floor treatments reduce heat loss (see also chapter 1).

- Is there a need to control sound from the outside? This might be a requirement for homes, high-density living quarters, and nonresidential interiors in high-traffic areas or locations near airports. An interlining of batting will muffle noise from the outside. Inside noise may stem from office machinery, televisions and appliances, music, and even too much conversation. It can be reduced with greater quantities of fabric at the window, the addition of fabric top treatments, and fabrics that are bulky and that provide air spaces to muffle sound.

- Are heating elements, such as baseboard heaters or forced-air registers, in the way of window treatments? The danger of a flammable fabric near a heat source must be considered. The damage to a textile from the forced air of coal- or oil-burning furnaces or from humidifiers must also be taken into account.

- Are often-used electrical outlets or light switches near the window? If so, the type or style of treatment may need to be altered to allow access to these features.

- Will window operation be affected by the treatment?

- Are there breezes the client desires to utilize that could be obstructed with certain types of coverings?

- Does the client own pets that might damage the window treatment? For example, cats or birds might climb the draperies or claw them to shreds; dogs or cats might lie next to the draperies, covering them with hair.

- Does the client wish to hang plants in or near the window? If so the treatment must stack off completely and/or do little to reduce incoming light.

- Is there an architectural or decorative theme that should be carried out? If the interior is to be an adaptive reuse, or reproduction or restoration of a historic period, then the designer must research style, colors, textures, patterns, and trimmings that may be required.

- Are there valuable or vulnerable furnishings that may be sun damaged or hurt by changes in temperature? An example might be a grand piano, which often is placed by a window, where it may look stunning but where it may easily be hurt by temperature fluctuations. In this case an automatic sensor might close shades or draperies to protect against direct sun or cold temperatures.

- Is there a need for fabrics and hardware that can withstand multiple openings and closings, such as in hotels and resorts? If so, special or architectural hardware can be specified. For instance, a wand draw will be a good alternative to a cord draw.

- Does the formality of the interior dictate a sumptuous or an elegant treatment?

- Is silk a fabric desired by the client? If so, a carefully selected lining fabric will be imperative to protect against sunlight deterioration.

- Are there environmental conditions that would dictate special materials or fabric finishes? These might include antimicroorganism treatments in locations where high humidity might cause a fabric to mold and mildew, or in medical facilities where codes strictly forbid materials that might be incubators for microorganisms. Smoke or air impurities can be very damaging to the fabric, particularly to its color.

- Do safety regulations or building codes in offices or other public facilities require flame-resistant or flame-retardant materials? Fabrics can be given flame-retardant finishes, but a sample should always be tried first. The fabric may change shading or hue slightly and may become "tender" (weak and easily destroyed by cleaning or handling).

- Does the fabric need to last a certain number of years? Then there would be a need to research life-cycle costing (the expected life span or length of wearability in years divided into the cost of the installed treatment). This will yield the cost per year and may be used to compare different types of treatments.

- Does the location of the window preclude easy access to the window treatment for dusting or removal for cleaning?

- Does the purpose of the interior or location of the window dictate motorized window coverings? Examples might include media rooms where daylight needs to be eliminated, institutions or bedrooms where invalided people need to control window treatment opening and closing, skylight coverings that cannot be reached by hand, or nonresidential situations where glare control or insulation needs to be automated.

There is almost no limit to the number of questions to be asked in regard to window and interior needs. The more information that can be gleaned before the treatment is selected, the better the solution invariably will be. It may, of course, be impossible or impractical to meet each and every need. For example, if the window is an energy-wasting culprit yet the client needs natural light or prefers the view, not all needs can be met at the same time. A compromise is sometimes the best solution, such as closing off the window for part of the day or layering a treatment that will reflect some heat while allowing some view or light.

THE PRINCIPLES OF GOOD DESIGN IN WINDOW STYLING

As important as it is for the designer to be acquainted with the myriad window treatment possibilities that exist, it is essential that the designer learn and understand the principles of good window treatment design. Many a grand idea will fail in the wrong setting. Some glorious magazine treatments are held together with pins and are far from being operable or even practical.

The idea of good design goes beyond being pretty. Good design will please even an undiscriminating eye. It spans centuries, societies, and styles. Good design meets the functional need in a pleasing manner. It is appropriateness in a given setting; it is the application of time-honored principles to create a work of art—be it a painting, a sculpture, or a well-dressed window. Responsiveness to beauty is human nature's sixth sense; without beauty we feel deprived. Well-proportioned and appropriately designed room settings can uplift, inspire, and comfort. Simply stated, good design makes us feel good.

The *principles* of design can be used as tools to evaluate the needs as well as the finished result or end product. The *elements* (see pp. 37–39) are the materials or dimensions that are manipulated to accomplish the principles. Analyzing and utilizing the principles and elements are the keys to good design in any application, from a piece of fine art, to the successful selection and design of window coverings, to a complete interior. These time-tested concepts always will be applicable to window treatments. A knowledge of their application will aid the designer when advising and guiding clients and when making selections that should prove intelligent solutions to the needs and demands of windows.

The principles of design include proportion and scale, balance, rhythm, emphasis, and harmony. These are accomplished through the elements of design: space, light, color, texture, pattern and ornament, form and shape, and mass.

Proportion and Scale

The designer might first evaluate the window to determine if it is harmonious in scale (size) and in good proportion (relationship) to the room. The window covering can alter these proportions, making the window look taller, wider, longer, or all of these by draping the wall beyond the window frame in each direction. Proportion is a sensitive matter when one sizes up a treatment in relationship to the overall size of an interior. An over-scaled, elegant treatment of heavily fringed swags and cascades over the top of privacies, sheers, and tied-back overdraperies would overwhelm a 12- by 15-foot room with a standard 8-foot ceiling. Conversely some windows in large rooms will need to be dressed up to be appropriately scaled. The depth of the window treatment and the proportion of its parts often require a scale drawing to evaluate its appropriateness. A top treatment that is too deep will always look top-heavy and cumbersome, perhaps overwhelming the entire treatment, giving it awkward, ill proportions.

Proportion is vital to well-designed window treatments. Good proportion was defined by the philosopher/architects of the Golden Age of Greece (approximately 500 B.C.) as "unequal, but harmonious." These ancient Greeks discovered that pleasing, or *golden*, proportions could be established mathematically. For example, a *golden rectangle* (which is easily applied to window and window treatment shapes) (fig. 2–1) would have sides that measured 2 feet by 3 feet, 3 feet by 5 feet, 5 feet by 8 feet, or 8 feet by 13 feet. This is written out as 2 is to 3 as 3 is to 5 as 5 is to 8 as 8 is to 13, or the ratio 2:3:5:8:13 and so on, *ad infinitum*. These pleasing dimensions can be multiplied to determine other golden proportions. For example, a 2-foot by 3-foot window or window treatment has the same proportion as a 4-foot by 6-foot window because the lengths and widths of each window differ by a common factor—in this case 2 (2 times 2 is 4 and 2 times 3 is 6). Another example is found by multiplying 3 and 5 each by 2, resulting in a 6- by 10-foot window—again, very pleasing proportions.

It is interesting to note that in this sequence, the sum of the previous two numbers equals the next number, or, 2 + 3 = 5, 3 + 5 = 8, and so on. If each number were divided by its successor, then we would find that .618 is the equivalent of another golden proportion, the *golden mean*. The mean is a line of division separating two parts into unequal but harmonious

2-1 The vertical golden rectangle—a pleasing window treatment shape.

proportions and often is said to fall somewhere between one-half and one-third from the top of an area. So the placement of a *dado* (chair rail molding) on the wall is most pleasing placed in this location—.618 down from the ceiling. Likewise, when placing ties on curtains and draperies, the golden mean is a good rule to follow (fig. 2–2): somewhere between one-half and one-third, or .618, or roughly six-tenths of the distance from the top, or .382, roughly four-tenths (which reduces to two-fifths) up from the bottom of the treatment. The placement of ties is crucially important in the installation of window treatments. Well-proportioned golden rectangles and golden mean lines of division (such as tiebacks) can make the difference in creating successful and harmonious window coverings rather than awkward and clumsy ones.

The scale of the pattern is another point to consider. Large scale or texture in large rooms, small scale or texture in small rooms is a safe rule of thumb. It is true that, in some situations, large scale in small areas will add drama and small scale in large areas will visually increase the space. However, it takes much sensitivity and training to enable a designer to evaluate when the opposite of tried-and-true rules are applicable for the given setting.

2-2 Draperies tied back according to the golden mean—somewhere between one-half and one-third the length of the treatment.

a   Draperies tied back low.
b   Draperies tied back high.
c   Separated tiebacks on a wide window echo the lines of slender tiebacks, allowing light and softening the straight lines of the window.

The proportion of color also is crucial to window treatment success. A large-scale window treatment that covers a broad area should never be of an intense or overbearing color in relationship to the scheme. Rather, the window is of greatest value when treated as part of the background.

An open-minded, critical look at the scale and style of the furniture should reveal how large or small or how elaborate or simple the window treatment should be. Formal, elegant furnishings often seem to demand greater detail and ornamentation at the window in order to complete an ambience or feeling of depth and richness. On the other hand, unpretentious, simple furnishings usually require treatments that are equally "down to earth" and practical.

Balance

Balance is a state of equilibrium, evenness, or stability, and is divided into three types: symmetrical or formal, asymmetrical or informal, and radial. Balance achieved through *symmetry* means that on both sides of a central point, objects, furnishings, or window treatments are identical or mirror image. It also is seen in tied-back or straight-panel draperies that evenly flank a window. This approach is decidedly formal and has been used for centuries with pleasing results to establish importance and dignity.

Asymmetrical balance is where two objects, or two sides of a single object, are somewhat different yet carefully balanced through visual judgment. This might be seen at the window as a nonuniform pattern on a shade or flat curtain or a painted design on a shoji screen. Asymmetry was popular during the Empire period, as illustrated in chapter 4, and the effect was often rich and majestic.

Radial balance means that objects "radiate" out from a central point as spokes or concentric circles. This type of balance is seen in the lines of fanlight windows and can be emphasized with shirred fabric or pleated shades that fan out. Radial balance is gracious and lovely and offers interest to an interior.

Rhythm

Rhythm is a principle of design that is defined as a connecting visual element. Rhythm "carries the eye along" in interior design much as the beat of music carries a melody. There are several kinds of rhythm—for example, *rhythm by transition*, where connecting colors, lines, or elements (such as trim or gracefully rounded top treatments) make the eye move gently along, or *rhythm by gradation*, where shapes decrease in size (as in the folds of a swagged top treatment). Gradation also can mean that colors become gradually darker or lighter and can be seen in layers of draperies where the sheers are slightly lighter and the trim on the overdrapery is slightly darker. Rhythm can be established by *repetition*, where a color, fabric, valance, or window treatment is used repeatedly in the room. When the fabric is repeated in upholstery on the walls, for example, then the rhythm becomes even more transitional, connecting the points with greater emphasis.

Rhythm also can be staccato, like a lively musical beat. This can be seen at the window as a pattern that repeatedly contrasts light and dark, or in shapes that are vivid and exciting. Right angles seen in window grids or panes provide *rhythm by opposition*, a kind of repetitive, abrupt change of direction that moves the eye in jumps from one point to the next. Rhythm is most effective when it is planned and organized and when the jump is not a great distance. A vivid contrast in the pattern or trim on one window treatment that is repeated only far across the room in another treatment (where the eye has to "leap" to continue the rhythm) may not provide the continuity that rhythm is intended to give.

Emphasis

Emphasis is the arrangement of materials and patterns to create a center of interest, commonly called a *focal point*. In large rooms there may be several focal points, but one must be more demanding of attention or more dominant than the others. The window treatment intended as a focal point should be beautiful without being obvious or overbearing. It should echo the theme of the room's architecture and furnishings. Where inherent areas of emphasis might dictate that the window *not* be a center of interest, then the window should be treated as a background element that supports the architecture and furnishings, colors, or artwork.

Harmony

Harmony is a principle of design made up of two subprinciples: unity and variety. For example, a window treatment can unify a room through a matching or blending of colors, fabrics, textures, proportions, and repetitive shapes or patterns. Yet too much unity is boring, and variety within the unity is an important point in establishing harmony and should be kept in mind. Blending rather than matching, contrast rather than continual repetition, can be accomplished through the variety of compatible or coordinated fabrics, and the overall design of the treatment. Within a home or nonresidential setting, there may be a variety of treatments selected and specified, but there must be unity within that variety. This might be seen in the selection of a general theme or look in the use of miniblinds throughout, with other treatments layered over the top, or in a color scheme with variations revolving around a single color or a small set of colors.

THE ELEMENTS OF GOOD DESIGN IN WINDOW STYLING

The elements of design are the tools by which the principles can be accomplished and seen in evidence. The elements include space, light, color, texture, pattern and ornament, and form or shape.

Space

Space can be visually and physically altered through the window treatments. More pattern and intense color will close in a space; less or lighter values of color, as well as textures, rather than pattern, will open up a space. Dark sheer fabrics or dark blinds will visually advance, whereas colorless sheers will allow view and light, which extend the apparent space. The amount of trimmings and curves or angles also is a variable in creating or restricting space. Long, uninterrupted lines and low contrast will visually increase space.

Light

Light can be literally altered through the selection of color at the window. Dark or intense colors will cut down on the amount of natural light and will absorb interior light. Shutter louvers and blinds can restrict light into the interior, and metallized fabric shades, which are translucent, can screen light as well.

Color

The color of the fabric, particularly in diaphanous (sheer or semisheer) textiles, will cast that color throughout the room. For example, an orange sheer will bathe the entire room in orange light. Stark white can even cause the light to be bluish and perhaps cold and unfriendly. Small samples of sheer fabrics need to be bunched together to imitate the three-times fullness of the finished drapery in order for the designer to evaluate the color of the light.

The amount of area covered with a fabric also will affect the color. Many yards of a colored fabric will appear darker and more intense than a small area of the same fabric, producing a sometimes surprisingly dramatic or heavy effect. This should be anticipated by the designer in advance, and perhaps sketched and colored to help him or her visualize the final color effect.

A dramatic solid color, brightly colored pattern, or intense contrasting trim color can attract unwarranted attention to the window covering. Unless the fabric is repeated or lavished elsewhere, the impact of colored fabric, pattern, or trim may be overstated or overwhelming. Fine interior design always keeps color use and distribution under control, leading the eye around the room and using it for emotional impact where it is most effective. Neutral colors (white, off-white, beige, brown, and gray) and neutralized colors (toned down or dull light, medium, or dark values) of the scheme often are wise choices at the window. The less a window treatment "demands" of the eye, the more lovely and long-lived it will be.

There are, of course, exceptions to this rule. Where a room genuinely calls for richness in color or pattern, then by all means it should be used at the window. An example of this is the effective window treatments often seen in English country estates, where very large rooms with tall ceilings have large-scale windows looking out onto misty expanses of sometimes lonely landscapes. The vividness of rich color and pattern at this type of window gives comfort and companionship to the occupants and adds needed visual warmth as well as fills up some of the space.

Texture

Texture is the surface smoothness or roughness created through the type of yarn used and the construction (knit, weave, or finish). Smooth, shiny textures generally are more formal, more clinical, more reflective, lighter in value, sleeker, and somewhat more sophisticated. Rough or nubby textures absorb light, show less dirt, look darker and more casual, refract glare, and absorb more sound. Each texture calls for an evaluation in terms of its relationship to the setting requirements.

Pattern and Ornament

Pattern and ornament are two separate but closely related elements of design. Pattern is a woven or printed design that either consists of motifs grouped or massed together or is a separate, isolated component of the overall design. Pattern at the window can be effective when the design or motifs are right for the style of the room and when the window treatment should be given emphasis.

For example, when a patterned fabric echoes the style of furnishings or is authentic or appropriate to the period or ambience, then pattern at the window is desirable. Certainly the elegance of Queen Anne furnishings justifies the use of a Renaissance or Georgian brocade or damask; Chippendale furnishings lend themselves to oriental-inspired patterned fabric; and Neoclassic motifs are called for in rooms that are adaptations of Federal or Empire themes. Again, appropriateness must be judged on an individual level.

Pattern can add drama and excitement and can attract attention to the window treatment, creating a focal point in a room. Greater emphasis can be achieved by framing a pattern or by outlining it with quilting, perhaps on a top treatment or shade. Pattern may even establish the feeling or mood in interiors and can lend charm in small areas, for example, with contrasting or coordinated designs in ruffles or fabric ties, trims, or banding.

The amount of pattern used is a matter of careful discrimination. Too much pattern, too many patterns (particularly conflicting patterns), or pattern at the window that is overscaled for the room may restrict natural light or perhaps contribute to a feeling of confusion in the setting. And yet pattern that is used appropriately with these considerations in mind can be richly rewarding and serve well to carry out an interior design theme.

Ornament is embellishment or decoration. The pattern within a fabric is a form of ornamentation, as are decorative accessories, such as holdbacks and decorator rods. The degree of ornamentation needed for the room should be a point of careful consideration. In formal, high-fashion, or complex treatments, ornament may serve well to carry out a theme. In simple treatments ornament may destroy the effect and seem arbitrary and unnecessary.

Another form or ornament that is highly desirable in formal treatments is *passementerie*—trimmings such as fringe, gimp, tassels, and decorative braid. Certainly every interior designer who specifies historic treatments recognizes the importance and richness trimmings can give to a treatment. And the sensitive selection and placement of trimmings will enrich the beauty of the fabric as well.

In less formal treatments ornament also may take the form of ruffles or banding added for charm, softness, or character. There are some fringes, braids, and trimmings on the market that are very appropriate and desirable for less formal treatments. Color should be a matter of discrimination in all ornamentation. Bold contrast of ornament can be dramatic, but it also stands a chance of weakening and cheapening the treatment's effectiveness in the interior.

Form or Shape

Form or shape concerns the outline of a filled-in *mass*, or third dimension. In window treatments form or shape is very important because the lines have the potential to be visually pleasing or disturbing. For example, tied-back draperies were originally draped on long, slender windows. The results were quite tasteful. However, when a tied-back drapery is used on a wide window and meets in the center of the window, then the form or shape is so severe that it is *not* pleasing. Often top treatments are used to achieve a specific shape, and the shape of the pelmet (shaped fabric valance), valance, cornice, or lambrequin may echo the shape of an architectural feature or a piece of furniture (the back of a chair, for example).

THE ROLE OF WINDOW TREATMENTS

Each window treatment design plays a crucial role in setting the stage for the theme, the look, and the style of the entire room. Window treatments may be handled in three basic ways—as part of the background, as supportive of the theme, or as a focal point.

The Treatment as Part of the Background

Obviously, the window with no treatment at all falls into this category. So do many hard and soft treatments of metal, wood, and fabric. Such treatments attract no attention on their own, though they are pleasing to view if one happens to look at them (fig. 2–3). They usually will be similar in color and texture to the walls. They may seem almost part of the wall and act as a subtle backdrop for the room's furnishings.

The Architecturally or Decoratively Supportive Treatment

Treatments architecturally or decoratively supportive will carry out a theme (fig. 2–4). Although not demanding of attention, the window covering will make a stylistic statement. The treatment may unify a room, make it more cozy and inviting, or perhaps visually close in the space. Supportive treatments add interest and variety in color, texture, and pattern.

2-3 A background treatment such as plain draperies or louvers on a matching wall attracts no attention.

2-4 A supportive treatment follows through on an architectural or decorative theme or element.

The Treatment as Focal Point

As noted, unless a room is large and divided into various furniture group-ings, a general rule of thumb is to have one focal point per room. If, for example, a 14- by 20-foot living room contains a lovely fireplace wall, it may be unwise to compete with this built-in permanent focal point by decorating a window on another wall with an elaborate treatment. The crucial consideration is the effect the focal point will have on the room's occupants. People who are seated facing an ornately draped wall may be impressed initially, but they may find that the treatment is unable to sus-tain their interest for long; a wall of artwork might be a better choice for a focal point in this case. A window treatment is an effective focal point when it is part of a natural architectural focus, such as the framing of an elaborate window (fig. 2–5). It is not a good choice when the focal point lies beyond the window, since the treatment will likely conflict with the view rather than support it.

It is wise to evaluate any aesthetic restrictions. Certain patterns, colors, or textures might negate the impact of the treatment itself. The long-term power of the understatement is far greater than the short-term value of the overstatement. Never lose sight of the *window* under the treatment. It should be respected and utilized for all it is worth.

2-5 A focal-point treatment becomes the center of atten-tion. Here the complex and elaborate treatment frames an equally majestic window and is compatible with the scale of the room.

FROM THE OUTSIDE LOOKING IN

Windows look out, but they also look in. A window treatment may be lovely from the inside yet leave much to be desired from the outside. For example, a colored sheer that contrasts with the color of the exterior building material is likely to be offensive, as are side-by-side stereotyped girl's and boy's bedroom windows or any window treatment that draws undo attention from the exterior.

The ancient Greeks believed that anything "obvious" insults the intel-lect; likewise, a window treatment should not be obvious from the exte-rior. It is wiser to keep treatments similar (though not necessarily exactly the same) and structural or simple to the exterior view.

From the exterior, window coverings often reveal the style of furnishing and the level of formality. Fabric sheers will look decidedly more formal than miniblinds, and shutters will look more frank and adaptive than sheer lace curtains. The window covering type, style, and color should be har-monious not only with interior furnishings but also with the exterior style of the home.

Well-designed treatments will support architectural style. This is not to say that a window in a Georgian-style building must be given a strictly historic Georgian treatment, nor must modern architectural windows be filled only with miniblinds. It is to say that the character of the architec-ture, whether residential or nonresidential, should be repected and main-tained.

Chapter 3   POPULAR WINDOW STYLES: HOW TO TREAT THEM

In addition to offering scenic benefits, ventilation, light, and protection, windows can and should be an important complement to any interior design. Windows ideally are a means of documenting historic style and adding character or charm to a building. The following is an alphabetical cross section of window styles and some basic design considerations and challenges they present. Specific measurement and treatment information for each window is presented later in the chapter.

A CROSS SECTION OF TODAY'S WINDOWS

Arched Windows

American architectural design has been influenced by the native architecture of many countries, especially that of Western Europe and Asia. One such architectural feature is the arch. Figure 3–1 illustrates the major styles of arches, from antiquity through modern times. Arches were not initially intended as windows; the practice began to emerge during the Renaissance when glass, such as crown glass (see chapter 1), became available for glazing. Today arches often are used to give historic authenticity to a home or building or to lend a flavor. The Spanish arch and the Roman keystone arch are two of the most popular, along with the segmental or elliptical arch of the Neoclassic era. Semicircular arched fanlights and sunburst windows flourished during the Georgian Era, as did elliptical fanlights during the Federal era (see also chapter 4).

Attic Windows

Attic windows are a type of skylight designed to provide up to 37.7 percent more light than the traditional dormer window. Attic windows are placed in and are parallel to the roof line (fig. 3–2). Unlike skylights they are glazed with glass rather than with hard plastic. They operate on a central pivot principle that allows them to be opened.

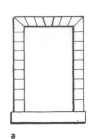
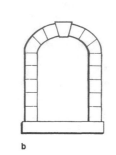
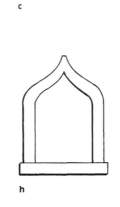
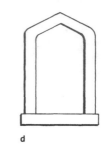
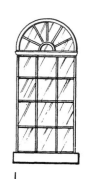

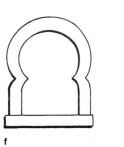

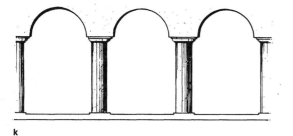
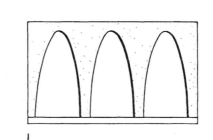

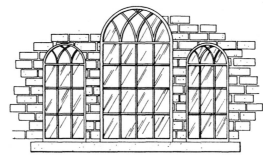

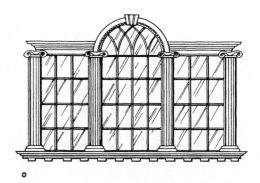

3-1 Types of historic arches.

- **a** Flat keystone.
- **b** Round Roman.
- **c** Gothic.
- **d** Tudor.
- **e** Elliptical or basket-handle.
- **f** Moorish or horseshoe.
- **g** Persian or onion dome.
- **h** Ogee or ogive.
- **i** Elliptical fanlight.
- **j** Round fanlight.
- **k** Spanish colonnade of arches supported by pillars, or columns.
- **l** Spanish stucco arcade, or series of arches.
- **m** Classic Palladian arch arrangement—a Roman keystone arch flanked by post-and-lintel architecture; here detail is Georgian classicism with Doric columns and complex molding.
- **n** Palladian arch arrangement, with tracery in the arch of each window.
- **o** Palladian window arrangement, with Ionic columns, center tracery in the arch, and enlarged side windows.

Attic windows were popular in Europe, particularly in Scandinavia, long before Americans began to appreciate them. They offer a precise, contemporary look that enhances modern home architecture. The use of attic windows in America may be a result in part of increased building costs, which have encouraged more people to remain in their present homes or offices by extending space within them. Attic windows make livable space out of attics without the expense of constructing dormers. They do not project as do dormers or even skylights. This means that attic windows make usable space in existing or new architecture without any undue attention to the roof plane. Attic windows also have become a popular architectural feature for use in greenhouses or solariums or when the attic is removed in remodeling and the ceiling is extended vertically to the angle of the roof.

Attic windows operate to give ventilation. Therefore the designer will not want to encumber any desired ventilation with heavy treatments. Light control may be a consideration during the times when direct sun shines in, depending on the size and number of attic windows. Privacy is rarely a major concern, since these windows are high and angled.

3-2 Cross section of attic or roof window installed into an angled roof. This window is set flush into an angled ceiling to look like a clear skylight. A pivoting mechanism allows for top and bottom ventilation.

Awning Windows

Awning windows are a variation of casement windows, hinged on the top to swing outward (fig. 3–3). They usually are small, horizontally placed, and rectangular. Frequently they are combined with fixed glass or are stacked vertically in units. Awning windows may be individually framed or may close on one another for a less restricted view. They often are stacked to allow ample ventilation or are grouped in horizontal ribbons high along a wall for privacy.

Awning windows are particularly nice for ventilation at a low point in the room, with stationary glass placed above. They provide excellent ventilation when fully opened. Another advantage is that they may be left open even during a rainstorm. Awning window sizes range from approximately 3 by 2 feet to 4 by 3 feet.

Treatments for awning windows have few restrictions. Since the glass swings out, the paramount concern is to allow access to the crank for operation. Any blind, shutter, shade, drapery, or curtain that can be stacked off the glass for operation will do well. Because these windows are useful for ventilation, the treatment may be one that would allow the air to circulate freely through it.

3-3 An awning window swings out, allowing excellent ventilation and preventing rain from coming into the interior.

Basement Windows

Basement windows are similar to awning and hopper windows in size and design, but they are top-hinged and swing inward (just the opposite of awning windows). They usually are of simplified design intended for installation in less demanding situations, such as masonry and concrete foundations or possibly as clerestory windows high in the wall (fig. 3–4).

The designer will need to consider treatments for basement windows that stack off the glass entirely or that mount onto the frame of the window. Note that any frame-mounted treatment will hang downward and out from the treatment when it is opened, unless there is a hold-down bracket or some other means to hold the treatment to the glass.

Bay and Bow Windows

During the Renaissance a window style developed throughout Europe called the *bay*, or projecting window. *Bay* refers to a common area in a

3-4 A basement window, which is open at the top and hinged at the bottom, swings in, catching breezes and funneling them upward.

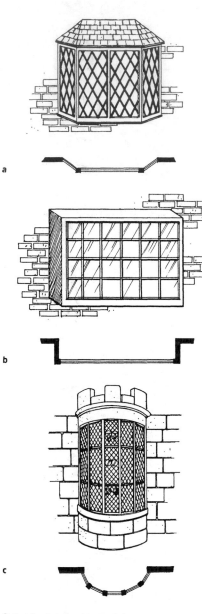

medieval house that was used for cooking, living, and sleeping. Most homes consisted of only one bay plus a loft for extra sleeping accommodations. A two-bay house could be divided by a wall or curtain, transforming the bay into a "room." When large manor houses were built during the Renaissance, bay windows were the size of small rooms, projecting straight out from a large hallway, library, or gallery, with glass on three sides of the projection. These windows were used on the main and upper floors and often were stacked one above another. As the style evolved the bay was given angled sides, and it eventually rounded into the *bow* window, which gained greater favor in France than in England. The bay window was and still is a favorite architectural device for extending interior space, expanding view, and increasing light and ventilation (fig. 3–5).

Bay windows always utilize an odd number of window segments. A typical bay is a three- or five-unit angled arrangement on the ground floor. A *projecting bay* is either three windows set at 90 degrees to each other

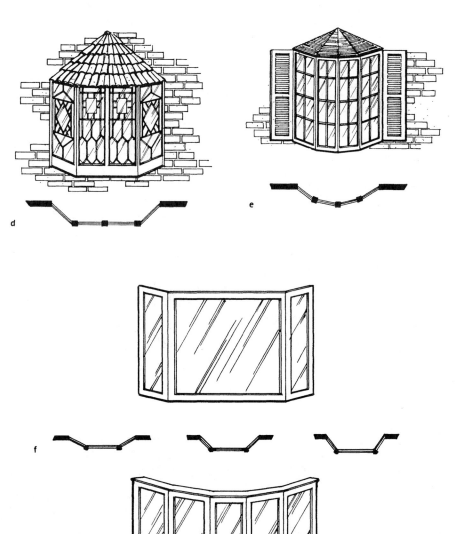

3-5 Historic bay and bow windows.

a Bay window with medieval diamond-shape panes and hipped roof. The cross section below shows angles.

b This bay window has solid sides and a 90-degree projection from the wall.

c Historic oriel bay, often seen on castles, which extends from the second story to the ground. The cross section shows that this example is actually a bow window by nature of its roundness.

d Old World second-floor corbel bay with no extension below. This example shows leaded and stained decorative glass and a tile dovecote roof.

e Rounded French bow window with angled dovecote hipped roof. Shutters add authenticity and charm to this symmetrical arrangement.

f Contemporary bay window. Shallow-, medium-, and deep-angle options are shown in the cross sections.

g Contemporary bow window. Cross sections with four, five, and six glass segments are shown below.

or a single window with solid sides boxed out. A bay on the second floor is called a *corbel bay,* and, if it is part of a turret (a tower with two or more stories) that extends to the ground floor, it is known as an *oriel bay.*

The bow window has an odd or even number of window segments arranged in a semicircle. Both the bow and the bay can be deep (set at a 45-degree angle from the building) or shallow (set at a 30-degree angle). The bow window is generally viewed as more formal, but both bay and bow windows are increasingly favored in traditionally styled architecture.

Typically the bay or bow consists of fixed or a combination of fixed and operable glass. Even when ventilation is the objective, it is common that only the side portions are operable. When all the segments of the bay or bow window are operable, ventilation can be significantly increased in the room. However, fixed glass often is used in bay and bow windows. Bay and bow windows can be ordered as preconstructed units or can be custom-built by a contractor to design or architectural specifications.

Bay and bow windows are more costly than windows that are set flush with the wall. They are far less energy-efficient—in winter they allow more heat to escape; in summer the direct sunlight magnifies glare and solar heat gain. These complications preclude planning for orientation and climate (see chapter 1).

Treating a bay and bow window can be a challenge. Some of the possibilities for installing pairs of draperies and one-way draws at bay windows are discussed later in the chapter under "Measuring and Treating Specific Windows."

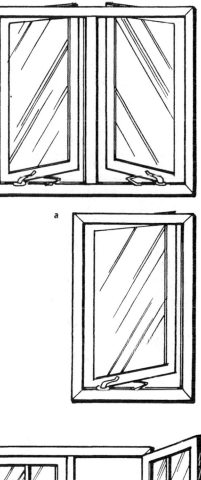

Casement Windows

In a broad sense this category could include awning, basement, hopper, and jalousie windows, since *casement* generally refers to a "swinging," hinged window. However, casement windows specifically are those that are hinged on the side and swing out. An important historical style, casement windows have long been favored in many regions, from Scandinavia to the Mediterranean. Indeed, they are the most universally common of all types of windows. Simple, tight-fitting features have made them readily adaptable to many parts of the world (figs. 3–6 and 3–7).

Today, casement windows are seen largely in two or three styles of architecture: French, English Tudor adaptations, and contemporary. The French have traditionally preferred long and slender casement windows that are one or two panes wide. This type of French casement window, enlarged to door-sized dimensions, results in a French door (see figs. 3–7d and 3–8c.) The addition of grids (true wood dividers or leaded glass dividers, wood or metal snap-in grids, or flat metal grids sandwiched between the glass) gives wood or metal casement frames a variable look of authenticity. (True dividers, or separate panes, are far more authentic and rich-looking than flat metal grids.)

Casement windows are operable windows. In a pair only one may open and the other may be fixed or stationary glass, or a pair of operable casements (both windows open) may meet at a center dividing bar. Casements may flank a fixed glass window, or perhaps a single casement may be used alone.

Casements have many advantages. Because they are side-hinged, both sides of the glass may be cleaned from inside the building. This is especially easy if the window is fitted with "projecting action," a sliding friction hinge that moves the hinge rail toward the middle as the frame is cranked open. Casements can catch air currents moving along near the exterior,

3-6 Casement windows.

a *Side-hinged single and double casement windows.*

b *Side-hinged casement window used around the world, notably in Europe and in Central and South America.*

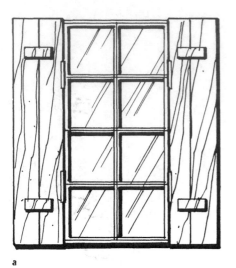

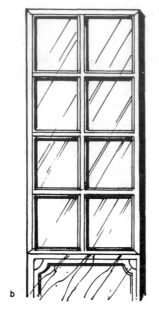

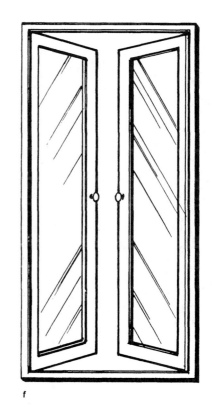

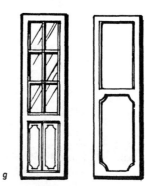

3-7 French casement or fixed-glass windows and doors.

- **a** Casement window with plank shutters.
- **b** Fixed or stationary glass with raised panel beneath.
- **c** Segmental-arch window with matching louvered shutters.
- **d** French casement door.
- **e** French door with long, narrow pairs of lights, or panes.
- **f** French rim doors.
- **g** Glass-and-wood-panel door variations.

and the entire length of the window may be opened for uniform ventilation. When closed, casements have the tightest fit of all the operable windows.

The designer must first look at the operation of the window, as well as how often it is opened, and give priority to window access by choosing a treatment that will stack out of the way.

Clerestory and Cathedral Windows

Clerestory windows are set high in the wall as a "strip" or "ribbon" of glass. These windows may be for light only or for light and ventilation. Light from clerestory windows is broad and even, and it penetrates deep into the interior. Generally these windows will not need any treatment at all because privacy is rarely a concern and light is desirable. When a treatment is desired, it generally will be a light-softening treatment, such as a casement drapery, horizontal or vertical blind, or shade. Operation of the treatment is a prime concern for the designer. The controls need to be extended to reaching height, and an automated or remote-control treatment may be a very good choice for high windows.

Cathedral windows are high-set angled glass in a pentagonal shape (see fig. 3–13a; note that two of the trapezoidal shapes shown in fig. 3–13b form a cathedral window). They are sometimes called A-frame windows. The cathedral window is a contemporary version of the Gothic arch and similarly points heavenward (see fig. 3–1c). These windows often end high on the wall even if they extend low into the room. Some have a cross bar where the angle begins. If so, this is a logical point from which to install window coverings, leaving the angled portion free.

It is possible to cover cathedral glass: Draperies and curtains can be custom-made with angled headings, and nearly any hard treatment—shutters, blinds, woven woods, pleated shades, Shoji screens, and so on—can be angled. The expense of creating the angle may be cost-prohibitive in some cases, however. One option open to the designer is to treat glass beneath (lower than) the cathedral window first, then add a coordinating treatment to the cathedral glass later, after a postoccupancy evaluation.

Door Windows

There are several types of door windows (fig. 3–8), but the two most frequently used are the sliding glass patio door and the French casement door, or hinged patio or atrium door. The sliding glass door is simply an enlarged version of the horizontal sliding window. Its main advantages are twofold: It functions as both a door and a window, and it extends visual space to make the indoors larger and bring the outdoors inside. Figure 3–8 indicates the options of stacking fabric off a patio door partially and fully.

Many levels of quality exist in patio doors. A single-glazed door of lesser quality can be a source of considerable heat loss or gain due to aluminum frames that conduct heat and cold or due to poorly fitting frames that leak air via convection. High-quality sliding doors provide good insulative value. Some have optional divider bars that snap in for a traditional look (fig. 3–9), and the higher-quality companies offer automatic spring-closing sliding screens. Sliders come in single, double, and triple arrangements, of which one or more may be operable. The standard sizes range from as narrow as 3 feet for a single unit to 12 feet for a triple unit. The average double unit is 6 to 8 feet in width.

3-8 Door windows.

a   Sliding glass patio door with two sections.

b   Sliding glass door with three glass panels. The center panel is operable.

c   Classic French doors come in variable widths.

d   Panel storm door with glass.

e   Colonial-style storm door.

f   Wood-panel door with traditional transom lights set into the door itself.

g   A rim door—steel- or wood-framed with inset glass panel.

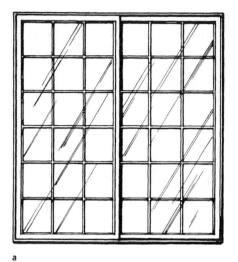

a

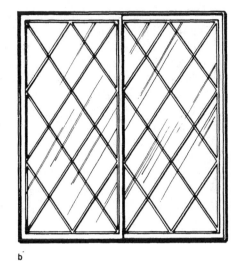

b

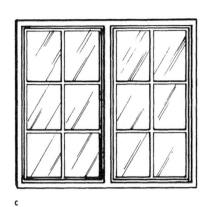

c

d

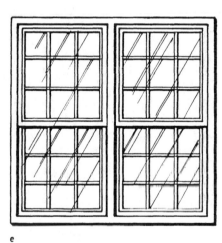

e

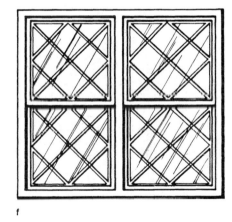

f

g

h

3-9 Snap-in grids.

a   Snap-in grids on sliding glass patio doors.

b   Diamond-shaped snap-in grids on sliding glass patio doors.

c   Snap-in grids for fixed-glass or casement window.

d   Medieval diamond-shaped grids for casement windows.

e   Double-hung sash windows with snap-in grids.

f   Double-hung windows with medieval diamond-shaped grids.

g   Diamond-shaped snap-in grids in awning pair.

h   Snap-in rectangular grids in strip or awning pair.

French casement doors are hinged on the sides like a casement window. They usually swing outward but may be specially installed to swing inward so may be used between rooms of the home or building; indeed, high-quality French doors add richness to an interior. French doors usually are available from major door manufacturers in standard door sizes. They may be glazed with a single sheet of glass or with glass that is two or three panes wide in smaller rectangles.

Snap-in grids over a single sheet of glass also can create the look of small panes. Many doors have beautiful combinations of wood panels and glass panes.

The casement is generally two to three times more costly than the sliding glass door, depending on the quality of each type of door. Two major advantages to the casement is the look of quality in the solid wood or steel frame and the appeal of the grids. Another advantage is that when both casement doors are operable, the total area may be opened for ventilation, traffic flow (circulation), or view; sliding glass doors generally have only one operable panel. Wood French doors are far less energy-efficient than the newer steel patio or atrium French doors. Wood doors tend to warp, losing their seal. However, wood doors are designed to open in pairs, exposing the full 5- or 6-foot-wide area. As such wood doors are especially beautiful between rooms or opening into a solarium or enclosed patio, and can be finished in a natural grain or painted. Insulated steel patio doors often are arranged in units where only one is an operable door and the other "door" is fixed glass. These may hinge so that the operable door opens away from the stationary door (is hinged next to it), allowing only one door to open for ventilation. These doors are frequently used in sets of three: two stationary units and one operable unit.

Challenges and solutions to treating casement doors are found later in this chapter under "Measuring and Treating Specific Windows."

Dormer Windows

A dormer is a window that protrudes from the roof, necessitating that the roof line be cut open and the window boxed out. Figure 3–10 illustrates the variety of dormer window styles. The style often depends on the way the window is framed or boxed, or on the roof line it is given. Dormers are thus referred to by the name of the framing or roof, such as gable dormer, hipped dormer, turret dormer, or inset dormer.

Dormer windows may have evolved out of the need to use attic space. During the Middle Ages in France, for example, attic spaces were not counted for taxation, so the clever French simply extended the roof down over the top story. Thus a window breaking through the line of the eaves (sometimes called a "break-through-the-cornice dormer") was born.

The dormer often is a small interior area, and the designer will need to evaluate existing wall space to determine if the treatment can be stacked off the glass. Frequently the treatment is left on the glass as a screening treatment because privacy is a lesser concern (due to the height and angle of view from the ground). Keep in mind the style of treatment from the outside of the building. It should be consistent and compatible with other window treatments.

English Sash Windows

For well over five hundred years, the English have taken pride in the arrangement of small panes of glass set in their walls. When glass finally became widely available, the small panes, usually of brilliant crown glass

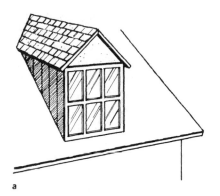

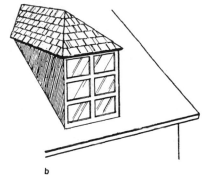

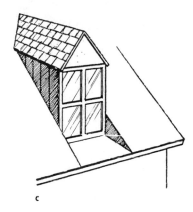

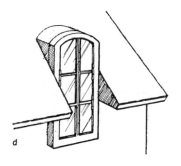

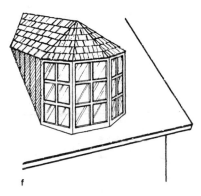

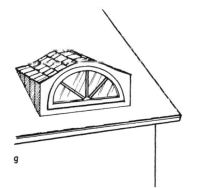

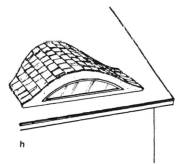

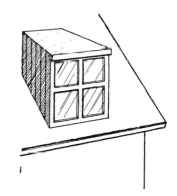

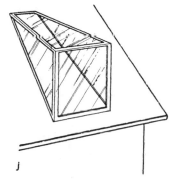

3-10 Dormer windows.

a Gable dormer, with roof on two sides.

b Hipped dormer, with roof on three sides.

c Inset dormer, set back into the roof.

d French segmental-top casement window. Note that the dormer breaks the line of the eaves.

e Rounded- or keystone-arch dormer with tracery placed in the arch.

f Turret dormer showing angled front and angled dovecote hipped roof.

g Fanlight dormer.

h Eyebrow dormer—a slender version of the fanlight dormer.

i Shed, or "lean-to," dormer with sloped flat roof.

j All-glass contemporary shed dormer.

k Extended shed dormer.

(see fig. 1–1), were cut into rectangular shapes and set in rectangular arrangements. These windows were copies of Italian Renaissance models and fit beautifully into the facades of English Renaissance, Baroque, Georgian, Neoclassic, and Victorian architecture. Americans incorporated this window style into Colonial, Georgian, Federal, Greek Revival, and some Victorian architecture as well.

The *sash* is the frame that holds the smaller rectangles. The unit may be stationary, or it may be a single- or double-hung sash window (fig. 3–11). The individual panes are also called "lights" or "lites" and the arrangement is referred to by the number of panes situated across, then down. For example, figure 3–11 shows sash arrangements in three by four, four by four, three by six, and four by six lights. Since the advent of the modern era, the sash window often has been installed in sheet or plate glass or in larger panels or glass. Aluminum frames and those in colors such as white or bronze also give a contemporary look to sash windows.

A single-hung sash window has an operable lower window that can be raised and lowered. In a double-hung sash window both sashes are operable. A double-hung window allows for better circulation, since cooler air can enter through the lower opening, where the lower sash is slightly raised, and warmer air can exit through the upper opening, where the upper sash is slightly lowered (fig. 3–12). Wood, metal-encased wood, and aluminum or metal sash frames are readily available today. Wood is traditionally the favorite, but it is costly; heavy to operate; requires painting and upkeep; and is vulnerable to warpage, shrinkage, and rotting. Aluminum windows are far less costly and require little or no upkeep, but they may be less desirable from an aesthetic standpoint. Energy efficiency is a variable according to quality of product and installation and the age and condition of the individual window.

Considerations for treating sash windows depend on the location; the orientation; the placement in the wall; the purpose or function of the room; the condition of the window and layers of glazing (single, double, or triple); and the need for ventilation, light, privacy, and aesthetics.

Fixed Glass

A fixed-glass window usually consists of a frame and a stationary glazed sash. Since it is stationary, a fixed window is used where ventilation is undesirable or unnecessary; where the window is out of reach; where a view is to be framed without being interrupted by a divider bar; or where it may most advantageously be combined with an operable unit, such as a casement or sliding window. Fixed windows are less expensive than operable units because they are simpler to construct and have no moving parts.

Standard fixed-glass windows are available in sizes ranging from 2 feet wide by 2 feet high up to 10 feet wide by 8 feet high. Larger versions of the fixed window are called *picture windows* for residential use and *curtain-wall construction* for nonresidential architecture. Snap-in grids or flat metal grids between layers of fixed glass give the look of a traditional English or French window with the convenience of a fixed piece of glass.

Fixed glass also can meet the needs of custom glazing where unusually shaped windows are an important facet of the architecture (fig. 3–13). Nonstandard shapes require custom glazing—either the combination of standard parts into uncommon arrangements or locations or glass cut and glazed into custom-built frames. Custom glazing demands the direction of a qualified architect, structural engineer, or building contractor who understands the requirements and limitations of the building and with whom

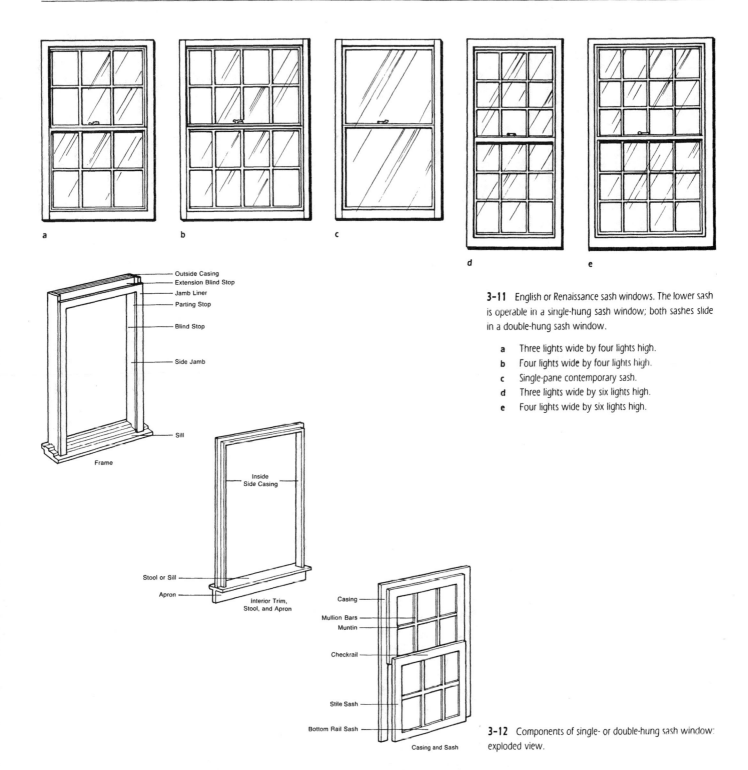

a   b   c   d   e

- Outside Casing
- Extension Blind Stop
- Jamb Liner
- Parting Stop
- Blind Stop
- Side Jamb
- Sill
- Frame

- Inside Side Casing
- Stool or Sill
- Apron
- Interior Trim, Stool, and Apron

- Casing
- Mullion Bars
- Muntin
- Checkrail
- Stile Sash
- Bottom Rail Sash
- Casing and Sash

3-11 English or Renaissance sash windows. The lower sash is operable in a single-hung sash window; both sashes slide in a double-hung sash window.

a   Three lights wide by four lights high.
b   Four lights wide by four lights high.
c   Single-pane contemporary sash.
d   Three lights wide by six lights high.
e   Four lights wide by six lights high.

3-12 Components of single- or double-hung sash window: exploded view.

the designer should feel free to collaborate on matters of design, aesthetics, and interior window treatment considerations.

Glass in a custom window may be glazed in other innovative fashions. One example is the geodesic dome (triangular panes fitted to create a dome) invented by architect Buckminster Fuller. Other examples include the many variations of greenhouse windows (which may incorporate some operable windows), window columns, custom skylights or ceiling glass, angled installations, and domes. Fixed glass also is used in the interior, between rooms in nonresidential situations where one-way glass is called for or where tinted glass deadens office sound without visual impairment.

3-13 Fixed glass in unusual shapes.

a   Pentagonal window.
b   Trapezoidal window.

a   b

Local glass companies will be glad to advise the designer on the types, limitations, and arrangements of fixed glass and perhaps to recommend a professional who could supervise installation.

As with sash windows the interior requirements or considerations for fixed glass will vary with each installation. Larger windows requiring treatment may need only light or glare control, whereas privacy and insulation or shading may be serious considerations in other windows. A major advantage to fixed glass is that the designer need not be concerned with operable portions, hardware, or ventilation when specifying a window covering.

Greenhouse Windows

The greenhouse window is similar to a bay or bow in that it protrudes from the building to catch sun. There are many sizes and shapes of greenhouse windows, and both fixed and operable glass may be used. Greenhouse windows may be vertical only, but most are vertical coupled with a curved or angled glass "roof." Figure 3–14 illustrates three sizes of greenhouse windows. Figure 3–14a shows the manufactured or prefabricated greenhouse window that is large enough for only two or three shelves of plants. It will bring additional light and cheerfulness to the interior and is popular for replacement windows in remodeling projects as well as in new construction. Figure 3–14b shows a barrel-curve greenhouse that also is manufactured and sold as a room-size "living" greenhouse. Figure 3–14c shows the cross section. Figure 3–14d illustrates a custom-constructed greenhouse complete with masonry wall and floor, which act as a "thermal mass" to absorb heat from the sun and then slowly release it into the interior at night. Deciduous trees block excess sunlight in summer; they allow it to penetrate in winter. Greenhouse windows are popular for adding a "gardening greenhouse," which can open off nearly any room in a residence. Greenhouse windows can create a pleasant solarium, sun room, Florida room, or Arizona room. They may enclose a swimming pool, patio, or other casual living area. They often are used in restaurants and commercial buildings.

The major concerns that face the designer where living greenhouse windows are concerned are twofold: winter insulation and summer shading. (See chapter 1 for information on window treatments that meet these two requirements.)

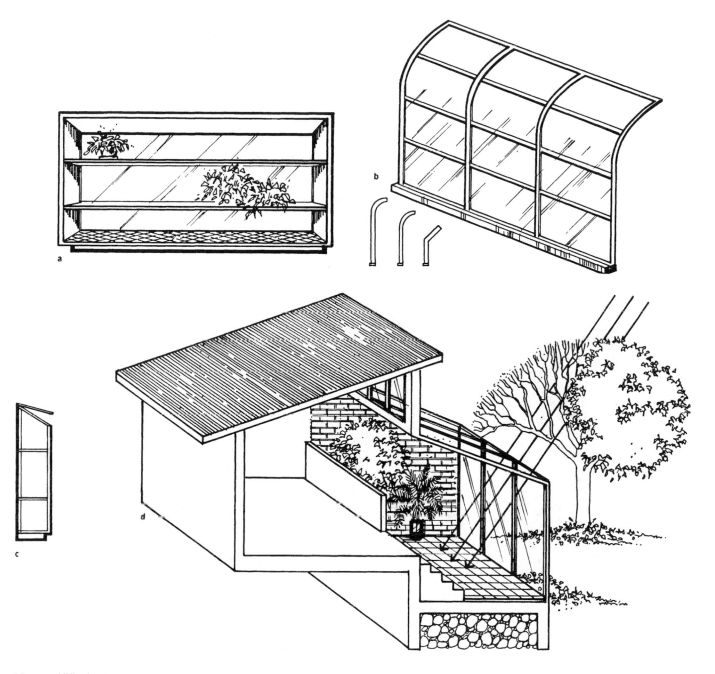

Hopper Windows

Hopper windows are also referred to as inverted awning windows. *Hopper* means a box, container, or opening that funnels or functions as a chute, like the old coal chutes. In this respect a hopper window allows ventilation fully as only a hinged or swinging window can. Hopper windows are used infrequently because they encumber interior window treatments and are safety hazards if someone were to bump or run into them. Window treatments should either stack off the glass or be mounted onto the window frame with a hold-down bracket (fig. 3–15).

Jalousie Windows

Jalousie (pronounced zhal'-e-zee or jal'-e-see), derived from the French word for "jealousy," is a set of louvered slats like small stacked awning

3-14 Greenhouse windows.

a   Window size greenhouse with metal grid shelves for plants and flow-through ventilation.

b   Factory-made room-addition-size greenhouse window. Vertical cross sections of curved and angled options are shown below.

c   Cross section of small greenhouse window with raised ventilating lid to allow excess heat to escape.

d   Custom-designed greenhouse with fixed glass set in straight and angled frames. Clerestory windows light the interior of the building. Brick wall, tile floor, and deciduous trees allow for passive solar heating.

3-15 Hopper window, opening inward. This is the opposite of the awning window, which opens outward.

3-16 The jalousie window is a series of glass louvers that funnel ventilation.

3-17 Round windows.

a Gothic trefoil tracery, seen in medieval cathedrals. These windows were originally set in stone with stained glass.

b Gothic quatrefoil tracery.

c Rounded keyhole window.

d Round porthole window with nautical motifs inscribed in the frame.

e Porthole window with divided lights.

f Octagonal porthole window with wood frame and symmetrical lights.

g Half-round window—keystone fanlight.

h Oval half-round—patterae, or elliptical fanlight. This one has a spider-web divider pattern.

windows. Jalousie "blinds" were used throughout Europe (particularly in France) by those who needed a hiding place where they could spy on lovers or scheming power seekers. As figure 3–16 illustrates, this window has ventilation control as its main asset. If the louvers project as far into the room as out to the exterior, they may interfere with treatments set very close to the glass. Select a treatment that will allow a flow-through breeze or that can be stacked off the glass to allow the window to function.

Round Windows

The circle has been favored in nearly every culture as a sacred symbol. Its absence of a beginning and an end is seen as a representation of eternity. This familiar shape naturally found its way into European buildings in the form of windows, possibly as a spin-off of the rounded arch that was so thoroughly imprinted in European history by ancient Roman conquest. Figure 3–17 illustrates several types of round windows. Americans often have installed round windows in their homes and public or commercial architecture. Their popularity may be partially due to the relief that a curved line gives to the unrelenting straight lines of most buildings.

During the Federal period, the bull's-eye mirror was introduced, a convex mirror gold-leafed and topped with an American eagle. This bull's-eye shape has become quite popular in modern architecture, with both convex and flat glass. Flat glass bull's-eye windows are ideal for art glass (fig. 3–17d).

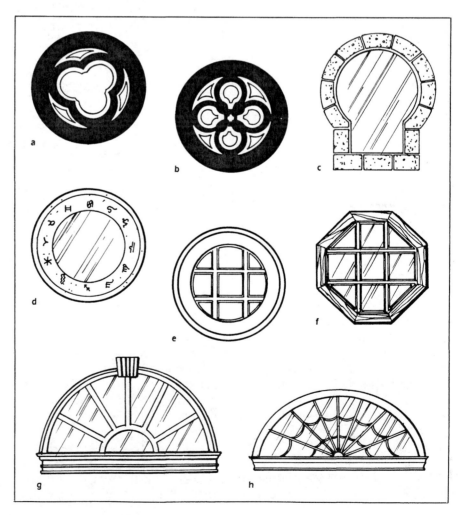

Nineteenth-century steamships brought Americans not only the port-hole, but every imaginable exotic window shape, as seen in the conglomeration of styles known to us as Victorian. Round windows still are utilized today, often as small windows in small rooms or over stairwell doors in the second story. Hexagonal windows, a six-sided variation of round, continue to be in favor as well.

The designer will need to evaluate whether a particular round window requires a treatment at all. If stained glass is set into the rounded frame, then a window treatment is not likely called for unless it is wanted for privacy at night.

Sidelights and Transoms

A sidelight is a narrow strip of glass next to a door. A pair of sidelights flank the door. A transom is glass that covers the area over the door. Transom glass is flat, and when it is arched, it is termed a fanlight or sunburst transom window. Figure 3–18 a–b shows some traditional arrangements of sidelights and flat transom glass, seen as Georgian and Federal fanlights and art glass sidelights. Figure 3–18c illustrates a

3-18 Sidelights and transoms.

a Traditional sidelight-and-transom arrangement.

b Double transom and raised wood panel with sidelights.

c Wide contemporary sidelights and oversize transom.

3-19 Skylight styles and installation types.

- **a** Rounded-dome skylight.
- **b** Rounded-dome skylight.
- **c** Flat-dome skylight.
- **d** Tilt-dome skylight.
- **e** Pyramid-dome skylight.
- **f** Barrel vault–dome skylight.
- **g** Ceiling-dome skylight installation.
- **h** Operable roof skylight.
- **i** Straight-shaft skylight installation.
- **j** Splayed-shaft skylight installation.
- **k** Ceiling-dome skylight installation.
- **l** Tilt-shaft skylight installation.

contemporary arrangement of clear sidelight and transom glass. Stained or art glass could be very effective in this situation.

Sidelights and transom lights (or lites) are designed to bring natural light into a building or home, specifically into the entry or reception area. As such they may or may not need any treatment.

Skylights

Skylights include pivoting and stationary types of glass, Plexiglas, or plastic placed in the roof and in the ceiling for added natural illumination and perhaps ventilation (fig. 3–19). The skylight admits light to otherwise dark interiors and provides privacy at the same time. Skylight domes are most often made from strong plastic; they may be clear or translucent. Domes may be stationary, cranked open by hand, or operated with a motorized device. Sizes vary from standard 14 by 14 inches to 70 by 140 inches.

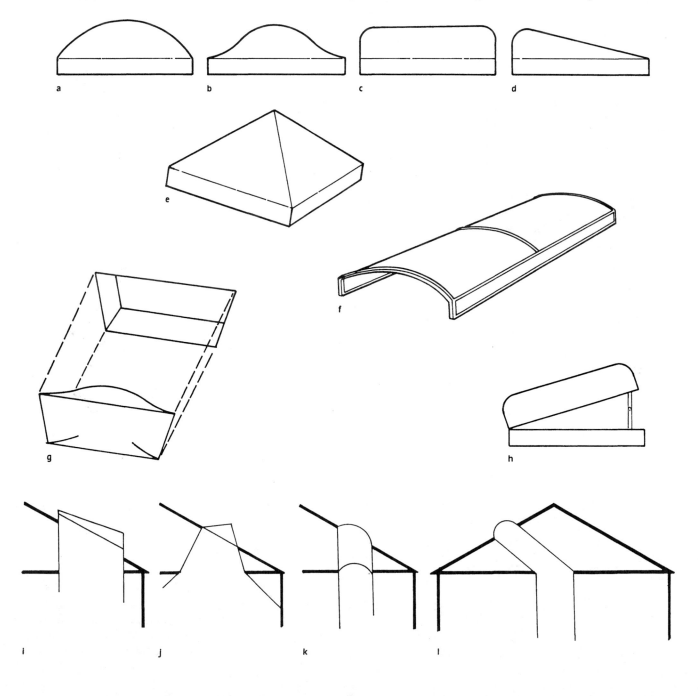

The wide variety of dimension and installation possibilities can be multiplied even further by grouping standard sizes. Exciting options are available that incorporate standard parts in custom installations. When skylights are enlarged in this way to cover a large roof area, they become dramatic architectural components. Larger units open to expose an entire room to the sky.

Rarely will the designer be called on to cover skylights. However, as in attic windows and greenhouse windows, some screening or insulation/shading may be necessary. The treatment will need to be anchored and set into a track or frame. Options would include miniblinds or pleated shades, insulated Roman shades, or another insulative fabric treatment set into tracks. Louvered shutters are available that may be automated to open and close to control direct sunlight. (See also the discussion of attic windows and greenhouse windows and suggestions on window coverage for skylights later in this chapter.)

Sliding Windows

A sliding window is similar to a sliding glass patio door and also to a sash window. Typically we think of sliding windows as aluminum- or metal-framed windows (although they also are made of wood) that move either vertically or horizontally within the window frame (fig. 3–20). Sliding windows became popular during the mid-twentieth century as large expanses of glass were used more often in modern architecture. Whereas sliding (or gliding) vertical windows may well be traditional sash windows with grids or true divider lights, horizontal sliders may have three horizontal sashes. In a two-sash unit, either or both sashes may operate; in a three-sash unit, two sashes may operate, with the center glass fixed. One advantage of the horizontal slider is that there is no projection inward or outward. Another is that it may be placed high for privacy and maximum light penetration. A disadvantage is that only part of the window space may be opened for ventilation.

The quality of vertical and horizontal sliding units varies with the manufacturer. Excellent-quality sliders will be made of vinyl- or metal-clad wood or of strong, tightly fitting aluminum; they operate smoothly and easily. An extrusion between the inner and outer aluminum frames prevents heat loss or gain by conduction in good-quality frames (fig. 3–21). Metal sliding window frames may be colored white or bronze, or the natural aluminum color may be retained.

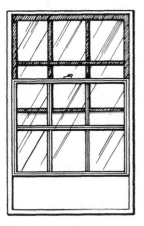

a

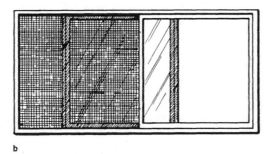

b

3-20 Sliding sash windows.

a Vertically sliding sash window. Grids are optional.

b Horizontally sliding, or gliding, window. Screen is shown behind open left sash.

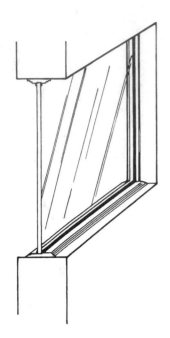

3-21 Extrusion between inner and outer aluminum frames prevents heat loss by conduction.

Sliding windows are relatively free of window treatment problems. The two main considerations are that, since they are meant to operate, the treatment must allow access to the sliding panel; and, since they are ventilating, the treatment should not obstruct breezes. Another potential consideration is that older or "cheaper" sliders may fit poorly or be leaky, or, in the case of wood, they may have begun to rot. The designer may suggest window replacement, storm windows, or an insulative treatment, depending on the seriousness of the energy loss and the resulting discomfort to the occupants of the interior space.

CUSTOM AND STANDARD GLAZING

Generally speaking there are two types of windows: fixed, and operable or ventilating. Fixed glass includes the above categories of angled glass. Ventilating windows operate either by swinging (as with casement, attic, awning, hopper, basement, or jalousie windows, or French patio doors) or by sliding (as with sash or horizontal windows, vertical sliders, or sliding glass patio doors).

Custom glazing means that the shape or size of the window is unusual and is constructed as a one-of-a-kind installation. While all windows are custom-made to order, very unusual sizes or shapes can be quite costly, as is any nonstandard building component. However, a custom look is readily obtainable through the combination of standard window sizes and types. Standard sizes are those that have even dimensions, such as 3 feet by 5 feet or 4 feet 6 inches by 6 feet.

New or replacement windows may have certain options that will enhance ease of maintenance, convenience of operation, or safety. Some of these window options are tempered glass; one-way glass; tinted, bronzed, or reflective glass; low-emission glass; double or triple glazing; winter or summer storm windows; safety locks; removable or roller screens; self-closers on patio doors; snap-in traditional grids or grids between the layers of plate glass; and various types of hardware.

Figure 3–22 illustrates some combinations of fixed and operable glass to create a custom look with standard sizes. Figure 3–22a shows a large fixed glass with one smaller fixed window beneath and two ventilating windows, one on each side. The small ventilating windows may slide or swing and offer ventilation out of the line of vision and low in the room, where it is desirable. Figure 3–22b shows a smaller version of the first window combination. Here, one large fixed glass tops horizontal sliders. Figure 3–22c illustrates twin single- or double-hung sash windows. Snap-in grids, such as those seen in figure 3–9, give this a traditional look. Figure 3–22d shows an enlarged version with a central fixed window flanked by matching sash windows.

Fixed, sliding, or awning windows create a ranch-strip window; placed very high, they form a clerestory window arrangement (fig. 3–22e). A series of these windows makes a "ribbon" of glass.

Figure 3–22f illustrates stacked awning windows. The top sash may be stationary glass; with snap-in grids the look could resemble traditional sash windows.

A casement window is seen on each side of the fixed window in figure 3–22g, and a variation of the casement, the awning window, is placed in the center of an arrangement of stationary panes in figure 3–22h. Figure 3–22i illustrates a hopper window and a basement window.

Figure 3–22j is an arrangement of glass surrounding a rim (single patio) door. Single-pane sidelights and door are topped with matching transom plain glass for a contemporary setting. Art glass could be placed here to add design to the window.

Figure 3–22k shows a stacked-glass combination for a two-story open area. Two stationary rim doors flank a single patio (swinging) rim door, and the trio is matched vertically with a fixed cathedral window arrangement. Figure 3–22l is a variation of this theme: a fixed-glass window below a custom-angled glass window. Window treatments for this often are installed from the horizontal divider between the upper and lower windows.

There is an almost limitless combination of windows available today for new and remodeled architecture, and these represent a cross section of styles. The designer who is sensitive to the aesthetic appeal of windows, as well as to the considerations for using, enjoying, and treating each, will be better equipped to provide expertise in selecting appropriate window coverings in every individual situation.

HOW MUCH COVERAGE IS RIGHT?

Regardless of the type of window, before you treat it, a decision must be made about the amount of coverage. Window treatments can be used to cover windows in a number of different ways, from scant coverage that includes the window only to treatments that cover much or all of the surrounding wall space. Whereas the majority of hard, or factory-made, window coverings (shades, blinds, shutters) are specified to cover only the area of the window, fabric treatments have the ability to alter the apparent size of the window because of the variety of styling possible (fig. 3–23). This means that the designer must make certain decisions before he or she figures fabric yardage. Often the client will be a part of this decision process because it affects the amount of yardage used and therefore the cost of the entire treatment. The designer should evaluate the aesthetic and practical needs of the window, then counsel the client concerning preferences for extending the treatment beyond the window's width, height, or length. In addition the fullness or amount of fabric used within the set dimensions may be scant or generous, and each approach has distinct advantages and disadvantages. Coverage options are listed below.

Widthwise, window treatment options are to cover:

- The window only, ending inside the frame or at the frame edge.

- Just slightly beyond the window on each side.

- Enough of the wall to stack off. (*Stackoff* is the wall-space area required for opened draperies, blinds, shades, and so on; *partial stackoff* means that a portion of the treatment is on the wall and a portion is on the window, where some of the glass is always covered. This option saves money since the required yardage is less than for treatments that stack off the glass completely.)

- Enough of the wall to clear the glass completely (see chapter 6 for stackoff or stackback charts and calculation methods).

- Enough of the wall to stack off the glass completely when the draperies (or other treatment) are opened. This allows full light and view from the window and can fully expose surrounding architectural detail, such as moldings. It also will probably involve more yardage and expense. If a double-hung (layered) treatment is stacked off completely, the underdrapery or undersheer does not need to cover

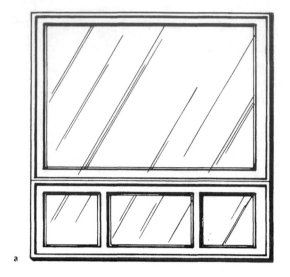

a

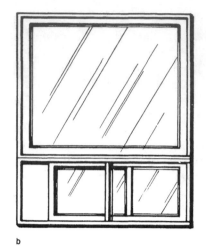

b

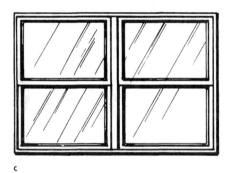

c

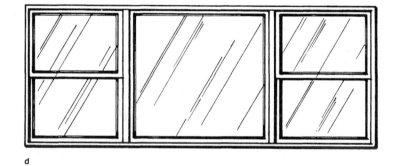

d

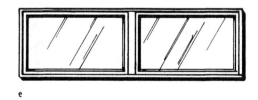

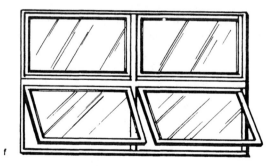

e

f

g

h

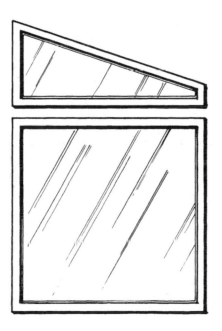

3-22 Combining fixed and ventilating windows using custom sizes and standard or stock windows.

a   Fixed glass with one fixed and two ventilating windows below.

b   Fixed glass with ventilating sliders stacked below.

c   A twin set of single- or double-hung sash windows.

d   Twin sash windows flanking a square fixed-glass window.

e   Fixed or awning windows in a strip, or ranch strip. If placed high, they form a clerestory window.

f   Awning windows below fixed glass or other awning windows.

g   Casement pair flanking fixed glass.

h   Stationary panes with one center awning window for ventilation.

i   Hopper (in-swinging awning) window below fixed glass (*left*). Basement (in-swinging) window below fixed glass (*right*).

j   A glass door arrangement: rim (single patio) hinged door with glass sidelights and transom lights above.

k   French patio (rim) door trio topped by a custom A-frame, or cathedral, window arrangement.

l   Fixed glass below a custom-angled window.

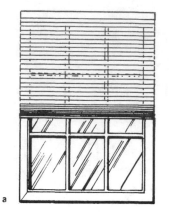
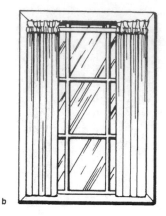

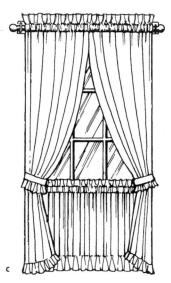

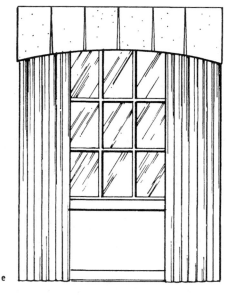

3-23 Altering the visual dimensions of the window.

a Maintaining the actual size of the window with mini-blinds.

b Making the window appear smaller with curtains inside the frame.

c Making the window appear larger with a café curtain below.

d Making the window appear higher with a valance to the ceiling.

e Making the window appear wider with draperies stacked off. The valance spans the distance.

f Making two windows appear as one.

the wall but may end 4 to 7 inches beyond the frame. This will save about 3 yards of fabric for every 20 inches of stackback. The installer should be instructed to connect the last drapery hook to the end bracket with a cord, (assuming a double traverse rod is in use) so that the side edge of the underdrapery is not pulled into the window when it is drawn closed. This technique will work if the overdrapery fabric is opaque.

- Wall-to-wall, where the window and all surrounding wall space to the corner of the room are covered. The advantage here is the possibility of a wider look, more visual softness through more fabric, more sound control, and a more sumptuous appearance. It also can eliminate small, awkward, or unequal sections of undraped wall, giving greater continuity to the flow of fabric and perhaps unifying the furnishings of the interior.

- More on one side than on the other. This may be the case when the window is off-centered on the wall and where the unbalanced wall space can benefit by being less noticeable.

Heightwise the treatment may:

- End inside the window frame, where stacking takes place on the glass. This always is the case in an inside-mount treatment, which leaves the edges or frame of the window fully exposed at all times.

- End on the window frame where one exists.

- Extend the standard 4 inches above the window. This will allow the heading of a drapery to be above the window line. Otherwise the incoming light would cause the heading to be an obvious and unnecessary line in the treatment.

- Extend above the window from 4 to 12 or more inches above the window. This will have application where the ceiling is unusually high (9 to 14 feet) and where taking the treatment all the way to the ceiling would create an awkward proportion. Four to 12 inches above also is a good choice for placing draperies installed on wood or metal "decorator" rods, because decorator rods should not be placed next to the ceiling. They look much better just above the window.

- Be installed next to the ceiling. A 1/2-inch clearance is standard to avoid rubbing the headings against the ceiling. This would wear out the fabric prematurely.

- End just above the window, and a top treatment might be installed to cover the space above the window and possibly to the ceiling. This will actually save yardage, and it also will make it much easier to remove and rehang draperies and to repair or replace the traverse rod.

Lengthwise, the options for window coverings are to extend fabric:

- Within the window frame, ending at the sill.

- To the bottom of the frame or molding.

- To the bottom of the apron (the flat piece of wood below the windowsill).

- Four inches below the bottom of the window. (This takes the line of the hems out of the light of the window and generally matches the hemline with the sill.)

- To a point just above baseboard heaters. Fabric should not be allowed to hang close to a heat source that could ignite it. Remember that cellulosic fibers (cotton, linen, rayon, and acetate) will be far more combustible than wool or synthetic fibers (acrylic, polyester, olefin, and saran). Modacrylic is inherently flame resistant.

- To the floor. Allow a ½-inch clearance so that the fabric will not rub against the floor. Check the sample to see whether the fabric will be dimensionally stable (not subject to elongation, stretching, shrinking, or hiking). Where forced-air heating vents are placed under the window, suggest to the client that clear plastic deflectors be used to direct the air away from the fabric and into the room. Forced air carries dust and impurities, which may soil, stain, or destroy the fabric.

- Onto the floor, where it is pooled or puddled. Historically, fabrics that flowed onto the floor signified the wealth of the owner, particularly when silk or very fine damask or brocade was used. Today, nearly any fabric can pool onto the floor. The caution would be that it *is* a historically formal treatment, and the use of casual or printed fabrics in this manner may be aesthetically questionable.

Scant Coverage

The advantages to scant coverage are that there is less cost involved in fabric and labor; a shorter, less expensive rod will be needed; and the cost of installation will be reduced. It creates a simple, structural treatment, a quaint provincial look that may be desirable in some settings. Examples include the French café curtain and the New England tab curtain. These and other similar treatments suggest a simple, uncluttered theme with just enough fabric at the window to soften the lines of the architecture. The client also may prefer a frank exposure of the surrounding architecture, which can be accomplished with a simple Roman shade, for example, or with a curtain shirred onto a plain curtain rod. This type of treatment will become a structural part of the background elements.

Generous Coverage

Greater coverage can mean more fullness in the fabric hung at the window. The pleats are deeper—more fabric is tucked into each fold. This provides a richer, more "custom" or "designer" look to the drapery fabric, which usually leads to greater customer satisfaction. More depth to the fabric also lends a quieter feeling to the interior, as it muffles noise. Greater coverage also means more fabric used beyond the window frame. When the drapery is higher, wider, or longer, or when top treatments are added to the scheme, the fabric lends security, visual and acoustical softness, texture, color, and perhaps pattern that can give character, charm, or loveliness to the interior. Other ways to increase the rich effect of more fabric include making deeper hems and headings and layering the fabric with privacy draperies, sheers, and overdraperies that are perhaps tied back. Draperies can be flowed, puddled, or pooled onto the floor, which gives a generous effect. Top treatments of fabric—valances, pelmets, and upholstered cornices or lambrequins—also are effective means of bringing more textile into the interior.

GUIDELINES TO WINDOW MEASURING

Once the decision is made as to how much window should be covered and how much fullness is desired or needed, the measurements can be taken (fig. 3–24). Many designers take measurements with great skill and accuracy. Others prefer to take measurements, then include in the price a fee that pays for the installer or a workroom representative to confirm them. This also makes the workroom or installer, not the designer, liable for any measuring errors.

The following guidelines are for measuring apply to a hard, factory-made treatment; a custom fabric treatment; or a combination of both.

- If possible, mount any hardware before taking measurements. New hardware can replace old hardware in the same position on the wall if the new treatment does not require different stackback. New hardware will be installed according to the measurements of the draperies.

- A steel retractable tape measure at least 10 feet long is essential. A cloth tape measure can stretch, giving inaccurate measurements. Rulers or yardsticks have to be moved along and the new reading added to the previous reading, thus paving the way for errors.

- When measuring always record a total of inches, not feet plus inches. This will eliminate some errors.

- Even if all the windows look the same or are specified to be the same size, measure each one individually. Slight variations in measurements can be critical, particularly for inside-mount (inside the frame) treatments, such as miniblinds, shutters, and pleated fabric shades.

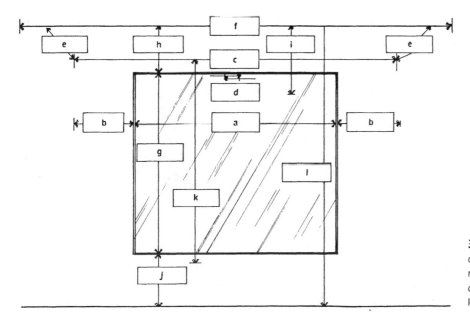

3-24 Diagram for standard window measurements: Window width (A); stackoff (B); rod width (C); overlap width (D); return depth (E); finished width (F); window length (G); window to ceiling (H); valance length (I); sill to floor (J); finished length (K); ceiling-to-floor finished length (L).

- Write down the measurements for each window as it is measured, and write down *each* measurement as you read it. When two or more measurements are written down at once it is too easy to reverse the numbers. For example, if a window measures 42 by 36, it might be written down as 46 by 32, which spells disaster. When two windows are measured before any record is made, then it is possible that *two* treatments will be the wrong size. Treatments that have to be altered or taken apart and resewn because of errors in recording can possibly cost the design firm all the profit of the job. Errors not only absorb the profit but also destroy the designer's credibility.

- Write down the width first, then the length, and do this with absolute consistency. It is too easy to reverse the numbers, unless you get into the habit of always doing it the same way.

- When measuring a width that is wider than one's armspan, someone else should hold the beginning end of the tape while the measurer measures and reads increments. Be certain that the tape is level.

- Write clearly and legibly in a notebook, not on a scrap of paper, which can easily be lost or misplaced.

- The date, client's name or job number, and location should be recorded. Any special considerations, such as angled ceilings, uneven floors, or out-of-square windows, should be jotted down.

- Proper identification of each window is important. In office buildings, each room should be assigned a number, or the orientation or location should be carefully noted. (For example, "first floor, southwest office.") In a residential setting the room and the window within that room should accompany the measurement in the notebook. An example might be, "living room, fireplace wall, north-side window." This will be especially helpful when many windows are covered with the same treatment. A drapery installer, for example, will be grateful if he can quickly pinpoint which draperies are to be installed in which room, and at which window. Treatments that are installed in the wrong place can cause a client to lose confidence in the designer rather than in the installer.

- The designer should consider contracting the installer or workroom personnel to remeasure before the goods are constructed. It might be worth the peace of mind to know that there is another responsible party involved.

- If carpeting is to be installed, a sample of the new carpet thickness and pad thickness should be measured and the measurement deducted from the overall measurement. When transferring the information to the worksheet, it should be noted whether the deduction *has* or *has not* been made.

- Mechanical features such as light switches and electrical outlets, door knobs, and heat registers should be noted. The treatment should not touch or cover any of these.

- Everything that might affect the construction, installation, and operation of the treatment should be measured and entered into the notebook. This includes window and pertinent measurements: stackoff on each side, ceiling to floor, windowsill to floor, ceiling to window top, window to light switch, outlet, and baseboard heater or register. Included also should be the inches of projection from the wall (drapery return) for each layer, the inches for overlap, and such factors as whether or not one panel must be wider than the other, or if the panel is to be a one-way draw. While it is true that some measurements are not actually needed, it is wise to be thorough, since more often than not a measurement is forgotten that *was* needed. It is a poor use of valuable time to return to an interior just to take one measurement that was overlooked. This book contains sample forms that can serve as checklists for taking measurements (see chapter 6).

- Off-center windows that are to be draped from one corner of the room to the other (wall-to-wall) need uneven pairs ordered as separate panels; an even pair in this case will not meet in the center of the window. It should be clearly recorded which panel is the left (with a left-return measurement) and which is the right (with a right-return measurement).

- When measuring operable windows that swing or slide open, the drapery or other treatment must clear the glass to allow the windows to open and close.

- When measuring the window and adding in the stackoff, the window size must be clearly indicated and the width of the stackback noted separately. If the stackback is inadvertently added in twice, both the treatment and the cost will be overscaled.

- When you record the measurements, the flat measurements should be written, then the stackback, overlaps and returns, and allowances and clearances accounted for. "Deduction not taken," or "take deduction" should be entered. Perhaps an abbreviation system can be worked out, such as "ded. n. tak." or "tak ded." Consistency is important, however. It is best to *always* take and write down flat measurements, rather than wonder later whether you have taken the appropriate deductions.

MEASURING AND TREATING SPECIFIC WINDOWS

In addition to the general measuring tips listed above, specific windows require more information. Although there is nearly an unlimited variety of decorating styles, there is a limited number of standard areas of coverage that apply to each style of window. Coverage and measuring tips for the types of windows found earlier in this chapter are listed here, along with recommendations for window treatments.

Arched Window Treatments

To measure an arched window, determine the width of the arch and the height at the center of the arch, as seen in figure 3–25a. A template or actual-size paper pattern also is helpful for accuracy.

Arched windows or fanlight/sunburst transoms or windows are handsome architectural elements. As such they often are left uncovered. When the choice is made to cover a rounded window, the treatment should follow the line of the arch. Options include fan-shaped shirred fabric that is sheer or semisheer installed on bendable custom rodding (with or without a ruffled edge) (fig. 3–25b).

3-25 Arched windows.

a Measuring width (A) and length (B).

b Shirred fabric or pleated shade.

c Pleated drapery in an arched window.

d Shaped pelmet with tiebacks—a formal treatment.

e Bishop's sleeve or tear-drop (poufed) tieback curtains with shirred or smocked heading.

f Wood shutters in fanlight shape below arch.

g Swag and cascade showing an option of fringe and tiebacks or no fringe and no drapery beneath.

h Miniblind in arch.

Pleated draperies can be made to follow the line of the arch as well; however, when the draperies are opened, the hemline will fall onto the floor progressively because the fabric is longer in the center (fig. 3–25c).

Pelmets, valances, and upholstered cornices also may fit into the arch. The bottom edge can be curved or straight, or designed to fit the architecture or furnishings in the room. (Refer to chapter 4 for styles of top treatments. These can be adapted to fit arched windows.) Keep in mind that the glass will be permanently covered when a top treatment is installed in an arch. However, the graceful curve of the arch is preserved (fig. 3–25d).

Swags and cascades make lovely choices for very formal arched windows. The swags usually are best proportioned when they overlap at the top, giving a slightly asymmetrical look to the arch. When cascades are placed underneath the festoons, the shape of the arch is better emphasized than if the cascades are placed on top of the swags. The cascades could be as long as desired, or tied-back draperies could be placed beneath the top treatment (fig. 3–25g).

Another beautiful treatment is the bishop's sleeve, or tear-drop, drapery, which is tied into several poufs. This treatment can have a variety of headings—pleated, shirred, or smocked, for example. Lengthwise this treatment may puddle onto the floor (fig. 3–25e).

Several factory-made treatments are lovely for arched windows. Louvered wooden shutters can be custom-fitted to arches (fig. 3–25f). The louvers can be stationary or movable. This is a rich and handsome treatment, satisfactory for residential and nonresidential design. Pleated shades also are excellent on arched windows because the lightweight polyester fabric naturally lends itself to a half-round shape (see fig. 3–25b). Woven woods, vertical louvers, and miniblinds all can be custom-fitted to arched windows as well (fig. 3–25h). Of these, the vertical louvers are likely to be operable, while woven woods and horizontal blinds will probably be stationary installations.

Keep in mind that treatments for arched windows are more costly to construct or fabricate than those for straight-top windows.

Attic Window Treatments

Measurements for attic windows are fairly simple, requiring just the width and length of the window or the frame. If the treatment is to slide off the window to one side, both sides, or above or below the glass, then check at this point to be certain there is adequate wall space for stacking or sliding (fig. 3–26a).

Window treatments for attic windows are restricted to those that can be attached to the angled plane. Also, the clean, contemporary lines of attic windows lend themselves to simple, handsome, structural treatments. These treatments are sliding shutters (fig. 3–26b); screens—shoji or lattice, for example (fig. 3–26c); or fabric panels. Other suitable treatments include miniblinds with hold-down brackets or set in a track system, pleated shades in a track (fig. 3–26d), Roman or pouf fabric shades, or woven-wood Roman shades in a track system (fig 3–26e). Miniblinds will be a good choice where light control and frequent adjustments are desirable; pleated shades will keep excess heat buildup under control and will provide some winter window insulation as well. Roman shades can add decorative or structural fabric to the room, a plus where fabric softness will be a benefit. Fabric shades also can be specified to be insulative and installed on a sealed track, a decisive factor when the attic space is too cold in the winter or too hot in the summer because of the glass area.

Awning Window Treatments

Measuring awning windows requires only width and length measurements, plus any stackoff area needed around the glass (fig. 3–27a). As noted, awning windows are top-hinged casement windows that swing out. Because the glass is exposed to the outside, the treatment should *not* be mounted inside the sash but on the window frame or on the wall, and it should be able to clear the glass area so as not to obstruct ventilation.

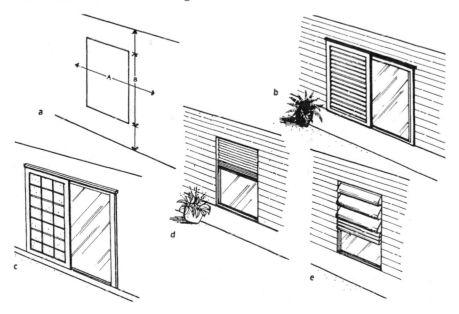

3-26   Attic windows.

    a   Measurements: width (A) and length (B).
    b   Sliding shutter with nonmovable louvers.
    c   Shoji screen on track.
    d   Pleated shade installed on track.
    e   Soft, folded Roman shade installed on track. Shade could be lined or interlined and insulative.

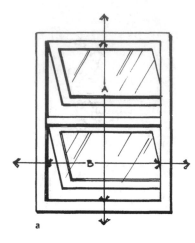

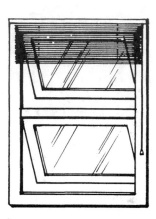

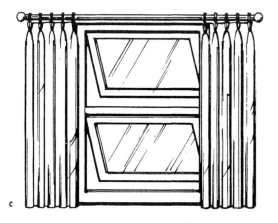

3-27 *Stacked awning windows.*

a *Measurements: length (A) and width (B).*

b *Miniblind stacked above the window. The treatment could also be a pleated shade, a custom fabric shade, a woven-wood shade, or a roller shade, any of which could be topped with a valance.*

c *Pleated draperies stacked to one side on a contemporary decorator rod.*

Good choices would be miniblinds that stack above the window (fig. 3–27b), shutters that can swing off for access to the hardware, roller and fabric shades that stack to the top of or above the frame, vertical louvers that stack to the side of the glass, and draperies that can stack off the glass (fig. 3–27c). Where ease in operating the window is not a consideration, then any of the treatments seen in figure 3–38, sash windows, will be good possibilities for awning windows.

Basement Window Treatments

As noted, basement windows are bottom-hinged casement windows that swing inward, allowing air currents to enter at the top of the room. The measurements will be taken either from the sash (frame that holds the glass) or above and wider than the treatment so the covering can stack off completely with no obstruction by the hardware to opening the window (fig. 3–28a).

Treatments that can be secured onto the casement trim are good choices—such as curtains shirred top and bottom (fig. 3–28b) or miniblinds with hold-down brackets (fig. 3–28c). Roller shades also could be affixed to the casement trim (sash) at the top and secured with a hook onto the finger pull at the bottom (fig. 3–28d). Soft treatments that can stack to the side will work as long as there is room above the window to mount the rod (fig. 3–28e). Sometimes basement windows are mounted so near the ceiling that no room exists above them to mount hardware.

Bay and Bow Window Treatments

Bay and bow windows are not as difficult to measure as it often seems. After a decision is made as to how to drape or treat the windows, then

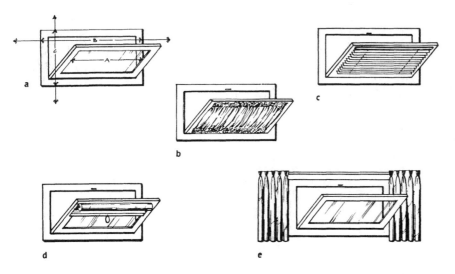

3-28 Basement windows.

a Measurements: sash width (A) and frame or rod width (B) with stackoff length (C).

b Curtain shirred on top and bottom and affixed to sash frame.

c Miniblind with hold-down bracket installed on sash frame.

d Roller shade installed on sash frame.

e Draperies on conventional traverse rod stacked off the glass and mounted above the window.

measurements should include the width and length of drapery for each window and the depth and overall opening size. Angles for each bend are needed to install custom rodding and for double-checking calculations by the workroom for draperies or top treatments, such as cornice boards that continue around the window. Figure 3–29a indicates measurements needed for bay windows, which include the width of each window; the various lengths for the selected treatment; and, if draperies are selected, the angles for use in ordering custom rodding (measure with a protractor). Figure 3–29a also indicates options (bird's-eye view) of stacking draperies: (I) shows the side windows with a one-way draw and a center-meet pair in the middle (three rods, one each of a close-right and close-left one-way rod and one conventional traverse rod); (J) has three sets of center-meet draperies (three separate conventional traverse rods); (K) shows custom rods that bend around the angle and meet in the center ((I), (J), and (K) will have drapery fabric stacked permanently onto the window, even when the draperies are opened); and (L) shows custom rods that stack the drapery onto the wall and traverse around two bends on each side to close over the glass.

Figure 3–29b illustrates a drapery that stacks off as in figure 3–29a(L) and has a fabric valance that follows around the glass to cover the rod. The glass itself could be covered with shutters, shades, blinds, screens, or shirred semisheer fabric.

Traditionally, tied-back curtains (Priscilla or country curtains) are a residential favorite (fig. 3–29c). Sheer and semisheer Priscilla curtains are charming for casual or cottage settings.

Fabric shades, such as Roman shades, also work nicely in bay or bow window arrangements, and the look can be quite different, as seen in the comparison of these two styles of shades in figure 3–29 d–e. Café curtains, shirred draperies, and valances are all good choices and can be installed on bendable curtain rods.

Bay or bow window sections may be treated separately with miniblinds, pleated or roller shades, shutters (fig. 3–29f), woven woods, or lattice screens. Using hard treatments alone at the window gives a clean, contemporary look to the interior; such unencumbered windows allow light for plants and people, and the treatments permit the user to control the direction of light or to cover the window for privacy. Hard treatments can be layered over with a valance that spans the distance or is hung straight across the opening. Softening also can be achieved, with side panels installed on the wall or hourglass tiebacks, as in figure 3–29c. Café curtains

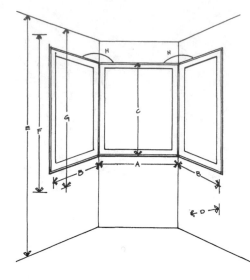

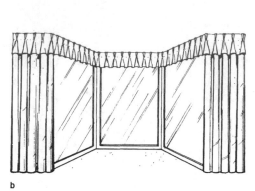

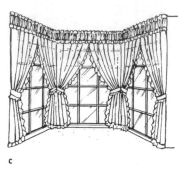

b

c

a

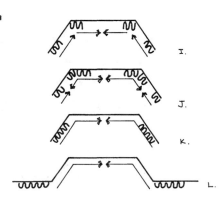

e

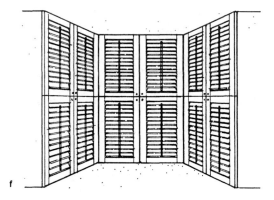

f

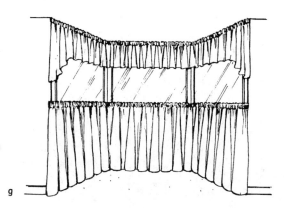

g

3-29 Bay or bow windows.

a   Measurements: window widths (A and B); window length (C); projection depth (D); ceiling to floor (E); 4 inches above to 4 inches below (F); ceiling to 4 inches below (G); angles of each bend (H); conventional traverse drapery options (center draw on middle window, or one-way draw on each side window) (I); center-draw option on each window (J); center draw on custom bendable traverse rodding (K); center draw extended to wall beyond window to stack off glass (L).

b   Continuous valance with draperies stacked on the wall. (See fig. 3-29a(L).)

c   Cottage Priscilla curtains of a semisheer fabric. They would require an undertreatment, such as a shutter, shade, or blind, for privacy.

d   Custom Roman shades.

e   Simple pouf shades with a tailored, box-pleated heading. This treatment could be made more decorative with ruffles and shirred headings.

f   Three sets of double-hung movable louvered shutters. Shutters take up little room and provide both light control and privacy.

g   Shirred café curtains with shirred valance ending in a soft cascade. A shade or shutter beneath the valance could be drawn for nighttime privacy.

are appropriate in informal settings where privacy is needed at eye level when the occupant is in a seated position, and where light is desired from above (fig. 3–29g).

Complete privacy could be obtained by installing roller, pleated, or woven-wood shades or miniblinds beneath the shirred valance. Where a bay or bow includes a window seat, it is charming to make the seat fabric match or coordinate with the window treatment. (See also chapter 8.)

Casement Window Treatments

Side-hinged casements are operable windows that allow very good ventilation because they can fully open. A casement window that is frequently opened and closed needs a treatment that will not restrict operation. The crank or lever hardware also must be accessible. Figure 3–30a indicates the necessary measurements for casement windows.

Proven options include the shirred curtain attached to the frame at the top and bottom of the window, which allows the frame to swing without interference from the fabric (fig. 3–30b). The disadvantage of this treatment is that the fabric cannot be drawn off the glass. Typical fabrics used are sheers and semisheers in fine weaves. Crane rods swing on an arm or a crane, allowing a fabric to cover the glass only but providing the option of exposing the glass for light or view (see fig. 3–35e). A crane-rod treatment is pleated or shirred on the top only.

Stacking treatments, such as fabric shades and miniblinds, may be mounted on the frame, within the casing (fig. 3–30c), or above the window.

3-30 Casement windows.

a   Measurements: single casement width (A); double casement width (B); stackoff width (C); window-frame mount measurement (D); 4 inches above to 4 inches below (E); ceiling to 4 inches below (F); 4 inches above to floor (G); ceiling to floor (H); sill to floor (I).

b   Semisheer fabric shirred onto casement "sash" at top and bottom.

c   Miniblind spanning both windows.

d   Scalloped curtains hooked to wood rings for a country, hand-draw treatment.

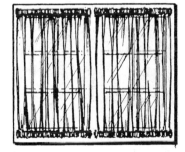

b

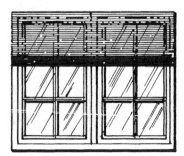

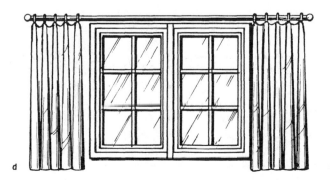

a

d

Pleated draperies or vertical louvers should ideally stack off to the side as fully as possible, and top treatments should cover only the window frame and allow as much of the glass as possible to be exposed. Keeping the treatment off the glass encourages ventilation and allows free access to operating the window. Also, because casement windows typically are not large, keeping the treatments off the glass will visually increase the size of the window and permit all possible natural light to enter the room. Draperies and curtains also may be mounted on the wall outside the window frame (fig. 3–30d) and tied back, with an additional shade or blind set inside the casing or on the frame for nighttime privacy. (See also figure 3–35 for French casement door treatments that are appropriate selections for casement windows.)

Cathedral and Angled Window Treatments

Angled windows—such as those in triangular, pentazoidal, and trapezoidal shapes—are fixed-glass windows that usually are set high in the wall and follow the plane of slanted ceilings; they are also called cathedral windows. Angled windows often are left undraped because of the expense in making custom soft and hard treatments to cover them and because their high placement lessens the need for privacy. To measure angled, triangular, pentazoidal, and trapezoidal windows, supply inches for each side, degree of each angle, a sketch, and, if possible, a paper template for the workroom's or manufacturer's use. If the treatment will need operation controls, also furnish the sill height (floor to bottom of window) (fig. 3–31 a–b).

Pleated and shirred draperies can be constructed with angled headings (fig. 3–31c). Shutters can be custom-constructed to fit slanted and cathedral windows and can be made fully operable or movable (fig. 3–31d). Pleated

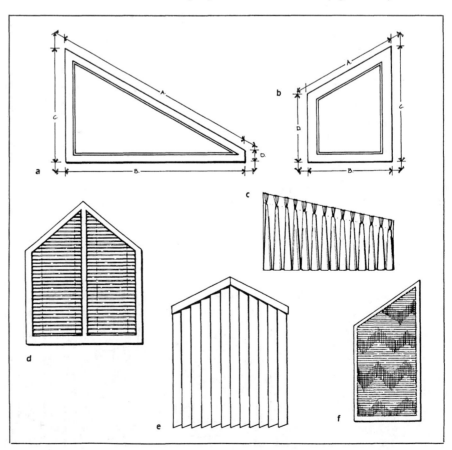

3-31 Angled windows.

a Measurements: angled window width (A); bottom window width at sill (B); long-side height plus 4 inches above and below (C); short-side height plus 4 inches above and below (D).

b Measurements for cathedral windows. (See fig. 3-31a for description.)

c Drapery pleated on an angle.

d Miniblinds or shutters. This also could be a pleated fabric shade.

e Vertical-louver blinds (two one-way-draw blinds).

f Woven-wood shade.

shades can be made to draw open in the rectangular area below the angle, and the vertical louver blind is fully operable in an angled window (fig. 3–31e). Pleated shades can be drawn open to the lower end of the headrail, as can some angled woven woods. Woven woods also make handsome permanent light-filtering or room-darkening coverings (fig. 3–31f).

Keep in mind that angled treatments are specialty items that require a surcharge that can be up to hundreds of dollars beyond the cost of a rectangular shade or blind of the same dimensions.

Clerestory and Ranch-Strip Window Treatments

Clerestory (fixed-glass, sliding, or awning) windows and ranch-strip (horizontal sliding) windows are set high in the wall for light and privacy. Clerestory windows are ribbons of glass set in very tall walls above eye level, and are installed for light (a sort of vertical skylight). Ranch-strip windows are ribbons of glass at eye level, typically seen in residential bedrooms. Figure 3–32a illustrates the measurements required for clerestory and ranch-strip window treatments.

There is ample space beneath a clerestory or ranch-strip window for furniture. Draperies may go just beyond the glass (4 inches above and below), stacking off onto the wall as needed or desired. Generally a center-draw drapery is best, since fabric stacked off on one side creates an awkward proportion of fabric-to-wall area. In fact, if the drapery is to stack off completely, then the rod has to be quite long, and the ribbon becomes even more pronounced, making awkward proportions, as seen in figure 3–32b.

If a top treatment is desired, the area from ceiling to glass should be measured. The window also may be draped to the floor and possibly from the ceiling. However, this treatment creates a disproportionate amount of fabric in relationship to the window area and may look encumbered.

Shutters, miniblinds, vertical-louver blinds, and pleated and woven-wood shades are all good choices for ranch-strip windows. Since these windows are rather frank and structural, they do not readily lend themselves to fancy treatments. Figure 3–32c shows a valance extended along the window, under which are three separate woven-wood or fabric shades (in this case, to match the three window panes). Figure 3–32d shows sleek vertical louvers at the window. In very high installations the controls will need to be ordered long enough to reach from a standing position.

The typical size of clerestory and ranch-strip windows is 6 feet wide by 2½ to 3 feet high. They are not easy to treat; hence the treatment should always be sketched and visualized in proportion to empty or furnished wall space and in scale with the size of the window and room.

Corner Window Arrangement Treatments

Windows placed in the corner of a room are some of the most challenging to treat. The drapery treatment most commonly and effectively used is a one-way draw on each side, which is closed toward the corner. However, this leaves the corner devoid of fabric; a two-way draw on each or on one window will solve that problem. If the window is tightly pushed into the corner, then the two-way draws may leave some stackback on the glass. Another option is to hang a stationary panel in the corner and draw the draperies from separate one-way rods to meet the panel. Standard rods do not center-draw for corner window arrangements, although specialty rodding that draws to the center with one cord can be put together by a professional installer. Figure 3–33a shows areas to be measured for a typ-

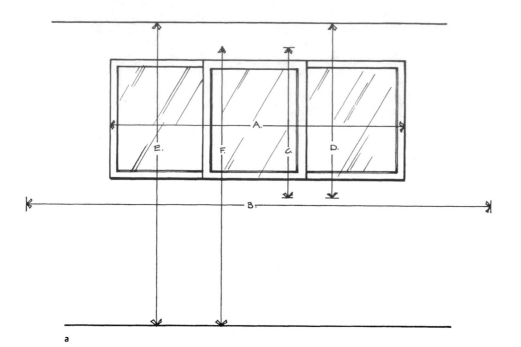

a

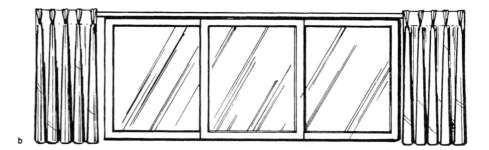

b

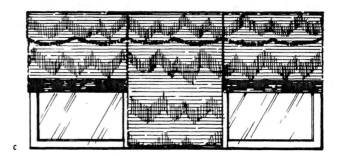

c

3-32 Clerestory windows.

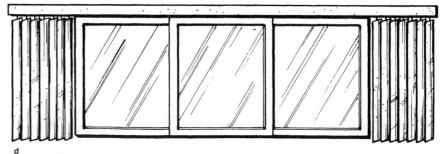

d

a Measurements: window width (A); stackoff drapery measurement (B); 4 inches above and below (C) ceiling to 4 inches below (D); ceiling to floor (E); 4 inches above to floor (F).

b Simple pleated draperies drawn off the glass. Fabric can add variety here, and a valance can span the distance.

c Three separate woven-wood shades under scalloped valance.

d Textured vertical louvers stacked off the glass.

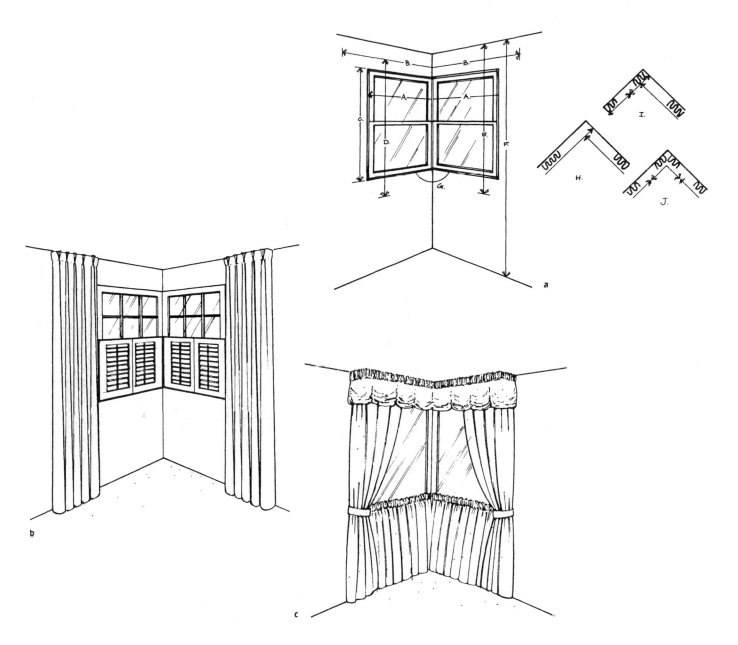

3-33 Corner windows.

a Measurements: window widths (A); stackoff widths (B); window length (C); 4 inches above to 4 inches below (D); ceiling to 4 inches below (E); ceiling to floor (F); 90-degree or other angle measurement (G); one-way draw for each window (H); center draw and one-way draw (I); center draw for both windows (J).

b Ceiling-to-floor draperies with one-way draw on each side and single-hung café shutters on each window.

c Scalloped pouf valance with low café curtains and long tiebacks.

d Flat valance or pelmet with center-draw drapery on each window.

ical corner window arrangement and some options (bird's-eye view) of stacking draperies: two one-way draw panels to make one pair; one pair and one panel; and two pair.

Many hardline treatments work well on corner arrangements because they take little room for stacking (fig. 3–33a). These include horizontal blinds, shades, shutters, and other treatments that fit the glass area. Figure 3–33b shows café or single-hung shutters with a one-way draw drapery on each window that stacks entirely off the glass. Vertical louvers, like draperies, may extend above, below, and beyond the glass area, drawing toward the center as described above. However, this treatment would expose wall space when the louvers were tilted to an open position.

Top treatments may be continuous over draperies or curtains to unify the windows and the treatment. Because the space below corner windows is considered awkward, café curtains might be installed to cover the wall area. However, this is a rather decorative treatment (fig. 3–33c).

Another option would be to mount a lambrequin around the pair of windows, or at least run a cornice, a valance, or a pelmet above the hard treatment (fig 3–33d). Layering a semisheer fabric on top of a hard treatment would be yet another good possibility that would visually unite corner windows.

Door Window Treatments

Doors with windows need to be covered for privacy or to filter light and diffuse glare. Most treatments are mounted onto the door 1, 2, or 3 inches away from the glass on each of the four sides (fig. 3–34a). Where light should be diffused but privacy is not a problem, a shirred treatment will soften and make a door window more lovely. Figure 3–34b shows a curtain shirred at top and bottom and tied in the center to form the classic hourglass shape.

3-34 Windows in doors.

a Measurements: window width plus 1 to 4 inches on each side (A); length plus 1 to 4 inches on top and bottom (B).

b Hourglass curtains shirred at top and bottom.

c Pleated shade or miniblind. This could be a woven-wood or a roller shade, or even a shutter.

d Tiered shirred curtain (hand drawn to expose glass). Hardware could be decorative brass café rods.

e Roller shade under semisheer crisscross curtains.

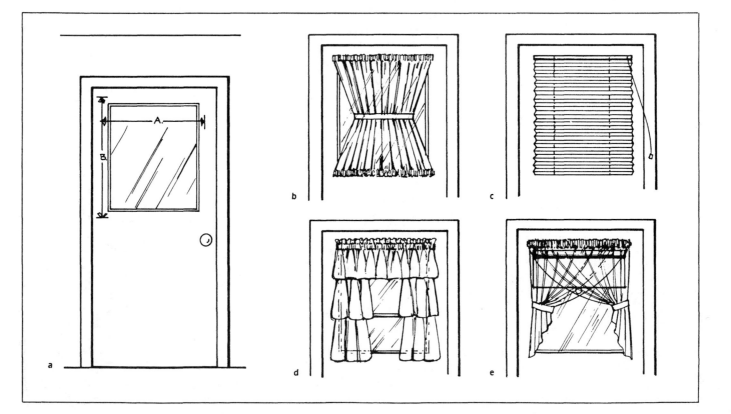

Pull shades, fabric or pleated shades, miniblinds or micro-miniblinds with hold-down brackets, and woven woods are good possibilities for hard treatments that give an air of practicality to a room (fig. 3–34c). Soft treatments that are charming include tiered (overlapping) curtains that can be shirred, pleated, or scalloped (fig. 3–34d) and crisscross curtains (fig. 3–34e).

French Casement Doors

French doors are enlarged versions of casement windows. Since people pass through the openings, it is imperative that the treatment be either attached to the glass or stacked sufficiently off to the side or above to allow for traffic. Figure 3–35a indicates necessary measurements for French doors or casement patio doors. Note the doorknobs are next to each other on adjoining doors. This is the traditional and historically correct French door. However, it is the least energy-efficient door. Today, casement patio doors have one or more stationary panel and one door hinged to open, with the doorknob on the outside edge of the frame to allow a tighter seal.

Curtains of semisheer fabric shirred top and bottom and covering just beyond the glass area are considered classic French door treatments (fig. 3–35b). Brise-bise curtains leave the top portion uncovered to invite sunlight and view, and they are timeless, lovely treatments for French doors (fig. 3–35c). These curtains provide daytime privacy. They do not give privacy at night, however.

Miniblinds (1-inch louvers), micro-miniblinds ($\frac{1}{2}$-inch louvers—fig. 3–35d), and fabric pleated or Roman shades work very nicely on the door itself. Since most people consider French doors beautiful, they generally want to leave them exposed as architectural elements. In this case the designer may specify a treatment that stacks up above the door frame or off to the side.

Another viable option is the crane or swinging-arm hardware discussed under "Casement Windows" (fig. 3–35e). Clearance is necessary in front of the glass to allow the 180-degree swing of the hardware and fabric. Vertical louvers or pleated draperies that draw horizontally need to stack off the door so that the door can be opened, and valances should not have deep scallops that would impede the occupant's passage (fig. 3–35f). Figure 3–35g shows a fluted wood rod with patterned fabric shirred on one side and another option shown on the other side: pleated draperies hooked onto wooden carrier rings. This would mean a hand-draw, but it is a charming and authentic Country French treatment, as seen in figure C–12 in chapter 4.

Sliding Glass Patio Doors

Measurements for sliding glass doors are seen in figure 3–36a. These doors often are challenging to treat with fabric. A one-way draw is the most logical choice in many cases because next to the operable glass door usually is a light switch that should not be covered. The great stacking distance required for a one-way draw eats up wall space and increases costs. One alternative is to leave part of the fabric stacked back on the stationary section of the glass door (fig. 3–36b).

Center-draw and tied-back draperies are possible, yet the fabric often is caught in the door as it is opened and closed. This soils and tears the fabric. It is acceptable, however, if the sliders are rarely used.

Vertical louvers are well suited for sliding patio doors because they require relatively little stackback area and may be stacked on one or both sides of the glass (fig. 3–36c).

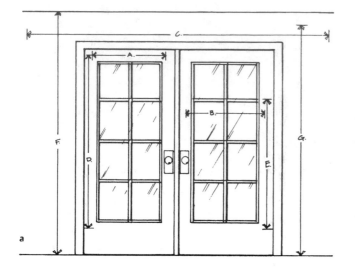

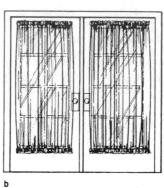

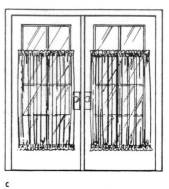

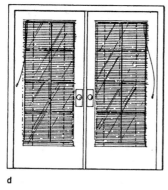

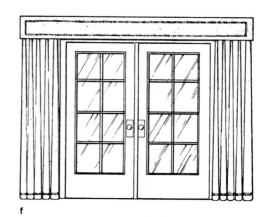

3-35 French casement door windows.

a   Measurements: frame-mount window width (A);
       frame-mount width for brise-bise shirred curtain (B);
       rod width, including stackoff for draperies (C); frame-
       mount length (D); brise-bise curtain length (E); ceiling-
       to-floor length (F); 4 inches above to floor (G).

b   Curtain shirred at top and bottom.

c   Brise-bise curtains, which provide privacy. The top is
       left untreated, for light and view.

d   Micro-miniblinds extended slightly wider and longer
       than the glass.

e   Swinging-hinge "crane" rods for shirred or pleated
       draperies.

f   High valance or pelmet with braid or gimp trim. The
       draw draperies shown underneath stack off the glass
       and are edged with trim for a formal, tailored look.

g   An authentic Country French treatment using a fluted
       wood pole rod with pleated curtains on wooden
       rings. (Alternatively, ruffled, shirred curtains may be
       used.) This treatment is hand drawn.

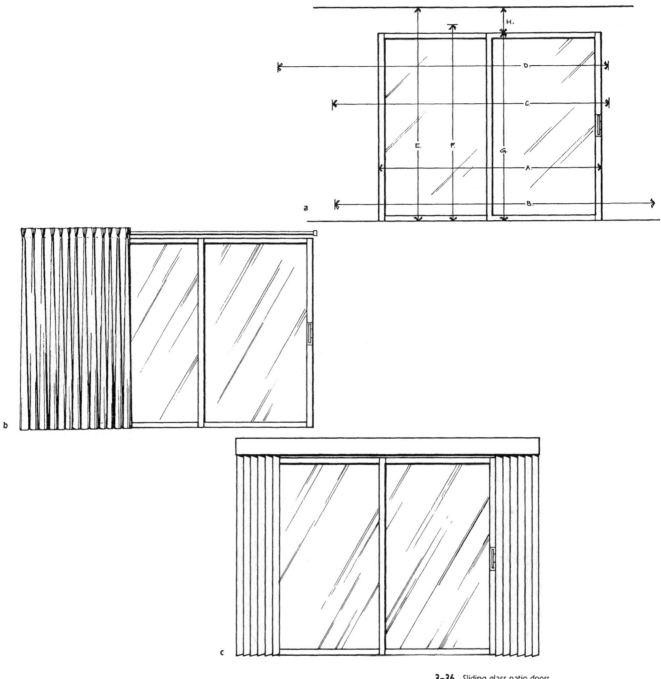

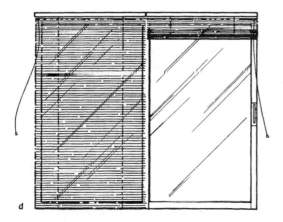

3-36 Sliding glass patio doors.

a Measurements: window width (A); stackoff width on both sides (B); partial stackoff on stationary glass side (C); rod width stackoff, all on stationary glass side (D); ceiling to floor (E); 4 inches above glass to floor (F); window frame to floor (G); ceiling to top of treatment (H).

b Drapery drawn to one side and partially stacked on the glass.

c Vertical louvers stacked off the glass.

d Hard treatment installed separately on each panel: miniblinds, pleated shades, or woven woods can be installed under a continuous valance. The treatment must stack above the window so heads do not bump against it when people walk through the door.

Treatments that stack above the glass, such as fabric shades or mini-blinds, are good choices if the treatment stacks far enough above to allow head room (fig. 3–36d). The disadvantage of these treatments on sliding glass doors is that the treatment must be completely opened to access the doorway and is quite a nuisance; horizontal-draw treatments can be partially opened to allow pass-through traffic.

Although sliding glass doors offer clear vistas and expansive light and are desirable for the structural design, they also can be somewhat dangerous. The bank of clear glass often fools people into thinking that the door is open, and many people have been injured from walking into or through sliding glass doors. Grids snapped into the glass can make the glass more visible, as can decals or etched-in designs. Stained-glass panels on the top slider can add beauty and curtail accidents as well.

Dormer Window Treatments

Dormers pose window-covering problems because of the lack of wall space around the window to allow a treatment to stack off. Coverage may cover the window alone, or go from wall to wall, from ceiling to sill, to 4 inches below the window, or to the floor. See figure 3–37a for dormer window measurements.

Layered treatments—such as tiered curtains (fig. 3–37b); double-hung draperies (overdrapery and underdrapery); blinds (fig. 3–37c); or shutters or pleated, roller, or custom shades (fig. 3–37d) topped with fabric or top

3-37 Dormer windows.

a Measurements: window width (A); wall-to-wall width (B); window length (C); ceiling to floor (D); ceiling to window (E); window to floor (F); ceiling to sill, and to 4 inches below frame (G).

b Pleated valance topping tiered curtains.

c Blinds with surrounding stencilwork.

d Custom-pleated shade with scalloped hem.

e "Victorian attic" lace treatment layered and ruffled.

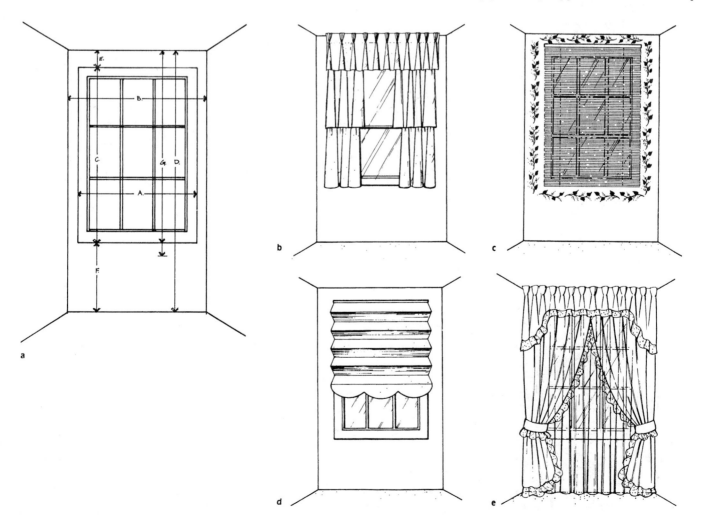

treatments—are all good solutions for dormer windows. Keep in mind the architecture and decorative style of the room, as well as the view from outside. It is tempting to design cute, lacy, or ruffled "Victorian attic" treatments to complete charming dormer settings (fig. 3–37e). If this type of treatment is right for the interior design and decoration, be certain that it also will be appropriate for the exterior style of the building and other windows viewed from the outside.

Crane hardware can swing curtains off the glass and against the wall. A tieback holder can keep fabric inside the dormer area.

English Sash Windows

As illustrated in figure 3–38a, sash windows (traditional double-hung Colonial windows) may be handled as follows: The treatment may cover the window alone, extend to the edge of the frame, extend down to the apron in length, extend above and below the standard 4 inches, or extend to the floor. The treatment may extend wider than the window, so that part of it covers the window and part stacks off the glass when opened; or the treatment may stack off the glass completely, giving an impression of a larger window area. The treatment also might extend from ceiling to floor, or ceiling to sill, apron, or 4 inches below. Figure 3–38a indicates the measurements needed for sash windows.

Classic styles of casual treatments for sash windows include café curtains (fig. 3–38b), cottage curtains (fig. 3–38c), or New England tab curtains (fig. 3–38d). Shutters are timeless at a sash window and can be a casual or formal treatment. Figure 3–38e shows single-hung café shutters topped with a valance for a casual setting, and figure 3–38f shows double-hung shutters with loosely swagged fabric reminiscent of the Empire period.

Other sash treatments that are more formal include draw or tied-back draperies that may be layered with undersheer curtains or sheer draw draperies (fig. 3–38g). Here the choice of fabric will determine the level of formality. A cheerful printed chintz will definitely be less formal than a shimmering textured silk or smooth satin fabric used in the same tied-back treatment. Valances, cornices, and pelmets work nicely on sash windows because sash windows are narrow and the top treatments are usually well proportioned if they are not too deep (fig. 3–38h). These are a good choice for formal, historically inspired interiors. A single swag with optional cascades perhaps epitomizes the most classic of the sash window treatments (fig. 3–38i).

Roller and custom fabric (Roman or pouf) shades (fig. 3–38j), miniblinds, and fabric pleated shades are all good choices for the sash window because they can be made as dressy, structural, formal, or informal as desired. In fact, the sash window is probably the easiest to treat because it inherently has good proportions and nearly every treatment can work successfully. Pay particular attention to the style of the architecture and the furnishings when selecting a window covering for sash windows.

A good rule of thumb is to scale the window treatment to the size of the window. If the sash dimensions or panes are small, for example, then the overall size and proportion of the treatment, pattern, and trimmings should not overwhelm them.

Fixed-Glass Treatments

Fixed-glass and picture windows often are treated so that the full benefit of the glass and the view are unencumbered. A treatment that extends from ceiling to floor and stacks completely off the window exposes the glass

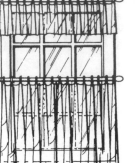

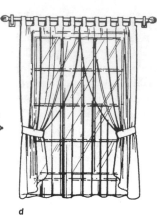

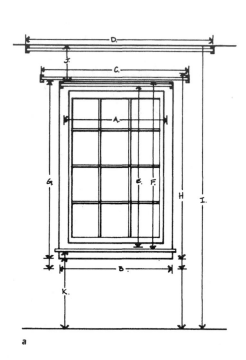

a

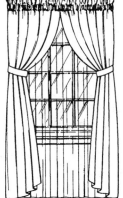

f

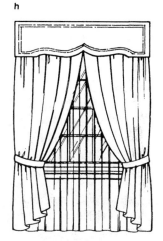

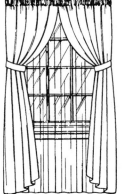

g

h

i

j

3-38 Sash, fixed, single-hung, or double-hung windows.

a Measurements: window width (A); window frame, with curtain rod placement (B); partial stackoff width and rod placement (C); width and rod placement for complete drapery and curtain stackoff (D); window length, mounted on frame (E); window frame to sill (F); window frame to apron and to 4 inches below (G); 4 inches above to apron, and 4 inches below (H); ceiling to floor (I); ceiling to top of window frame (J); apron to floor (K).

b Scalloped café curtain and valance on brass café rod with rings.

c Tieback cottage curtains shirred onto wood or brass rod, with ruffled heading and ties.

d New England tab curtains, shown here tied back.

e Ruffled and shirred cascade valance softens the top of a window where café or single-hung shutters are installed halfway.

f Double-hung shutters with contemporary Empire swag. The options show fabric pooled onto the floor (*left*) or ending in a cascade taper (*right*).

g Sheer undercurtains and high tiebacks, shirred and ruffled on a wide curtain rod.

h Historic upholstered cornice with tailored tiebacks and undersheers.

i Single swag over cascades. The cascades may be placed on top of the swag and may consist of only one swag (asymmetrical treatment).

j Pouf shade with ruffle. The heading has a pencil pleat.

and softens the large area with a compatible amount of fabric. The measurement from the ceiling to the glass or window frame, and from the window frame to the floor, may be useful here. Since fixed glass does not pose the problem of access to hardware and movable sections of glass, the treatment can fit inside the window, opening from the top or bottom, from one or both sides. The amount of stackback can be varied, with some left on the window if the wall space or budget is restricted. Figure 3–39a shows the areas to measure for picture and off-center windows.

In wide expanses of fixed-glass or picture windows, the client may want a top treatment to soften the hard line of the window. Use caution here. The long expanses of fabric, curves, or trimmings may possibly overwhelm the window and destroy the structural effect intended by the architect. This is especially true if the top treatments are too deep, say, more than 18 to 22 inches. It is wise to sketch out both fancy and simple top treatments. Consider the rightness or compatibility of the top treatment with the architecture and the room's furnishings. Remember that picture windows were designed to be a structural approach to interior architecture. It is best to complement subtly rather than to alter radically the intent of the window style.

Most fixed-glass and picture windows are enhanced by the use of simple and structural hardline treatments, such as miniblinds, vertical louvers (fig. 3–39b), standard blade-size shutters, or plantation shutters, which have very wide blades (fig. 3–39c).

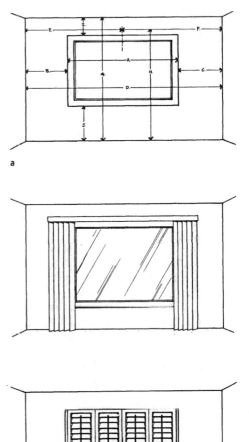

Greenhouse Window Treatments

Figure 3–40a illustrates the smaller version of a greenhouse window, which is most popularly used over a kitchen sink and comes in standard sizes. This window will be measured just as a rectangular sliding window would because the size and shape of the opening is similar and the treatment cannot be placed inside the window. There may be little need to cover this window for daytime light control or privacy if it is filled with plants, yet there may be a need for nighttime privacy.

Miniblinds are a very good choice, as are woven-wood and pleated fabric shades, because they can stack above the window to expose the plants and the light and because they are a frank, structural expression compatible with the structure of the greenhouse (fig. 3–40b). Vertical louvers will work if there is space for the wide louvers in the window frame or mounted onto the wall on each side (fig. 3–40c). Each of these louvered or slatted treatments allows air circulation and prevents heat buildup. Roller shades are a simple and inexpensive covering (fig. 3–40d), yet they should not stay closed during the day because the heat can be trapped in the window, killing the plants.

Hopper Window Treatments

Figure 3–41a shows a hopper window that opens into the interior. Measuring this window requires that the treatment stack off entirely to the side or far enough above to allow the window to be operated. A treatment that can mount on the glass frame is a good choice (fig. 3–41b). Possibilities here would include miniblinds, pleated fabric shades, woven woods, roller shades, and curtains. These and custom fabric shades can be mounted above the glass (fig. 3–41c). Treatments that can stack off the glass to the side include shutters, draperies (fig. 3–41d), and vertical louvers.

3-39 Picture and off-center windows.

a Measurements: window width (A); left wall width (B); right wall width (C); wall-to-wall width (D); left panel width (E); right panel width (F); ceiling-to-floor length (G); 4 inches above window to floor (H); ceiling to window (I); window to floor (J).

b Picture window with vertical louvers stacked evenly on each side.

c Plantation shutters with extra-wide (3 ½- to 4-inch) louvers.

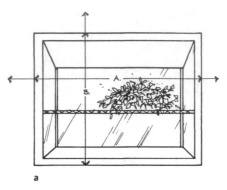

a

b

3-40 Small greenhouse windows.

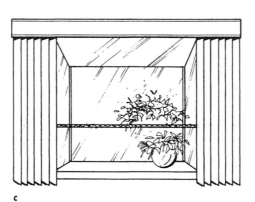

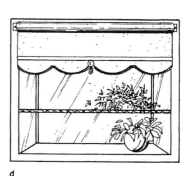

c

d

a Measurements: window and stackoff width (A); window length and stackoff height (B).

b Pleated shade softened with shirred lacy swag, allowing air to circulate to the plants.

c Vertical louvers stacked off the glass make the greenhouse window appear wider and higher.

d Scalloped roller shade. Take care to keep shade in raised position when sun is shining, to avoid heat buildup.

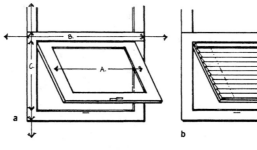

a   b

3-41 Hopper windows.

a Measurements: casement sash width for treatments mounted on the glass frame (A); window width and stackoff width (B); window length, plus length for stacking above and below (C).

b Hard treatment mounted onto a glass frame.

c Custom fabric shade mounted above.

d Draperies stacked off glass.

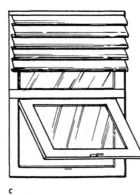

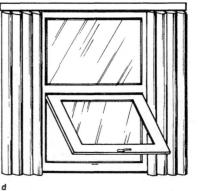

c   d

Jalousie Window Treatments

The jalousie window sometimes is used in the door as well as in a window; measurements are shown in figure 3–42a. Since the glass pivots so that half moves outward and half inward, the treatment either needs to stack above or off to the side (fig. 3–42b) or needs to be held away from the pivoting glass so as not to interfere with the operation of the glass, as suggested with the shirred curtain in figure 3–42c.

Off-Center Window Treatments

An off-center window is one that is placed in the wall such that unequal and often awkward wall space exists on each side. Off-center windows may require some extra measurements (see fig. 3–39a). When the fabric is to extend to the corner of the room on each side and an even pair of draperies is specified, then the draperies will not close in the center of the window and may leave some fabric hanging in the window on one side when drawn open. This means that the draperies will need to be ordered as two panels of different size rather than as one equal pair. One panel will draw from right to left with a right return only; the other will draw from left to right with a left return only; and the finished width measurement will be different (one larger than the other to cover the desired wall area). The designer should specify that these two panels constitute one pair, and that pleat spacing should be the same on each panel (fig. 3–43).

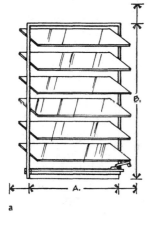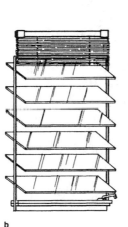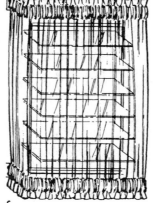

3-42 Jalousie windows.

  a Measurements: window frame width and stackoff width (A); window length, plus length for stacking above and below (B).

  b Hard treatments that can stack above the glass include miniblinds, pleated shades, woven-wood shades, and roller shades.

  c Shirred (or pleated) curtain installed on rods that hold it away from the pivoting glass for clearance. Treatment may also stack to the side(s).

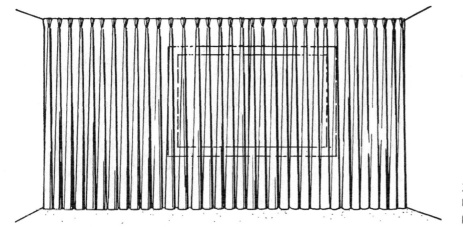

3-43 Off-center picture window draped wall to wall. The left panel is wider than the right panel so that the drapery pair will meet at the center of the window.

Rounded Window Treatments

Figure 3–44 a–b indicates the measurements needed for a rounded and for an octagonal window. However, it always is wise when measuring these windows to make a template of kraft paper and include it with the treatment order form or with the specification sheet or work order. Good possibilities for round windows include shirred fabric with a rosette or covered disc (medallion) in the center (on both sides of the center point, inside and outside); a similar look can be achieved with pleated fabric shades (fig. 3–44c). Miniblinds can be made to fit odd-shaped windows, yet the cost is quite substantial. Round and octagonal windows are ideal places for stained, beveled, or etched glass, because the windows themselves are intended to accent the interior and exterior with round or angled relief (figs. 3–44 d–g).

Sidelight and Transom Window Treatments

Measurements for a traditional sidelight and rectangular transom are illustrated in figure 3–45a. A rounded or arched fanlight or sunburst window should be measured and treated in the same manner as a round window. It is rare to cover a rectangular transom window; because it is high, privacy generally is not a concern, and light is desirable for entrance areas. However, it usually is judicious to cover sidelights to ensure some privacy. The shirred-top-and-bottom treatment is a lovely choice because it diffuses light, ensures daytime privacy, and gives a mellow, soft glow at night when the fabric screens light (fig. 3–45b). Miniblinds and the more delicate micro-miniblinds are nice as sidelight treatments; the louvers can be tilted to assure privacy at night (fig. 3–45c). Stained or beveled glass is a favorite treatment on sidelights because it adds beauty to the entry, gives some privacy, and can be effective in carrying out a decorative theme both inside and outside the building (fig. 3–45 d–g). Shutters also work well.

3-44   Round windows.

a   Measurements: horizontal (A); vertical (B).

b   Measurements for an octagonal window: width (A); length (B); angles (C). (Making a template or pattern by tracing the exact window shape also is recommended.)

c   Shirred fabric treatment with central medallion. Pleated fabric also works well here.

d   A round window is "created" inside a square one with stained glass. This design is a contemporary version of oriental-inspired Art Nouveau glass.

e   This round window is filled with simplified oriental branches and blossoms.

f   Flowery plant forms and warbling birds fill an octagonal stained-glass window.

g   A large-scale art-glass flower lends drama to this octagonal window.

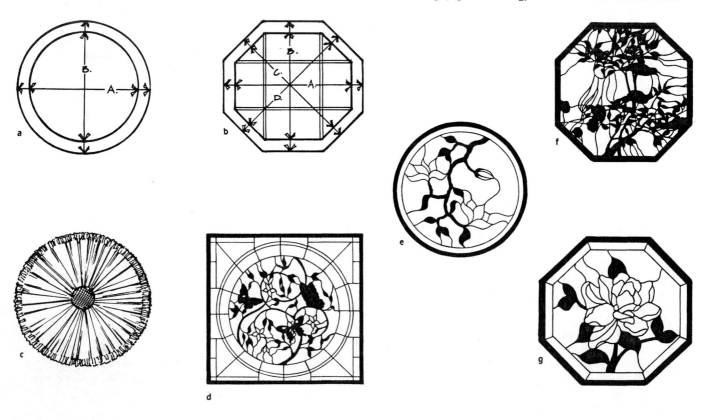

3-45 Sidelight and transom windows.

a   Measurements: window width and frame-mount treatment width (A); sidelight treatment length(s) (B); glass and extended transom width (C); transom treatment length (D). (Arched fanlight transom windows should have a template or pattern made to their exact shape.)

b   Shirred curtain on sidelights and transom.

c   Micro-miniblinds give a delicate look to sidelights.

d   Art glass is a favored treatment on contemporary sidelights and transom lights. Here a fleur-de-lis–inspired pattern adds elegance to the entry.

e   Delicate floral beauty is seen in this asymmetrically designed stained art glass.

f   A trio of iris grace a short sidelight.

g   The motif of art glass in a door window is continued in the transom light above.

Skylight and Solarium Greenhouse Treatments

Skylights and solarium greenhouse windows should be covered when there is too much sunlight or too much heat loss, or when glare or privacy is a concern. Figure 3–46a indicates the necessary measurements, which, incidentally, might require a ladder to obtain. The treatment in all cases will require a track, and four treatments have been popular and effective: the miniblind, the pleated fabric shade (fig 3–46b), the louvered wide-blade shutter (fig. 3–46c), and the quilted or insulated-fabric shade (fig. 3–46d). These treatments can be motorized to be switched on in a wired location, programmed to close according to the amount or direction of the sunlight, and even operated by remote control.

Sliding-Window Treatments

The sliding window, measured according to figure 3–47a, is a relatively easy window to treat. In fact, any of the clerestory or ranch-window treatments (see fig. 3–32), casement treatments (see fig. 3–36), or sash treatments (see fig. 3–38) may be highly recommended. Sliding windows are located lower in the wall and usually have more pleasing proportions than ranch-strip windows, but they function in the same way. They imitate the look of casement windows without the concern for crank-type hardware. And they often are fitted with grids to give the traditional look of the sash window. Sliding-window treatments require only that the treatment be able to stack to the top of the glass or off to the side so that the window can be operated and desirable breezes will not be deterred. Figure 3–47b shows a custom fabric shade; figure 3–47c shows a drapery treatment with a valance.

Treatments for Multiple Windows

Measurements for multiple windows (fig. 3–48a) can be handled in two ways: Each window can be treated separately or measurements can be taken from the center of one window to the center of the next. Hourglass tiebacks are a favored treatment because they introduce curved or angled lines at the window, softening the repeated vertical lines (fig. 3–48b). Each window can be treated with a separate pair of draw draperies (rods will be mounted side by side, and no returns should be specified). It is possible to make one panel serve as both a left- and a right-hand panel of adjoining windows (fig. 3–48c), although it will be more difficult to reach the traverse rod cords behind a wider panel of fabric than if there were two panels side by side. An alternative is to drape the intervening wall space separately with stationary pleated or shirred panels or lambrequins, and specify that sheers, draperies, or hardline treatments be installed into the window frame (fig. 3–48d). The entire wall also may be treated as one window, providing there is enough wall space to stack off the fabric drapery, woven-wood drapery, or vertical louvers (fig. 3–48e).

Each window might be filled inside, on the frame, or beyond the frame with a hardline treatment such as blinds, shutters (fig. 3–48f), or shades. Vertical louvers also could cover the series of windows as one treatment.

The measurements needed will depend on the treatment selected. A good method is to sketch the arrangement of windows, then fill in every measurement that might be required by a workroom, manufacturer, or installer.

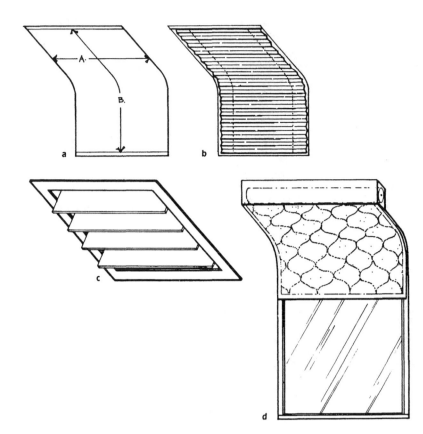

3-46 Skylights and solarium greenhouse windows.

  a Measurements: width of desired treatment (placement of track) (A); exact finished length of treatment, top to bottom (B).

  b Pleated shades or miniblinds on a motorized track.

  c Wide-blade shutters may be operated by remote control or programmed to direct the sun's rays or to close when temperature drops.

  d Quilted insulated-fabric shade. This installation offers visual and acoustical softness as well as insulation against excessive heat and cold.

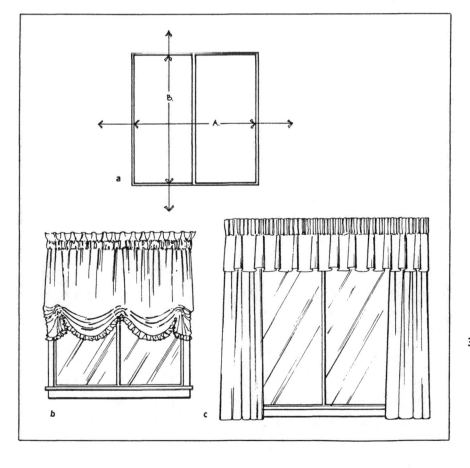

3-47 Sliding glass windows.

  a Measurements: width of window plus stackoff (A); window length plus desired above- and below-window measurements (B).

  b Custom fabric shade can stack above the glass.

  c Drapery with valance can be made to look formal or informal, historic or contemporary.

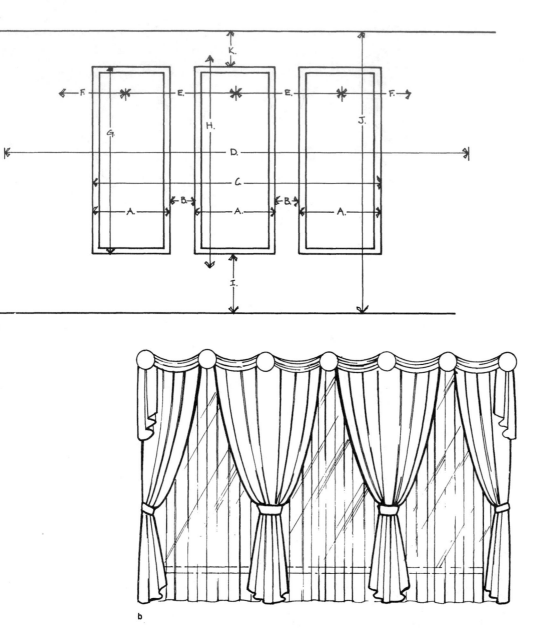

a

b

c

3-48 Multiple windows.

a Measurements: individual window widths (A); wall space between windows, if any (B); complete unit width (C); complete unit plus stackoff width (D); hourglass curtain width (add overlaps) (E); side-panel tieback width (F); window length (G); 4 inches above to 4 inches below (H); sill to floor (I); ceiling to floor (J); ceiling to window (K).

b Hourglass tieback curtains. Underneath may be shades, blinds, or curtains inside each window.

c A pair of draw draperies on each window.

d Lambrequin frames. Inside options include hard treatments such as blinds, draperies, or curtains.

e Woven-wood "draperies" on a spring traverse rod.

f A series of shutters with movable louvers.

THE GAMUT OF WINDOW-COVERING CHOICES

The suggestions above certainly do not constitute all the possible choices for window coverings. Indeed, there is no limit to the creative and distinctive possibilities, particularly those in which different materials and styles of treatments are combined. Each window setting and list of requirements should be evaluated before the treatment is chosen.

In addition to this overview, the following chapters present a great many of the classic window treatments that have proven their worth in a practical, aesthetic, or historic sense. With an understanding and knowledge of these time-tested treatments, the professional should be prepared to specify those that will meet the needs of both the client and the interior.

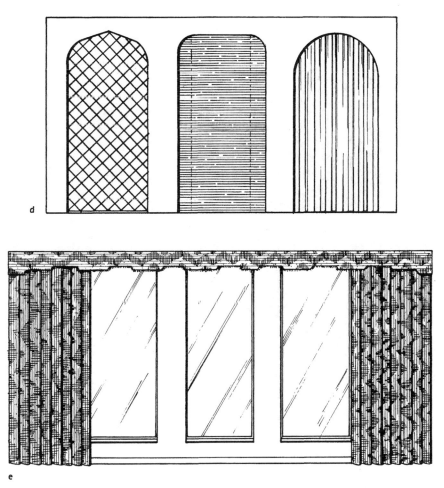

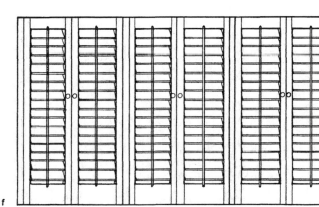

Chapter 4   PERIOD WINDOW TREATMENTS

The window treatments we select and specify today are the result of a rich and diverse history of many cultures and centuries. In fact, as we look at the interior design of today, we see that it cannot be fully separated from its historic prototypes. This is partly because the architecture of other eras is still lovingly preserved and often occupied, and partly because styles from other periods and places are so revered that they are continually being revived, adapted, and re-created through the selection of furnishing elements and designs that are uniquely combined to create a feeling of rightness. Even in contemporary modern interiors we often see unexpected but welcome fragments of other eras, such as authentic or reproduced fine artwork, furniture or accessories, fabrics, and period rugs.

The rich diversity that makes up our interiors often is a challenge to interior designers. When a period window treatment is called for, all the other elements of the interior—the architectural background, the furnishings, the colors, and the textiles—must be carefully considered and selected to be harmonious. This can be quite difficult, unless the designer has a knowledge of the specific elements found in each major historic period.

A historic period, or era, is a time frame when changes in interior design and decoration paralleled changes in society, trade and travel, industry and mechanics, and research and technology. Most influences that dictated colors and motifs or designs were social and political: they included times of peace and prosperity, of new beginnings or rediscovering ancient civilizations, of social or military upheaval. All these influences combined to create a style that was generally consistent in one or more countries for a sustained time, and that has consequently been admired and protected until our present age. In every major city in the Americas and Europe, a selection of preserved or restored homes and public architecture is open to the public. We visit them as museums and tributes to the styles of other eras. Designers continually look back to these styles for inspiration, for a sense of rightness and refinement, or to obtain the elegance or graciousness of another age, and then skillfully weave together selected elements to create contemporary interiors rich in reflections of the past.

Looking to the past is important to us today. One reason is the people, now gone, who spent their time, talents, efforts, and even entire lives developing beauty for their era. By living and working around architecture, furnishings, and textiles of the past, we are able to more deeply appreciate these persons' dedication and their heritage freely given to us. Another reason is that good design spans the centuries, and fine design—whether it be in the furniture, the fabric, the window treatment, or the entire interior—can become more appreciated and beautiful, or classic, with the passing of time. Yet another reason why period interiors are significant is that the careful development of a style brought together elements that were compatible, harmonious, and well proportioned. With careful study we can sense the rightness of each element within a period or historic setting and then translate that feeling to the interiors we are creating. This can be the most exciting element of all: to consider that the results of our efforts can bring about interiors that may equal the beauty, grace, integrity, or charm of admired interiors of yesteryear.

Although many styles exist beyond those discussed and illustrated here, this survey represents the historic periods most important to the American- and European-influenced interior designer. Further, these are the periods that followed the development of Western European and American decorative arts from the Italian Renaissance through the Modern period—including the classic influences of China, Japan, and Spain, whose histories and interior elements span centuries rather than just a few decades.

Each period evaluated in this chapter includes the following information: its time frame; the source names by which it is known (including influential people such as monarchs, architects, or designers); a description of the characteristic interior architecture, colors, and textiles; and an examination of the window treatments used in each period. More details on architecture, furnishings, color, and textiles can be found in books specializing in those subjects (see the bibliography at the end of this book for suggestions). Each period discussed here is illustrated by a color rendering of a typical interior in an upper-class home. Traditionally the lower and middle classes have looked to the nobility and upper classes for the establishment of styles and trends; and the interiors of the relatively wealthy, as well as public and church architecture, are the ones that have been preserved for the future.

Also included in this chapter are inkline illustrations of classic window treatments belonging to each period. These suggestions can be adapted to contemporary settings. The designer should feel free to alter an authentic treatment to fit a contemporary interior by varying the type, style, and color of the fabric and the trimmings; the width and depth of the treatment; and the exactness of the curves and angles and lengths of the straight lines. In short, any change made to an authentic treatment will serve to individualize that window covering for its intended setting.

The following list is an overview of the historic periods that will be discussed in this chapter:

- *Oriental:* China (1368–1912) and Japan (1392–1603, preserved and revived today)

- *Spanish Colonial:* Spain and the New World (1492–1940)

- *Renaissance:* Italy (1400–1600), France (1589–1643), England (also called Late Medieval, Early Renaissance, Elizabethan/Tudor, or Jacobean/Stuart, 1558–1649)

- *Baroque:* France (1643–1730), England (also called English Early Georgian, 1660–1714)

- *Early American or American Colonial:* (also called English/American Colonial, 1608–1790)

- *American Early Georgian:* (simplified English Baroque with elements of Early American Colonial, 1700–1750)

- *Rococo:* France (1730–1760), Country French or authentic French Provincial (simplified Rococo, 1730–1760) (This style also was highly developed in Austria and Germany.)

- *Georgian:* English Middle Georgian (1714–1770), American Late Georgian (1751–1790) (strongly influenced by Thomas Chippendale II, called Chinese Chippendale)

- *Neoclassic:* France (1760–1789), England (1770–1820), America (also called Federal, 1790–1820) (All these periods show the influence of the sixteenth-century Italian architect Andrea Palladio.)

- *Empire:* France (1804–1820), England (also called Regency, 1810–1837), America (1820–1860)

- *Victorian:* England (1837–1910), America (1840–1920), Art Nouveau, (1890–1910)

- *Modern:* Scandinavia (1900–present), America (1919–present), Art Deco, (1909–1939)

CHINA (1368–1912)

Source Names

The Ming and T'a Ch'ing Dynasties

Interior Architecture and Furnishings

The homes of the royalty and the very wealthy, along with religious buildings, were made of wooden post-and-beam construction. Usually dark-brown Persian cedar was used for the wood, and it either was painted with colorful designs or was beautifully carved or pierced. Figure C–1 represents a composite of the interior architecture and furnishings of Chinese designs, which are admired and re-created even today. The pierced latticework (carved through to achieve a lacelike quality) is used to frame a niche. In the niche is a beautiful polished chest, or credenza, with Chinese brass medallion hardware and a slightly flared "wing" on the top surface, inspired by the pagoda roofs of religious shrines. The brass vase on the chest may have served as an artwork, as a container for flowers, or (if covered) as a sacred depository for an ancestor's ashes. The artwork on the wall is a watercolor, painted on silk or mulberry paper, which gives a mystical quality to the characteristic nature themes of flowers, trees, birds, and unusual, steep mountains dotted with summerhouses and people.

The Chinese rug has a deep, lush pile in royal Ming blue and white. Rugs such as this one are available and popular today and priced to be affordable. They have simple medallions on an open background, with fretwork borders. Other motifs are flowers, dragons, cranes, and various conventionalized or abstract designs, such as clouds, geometric forms, or asymmetrical flora (branches of cherry blossoms, for example).

The chair is carved wood with a *banti,* or slightly turned-in foot, on the leg. The seat and back are flat; some Tsu chairs have simple straight slat backs with curved arms and back frames. The size of Chinese furniture is similar to the size of Western furniture; the chairs and chests are tall, for example, and are dignified in appearance. Woods such as rosewood and teak, polished to perfection, are in themselves works of art.

Colors

The colors used in classic Chinese interiors often are predominated by the well-known Ming blue and white. In fact the term *china* used for dinnerware was derived from Ming blue-and-white porcelain imported from China as early as the seventeenth century. Red (often called Mandarin or Manchu red) is another favorite Chinese color. It symbolizes good fortune and long life. A soft gold frequently is seen in paintings and textiles, such as the gold used in the chair seat and painting in figure C–1. Cream or off-white is used lavishly, as seen in the walls and screen.

Many other exotic colors originated in China. These include jade green (from greenish off-white to dark, rich green), peacock blue, lacquer black, peony (vivid) pink, chrysanthemum yellow, and the spectrum of soft yellows or "spun-honey" golds.

Textiles

Silk was discovered in China, according to legend, around 2640 B.C. by the empress Hsi ling-Chi, who began the sericulture industry of cultivating silkworms and spinning the cocoon filaments together to form silk thread. The Chinese kept the origin of silk a secret, and for centuries silk imported by Europe was surrounded by rumors of its origin—for instance, that it came from clouds, fine soil, or spider webs. Exquisite and luxurious hand-embroidered, printed, or painted Chinese textiles have given silk the title of "queen of fibers."

The Chinese also invented batik, the method of resist-dyeing silk and cotton. Intricate handwork, cutwork (cut-out holes with extensive embroidery), and lace textiles are famous Chinese fabrics whose techniques have been preserved and reproduced through the centuries. Cotton was used extensively in China, and wool was prevalent in Chinese rugs, which gave insulation to the interior.

Window Treatments

Although some silks and cottons were used as draping fabrics, most were hung around or at beds and were rarely used at the window. Instead, the Chinese rice- or mulberry-paper sliding screen, such as the one in figure C–1 was used extensively, with intricate fretwork designs. Other fretwork designs are seen in figure 4–1. Note the simplified, contemporary versions of Chinese screens in figure 4–1 c–e.

Another treatment that originated in China was the roll-up bamboo shade, used to screen and filter light and provide some privacy (fig. 4–2). Both of these classic Chinese treatments offer an element of intrigue because they are translucent. This shadow/screening effect in part represents the fascination we have for China, so long closed to foreign trade, a country whose secrets and beauties we are still discovering. Figure 4–3 shows shutter frames filled with inserts of fretwork, wood, and bamboo shade fabric—a contemporary and handsome adaptation of old Chinese themes.

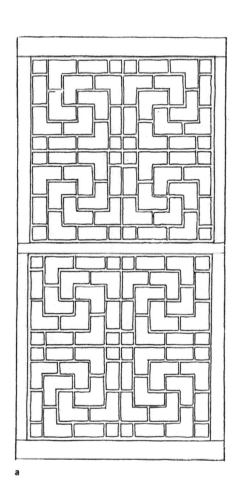

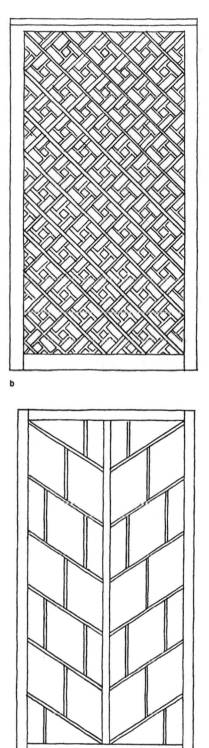

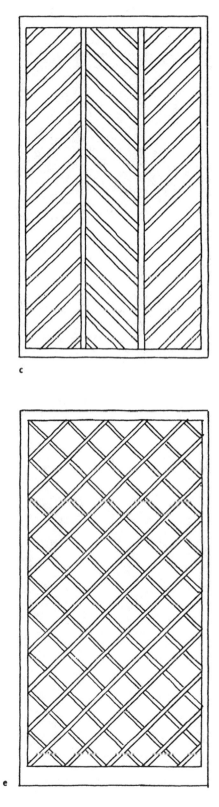

4-1 Chinese screens.

a   Authentic Chinese latticework screen.
b   Authentic Chinese latticework screen.
c   Contemporary adaptation of Chinese screen.
d   Contemporary adaptation of Chinese screen.
e   Contemporary adaptation of Chinese screen.

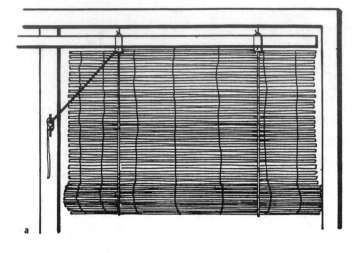

4-2   Chinese shades.

a   Chinese roll-up bamboo shade. Sometimes called Bali blinds in the South Pacific, where they have been used to filter light for centuries.

b   Contemporary Chinese-influenced bamboo shades mounted on a spring roller and topped with a valance. These sometimes are called matchstick shades or blinds because of the individual, though nonmovable, slats.

4-3   Chinese-influenced shutter or screen inserts.

a   Fretwork.
b   Woven wood.
c   Bamboo.

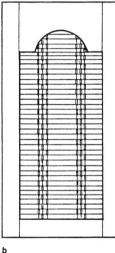

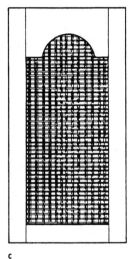

a   b   c

JAPAN (1392–1603)

Source Names

Muromachi and Momoyama periods

Interior Architecture and Furnishings

Japanese architecture is mainly wood, frankly exposed and used in structural designs with predominant horizontal lines. In palaces the wood was ornately carved; in the homes of the wealthy, the decoration resulted from simple posts and beams and carefully arranged latticework. Open floor plans made rooms look larger. Rooms were divided by shoji or fusuma partitions or lacquered coromandel wood screens (hinged, free-standing lacquered panels with decorative designs applied in colored lacquer or mother-of-pearl inlay). Wall composition was somewhat cubist, with long planks of hinoki cyprus used to frame wooden walls. Interior walls were few in number and often consisted of sliding fusuma partitions (made from plain or painted mulberry paper or wood), which were block printed or hand painted as seen in figure C–2.

Decoration and furniture were sparse, although every home had its *to-konoma* (a niche the size of a clothes closet), where rice paper or silk scrolls were hung and beautiful floral arrangements, or *ikebana*, were rotated regularly. The wood floors were covered with *tatami* mats (mats woven of rice straw or reeds of varying thicknesses). *Tatami* mats can be seen in figure C–2, along with a wood-strip ceiling with a hanging rice-paper lantern and a low table with *banti* legs. The square pillows, or *za-buton*, were used for chairs. When dinner was over, the table and chairs could be removed and sleeping mats rolled out to transform the area into a bedroom. The out-of-doors was an integral part of the interior, as seen through broad, unglazed windows. An *engawa*, or veranda, made it possible to sit outside and enjoy the symbolic and beautifully inspiring Japanese garden.

Colors

Although vivid colors were used in temples and shrines, the colors in Japanese homes were subdued and often based on the natural color and value of interior and exterior elements: the wood, the *tatami* mats, the garden, the flowers in the *tokonoma* vase, and the watercolors in the hanging scroll. Colors also were used in textiles, as shown in figure C–2 in the *zabutons*.

Traditional Japanese color schemes are based on the ancient aesthetic philosophy *shibusa* (*shibui* is the adjective form). *Shibui* colors are used in the same ways and ratios as nature uses color. They are subtly blended and not matched, with shading, texture, and understated printed or woven pattern used to interrelate hues. Pattern is complex yet has an unfinished look that gives depth, richness, and intrigue to textiles and color schemes. Color value is carefully distributed: the darker, more somber colors appear lower to the ground, producing a sense of security; lighter colors appear above the "horizon," much as color appears in nature. Thus, value is progressively lighter from floor to walls to ceiling. In addition, large areas are dull, neutralized, or of low intensity and have a matte finish. The smaller the area, the brighter the color and shinier the surface may become. Only tiny areas of glitter are allowed, but they are crucial: without little areas of bright and shine, the *shibui* color scheme is uninteresting. The overall look is one of mellow patina and time-tested, exquisitely beautiful design.

Textiles

As in China, silk was the most loved and used of the Japananese textiles, although cotton and linen also were prevalent. Designs were embroidered, woven, or printed, and the fine arts of batik and tie-dye date back many centuries in Japan. Motifs were less religious and symbolic than in Chinese textiles. More common, for example, were Japanese women in elaborate headdresses and long, flowing silk robes, plum and cherry blossom branches, and flowers arranged asymmetrically. Family crests, based on a circle, often were used for motifs as well.

Window Treatments

The sliding screen used in China also was the mainstay of Japanese window treatments. In Japan the screens are known as *shoji* (shō'zhē), and consist of a wooden lattice glazed with fine oriental paper and a wood hipboard, or solid wood panel, on the lower portion to protect the screen against rain or snow. As shown in figure C–2, shoji screens were traditionally used as window glazing (where today we would use sliding glass doors).

Fusuma screens, a variation of shoji, have painted or block-printed designs on layered paper. Originally used as room dividers, fusuma now appear both at the window and as partitions in some modern interiors.

Shoji screens are made of natural cedar frames with panes or grids glazed with mulberry or rice paper. They are used in both residential and non-residential interiors in Western settings today and are admired and appreciated for their subtle beauty and clean structural lines. The shadows of translucent shoji screens are intriguing, and the patterns formed by the grids can be simple or complex (fig. 4–4).

Shoji screens can be free-standing, and the grids may be large or small squares with a solid wood portion or a window. Windows have sliding shoji frames to open or close the opening. The panes, or lights, can be horizontal or vertical rectangles. Complex patterns may be based on a square, a horizontal or vertical rectangle, or a diagonal pattern. An asymmetrically designed panel may be balanced with an identical screen for symmetrical balance or with a slightly different screen for asymmetrical balance.

Sliding shoji should ideally be set into tracks that are recessed into the floor and ceiling or frame. Transom screens can be particularly beautiful because the transom can be more complex and does not have to match the shoji screen below (figs. 4–5 and C–2).

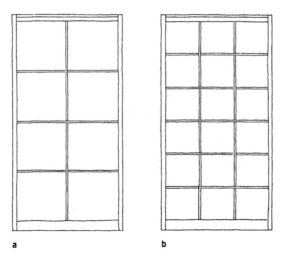

a   b

4-4 A sampling of shoji screen designs.

a   Large square-grid arrangement.

b   A grid configuration of three squares by six squares.

c   Smaller squares with horizontal sliding "window" and low hipboard.

d   Small horizontal-rectangle grid.

e   Classic shoji with vertical rectangles.

f   Decorative panels set into grids, with low hipboard.

g   Long horizontal lines, with complex pattern in the lower portion.

h   Interlacing horizontal slats with fine-mesh lattice in the lower portion.

i   This complex lattice arrangement may be duplicated in mirror image on another panel to create a large, symmetrical pattern.

j   Rhythmic pattern in long, horizontal overlapping shapes.

k   This diagonal lattice produces large geometric shapes.

l   Curved pieces imitate growing bamboo.

m   Asymmetrical patterns. The empty lower portion is an optional window area.

n   Symmetrical pair with interesting lattice above and diagonal fine-mesh design below.

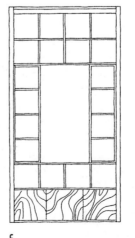

c   d

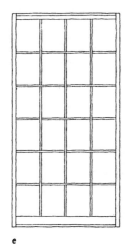

e

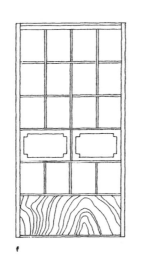

f

g

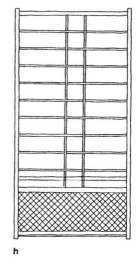

h

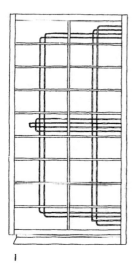

l

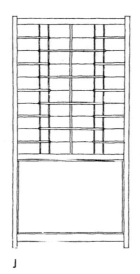

j

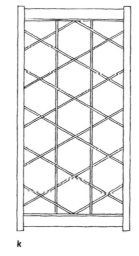

k

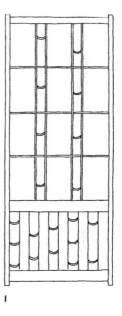

l

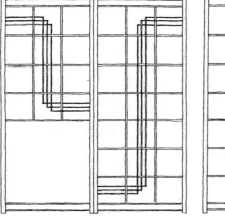

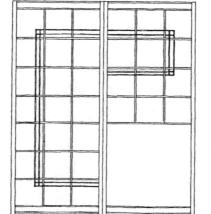

m

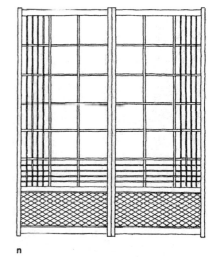

n

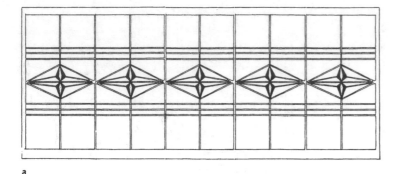

a

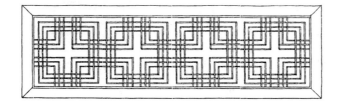

b

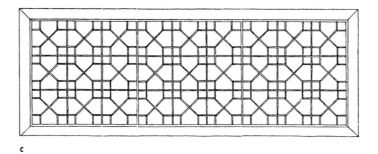

c

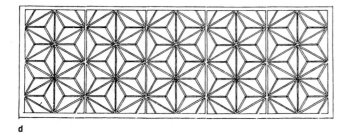

d

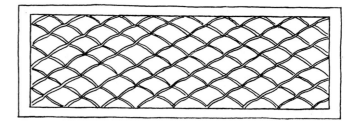

e

4-5 A selection of shoji transom designs. (The transom is a piece that covers the area above the shoji panels.)

- **a** Diamond patterns set into rectangles.
- **b** Concentric, overlapping squares.
- **c** Geometric lattice with strong rhythmic pattern of interlocking octagons.
- **d** This striking star pattern would require great expertise to accomplish.
- **e** A wave- or cloud-inspired pattern.
- **f** Carved phoenix or bird of paradise in an oriental cedar tree is part of a pierced decorative panel for the transom area.

f

SPANISH COLONIAL (1492-1940)

Source Names

Influence of the Islamic Moors (dating from 800 to 1500 A.D.), specifically the Sunni sect, whose prolific geometric designs stemmed from a zealous belief that people must not create motifs that imitate nature. Only God (Allah) was entitled to make living, natural designs. Spanish Colonial was also influenced by the Mudejar period of Christianized Moors (dating from 1300 to 1600).

Interior Architecture and Furnishings

Many styles evolved throughout the history of Spain. Described here is the style that came to the Spanish colonies in the Americas beginning with Christopher Columbus and following the conquests of the Spaniards, whose influence in the United States is felt most strongly in Florida and the deep Southeast and in the great Southwest and the Pacific West. The dates above indicate that the period style was used until the 1940s; it was revived with great popularity during the Beaux Arts period from about 1900 to 1940. However, as with the oriental styles, Spanish Colonial is classic and is as welcome today in warm climates as it was nearly four hundred years ago when it first came to America.

Figure C-3 illustrates a typical Spanish Colonial interior. Traditional flooring materials included tile, brick, and rust-colored clay, or terra cotta. Here the flooring has been polished or waxed, but floors often were left rustic and unfinished. Small squares, rectangles, or complex Moorish ogive brick or tile patterns would have been equally appropriate, as would tiles hand painted with geometric or Moorish patterns.

Walls and ceilings in Spanish Colonial interiors were rough stucco, white or tinted a slightly reddish or yellowish hue. Heavy beams supporting the ceiling were exposed and were squared off (as seen in figure C-3), or left round. The Spanish Colonial interior copied Southwest native American architecture by leaving these supportive beams round and unfinished. Also shown in figure C-3 is a stone Spanish arch supported by Doric columns and a wall bracket. In the background of figure C-3 is a carved geometric door panel, which was typical of Spanish doors, window shutters, and wooden casepiece furniture.

The simple straight chair shown in the illustration is typical of Spanish furniture in that it gives a nearly austere impression. However, plants, both those inside and those viewed through doors and windows, bring life to the Spanish Colonial interior.

Colors

Spanish colors are dramatic and of high contrast. For example, the stucco is naturally light, and the wood is generally very dark. The floors lend a natural rust hue to the palette. Colors may be vivid in small areas—as in paintings and accessory textiles—or they may be sun-drenched or faded, perhaps literally so, from exposure to the unrelenting sun of Spain and the early Spanish colonies. Golds, blacks, reds, oranges, and some greens constituted a favored palette, either vivid or faded.

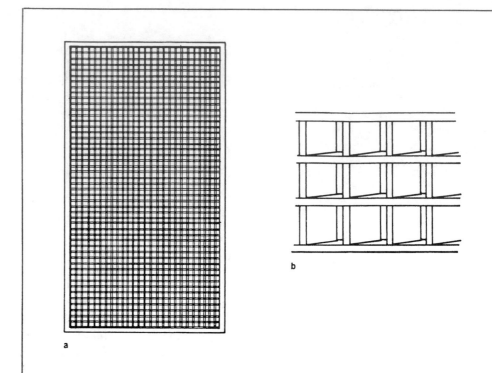

Textiles

Spanish textiles from this period were durable and notably masculine. They included leather, as shown in the chair in fig. C–3; matelassé; brocatelle; tweeds; and velvets made from wools, linens, cottons, or similar textured fibers, such as nylon. Some semisheers were used, and in formal Spanish settings, elegant Renaissance fabrics appeared in pelmet or cornice top treatments (see next section). Spanish Baroque treatments may be compared to French and English Baroque treatments discussed below (see figs. 4–9 through 4–11).

Window Treatments

Because the sun in Spain and the Spanish colonies tended to damage and wear out fabrics quickly, the traditional coverings made popular in the Americas have been shutters (much like the paneled door in figure C–3) or screens. At the window in figure C–3 is a folding, free-standing screen; some screens were sliding or stationary. Figure 4–6 illustrates several latticework screens. Figure 4–7 shows three variations on the insert shutter.

Yet another typical Spanish window treatment is the hand-wrought railing, seen beyond the window in figure C–3. Wrought iron is used today on the exterior of the window not only for authenticity but for protection against intruders. It has been used traditionally as a free-standing, glare-diffusing treatment on the interior of the window. *Note:* see the description at the end of this chapter of the Spanish Colonial adaptation known as the Southwest Adobe, or desert, style, popular in the 1980s and 1990s.

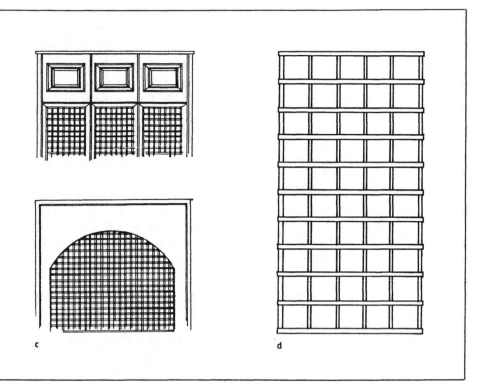

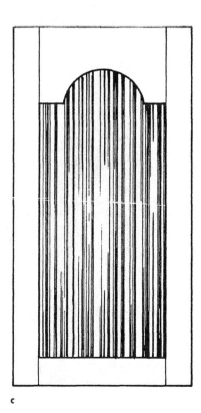

4-6 Shutter-framed screens with Middle Eastern lattice designs.

a   Screen with close-set lattice.

b   A closeup view revealing the depth of traditional screens, which served as light diffusers and as a "blind" (enabling the occupant to see without being seen).

c   Variations on the frame of the screen itself: the raised-panel frame (*top*), and the segmental or elliptical arch frame (*bottom*).

d   A contemporary adaptation with spaced lattice strips.

4-7 Shutter or screen inserts from the Near East, Spain, and Mediterranean.

a   A metal grid or "mesh."

b   Pierced wood inset in Moorish design.

c   Fabric shirred on a dowel onto the back of the shutter frame.

ITALIAN RENAISSANCE (1400–1600)

Source Names

Andrea Palladio, the great Renaissance architect, profoundly influenced later British and American designers. Representative of this period are the Florentine and Roman Renaissance pallazzi he designed for the Medici and Borghese families, Renaissance patrons of the arts.

Interior Architecture and Furnishings

Renaissance means a rebirth or reawakening, and all the arts of the Italian Renaissance reflected a resurgence of the classical forms of ancient Greece and Rome. Interior architecture included columns, pilasters (columns cut in half lengthwise and placed on the wall), complete entablatures (cornices and wood trim next to the ceiling), moldings, and pediments (triangular forms set above doors). These forms also were used to make exterior porticoes, or covered porches, hallmarks of Palladian Renaissance architecture. Classical forms are used at the window as well, where a pair of Roman arches and a circle inspired by the Roman dome form the window in figure C–4. Note the typically green bull's-eye of crown glass with which the windows are glazed.

Carving, or relief, was popular. In figure C–4 we see wood carving on the door, on the dado (lower portion of the wall), and above the door in the round Roman arch, which frequently was incorporated into the interior architecture. Wood also is shown as a cornice (molding) next to the ceiling. The ceiling is wood, set in a coffered design, with squares formed with wood trim. Some coffered ceilings were quite elaborate.

Plaster walls were common, and plaster also was used as an exterior building material over blocks of stone or brick. Marble was popular as wall material, and figure C–4 shows another common use—flooring. Doors open to a marble-paved balcony with a twisted column, which would often have been straight; foliage, vines, and plants were enjoyed much of the year, according to the climate, for much of Italy is warm year-round.

During the Renaissance furniture began to evolve into styles and pieces that have endured. Shown in figure C–4 are the Dante chair and the poster bed. Low chests, similar to dowry or hope chests, were designed and used for storage and sitting. Most furniture was of heavily carved dark wood; little upholstery or cushioning was used at first. (More fabric is seen as upholstery and table covers in figure C–5, which illustrates a French Renaissance decor.) The scale of furniture was relatively heavy, as the structural members, turned legs, and shaped stretches were substantial and strong.

Colors

Colors were clear and vivid during the Italian Renaissance. Those used in paintings (both on canvas and as frescoes on walls and ceilings) were rich and realistic. Perhaps the four most important families of color, as shown in figure C–4, were warm red, blue, green, and gold. Colors have been given such names as Pompeii red (a brilliant orange-red), bright copper (rust), garnet red (a rich blackened red), dull brown (taupe), rich brown (a dark, warm brown), golden ocher (a medium yellow-orange), metallic gold (seen in gilt ornament), medium and deep malachite (grayed, yet strong, greens), ceramic blue (blue-green), della Robbia blue (a slightly grayed blue leaning toward violet), and deep cobalt (a slightly grayed royal blue). All the colors seen in marble were integral to the Italian Renaissance. These include the spectrum of soft gold-yellows and cream, called marble cream and ivory white, with veins of color ranging from gray to blue to green to red to violet.

Textiles

Velvets were important in the Italian Renaissance, and many types of rich, exquisite velvet were developed, some of which are stunning even today. Damask, brocatelle, and brocade also were famous during the Renaissance for their elegant beauty. Fabrics woven of cotton, linen, wool, and particularly silk were exported to Europe and later to America. These also included tapestries, detailed laces, and even lamé (fabric woven with silver and gold thread). Artistic expression in textiles included such motifs as the elongated S-shape, the pomegranate, and the artichoke, the tops of which burst into an amazing array of foliage—sometimes tiny thistles, sometimes pineapple spikes, and later on carnations and roses. Bold, naturalistic floral forms in large scale greatly influenced later textiles in the Baroque and Georgian periods. The oriental rug, as shown in figure C–4, became very important for decoration, prestige, and softness over the stone or brick floors. This set a standard for the European styles to follow, which began to copy the Renaissance by including oriental rugs in fine interiors.

Window Treatments

As shown in figure C–4 the shutter was an important element in interior design. Most windows were relatively small; shutters could be stacked off the window completely and closed for privacy, protection, and insulation. In the villas and estates of the wealthy, the windows were draped with the rich tapestries, velvets, and brocades that are represented in the bed fabrics in figures C–4 and C–5. The pelmet seen around the bed also could have been used at the window. The window treatment shown in figure C–5, an example of French Renaissance decor, was also very typical of Italian window treatments.

Figure 4–8 illustrates many of the ornate top treatments of the Italian and French Renaissance, which were flat pelmets combined with carved wood; urns or vases (real ones or wood imitations) often were placed atop the pelmet. Cornices and pelmets began as simple, flat treatments and evolved into ornate, carved or curved styles, heavily trimmed with banding, braid, decorative ropes, fringes, and tassels. Trimmings usually were of silk and gave considerable richness and detail to the treatments. The wood was stained, painted, or even gilt with gold leaf. Fabrics used at the window were relatively flat panels without fullness, either hung straight or tied back low with heavy rope braid and tassel trimmings. The fabric itself often was heavy or very lavish, so that fullness was not important to achieve a rich effect. The lengths of fabric at the window would be only one width used as a stationary panel on each side of the glass.

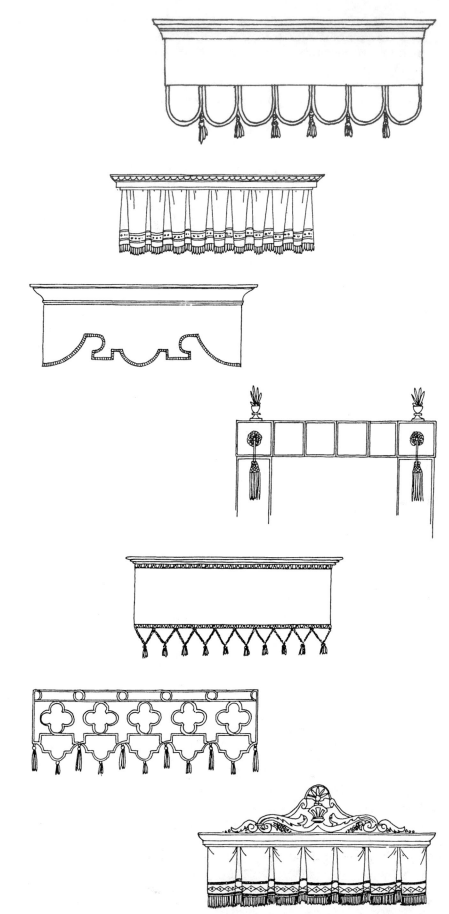

4-8 Window treatments of the Italian and French Renaissance. Heavy shutters of formal fabric hung in relatively flat panels topped with wood cornices and fabric pelmets. Top treatments were straight or had shaped tops sometimes decorated with urns or vases. Bottoms were of fringed or scalloped draped fabric. Trimmings and tassels were used extensively. Exposed wood may have been gilded. The look was heavy and dignified.

C-1

C-2

C-3

C-1 Classic Chinese interior with sliding paper screens and wood fretwork designs. Note the cut-out "window" and the transom above the screen.

C-2 Japanese shoji screens at the window open to provide a view of a beautiful Japanese garden. The interior partitions are fusuma screens.

C-3 Spanish Colonial interior with screens at the window and wrought iron outside the window.

C-4

C-5

C-6

C-4 Italian Renaissance interior showing solid-panel shutters stacked off windows that are arched and glazed with greenish crown glass.

C-5 French Renaissance interior with heavy velvet or brocade draperies in nearly flat panels. The pelmet is trimmed with gold braid and fringe and topped with carved wood urns.

C-6 English Medieval/Early Renaissance interior featuring a bay window set with small diamonds of brilliant crown glass. The crewel embroidery fabric is attached with leather straps onto a wood or metal rod and drawn closed with a braided tassel.

C-7

C-8

C-9

C-7 French Baroque interior illustrating a silk-damask fabric in a Renaissance pattern. The florid hue was a favorite of the "Sun King," Louis XIV. Draperies were full, tied-back low, and topped with an ornate pelmet and shell decoration.

C-8 English Baroque interior featuring a straight silk fabric to the floor. A sheer fabric softens the light entering the room, and the fringed pelmet gives a stately, dignified impression to the whole.

C-9 Early American Colonial interior with a plain muslin or homespun fabric in a New England tab curtain treatment, which is made by sewing strips of fabric onto the curtain and then threading the tabs over a wood dowel. This treatment may have been a carryover from the English Medieval period.

C-10

C-11

C-12

C-10 American Early Georgian interior showing raised-panel shutters softened with a single swag and cascade. Fabric was imported, costly, and scarce, so the treatment is simple.

C-11 French Rococo, or Louis XV, window treatment in turquoise tieback draperies, embroidered pelmet with a shaped top and bottom, and similarly shaped and embroidered ties. The French casement window also is curved, with Rococo dividers.

C-12 Country French windows showing two types of treatment—a printed fabric attached to wood rings on a wood pole rod, pulled open and closed by hand over the French door, and white shutters on the smaller window.

C-13

C-14

C-15

C-13 English Middle Georgian room reflecting Chinese Chippendale styling in a "Georgian gold" color. The pelmet is capped with carved or pierced wood filigree in Chinese designs. The tieback draperies are full, yet separated and slender. Sheer fabric provides daytime privacy.

C-14 American Late Georgian room in a peach hue trimmed with white. The straight draperies and the Chinese Chippendale-inspired cornice are in a beautiful peach-and-blue floral pattern.

C-15 French Neoclassic, also called Louis XVI, interior showing a translucent fabric with soft swags in the valance. The sheer fabric is stacked off the glass to reveal formal French gardens.

C-16

C-17

C-18

C-16 English Neoclassic room showing the influence of Robert Adam. The draperies are long and slender, tied back low. The fabric valance combines curves, pleats, and cascades in a restrained design.

C-17 American Federal interior in Federal blue with slender upholstered cornice board and tieback draperies patterned in a refined stripe.

C-18 French Empire window treatment features a deep green favored by Napoleon. The heavy look of the asymmetrically swagged draperies and valance was inspired by Roman military tents and classical Roman fabric and motifs.

C-19

C-20

C-19 American Empire drapery in a small-print, light-colored fabric topped by a heavy swag and cascade valance with a squared jabot in the center. A gilt cornice tops the valance.

C-20 American or English Victorian interior. The lace curtains are layered with patterned rose-colored draperies. The valance combines swags, cascades, and inverted box pleats and is trimmed with fringe and topped with a gold cornice.

C-21

C-22

C-21 Scandinavian Modern interior with expansive plate glass that is softened with only a casement fabric drapery.

C-22 American Modern interior with miniblinds in the angled clerestory windows and vertical louvers below. Outside, an extended overhang blocks direct sunlight.

FRENCH RENAISSANCE (1589-1643)

Source Names

Kings Francis I, Henry IV, and Louis XIII, heavily influenced by and imported from the Italian Renaissance

Interior Architecture and Furnishings

The French Renaissance rooms belonging to nobility or the upper classes were formal and dignified, with large panels of heavily molded wood that was carved and perhaps painted. In figure C–5 wood is used extensively, seen in a semicoffered beamed ceiling, wood walls, and carved panels. Coffered ceilings became more ornate and very heavily carved late in the period. Also shown in figure C–5 are typical marble floors, which sometimes were replaced with plank or parquet wood because the French climate is cooler than the Italian, and marble is a cold flooring. Windows were stationary or casement types glazed with small panes in long, narrow rectangles or in more decorative patterns, as seen in figure C–5. Again, a greenish tint was often typical of early glass, and the effect was translucency rather than transparency. The general feeling of French Renaissance rooms echoed the classic detail and sumptuousness of the Italian Renaissance.

Furnishings shown in figure C–5 were influenced both by the furniture of the Italian Renaissance and by the styles of Flemish artisans. The Flemish were Protestants who initially came to northwest France following the Edict of Nantes, which granted them religious freedom but was later revoked. The round (bun) feet, curved stretchers, and twisted turned legs were Flemish influences.

Colors

The colors of the French Renaissance naturally were influenced by the Italian Renaissance palette. In France the spectrum was compounded with orange hues, brownish yellows, and lighter greens. In figure C–5 the red-orange velvet used as window treatment and upholstery is combined with gold and trimmed with gold braid, fringe, and tassels. Light green is seen in the marble floors.

Textiles

Velvets were a favorite during this period, as represented in figure C-5. These were plain or cut, sometimes in wide stripes and shaded colors. Silk damask, brocade, brocatelle, tapestry, and cloth woven with accents of gold and silver thread also were seen. The bold and heavy patterns of the Italian Renaissance were imported from Italy, and with the help of Flemish artisans, Henry IV founded the French luxury textile industry. As the French patterns developed, they favored symmetrically scrolled motifs of fruit, flowers, and stylized leaves.

Window Treatments

Solid shutters inside and/or outside helped occupants to maintain privacy and to protect themselves from colder French winters. Popular treatments were upholstered pelmet or cornice (wooden) boxes with prominent straight lines. Ornate embroidery and passementerie were used as detail on top treatments and on drapery side and bottom hems. Draperies, somewhat flat and rigid, hung in pairs or to one side, straight or tied back. (See fig. 4–8 for window treatments characteristic of both the French and Italian Renaissance.)

ENGLISH LATE MEDIEVAL AND RENAISSANCE: ELIZABETHAN (TUDOR) AND JACOBEAN (STUART) (1558–1649)

Source Names

Elizabeth I (House of Tudor), James I, and Charles I (House of Stuart)

Interior Architecture and Furnishings

In the early part of the period, floors were paved with slate (a gray metamorphic stone) or other stone, or with random wooden planks. Figure C–6 shows slate used on the floor. Early ceilings were plaster and strapwork or wood beams with stucco infill, called half-timber construction, as seen in figure C–6. The great English halls in manor houses or public buildings boasted ceiling beams that trussed upward in hammer-beam construction into giant Gothic arches. These beams often were elaborately carved in patterns of oak-tree stems, leaves, and acorns. Medieval thick stone walls—painted with frescoes and adorned with hanging tapestries, or arras—later gave way to post-and-lintel construction with rough stucco between the exposed half-timbers. The Elizabethan period first used wood as a wainscot (lower portion of the wall) carved in such Gothic motifs as geometric patterns and linen fold. Geometric diamond-shaped carving is seen on the wall, and linen fold is seen as a wainscot beneath the window in figure C–6, representing the earlier portion of the period. Also seen in the interior is an example of strapwork, carved into the transom area above the Tudor windows.

Later in the period wood walls reflected the style, if not the proportions, of the Italian Renaissance brought to England: included were pilasters, overmantles, and raised-panel rectangular walls. Ceilings became more complex as they became coffered (constructed with three-dimensional square patterns) late in the period.

Early windows of this period began as narrow Medieval Norman openings, seen in the castle or "keep." These had round or lancet (very narrow Gothic) shapes. Next came wider Gothic forms filled with stone tracery, and still later heavily leaded windows with small glass panes set into large and beautiful bays, occasionally flanked with pilasters and crowned with Tudor arches. Figure C–6 shows a moderate-size window with Tudor arches and small panes of crown glass set in lead strips, or caming.

Colors

Although colors were inspired by the vivid and rich hues of the Renaissance, pure colors were rare in England. This may have been because early on, England, somewhat isolated, had limited access to luxurious fabrics and brilliant dyestuffs. It also may have been a reflection on the colder climate, the less prosperous economy, and the relative staidness of the English people. Figure C–6 shows bits of color in small proportions at the window; the larger portions of the room are colored with wood and the blue-green of the slate floor.

Textiles

Fabrics were primarily woolen until the reign of Elizabeth I, which brought rich East India Trading Company and Italian Renaissance materials across the English Channel. The lavishness and astounding scale of Italian Renaissance designs eventually appealed to English tastes, and late in the period, England began to clamor for damask, brocatelle, and velvet.

Everything was covered with pattern. Strapwork designs adorned the beautiful embroideries that were still more important than woven fabrics. English garden flowers floated inside each division. The Jacobean period frequently is called the Age of Embroidery. Crewel embroideries on plain linen or woolen cloth stitched out English versions of Tree of Life or Chinese river themes—trailing vines and large flowers of many varieties ideally suited to the display of intricate stitches. Flamestitch designs also were used in woven textiles at the window and as upholstery fabrics.

Window Treatments

The earliest treatment that has been documented in the Medieval English period was leather threaded onto an iron rod. Shown in figure C–6 is a crewel embroidery fabric with "rings" attached (fabric or leather strips). It is strung onto the metal or wood rod that wraps in close to the glass in the projecting bay window. This type of treatment could be drawn closed by pulling the leading edge with a braid or heavy tassel (the clear plastic wand seen in many hotel window treatments had its inspiration here). In cold seasons solid-wood shutters were used.

FRENCH BAROQUE (1643–1730)

Source Names

Louis XIV, the "Sun King". The term *baroque*, French for "irregular," was taken from the Portuguese word *barroco*, meaning an imperfect pearl. Baroque was a period of much ornamentation, with furnishings and accessories curved and flamboyant.

Interior Architecture and Furnishings

Although the interior shown in figure C–7 is of modest size, Baroque châteaux and palaces often displayed awesome scale and splendor. Louis XIV patronized builders and craftsmen of the fine and decorative arts to construct and decorate buildings, such as his palace at Versailles, the most widely copied building in the world. Baroque France became the leader of the Western world to which every country looked for inspiration for art and ornate interior decoration. In figure C–7 we see extensive use of wood wall paneling in rectangular shapes with classical details, often gilded and ornately carved. Floors were oak parquet or marble in black-and-white squares. Figure C–7 shows a highly polished and refined parquet floor. Ceilings usually were coved and embellished with curved, Baroque designs in cast plaster. They were high whenever possible. Also seen in figure C–7 is a Louis XIV chair with straight back, tapered legs, roll-under arms, and scrolled X-stretchers. In the court Baroque furniture often was gold leafed.

Window panes became larger with the advent of cast plate glass (see chapter 1), and gardens seen through the windows were formal and manicured. Figure 4–9 shows a French window treated with period splendor.

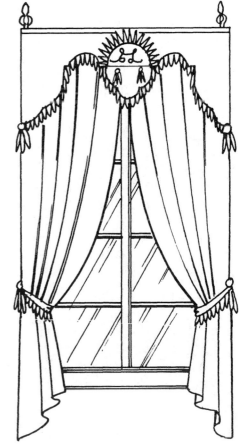

4-9 Back-to-back *L*'s represent the "Sun King," Louis XIV, on the medallion of this Baroque window treatment.

Colors

"Florid," or flushed with rosy red or pink, is an apt description of Louis XIV Baroque interiors. This is illustrated in the more modest interior of figure C–7, where the draperies are of a favored red hue. Golds and silvers were used in fabrics and as leafing or gilding of furniture or architectural trim. Other favorite colors included Medici blue (turquoise), Medici green (a deep mint green), and palace cream (pinkish yellow). White trimming was frequently employed. Colors were vivid and intense in large-scale court interiors but more subtle in smaller interiors, as seen in figure C–7. Note, for example, the upholstery of the Louis XIV chair, which is a tapestry colored with reds, blues, golds, and greens on a somber black background.

Textiles

Typical of the period are needlepoint, tapestries, damasks, brocaded and plain velvets, and heavy silks. Motifs included repeated trellises and baskets, fountains, heavy garlands of fruit and flowers, huge scrolls, and back-to-back *L* letters (for Louis—see fig. 4–9). All patterns were bold and florid, displaying a dazzling interplay of light and shadow. Gold and silver threads were woven into fabric for the "court" (the nobility), adding glitter and rich effects to already sumptuous textiles.

Window Treatments

Typical are draperies that were tied back low, as shown in figure 4–9. A variety of elaborate top treatments were used throughout the period. Generally the lower edges of pelmets were scalloped and sculptured, and the tops were straight or shaped to match the lower edges. Back-to-back or crossed *L*'s, seashells, or sunburst motifs were employed at top or cornice boxes. The ties were braid cord, often tasseled either on the outside or inside of the tie. Figure 4–10 shows a variety of Baroque top treatments, which progress from stiff, formal treatments influenced by the French and Italian Renaissance to the softer, fuller, and more elaborate treatments by interior designer Daniel Marot. These top treatments were used in both France and England. The window shown in figure C–7 features a red ornate fabric and treatment, heavily fringed. Note the gilt seashell at the top.

ENGLISH BAROQUE OR ENGLISH EARLY GEORGIAN (1660–1714)

Source Names

Charles II, James II, William and Mary, and Anne (all House of Stuart). Architect Inigo Jones brought the classic elements from Italy, and Sir Christopher Wren made London famous during this time with his Baroque-style churches and interiors. Window treatments by Daniel Marot also were seen in English Baroque interiors.

Interior Architecture and Furnishings

Some common elements of English and French Baroque can be seen by comparing figures C–7 and C–8. In England the walls were wood paneled, left natural in color, and enlarged to cover the wall from the dado (chair rail and below) to the cornice (molding at the ceiling), with wood panels also seen from the dado to the baseboard (the wainscot). Wood carvings

4-10 Baroque top treatments evolved from a somber, dignified, straight-top, scalloped-bottom style to a curved style that used more fabric toward the end of the period. The pouf valances are credited to French designer Daniel Marot.

shaped as festoons in high relief and with precise floral detail added richness to the warm wood. Grinling Gibbons was the most famous of the wood carver/decorators. Heavy, protruding molding framed the panels and topped the doors and niches in triangular, segmental, broken, or scroll pediment forms or in large shell motifs. (Figure C–8 shows a segmental form.) Late in the period wallpaper became popular. Floors were plank oak and even exotic woods, often topped with luxurious oriental rugs. Plastered ceilings were plain or coved and decorated. Seen in figure C–8 is a ceiling with plaster molding in an ornate pattern.

Windows that became known as English (Late Renaissance) "sash" windows were introduced from the Italian Renaissance and gained great favor during the Baroque period. In figure C–8 the window panes are much larger than in English Medieval and Early Renaissance period interiors, and they are arranged in a formal, rectangular manner, with the entire window area increased dramatically in size.

The furniture of this period was named after William and Mary (joint sovereigns) and their successor, Queen Anne. It endures today as a favored traditional style. The classic Queen Anne chair shown in figure C–8 has a splat back with a fiddle-shape frame, delicately curved arms, and cabriole legs, which appear as separate pieces anchored to the frame. Court furniture often featured detailed carving on the knees, feet, and frame backs of chairs.

Colors

Although English Baroque colors were rich, they were generally more subtle or darker than those of the French period. The English taste began to express itself during this period. Popular hues included Stuart ivory (creamy orange), Dutch blue (a turquoise blue brought from Holland by William and Mary), and Georgian blue (a deep greenish blue). This last color is seen in the draperies, chair, and oriental rug in figure C–8. Other colors were Queen Anne green (dark spring green), light Georgian green (grayish yellow-green), Georgian gray-green (a medium-light greenish gray), and silver gray (deep gray).

Late in the period colors softened and lightened, as seen in Queen Anne chintz and cotton cloth printed with cheerful garden flowers on a white or tinted background. Pinks, teals, blue-violets, and softened golds or mustard yellows were among the favorite chintz colors. This style continued into the next period.

Textiles

In more elegant interiors fabrics such as brocade, brocatelle, damask, and velvet were used extensively. Some crewel embroidery was still in use early in the period, but as Charles II imported elaborate, lavish designs from France, fabrics became much more sophisticated.

William and Mary contributed the Dutch flair for comfort. Late in the period, Queen Anne made popular simple block-printed or silk-screened cotton fabrics—chintz and cretonne decorated with English garden flowers, Chinese motifs, and cockle shells—which were prevalent in less formal rooms. Fabrics were printed with flowing lines and foliage evoking summer climbing vines with resplendent sprays of flowers. In addition, English ladies produced petit-point (needlepoint) fabrics used for upholstery.

Also seen in figure C–8 is a large and intricate oriental rug that adds visual, acoustic, and physical softness to the room.

Window Treatments

Draperies became lavish and beautiful in the English Baroque period. As seen in figure C–8 the fine teal-blue silk at the window is pleated full and flows in puddles onto the floor—a symbol of wealth and opulence. The hardware rods are concealed with a pelmet that is shaped and heavily trimmed with fringe. Also seen are sheer "glass curtains," which gave daytime privacy and much needed fabric softness to the interior.

The Baroque period largely used symmetrical pairs of draperies, either straight or tied back, sometimes trimmed with rope braid. English Baroque rooms frequently were given a heavy cornice molding at the ceiling, and the molding often was boxed out over the window to make a true architectural cornice top treatment (fig. 4–11a).

Another highly successful treatment was the pouf or balloon shade, also called the Parisian, Austrian, or Viennese shade, or the Marot shade after its French designer, Daniel Marot (see fig. 4–10).

An adaptation of the puddled straight draperies is shown in figure 4–11b. This floral-patterned fabric represents the gamut of wonderful English block prints that became well known and appreciated in many of the isolated country estates. The lavish color and pattern provided interest, comfort, and visual warmth during the often cool and inclement weather.

EARLY AMERICAN OR AMERICAN COLONIAL (1608-1790)

Source Names

Early American actually is a vernacular Country English Medieval style, as it developed in America from the memories of those who left England in the Medieval/Early Renaissance period. However, this style is uniquely its own. American Colonial incorporates the time frame prior to the Revolutionary War, and so this period overlaps the Baroque periods of England, France, and other European countries. Here is described the interiors of a lower-income group of people, farmers; the following section, detailing the American Early Georgian period, describes interiors of the well-to-do.

Interior Architecture and Furnishings

As seen in figure C–9 the common wall treatments were exposed stucco (sometimes with half-timber framing exposed, as in the ceiling of figure C–6) and a palisade wall, which consisted of board and batten (wide planks topped with strips to cover the joints). The palisade wall is shown around the fireplace in figure C–9. There was, understandably, no architectural embellishment.

The earliest floors were of earth; then stone; and then broad, random planks. The wooden ceilings were made of a large "summer" beam, which was the main support, or load-bearing, beam crossed with smaller beams. The wood ceiling planks shown in figure C–9 made up the floors of upstairs rooms. These houses often were small, and the dark, warm colors gave interiors a cavelike coziness.

Originally, small casement windows with diamond-shaped panes were prevalent (see fig. C–6). These were often glazed with heavy oiled paper. When glass became more available, about the time of the Revolutionary War, casement windows were largely replaced with the sash windows illustrated in figure C–9.

4-11 English Baroque.

a This wood cornice top treatment is in a typical English Baroque style.

b The printed floral fabric valance and drapery pooled onto the floor reflect the Baroque look of the English country estate.

Another architectural detail shown in figure C–9 is the plank door, hinged with wrought-iron hardware. The fireplace, lined with brick, is very large because it was also used for cooking (note the plates and mugs that line the mantle). The chair is a bow-back Windsor, an adaptation of the English Windsor.

Colors

Somber colors—ecru, parchment, and gray, the hues of natural fibers—were used when no dyes could be obtained. Warm, earthy colors were derived from vegetation. These included indigo blue (deep violet-blue), cranberry red (deep dull red), mustard yellow (mellow orange-yellow), olive green (dull yellow-green), parchment (yellow ivory), flax (light gray-cream), and black.

Textiles

Practically every New England home eventually included a loom. New Englanders learned how to make stripes, checks, and even smaller diaper (tiny diamond-shaped) "dobby" patterns. They spun their yarn from wool, linen, or cotton. Tweed, homespun (seen in the curtains in fig. C–9), and muslin were common fabrics that often appeared in nubby textures reflecting the primitive conditions. Richer fabrics of the era are discussed in the sections on the Georgian periods, which follow.

Since the majority of homespun and hand-woven textiles were used for utilitarian purposes and for clothing, little fabric was left for interiors. Recycling fabric was a necessity. The braided rug on the floor in figure C–9 was made from strips of cast-off clothing. Today, nubby, striped, checked, or calico (small-printed) fabrics and rag rugs give authenticity to Early American or contemporary American Country interiors.

Window Treatments

Quite often the window would be untreated in Early American interiors because of the need to use precious fabric for toweling and clothing. Also, the relative isolation of houses assured privacy even without window treatments. During the winter months, cold air was kept out with solid-panel interior and/or exterior shutters. Colonial curtains were simple and relatively flat, like the classic New England tab curtain seen in figure C–9. Other New England curtains that evolved during and after the Colonial period are illustrated in chapter 5. A shirred valance, used to soften the hard lines of the sash windows, sometimes was the only treatment.

German, or Pennsylvania Dutch (Deutsche), and Dutch Colonial homes often had roller shades at the window. The original roller-shade fabric is called Holland cloth and is a sturdy, heavy material that often was oiled to produce a plasticlike surface. This has evolved into the vinyl shades of today. Stencilwork is another legacy of the Pennsylvania Dutch that continues to give charm to interiors. Stencilwork is rarely even and perfect; the slight irregularities in placement and coloration are part of the appeal. Figure 4–12 shows a simple roller shade stenciled with contemporary American Country geese. A shirred valance is illustrated on an otherwise bare window in figure 4–13a, trimmed with a stencil pattern on the wall. Figure 4–13b shows a sampling of authentic stencil borders used in American Colonial interiors.

4-12 American Country stencil pattern inspired by Early American designs. This one includes a bit of folk art in the painted country geese and stenciled border on the roller shade. The shade, originally of Holland cloth, was brought to America by Dutch settlers.

4-13 Early American folk decorations.

a   A Pennsylvania Dutch (Deutsche) stencil pattern applied around a sash window. The shirred valance adds fabric softness.

b   A selection of authentic American Colonial border stencil patterns reflecting the charm of the human touch. These were used around windows and doors, and along walls, near the ceiling, as a replacement for a cornice molding.

AMERICAN EARLY GEORGIAN (1700–1750)

Source Names

The Georgian period is the more formal part of the Early American or American Colonial era. As the name suggests, it coincided with the reigns of the three kings who ruled England during the pre–Revolutionary War years of the eighteenth century: George I, George II, and George III. Early Georgian is a simplified, scaled-down version of English Baroque, overlapping and following that period by about forty years.

Interior Architecture and Furnishings

Figure C–10 illustrates a typical Early Georgian interior with a broad-plank floor. Wood floor planks gradually became smaller and more refined as the period progressed and were covered wherever possible with oriental rugs, originally called Turkey rugs after one of the principal countries from which the rugs were imported by returning sea captains. Eventually, the more coarse Turkish and Caucasian rugs were replaced by fine Persian rugs, as seen in figure C–10. (Small Turkish rugs were less costly and used in the more formal settings of Early American interiors.)

Plain plaster or wood ceilings and uncomplicated crown moldings, some entablatures and pilasters, and wood walls were acceptable background treatments. Fireplace walls and wainscot or dado moldings were all constructed from wood, pine being the most common. Walls above the dado were of semi-smooth stucco or plaster and were occasionally covered with paper in a Renaissance or Baroque pattern.

The fireplace in figure C–10 is formed with a simple "bolection" molding and lined with blue-and-white Delft tile imported from the Netherlands. Fine porcelain is seen on the mantle, and a long mirror in the Queen Anne style appears on the overmantle.

The window is of the type often called the English sash (see chapter 3), which often was set deep in the wall with a window seat beneath the sash. The chair is similar to the English Baroque Queen Anne chair in figure C–8 but more simple and unembellished.

Colors

The warm colors of wood were an important feature in the Early Georgian color scheme. Although colors were somewhat influenced by the English and French Baroque colors, American Early Georgian hues stressed refinement, and few strong colors were used. The palette was light and medium in value, with only a few dark hues. All were grayed. The most common colors included Virgina green (a grayed spring green, or celedon green), dove gray (a medium-value gray, leaning slightly toward violet), Colonial green (a grayed, slightly bluish green), cupboard red (a dull orange-red), Williamsburg green (gray-green), and Williamsburg blue (a medium-value gray-blue).

Textiles

The fabrics seen in the Early Georgian period were similar to English Baroque textiles, which were inspired in turn by the grand Italian Renaissance patterns. Among wealthy Americans fabrics, including a variety of damasks and brocades, brocatelles, and velvets, were largely imported and nearly cost-prohibitive. Therefore they were used sparingly where they would have the most impact, such as on the chair seat and as a simple swag and cascade at the window in figure C–10.

Window Treatments

As seen in figure C–10, a characteristic window treatment consisted of raised-panel shutters that could be closed completely for privacy and insulation. Here, the swag and cascade top treatment made effective use of the prized, scarce fabric. Figure 4–14a illustrates a stacked double-hung shutter arrangement that often was seen in both homes and public architecture. Figure 4–14b shows a fringed single swag and cascade with Venetian blinds for privacy. Seen in figure 4–14c are two swags—one alone and one with a set of short cascades—two shaped pelmets, and a very streamlined version of a Marot poufed top treatment, surrounded by a wooden "dog-ear" Georgian molding.

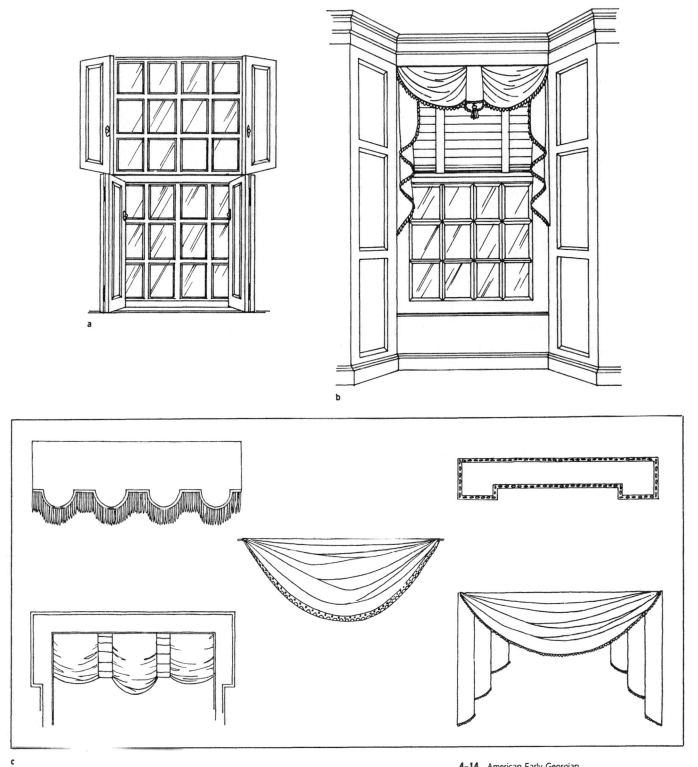

4-14 American Early Georgian.

a A typical hard treatment of the American Early Georgian era: double-hung (stacked) raised-panel shutters.

b The introduction of a top treatment and wood Venetian blinds. Fabric was costly and scarce so it often was used in top treatments only.

c A selection of top treatments that may have been used over shuttered windows.

FRENCH ROCOCO (1730–1760)

Source Names

This period also is known by the name of the reigning French king, Louis XV. Patrons of the arts who were largely responsible for the colors, designs, and tastes of the Rococo period were Madame de Pompadour and later Madame Du Barry. Excessive use of rock and shell designs, originally called *rocaille,* gave rise to the term *Rococo.*

Interior Architecture and Furnishings

The Rococo period followed the French Baroque. Straight lines were all but eliminated. The classical orders and entablature disappeared, replaced by simple architrave (similar to a door-frame molding) at the ceiling. Ceilings often were coved. Scale was reduced to human dimensions, and a feeling of intimacy and femininity prevailed. Fine detailing highlighted an era of luxury, romance, and extravagance. In figure C–11 the wall paneling, or boiserie, has slightly asymmetrical, free-flowing, generously curved molding. Boiserie often was gilded with gold leaf in more formal and court settings. Curves are seen in the overmantle mirror and in the stone fireplace as well as in the Louis XV open armchair, or fauteuil.

The transition from Baroque to Rococo was heavily swayed by Chinese designs imported in the form of textiles, wall coverings, and objets d'art.

The floor in figure C–11 is refined, polished parquet; the area rug is an oriental woven in Rococo colors, a French Savonnerie (hand-knotted pile), or a flat French Aubusson tapestry. Today pile rugs similar to this are commonly woven in India and China and are termed Indo-Aubusson rugs.

The window frame is divided into two lights in a typical French Rococo arrangement. Even the window dividing bars are curved in Rococo fashion. The Rococo theme is further carried out in the wall sconce—an asymmetrical gilt candleholder.

Colors

The colors introduced during the Rococo period are closer to modern tastes, with a refreshing subtlety of muted tones and pastels. The soft hues lent an intimate, soft spoken, and cultured sophistication to the playful curved lines and excessive gilt ornament. They included blues, bluish greens, yellowish greens, pinks, golds, and off-whites. A pinkish-yellow off-white called palace cream is seen in the walls of figure C–11. Another favored color was cloud white (a very pale green). Greens also included powder green (a grayed, lightened yellow-green), French gray (a bluish-green gray of medium-light value) and apple green (a crisp, bright yellow-green); oriental gold was a greenish gold taken from oriental artwork.

Blues included Sèvres blue (a medium-value soft turquoise named for the porcelain factory), Pompadour blue (a medium-value hue slightly on the violet side and slightly grayed), and French turquoise (seen in the draperies and area rug in figure C–11). French lilac was a fairly clear blue-violet of medium value.

Pinks included powder pink, a soft, very light grayed pink; and rose Pompadour, a stronger, deeper pink, as seen in the rug in figure C–11. Du Barry red was a more vivid, coral version of rose Pompadour.

Textiles

Court and upper-class "bourgeoisie" textiles were smooth silk and cotton woven into very fine brocade, satin, damask, and velvet. Textures were lustrous and sometimes slightly irregular, as evidenced by the brocatelle and hand-embroidered *broché* (brocade) fabrics of the time. Very fine petit point was a favored upholstery fabric. Sheers and semisheers were introduced, and crisp yet soft silk textures were favored. Fabrics occasionally were interwoven with gold and silver threads.

Window Treatments

As shown in figure C–11, draperies and pelmets followed the traditional Baroque curve. Beneath the turquoise draperies tied back with shaped ties is seen a sheer Parisian shade rather than a sheer drapery. The pelmet is embroidered with a boiserie design. Figure 4–15a illustrates a full treatment of fringed tieback with crescent-shaped ties. Note that the sheer Parisian shade also is fringed, and the pelmet shows an embroidered shell motif and coved top corners. Figure 4–15b shows two sets of top treatments of varying width, to accommodate windows of increasingly larger size.

Shown in figure 4–15c is a series of top treatments that reflect the curved, graceful lines of the Rococo period. The embroidered designs are based on Chinese motifs and oriental compositions.

COUNTRY FRENCH OR FRENCH PROVINCIAL (1730–1760)

Source Names

This style is the version of Court French Rococo that was adapted to the interiors of the French countryside, where wealth was generally lacking but good taste and style were not. Country French or French Provincial is claimed by some to possess the real charm of the Rococo period, with its unpretentious design and natural materials. It is essentially a toned-down version of Court Rococo without the gilt and ostentation. According to some American furniture manufacturers, French Provincial is a more formal style than Country French, characterized by white-painted furniture with touches or trim of gold leaf, feminine colors, and more formal fabrics. However, this intrepretation is strictly American and is not authentic. Real French Provincial or Country French is described here as the earthy, natural aspect of Rococo, as illustrated in figure C–12.

Interior Architecture and Furnishings

Figure C–12 expresses the essence of Country French interiors. On the floor is seen hexagonal-shaped terra-cotta quarry tile, which also may have been square tile, or brick, or broad plank wood that was not refined but had much character. Interior brick floors were set in basketweave and herringbone patterns, sometimes framed in wood. Seen in figure C–12 are cream-colored walls of stucco. Stucco was the material between frankly exposed half-timber beams on the low ceiling. Fabric such as ticking, Toile de Jouy (see under "Textiles" below), or wallpaper was sometimes employed as wall coverings.

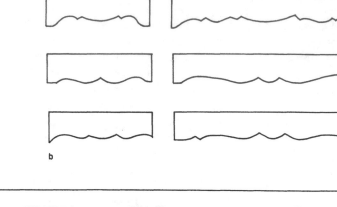

b

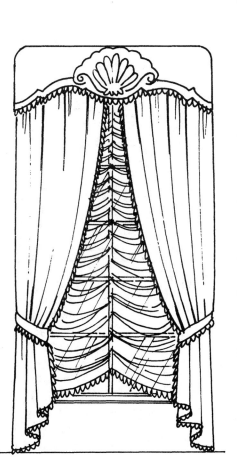

a

4-15 Rococo.

a   Rococo or Louis XV–style treatments were lightly scaled, with delicately curved top treatments, shell motifs, and refined fringes. Austrian shades were popular in this period.

b   The extending size of Rococo top treatments to accommodate wider windows.

c   Rococo top treatments included fabric valances and pelmets, as well as curved, upholstered cornices.

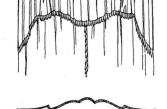

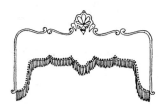

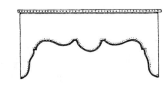

c

Also shown in figure C–12 is a Rococo fireplace, scaled down but very similar to the stone fireplace in figure C–11. In the provinces the mantle would likely have been of wood, carved and left natural or sometimes painted to imitate the more costly stone of the French court interiors. The overmantle here is brick, and on either side of a unicorn tapestry is a Rococo candelabra and a pair of simple candles, imitative of the fine gilt sconces and candelabra of the court.

The small window next to the fireplace is a French casement, and the large glass is a pair of French casement doors (see chapter 3). These have been painted white, but they may easily have been stained or left the natural color of the wood. French windows framed with vertical posts were either rectangular or framed in a segmental (elliptical) arch at the top (see chapter 3).

In the foreground of figure C–12 is an armless side chair with Rococo cabriole (curved) legs. The upholstery is attached with exposed brass-headed nails. The Country French Rococo table is filled with traditional fresh flowers, French bread, wine, cheese, and fruit. In the background is a French ladder-back chair with a rush seat. Other natural fibers are seen in the broom and the baskets. The French love of outdoor beauty is manifest in the potted geranium, floral printed drapery fabric, and well-tended yard beyond the French doors. Some wrought iron and tin also were used for accessories, as seen in the lantern hanging on the wall.

Colors

The colors examined in the French Rococo period all apply to Country French interiors, with an exception. Practicality dictated that very pale colors would not stand up to the less refined country life-style. The colors are, then, related in identity, yet deepened and often set on cream, dark, or colorful backgrounds. Neutrals such as gray, brown, beige, and even black were used. Black is shown in the seat of the side chair and in the unicorn tapestry in figure C–12. Toned-down red, blue, green, and gold often were seen in fabric.

Textiles

Country French fabrics are widely known for their charming floral, striped, and checked patterns. Fabric designer Christophe-Philippe Oberkampf printed French country scenes in one color—black, red, blue, or green—on a cream-colored muslin ground cloth. Because this fabric originated in the town of Jouy, near Versailles, it is known as Toile de Jouy. Toile de Jouy scenes included "men and maids at play," châteaux, gardens, isolated architectural ruins, carriages, agricultural landscapes, and people at work farming. Often they included Chinese "chinoiserie" motifs, such as floating pavilions, and oriental garden paths and flora.

Also popular were woven ticking (navy stripes on a cream background), houndstooth (a checkered woven pattern), and herringbone (a reverse twill or chevron pattern). Tapestries, like the one in figure C–12, were durable textiles used both as wall hangings and upholstery. Printed fabrics were polished cotton, chintz, coarser cretonne, or Oxford cloth or poplin.

Window Treatments

As seen in figure C–12 two types of treatments were popular during this period—shutters and curtains. Shutters, painted or stained, often were mounted both on the inside and on the outside of the building, allowing

4-16 Simplified treatments of the French provinces have become classics. Louvered and solid wood shutters and/or curtains, often shirred onto a wood rod, softened the interior.

light but providing privacy. White and natural were popular choices for interior shutters, while exterior shutters were painted darker values of the period colors (cranberry, blackish turquoise, olive green, and charcoal gray, for example). The exterior shutters may have been nonmovable louvers, raised panels, or plank shutters (see chapter 7).

The curtains shown in figure C–12 are pleated and attached to wooden rings that necessitated hand-drawing. Today dowel rods are available in unfinished, white, or stained wood and can be painted any color or covered with a matching fabric. They also come in plain and fluted varieties. Figure 4–16 shows a shirred curtain treatment for a small window. Authentic dowel rods of the period were left the natural color, stained, or painted. Very seldom were top treatments used in Country French interiors, and they were relatively simple and unaffected when they were seen. Draperies in more formal Country French settings may have had top treatments and been tied back in more elegant fabrics.

ENGLISH MIDDLE GEORGIAN: CHIPPENDALE (1714–1770)

Source Names

The house of Hanover was on the throne during the English Palladian period, which included the reigns of King George I, King George II, and part of the reign of George III (hence the name Middle Georgian). *Palladian* is the adjective describing "classical" architecture and detail by the Italian Renaissance architect Andrea Palladio, whose influence was strongly felt in England and America through contemporary period architects. The man of greatest influence, however, was Thomas Chippendale II, who in 1754 published *The Gentleman and Cabinet-Maker's Directory,* which had profound importance in both England and America. Chippendale took the best of several sources he admired—Louis XIV and XV (Baroque and Rococo), Italian, Gothic, and Chinese—and produced designs so widely copied that even today they are preserved in numerous restorations and re-created in countless modern interior adaptations.

Interior Architecture and Furnishings

Of the amalgamation of styles, figure C–13 illustrates this period as largely Chinese Chippendale. English Palladian is, of course, a mixture of styles. The classic elements of cornice-with-dentil-trim molding at the ceiling and the raised-panel dado painted white were common in English Palladian interiors. The trim may have been a warm cream or even natural wood (pine for walls and mahogany for furniture). Wood floors had straight, medium-width planks and were occasionally topped with oriental rugs. On the wall in figure C–13 is seen a hand-blocked or hand-painted Chinese wallpaper with almost mystical mountains and gnarled oriental trees. Where wallpaper was not used, the painted pine paneling was arranged in raised-panel fashion.

The bed and pelmet "crown" shown in figure C–13 also are in a Chinese Chippendale style, complete with a pagoda roof. Yet we also see the influence of Rococo styling in the filigree detail. The chair has a Chinese influence in the back fretwork. The large English sash window is generous in scale.

Colors

Seen in figure C–13 are some of the notable colors of the period. The draperies are Georgian gold, and the wall covering is Georgian gold and golden taupe (a warm yellowish brown). White is seen on ceiling and dado, in the sheers, and as the background of the bed fabrics. Other important colors were olive green (called deep Georgian green) and soft Georgian green (a medium-value moss or sage green); greens are a historic favorite in England. Popular hues also included English rose (a clear peach especially popular in America) and Chinese reds, as shown in the oriental rug in figure C–13.

Textiles

Silk fabric was preferred during the Palladian era, woven into damask, brocatelle, brocade, and cut velvet. Still in limited use were the Italian Renaissance patterns; however, Chippendale's Gothic, Rococo, and Chinese designs (called chinoiserie) increased the variety of fabric motifs. Exquisitely embroidered fabrics also gave richness to English Palladian or Middle Georgian interiors.

Chintz and toile fabrics inspired by Rococo chinoiserie designs were used extensively in English Country estate interiors. Crewel embroidery also became more popular as the English interpretations of oriental patterns became more airy and lightly scaled.

Window Treatments

As shown in figure C–13 straight sheers and tieback draperies were often seen with an elaborate pelmet. Here they are crowned with Chinese Chippendale carved filigree. The effect often was ponderous and somber, with an occasional note of frivolity, which describes the overall look of this English period.

Figure 4–17 illustrates a selection of window treatments of the English Middle Georgian Chippendale era, which was copied in the colonies as the American Late Georgian style. Note the Chippendale-inspired top treatment over long, straight draperies that pool onto the floor. This is accompanied by a selection of four top treatments that each reflect a Chinese or Rococo influence.

In a less formal room crewel embroideries (with oriental motifs) or printed cotton or linen fabrics might have been shirred onto a wooden rod and topped with a shirred valance with a shaped hemline.

Figure 4–18 shows three examples of art glass (called fanlight or sunburst widows) set into round, keystone arches. The arch, a Palladian trademark, was not filled with glass during the Italian Renaissance. (Also see fig. 3–1 m–o for beautiful Palladian window arrangements.)

AMERICAN LATE GEORGIAN (1751–1790)

Source Names

In America the style called Late Georgian copied English Palladian/Middle Georgian. Architectural patterns were derived from James Gibbs and Palladian designers.

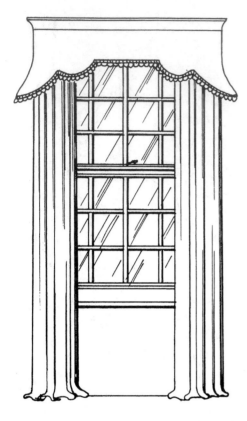

4-17 Draperies and top treatments of the English Middle Georgian and American Late Georgian periods show a strong influence of Chinese Chippendale. The cornices, or pelmets, were capped with wood that was painted, stained, or gilded.

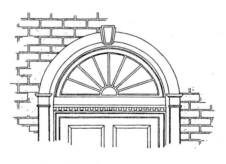

4-18 Georgian semicircular fanlight or sunburst transom windows—seen here above doors and set into classic architectural detail—became an important decorative art-glass form.

Interior Architecture and Furnishings

As compared with the floors of the American Early Georgian period, the wood floors of the Late Georgian period were scaled down and polished to a mellow gleam. Walls were of painted wood or plain, unadorned plaster and often had interesting moldings that produced the look of rectangular panels.

Figure C–14 shows that demand for refinement increased with wealth in the colonies. Designs by Wren and Gibbs were eagerly sought, although local craftsmen simplified and often misinterpreted the scale of the Renaissance cornices, entablatures, pilasters, and columns. Moldings, for example, often appeared top-heavy. Crown moldings, some with dentil trim, and chair-rail moldings were common decorative elements. Hand-painted Chinese wallpapers or large-scale meandering floral fabrics or wall coverings (seen in figure C–14) adorned more formal rooms. Marble was used around fireplace openings, and real or *faux* (imitation) marble adorned some walls or squared pilasters. Widespread use of fine classic detail spread to the homes of the less wealthy in the latter part of the century. Ceilings were of plain plaster or occasionally cast-plaster forms that were inspired by Palladian and Neoclassic English styling.

As seen in figure C–14 classic forms such as pediments were used. Above the stained-wood door is a "broken" pediment, and heavy use of moldings not only reflects Palladian interiors but is also reminiscent of Baroque detailing. The lower portion of the wall, the dado or wainscot, is of painted raised-panel wood, above which is a beautiful floral fabric or wall covering that is similar to the Chinese coverings imported to England from the Orient. Other wall coverings were hand-painted murals depicting scenes from past civilizations, such as Cortez among the Aztecs or ruins of ancient Rome or Greece. The latter became fashionable with the excavation of Pompeii during this period. Larger and more costly oriental rugs appeared on finely polished wood floors as a symbol of new wealth and status.

Furniture was largely Chippendale, with some Queen Anne pieces still quite popular. In figure C–13 we see a Chippendale chair with a cabriole leg. At the foot is Chippendale's famous claw and ball (the Chinese dragon clutching the "pearl of wisdom"). The table next to the chair is a Chippendale "pie crust" tilt-top table, and both are examples of the fine craftsmanship that was available from the furniture makers of both Europe and America. Philadelphia cabinetmakers executed highboys (tall chests on cabriole legs) and other furniture with amazing carved detail and fine workmanship.

The rounded windows illustrated in figure 4–18 and the Palladian window arrangements shown in figure 3–1 m–o were important architectural components. Figure C–13 also shows an English sash window of larger, perhaps slightly exaggerated proportions, through which is seen colonial gardens and Late Georgian architecture. Note that the frame and all the woodwork is painted white, with the exception of the wood door and a chair-rail molding, which is stained a wood color. This combination also was seen in stair balustrades: the balusters or spindles often were painted white and the handrail stained and polished.

Colors

Colors of the English Middle Georgian (Chippendale) period were used in American Late Georgian interiors as well. In America two avenues of color were common. One was the vivid oriental colors espoused by the Chinese Chippendale style—rich reds, golds, and touches of blues (see fig. C–12).

However, these colors generally were not used in large amounts or necessarily next to each other. A drapery at a window may have been gold, with red seen in a chair seat; an oriental rug may have tied the two together. In a few rooms red, blue, and gold appeared together in greater quantity, but this scheme was the exception rather than the rule, and it would have likely included white or light-cream walls and mahogany-colored wood trim characteristic of the period.

The other avenue of Late Georgian reflected the trend in the latter part of the period to lighten color. This was undoubtedly influenced by the colors discovered at Pompeii. The peach color called English rose is seen in figure C–14 as Vernon rose (named for Mount Vernon, home of George Washington) and is also known as Georgian peach. A favorite color toward the end of the period, Vernon rose sometimes was accented or combined with a green or blue. This may have been Charleston green (light olive), blue room (a medium-dark, grayed teal blue), Vernon blue (an American version of Adam green that is a clear, greenish turquoise), Washington gold (buff, or a slightly greenish yellow-beige), or Vernon gray (a light gray-violet).

Textiles

Rich textiles, still reflecting Italian Renaissance designs and colors, often were imported to America during the late Georgian period. The patterns gradually gave way to the more Rococo and Chinese influences, with lighter values and softer colors, as seen in figure C–14. Although the finest fabrics—woven silk, damask, velvet, and brocatelle—were still imported from Europe, the textile-manufacturing system in America had come into its own. By the 1860s cotton and linen factories were copying the crewel and chintz designs of the English Palladian period. As the period progressed, the textures became smoother and yet more refined.

Window Treatments

Where they could be afforded, pairs of long draperies, sometimes pooling onto the floor, were used. Tied-back fabrics were finished with silk tassels and fringes in formal settings. Top treatments largely reflected Chinese Chippendale designs, and the English Middle Georgian window treatments illustrated in figure 4–17 were used in America, although the complexity of the design was sometimes simplified in the States. The wood-slat blind, known as the Venetian blind, also was used during the Late Georgian period, perhaps with only a top treatment, as shown in figure 4–14b. Raised-panel shutters were the other means of establishing privacy where long draperies were not used. These shutters were stacked off into the deep-set window wall and appeared to be a part of the architecture when they were opened.

FRENCH NEOCLASSIC (1760–1789)

Source Names

This period appeared simultaneously in France, England, and America. In France it also is known by the name of the reigning monarch, Louis XVI. The abrupt change that came about between the Rococo/Georgian period and the Neoclassic period was due to the excavations of Pompeii and its sister city, Herculaneum. The chief archaeologist, a German named Johann Winckelmann, published a monumental series of works between 1762 and 1767 that fascinated the world of architecture and interior design, causing the transition to delicate, refined Neoclassicism. It should be noted that although this period bears the name of Louis XVI, who reigned from 1774 to 1789, it began fourteen years before the death of Louis XV. Textile designers of importance were Philippe de la Salle and Jean-Baptiste Huet, both of whom produced designs for this period and for the following Empire period.

Interior Architecture and Furnishings

As depicted in figure C–15 the lines of the architecture became straight and small scaled. In France the rooms themselves were constructed on a smaller scale whenever possible, although high ceilings and tall French windows were common. In addition, the rooms were not always square. Round, elliptical, and even hexagonal or angular rooms had been discovered in Pompeii and became very popular in Europe and America. A round room from a contemporary period is seen in figure C–16.

Figure C–15 illustrates the period treatment of walls, which were of wood painted off-white and decorated with delicate, symmetrical rectangular panels, often in a contrasting color or with an accenting stripe near the molding. The fine cast-plaster classical decorations and straight moldings of French rooms sometimes were trimmed in silver or gold leaf. The walls of more elegant homes were ornamented with stucco bas-relief or cast plaster painted with classical figures; arabesques (fine vertical detailing); garlands; or natural flowers in swag or festoon form, with fluttering bow ribbons. Classical elements included cornice molding with dentil trim, friezes, columns, and pilasters decorated with arabesques. Other Neoclassic forms included acanthus (Grecian thistle) leaves, wreaths, and rosettes.

Seen in figure C–15 are prominently straight lines given relief with delicate festooning around the ceiling. An oval *patterae* is painted above the door with a book and foliage, representing knowledge of antiquity through book study. The oval is surrounded with cast-plaster garlands. The overmantle mirror also is topped with cast-plaster vases and ancient Roman motifs. The fireplace is flanked with small-scale rounded half-columns, called pilasters, topped with gold-leafed Ionic capitals. The mural painted next to the window represents the beautiful gardens of ancient Herculaneum, whose inhabitants lovingly cultivated and tended climbing vines on classic columns. This scene looks across the Bay of Naples on the southwest Italian coast to Mt. Vesuvius, which towered above Pompeii and in 79 A.D. buried it in hot ashes, remarkably preserving the city. (Herculaneum was destroyed by earthquakes and mud slides.)

The floor seen in figure C–15 is finely scaled wood parquet. Some rooms were laid with marble, here seen in the fireplace hearth. The rug is a French Aubusson. The window is a French casement door with rectangular panes looking out to a formal French garden.

Furnishings shown in figure C–15 are a pair of Louis XVI, or Neoclassic, fauteuil chairs with open arms; tapered, fluted legs; and an oval back. The *bouillotte* table also has straight legs and an oval top with tiny gold gadrooning, or repeated festoon ornamentation. On the wall is a gilt sconce with candle lamps. The sconce is straight with a fluttering ribbon at the top. Accessories on the mantle represent decorative art from the classical Roman period.

Colors

Although the colors found in Pompeii were vibrant and bold, they did not find acceptance until the Empire period. Colors of the French Neoclassic period were largely dictated by Queen Marie Antoinette's taste, and they were very subtle indeed. These included chalk green (a soft mint green), chalk beige (a dark, warm beige), flesh pink, as seen on the upper walls of figure C–15, and gray–ivory, as depicted on the lower wall portion. French rose is seen in the draperies, chairs, and rug. Pale ivory is the background color of the mural. Gray-blue and azure blue are seen in the rug, the mural, and the chairs. The entire room is trimmed in white and gold. Some Neoclassic French rooms were done completely in silver-blue and some in very pale golds; both schemes were largely devoid of color. Figure C–15 depicts the richer and prettier color scheme of the French Neoclassic period.

Textiles

Brocade, smooth satin, armure (tiny woven designs), lampas, and fine velvets were most common. Silk fabrics, with their smooth, dry hand, were in demand. In addition to the other classical motifs, stripes with intertwining flowers or ribbons were typical, and a lightly scaled, refined feeling of detailed delicacy was present in all textiles. Semisheer and lightweight, translucent fabrics were popular at the window, as seen in the overdraperies and top treatment in figure C–15. Draw sheers also were frequently seen as glass curtains.

Window Treatments

The refined fabrics described above lent themselves to lightly scaled treatments of straight or narrow tieback overdraperies. As mentioned above, ceilings were frequently very high, and tall, narrow windows were well served by long, slender tieback draperies. In figure C–15 the draperies are separated to give that effect. Sheers and translucent semisheer fabrics were used for draw underdraperies or as Austrian shades similar to the Rococo treatment shown here.

Top treatments of the French Neoclassic period were delicately scaled and often detailed with embroidery, fringe, and fluttering ribbons and tassels. In figure C–15 a simple top treatment similar to an Austrian shade is shown with small-scale trim. Figure 4–19 shows a selection of lovely Neoclassic pelmets and fabric valances.

ENGLISH NEOCLASSIC (1770–1820)

Source Names

The Neoclassic period in England had the same roots as the French period it overlapped and followed. In England the reigning monarchs were George III, who ruled until 1811, and George IV, who set the tone for the severe Neoclassic style known as *Regency* when he ruled England as regent between 1811 and 1820. The most influential architect, designer, and cabinetmaker of the era was Robert Adam, who had spent an extended period of time in Italy making reduced-scale drawings of interior and exterior architecture, details, and motifs of the classical Roman era, and then brought his designs back to northern Europe to transform Palladian Britain

4-19 The French Neoclassic style is associated with the reign of Louis XVI. Treatments combined straight lines with festoons, fluttering ribbons and bows, and classical elements. Lovely fringed, often slender tiebacks were popular.

into Neoclassic Britain. Preserved Adam-Neoclassic interiors are among the most beautiful. Furniture designers Thomas Sheraton and George Hepplewhite produced designs that filled Neoclassic interiors both in England and in America. Thomas Chippendale III also created beautiful Neoclassic furniture. It was the Age of Satinwood.

Interior Architecture and Furnishings

Figure C-16 represents an Adam-Neoclassic interior. It is evident from the size of the chair that the scale of the room is enormous. High, vaulted ceilings were not uncommon; and the elliptical shape, although not pervasive in interior architecture, was an important element. The curved part of the ceiling is filled with arabesques and medallions of Wedgwood Jasperware, which also adorn the mantlepiece. Above the arabesques is a running *rinceau* pattern of cast plaster, and beneath the arabesques is a frieze of scrolls and anthemion motifs. All these designs were adopted from the classical Roman era. The ceilings of smaller interiors were plaster, plain and flat in modest homes and ornamented with anaglypta (decorative cast-plaster forms) in luxurious ones. Walls were predominantly plaster, painted in colors and trimmed with white or cream. Molded reliefs were painted white to contrast with colored backgrounds. Slender pilasters, complete entablatures, Greek details, and wall niches with Greek and Roman statues or busts were common. Doors had rectangular panels defined by applied moldings and flanked by pilasters.

Note the marble hearth and Venus-like statuette on the mantle in figure C–16. A semicircular cast-plaster or carved Roman arch is seen above the mirror, and the elliptical firescreen and hearth fender echo the shape of the room.

Wood floors were prevalent in this period, as in other periods, yet also installed were floors of marble and other stone with inlaid elliptical sunburst patterns and other classical Adam designs. The high window reveals the serene and picturesque grounds of an English country estate, where much of the Adam architecture outside London was executed. Although this window is a large-scale, long English sash (note that the window ends at the floor), Palladian window arrangements and elliptical fanlight transom art glass also were important to the architecture.

Colors

Represented in figure C–16 is a color scheme sometimes employed by Robert Adam—a stunning combination of Adam pink (a pinkish coral) and Adam gray (a taupe-gray seen on the upper walls). Here the contrast is part of the drama, with values ranging from medium to very dark, and colors set off by white trim. Perhaps Adam's most famous colors were his light Adam green, a clear, slightly blued or softened green, and deep Adam green, an avocado color used repeatedly and prolifically in England since this period. Adam yellow, a clear lemon yellow, and British gold, an avocado-gold, were used for upholstery and accent. Other tones preferred by Adam were opal pink, opal blue, and opal green, which were soft, light, grayed colors.

Inspired by Adam's colors and the famous Portland vase, Josiah Wedgwood developed his Jasperwear, modeled after that classical Greek porcelain prototype (now in the British Museum) with light, bas-relief figures on a darker background. These colors became very important to Neoclassic interiors and included pale Grecian blue (a medium-light–value violet-blue), British blue (deep aqua), Wedgwood blue (light royal blue), Grecian lilac (a medium-value gray-violet), Jasper yellow (a dull orange-yellow, like eggnog), and Regency red (a dull, light brick red or deep coral).

Textiles

Like the French, the English prized refined silks, including plain satin, brocade, lampas, damask, and fine-textured velvets. Mass-produced toile and block- and screen-printed cottons and linens were used for informal rooms. These fabrics displayed the classical designs described above, including Greek fretwork, disciplined fine stripes, landscapes of classical ruins, and motifs of honeysuckle, festoons, and tiny husks. Medallion patterns bore dancing nymphs, floating fabrics, doublets of griffins, or rams' heads. Other formal motifs included flaming torches, Cupid's bow and quiver, candelabra, and urns. Note the woven Wilton or Axminster area rug in a pattern that reflects Adam designs.

Window Treatments

As shown in figure C–16, tieback draperies were so slender they were nearly straight. Also seen are restrained sheer Austrian shades (raised) and a softly shaped and pleated fabric valance that ends in cascades at the sides. Figure 4–20 illustrates Neoclassic top treatments that may have been used in France as well as England, although extreme delicacy and an element of frivolity were more characteristically French, whereas a frank and restrained look was more English (see fig. 4–19). Undertreatments for privacy, warmth, and protection of the delicate fabrics included raised-panel shutters (seen recessed in fig. C–16) and Venetian blinds.

AMERICAN FEDERAL OR NEOCLASSIC (1790–1820)

Source Names

The American design era that followed the French and English Neoclassic period sometimes is called Neoclassic. More often, however, it is known as Federal, a title inspired by the birth of a new nation. Two of the period's best-known architect/designers were Samuel McIntire and Charles Bulfinch, both of whose work is seen extensively in New England, Washington, D.C., and bordering areas.

Interior Architecture and Furnishings

Interiors in the Federal period, represented in figure C–17, were much more simple and restrained than those of France or even England. Seen here are plain plaster walls, which were occasionally wallpapered; simple cornice moldings, sometimes with dentil trim; a raised-panel dado; and cast-plaster anaglypta in the Adam manner. The fireplace has a true Adam mantle complete with center block, classic festoon detailing, and pilasters with a simple Ionic capital. Over the door is seen a bracketed cornice with fine detail work. The window is much smaller than in the English Neoclassic style, but it still is an English sash, with raised-panel shutters recessed into the window well. Wood floors continued in popularity, covered over with French Aubusson or English Wilton or Axminster carpets.

In the background of figure C–17 is a Sheraton/Hepplewhite "shield-back" chair with a sheaf-of-wheat design; the rectangular cornice mirror above it echoes the door treatments.

Often, elliptical arches or fanlights separated rooms, and elliptical fanlights or rectangular transom lights, flanked by sidelights, were leaded into scrolled designs (fig. 4–21). These arrangements make up some of the most beautiful entrances in America.

Colors

Colors were similar to those of France and England and overlapped the Late Georgian era ("the second avenue" of Late Georgian color) but specifically the following were prevalent: Federal blue (seen in fig. C–17), Newport yellow (a creamy, rich yellow), Salem white (yellowish off-white), Virginia green (a spring or moss green), Vernon gray (gray-violet), Vernon blue (greenish turquoise), Vernon rose (a lighter, grayed coral), Washington gold (the famous buff of George Washington's uniform), and Colonial green (a deep seafoam green). Rooms painted in these colors were invariably trimmed in white or cream.

Textiles

The same fabrics were used as in France and England: silk, plain satin, damask, brocade, lampas, and some velvets for formal rooms. The motifs

4-20 The Neoclassic period in England saw interiors de-signed by Robert Adam. Delicately swagged fabric top treat-ments complemented the Neoclassic interpretation of interior architecture in England and France. These styles were widely copied and adapted in America during the Federal Period.

seen in American Federal were fine and wide stripes, some floating ribbons, small-scaled ovals, classical designs, pineapples (the Colonial symbol of hospitality), and Chinese-inspired details. Printed cottons began to be used, particularly those inspired by the French Empire period, which the Federal period overlapped.

Window Treatments

Seen in figure C–17 is a very conservative upholstered cornice. Straight and narrow, it tops tieback draperies and recessed raised-panel shutters. The double-tieback treatment with a single swag or festoon in figure 4–20 is characteristically Federal, inspired by Greek clothing worn by women depicted on ancient vases and pottery. Late in the period layered fabric was used, for example, a semisheer or sheer cotton or wool hung straight or swagged and tied back to one side. On top of this might have been another layer tied back to one side, topped with a swag or single festoon and perhaps a cascade only on the side where the drapery was tied back. This elegant treatment generally was fringed, reflecting the Empire influence that was already under way in France (see fig. 4–22).

FRENCH EMPIRE (1804-1820)

Source Names

The period from the execution of the French nobility to the time when Napoleon proclaimed himself king is known as the Revolution, or Directoire, period in France. The motifs of this interim were carried over to the French Empire, so called because Napoleon, who was a military genius of a conquering spirit, was determined to establish an empire equal to or greater than the republican Roman Empire. In England this period coincided with the Regency period, and in America it is known as American Empire. The source, however, was decidedly French.

Interior Architecture and Furnishings

Figure C–18 shows an interior that represents some important architectural and decorative elements of the French Empire. Wood panels in geometric shapes form wide, solid French doors. These panels may have been carved or embellished with anaglypta in motifs of agricultural imple-

4-21 Art glass from the Federal and Greek Revival/American Empire eras.

a Transom light and sidelight art glass.
b Elliptical sunburst on fanlight and sidelight art glass.

a

b

ments, sheaves of wheat, symbols of the revolution, or designs taken from classical Rome. The plain plastered walls are painted around symmetrical mirrors. Late in the period delicate figures adapted from the classical eras were painted on walls or ceilings. Walls also may have been painted to imitate marble or covered with scenic wallpaper or even wood panels. Napoleon had some walls draped with fabric, pleated and falling in soft folds, to resemble a Roman military tent.

The painted ceiling in figure C–18 is designed to appear as a dome; the rounded walls and domed effect copied a rotunda, or round receiving area in Roman public architecture. The rounded Roman arches often were decorated with reclining classical figures in bas-relief and gilt. Figure C–18 shows cornice and dentil trim molding at the ceiling, edged with gold leaf.

The marble floor in figure C–18 has a black-and-white-checkered pattern; wood sometimes was seen. Most rooms were softened with a French pile Savonnerie rug in Empire colors and designs made popular by Napoleon's preferences. Next to the window is an Empire or Directoire chair. The splayed legs (flaring out) were adapted from the Klismos chair of ancient Greece.

Colors

The colors shown in figure C–18 are symbolic of Napoleon's personal taste. The rich, deep Empire red, green, and gold were strong hues, sometimes used lavishly, that were revealed by excavations at Pompeii and seen in mosaic tilework. Other colors of the period included amethyst (a vivid lilac), deep ruby (a browned red), tobacco brown (a dark reddish brown), Empire yellow (a bright bumblebee yellow), azure blue (a rich sky blue), salmon (a peachy coral), gray-blue (a medium-light–value blue), and pale ivory (a peachy yellow).

Textiles

The Empire period increased the demand for smooth satins. Moiré (textured with a watermark design) and polished satin were quite popular, and some brocade, brocatelle, and lampas were in demand. Sheer wool fabrics, such as fine nun's veiling, were used as underdraperies. Printed fabric appeared on the scene in great quantity with the invention of the roller printing machine, and the Jacquard loom produced quantities of woven textiles. Designs on fabric included wide stripes, urns, torches, acanthuses, anthemia, and lyres, borrowed from Roman models. Swags or festooned designs appeared on many printed and woven fabrics. Often a smooth satin plain ground, called an open field, would have a small motif, such as a honeybee, a laurel wreath, or a star, or the fabric would be woven into broad stripes. The textiles Napoleon favored were bold and brilliant in texture and design. Pattern sizes ranged from tiny to very large.

Window Treatments

The two key words that describe Empire treatments are *layered* and *asymmetrical*. As pictured in figure C–18 the tiebacks do not center-meet. One is more narrow and tied back higher than the other, and the heavier side has yet another deep, swagged fabric layered on top. The top treatment was most frequently draped in an unconstructed manner over the top of a metal rod. This treatment is heavily fringed and tasseled, and the rod and decorative metal ornaments are gilded. Figure 4–22 illustrates two complete Empire treatments, each tied back to one side. One has Roman

4-22 French and American Empire window treatments were asymmetrically draped with layers of silk, wool, and cotton. Elegance was achieved through heavy draping and trimmings. Rods often were exposed wrought-iron spears or ropelike shaped metal.

motifs on the frieze and a cornice and dentil trim above the top treatment; the pilasters have Egyptian column capitals. This treatment is layered beneath with shutters. The other full treatment has one straight panel and one tied-back panel held with a chain and metal rosette tieback holder. It also was common practice to layer a straight or tied-back sheer beneath the fabric, and the sheers themselves sometimes were patterned with small designs. Figure 4–22 also shows a fine selection of swagged Empire top treatments. Some of these have rods in the shape of arrows (symbols of the revolution), and several are draped in a style reminiscent of Napoleon's military tent interiors. Fabric at the window in Empire interiors was sumptuous.

AMERICAN EMPIRE (1820–1860)

Source Names

The American Empire closely followed the designs, colors, motifs, and furniture of the French Empire. America was sympathetic to France, which at this time had just undergone a revolution and overthrown a monarchy, much as America had symbolically done. The French also were striving for a democracy, although in this they were less successful than the Americans. In America these interiors largely were seen in antebellum Greek Revival homes and public architecture. The foremost furniture designer was Duncan Phyfe.

Interior Architecture and Furnishings

Figure C–19 represents an American Empire interior. Architecture here reveals plain plastered walls, a low chair-rail molding, and a deep cornice. The pillar in the foreground sports a Corinthian capital of stylized acanthus leaves. Fireplaces in American Empire rooms most often were of black marble, and the pillar seen here represents the heavier scale of the period. Above the mantle is a bull's-eye mirror capped with a Federal eagle. The carpet is a woven Wilton or Axminster. This was the first time broadloom carpet was available and installed wall-to-wall. The window is large and low to the floor, as was typical in formal rooms. The scale of the room itself gives a feeling of spaciousness.

The harp was a status symbol. Every important parlor was expected to have one.

Colors

The colors used in the American Empire period followed almost exactly those of the French Empire. Figure C–19 indicates that red and olive green were color scheme adaptations that were particularly popular. Yet this room shows only one facet of American Empire. The pure French Empire rooms in the White House—the Red Room and the Green Room—are of far stronger intensity than the interior shown in this illustration. On the other hand some American Empire rooms were done in very pale, dull colors, moving predominantly to the grayed mauves. This interior rests somewhere between those extremes. Refer to the section on French Empire colors for specific names and descriptions.

Textiles

The textiles of this period also echoed those used in France: smooth satins and cottons, woven Jacquards, printed fabrics, and motifs that matched the French designs. Seen in figure C–19 is the Napoleonic star woven into the carpet and a tiny motif in the chair fabric.

Window Treatments

Figure C–19 shows a printed (or perhaps woven) light fabric at the window, topped with a ponderous and dominating swagged treatment. The green fabric is backed with gold and heavily fringed. The center tab or straight-bottom jabot has an embroidered design and a conspicuous tassel. The cornice above the fabric is gilt and resembles the ropelike design of the metal hardware seen in some of the examples shown in figure 4–22. American Empire top treatments tended to be very deep, swagged, and sometimes overbearing. Yet some top treatments were lovely because of the depth and richness of the fabric, the festooning, and the trimmings. For example, vertically striped fabrics used as top treatments could be quite dramatic and effective in making a strong statement. Greek Revival homes also were heavily influenced by French Rococo Revival furniture, and top treatments for these interiors usually were shaped pelmets in simple and tasteful fabrics or in strongly patterned fabrics, such as cut or patterned velvet, that were heavily fringed.

AMERICAN AND ENGLISH VICTORIAN (1837-1920)

Source Names

The Victorian era was named after Queen Victoria, who reigned for sixty-four years during the Industrial Revolution. Her consort, Prince Albert, was a great patron of the arts. He sponsored a series of exhibitions designed to arouse interest in the manufacturing of art, which led to the Crystal Palace at the London exhibition in 1851. This huge extravaganza spread Victorianism everywhere.

Interior Architecture and Furnishings

During the Victorian era there were many exterior styles, yet only three interior styles became well known and copied. These were Rococo Revival, Renaissance Revival, and Classic Revival. Two architect/designers became famous: John Belter (Rococo Revival) and Charles Eastlake (Renaissance Revival).

The Victorian era was a time of revivals of many sorts. The English Regency style, which came at the beginning of the English and American Revival periods, drew heavily on Gothic, Italian Renaissance, Indian, Chinese, and French prototypes. Other influences were Egyptian, Turkish, Moorish, Greek, Byzantine, Persian, and Venetian. All these styles eventually melted into the eclectic Victorian hodgepodge of excessive, overbearing design. Although furniture designer William Morris and others instituted guilds—such as the Arts and Crafts movement, which promoted hand-crafted furnishings and decoration—the masses, clamoring for more of everything, found craftsmanship too costly or scarce. The Industrial

Revolution, then, facilitated the excessive ornamentation that was so in vogue and financed the travels of newly rich industrial magnates, who brought styles from around the world home to the nest.

The permeating philosophy of the Victorian Era was "more is better." Many busy designs competed in each room. Sometimes the effect was cozy and charming, even endearing; other times it was ostentatious. Figure C-20 illustrates a Rococo Revival interior with a dominating Wilton carpet in dark colors and flowing, complex pattern. Although the walls here are painted, Victorian walls often were covered with a floral or scenic wallpaper that competed with the patterned carpet. Toward the end of the period, the carpet may have been covered with oriental or bearskin rugs (reminders of travels). Where cornice molding was seen in other periods, the trim here is pierced filigree, which was made of cast plaster. A matching filigree medallion is seen in the center of the ceiling, with a gaslight chandelier suspended below. The mirror and carved fireplace mantlepiece reflect the Rococo period in excess, and the chair seen here is a Rococo Revival piece, quite popular in the Deep South during the antebellum period, and a general Victorian favorite. The hearth is marble, as were the tops of most occasional tables, and the opening of the fireplace was almost always rounded.

Colors

Victorian colors spanned a very wide spectrum from bright to dull. Fuchsia and light green are seen in the drapery and wall paint in figure C–20, and dark somber reds, blue-greens, and cream colors appear in the carpet. Variations of red included Victorian rose (a dull dark pink), fuchsia (a bright violet-pink), Victorian mauve (a very dark, grayed violet), gray-mauve (just as it sounds), wine red (a very deep burgundy), taupe (brownish gray), and cedar rust (orange-brown). Greens were second in popularity, including Stuart green (a bright forest or kelly green), dark olive (similar to avocado), sage green (a dull, dark grayed green), and various blue-greens, such as the one seen in figure C–20, which is a lightened version of Chinese blue (teal or greenish blue). Tobacco brown (very dark brown) also was seen as a holdover from the Empire period. The overall color effect of most Victorian interiors was dark and somber, with small areas of intense color.

Textiles

In the Victorian era many different textiles were used. Perhaps the most popular was velvet, especially antique and floral cut velvet. Another much-used fabric was printed cotton in a vast array of designs, most of which were borrowed from other periods or combined into busy and unrelated patterns. Silklike fabrics appeared in the form of real silk or rayon, "poor man's silk." Both formal and informal fabrics favored floral motifs, such as roses and bouquets. The cabbage rose (in full flower) was perhaps the most common, appearing in carpeting, wall coverings, and fabrics. Patterns often were overscaled, elaborate, and repetitious. Sheer fabrics came onto the market, and lace panels were seen at nearly every window.

Window Treatments

The window treatment seen in figure C–20 was typical of the more formal Victorian parlor. It consists of heavy overdrapery and a large-scale top treatment with added ornamentation in the form of deep fringes and gilt

4-23 The English and American Victorian era saw heavy use of swagged top treatments layered over the top of lace curtains and cumbersome overdraperies. The important interior styles were Rococo Revival, Renaissance Revival, and Classic Revival.

metal trimming. Figure 4–23 illustrates a sampling of Victorian top treatments of varying degrees of ornateness.

The lace sheers tied back in figure C–20 may have hung straight, with the overdraperies tied back, as seen in the full window treatments in figure 4–23. Metal tieback holders were very popular. Both sheers and overdraperies were patterned in large, unrelated designs, and both competed with the patterns in the upholstery, wall coverings, and carpet.

As noted, Victorian is a culmination of many styles. Refer to the selection of fabric tiebacks and tieback holders in figure 4–24. It will be apparent at this point that some styles are decidedly Renaissance, some Baroque, some Rococo, some Neoclassic, and some Empire. Several of these ex-

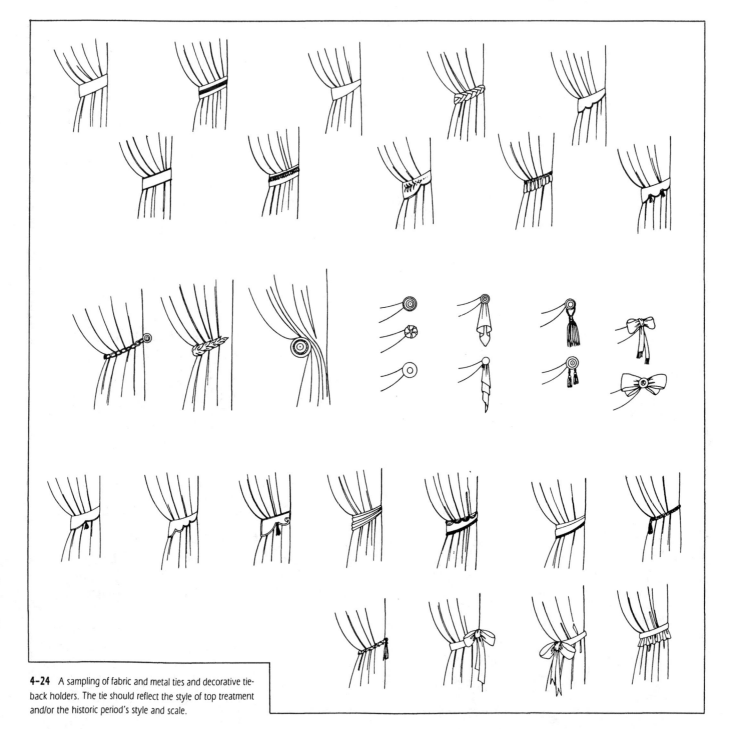

4-24 A sampling of fabric and metal ties and decorative tieback holders. The tie should reflect the style of top treatment and/or the historic period's style and scale.

amples might be used in more than one period. Above all the tie should coordinate with the top treatment, or, when no top treatment is used, the tie should reflect the general feeling of the drapery treatment and the interior.

With the Industrial Revolution came the first traverse rods with cords and pulleys. In less formal rooms these new draw draperies usually were made of a printed cotton with semisheer or lace curtains underneath. Shutters or Venetian blinds occasionally were used next to the glass.

The excessive coverage of windows often rendered the Victorian interior dark. Today revived Victorian homes often are stripped of their heavy velvets, damasks, and printed cottons, and the architecture surrounding the large window is left bare, with minimal coverage. This is especially true where the stripping process reveals stained glass, a busy but artistic heritage of the era.

Victorian stained glass is considered both an art-glass window and a window treatment. Victorian art glass is prized today for its historic significance and interest if not for its good design. In modern interiors a bit of nostalgia often is a refreshing counterpoint. Figure 4–25 illustrates a selection of Victorian stained or art glass set within and reflecting borrowed architectural window shapes, such as Gothic, Tudor-arch, segmental Neoclassic, round, and transom windows.

4-25 A sampling of Victorian art glass.

a A modified Gothic arch with medieval quatrefoil tracery.

b A Tudor arch with borrowed Art Nouveau fleur-de-lis design.

c Classic Greek Revival urn motif.

d Keystone-shaped window with flowing composition.

e Late Victorian stained-glass transom—busy in line, color, and pattern.

Artisan Louis Comfort Tiffany brought into fashion the naturalistic forms and designs of the Art Nouveau style (1890–1910) through his stained and painted art glass. Art Nouveau had its beginnings in the Arts and Crafts movement founded and advocated by William Morris and John Ruskin, and it permeated printing, posters, architecture, furniture, and interior design.

Art Nouveau motifs were taken almost exclusively from nature: vines; leaves; stems with budding, blooming, and seeding flowers; ocean waves; twisting smoke; flowing tresses of women's hair; and the feminine form (rounded and soft). Japanese design strongly influenced Art Nouveau. Prevalent were oriental motifs, especially the cherry blossom, the peacock, the dragon fly, and the lily pad. These designs followed the lines of nature with winding foliage and curving yet stylized forms. The colors were soft, hazy summer colors of natural foliage and evening sunsets—a spectrum that was so muted and varied that individual names were not created. Art Nouveau stained glass is seen in figure 4–26. It remains appreciated and used today.

4-26 Stained or art glass of the Art Nouveau style, which was used at the end of the Victorian era and is still appreciated today. Note the graceful, flowing lines based on nature, converging and then opposing in near-perfect symmetry or in beautifully balanced asymmetry. Seen here is the peacock, a favorite Art Nouveau motif. Also seen are three pairs of stained glass with motifs based on flowers, stems, and leaves.

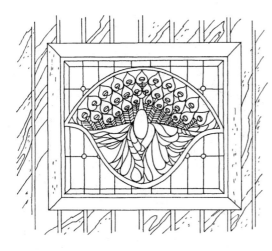

SCANDINAVIAN MODERN (1900–PRESENT)

Source Names

The Scandinavian countries—Denmark, Sweden, Finland, and Norway—have made a remarkable contribution to the modern world in fine interior design and superior-quality craftsmanship. Perhaps one reason why Scandinavian design is a world leader is that the Scandinavian countries never went through the rigors of the Victorian era. They came relatively unscathed from a wonderful folk style of architecture and furnishings directly into the age of the machine in the early 1920s, about the time that the Bauhaus was founded in Germany. The Bauhaus brought together artists, architects, craftsmen, and furniture/interior designers to design for the machine, using "modern" materials such as steel and glass. The Scandinavians adopted what was good from the Bauhaus and kept traditions of handcraftsmanship and natural materials such as wood and leather, adding new man-made fiber textiles and designs. The result was a unique combination that has won approval and appreciation around the world.

A host of designers from Scandinavia have made valuable contributions to the modern scene. These include Eero Saarinen, Gunar Asplund, Alvar Aalto, Finn Juhl, and Hans Wegner.

Interior Architecture and Furnishings

Figure C–21 illustrates a modern interior that reflects the Scandinavian appreciation for natural beauty and for materials that arc both natural and man-made. The scale of living in Scandinavian countries is small, and the need to extend space has been accomplished with large plate-glass or float-glass windows (see chapters 1 and 3). Here we see the glass framed in bronzed steel. The scene outside is of a meadow, indicating that this building may be a small country home. Extensive glass and a wall extending to a patio give the impression of a bigger interior. (This concept has been a great influence to modern design.) Double or triple glazing renders large expanses of glass more practical for the Scandinavians, who delight in making the exterior a visual extension of the interior. Sliding glass doors are common, as are attic windows (see chapter 3).

Wood is perhaps the chief building material, with pine, birch, fir, spruce, oak, and teak most common. Wood is used in strips or beams on ceilings, as flooring, and for walls. Other prevalent wall materials are brick (as seen in figure C–21), tile, and rough plaster. The floor also may be of tile (as here), slate, fieldstone, or brick (set in various patterns, such as basket-weave and herringbone).

The chair seen in figure C–21, the Pension chair by Alvar Aalto, is just one of dozens of internationally recognized classic Scandinavian designs. Scandinavian furniture is known for superior craftsmanship and exquisite structure. Lines are simple, as seen in the wooden table against the brick wall in figure C–21. Furniture is always well proportioned and designed for beauty as well as for comfort. Art and accessories alike set standards of excellence in modern design.

It should be noted that the modern Scandinavian interior co-exists happily with rustic cottages and folk art, which is part of the charm and appeal of the period. It is never without the touch of the human hand. Traditional folk art or contemporary handcrafted artwork (pottery, painting, prints, and textiles) are integrated into the interior, giving charm, appeal, and livability.

Colors

The Scandinavians brought to the Western world in the 1950s a surprising combination of blues and greens evoking the sea, sky, and forest. Since then we have looked to Scandinavia for successful and livable colors, which have taken two directions. One is the natural colors found in materials such as stone, brick, wood, leather, and quarry or ceramic tile. The other is vivid primary colors, used in discriminating combinations and smaller areas of intensity, such as in the small artwork seen on the wall in figure C–21, in printed or solid fabrics, and in fresh flowers.

Textiles

Natural materials such as leather, wool, and cotton are very important to Scandinavian interiors. Also used are modern man-made fibers such as nylon, acrylic, and polyester, which make durable and practical interior fabrics. The Pension chair in figure C–21 is upholstered with tough woven webbing made of a man-made fiber.

Fabrics used at the window include lightweight casements in interesting textures such as semisheers, batiste, and textured sheers with novelty yarns and weaves. Printed cotton fabrics such as broadcloth, poplin, sailcloth, serge, and sateen feature lively graphic interpretations of familiar Scandinavian motifs. These motifs include field flowers (the tulip is perhaps the favorite); ocean waves; boats; geometric shapes; animals and birds; and nature shapes such as trees, leaves, and snowflakes.

Seen on the floor in figure C–21 is a *flokati* or Greek goat-hair rug. Shag rugs called *rya* and *flossa,* and flat *rollikan* tapestry rugs also are used in Scandinavian interiors, reflecting folk crafts in contemporary colors and designs.

Window Treatments

The large expanse of glass seen in figure C–21 is draped with a semisheer casement fabric that is effective in screening glare and softening the visual and acoustical effects of hard materials. A textile such as this one allows all possible light to enter, an important feature in long northern winters.

Another classic Scandinavian treatment is seen in figure 4–27. This is a set of sliding nonmovable louvered shutter panels that are handsome, give privacy, and still allow some light to enter. A variation of this treatment is the sliding fabric panels that are widely used in Scandinavia. They usually are printed in subtle patterns and pull open and closed with an attached wand.

Not all contemporary interiors in Scandinavia are modern. The folk interior, which originated from the log cabin, has given us charming treatments that are at once historic and contemporary in classic, rustic settings. Figure 4–28a illustrates a set of solid-panel shutters covering the lower half of the window which are painted with authentic Norwegian rosemaling (floral patterns based on C and S curves). The top of the window is softened with an eyelet or embroidered shirred valance. Figure 4–27b shows rosemaling around the window. Tambour curtains (hand-embroidered semisheers) are complemented by the traditional accessories of colored glass and a vase of tulips.

Other contemporary Scandinavian window treatments parallel those of America—namely, miniblinds, vertical louvers, pleated shades, and pulley-roller shades. (Indeed, pulley-roller shades originated in Scandinavia.) See chapter 7 for further information and illustrations of these treatments.

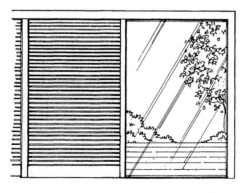

4-27 Contemporary Scandinavian fixed, sliding-panel louvered shutters. Sliding-panel fabric is another important Scandinavian window treatment.

4-28 Norwegian rosemaling.

a Rosemaling on solid-wood raised-panel shutters. An eyelet valance echoes the scroll motifs below and softens the hard materials at the window.

b Rosemaling surrounds the casement window of a rustic Scandinavian cottage. Scalloped tambour curtains (hand embroidered) are hung inside the window frame. Colored glass and fresh tulips at the window complete the authentic Scandinavian look, where folk art and modern elements mix pleasingly.

AMERICAN MODERN (1919–PRESENT)

Source Names

Revolutionary in spirit and approach, the Modern era in Europe and America broke ties completely with all Victorian philosophy. Modern has its roots in the Bauhaus school of design which existed first in Weimar and then in Dessau, Germany, from 1919 to 1944. Walter Gropius and Mies van der Rohe, two successive directors, came to America and proclaimed the "form follows function" theory, embraced by modern architects such as Richard Meyer, Philip Johnson, and the architectural team of Skidmore, Owings and Merrill. Another notable twentieth-century architect, Le Corbusier, declared, "A house is a machine for living in." Frank Lloyd Wright, known as the father of modern organic architecture, felt that natural materials should be left natural, and that the house or building should seem as though it rose from and was a part of its environment. Wright was strongly influenced by traditional Japanese structural architecture and design. These philosophies all found room for acceptance in America; generally Modern interiors can be described as structural and sometimes stark, with open spaces, long lines, unusual angles, geometric shapes, and unabashed simplicity. Paramount was the use of natural and man-made materials in harmonious juxtaposition, including expansive use of curtain-wall construction (glass walls). In fact glass walls, glass doors, and even glass ceilings are hallmarks of the Modern style.

Figure C–22 illustrates a Modern interior in an alpine setting, where large areas of glass topped by angled windows frame the view and create interesting, dramatic lines. The ceiling is wood ("woodsy-Modern" is one version of contemporary Modern), and the fireplace wall, also wood, has

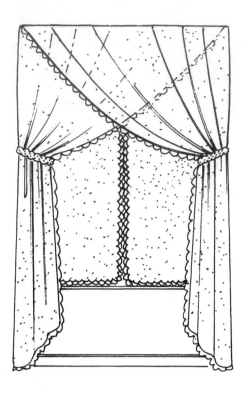

a simple fireplace facing and an abstract, noncommittal painting above it. Seen on the wall-to-wall taupe carpet are a pair of Barcelona chairs and a Barcelona table designed by Mies van de Rohe in the early part of the Modern period. These examples epitomize the fine design sought by the Bauhaus architects out of machine-made and natural materials (glass, steel, and leather).

Outside the large doors in figure C–22 is seen a deck that wraps around the building, inviting the occupant to step outside onto an extension of the interior. A broad architectural overhang prevents too much sun from penetrating the room.

Textiles

Figure C–22 shows how hand-woven texture has been used most appealingly as visual relief from the abundance of hard surfaces. Indeed, texture is as important to the Modern interior as is color. Contemporary textiles are becoming increasingly sophisticated; they offer weave and dye variations that are strikingly innovative. At the window we find casements that are woven, knit, and needle constructed. Extra-wide widths are now common in a variety of weights, patterns, and types of fabric, from opaque to semisheer to contemporary lace and patterned sheer to very sheer.

Colors and Window Treatments

Color trends are established every year by organizations made up of professionals who design, manufacture, and market the goods we buy for our modern interiors. Thus the Modern style of today may be influenced by selling forces rather than by designers, social trends, or important personalities of past historic periods. The important colors used in each decade, beginning with the 1920s, are covered below, with an examination of fabric and treatment of each stage of the Modern era.

The Twenties

Seen in figure 4–29 is a typical treatment that used lace panel curtains carried over from the Victorian era as a main element. The curtains would have hung straight, tiered, or crisscrossed and faced the room when used alone. When lace was employed as undertreatment, the fabric faced the outside. Colors carried over the drabness of the Victorian period. They were earthy—soft, grayed, and muted—but some bright colors were seen in small quantities, reflecting the "anything goes" philosophy of the Prohibition era.

The Bauhaus was in its early years during the 1920s, and its philosophy was to use glass extensively but to leave this marvelous material frankly exposed and untreated at the window. For example, Frank Lloyd Wright set his windows in horizontal bands, or ribbons, and used only geometric forms (small squares and rectangles) as art glass that was integrated into the overall design plan of the building. Plain fabric or Venetian blinds were used occasionally where the Bauhaus or International Style dictated interior design.

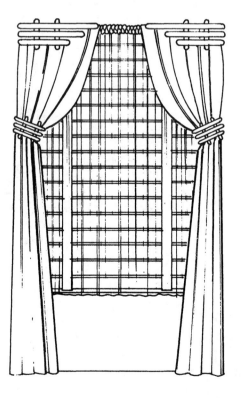

4-29 The 1920s treatments often used lace panel curtains carried over from the Victorian era as a main element.

4-30 Venetian blinds were popular in the 1930s. Here, short sheers are shirred over the top of privacy blinds and overdraperies are tied back high. Accompanying metal ties and decorative rods establish the Art Deco style.

The Thirties

Figure 4–30 shows Venetian blinds, which became very popular in this decade for privacy and light control. Overdraperies were fuller and better tailored thanks to specifications made by the new professional designer.

Drapery and curtain rods became more functional as well; decorative ones often reflected Art Deco lines.

The Art Deco period dates from 1909 to 1939, but it really came into its own during the 1930s. Motifs were sleek, sophisticated, elongated women's forms with high-fashion clothes and accessories. Fountains, leaping gazelles, sunbursts, and lightning designs symbolized a machine-crazed society in which speeding cars, airplanes, trains, and travel were paramount. In 1923 Tutankhamen's tomb was discovered, popularizing Egyptian forms for a while. Egyptian pyramids and South American ziggurat (stepped) pyramids also were favored. Rectangular forms and designs had rounded corners. The high-tied-back draperies in figure 4–30 resemble the era's slender and flowing evening gowns.

Figure 4–31 illustrates some of the art glass of the era. These designs may have been executed in stained glass or etched onto glass windows, interior doors, or mirrors.

4-31 Varied patterns of the Art Deco style that apexed during the 1930s.

a The popular sunburst motif in stained glass creates interesting radiating lines and patterns.

b Concentric pyramid shapes and semicircular forms establish a rhythmic pattern.

c Egyptian lotus buds and palm frond motifs are central to this design, capped with the Art Deco chevron.

d Repetitive curves and gracefully rounded corners contrast with central zigzags to create vertical and horizontal symmetry.

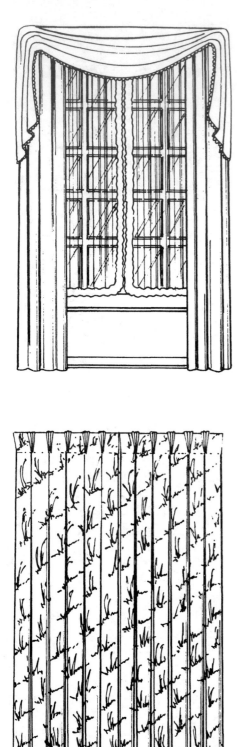

The Forties

An illustration of a treatment of the 1940s is seen in figure 4–32. Hardware was used less decoratively because metal was needed for World War II munitions. Draperies in formal settings were full and lovely, and straight draperies were preferred over tieback ones. In the illustration we see shorter, sheerer undercurtains that have a modest ruffle around the edge. A beautiful finger festoon is shown with a fine-scale trim. This festoon is formed with a bracket that looks a bit like a comb with giant teeth where the fabric is held discreetly in place at the upper corners.

The 1940s offered little color. Since all resources went to supporting World War II, color was considered extravagant and inappropriate. There was an abundance of whites, army drabs, and grays, as well as blues and reds on the darker, duller side.

The Fifties

The 1950s were heavily influenced by the Danish Modern style, and printed fabrics, especially floral and Scandinavian motifs, flourished in both long and short draperies (fig. 4–33). The extensive use of large areas of plate glass (curtain-wall construction) curtailed the use of undersheers; it was believed that they encumbered both the view and this new Modern architecture. Often the draperies were only overdraperies pulled closed at night, or sometimes casement fabrics, to diffuse glare when necessary and cut down on solar-heat gain.

The 1950s brought reserved introduction of a new spectrum of rose colors, such as a grayed, medium-value pink, rose beige, sandstone (pinkish beige), flesh, rose (a dirty, dull pink), peach, warm yellow (pinkish yellow), and medium coral (dull pink). Light blue-green, medium blue-green, medium blue-teal, medium green, light green, light jade green, light aquamarine, medium-warm gray, light gray, and nutria (pinkish brown) composed a palette that offered little contrast in value. Some vivid colors were introduced and used without much sophistication; they bore such names as flame red (coral), chartreuse (a bright yellow-green), sulphur yellow, avocado (a bright, browned green), fern green (a medium-value avocado), Bristol blue (a bright turquoise), hyacinth, vermilion (dark coral), flamingo (medium coral), melon (light coral), and sunset orange (a bright pinkish orange). These colors laid the foundation for the next two decades of bright-color experimentation.

Figure 4–34 shows an example of art glass representative of the early Modern era and popular during the 1950s and 1960s. The angularity is taken from artist Piet Mondrian's studies in cubism and from the De Stijl movement's use of bright primary colors outlined in black.

The Sixties

The late 1960s and early 1970s saw a general increase in color brightness and purity for larger areas in interior design. The medium-to-light bland color schemes of the 1950s and early 1960s were replaced with vibrant colors, such as electric blue, fire-engine orange, shocking pink, vibrant yellow, and Spanish red, edged and contrasted with black. All these colors bordered on psychedelic intensity and were seen in broadloom carpeting, loose-weave casement draperies (fig. 4–35), and upholstery. Influences came from India, from Spain and the Mediterranean (largely our interpretation), and from experimentation with new man-made fibers and dyestuffs. Many of these colors were used with little restraint and good taste. But as a foil to the bland 1950s to 1960s era, they formed the basis for learning by contrast.

4-32 In the 1940s draperies in formal settings were full and lovely and often were coupled with short, sheer undercurtains. Seen here is a finger festoon edged with fine fringe. Straight lines, as shown in the draw draperies, were in vogue.

4-33 A stylized version of Scandinavian natural designs in printed fabric. Large bouquets of flowers were another popular motif.

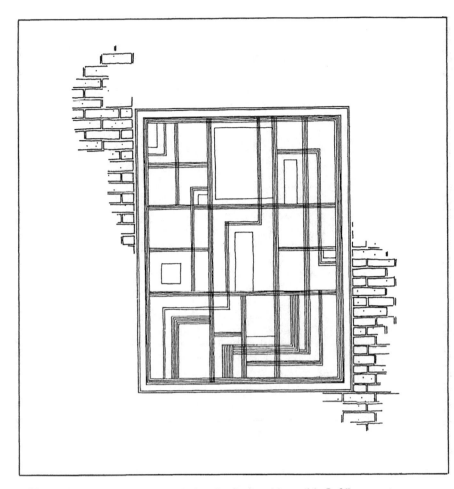

4-34 Early Modern painted, stained, or etched art glass that is reminiscent of the De Stijl movement.

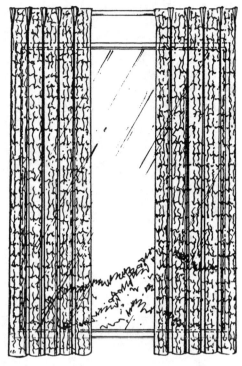

4-35 From the 1960s to today, Modern-style treatments have included the use of light-diffusing, semisheer casement fabrics. Seen here is a casement from the 1960s, when garish colors and novelty yarns produced a colorful glow at the window. Heavy yarns often caused the drapery hems to sag in an uneven line at the bottom.

The Seventies

The 1970s brought new color and design directions to interiors. One was the back-to-nature rage, resulting from the social defiance of the hippie generation, which forsook what it saw as the decadence of a materialistic society and opted for a life of "natural living" with few modern conveniences. This influence was so pervasive that it dictated natural texture, little or no color outside brown and beige, and natural materials such as beads and macramé.

Another direction was a return to our "roots," influenced by the bicentennial year 1976, when America rediscovered the beauty of traditional and colonial design. At first the traditional colors of the colonial periods to which we looked were interpreted in vivid intensities: vibrant red, white, and blue, for example. Late in the 1970s, however, traditional colors softened to authentic ones and eventually were blended with neutrals to produce the gamut of "pastels" that was so widespread during the mid-1970s to mid-1980s. Pastels included nearly every conceivable off-white in a vast array of light-to-medium values.

A lesser influence that began in the 1970s and became more important during the 1980s resulted from the normalization of relations with mainland China, which made it legal to import goods that had long fascinated Westerners. Colors such as peacock blue (vivid green-blue); orchid violet; chrysanthemum gold; peony pink; porcelain blue-and-white (the Ming combination); and light, grayed jade green became fashionable—at least in small quantities and for richer-looking interiors.

As far as windows were concerned, art glass continued its popularity as an alternative window covering. Figure 4–36 shows art glass in several modern forms. Figure 4–36a illustrates an inverted "rainbow" of colorful glass, a holdover from the De Stijl aesthetic. Figure 4–36b shows a seventies interpretation of Art Nouveau; plant forms in straighter "Modern" lines. Figure 4–36c reflects the motifs that results from the Early Modern Frank Lloyd Wright influence in stained glass combined with a feeling of hanging beads and macramé. Figure 4–36d is of an art-glass stylized eagle representative of the deepened appreciation for things natural, and breaking away from the predominantly straight lines of the Early Modern era.

The miniblind, introduced in the 1970s, may have been a result of a desire to get back to basics. Since its introduction to the marketplace (see chapter 7), nothing has so pervasively swept the world of window treatments. Its clean lines, affordability, and no-nonsense approach fit well with the modern, natural look of the 1970s. And the miniblind is as viable today as when it was first introduced.

4-36 A variety of Modern art glass from the 1960s and 1970s.

a An inverted rainbow creates a prismlike effect as it frames a plate-glass window.

b Asymmetry produces interest in this stylized plant-form design, which is a straight-lined interpretation of the Art Nouveau theme.

c This art glass echoes the linear designs of Frank Lloyd Wright and resembles the beadwork window treatments of the era.

d A stained-glass eagle reflects an innovative interpretation of nature in the 1970s.

Another important treatment of the era was the woven-wood Roman shade (see chapter 7), which began with vibrant yarns in the color schemes of the late 1960s and early 1970s (red-and-black, orange-and-yellow, gold-and-green) but softened in color and pattern in the next decade.

The Eighties

The period overlapping the 1970s and 1980s saw a surge in nonresidential building construction. This meant more people (both men and women) in the marketplace and a heavy emphasis on hardline treatments, such as miniblinds and woven-wood shades. During this time the vertical-louver blind was re-introduced (see chapter 7). It had been on the market since the early 1960s but had not been well received then. The miniblind paved the way for a new decade of hard window treatments. The vertical louver blinds did not catch dust and offered the lines of draperies without the upkeep.

The early 1980s saw the beginning of multiple trends in window coverings. After a period of miniblinds and verticals, the return to softer coverings was inevitable. Part of this was due to the trend toward home offices, greater flexibility in working hours, and the resurgence of the home as a sanctuary away from the hectic working world. Even workspaces had become somewhat saturated with hardline treatments, and the market was ready for softer materials, which began with the pleated shade, first imported from the Netherlands with no pattern and in a limited range of colors (see chapter 7). Pleated shades are heat-set polyester intended to screen glare at the window, and so were first viewed as utilitarian, not beautiful, treatments. The late 1980s, however, saw the introduction of not only lovely colors and a host of subtle patterns for pleated shades but also many options in size, opacity, and ways to use this innovative fabric.

With the stability of the miniblind and its relatives—the 2-inch blind and 1/2-inch micro-miniblind, the vertical louver, the updated woven-wood shade, and the pleated shade—other treatments, such as 1-inch and extra-wide plantation shutters (see chapter 7) also were made popular. Roller shades from Europe that were constructed with a pulley system made a small showing, along with flat panels of fabric installed on a track system.

In 1981 another event fired our imaginations: England's Prince Charles married Lady Diana Spencer, and the world was caught up in the royal romance. This caused us to gaze more acutely at the tradition of British design and specifically at the English drawing room, where fabric was generously draped at the window. Fabric top treatments could be duplicated even for those without royal blood. This, in combination with the beautiful style of the Georgian period (still appreciated from the bicentennial year), created a trend of soft window treatments graciously draped over the top of hard treatments. The result was wonderful: the advantages of hard treatments plus the softness and luxury of fabric (see chapter 8). This trend affected less formal interiors as well. Miniblinds were seen under casement fabrics, Priscilla curtains, valances, and soft treatments of every description.

From the scrutinizing look at the elegance of England (and perhaps as important, the concurrent historic periods of France and Italy), we turned to the American colonies, a simpler precedent, for inspiration. The 1980s saw a trend toward the New England colonial look (see fig. C–9), which was a springboard for American Country. This style became a combination of folk arts and crafts in honest, simple form and later included some of the fussiness of Victorian ruffled curtains in country cottages.

In the 1980s a mauve palette came into vogue, combined with other toned-down or grayed colors. Pink-and-gray was a standard color scheme

4-37 Beveled art glass (antique or new) used in a contemporary setting of the 1980s reflects the trend toward nostalgia and a deepened appreciation for styles of the past.

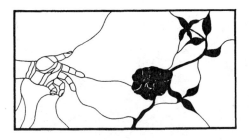

4-38 Architectural glass block was revived in the 1980s to provide both light and daytime privacy, as well as an interesting textural, geometric pattern.

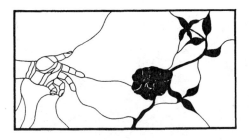

4-39 Contemporary stained glass is often thought-provoking. Note the reach of the hand toward the symbolic (and actual) beauty of the rose.

in both homes and public interiors. In fact the 1980s have been referred to as the gray decade, beginning with pastels in the earlier part and moving toward darker, richer colors in the latter part. The late 1980s warmed up with the trend toward peach tones, warm off-whites, and colors inspired by Italian marble, terrazzo, and Southwest desert hues, such as warm pinks. A new generation of prosperous working couples made rich-looking interiors quite fashionable. At the same time, pastels gave way to deeper earth colors, such as cobalt blue (a deep violet-blue), emerald green, amethyst, and the full spectrum of natural marble, terrazzo, granite, and sandstone hues and textures.

Another interesting development evolved during the 1980s. Soon after the bicentennial and royal wedding revitalized the Georgian period, an era of "postmodern" traditional design swept the country. It essentially consisted of classical elements simplified and painted white, set off by pastel-colored walls, much as the Federal period had done. Late in the 1980s the next period, American Empire, was revived, with updated, lightened versions of classic Duncan Phyfe furniture. The interior colors of these three updates (Georgian, Federal, and American Empire) followed the palette of traditional colors in rich, usually toned-down variations.

In the late 1980s, as noted, we began to adapt the Colonial styles of the southwest United States. The "Santa Fe" desert look appeared simultaneously with the updated American Empire style (because the Southwest had been settled during the Greek Revival/American Empire period) and formed a style called Territorial American Empire. The look is essentially a mixture of Spanish and Native American architecture with Empire furnishings. Rustic building and furnishing materials, primitive forms, heavy lintels over windows, and softly rounded but rough plaster adobe walls and components called for shutters, screens, pleated shades, and even bamboo shades at the window. This style helped to turn the late 1980s palette away from the gray-and-pink scheme toward warmer, neutral hues, predominantly yellowish pinks, where the texture and native material dictated the actual color. Looking farther south, to Mexico, we saw such colors as fiesta yellow (vivid egg-yolk yellow), cayenne red (hot-pepper red), claret (brick or blackish red), fuchsia (bright red-violet), turquoise (blue leaning toward violet), lapis (azure blue), opal green (a milky aqua—the opal gem actually varies from blue to green), malachite (an uneven or black-streaked rich green similar to kelly green), Indian coral (light pinkish orange), Mexican blue (a bold violet-blue with a medium-light value), and desert green (a light spring or mint green).

Wood slat blinds, particularly those with 2-inch slats, became popular in the late 1980s. Stained a wood hue or painted white or pastel, they offered the clean lines of miniblinds and the richness of wood shutters. Pleated shades, woven woods, miniblinds, and vertical louvers often sported loosely swagged, asymmetrical top treatments and side draperies.

Art glass of the 1980s is seen in figure 4–37, where the seemingly antique look of beveled glass was rescued from old buildings or re-created for the revitalized traditional look described above, under European influences. Figure 4–38 illustrates the revival of glass block from the 1950s and 1960s, this time combined with modern architecture and furnishings not only to become a structural source of light but also to be appreciated as an art form at the window. Figure 4–39 shows a revival of floral motifs, inspired by Art Nouveau and oriental meandering designs, this piece with the human hand reaching out for beauty.

A FINAL WORD ON PERIOD WINDOW TREATMENTS

This overview is but a sampling of major design and color trends as they affect window treatments. The color names listed are not necessarily exclusive because each window treatment, paint, fabric, carpeting, and wall-covering company will put different names on similar colors. They do represent an accurate feeling for the period but are by no means comprehensive. It also is important to note that color is determined by professional groups involved in fashion, home, and nonresidential design. These groups—the Color Marketing Group, the Color Association of the United States, and the International Colour Authority—independently coordinate colors on the basis of what they think will sell and establish color trends every year for the next eighteen months to three years. Available colors overlap: some are rising in popularity while others are declining, and it is fairly predictable that one color will have a heyday for only one to three years. Window treatments may wear out (physically or in emotional appeal) in as few as three to five years. However, understanding the classic elements that have been presented in this chapter will enable the designer to create interiors and window treatments that will endure in terms of appropriateness and general appeal for a greater length of time.

Today's designer can see current directions by observing social changes (including trends in apparel design and color) and political developments (both national and international). Most important the designer can keep abreast of current trends by subscribing to and scouring the best of the interior design and decoration periodicals and by paying attention to color trends in the fashion marketplace.

Chapter 5 SOFT WINDOW TREATMENTS

The term *soft window treatments* includes draperies, curtains, shades, and top treatments—all of which are made of fabric. Today the choices within these four major categories are broad and diverse because of the unique requirements of every window and interior design and because of the unlimited spectrum of contemporary fabric. We can find decorative and functional fabric in an almost overwhelming array of colors, patterns, textures, weights, and constructions. When individually selected or specified fabric is combined with a variation of a standard soft treatment, the result is a one-of-a-kind treatment that is not only right for the particular interior design scheme but also deeply pleasing to the occupants.

THE ROLE OF FABRIC

Fabric at the window has long been an important feature of interior design and decoration. The major trend of treating windows with hardline treatments alone (see chapter 7) has been amended to include fabric treatments in combination with hard materials; in many cases hard treatments have been replaced with soft fabric treatments. People generally *want* fabric at the window, even though it may require cleaning and upkeep and even though the cost may far exceed that of basic hard treatments. Fabric offers many advantages to the window, to the interior, and to the people who occupy the space. Fabric can do the following:

- Screen glare by softening intense directional light, thereby lessening the irritation of that light.

- Darken a room by decreasing the amount of direct and indirect light—a necessity during the summer cooling season, in hotels, and for daytime sleepers.

- Lower heating-fuel bills by keeping more warmth inside a room.

- Absorb sound from without and within. (Noise inside may be generated by a stereo, radio, or television, by conversation, by machines and appliances, or by walking on hard-surface floors. Noise from outside may come from traffic or machinery. These unwelcome sounds can be muffled with fabric at the window, particularly treatments that are layered or that provide bulky, lofty yarns with air spaces in the fabric.)

- Provide privacy for both day and night. (Sheer fabrics assure daytime privacy, and overdraperies or underdraperies supply privacy at night.)

- Give visual stimulation, comfort, and aesthetic satisfaction through color, texture, and perhaps pattern.

- Serve to document or adapt a historic period theme to a room.

- Carry out a decorative scheme by repeating a patterned fabric at the window or by coordinating with and complementing the color and design of a room.

- Increase the sumptuousness of a design scheme. (Generous yardage at the window gives a regal, elegant, comforting feeling to an interior.)

- Soften the hard lines of architecture or of existing hard window treatments.

- Complement the architectural style, lines, or scale of an interior.

- Provide a neutral, subtle background with texture rather than with pattern. (This approach is a good choice where the decoration will change frequently—for example, with the seasons—and where the interior design is intended to be simple and structural.)

- Establish a decorative effect and even create a focal point or center of interest.

GUIDELINES FOR SELECTING WINDOW TREATMENT FABRICS

In order to be considered a wise choice for a given installation, window treatment fabric must meet specific criteria. These criteria are evaluated in terms of environmental, aesthetic, functional, and user requirements.

Environmental requirements deal with the interior's architectural or spatial needs, the quality of the air, the direction and intensity of the light, and so on. *Aesthetic requirements* concern fabric color, texture, and pattern and the compatibility of the window treatment with the design of the interior where it will be seen. *Functional requirements* concern the way the fabric performs in the interior with respect to durability, dimensional stability, and so on. *User requirements* deal with aspects requiring decisions, money, or effort from the client.

Since every window and every situation is individual, fabric should be carefully selected to ensure that the best possible choice is made. Because the public has come to view designers as liable and has increasingly brought its grievances to court, the designer has a greater responsibility to make certain that every fabric specified meets the above requirements as thoroughly as possible. The following annotated considerations (which have been listed alphabetically for your convenience) may form a checklist for fabric selection. This will assist you in making choices that will best satisfy the demands of the client. (Note that some of the specific considerations will apply to more than one requirement category.)

Cleanability

Depending on the circumstances fabric may need to withstand repeated cleaning. It should do so without shrinking, fading, or becoming weak or "tender."

Color

Color is a most important consideration in the selection of window-covering fabric. Colored sheer fabric will bathe a room in the hue of the sheer, a fact often overlooked when the designer selects from a small, flat sample. Sheers typically are constructed at three-to-one fullness, intensifying a color with often surprising results. This can be potentially disastrous. If, for example, blue sheers are placed at a cold north window, the room may feel uncomfortably cold regardless of the thermostat; or, if orange sheers are used at a southern or western exposure, they may intensify the impression of heat.

Color can psychologically warm or cool an interior—a factor to be used as a design tool. The color of any fabric should be carefully selected to coordinate, complement, and support the interior. Caution should be used to avoid intense color or vivid, contrasting colored patterns that draw undue attention to the window. As a general rule subtle, understated, neutralized colors make more pleasing backgrounds. The exception to this rule is where large spaces, cold temperatures, or lack of interest might dictate bright, advancing, warm color.

Color can be manipulated at the window through the opening and closing of various fabric layers. The value of color also can be changed in this way. An overdrapery or underdrapery of darker fabric creates a dramatic deep value, while light colors produce an airy and more cheerful value. Thus, by layering different colors or values, much flexibility may be obtained.

Colorfastness

Colorfastness of the fabric is important in situations where there is excessive exposure to sunlight or harsh interior lighting. Colorfastness against fume or gas fading also may be a factor in certain settings. Brighter and darker colors will fade faster than lighter, neutralized colors.

Cost

Cost is a factor in two respects—first is the initial cost of the fabric, which usually must fit into a budget, particularly in contract work; second is the life-cycle cost, which is the initial cost divided by the number of years of expected use. A costly fabric that will wear long at the window may be more cost-efficient in the long run than a poorer-quality, inexpensive fabric. On the other hand some very expensive fabrics do not have a long life span. Many factors make up the cost of a fabric (see the section on purchasing fabric below).

Dimensional Stability

This simply means that a fabric will not stretch with gravity because of heavy, bulky yarns or fabric weight; it will not elongate with humidity; it will not shrink as humidity drops or as a result of wet or dry cleaning.

Dimensional stability factors inherent in the fabric itself include the type and quality of the fiber, the type and weight of the yarn, and the type of construction.

Drapability

Drapability is desirable for some types of treatments and undesirable for others. Light- to medium-weight fabrics that are soft usually hang graciously and drape easily. However, a too-soft fabric will hang limply and without body. Soft fabrics will not make crisp ruffles or trimmings; nor will too-stiff fabrics. Very stiff fabrics, such as some linens, do not fall gracefully into folds yet may be quite suitable for flat treatments such as shades and shaped valances. The relative softness is referred to as the *hand,* or feel, of the fabric.

Durability

Durability is the capacity of the fabric to function and remain beautiful for an expected period of time. A durable fabric will not easily fade, sun rot or deteriorate, or become weak or tender from cleaning. It will not be affected or change color due to environmental impurities (smoke, for example). It will not prematurely wear out because of repeated opening and closing of shades or draperies or because of handling.

Extra-Wide Yardage

Seamless widths of 105 to 118 inches are now readily available in sheer, semisheer, lace, warp-knit, and lightweight casement fabrics. The advantage of extra-wide yardage is that it may be railroaded (run horizontally in one length, rather than in vertical widths), which makes it possible to construct draperies, sheers, and wide or deep swags without unsightly seams. The draperies will then hang more nicely, be more dimensionally stable, and carry patterns (even horizontal stripes) with greater success.

Fiber Selection

A knowledge of fibers is essential to any window-treatment professional. The durability, dyeability, dimensional stability, and other important textile characteristics often lie in the quality of the selected fiber. Appendix 12 lists natural and man-made fibers and describes their inherent characteristics.

Flame Resistance and Special Finishes

These become necessary where codes or regulations and contract specifications dictate, and they should be applied to yardage by a fabric-finishing company. Flame-retardant treatments require a 10 to 25 percent shrinkage allowance. Fabrics that meet or exceed standards for fire retardance, colorfastness, abrasion resistance, and other regulations should have ratings listed in the sample books or pricing/documentation charts. If the information is missing, it may be obtained in writing from the manufacturers. The designer should always keep copies of the test result information on file and give a copy to the client as well.

Glare

Another consideration in fabric selection is glare. A semisheer casement or lacelike construction in a sunlight-resistant fiber is a good choice to control excessive directional light (see appendix 12).

Horizontal Stripes and Strong Plaids

These should be avoided whenever possible at the window. Yo-yo problems (hiking, sagging, and unevenness) will make horizontal lines wavy and disturbing (see also "Dimensional Stability" and "Pattern"). The yo-yo effect is almost unavoidable in tall or wide installations. Plaids are undesirable because the weaving tension on the loom may cause a plaid pattern repeat to vary slightly, making a perfect match alignment nearly impossible.

Humidity

Humidity levels affect dimensional stability. Higher humidity causes yarns to stretch, sag, and elongate. As humidity lowers, parts of the fabric can shrink or hike, causing an uneven yo-yo effect in the bottom hemline. In addition, some fibers may be affected by humidity, becoming weaker, stained, or discolored.

Insulative Qualities

This refers to the ability of fabric to help maintain the temperature of a room, either by blocking the influx of heat or by preventing warm air from escaping. This quality is, of course, important in extreme climates. Fabrics that darken or screen sunlight will be effective in hot climates or during the summer. Fabrics that block the path of convection or currents of air will be insulative as well. Opaque or metallic lining fabrics used as supplemental draperies or liners also will increase insulation at the window.

Iridescence

Iridescence is the quality of looking like one color in one light and another color in another light or at a different angle. An iridescent fabric may be rich, subtle, and sophisticated.

Opacity

Opacity is the quality that blocks out light or gives total privacy when the treatment is closed. Translucent fabrics screen out harsh light and give texture or pattern to light coming in, while providing daytime privacy. Translucent fabrics include many rachel knits, malimo weaves, and other semisheers. Transparent fabrics are "see-through," meaning that one can see toward the light source. Sheer transparent fabrics, such as ninon, chiffon, and marquisette, give daytime privacy but no protection at all at night when lights are on inside the room. Translucent and transparent fabrics often are layered with opaque fabrics.

Orientation

Orientation, or the direction windows face, and exposure to direct sunlight will be factors in fiber selection. North light is less damaging to sunlight-sensitive fibers (see appendix 12) than is east light. South and west light are the most damaging to textiles because they are the strongest and most constant.

Pattern

Pattern, the woven or printed design of the fabric, may vary in scale, or size, from small to medium to large to grand (extra large). A large-scale pattern is also accomplished with the massing (grouping together) of design motifs. Scale should be harmonious with the architecture and spacial dimensions of the interior. If other patterns exist in the room, then the scale may need to be dramatically different—much smaller or much larger—so as not to compete visually. The exception to this rule is where different patterns are designed to coordinate in type or design and match colors precisely.

The style, coloration, and effect pattern will have on the room also needs evaluation. Even the furnishings in the room should help dictate the appropriate selection of patterned fabric at the window.

Finally, the pattern repeat may have some bearing on whether a fabric selection is appropriate for an interior. The pattern repeat is measured vertically from the top of one pattern to the top of the next repeated pattern. Pattern repeats must be carefully matched on every soft window installation. Some fabric is expected to be wasted because the pattern must begin at the same point on every width of fabric sewn together. For example, the top of the pattern should be placed at the top of the treatment in ceiling-to-floor treatments, and the bottom of the complete pattern should be at the lower hem if the treatment ends 3 or 4 feet above the floor. The eye will follow along the top of ceiling-to-floor treatments and along the lower edge on shorter treatments. The complete pattern that begins or ends at these points will be visually harmonious. Pattern repeats also may be horizontal. In a horizontal pattern repeat, be certain that the fabric will not sag, hike, or yo-yo. Uneven horizontal pattern repeats are visually disturbing.

Privacy

This is a major consideration that often is successfully accomplished with layered fabrics. A sheer or semisheer fabric that screens and diffuses daylight will give daytime privacy but no nighttime privacy. As with tied-back draperies, which ideally are not let down at night, several types of fabric need a liner, shade, shutter, or blind to ensure nighttime privacy.

Resistance

Resistance to various environmental factors and dangers also is a criterion that includes many categories. Among these may be the need to resist fading, flammability, mold, mildew, bacteria, staining, deterioration from wet or dry cleaning, and insect damage.

Support Fabrics

Lining and interlining window treatments will protect window fabric from sun damage and will insulate against temperature extremes and noise. Lining fabrics may be used as a separate privacy drapery and may be hung next to the glass under sheer fabric, lace, or casement overdrapery. Some fabricators maintain that tied-back draperies and formal curtains drape far better with the weight of a lining fabric.

Lining fabric comes in many weights, from light to heavy. The fabric may be woven from one fiber or be a blend of up to three different fibers. It may be treated to resist water condensation stains, to insulate, or to be easy to clean. Check with the manufacturer or jobber for specific recommendations and guarantees of lining fabrics.

Lining fabric comes in a variety of colors, and can be economical for decorative or practical uses, such as for privacy draperies or for nighttime protection. Colored lining fabric will need to be checked against the color and material of the exterior architecture. Interlining, such as batting, muffles sound from the outside and inside and increases energy efficiency. However, interlining may cause draperies and shades to appear bulky and may perhaps make them difficult to operate. Also be certain that the lining will not be damaged by the sun and wear out prematurely.

Texture

Texture is incorporated into fabric in three ways: through the type and variety of the yarn, through the weave, and through printed pattern small enough to read as texture. Smooth textures generally are produced with fine, smooth, filament or combed yarns or with tight, fine weaving, and no pattern. Coarser textures come from bulky, lofty, or novelty yarns; loose, pile, or combination weaving; and woven or printed patterns. Texture should be compatible with the ambience, furnishings, and architecture of the interior. However, texture is an element that can bring interest and variety into a room. Too many textures that are similar can produce boredom; textures that are not related and compatible will yield confusion and disharmony.

Weight

Weight is closely related to opacity. Generally very lightweight fabrics are transparent or translucent and are suitable for glass curtains or sheer installations. Lightweight fabrics may be translucent or opaque, and they are flexible, suitable for many types of curtains, ruffles, top treatments, draperies, and shades. Medium- to heavyweight fabrics are often used for draperies and occasionally for shades and give the most privacy and insulative qualities.

Yarn Types

Yarn types vary considerably. Man-made and natural silk monofilaments and finely combed natural fiber staple are smooth and lustrous. Natural and man-made fiber staple, or short lengths, will be dull, lofty (light and bulky), and able to refract (break up, or diffuse) light. It is most often the yarn variety that determines the texture, interest, and surface quality in fabrics.

PURCHASING FABRIC: PRICING CONSIDERATIONS

Drapery fabric prices vary so dramatically that designers and clients may wonder why. Fabric retail prices generally range from $6 to $160 per yard, with some specialty fabrics (hand-embroidered, sequinned, or pearl-studded silks, for example) retailing for as much as $400 a yard. This wide range is in fact the result of production and marketing processes, which are explained here.

Fiber

Man-made fibers usually are less costly to produce than natural ones. Of the natural fibers silk is the most costly. Wool is next, followed by linen and cotton. Jute is the least expensive. Within each natural fiber type, levels of quality establish levels in cost. Often the quality of the fiber is not apparent in the finished fabric, but the highest-quality fibers usually are made into the most beautiful textiles. A few companies will always market them with pride and distinction, and the finished product will be worthy of fine residential or nonresidential interiors. Medium quality is the most widely available price and durability level. Lower-quality or shorter staple and lower-grade fibers generally make less costly fabrics but they also make less durable fabrics.

Yarn

Yarn production also affects price. Specialty, novelty, or fancy yarns require more time and labor to produce than do simple twisted yarns. Yarns that are coated or compounded will be more costly, and yarns that combine natural fibers with synthetic fibers generally will cost more than fibers that are purely synthetic. The length of the natural staple is a major factor in yarn quality and cost. For example, long-staple "line" linens are far more costly than the popular and coarsely textured short-staple "tow" linens. Likewise, fine, long-staple combed cottons are more expensive than shorter-staple fibers.

Fabric Construction

The type of construction has a bearing on the fabric cost. Simple plain weaves take less time, machinery, and labor to produce than more complex weaves, such as Jacquard or combination weaves. Likewise, a tight, densely woven fabric of fine yarns may take longer and cost more to produce than an open-constructed cloth of bulky yarn. In addition, pile-weave fabrics, such as velvet, require more yarn and perhaps more processing time. The denser (more compact) the weave, the more yarn will be used, thus hiking the cost. In contrast, nonwoven fabrics—such as warp knits, malimo, and arache needle constructions—or extruded fabrics (a sheet of fabric flowed directly from a man-made viscose liquid)—such as vinyl—are produced with great speed, which makes them less costly.

Coloring

Dye composition and processes can account for up to 50 percent of a fabric's retail price. The greater quantity of dye used or the more colors applied, the higher the price may be. The method of coloring also is a variable cost factor. Fibers may be dyed in the viscose or solution stage before being extruded into filaments (fibers formed from solution). This technique, called man-made fiber *solution or dope dyeing*, produces permanent colors that resist fading but is quite costly. Natural fibers may be dyed in their yarn state, called *stock dyeing*. *Yarn dyeing* is accomplished in several different ways, as is *piece dyeing* (coloring the woven piece goods).

Printing methods vary dramatically, from hand-blocked printing and hand-applied resist prints to fully automated roller printing, rotary silk-screen printing, or transfer printing. Some methods, such as flat-bed silk-screen printing and airbrush painting, utilize both hand and automated procedures. Appendix 13 contains definitions of these and many other fabric-coloring terms.

Finishing

Finishes also add to the cost of fabric. Although most fabric finishes are not visible, the majority are indispensable to the success of the fabric. Fabrics receive an average of six finishes, including standard or functional, aesthetic or decorative, and performance finishes. See appendix 13 for information on finish types.

Quantity

When great quantities of a specific fabric are produced, the cost to produce each yard decreases proportionately. Fabric manufacturers who purchase yarn and dyestuff in bulk will obtain better prices than with small orders. Looms, which take time to set up for each different piece, will be able to produce more in less time if a single run of fabric is continuous. This also requires less labor per yard once the looms, dyebaths, and so on are set up. Also, the longer a fabric can stay marketable, the less costly it is, because the mechanics of producing that fabric already are in motion. A steady stream of fabrics with new patterns, textures, and colors is very costly in terms of labor, supplies, and equipment not to mention the cost of making samples for designer use. A neutral, textured, or conservatively patterned fabric that remains popular may be produced in large runs without the risk of having to dump fabric that no longer has sales appeal. Designer fabrics, on the other hand, may be discontinued and replaced with a "new line" as often as every six months to one year. These fabrics are produced in smaller runs, forcing the cost per run to escalate.

Width

Cost per yard also is reflected in the width. A 36- or 48-inch-wide fabric often will cost less than a seamless 118-inch fabric. However, substantially less yardage is required for seamless fabric, and the absence of seams may possibly reduce the cost of production. This may make draperies of wider fabric less costly than those of narrower fabric.

Retail Source versus Wholesale Source

Fabrics purchased through interior designers or architects usually are more costly than those purchased through department stores or discount fabric stores. This is because large-volume stores or drapery specialty shops often purchase piece goods (bolts of fabric) at a lower price per yard and pass the savings on to the customers, repeating the fabric in many installations. Fabrics purchased through design professionals routinely reflect the cost of the design service. The more exclusive the design firm, the more costly the fabric is apt to be. Design firms purchase fabrics at a wholesale cost and typically mark them up 100 percent (for example, a $10 wholesale cost retails for $20); a smaller markup will yield less profit to the designer. The designer is free to mark up any percentage and may opt for discounts off retail or even may operate on a cost-plus percentage, depending on the quantity of fabric ordered. Residential fabric sales may be offered at retail less a percentage (20 percent is typical), while most large nonresidential orders will be sold on a cost-plus basis. Likewise, a fabric that is very costly will probably not be marked up to retail as readily as one purchased at a low wholesale cost. Piece goods for casement or semisheer draperies may be obtained at a wholesale cost of under $5 per yard, making quantities of yard goods very economical to the designer.

The wholesale source also dictates the retail cost to a degree. It is generally considered good business to deal almost exclusively with only a few sources for most window treatment fabric needs. Choose a wholesaler or jobber who can supply the design firm with a wide variety of fabrics—from solid to printed to woven to sheer fabrics—in the price range required to service the clientele. In this way a large volume with one dealer will yield better service and more cooperation for special needs. Add to this fabric companies that can supply specialty or exotic fabrics as your market demands. The major source company will likely give cost breaks and keep your fabric at reasonable prices, whereas specialty fabrics will cost more at the wholesale level (see also the section on exclusive fabric houses below).

Price versus Aesthetics

The purpose of lovely fabrics is to stimulate awareness and deepen the appreciation of visual beauty. No price can be put on the joy, the satisfaction, and even the thrill of living with or seeing stunning fabric. If such a fabric is cost-prohibitive for extensive drapery yardage, smaller amounts can be used in flat window coverings or wall hangings, in trimming a less costly drapery fabric, or for accessories such as pillows. However, if every fabric in an interior is "fabulous," the effect may well be overwhelming or perhaps pretentious. That is why background fabrics often are needed, to provide a handsome contrast for an exquisite fabric piece. Qualified interior designers and window treatment professionals should know how to create successful combinations that use the fabric allotment (budget) wisely and to the best advantage to create a beautiful interior.

Price versus Durability

It is a common misconception that the more costly the fabric, the better the service it will give. This is only partially true. Indeed, "cheap" fabrics will not give length of service and durability. However, middle-range fabrics vary in quality according to such factors as the fiber's quality; the yarn's sturdiness; the weave's density, tightness, and stability; and the textile's finishes. Moreover, high-end (expensive) fabrics often are durable because of the quality of the fiber, the weave, and so on, but they may be fragile if they are specialty fabrics (for example, fine silk). Very high-end fabrics often are one-of-a-kind pieces that will last a long time because they are protected with lining fabrics and underdraperies. Yet many high-end fabrics will have about the same life span as middle-range fabrics.

Fabrication and Installation

Some of the cost of custom drapery is wrapped up in the labor involved in fabricating and installing the treatment. In other words, the cost of constructing a complicated treatment, or one involving a fabric that is difficult to handle or fragile, may easily be more than the cost of a simple treatment involving a more common textile. Likewise, a treatment that is complex or involves special handling will command a higher installation fee.

Exclusive Fabric Houses

There are a large number of fabric companies that specialize in exclusive designer fabrics. These usually are based in New York City and sell only to the trade. If the showrooms are "open," clients are welcome when accompanied by their designers; if they are "closed," no retail clients may be admitted. Regional showrooms are found in larger metropolitan cities, and sales representatives keep the architectural or interior design firm supplied with samples. These samples are costly, and fabric lines are routinely discontinued to make way for new decorative fabrics. This is especially true of printed designer fabrics, many of which have exotic and unusual patterns. Exclusive fabrics that are neutral and textured are less likely to be discontinued. Although these may be on the market for several years, the type and quality of the fibers, yarns, and constructions may dictate higher prices.

Distributors

There also are many fabric companies that stock, sample, and sell cut orders to the trade; they may not be nationally prestigious or advertise on a high-profile basis, but they do serve effectively on a regional or national basis. In many cases the volume of fabric sold through distributing companies exceeds that of some of the better-known fabric houses. Fabric distributors have sales reps and their showrooms may be open or closed. They may have manufacturing facilities for the fabrication of custom fabric (softline) window treatments. Thus they can process orders without the necessity of the designer handling the yard goods. And they will fabricate customer's own material (C.O.M.). A distributorship also may handle or manufacture hard treatments, such as miniblinds, vertical blinds, pleated shades, shutters, woven woods, drapery hardware, trimmings, and ancillary goods (bedspreads and pillows, for example).

Fabrics carried by distributors frequently cost less than they do from national fabric houses. Distributors usually carry a complete range of middle-line window treatment fabric in all weights and constructions and some patterns in contemporary colors. These fabrics may form the backbone of the designer's source needs, with a select number of more exclusive fabric houses as sources for unusual or prestigious fabrics.

There are four general categories of soft window coverings: draperies, curtains, shades, and top treatments. Each has specific uses and qualities to offer an interior.

DRAPERIES

Draperies are made with pleats. They are hung with drapery hooks onto carriers of conventional, architectural, or decorative traverse rods or into the rings of wood rods or café curtain rods; or they may thread onto spring-system traverse rods. Generally draperies are either hung straight to the floor or tied back. Thus they operate, or "draw," by opening and closing with a cord or a wand or by hand. The exception is tied-back draperies, which sometimes are let down at night. However, tied-back draperies are trained to tie back at an angle and therefore should not be handled to any extent. Draperies draw in a pair and meet in the center (center-meet) or draw one way from left to right or from right to left. One-way draw draperies require one-way traverse rods.

Draperies that hang at a doorway rather than at a window are called portières. They may be pleated in any fashion or shirred. They may be placed on a traverse rod, but historically (and they were used extensively in the Victorian era), they were tied-back stationary panels made of a heavy fabric that were let down when privacy or insulation was needed.

Draperies can be made of any fabric. The selection will depend on the style, use, and needs. Sheer fabrics do best as diffusers of glare and as providers of daytime privacy. Medium- to heavyweight fabrics are excellent choices for overdraperies and plain tieback draperies. Lining fabrics are the right weight for privacy liners or underdraperies. If a drapery is given a ruffled edge or a banding, that trim should be a lightweight, semi-crisp, flexible fabric, not a heavy, stiff fabric or a sheer, slippery fabric.

Pinch Pleats

There are many styles of pleats for draperies. The most common is the pinch pleat, or French pleat (fig. 5–1). The pinch pleat is a cartridge or loop of fabric taken up and sewn into the heading (top 4 inches of the drapery) area, which is reinforced with buckram or crinoline interfacing for stiffness. The cartridge is then folded into three or four folds, or fingers, and bar-tacked at the base of the folds (see "Workroom Procedures and Equipment" below). A small technical difference is that the pinch pleat is creased into crisp folds; the French pleat is not creased and has softer, rounded fingers. There are several reasons for the popularity of pinch or French pleats:

- The uniform proportion.

- The smoothness with which the pleats allow the fabric to open and close on traverse or wand-operated rods.

- The relatively small stacking distance (stackback) required when opened.

- The soft and nicely sculptured folds that fall from the pleats.

- The possibility of hiding the seams that join the widths of fabric in the back or side of the fold.

- The versatility with regard to the fullness that can be taken into each fold (deeper, fuller folds produce richer, fuller draperies; more shallow folds produce flatter draperies).

- The relative simplicity of construction.

- The versatility with regard to the finished width measurements (by adjusting the depth of the pleat and the distance between the pleats various widths are possible).

- The versatility with regard to the finished length after fabrication, through drapery-hook placement in the back of the pleats.

Some designers dislike this pleat, finding it monotonous, unoriginal, and too precise, in contrast with a loosely flowing, "draped" look. Yet the many varieties of pinch pleats give the designer flexibility in selecting a

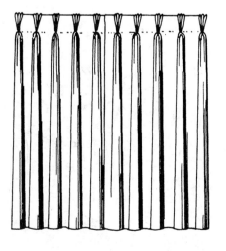

5-1 Draperies with the French, or pinch, pleat. This is the most widely used of all pleat styles.

specific or custom look for draperies. Figure 5–2 a–k illustrates some variation pleats, including box pleats, cartridge pleats, and slender architectural pleats.

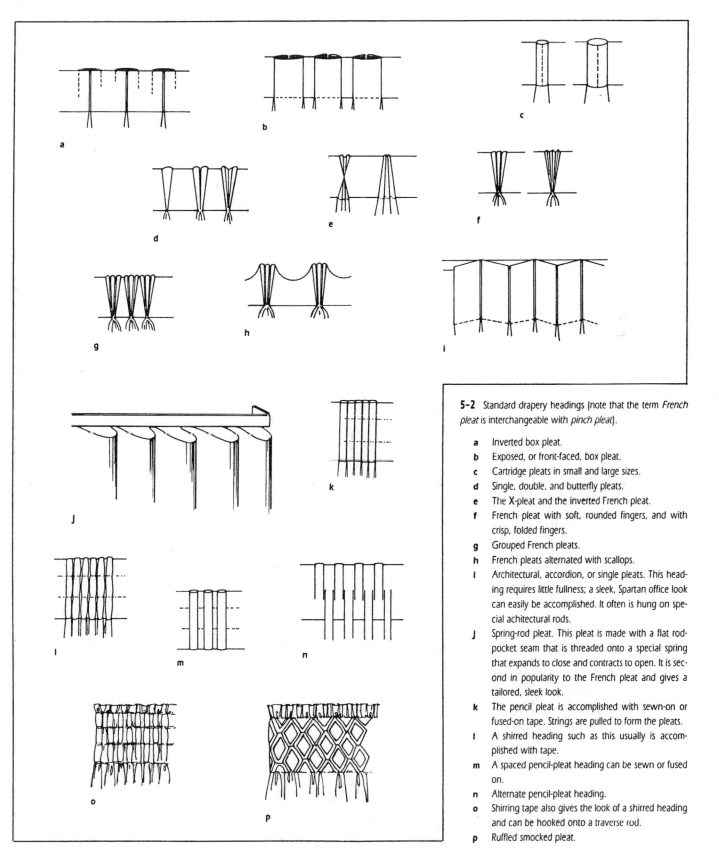

5-2 Standard drapery headings (note that the term *French pleat* is interchangeable with *pinch pleat*).

a   Inverted box pleat.

b   Exposed, or front-faced, box pleat.

c   Cartridge pleats in small and large sizes.

d   Single, double, and butterfly pleats.

e   The X-pleat and the inverted French pleat.

f   French pleat with soft, rounded fingers, and with crisp, folded fingers.

g   Grouped French pleats.

h   French pleats alternated with scallops.

i   Architectural, accordion, or single pleats. This heading requires little fullness; a sleek, Spartan office look can easily be accomplished. It often is hung on special achitectural rods.

j   Spring-rod pleat. This pleat is made with a flat rod-pocket seam that is threaded onto a special spring that expands to close and contracts to open. It is second in popularity to the French pleat and gives a tailored, sleek look.

k   The pencil pleat is accomplished with sewn-on or fused-on tape. Strings are pulled to form the pleats.

l   A shirred heading such as this usually is accomplished with tape.

m   A spaced pencil-pleat heading can be sewn or fused on.

n   Alternate pencil-pleat heading.

o   Shirring tape also gives the look of a shirred heading and can be hooked onto a traverse rod.

p   Ruffled smocked pleat.

Spring-Rod Pleats

The second most popular pleat today is the spring-rod pleat. This requires only a special rod pocket to be sewn into the top of the drapery. The rod pocket is then threaded onto a rounded zigzag-spring traverse rod. When opened the zigzag spring is tightly compressed; as the drapery is drawn closed, the springs relax and are spread out so that each fold is less deep. Draperies of this sort usually are referred to by the manufacturer's name for the draperies or by the marketed trade name of the hardware or drapery rods, such as Spring Crest, Beautipleat, and Beautifold.

The advantages of spring-rod pleats are the simplicity of construction, the ease of removal and cleaning as flat panels, the absence of buckram, and the disciplined, straight lines of the folds. Hardware is available as regular concealed or decorator rods. Disadvantages lie in the inability to adjust the position of the drapery on the rod and perhaps the severity or absolute regularity of the vertical lines through the absence of pleats (see fig. 5–2j). Also illustrated in figure 5–2 (l–p) are headings typically accomplished by sewing or pressing onto the heading area a specialized pleater tape, then drawing cords to gather and produce a pencil pleat or shirred, ruffled, or smocked pleat. Tape headings do not have the crisp, controlled look of pinch-pleat variations, yet their softness is desirable in settings where a less constructed look is preferred.

CURTAINS

Curtains are soft window coverings that generally are shirred (gathered onto a rod) or have headings attached to solid-wood rods, round or oval metal rods, or café rods rather than cord-operated traverse rods. Curtains may be either stationary fabric panels or slid open and closed by hand. They are flexible in that they can be short or long, layered or tiered, or used alone or in combination with other soft, or with hard treatments. *Curtain* is traditionally a term for informal treatments, such as café curtains. However, curtains also may be quite formal, as are shirred and elegant tied-back fabric treatments.

Even though curtains are generally thought to be shirred treatments, other headings might be included in this category. Indeed, there is a crossover of terminology between draperies and curtains. Generally draperies are installed on cord-operated traverse rods, although they may be stationary pleated panels. Curtains may be installed on traverse rods (as in a pleated café curtain, for example), and headings such as the pencil pleat; drawstring pencil pleat; shirred, spaced pencil pleat; alternate pencil pleat; ruffled shirring tape heading; and smocked heading may be called either curtain or drapery treatments.

Shirred Curtains

Shirred curtains have a variety of gathered headings. Figure 5–3 illustrates eight styles that are gathered onto a rod or a set of rods. The width and shape of the curtain rod will affect the overall look of the curtains (see chapter 6), and further variety may be achieved by using multiple rods (of the same size or different sizes), by spacing the rods, by varying the size of the ruffle, or by eliminating the ruffle. Curved rods also are available to affect the shape of shirred headings.

Figure 5–4 illustrates three additional types of headings commonly used for curtains. The New England tab curtain has strips of fabric or trimming

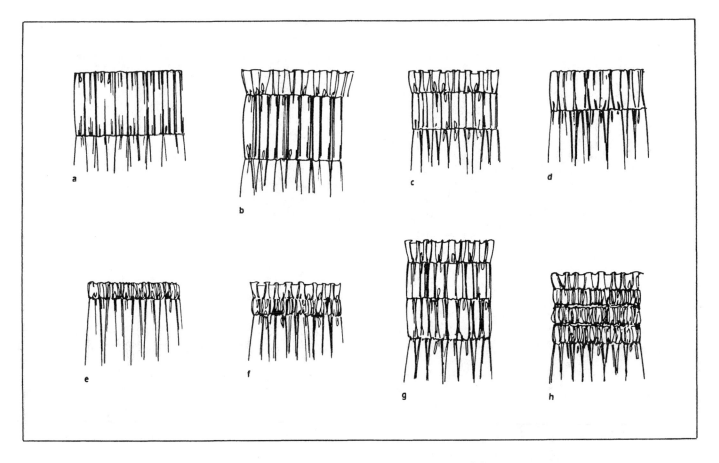

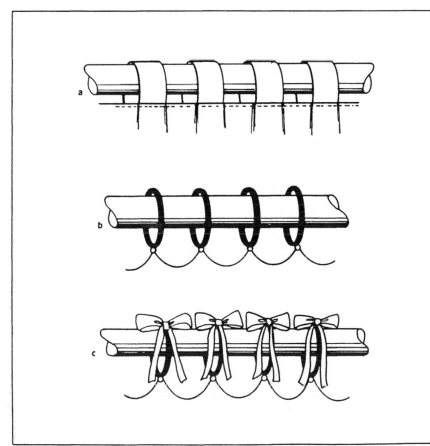

5-3 Shirred headings.

a Shirred heading gathered onto an extra-wide rod.

b Ruffled shirred heading on an extra-wide rod.

c Ruffled shirred heading on a wide rod, plastic round pole, or wood pole.

d Ruffleless shirred heading on a wide rod.

e Ruffleless shirred heading on a narrow curtain rod.

f Ruffled shirred heading on a narrow curtain rod.

g Double shirred heading. Two rod pockets are sewn and threaded onto two rods. This example has a ruffle.

h Triple shirred heading with ruffle. Three narrow rods are used.

5-4 Alternate headings.

a The tab heading is a classic from colonial New England.

b Flat, scalloped heading with rings sewn onto the fabric and threaded onto a rod.

c A combination scalloped heading with rings and bow-tie tabs or strips attached to the top of the rings.

sewn into a flat panel. A wood or metal rod is threaded through the tabs to give slight fullness. Curtain headings may be attached to wood or brass rings, and a traditional favorite for café curtains is the flat scallop. A variation of this is the pleated heading with a scallop cut out between each pleat. Figure 5–4 also shows bow-tie tabs, which could be made of trimming, of the curtain fabric, or of a contrasting fabric.

Cottage Curtains

Cottage curtain is a loose term that applies to all the styles in figures 5–5 and 5–6. They are named after the eighteenth-century "colonial" Cape Cod cottage, which was a scaled-down version of the grand Early Georgian–style home. These and other styles usually are of batiste, muslin, broadcloth, or even sheer fabric and are widely available through department stores and mail-order catalogs, usually at modest prices. They often are machine washable, if the manufacturer's care instructions are followed. They may also be custom-made, when the ready-made variety does not supply the colored or patterned fabric or style desired for a specific interior.

Many styles of curtains are comprised in this category. They include simple, straight shirred curtains (fig. 5–5a), and curtains shirred at the top

5-5 *Shirred and colonial curtains.*

a   Straight, shirred curtain with no ruffle.

b   Shirred top and bottom, this lovely and practical curtain may be used on operable doors and windows that are stationary.

c   Hourglass curtain, shirred top and bottom, with a fabric tie around the middle. This is a favorite treatment for glass-inset doors.

d   Tiered curtains. When used alone, the bottom layer is considered a café curtain.

e   New England tab curtains attached to the rod with strips of fabric rather than inserted into a rod pocket.

f   Colonial curtains, shirred, with no ruffle. Ball fringe is a traditional trimming.

g   Scalloped curtains shirred onto a wide rod.

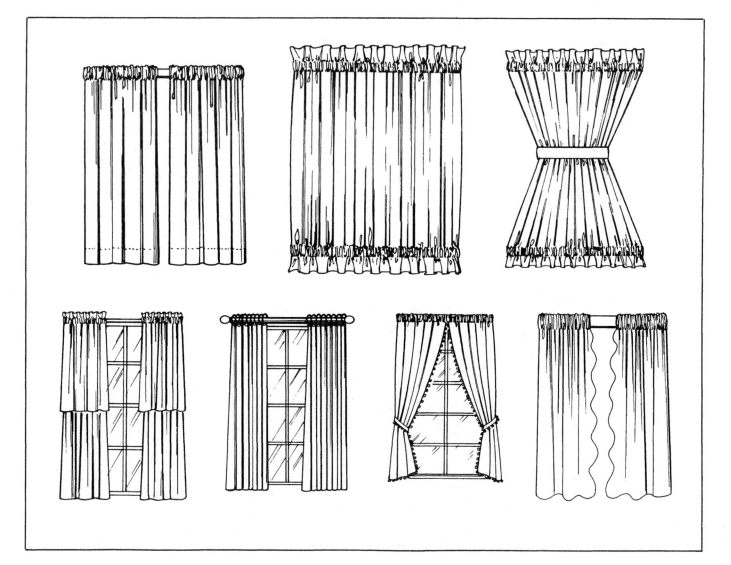

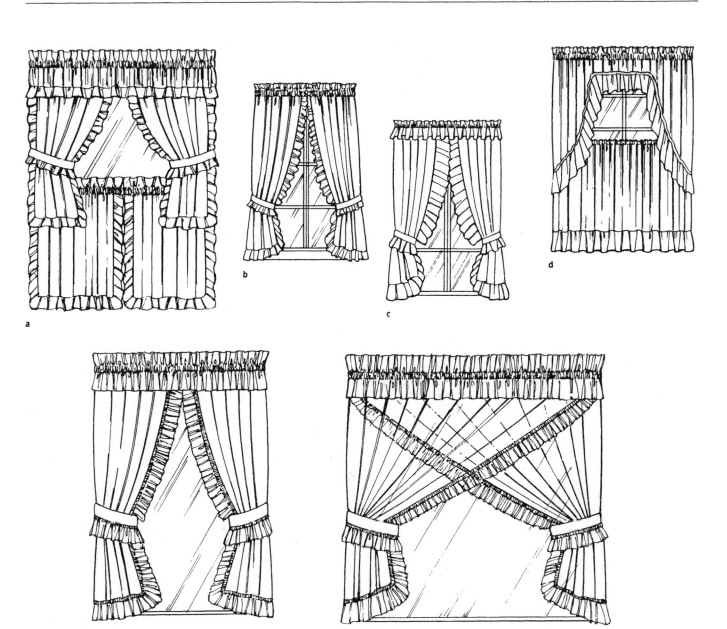

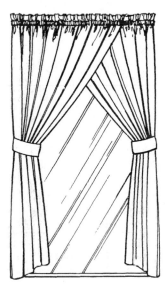

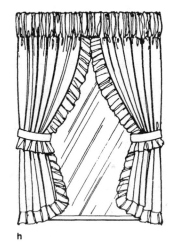

5-6 Cottage curtains. The illustrated styles may be found ready-made in standard lightweight fabrics or may be custom-made of coordinated fabrics.

- **a** Café "ruffle-round," or Cape Cod, curtains with tie-backs. Tiered curtains above are topped with a ruffled valance.
- **b** Window-size ruffled tieback curtains.
- **c** Wide-ruffled edging and ruffled valance on tieback cottage curtains.
- **d** Ruffled café curtain with ruffled, shirred cascade valance.
- **e** Center-meet Priscilla curtains with center-ruffled valance, ruffled curtain edges, and ruffled ties.
- **f** Crisscross Priscilla curtains with attached valance. This style usually is of sheer or semisheer fabric.
- **g** Contemporary version of Priscilla curtains shirred onto a special crisscross rod.
- **h** Contemporary Priscilla with extra-wide ruffles and a shirred valance or upholstered cornice.

and bottom, which are ideal for swinging doors and windows and inside-the-frame treatments (they often are of semisheer fabric) (fig. 5–5b). Hourglass curtains are shirred top and bottom and tied around the middle to form their distinctive shape; they are charming on doors where both softness and light are desired (fig. 5–5c). Shirred curtains may be tiered (vertically overlapping) and perhaps ruffled at the bottom (fig. 5–5d). Simple, straight curtains may have tabs rather than gathers (fig. 5–5e). Trimmings on shirred curtains traditionally used in Colonial New England include cotton ball fringe, seen in tieback fashion in figure 5–5f, or any number of appropriate trimmings could be selected to complement the fabric at the desired level of formality. Shirred curtains also may have a scalloped or trimmed edge, lending a soft appearance without the fussiness of ruffles (fig. 5–5g).

Figure 5–6 shows examples of ruffled cottage curtains and of ruffle-round, or Cape Cod, cottage curtains, which are panels and valance treatments with narrow ruffles around each panel and with ruffled tieback strips. Ruffles on curtains may be seen in the headings, on the inside edges, and along the bottom (fig. 5–6a). Ruffled ties also are appropriate to this type of curtain (fig. 5–6b), and deeper, fuller ruffles may justify an attached or separate ruffled valance (fig. 5–6c). Ruffled cottage curtains may be layered in a café and cascade-valance treatment (fig. 5–6d). Alternatively, the valance may be used without the "skirt" (bottom-tier curtain) to soften a naked window or window treated with a shade, blind, or shutter.

The Priscilla cottage curtain is a classic in Colonial interiors. Two varieties are center-meet and crisscross Priscillas (fig. 5–6 e–f). These curtains usually are sheer, semisheer, or muslin-weight opaque fabric with a self-attached ruffled valance, ruffles along the inner edge and bottom, and ruffled ties. Although Priscilla curtains usually are quite full (gathered 3-to-1 fullness), and so provide some daytime privacy while admitting natural light and adding considerable softness at the window, they are not meant to give nighttime privacy. A shade or blind will have to be added underneath for this purpose. An adaptation of the Priscilla is shown in figure 5–6g, which is a shirred crisscross curtain that resembles the treatments of the Empire period (see chapter 4). This treatment, shown with formal curtain styles, can also be informal and contemporary, depending on the pattern, texture, and weight of the fabric. Figure 5–6h is a version of the Priscilla with an extra-wide curtain-rod heading with no ruffle.

Contemporary variations of the Priscilla curtain that always are custom-made to fit the interior are shown in figure 5–7. These are country curtains, usually of a lightweight, fairly crisp cotton cloth and very full—up to 5-to-1 fullness—with deep ruffles sometimes trimmed with yet another, smaller ruffled layer. They may be tied back about a third of the way down from the top or up from the bottom and may be layered beneath with ruffled café curtains.

Tieback Curtains and Draperies

Tieback curtains and draperies soften a room with curved lines and provide a pleasant diversion from the stiff angular lines of most window architecture. The exact placement of the tie on the panel is a matter of individual sensitivity and discretion, but it should fall somewhere between one-half and one-third of the way from the top or the bottom of the treatment. The tie is attached to the wall if possible, with a projecting concealed or decorative tieback holder. A projecting tieback holder will hold the side of the curtain or drapery out from the wall so that the tie does not crush the fabric.

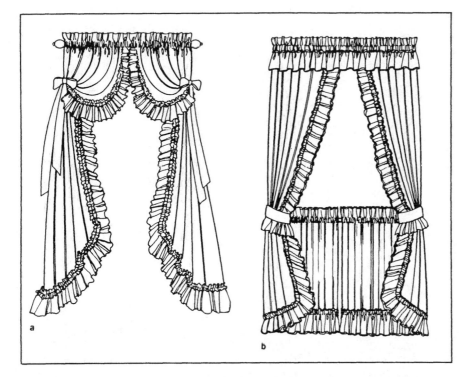

a Country curtains tied back high. This example has 5-to-1 fullness and an extra-wide ruffle with optional double-ruffle trim. Long bows attach to ties.

b Country curtains with ruffled café curtain layered beneath tiebacks.

Curtains that are tied back should not drop closed at night; they are trained to fall in a progressive diagonal arrangement, so they will not hang straight if they are dropped. Handling the fabric can soil and damage it. Also, the effort necessary to hand dress the folds back into place is time-consuming.

Since tieback treatments are intended to be permanent, they usually will require an undertreatment for privacy. Possibilities include shutters, blinds, shades, and privacy draperies.

The tieback is intended for narrow windows, and a window wider than 4 feet may need separated tiebacks (ones that do not meet in the center of the window) to give pleasant proportions. Not only do center-meet tiebacks on wide windows give awkward proportions, but they block a large amount of light, view, and ventilation. Therefore all illustrations in figure 5–6, except for the sheer crisscross Priscilla curtain, show narrow windows.

Formal Curtains

Curtains assume many levels of formality. Even the New England tab curtain, when long and hung on an attractive wood or brass rod, takes on a simple dignity (fig. 5–8a). Formal curtains may be tied back high or low (fig. 5–8b). Note the smocking, rather than shirring, used for the heading and ties in figure 5–8c. This particular treatment could be made more or less formal according to the furnishings and colors of the interior.

One of the more formal tieback curtain styles is the Bishop's sleeve (also known as the pouf, or balloon, or tear-drop) tieback seen in figure 5–8 d–e. This treatment allows generous lengths of fabric to be hiked up under the tier above it and may be tied with long bows or other trimmings. Originating in the Neoclassic/Federal era, and particularly popular in France at that time, it is a characteristically slender treatment that lends itself nicely to arched windows.

Curtains and draperies do not have to be tiebacks in order to be considered formal. Figure 5–8f illustrates vertical panels that puddle onto the

5-8 Formal curtains.

a Long New England tab curtains, tied back, have a tailored look.

b Long shirred curtains, tied back about one-third the distance from top to bottom.

c Long tieback curtains with smocked heading and ties.

d Bishop's sleeve, pouf, or balloon tieback curtain panel.

e Bishop's sleeve curtains on an arched window. The use of exquisite fabrics makes this a sumptuous treatment.

f Straight-panel curtains with shirred and festooned top treatment. The extra length puddles onto the floor, in a rich and elegant use of stationary fabric.

floor. Historically only the wealthy could afford such generous lengths of fabric. Spilling fabric onto the floor was an indication of a person's economic status, particularly when the fabric was exquisite and expensive. Today it is still evidence of luxury and a fine aesthetic sensibility. It is important to note here that when these formal treatments are pleated, the correct term for them is *draperies*.

FABRIC SHADES

Shades constitute a variety of looks and styles in fabric treatments, from fussy and feminine to tailored and sleek. Shades made of fabric are far more costly than vinyl or plastic shades, but they have much to offer as well. Fabric shades have a three-dimensional quality because fabric itself is not flat. There is also the possibility of using fabric sumptuously, thereby softening the typical straight lines of the room. Of course the inherent nature of fabric is the most important reason for using it: fabric gives texture, color, and pattern that can unite a room in a visual and tactile way.

Fabric shades generally draw up from the bottom, allowing light at the lower levels. Most shades can be stopped at any point, controlling the amount of light that enters the room. Fabric shades make appropriate and lovely undertreatments for overdraperies such as tiebacks or simply for top treatments (discussed below). They can soften, humanize, and give comfort to the interior.

There are three basic types of fabric shades: (1) Austrian, Parisian, pouf, balloon, and cloud shades; (2) Roman shades; and (3) flat roller shades. Each is discussed and illustrated below.

Austrian and Pouf Shades

Austrian shades made their debut during the Rococo period, and they have historically been the most popular of the fabric shades. They are seen in many formal settings, from opera houses and grand theaters in the cultural centers of Vienna and Salzburg, where they originated, to formal homes around the world.

The graceful look of Austrians is achieved by vertical shirring every 3 to 12 inches, so that the fabric falls into soft scallops. As the shade is drawn up, the gathers become fuller and tighter but do not fold (fig. 5–9a). These shades can be either flamboyant or feminine, giving the window treatment a rich effect. They often are edged with fringe.

Austrian shades may be stationary panels or may operate vertically, and very short Austrian shades make lovely valance treatments. The only difference is that operable units have rings on the tape through which cords are strung and tied together to raise and lower the shade. The operation also may be mechanized or automated. Austrians usually are mounted onto a narrow board that is secured into the window frame, wall, or ceiling.

5-9 Austrian and pouf, cloud, or balloon shades.

a The vertical gathers of Austrian shades become fuller as the shade is drawn up. Bottom fringe is optional but commonly used.
b Box-pleated pouf, balloon, or cloud shade.
c Large poufs with smoothly tailored box-pleated heading.
d Smocked heading on a fringed balloon shade.
e Shirred, ruffled balloon shade with ruffled hem.
f A very decorative variation on the balloon shade, with pleated heading and shaped, ruffled bottom and sides.

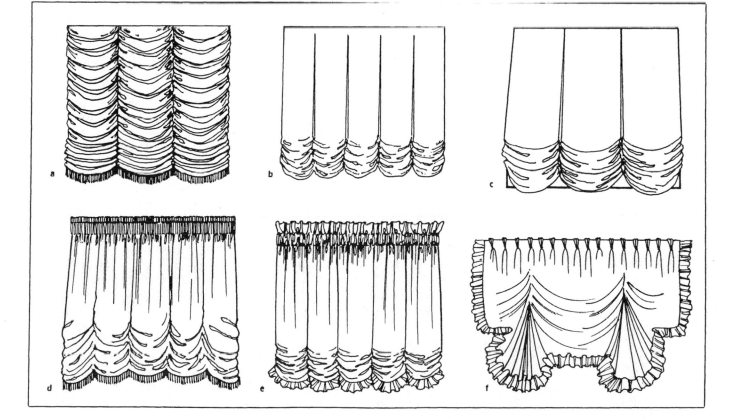

Usually made of sheer, semisheer, or lightweight opaque fabric (except in theaters where the fabric is medium/heavyweight), Austrians often are used as glass sheers in place of sheer draperies or curtains. In this case they will need overdraperies or an undertreatment to ensure nighttime privacy. Since the fabric usually is installed next to the glass, the shades will be readily seen from the outside of the building. Therefore the designer should be certain that the style and color will be compatible with the exterior building design and with other window treatments visible from the same viewpoint.

Pouf shades are similar to Austrian shades in that they have scalloped hems that draw up from the bottom in a gathered fashion. This shade, however, offers a less constructed look and an almost unlimited number of variations because of the many headings that can be used; the choices of fabric weights, textures, patterns, and trimming methods available; and the various ways they can draw up. Operable poufs are mounted onto wood strips; stationary poufs are shirred or attached with hooks onto curtain rods. Because of these options many alternative names exist, including Parisian shades, balloon shades, and cloud shades (the last two names are more commonly used to describe pouf shades). Figure 5–9 b–c shows box-pleated pouf shades, also called inverted-pleat poufs, flat-pleat poufs, or flat-top poufs. This style usually is mounted onto wood and presents a streamlined look, with the scallops or festoons appearing only at the bottom. The hem often has no ruffle because of the simple, structural approach.

Figure 5–9 d–f shows some other types of pouf shades that are more decorative. These are smocked or pencil-pleat, shirred, and pleated shades—variations of the original Parisian shade, which is similar to the Austrian but is tightly gathered along the top rather than sewn with Austrian tape. These types also are called festoon shades or blinds, shirred pouf shades, or balloon or cloud shades. The possibilities for individualizing them are nearly endless. The top may be shirred or have French/pinch pleats, pencil pleats, or any of the pleats shown in figure 5–2. Cotton prints are a favorite for a "country" look, whereas fabrics such as sheer, batiste, satin, taffeta, and moire are preferred for more formal or dressy settings.

Another way of individualizing pouf shades is to vary the placement of the rings on the back where the cords are threaded (fig. 5–9f). It is important, however, for the designer to understand that there must be symmetry in drawing up the shades. When designing an original idea for a balloon shade, it is smart to consult with the workroom to confirm the feasibility of the design operation before promising that treatment to the client. Balloon shades may be ruffled with piping (welting) or trimmed with fringe or braid and can become quite decorative, depending on the fabric and the trimmings.

Pouf shades can blend with different levels of formality but often give a light, airy feeling to the window treatment, unless, of course, the fabric is very dark and somber. They may be mounted inside the window frame or outside on the wall or they may be hung from the ceiling. Outside mounts will cause a "light strike" (where light leaks into the room around the edges of the shade), unless the shade can be attached to the wall with magnets or slides inside a track. If the shade is attached to the wall as it is lowered it will be more energy-efficient. In addition, these shades can be lined and interlined to be made insulative. Keep in mind that very sheer fabrics provide neither privacy nor insulation and that pouf shades should be lined with or made from an opaque fabric to hide the rings or tape. Lining will protect the fabric and will make the shade a neutral color from the exterior view.

Roman Shades

Roman shades are flat fabric shades that fold up from the bottom (or down from the top when specified that way) in an accordion fashion. They are similar to Austrian and pouf shades in that they are drawn up with cords strung through small plastic rings. Roman shades, however, draw up in neat, even folds rather than in poufs. This gives them a tailored, structural look, unless the fabric used is very decorative. The width of each fold may vary from about 2 inches to 4 inches. The folds may have a loose, unconstructed, soft look (fig. 5–10 a–b), or they may be crisp (fig. 5–10 c–d). Like balloon shades Roman shades may be insulated to be energy-efficient (see fig. 5–10b).

Three types of Roman shades are the flat Roman, the pleated Roman, and the gathered Roman. The flat Roman appears flat when lowered, with or without small tucks at each fold seam, and the folds fall only to the front when it is raised. The pleated, or double-pick-up, Roman appears pleated when lowered, and the folds fall both to the front and to the back as it is raised. Pleated Romans use more fabric and give a slightly fuller look. The gathered Roman (fig. 5–10e) is shirred along the sides and perhaps in vertical rows. Its folds fall to the front when it is raised.

The cost of fabricating Roman shades is based on the square footage, and the cost of sewing often is higher than that of the fabric. (Draperies and curtains, on the other hand, require a lot of material and cost relatively little to fabricate.) Sewing costs may be obtained from the workroom in advance.

Advantages to Roman shades lie in the sleek, tailored look of flat fabric, which can be drawn up to a small stacking distance, frankly exposing the architecture or view and blending with the structural interior design. Ro-

5-10 Basic Roman shades.

a Soft Roman shade with valance.

b Insulated Roman shade. The look is puffy and cushioned.

c Crisp Roman shade with large, precise folds.

d Pleated, or double-pickup, Roman shade. Smaller folds fall both to the front and to the back as the shade is raised.

e Gathered Roman shade with shirred sides, top, and hem.

mans also are a good choice to go under stationary treatments—panels or tiebacks, for example—that do not give nighttime privacy. And of course, they can aid considerably in temperature control when they are made to be insulative.

Flat Roller Shades

Flat roller shades fall into two methods of operation: those that are drawn up onto a roller at the top of the window and those that roll up from the bottom. Rollers at the top may be spring-tension rollers, or they may be operated with a ball-chain cord. The latter is more costly, but it gives better control at the point where the shade stops and it will not break as easily. The cord also may be operated up to 3 or 4 feet away (to the side or in front of the window), since it is free-hanging. This makes it much easier to operate the roller shade when it is located behind a piece of furniture.

Fabric for roller shades usually is laminated or head-affixed to a stiff lining material, or the fabric itself may be stiffened with special starch preparations. This is a service offered by most workrooms.

Rollers may be "reverse" mounted, where the roller is behind the shade rather than in front. When the roller is in front, a valance often is specified. Figure 5–11 a–c shows a fabric shade that rolls up from the bottom, a spring-tension shade, and a cord-operated fabric shade.

A variation on the flat roller shade but without the roller is the flat-panel shade, sometimes called a handkerchief curtain (fig. 5–11 d–h). The treatment consists of a pair of fabric pieces. One is the face fabric and usually is decorative—printed or bold colored, for example. The lining fabric is of a contrasting color or white or has a contrasting pattern or scale. The fabrics are sewn together in a pillowcase lining manner, meaning that they meet evenly at the edges. The top, or heading, has a rod pocket, and a rod or dowel is threaded through with no shirring; this is a flat treatment. Another method of installation is to affix half of a loop-and-fastener nylon tape (such as Velcro) onto a mounting board or onto the window frame. The companion tape is sewn or glued onto the fabric lining. The fabric is then tied back to expose part of the lining.

This is a simple and inexpensive window shade. It can be subtle or bold, floral or graphic. It is easy to let down at night for privacy and can provide some insulation against heat and cold as well as noise. Insulative features may be enhanced with an interlining or batting, or by fastening together the fabric pair to prevent air movement (convection) from the room to the glass.

Figure 5–11f is a crisscrossed flat-panel shade, shown here with a fold-back or banded area in strong contrast. A flat panel tied loosely to the side is illustrated in figure 5–11g. A sliding track with panels that close one after the other is shown in figure 5–11h; this is a clean, functional approach we have adopted from modern Scandinavia.

Shade Valances, Skirt Hems, and Trimmings

These are some of the key ways to customize the fabric shade. From Austrian pouf to Roman to flat shades, each fabric shade may be topped with a valance. A valance is a piece of fabric that echoes the style and fabric of the "skirt," or the shade itself, and serves to cover otherwise exposed mechanisms and to give a finished effect. For flat shades the valance may be scalloped or shaped in a variety of patterns, and perhaps the skirt hem may be shaped to match the valance. Trimmings for fabric

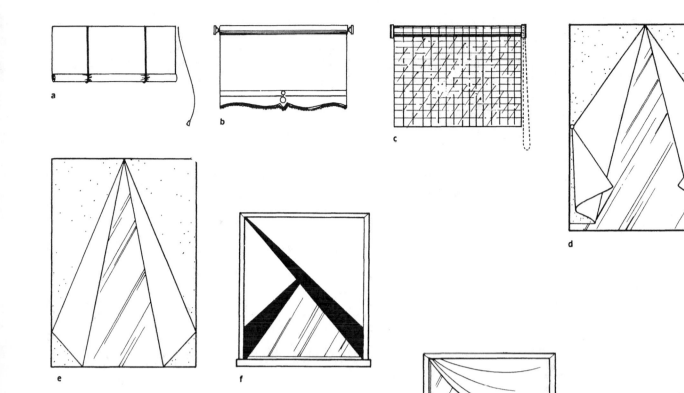

5-11 Flat roller shades. These shades are stiffened or laminated.

a Bottom-roll-up shade with exposed cords similar to those seen in bamboo shades.

b Spring-roller fabric shade with optional scalloped and trimmed hem.

c Fabric shade with chain-drawn roller mechanism.

d Handkerchief or tieback panel shade. Usually made with a colored or decorative face fabric and a lining in a contrasting color.

e Handkerchief panel shade variation with sleek angular lines. This treatment permanently blocks most of the light and view from the window but is simple to let down at night.

f Crisscrossed flat shades, also called lined handkerchief panels or curtains.

g Self-tied handkerchief panel.

h Sliding fabric panels are a cross between flat panel shades and shoji screens. The baton, or wand, is used to draw them, one after another, across the window opening.

shades and valances take the form of braid, gimp (narrow braid), fringe, piping, welting (cord covered with fabric), banding (strips of fabric sewn or laminated and then heat-pressed onto the skirt or valance), or ruffles. Ruffles on fabric shades may be narrow or deep, single or double, and sewn down the center symmetrically or with one part of the ruffle wider than the other. Ruffles and bandings may be of contrasting fabric.

TOP TREATMENTS

Top treatments, which include cornices, pelmets, and valances, have many reasons for being included in a window treatment. They may:

- Frame, or finish, the window treatment.
- Tie the window treatment structurally to the architecture.
- Soften the window covering with additional fabric or with curved lines. (This often is important with hard window coverings.)
- Make the windows and the room look higher by appearing above the window line.
- Cover hardware, awkward wall space, or architectural flaws.
- Cover pleats or other headings of draperies or curtains, or even shade headings.
- Establish a period theme or a particular ambience, mood, or contemporary theme, thus setting the stage and providing an appropriate background for furniture and accessories.
- Add ornamentation or decoration to the room.
- Enhance a focal point by drawing attention to the window arrangement, thereby increasing interest in the window treatment.
- Add formality, elegance, richness, or sumptuousness to the room.
- Lend grace and sophistication to the interior scheme. (This can be done even with simple, understated treatments.)
- Absorb sound with the incorporation of fabric top treatments.
- Increase energy efficiency by stopping the flow of warm air from reaching the cold glass above the treatment and forcing cold air to the bottom. (In summer rising air heated from the inside of the glass, which can reach as high as 300 degrees Fahrenheit, will be deterred from entering the room—see also chapter 1).

However, top treatments will not always be desirable in a particular room. Some restricting factors that may curtail their use include:

- The simplicity, structural approach, or style of the room. (It may not call for the extra softness, decoration, or ornamentation.)
- Restricting architectural features. (A low ceiling, in-swinging casement windows, or perhaps gabled or angled ceiling lines would compete with or be visually threatened by the addition of a top treatment.)
- The possible overworking of a fabric or color scheme.

- The possibility of overbearing pretentiousness in a room that is generously furnished.

- An unusually large, awkward space between window and ceiling.

None of these guidelines, however, is cast in stone. In fact, there are no clear and simple rules as to when to use a top treatment, or which style belongs to a particular interior, or indeed whether one is appropriate at all. This places a great deal of responsibility on the shoulders of the designer to make a wise and justified decision. Two of the best aids in this light are (1) a scrapbook and (2) sketches.

Organize a collection of magazine pictures of top treatments in a scrapbook or binder. Put them in categories: all cornices, all swags, all pelmets, all pleated styles, all shirred styles, and so on. Study these to see which of the treatments have been most effective in supporting and enhancing the overall interior. Do not hesitate to show this binder to your clients; it is largely true that people do not know what they want, but do know what they like when they see it. Understanding this may save the professional much frustration in trying to create a look that may not be right for those persons who are unable to express their tastes in words.

This pictorial approach also is obtained through sketching. A designer should always develop a skill for not only visualizing and specifying beautiful treatments but also presenting the ideas in graphic form. Develop a keen eye for proportion. This can be accomplished by study, evaluation, and repeated practice. Carry a sketch pad and pencil to the site and use an architect's scale, if necessary. Put the treatment on paper for the client (and for yourself) to a scale such as $1/2$ or 1 inch to 1 foot. Do not overwork the sketch, and do not worry about drawing in every pleat or detail, but do give an accurate representation of what the finished treatment will look like. This will be a boon in every respect: educating, selling, visualizing, evaluating, and specifying.

Cornices and Upholstered Cornices

Top treatments are made primarily of one or two materials: wood and/or fabric. Wood top treatments are referred to as *cornices*. When they are padded and covered with fabric, they become upholstered cornices. Wood cornices or upholstered cornices that extend partway down the sides or to the floor are referred to as lambrequins or cantonnieres. Figure 5–12 illustrates some lengths of cornices and lambrequins and a few possibilities for styles. See also chapter 4 for many cornice styles.

Cornices generally are constructed by large workrooms or manufacturing plants and perhaps by smaller workrooms (see "The Making of Soft Treatments" later in this chapter. It is best to have cornices constructed by a manufacturer that specializes in them; their workmanship and guarantees will be very good, and this always reflects on the designer or window treatment specialist. Prices usually are structured by the running foot, and price charts will be available from the manufacturer for various detail work.

The advantages of cornices as top treatments include:

- The historic accuracy of styling the wood frame to reproduce classic and favored period styles.

- The latitude of shaping the bottom (and/or top) of the wood to

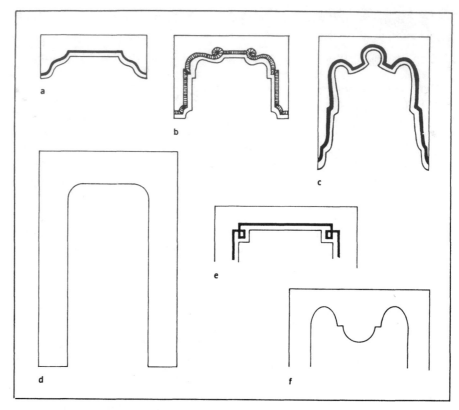

5-12 Upholstered wood cornices and cantonnieres.

a   Classic short cornice style, upholstered, with narrow banding or trim.

b   Upholstered cornice with wide banding and sides extending down approximately one-third the length of the treatment or window.

c   Elaborate long cornice or cantonniere with trimming.

d   Simple lambrequin or cantonniere style that extends from above the treatment to the floor. Top and side pieces prevent heat from escaping out the window or into the room.

e   Angled oriental-style trimming in a simple lambrequin top.

f   Curved design for a lambrequin heading.

match architectural detail or furnishings—the back of a chair or the motif in another furniture piece, for example.

- The possibility of staining, painting, or antiquing wood to match or blend with existing architectural trim.

- The richness and ambience of wood grain.

- The solid nature and character of wood as a structural building material, allowing depth and height in size and shape.

- The flat nature of the board, which can be padded and upholstered. (This gives emphasis to the flat fabric pattern or texture.)

The disadvantages of cornices include:

- The inflexibility of depth or changes once the wood has been cut and constructed to a specific size and shape.

- The cost. (Cornices typically are expensive because of the wood and labor involved, and even more so when fabric, padding, and trimming are added to the top treatment.)

Other Top Treatment Materials

Top treatments may incorporate other materials: wood trim, decorative iron work, and mirrors, shiny mylar, or other reflective or brushed metals. Plastic frames imitative of Victorian moldings or even wallpaper borders may be used as top treatments or as trim to frame the entire window.

Trimmings are often used on both cornices and fabric top treatments (see the following section). A general term for trimmings is *passementerie*, meaning the gamut of welting, piping, gimp, braid, rope, and fringe. Other types of trimmings include contrasting ruffles, ruching, and banding.

Fabric Valance Top Treatments

Valance is a word that loosely means any top treatment made of fabric. It covers these categories: swags, or festoons, and cascades; pelmets; pouf valances; shirred valances; and pleated valances.

Fabric top treatments are desirable for several reasons:

- Valances provide softness in line and material at the top of the window.

- They provide continuity of color, pattern, or texture, as the fabric frames the sides and top of the window.

- Fabric can hide hardware for draperies and curtains, can cover the window frame, and can cover part or all of the often-awkward space between the glass and the ceiling.

- Fabric above the glass can match fabric on the wall or on upholstery and serve to carry out a decorative theme.

- Fabric valances are flexible and can assume many decorative shapes through draping, pleating, shirring, and so on that are not possible with wood or other hard materials.

- They are available in a range of prices, depending on the yardage required and the degree of complexity involved in their construction.

- Valances can run the gamut of styles, from structural and tailored to fancy, leaving room for individual expression and creativity.

- Fabric above the glass can add character and depth to the interior design scheme.

Swags (Festoons) and Cascades

Swags, or festoons, are probably the most favored of all top treatments. In nearly every historic period, they have graced windows to a lesser or greater degree of formality. This is the aspect that has gained them such popularity, yet not only can swags span the levels of formality, but they also can be dressed into loose, flowing fixations or into strict and exacting arrangements.

Swags can be accomplished with a single length of fabric draped over a rod (fig. 5–13a) or constructed with neat, precise folds. They may be used singly (fig. 5–13b) and extended into a finger festoon, with tucks on the sides rather than on the top (fig. 5–13c). This style is especially lovely when trimmed with matching or contrasting fabric rosettes (fig. 5–13 d–e).

Cascades are folded fabric "tails" that were once a natural extension of the fabric draped over the rod, but today are constructed separately and sewn on, or tacked individually onto a board. Cascades may be doubled to become a *jabot* or simplified into *tabs* (fig. 5–13 f–g). Figure 5–13 h–i shows an asymmetrical swag and single cascade. Note that the cascade may be placed in front of or behind the swag. Cascades may be long (fig. 5–13j), perhaps even to the floor, although a general rule of thumb is to extend them one-fifth, one-third, one-half, or two-thirds the length of the window.

A variation of the single swag is shown in figure 5–13k, where the center of the swag is "lifted" and topped with a rosette or metal ornament.

Grouped swags may be symmetrical, as shown in figure 5–13 l–m. An odd number (here, three) is required to make these arrangements, and the

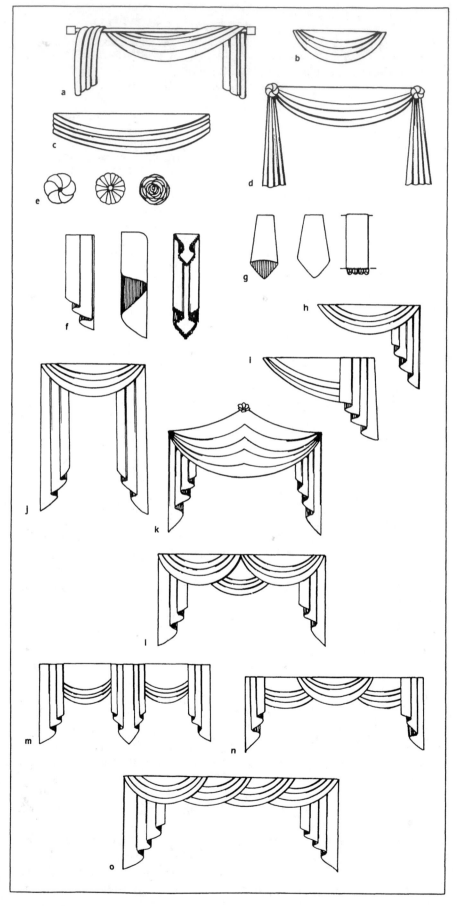

5-13 Swag, festoon, and cascade top treatments.

a Draped festoon hung over a rod or dowel. The draped fabric on the sides may end in cascades, seen here, or may extend to the floor.

b A single swag, scaled for a narrow window. Pleats or tucks are on the top.

c Finger festoon without cascades. This may be mounted on festoon hardware or constructed as fabric over a wood cornice.

d Rosette festoon. This may be a finger festoon with attached rosette trim.

e Three styles of fabric rosettes, used for trimming top treatments.

f Small cascade, large cascade, and jabot with a tab overlay and fringe trim.

g Examples of tabs, used to trim or overlay top treatments.

h Single swag over an asymmetrical cascade.

i Asymmetrical cascade over a single swag.

j Single swag with long cascades beneath.

k "Lifted" swag over cascades. The swag would be effective even without the cascades.

l Symmetrical swags with cascade and center swag behind.

m Symmetrical swags and cascades with center jabot.

n Cascades and center swag over symmetrical swags.

o "Running swags" over cascades. The cascades may be on top of the swags. Running swags often are used where even numbers of swags are required.

center swag may be in front of or behind the others. Five, seven, or more swags also will work in this manner, and they may overlap so every other swag lies beneath adjacent swags. Also, the cascades may be placed on top of or beneath the outer swags.

In figure 5–13n two swags are covered with a jabot (zha-bō′)—a double cascade with center tail. This is a very formal, symmetrical treatment that can include any number of swags desired.

Another swag treatment is seen in figure 5–13o. This is called a running swag and may be used for an even as well as odd number of swags. Each swag overlaps the one next to it in one direction. Again, cascades may be placed in front of or behind the grouping.

retroperitoneal inflammation

Pelmets

Pelmets are flat fabric treatments that are lined (and sometimes interlined) and usually are somewhat stiff. They tend to be shaped or scalloped but may be cut straight across both the top and the bottom (fig. 5–14a). Pelmets can be quilted to emphasize a pattern or to give a design to a plain fabric (fig. 5–14b). They may have extra fabric tucked into pleats at the corners while the body, or facia front, is flat. *Pelmet* is a term that is perhaps more commonly used in England than in America, but it seems to be gaining favor among professionals in the United States. The word describes a particular group of top treatments and, as such, is very useful to the interior designer or decorator.

Shapes for pelmet valances may be derived from a host of inspirations: an exterior or interior architectural detail, a motif from a historic period

5-14 Pelmet and pouf or balloon valances.

a   Shaped pelmet valance with banding on the face.
b   Custom-quilted shaped pelmet.
c   Austrian valance with trim.
d   Box-pleated balloon valance.
e   Shirred, ruffled balloon valance.
f   Bloused, shirred pouf valance.

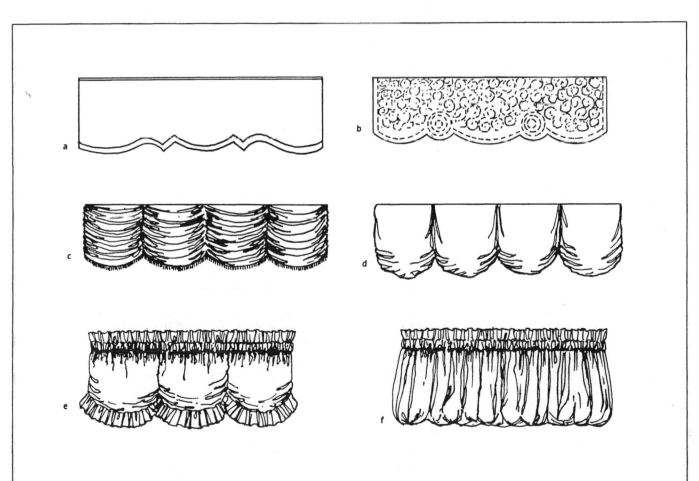

(or even a family-crest symbol), the back of a chair or other prominent piece of furniture, or a pattern within the fabric itself. Chapter 4 contains illustrations of pelmet styles from each of the major historic periods. These are but a sampling and may be altered or serve as inspiration for adapted or unique top treatment styles.

Pelmets often have small puckers or wrinkles. This is not a fault of the workroom. Sometimes shaped pelmets simply do not lie perfectly flat or smooth because of the curves and angles of the scalloped hem, and because two or more fabrics sewn together will not hang exactly the same way. Most historical pelmets are slightly wrinkled and puckered. However, if the client views this as a problem, then the pelmet can be custom-quilted. Remember that quilting takes up fabric, requiring 20 percent more fabric to be supplied to the workroom to make the pelmet valance. Another means of diminishing the puckers is to add trimmings, such as fringe, banding, welting, or ruffles.

Pouf Valances

Pouf valances may be seen in any of the pouf shade styles shown in fig. 5–9. Figure 5–14 illustrates four basic types: the Austrian, which may be plain or trimmed with fringe (fig. 5–14c); the box-pleated pouf or balloon valance (fig. 5–14d); the shirred balloon valance (fig. 5–14e); and the "bloused" valance (fig. 5–14f). Austrian valances are lovely in sheer or lightweight, soft fabrics. This style is more feminine than the poufed valance with a flat box-pleated heading, which can be made of any lightweight or medium-weight fabric. It is especially handsome in a crisp chintz, which produces a light, airy effect. Shirred balloon and bloused valances are also more feminine and may be ruffled to enhance their delicate look.

Shirred Valances

Shirred valances are one of the most versatile types of top treatments and among the simplest to construct. They are gathered onto a curtain rod that is inexpensive, simple to install, and allows flat, straight or shaped panels to slide easily on and off again for cleaning or replacement. Shirred treatments take a modest amount of fabric and are an economical way to soften a window. Figure 5–15 illustrates examples, many of which would do nicely over a blind or shade.

Shaped shirred valances include those shown in figure 5–16. The level of formality of this group of valances will vary with the fabric and the setting. However, a general rule of thumb is that when a ruffled edge is sewn onto a valance, the effect is more of a country curtain and therefore more casual.

Double-shirred top treatments are illustrated in figure 5–17. These can be accomplished with narrow rods (fig. 5–17 a–b) or wide rods (usually 3 or 4 inches in diameter and known by brand names) (fig. 5–17 c–d). The shirred treatment may have a ruffled top and bottom or no ruffle at all. Special rodding makes it possible to form segmental and fanlight-shaped shirred valances (fig. 5–17 e–f), and the square-top segmental-arch valance (fig. 5–17g) may even be attached onto a wood board or frame as well as onto rods.

Pleated Valances

Pleated valances also add great dimension to top-treatment design. Figure 5–18 illustrates some of the classic styles. The straight French-pleated valance is seen in figure 5–18a, and the bell-pleated or scallop-pleated valance

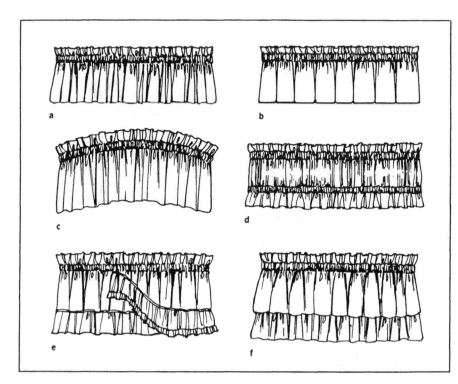

5-15 Shirred valances.

a   Straight shirred valance.
b   Box-pleated shirred valance.
c   Shirred valance on a curved rod.
d   Ruffled, shirred valance.
e   Overlapping, tapered ruffled valance.
f   Bloused valance with shirred skirt attached beneath.

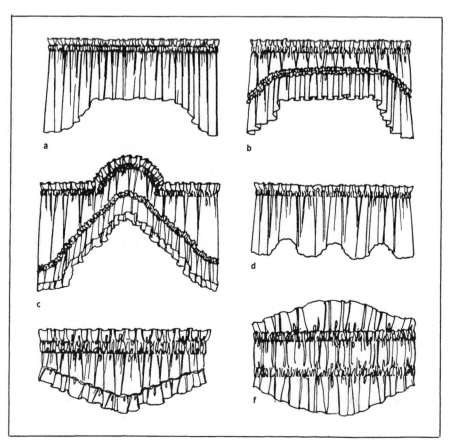

5-16 Shaped shirred valances.

a   Shirred cascade valance.
b   Ruffled, shirred cascade valance.
c   Ruffled, shirred cascade valance threaded onto an arched curtain rod.
d   Scalloped, shirred valance.
e   Ruffled swag valance on a wide rod.
f   Ruffled swag valance with crown ruffle heading.

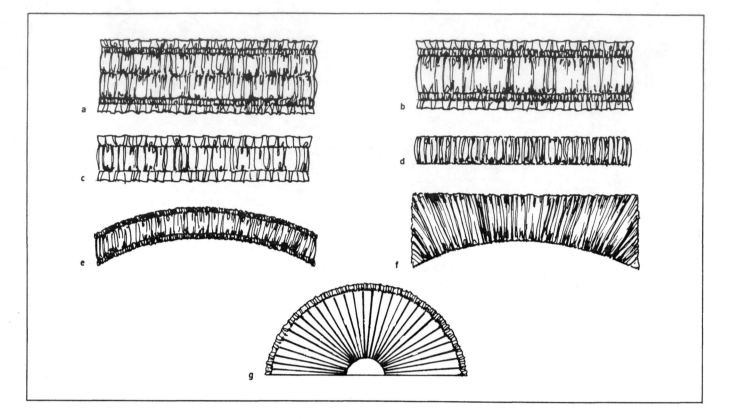

5-17 Double-shirred top treatments.

a Double-gathered valance with shirred top and bottom. This may be sewn with a rod in the center.

b Valance shirred top and bottom.

c Ruffled, shirred valance on an extra-wide rod.

d Ruffleless shirred valance on an extra-wide rod.

e Segmental shirred valance on bendable rodding.

f Square-top valance or cornice shirred on all sides.

g Fanlight shirred valance.

5-18 Pleated and tabbed valances.

a French-pleated valance.

b Bell-pleated, or scallop-pleated (spaced), valance.

c Shaped valance with grouped pinch pleats.

d Festooned valance with tabs or pleats.

e Flat shadow-pleated valance.

f Box-pleated valance.

g Valance with box pleat in center and layered box pleats at corner.

h Flat valance with tabs.

in figure 5–18b; figure 5–18c shows the concept of grouped pleats plus a shaped center portion (the scallop may be altered or the hem left straight). A swagged effect is seen in figure 5–18d with tab pleats. This valance could be constructed as a simplified Austrian with the tabs placed over the top. Flat pleats are used in the valance in figure 5–18e; box pleats are seen in figure 5–18f, with figure 5–18g showing a flat valance with layered box pleats on the corners and a single, wide box pleat in the center. This treatment also could have a curved or slightly scalloped hemline. Figure 5–18h is a flat valance with layered tabs placed in a symmetrical arrangement on the face of the valance.

The styles of top treatments illustrated in this book are meant to be used as a springboard for creativity and appropriate individual design. New variations on these classic styles continually appear in monthly design periodicals, and there will likely never be a time when all the feasible styles have been exhausted. By sketching possibilities and combining aspects of these designs you can find an individual look. One word of caution, however: Always feel free to consult with the workroom during the design stage. Cooperative collaboration will not only enable you to create with more confidence but will also help to ensure the success of the finished top treatment. Always keep in mind three things:

- The *appropriateness* of the style with respect to the interior architecture and design, including the style of furnishings.

- The *feasibility* of the style with respect to construction, hardware, installation, and cleaning.

- The overall *proportion* of the top treatment, including its relationship to the size, scale, and function of the rest of the window covering.

Passementerie and Trimmings

Passementerie refers to such trimmings as braid, gimp, fringe, tassels, and even beads. The addition of passementerie to a fabric treatment, cornice, or valance gives richness and formality to the window and hence to the interior. Passementerie comes in a wide selection of manufactured styles and colors. Suppliers make sample books or folders available to the interior designer, and yard lengths can easily be obtained to try out a particular fabric.

The highest-quality passementerie usually is of silk, and much of it is imported from Europe, where exquisite trimmings have been a standard finishing touch in formal settings for centuries. Colors in high-quality fringes often are subtle and blended, combining two or more colored threads to achieve depth and richness. Rayon imitates silk to an amazing degree and costs considerably less; rayon trims are more simple, and fewer colors or nuances are integrated into the fringe. Cotton trims are less formal and less costly. In the United States many companies produce trimmings in a wide price range. However, trimmings will add to the overall cost of the treatment and, as such, are called "add ons." A creative designer or decorator may even look to other sources for trimmings. Perhaps items from gift and floral shops or even Christmas ornaments might make interesting additions. Figure 5–19 shows a selection of passementerie styles.

Trimmings beyond passementerie are shown in figure 5–20. These are custom-made of fabric and thus can be constructed and sewn or glued on in unlimited ways. The basic categories of trimmings are piping, or welting; banding; and ruffles.

5-19 *(right)* Passementerie.

a   Single-tassel fringe with gimp braid.
b   Single-tassel fringe with gimp braid.
c   "Rat-tail" loop fringe.
d   Cottonball fringe—an informal style.
e   Fine looped fringe.
f   Moss-edge fringe.
g   Fine scalloped fringe.
h   Multitasseled fringe.
I   Two examples of wide braid.
J   Two examples of narrow braid.
k   Two styles of gimp.
l   Rope cord and braided cord trimming.

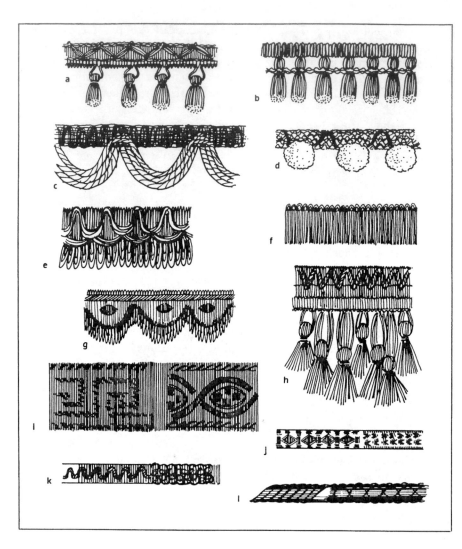

5-20 *(below)* Custom-sewn fabric trimmings.

a   Piping or welting sewn around cotton cording.
b   Piping sewn next to a ruffle in a soft window covering.
c   Double piping edge.
d   Fat piping sewn onto a tapered fabric tie.
e   Ruched (gathered or pleated) fabric piping.
f   Wide banding top-stitched in place and narrow fabric banding in a contrasting color held in place with heat-sensitive fusing tape.
g   Layered banding—narrow over wider banding in two contrasting colors or patterns.
h   Two contrasting-colored ruffles of the same depth.
I   Two ruffles of different size top-stitched in place to equal four ruffles.
J   Ruffle gathered and top-stitched in the center and ruffle top-stitched to one side.

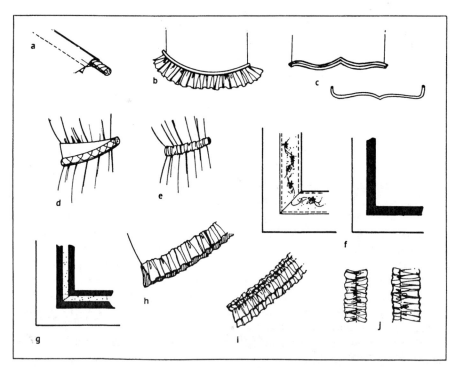

Piping, or welting, is cotton cord covered with fabric (fig. 5–20a). Narrow cording usually looks more dainty or tailored. It often is sewn into the seam next to a ruffle (fig. 5–20b). Double piping makes wonderful detail work and is rather rich yet dignified (fig. 5–20c). Fatter cording makes piping that is less formal and can add a custom look that is unexpected, charming, and particularly appropriate for large-scale treatments (fig. 5–20d). Piping also is used at the bottom of cornices or pelmets, on ties, and wherever details need defining. It is an ideal way to accent with a contrasting color, or even a contrasting pattern, in a subtle, understated way. Piping also may be ruched, or sewn on in pleats or gathers (fig. 5–20e).

Banding is fabric that usually is cut on the bias, then folded under on each side, pressed, and stitched, glued, or fused in place. Top stitching can be done with a matching or contrasting color of thread and will cost more because sewing takes longer than gluing or fusing; gluing is done with special adhesives, and fusing is done by ironing on special tape. Fusing tape has a substance on both sides that melts into glue when heated. The tape is ironed onto the banding, which is then positioned on the face of the fabric and ironed down. Labor to affix banding is charged by the foot. This cost is in addition to the fabric needed.

Banding can be wide or narrow (fig. 5–20f) and can even be layered, with a narrow banding on top of a wider banding (fig. 5–20g). In this way two different fabrics can accent the treatment. Banding may also overlap to form a wider banding.

Banding usually is positioned 1 to 3 inches from the edge of the treatment and is favored for tailored treatments—such as Roman shades, straight pelmets, and straight shirred or pleated valances—and along the leading edge and hemline of curtains and draperies.

Ruffles give softness and femininity to a fabric treatment and, like banding, can be sewn of the same or of a contrasting fabric color or pattern. Ruffle trim can be wide or narrow and can be layered: two ruffles can have the same depth (fig. 5–20h) or one can be wide and the other narrow (fig. 5–20i). Further, ruffles can be constructed so that the gathering is in the center, off to one side, or to the edge (fig. 5–20j). Ruffles are favored at the hemline of pouf shades, shirred valances, and cottage curtains. They generally dress down a treatment, but their degree of formality is determined by the selection of the fabric color, texture, and pattern. Fabrics that are ideal for ruffles are lightweight textiles that have a certain amount of body or crispness, such as chintz. Stiff and heavy or thin and sheer fabrics are not good choices for ruffles. It might be wise to consult with the workroom for advice before making a final selection for trimming fabrics.

THE MAKING OF SOFT TREATMENTS

Many good books have been written on the making of soft window coverings, and the bibliography at the end of this book lists several reputable construction guides. Although it is beyond the scope of this text to examine the details of constructing soft window treatments, the procedures employed by most workrooms are given below. An understanding of these procedures will help designers and window-covering professionals specify treatments with greater accuracy. Those who order soft window coverings will be working with one or both of the typical workroom arrangements: the small workroom and/or the large manufacturing workroom. Each has distinct advantages and disadvantages.

The designer may use the small workroom for jobs with custom detail work and the large workroom for more standard drapery treatments, although good workrooms can handle almost any type of treatment. The costs of making soft coverings tend to be parallel in each workroom, and a cost breakdown of labor usually is printed out by the large workroom. The quality may be somewhat similar, and possible differences are discussed below. Regardless of their size, it is important that the designer select workrooms based on the quality of workmanship, reliability, service, and delivery. To discover this initially the designer could ask the names of other design or decorating firms that use the workroom and then talk to these people about the service.

The Small Workroom

The small workroom often evolves when a person with a talent for sewing has the desire to be in business for him- or herself. It frequently is a part of the person's home, extended to a basement or garage or built on as a home business. If the business grows, then a separate building or location may naturally house it. The small workroom consists of only a few workers (sometimes one or two, but usually three to five), some of whom may be part-time employees. The space often is small and crowded with fabric and equipment, and the impression may be one of disorganization. This can be quite deceiving, however, because the small workroom has the potential to produce exquisite custom work. The workers usually take intense pride in their craft; when a shop or workroom with high quality is discovered by the designer, it is of great worth to the designer's reputation as well. Another advantage is the personal attention given to each job when the drapery workroom owners and personnel know the designer. If the relationship is a pleasant and friendly one, then the workroom will be interested in keeping the business of the design or decorating firm.

Yet another advantage to the small workroom is the scope of creativity possible when the designer is familiar with the particular skills of the workroom personnel. Custom quilting may be a specialty, for example. Or the workroom may produce particularly beautiful top treatments with close attention to banding, welting, or other detail. True custom tailoring becomes relatively easy to work out when there is open communication between the designer and the person who will be fabricating or overseeing the fabrication; the one-on-one consultation is a valuable aid to designers who create individual custom window coverings. Consequently, jobs with special requirements or unusual types of treatments or installations are more feasible with the expertise and personal attention the small workroom affords.

Also, if it becomes necessary to "push through" a rush job, the small workroom may be able to rearrange orders and priorities to make the accommodation, particularly if the working relationship is amiable and reciprocal. The small workroom may have qualified installation as a part of its service, and, if the team works together frequently (it may be a husband–wife team), then the installer often is readily available to confirm measurements or to consult on challenging installations prior to fabrication. The advice of an expert installer is of great value to the person who selects and specifies window coverings. If installation is a service of the workroom, then the workroom may be willing to schedule installation with the customer as well.

The disadvantages of working with a small workroom might include the workroom's inability to execute certain types of window treatments or details due to lack of training or proper equipment. Or it might not be able to handle large volumes of drapery orders in short lengths of time. Another potential problem is that the small workroom works almost exclusively with "Customer's Own Material" (C.O.M.). This means that the responsibility falls on the designer or person placing the order to see that the right material is delivered to the workroom. If the treatment is fabricated and flaws are later found in the fabric, it is the designer, not the workroom, who is responsible for replacing any of the fabric or the labor.

The Large Workroom or Manufacturer

Manufacturing plants or large workrooms are in every metropolitan area; frequently designers can choose from among several. Manufacturers also fill orders long distance from more isolated areas where few workrooms exist.

Although a large workroom may have grown out of a small workroom, there are still major differences. The manufacturer usually is located in a manufacturing plant facility, in a business district or light industrial area that is relatively convenient to a sizable population. The manufacturing plant will employ up to dozens of workers, all of whom have specific tasks, often for the duration of their employment at the plant. As a result, most become proficient at a particular job and are able to produce their work quickly. Soft window treatments follow an organized course from the light table to the hand-folding of the finished product. Orders are filled in sequence as they are received. The time that elapses from order placement to finished goods will vary according to the manufacturer's workload; the heaviest volumes usually are processed before and during the November/December holidays and in the spring. The fabrication time frame generally is two to six weeks, with faster delivery possible during less busy times of the year. It is advisable to get an estimate on the delivery date from the workroom, if a deadline must be met. If the designer brings repeated business to the large workroom, it may be feasible to rush an order, just as with the small workroom.

The large workroom has specialties, such as contract draperies or custom residential work, although many workrooms process both. Other treatments produced—such as top treatments; Roman, Austrian, and pouf shades; and energy-efficient treatments—will vary from plant to plant. One advantage often associated with large manufacturing facilities is that they may distribute fabric as well. If they do then the person placing the order does not have to worry about delivering fabric to the workroom. He or she simply fills out the order from information out of the sample books. They may even offer periodic sales or promotions on certain fabrics as an incentive to the design or decorating firm.

The finished product is delivered in the plant van or shipped via a surface carrier. If there is an inherent flaw in the fabric, the large workroom carrying the goods usually is willing to replace the treatment at no cost or at a reduced cost to the designer. In addition, large manufacturing plants often have a reputable line of drapery hardware, further simplifying the ordering process. The hardware can be delivered with the finished product, if so specified. Large workrooms usually will accept C.O.M. as well, and they may have installation services for local jobs or may keep a list of qualified installers.

The disadvantages of the large workroom lie in the lack of personal attention given to each order and the lack of close association between fabricator and specifier. It also is more difficult to rush orders through. Likewise, if the plant is backlogged with orders, the wait may be increased. As far as the quality is concerned, it will, of course, vary from plant to plant. Some facilities do not offer the fine custom handwork or tailoring that can be found in small workrooms.

Workroom Procedures and Equipment

On arrival at the workroom, the fabric for each job is tagged with the date, the design or decorating firm name, and perhaps an account number. It is then "sidemarked" with the customer's name and perhaps assigned a job number. The finished dimensions also will be written on the tag. The fabric ideally will be inspected over a light table for flaws before it is cut. If the fabric is cut before it is inspected, the fabric company will not accept a return on flawed goods.

The fabric is next divided into cut lengths, or the finished length of the treatment plus the workroom allowance for headings and hems. Careful attention is given to cutting the fabric in equal pattern repeats. Next, the fabric is tabled (laid on a table) to check that it is square (threads are straight and on grain). If the fabric is skewed (one selvage is ahead of the other) or bowed (the center is ahead of the selvages), then it may be stretched by two people pulling on the bias (diagonal) to square the grain. It is clamped to the table where the finished length is pinned and then marked (the latter part of this procedure may take place after the fabric is serged; see below). If half-widths are required, the tabled fabric is cut lengthwise.

The fabric cuts or widths are then serged. The serger is a machine that seams two widths together rapidly with a secure, straight, and overlocking stitch that prevents the edges from fraying. The serger also cuts off the selvage (more tightly woven sides of the fabric) just before the stitching, because the selvage may cause the seams to pucker, particularly when they shrink during cleaning with wet or dry heat. Fabric widths are serged to the number of widths required for each panel. The panel, consisting of one or more widths, may be a one-way draw drapery; two panels make up a pair.

If the fabric is to be lined, it is sewn in at this point with right sides together, then turned right side out. The lining is cut to be slightly narrower than the face fabric, so that the face fabric wraps around to the back and the lining has no chance of being seen from the front. If the face fabric must not be seen from the outside of the building, the order should specify a pillowcase lining, which means that the lining and the fabric are cut the same size and meet evenly at the edges. An illustration would aid the workroom in following this instruction.

Next, the hems and headings are marked to an exact length. The bottom hem typically is turned under twice for a double 4-inch hem. This is pinned and pressed into place with a steam-pressure iron. The bottom hems are then blind-stitched (with a special machine that hems without the thread showing on the face of the fabric), and weights are sewn into the bottom seams and corners. In the case of sheer fabrics, the weights may be of the bead variety, which run the length of the hem and are less noticeable than larger, geometric weights.

Side hems are then blind-stitched to a typical 1- or 1½-inch width. The corners usually are folded into a miter and hand-stitched in place. The buckram or crinoline (usually 1-inch-wide stiffened interfacing) is next sewn on, typically onto the face of the fabric, then turned to the back, and perhaps turned under once more, depending on the bulk of the fabric. It is pinned in place and marked for pleat spacing (the distance between the pleats). The spaces may be figured longhand, via computer software, or with spacing and marking machines. Many workrooms use marking machines that do the figuring and clamp the spacing to be marked by the fabricator. Some workrooms use a special marking pen visible only under ultraviolet light. A small ultraviolet light is clamped onto the sewing machines to reveal these marks; none can be seen on the finished product. This is particularly helpful if the draperies should need to be repleated because of mismeasurement.

Next, the fabric is machine-folded into pleat pockets (large folds of fabric from which smaller folds, or fingers, will be created). The machine stitches and reinforce stitches the fold in place, giving strength to the pleat.

The pleat is now folded into a specific type. If it is to be a French pleat, the pleat pocket must be broken into fingers and stitched in place. The bartack machine sews a repetitive single stitch in one spot at the base of the French pleat. This allows the top of the pleat to flare out and the fabric beneath the pleat to fall into a large, graceful fold. If the draperies are to be tiebacks, they are folded flat (in folds about 2- to 3-feet-wide), so they may be hand-dressed (arranged by hand) into the proper angle and tied back. Shirred draperies and curtains also are folded flat. Pleated draperies that will hang straight are fan-folded. This is a two-person operation in the small workroom and usually done on a vertical machine in the manufacturing plant. The folds are secured with a self-sticking paper strip or soft cloth tied around the draperies near the bottom, at the top beneath the pleats, and in one or more places in the body of the drapery, depending on the length. The folded draperies are hung in the center of a cardboard-doweled metal hanger about 5 inches wide. They are then covered with plastic, such as the plastic dry cleaners use, to prevent soiling. Most draperies will hang in the folds in a nicer way if they are allowed to stay tied up on the hanger for a few days.

THE DESIGNER'S ROLE

The interior designer, decorator, specifier, window treatment specialist, or salesperson who orders fabric window coverings bears a major responsibility for making certain that these coverings are made to the correct dimensions. Measurements must be exact, and the computation for yardage must not be short. Work orders must be filled out according to the procedures and expectations of the workroom, as must the installer's worksheet. Errors may be made by the fabricators, but these are not common. Many of the mistakes are made by the person filling out the work orders. It cannot be overemphasized that exact figures and prices are crucial to the success of the window covering and must be checked and double checked. It behooves the professional placing the order to fill in all areas of requested information, including shipping data, customer name and address, date of order and expected delivery date (never "As Soon As Possible," or ASAP), and whether rods (hardware) are to accompany the finished order (always cross-reference work order numbers with purchase order numbers in this case). Enclose with the order reduced illustrations or full-scale patterns for top treatments, sizes, and dimensions, and write additional instructions for special needs clearly and concisely. If the workroom has occasion to contact the professional concerning an order, it is sound business practice to be courteous to the workroom personnel. Never assume that all errors are the workroom's fault, because the designer often is to blame. Remember that every order is a learning experience, and, since errors are very costly to the designer, it is important to be doubly careful when placing the order.

Quality Checks: Pleated Draperies

Pleated draperies are perhaps the easiest soft window treatment to judge for good quality. Custom-pleated draperies are more costly than stock ready-mades or department store made-to-measure draperies. This cost difference is reflected in two ways: the quality of the fabric and the quality and fullness of the construction. While it is certain that part of the lower cost of ready-made draperies is due to the bulk purchase of piece goods (hundreds of yards at lower costs), it also is true that, for the most part, the fabric selected for custom treatments will be of higher quality. The quality and the type of fabric used in custom draperies is a matter of individual selection. It costs just as much in labor to fabricate a low-end (cheap and poor-quality) fabric as it does to use a quality fabric. It therefore stands to reason that using the better-grade fabric will be the best investment over the long run.

Below is a checklist of quality points for soft window coverings:

- Check for fullness and spacing. Spacing is the horizontal length in inches between the pleats. Quality draperies are "generously full." This means at least 2 to 2 1/2 times the fullness of a flat fabric panel, which makes spacing between the pleats 2 1/2 to 4 inches. The greater the space, the less fullness in the draperies. The other factor in fullness is the depth of the pleats. The deeper the pleat, the greater the fullness and the deeper the fold of fabric hanging from the pleat. There are times when the drapery may need to be less full, such as when the fabric is very bulky or when the stackoff needs to take up less space. A drapery that is less full will take up fewer stacking inches. Most often, however, a full drapery will look more custom and rich than one that is skimpy.

- The spacing should be very similar between each pleat. Some allowance is made to enable seams to be hidden at the back of the pleats, yet the spacing should be consistent. This spacing should be similar in companion draperies in the same interior, if possible.

- None of the bartack threads that hold the pleats into their fingers should be loose or hanging.

- Pleats should be crisp and not crumpled. Always ask what kind of buckram will be used to construct the draperies. There are many quality levels, and the better qualities, whether woven or non-woven, will more likely hold their shape after successive cleanings. The cost difference between lower and higher qualities is very slight.

- Seams should be inspected for quality. The selvages should be trimmed off (except for open-construction fabrics with many holes or openings in the fabric design), and the seams should be sewn with an overlock stitch (done on a serging machine). If the selvages are not trimmed, the seams probably will pucker.

- Seams should be smooth and inconspicuous from the face of the fabric; they should always be planned to be at the back of the pleat so that they fall in the depth of the folds.

- If there is a pattern, it should be as carefully matched as possible at the seams. Where more than one patterned drapery is hung, the pattern repeat should be lined up. In loosely woven or knitted textiles, there should be no stray yarns that were missed (not anchored in) by the sewing machine.

- Hems should be blind-stitched with a colorless monofilament or with a colored thread matched to the fabric.

- The stitches should not show from the face of the fabric; they should be as inconspicuous as possible. This applies to both the bottom and the side hems.

- The corners where the bottoms and the side hems meet should be folded into a diagonal miter and hand sewn with small blind stitches.

- The bottom corners—both the leading corners and the corners at the end of the draperies—should be weighted. Weights also should be sewn into the hems at each of the seams. Bead or rope weights should be sewn into sheer, semisheer, and casement textiles and should not be obvious. In many woven or knit seamless casement fabrics, the hem is very small, encasing only a rope weight. This is aesthetically pleasing because a semisheer patterned fabric hem would cause an unnecessarily heavy and busy look at the bottom of the drapery. Some of these seamless fabrics are prehemmed in this way by the fabric producer.

- The side hems should be 1 to 2 inches wide and folded twice to be doubled.

- The bottom hems should be at least $3\frac{1}{2}$ inches and doubled (turned under twice). The average is a 4-inch double hem, and 5 inches often make a more custom-looking hem. A single hem will not leave any real leeway for lengthening the draperies if they should shrink or be measured too short. Deeper hems are heavier and may make the draperies hang better. Some seamless sheer fabrics come self-hemmed in deep (up to 12-inch) embroidered hems.

- No threads should be hanging from any of the hems.

- Lining is recommended for vividly colored, dark, or printed fabrics that are vulnerable to fading. It also makes light- to medium-weight fabric hang better, particularly tieback draperies. Lining should be neatly sewn on, with the face fabric wrapped around to the back of the draperies so that the lining will not show on the sides or front. The bottoms of the drapery and lining fabric should be hemmed separately, with the lining shorter by about 1 inch. Lining fabric should be a durable fiber or blend of fibers that is resistant to sunlight deterioration. Quality lining that also resists water or condensation staining is recommended. A light, neutral white or off-white lining fabric generally is the best choice because a colored fabric is too obvious from the outside of a building. Colored lining fabrics should be used with concern for aesthetics both inside and outside the window.

Quality Checks: Shirred Treatments

The same quality checks apply to shirred treatments as to pleated treatments with regard to seams, hems, and lining. In addition:

- Headings on shirred treatments consist of a single rod pocket for a treatment with no ruffles or a double rod pocket for a treatment with a ruffle and another rod pocket for each additional rod and each additional ruffle. The rod pocket used for the ruffle should be hand stitched together at the ends and all threads trimmed off.

- The seams should be sewn in a neat, narrow straight line.

Quality Checks: Fabric Shades

- Fabric shades should be sewn with no puckered seams.

- Fabric shades should be weighted so that they drop smoothly, stay closed, and do not flare away from the window at the bottom. This often is accomplished with a metal rod inserted at the top of the hem or 1 to 3 inches above the bottom of lined fabric shades. Roman shades may have optional metal rods or weights inserted at each horizontal tucked seam.

- Except for sheers, fabric shades will hang well if they are lined. The decorative fabric will then be protected from the sun and its color, pattern, and texture will not be obvious from the outside.

Quality Checks: Top Treatments

- Quality upholstered cornices should be solidly constructed with no gaps between the cornice and the wall or ceiling.

- Fabric should be tightly applied and wrapped around the bottom so that no wood is exposed on upholstered cornices.

- No loose or hanging threads should be seen on either cornices or fabric top treatments.

- Swags should have deep folds that are evenly spaced and should be gracefully tucked or folded at the ends (sides or top) and not bunched.

- Swags generally are lined, except when made of a decorative fabric with a pattern that can be seen through from the front, or when cost is a factor.

- Swags should not curl up at the front of the bottom hem but should hang gracefully.

- Top treatments may be sewn in vertical panels, which usually exposes seams but avoids the chance of the fabric appearing a different color from the interchanging of yarn position. Vertical panels with seams hidden in the pleats and falling in the depth or back of the fold are far more pleasing than obvious seams at the front or top of a pleat and fold.

- Except for sheer treatments, all top treatments should be neatly lined. This is important particularly for pleated and shirred top treatments so that no horizontal lines from hems are evident.

- Some top treatments will need to be weighted at the corners to hang without flaring out at the lower edges.

- Welting, banding, or passementerie on cornices or pelmets should be attached straight and neatly.

- The thread used should be the same color as the trim and the stitches should be unnoticeable.

- Ruffles should be of a consistent depth and sewn on evenly.

FABRIC CARE AND MAINTENANCE

The actual life span of a drapery fabric depends largely on how it is cared for and protected. It is part of the designer's responsibility to educate clients about the proper care of the fabrics utilized for their window treatments. This should be in written form whenever possible, and a copy should be given to the client. Another copy should be placed in the designer's file with documentation that the original was indeed given to the client on a particular date. The instructions should include a disclaimer that will protect the designer against liability claims in case of fabric damage or premature deterioration.

Protection

Protection of the fabric mainly involves keeping it from being unduly exposed to direct sunshine, which will cause it to become "tender," or weak and fragile.

Protection can be accomplished in several ways:

- Have the fabric lined as it is sewn. This also may make the fabric hang better.

- Add a separate liner to the back of the drapery by hooking the buttonholes onto the same hooks as the overdrapery. This may cause the drapery to look more bulky and to operate more clumsily than it would with a sewn-on lining, but the liner will be easier to remove and less costly to clean separately.

- Install a privacy drapery of lining fabric on a separate rod so that it can be pulled closed to keep damaging rays from the fabric.

- Add a blind, shade, or shutters. Blinds can be effective as a privacy treatment as well. They take up less space when in use, require no extra hardware, stack in smaller areas, and generally cost less than privacy draperies.

- Use exterior shading devices, such as architectural overhangs, trellises, shade trees, awnings, rolling shutters, shades, or blinds. Some exterior window treatments can be electronically operated from inside the building; others may be electronically controlled with light- or temperature-sensing devices or with clock-operated mechanisms.

Preventing the sun's rays from striking and heating the glass is crucially important. A closed drapery that traps the magnified rays of the sun will be exposed to temperatures that may climb up to 300 degrees Fahrenheit. The heat, in combination with ultraviolet rays, will speed the rate at which damage to the fabric takes place. If the draperies in the room are the same size, they may be rotated to give equal exposure to various orientations. Thus one set of draperies will not wear out before another one.

Cleaning

Cleaning involves the removal of airborne dirt, dust, oil, and water. Cleaning airborne dirt and dust from draperies can be simple and inexpensive. The following methods may work for the client:

- Shake the draperies periodically. This will keep the dust loose so it cannot penetrate into the fabric.

- Vacuum the fabric, paying special attention to the pleats and headings where dust lands.

- Place one drapery panel at a time (with pins or hooks removed) into the clothes dryer on "air/fluff." Put a soft, damp cloth in the dryer as well and tumble for 10 to 15 minutes. As the tumbling action shakes the dirt and dust loose, the cloth will absorb the impurities. Wet cloths should not be used; they may spot the fabric. Remove panels immediately when the dryer stops, and rehang without delay. Hand dress the folds (work into place by hand). If necessary, the folds may be reestablished by tying the opened draperies near the top, in the middle, and at the bottom of each panel with strips of soft cloth or the paper strips used by dry cleaners.

Removing water stains might be possible through professional dry cleaning, but it is rarely guaranteed. Some fibers, particularly rayon and acetate, water spot permanently. Water spotting occurs in one of two ways: through rain coming in opened windows or through humidity condensation between the glass and drapery fabric. The latter usually takes place when warm, moist air hits a cold glass surface. This can be prevented by adding storm windows inside or outside—thus increasing surface temperatures of the glass in winter—or by controlling the humidity levels. Lining the fabric also is effective, and there are some fine-quality lining materials available that are guaranteed not to stain from water condensation or rain.

There are two avenues for removing particles from fabric: dry cleaning and wet cleaning.

Dry cleaning is done in special machines that look like front-load washers or dryers but use solvents rather than soap and water as cleaning agents. Primarily done by a professional cleaning establishment, it is most often recommended for fabrics that may stretch, shrink, fade, or lose color in wet cleaning. It also is best when special finishes have been applied, such as starch or glazing, flame retardants, insect repellents, or soil or moisture repellents, since dry cleaning will likely not remove these finishes as readily as wet cleaning. Finishes will be *durable* and withstand repeated cleanings, or *nondurable* and be removed within the first few cleanings. Dry cleaning is mandatory for silk, rayon, acetate, and wool and is generally recommended for all decorative fabrics.

Sometimes the fiber itself may wash well, but the soap and water will damage the buckram or crinoline or the trimmings. Fancy fringes usually are of rayon or silk and will therefore need to be dry cleaned. Dry cleaning works best when a few simple guidelines are followed:

- Deal with a reputable establishment that specializes in drapery cleaning.

- Look for cleaners with a no-shrinkage guarantee who come to the site, remove the drapery, take it to be cleaned, and rehang it.

- Advise the cleaners of the fiber content so that the correct cleaning process and solution will be used to minimize damage or setting in of stains.

- Avoid cleaning the fabric too often. Once every six months is the maximum frequency for draperies (unless circumstances dictate more frequent cleaning).

Although professional dry cleaning is safer than washing in most cases, there may still be progressive shrinkage and removal of finishes, and a deterioration of the fiber (see "When the Damage Has Been Done" below). Chemicals used in the cleaning process can change the value or hue of the fabric slightly with successive cleanings. This can create a real problem if the draperies go to the cleaners, while the valances or companion furnishings remain *in situ* (at the site). Also, with cleaning the fabric may become tender, causing it to wear out prematurely. If the client keeps the fabric clean, soft window treatments may never need costly professional care.

For contract situations it is advisable to procure the services of a professional maintenance company that will keep the draperies vacuumed and will take the responsibility to have them cleaned when necessary. The frequency of cleaning contract draperies will vary according to the cleanliness of the air and whether there is smoke, smog, airborne oil or grease (as in an eating establishment), plastic-released fumes, and so on.

Wet cleaning means washing by hand or in a washing machine. Small, informal curtains usually do best when machine or hand washed in warm water with gentle agitation and mild detergent in low quantities. Some will be safe in the dryer at medium or even high temperatures, although some will do best when rehung damp.

Cotton fabrics historically needed sizing and starch and pressing or ironing to bring back their crisp appearance. Today many curtains are made of permanent-press, care-free cotton/polyester, which retains shape and does not wrinkle as did the cottons or linens of the past. Further, sheers and casement (needle-constructed) fabrics often are made of polyester, which may be wet cleaned and hung to dry and do not loose body or crispness in the cleaning process. Polyester sheers, semisheers, and laces will wash better in water than they will dry clean because the heat of the dry cleaning (or the very high heat from clothes dryers) will "set in" oil stains. Polyester is *oleophilic* (absorbs oil) but *hydrophobic* (does not absorb water). Therefore it is not affected by soap and water cleaning, and laundry detergent is designed to remove oily dirt. Some fabrics may be machine washed in a short gentle cycle. Remember, however, that some buckram/crinoline will not hold up when wet cleaned, particularly if the water is hot: the sizing dissolves or melts away. It will then lose body, making the drapery headings sag and hang limply when rehung. These fabrics may be "swished" gently in a bathtub filled part way with tepid (slightly warm) water from the shower head, shaken to remove excess water, and immediately rehung. Avoid immersing or agitating the buckram, if possible (although it may be necessary to wet the heading in order to clean off the soil). Also, do not allow moist sheers to touch other drapery fabrics when they are rehung—this may damage or stain other fabrics. Wet cleaning may possibly be used for acrylic and modacrylic fabrics as well. If possible, test a small swatch or corner first to determine the performance of the fabric when wet then dried.

Additional Protection Measures

Avoid handling draperies whenever possible. Children should be encouraged not to touch, let alone play with, drapery fabrics. Minute amounts of skin oils are present even on hands conscientiously cleaned before touching the fabric. Handling tieback draperies each day to let down and re-hand-dress them is a sure way to soil them unnecessarily. Tieback draperies should be left alone. A draw drapery, shade, blind, or shutter should be used beneath tieback draperies for nighttime privacy and sunlight protection.

Keep the room and the air clean to protect draperies from dirt and dust assault. Controlling and venting oil from fried foods also will keep draperies cleaner and fresher. Oil is especially harmful; it forms a difficult-to-remove layer on the fabric surface that attracts dirt and then moisture. Smoke from cigarettes also is damaging to textiles.

When the Damage Has Been Done

There are times when draperies are sent to dry cleaners in apparently good condition yet returned in shreds—smaller, uneven, or completely faded. This often is not the fault of the dry cleaners but happens because the fabric has already become tender owing to eight invisible factors: the fiber(s) used, sunlight deterioration, dye and pigment fading, oxidation, fume fading, shrinkage, humidity, and water staining.

Fiber selection is a major factor of longevity in drapery fabrics. When draperies come back in shreds, the fiber may have been weakened because of the chemicals used in the cleaning, the natural aging process, or the poor quality of the fiber itself. In every natural and man-made fiber, various levels of quality and durability exist, and this is a factor largely unknown to the designer before specification. Where large installations justify the cost, fabrics may be subjected to tests that determine durability, sunlight resistance, flammability, and so on. In fact, several hundred tests are now available. These tests can be performed by the manufacturer but usually are conducted by independent testing service companies or agencies.

Sunlight deterioration is an invisible enemy that slowly causes fibers to disintegrate. The fiber quality determines the extent of susceptibility to sun damage. When a lining fabric is sensitive to sun damage, the lining may fall into shreds long before the draperies have begun to age. It may well be the *agitation* of the cleaning process that destroys the already weakened fibers. Again, this is not the fault of the cleaners.

Dye and pigment fading is a condition of color change or lightening. For example, it could be the yellowing of a neutral color, a change from blue to blue-green, or red fading to pink. Colors most susceptible to fading are in the yellow, red, and blue families. In both plain and printed fabrics, the folds closest to the glass will fade more quickly and will show signs of sunlight deterioration. This means the fading often is apparent in vertical streaks. The cause is generally the reaction of the dyes, not the fibers. Except in viscose dyeing (where the dye is added to the man-made fiber solution before it is extruded into fiber form), there is no such thing as a colorfast dye.

All dyes change to a lesser or greater degree when exposed to prolonged sunlight. Also, the more direct or brilliant the sunlight, the more quickly the dye will fade. In the case of silk, the fading may be caused by exposure to incandescent or fluorescent interior lighting. Fading also is due to chemical reactions of the dry-cleaning solutions with the dyestuffs.

This is particularly true of pigment prints, which are not water-soluble dyestuffs absorbed into the fiber but are coloring agents held onto the surface with resin binders. Pigments may appear "painted on," and often are white or bright colors. Pigments are more readily removed by dry cleaning because they lie on the surface, and the chemicals literally loosen the binding action, removing a portion of the coloring agent.

Oxidation is the process of uniting a substance with oxygen and perhaps humidity to form a reaction whereby electrons are removed from atoms or ions. Smog and airborne impurities, such as exhaust from cooking, furnaces, fireplaces, smoking, and automobiles, can unite with oxygen and humidity to create an acid that discolors and wears out the fabric.

Fume fading is closely related to oxidation. Atmospheric gases and fumes within the interior may react with dyes, particularly in acetate fabrics, causing a color change toward the red spectrum. The sources of atmospheric fumes include those listed for oxidation above or fumes may be emitted from plastics and other man-made materials.

Shrinkage is the tightening of the weave through yarn compacting in fabrics that have not been preshrunk. An estimate of shrinkage may be obtained from the manufacturer and given to the client in writing. Some fabrics may be preshrunk before the draperies are constructed. However, this often is not done because of the cost and possible removal of soil-retardant finishes. Delicate, exclusive fabrics are rarely preshrunk, although many mainstream fabrics are. When a fabric is not preshrunk, shrinkage up to 4 percent is common. Inform the client that some dry cleaners may have limited guarantees against shrinkage of drapery fabric. This service is offered with a take-down and re-installation fee.

Humidity changes may cause fabric to absorb airborne water, elongating the yarns and causing sagging. When the humidity drops, the fabric may hike in an uneven manner, called the yo-yo effect. Dry cleaning may accentuate this problem by further shrinking some of the yarns.

Water stains occur when a drapery is placed where condensation is occurring or when the fabric is exposed to rain through open windows. Sometimes water "marks" are camouflaged by soiling and become noticeable only when the soil has been removed by cleaning, but the stains usually are permanent. A preventative measure may lie in lining draperies with a fabric guaranteed not to water stain.

Taking the Risk

Although there are inherent risks in using fabric at the window, most people are willing to accept that fabric will not last indefinitely and continue to choose it because of its many advantages. The wise designer will inform the client that no fabric is infallible and that many factors may contribute to deterioration or eventual unsuitability. There is no way to predict with complete accuracy the life span of any treatment (although contract fabrics may be tested and issued guarantees) because so many of the variables (from invisible enemies to the care and maintenance given the fabric) will change with the function and occupants of the room and even with the season. Given this fact, a realistic expectation of the life span of a fabric lies in a healthy attitude about using and enjoying it, while keeping it clean and respected. Although certain fabrics, protected and cared for, may hang at the window beautifully for twenty or more years, it generally is recognized that the life expectancy of draperies is three to five years.

Chapter 6 CALCULATING, SPECIFYING, AND INSTALLING SOFT WINDOW TREATMENTS

When draperies, curtains, shades, and top treatments are measured and sewn to correct specifications, the result is successful. However, when the measurements, calculations, specifications, or installation are done incorrectly or sloppily, the result can be disastrous. Soft window treatments are perhaps one of the best money-makers in interior design because of the amount of yardage needed to make full custom draperies. A soft window covering that is the wrong size, for example, will need to be altered or thrown out. In either case the interior designer will be responsible for the error; he or she will lose the profit and go in the hole, or "eat the job."

Many tables, such as tables 6–6 and 6–7 appearing later in this chapter, aid the window treatment specialist in calculating drapery yardage; some are available as computing wheels. Manufacturing plants supplying fabric use pricing charts that show the telescoping widths (48 to 50 inches, for example) and various lengths. The designer simply needs to find the categories of width and length, then look up the finished price. These charts save the effort of calculating the yardage or cost of the treatment longhand. However, most charts or wheels are for pleated draperies or shirred curtains and do not take into account the variable of hems and headings. They also do not include hardware or installation.

The competent designer, decorator, or window treatment specialist should have a working knowledge of how to calculate yardages longhand because many situations call for custom calculations. The process of correctly specifying soft treatments and a basic understanding of hardware and installation are equally important, so that every treatment can be constructed and installed to the correct dimensions. Well-planned and well-executed soft coverings can make the business of window treatments financially successful and satisfying.

THE BASIC MEASUREMENTS

Accurate measurements are crucial for correct calculation and specification of any window treatment. These are discussed and illustrated in detail in chapter 3. The window measurements must supply the dimension in inches of at least the following:

- window width

- stackoff, or treatment extension on each side of the glass

- rod width (the window width plus the stackoff)

- overlap and returns, if applicable

- finished width

- finished length (including the area above and below the glass) of the treatment

This information will be used to calculate the number of widths (including the cut length of each width), the total yardage, the cost of labor to sew, the cost of hardware, and the cost of installation. It also is needed to fill out work orders or specification sheets and installation forms. Samples of these forms are found later in this chapter.

Calculations for each of the general categories of soft window treatments—draperies, curtains, shades, and top treatments—are found in this chapter. First, calculating draperies is outlined, and the explanation of each step follows. Many of the steps in calculating draperies are basic to the calculation of other soft treatments.

CALCULATIONS: PLEATED DRAPERIES

Of the many styles of pleated draperies, the French pleat is most common. Since the calculations for all pleated draperies are very similar, the procedure outlined below can be followed for nearly every type.

1. Measure the window width (ww).

2. Add stackoff (so) or stackback (sb) to find the total rod width (rw):
   ww + so = rw.

3. Add overlaps (ol) and returns (rt) to get finished width (fw):
   rw + ol + rt = fw.

4. Compute the number of widths or cuts (w):
   fw ÷ ratio = w, or
   (fw × fullness) ÷ fabric width = number of widths

5. Measure finished length (fl).

6. Add length for hems and headings (h/h) to finished length (fl) for cut length (cl):   h/h + fl = cl

7. Multiply cut length (cl) by number of widths (w) for total linear inches and divide by 36 to find total yardage (yd):
   (cl × w) ÷ 36 = yd

8. Determine any seamless (extra-wide fabric) yardage:
   (w × fullness) ÷ 36 = yd

9. Determine fabrication cost (fc), or number of widths times cost per width to sew: w × $ per w = fc

10. Add on yardage for trimmings, such as ruffles, banding, fringe, or braid, and the labor to sew per foot or per yard.

11. Select hardware and price it, along with cost of installation per width (rods and draperies) or per foot (shades and valances) or per tieback holder or bracket:

$ per yd + fc + rods + inst + tax = total $

12. Fill out fabric and hardware purchase orders, specification work orders, and installation orders.

Details of the above outline are as follows:

1. Measure the Window Width

The window width is the actual opening of the window horizontally. Draperies may cover just this opening or may go beyond the opening to cover the wall space on one or both sides. When draperies cover the opening only, some of the glass will be covered even when the draperies are opened, making the window appear smaller. Draperies that go beyond the opening increase the apparent size of the opening. In either case the window width is used to determine the wall space needed for stackoff.

2. Add Stackoff or Stackback

Stackoff or stackback is the area needed by opened draperies to stack off the glass. Complete stackoff is approximately one-third the window width for a medium-weight fabric at 250 percent fullness, for example. To find this, divide the window width by 3 and add that amount to each side of the glass. Lightweight and sheer fabrics might take less space, up to one-fifth the width of the window, depending on how full the fabric is pleated. Also, skimpy draperies will stack off to a smaller area than will those of generous fullness. Table 6–1 gives stackoff dimensions for a two-way draw or a pair of draperies. Table 6–2 lists one-way draw stackoff.

The advantages of complete stackoff include:

- maximum daylight exposure

- better proportion of the window because the glass is fully exposed

- the impression of a wider window because draperies stacked on the wall give the impression of glass behind the fabric

- no fabric hanging in the window when the draperies are open, resulting in a cleaner look from outside the building

- a richer, fuller look and a quieter interior due to increased fabric yardage surrounding the glass

Complete stackoff will not be used when:

- there is inadequate wall space on one or both sides of the glass

- the cost of the extra fabric to cover the wall is prohibitive

- the stackoff covers important wall space needed for furniture, art, or outlets or switches that must be left free for access

- the color or pattern is strong and the quantity would overwhelm the room

- a slender, historic treatment is specified

In the case of partial stackoff, the designer makes the decision how far beyond the window to extend the rod—usually 4 to 12 inches. Stackback

Table 6–1 Two-Way Draw Drapery Stackoff or Stackback: Medium-Weight Fabrics

Standard-Size Window Width [in.(ft.)]	Stackoff Each Side (in.)	Times Two Sides for Two-Way Draw Equals (in.)	Plus Window Width (in.)	Equals Total Rod Width (including Stackoff) (in.)
24 (2)	8	x 2 = 16	+ 24	= 40
30 (2 ½)	10	x 2 = 20	+ 30	= 50
36 (3)	12	x 2 = 24	+ 36	= 60
42 (3 ½)	14	x 2 = 28	+ 42	= 70
48 (4)	16	x 2 = 32	+ 48	= 80
54 (4 ½)	17	x 2 = 34	+ 54	= 88
60 (5)	18	x 2 = 36	+ 60	= 96
72 (6)	24	x 2 = 48	+ 72	= 120
84 (7)	28	x 2 = 56	+ 84	= 140
96 (8)	32	x 2 = 64	+ 96	= 160
108 (9)	36	x 2 = 72	+ 108	= 180
120 (10)	40	x 2 = 80	+ 120	= 200
132 (11)	44	x 2 = 88	+ 132	= 220
144 (12)	48	x 2 = 96	+ 144	= 240

Table 6–2 One-Way Draw Drapery Stackoff or Stackback: Medium-Weight Fabric

Standard-Size Window Width [in. (ft.)]	Stackoff One Side (in.)	Minus 4 or 6 Inches Equals (in.)	Plus Window Width (in.)	Equals Total Rod Width (including Stackoff) (in.)
24 (2)	16	–4 = 12	+ 24	= 36
30 (2 ½)	20	–4 = 16	+ 30	= 46
36 (3)	24	–4 = 20	+ 36	= 56
42 (3 ½)	28	–4 = 24	+ 42	= 66
48 (4)	32	– 4 = 28	+ 48	= 76
54 (4 ½)	34	– 4 = 30	+ 54	= 84
60 (5)	40	– 4 = 36	+ 60	= 96
72 (6)	48	– 4 = 44	+ 72	= 116
84 (7)	56	– 6 = 50	+ 84	= 134
96 (8)	64	– 6 = 58	+ 96	= 154
108 (9)	72	– 6 = 66	+ 108	= 174
120 (10)	80	– 6 = 74	+ 120	= 194
132 (11)	88	– 6 = 82	+ 132	= 214
144 (12)	96	– 6 = 90	+ 144	= 234

on one side only will be greater than when it is balanced on both sides. This often is used at sliding glass doors or corner windows. The drapery should not end at the glass on the nonstack side, however; it should be installed 4 to 6 inches beyond to prevent light strike and to assure privacy.

The window width measurement added to the stackback (both sides) will give the rod width or bracket-to-bracket measurement. Both the window width and the rod width need to be supplied to the drapery installer.

3. Add Overlaps and Returns

Overlaps are where the headings overlap at the top of the drapery rather than meeting at the center point. On a conventional traverse rod, the overlaps are attached to the master carriers (leading carrier arms of the rod that overlap each other—see fig. 6–10). The overlap is generally 2 inches on each side, or a total of 4 inches on a pair of draperies. The overlap keeps the draperies closed from top to bottom, as the fabric tends to flare outward. It eliminates a light strike, assures privacy, increases energy efficiency, and looks neat.

Returns are the end of the drapery headings that wrap around to the wall and cover up the rod projection, which is the depth of the end bracket (see fig. 6–10a). The depth of the return will depend on how many layers of draperies are specified. Rod projections vary slightly, and workrooms may make returns a little different than specified. Where a 4-inch return is ordered, it may be fabricated to $3\frac{1}{2}$ inches, for example.

Overlaps and returns (table 6–3) are totaled and added to the rod width (window width plus stackback) to find the finished width or pleated width.

4. Compute the Number of Widths

The draperies will require a certain number of widths sewn together to equal the finished or pleated width. The determining factor is the fullness desired. A skimpy, less full drapery will require fewer widths than a generous drapery. Table 6–4 is a simple way to quickly find the number of widths needed. It lists the number of inches in a width of fabric that has been *pleated* (to a particular fullness). Take that number and divide it into the finished or pleated width, then round up the answer to the next width. This method is very easy because it deals only in pleated widths and not in flat widths, since that is the way draperies are specified. For example, say that the pleated width is 68 inches and that the fabric is a standard 48 inches wide pleated down to a 250 percent ($2\frac{1}{2}$ times) fullness. Looking at the chart, note that 48 inches pleats down to 18 inches. The pleated width, 68 inches, is divided by 18, and the answer is 3.8. Rounding up is customary if a fraction remains of more than two-tenths of a width. This gives a more generous fullness, whereas rounding down results in a skimpier drapery. Here, four widths will yield that generous fullness.

The number of widths can also be obtained by multiplying the finished width by the desired fullness, then dividing by the width of the fabric (abbreviated fw × fullness ÷ fab. width = w). For example, a 60-inch-wide finished width multiplied by 2-times fullness equals 120 inches. This divided by 48 inches equal 2.5 widths, rounded up to 3 widths. Or:

$$60 \times 2 = 120 \div 48 = 2.5, \text{ or 3 widths}$$

This method works very well. However, it does involve more steps than the first method.

The number of widths is used to determine the labor to fabricate and to install treatments. Both labor costs are based on cost per width, usually regardless of length. Note, too, that when ordering fabric, it is wise to list the number of widths in case the fabric needs to be cut because of flaws.

Drapery and curtain styles typically are seen with the following fullness:

- 150 percent fullness: New England tab curtains, slightly shirred cottage curtains, slender architectural (accordion-fold) draperies

- 200 percent fullness: bulky fabric draperies, contract or architectural draperies, and draperies that need to stack to a smaller area

- 250 percent fullness: light- and medium-weight drapery fabrics and shirred curtains

- 300 percent fullness: sheer fabrics where greater fullness gives a custom look

- 400 percent fullness: country curtains (very full shirred and ruffled curtains)

Table 6-3 Overlaps and Returns

Placement of Drapery Layer	Overlap Needed (in.)	Return Needed (in.)	Rod and Drapery Clearance (in.)	Total (Add This for Overlaps, Returns, and Clearance) (in.)
Single-layer drapery	2 each side = 4	4 each side = 8	0	12
Underdrapery (sheers or privacy)	2 each side = 4	0	0	4
Overdrapery (second layer)	2 each side = 4	6 each side = 12	0	16
Third layer (center-meet tiebacks)	2 each side = 4	9 each side = 18	0	22
Third layer (separated tiebacks)	0	9 each side = 18	0	18
Valance over one layer	0	6 each side = 12	I each side added to rod width = 2	14
Valance over two layers	0	9 each side = 18	I each side added to rod width = 2	20
Valance over three layers	0	12 each side = 24	I each side added to rod width = 2	26

Table 6-4 Determining Pleated Widths

Medium-Weight Fabric Width Laid Flat (in.)	Will Pleat Down to This Measurement for:				
	150% Fullness (in.)	200% Fullness (in.)	250% Fullness (in.)	300% Fullness (in.)	400% Fullness (in.)
44–48	23	20	18	15	10
54	25	22	20	18	13
60	27	24	22	19	14
69	29	26	24	20	15
103	53	48	42	38	33
118	57	52	46	40	35

5. Measure Finished Length

The finished length is the exact measurement of the finished drapery. This will be a simple measurement, unless the drapery is to be installed floor to ceiling. Then a standard deduction of ½ inch is taken from top and bottom, or a total of 1 inch. This clearance prevents wear from the drapery's rubbing against the ceiling or dragging on an uneven floor or from fabric elongation (stretching).

Deduct another inch off the length for sheers under overdraperies, so that they will not be seen lower than the hem or above the heading. Exposed sheers have what is called a petticoat effect.

Deduct ½ inch rather than 1 inch when draperies are to be tied back, because they tend to hike when tied.

For privacy draperies beneath tieback draperies, deduct yet another ½ inch, so that the draperies will not show beneath the hem.

To summarize:

- For *ceiling-to-floor draperies,* deduct 1 inch for overdraperies and 1½ inches for sheers under overdraperies.

- For *ceiling-to-floor tieback draperies,* deduct ½ inch for overdraperies, 1½ inches for sheers under overdraperies, and 2 inches for privacy drapery under sheers and overdraperies.

6. Add for Hems and Headings

Hems are the turned-under bottom fabric that finishes the draperies. They generally are 4 inches deep, turned twice, for a total of 8 inches. Deeper hems, such as 5 inches or 6 inches can give a more luxurious, custom appearance. The depth of the hem is the decision of the designer or decorator.

Headings at the top encase the buckram or crinoline used to stiffen drapery pleats and also will require 4 to 8 inches of additional fabric length, depending on whether they are double or single wrapped. The way headings are made is the decision of the workroom, and the designer or window-covering specialist needs to know the heading allowance required by a particular workroom before the yardage is calculated.

Headings also can involve ruffles above rod pockets in shirred curtains (discussed below).

Table 6–5 lists some variations on cut-length requirements. In general, to protect against shortages, it is wise to add on 16 or 20 inches for hems and headings. The cut length is obtained by adding the inches needed for hems and headings onto the finished length. For example, a 94-inch finished length plus 16 inches for hems and headings makes a cut length of 110 inches.

7. Find Total Yardage

The total yardage is found by multiplying the cut length by the number of widths for total linear inches, converting that to yards by dividing by 36, and then rounding up to the next whole yard of fabric. For example, a 110-inch cut length multiplied by 6 widths equals 660 inches. This divided by 36 equals 18.3 yards, rounded up to 19 full yards, or:

$$110 \times 6 = 660 \div 36 = 18.3, \text{ or 19 yards}$$

Table 6–6 is a simplified chart for whole or rounded-up yardage based on finished length plus 16 inches for hems and headings, 250 percent fullness, and 45-, 48-, and 54-inch-wide plain fabric.

Table 6-5 Hems and Headings Variations for Cut Lengths

Draperies	Finished Length	+	Hems (in.)	+	Heading (in.)	=	Cut Length (in.)		
Lined pleated	FL	+	8 (or 10)	+	8	=	FL	+	16 (or 18)
Unlined pleated	FL	+	8 (or 10)	+	10	=	FL	+	18 (or 20)
Shirr only top and bottom (1½" hem/head casings)	FL	+	7	+	7	=	FL	+	14
Shirr top and bottom with ruffled heading	FL	+	9	+	9	=	FL	+	18
4"-wide curtain rod	FL	+	8 (or 10)	+	8	=	FL	+	16 (or 18)
				(5½" pocket—no ruffle. For ruffle, add 2 × heading to CL)					

Table 6-6 Whole Yardage Chart: 45-, 48-, and 54-Inch-Wide Fabric

Finished Length (in.) to:	Cut Length (in.) to:		2 Widths	3 Widths	4 Widths	5 Widths	6 Widths	7 Widths	8 Widths
		45" fabric	11–28"	29–50"	51–74"	75–94"	95–116"	117–138"	139–162"
		48" fabric	13–32"	33–56"	57–78"	79–102"	103–126"	127–148"	149–172"
		54" fabric	23–38"	39–64"	65–90"	91–118"	119–144"	145–170"	171–197"
30	46		3	4	5	7	8	9	11
36	52		3	5	6	8	9	10	12
42	58		4	5	7	8	10	12	13
48	64		4	6	7	9	11	13	15
54	70		4	6	8	10	12	14	16
60	76		5	7	9	11	13	15	17
66	82		5	7	9	12	14	16	19
72	88		5	8	10	13	15	17	20
78	94		6	8	11	13	16	19	21
84	100		6	9	11	14	17	20	23
90	106		6	9	12	15	18	21	24
96	112		7	10	13	16	19	22	25
102	118		7	10	13	17	20	23	27
108	124		7	11	14	18	21	24	28
114	130		8	11	15	18	22	26	29
120	136		8	12	15	19	23	27	31
126	142		8	12	16	20	24	28	32
132	148		9	13	17	21	25	29	33
138	154		9	13	17	22	26	30	35
144	160		9	14	18	23	27	31	36
18" valance, self-lined			2	3	4	5	6	7	8

Note: This table is based on a 16-inch allowance for hems and headings to determine cut length, 250 percent, or 2 ½ times fullness, and plain fabric. Pattern repeats are not figured into this table.

Pattern repeats also affect the cut length. Pattern repeats will need to match horizontally from one cut to the next, and this will mean that some waste is inevitable. To allow for this, fabric is ordered in *complete pattern repeats.* For example, if 110 inches is the cut length, and the pattern repeat is 25 inches (a typical large-size pattern repeat), then five complete pattern repeats are required per cut and some will be wasted. This will necessarily increase the yardage, so that five complete pattern repeats per width makes the new cut length 125 inches rather than 110. If six widths are used, then:

$$6 \times 125 = 750 \div 36 = 20.8, \text{ or } 21 \text{ yards}$$

A general rule of thumb is that when the draperies are ceiling to floor, the pattern repeat should begin at the top, where it is most noticeable. The partial repeat may then be at the bottom hem. In a short drapery the complete pattern repeat should end at the bottom, where the eye follows the line of the hem. This means that a partial pattern repeat may be needed at the top. In other words the whole pattern repeat is placed where it is noticed, and it is the responsibility of the designer to communicate the placement to the workroom.

When fabric yardage is short because pattern repeats are overlooked, extra fabric will need to be ordered to finish the draperies. If this happens be sure to clip to the purchase order a sample of the existing fabric so that dye lots can be matched. Ordering extra yardage often means a wait for the fabric and extra cost of the yardage, causing inconvenience to the customer and loss of profit to the designer.

8. Determine Any Seamless Yardage

Seamless yardage is fabric that runs 103 to 118 inches wide, and it usually is turned sideways and railroaded so that the width becomes the length and no seams are needed. When using seamless yardage simply take the finished width and look on table 6–7 for the total yardage required for the desired fullness (2–1 is 200 percent fullness, 2½–1 is 250 percent fullness, and 3–1 is 300 percent fullness). Even though the chart lists fractions of a yard, such as 9¼, many fabric companies fill orders only for complete yards, so it is customary to round up to the next whole yard.

9. Determine Cost to Fabricate

Cost to fabricate, also called fabrication or labor to sew, is calculated by the number of widths. The charge will be determined by the workroom and will be higher for lined than for unlined draperies. For example, if

Table 6-7 Seamless or Railroaded Yardage Calculation

Column	Exact Yardage for Fullness				Column	Exact Yardage for Fullness		
1	2–1	2 ½–1	3–1		1	2—1	2 ½–1	3–1
To 36″	2	2 ½	3		199–201	11 ¼	14	16 ¾
37–39	2 ¼	2 ¾	3 ¼		202–205	11 ½	14 ¼	17 ¼
40–43	2 ½	3	3 ¾		206–208	11 ¾	14 ½	17 ½
44–46	2 ¾	3 ¼	4		209–212	12	14 ¾	17 ¾
47–50	3	3 ½	4 ¼		213–216	12	15	18
51–54	3	3 ¾	4 ½		217–219	12 ¼	15 ¼	18 ¼
55–57	3 ¼	4	4 ¾		220–223	12 ½	15 ½	18 ¾
58–61	3 ½	4 ¼	5 ¼		224–226	12 ¾	15 ¾	19
62–64	3 ¾	4 ½	5 ½		227–230	13	16	19 ¼
65–68	4	4 ¾	5 ¾		231–234	13	16 ¼	19 ½
69–72	4	5	6		235–237	13 ¼	16 ½	19 ¾
73–75	4 ¼	5 ¼	6 ¼		238–241	13 ½	16 ¾	20 ¼
76–79	4 ½	5 ½	6 ¾		242–244	13 ¾	17	20 ½
80–82	4 ¾	5 ¾	7		245–248	14	17 ¼	20 ¾
83–86	5	6	7 ¼		249–252	14	17 ½	21
87–90	5	6 ¼	7 ½		253–255	14 ¼	17 ¾	21 ¼
91–93	5 ¼	6 ½	7 ¾		256–259	14 ½	18	21 ¾
94–97	5 ½	6 ¾	8 ¼		260–262	14 ¾	18 ¼	22
98–100	5 ¾	7	8 ½		263–266	15	18 ½	22 ¼
101–104	6	7 ¼	8 ¾		267–270	15	18 ¾	22 ½
105–108	6	7 ½	9		271–273	15 ¼	19	22 ¾
109–111	6 ¼	7 ¾	9 ¼		274–277	15 ½	19 ¼	23 ¼
112–115	6 ½	8	9 ¾		278–280	15 ¾	19 ½	23 ½
116–118	6 ¾	8 ¼	10		281–284	16	19 ¾	23 ¾
119–122	7	8 ½	10 ¼		285–288	16	20	24
123–126	7	8 ¾	10 ½		289–291	16 ¼	20 ¼	24 ¼
127–129	7 ¼	9	10 ¾		292–295	16 ½	20 ½	24 ¾
130–133	7 ½	9 ¼	11 ¼		296–298	16 ¾	20 ¾	25
134–136	7 ¾	9 ½	11 ½		299–302	17	21	25 ¼
137–140	8	9 ¾	11 ¾		303–306	17	21 ¼	25 ½
141–144	8	10	12		307–309	17 ¼	21 ½	25 ¾
145–147	8 ¼	10 ¼	12 ¼		310–313	17 ½	21 ¾	26 ¼
148–151	8 ½	10 ½	12 ¾		314–316	17 ¾	22	26 ½
152–154	8 ¾	10 ¾	13		317–320	18	22 ¼	26 ¾
155–158	9	11	13 ¼		321–324	18	22 ½	27
159–162	9	11 ¼	13 ½		325–327	18 ¼	22 ¾	27 ¼
163–165	9 ¼	11 ½	13 ¾		328–331	18 ½	23	27 ¾
166–169	9 ½	11 ¾	14 ¼		332–334	18 ¾	23 ¼	28
170–172	9 ¾	12	14 ½		335–338	19	23 ½	28 ¼
173–176	10	12 ¼	14 ¾		339–342	19	23 ¾	28 ½
177–180	10	12 ½	15		343–345	19 ¼	24	28 ¾
181–183	10 ¼	12 ¾	15 ¼		346–349	19 ½	24 ¼	29 ¼
184–187	10 ½	13	15 ¾		350–352	19 ¾	24 ½	29 ½
188–190	10 ¾	13 ¼	16		353–356	20	24 ¾	29 ¾
191–194	11	13 ½	16 ¼		357–360	20	25	30
195–198	11	13 ¾	16 ½		361–364	20 ¼	25 ¼	30 ½

there are six unlined widths and the cost to fabricate is $10 per width, then the fabrication is $60.

Labor to sew seamless draperies often is based on every 18 inches, which would be the pleated width of a 48-inch sheer at 250 percent, or 2½–1 fullness. Table 6–4 lists this and indicates that extra-wide fabric also may be used in vertical cuts, along with the pleated width for each fullness.

10. Add on Yardage for Trimmings

Yardage for trimmings depends solely on what type is used and where it is placed. Trimming, discussed and illustrated in detail in chapter 5, includes passementerie and custom fabric trims.

Passementerie is sold by the yard (tassels are sold individually). Yardage is calculated by adding up the number of inches needed for trimming a treatment, then dividing by 36 and rounding up to the next whole yard to find the total yardage. Or:

$$\text{Total inches} \div 36 = \text{total yards trimming}$$

For example, if fringe will be placed on the ties, down the front, and along the bottom of tieback draperies that are three widths wide, then add the finished length, the flat width of the three widths, and the length of two ties. The calculation would look like this:

- 84-inch finished length × 2 = 168 inches

- 3 widths of fabric at 48 inches each = 144 inches

- 2 ties each 36 inches = 72 inches.

- 168 + 144 + 72 = 384 total inches.

- 384 ÷ 36 = 10.6, or 11 yards.

Fabric may be cut into vertical or horizontal strips for piping, banding, or ruffles and banding may also be cut on the bias (diagonal). Calculate it as simply as possible. For flat banding the yardage is found by figuring the number of strips from a yard. For ruffles, the total in inches is doubled or tripled for fullness, then divided into yardage, and then further divided into strips.

For example: if the total yardage for a ruffle came to 20 yards and the width of the ruffle is to be 4 inches (2 inches doubled for hems), then possibly twelve strips of fabric could be obtained from one width of fabric (48 inches divided by the 4-inch strip), and only about 2 yards would be needed (20 yards divided by twelve strips per yard). If the calculation becomes frustrating, call the workroom and ask for help figuring the yardage. (A little practice in advance can give confidence in figuring banding and ruffles.)

Labor costs to fuse or sew on trimmings probably will be per linear foot. Sewing costs more than fusing, and every workroom will establish the actual price for applying trim (see fig. 6–3).

Ties are the fabric strips used to secure tieback draperies. Generally an extra yard of fabric should be ample to take care of one, two, or even three pairs of ties. The exact length and width can be figured: two-thirds the finished width of each panel for the length and 2½ to 4 inches wide. In this way the yard is cut into strips. Remember to charge the customer for the labor to sew up the pair of ties and to install the tieback holders and ties. Overlooking small charges can eat up the profit.

11. Select and Price Hardware and Installation

Hardware is selected from a catalog (discussed at the end of this chapter) and is ordered with a separate purchase order (or held in stock by the design or decorating firm) and delivered with the draperies for installation. Add the cost of installation per width, foot, or bracket.

12. Fill Out Forms

Sample fabric purchase orders, specification orders, and installation work orders (see samples later in this chapter) must be filled out before production can begin. When filling out fabric purchase orders, indicate the name, number, color, and total yardage. Also indicate the number of cuts or widths and the cut length of each. For patterned fabric indicate the number of complete pattern repeats needed per cut. Fabric rolled off bolts may be flawed, or the yardage may be too short for the entire order, and it may become necessary to cut. If 60 yards are ordered with no indication of the cut lengths or number of widths, then the designer is taking a great risk that the yardage will not be sufficient.

Specification sheets must be filled in completely, with painstaking accuracy. Errors on the part of the designer can be disastrous, causing ruined draperies and dissatisfied clients (see "Specifications" below).

CALCULATIONS: CURTAINS

Curtains are simpler to compute than draperies because they generally are sewn in flat panels with rod pockets or casings that are shirred or gathered onto a rod. Thus, stackoff, overlaps, and returns are not figured into the calculations. The important measurements are the desired *rod width, finished width,* and *finished length.* From the rod width the number of widths can be calculated as for draperies (see table 6–4); the yardage also is figured this way.

Keep in mind that fabric yardage for headings depends on the size of the rod, whether there is to be a ruffle, and how deep that ruffle will be above the rod (see table 6–8). Hems may be smaller for shorter curtains, but, generally, 4-inch double hems are a safe measurement.

Beyond the simple curtain that is shirred onto a rod, there are many other styles, as seen in chapter 5. Some of these are less full, such as the flat café and the New England tab curtain, which may be only 150 percent, or 1½ times fullness (see table 6–4).

The number of widths of curtain also can be found by multiplying the finished width by 1.5 (the desired fullness), then dividing by the width of the fabric. If this method is used, then the side hems should be added to the finished width before multiplying (an additional 6 inches per panel). Total yardage calculation is the same for curtains as for draperies. Multiply the number of widths by the cut length for total inches. Divide by 36 for total yardage, then round up to the nearest whole yard. Trimmings and ruffles are also calculated as for draperies.

Curtains and valances shirred onto rods will need specified lengths to suit the type of rod being selected. Table 6–8 lists the most common sizes and types of rods used to shirr curtains and valances and suggests ruffle headings proportional to the rods. The designer will need to realize that the overall length of the curtain will be *increased* in proportion to the extra inches needed for the rod. For example, according to the table, a curtain shirred onto a 2-inch wood pole will need a rod pocket 4½ inches

Table 6-8 Curtain Rod Pocket and Ruffle Heading Sizes

Rod Type	Rod Pocket Size (in.)	Ruffle Heading (in.)
Oval Rods		
Standard oval curtain rod	1 ½	1 ½
2-inch oval curtain rod	3 ½	2
4-inch oval curtain rod	5 ½	3
Round Rods		
1 ⅜-inch-diameter wood pole	3	3
2-inch-diameter wood pole	4 ½	4
2-inch-diameter PVC (plastic pipe)	4 ½	4
3-inch-diameter PVC (plastic pipe)	4 ½	5

wide. The new finished length, then, would be 2½ inches longer than the vertical finished length, to accommodate extra fabric for the rod pocket. Also note that the ruffled heading is placed above the rod. The depth of a ruffled heading of curtains and shirred valances is specified at the discretion of the designer. Sometimes a ruffle is not used, but, when it is, it should be in proportion to the size of the rod. Table 6-8 gives suggestions for good proportions for ruffles according to rod diameter. Use this information in conjunction with table 6-5. Note that the round rods require a rod-pocket size about double the diameter of the rod.

Country curtains, such as those seen in figure 5-7, are extra full: 4-1, or 400 percent fullness, and the ruffles are up to 5-1, or 500 percent fullness. Since the yardage for country curtains is difficult to calculate, table 6-9 lists the rod size, flat curtain size (before shirring), number of widths needed, and yardage for the curtain and one ruffle and for optional double ruffle and lace.

CALCULATIONS: FABRIC SHADES

Chapter 5 lists and illustrates the types of fabric shades: Austrian shades, pouf shades, Roman shades, and flat fabric shades. Calculations for yardage and labor to sew for each type vary accordingly.

Austrian Shades

For inside installations deduct ½ inch from the exact width, for a ¼-inch clearance on each side to prevent the shade from rubbing against the window frame. Since the scalloped hem will cause a light strike or exposed glass on an inside mount, an outside mount is preferred where possible. Remember that the Austrian shade typically has no return.

An outside mount can be extended beyond the window frame 4 to 6 inches overall (2 or 3 inches on each side) so that light strike is diminished. Austrian shade length usually is extended 4 or more inches below the window to eliminate exposed glass area through the scalloped hem.

To determine the number of widths, figure that for every 20 inches of board, one width of 48-inch fabric is needed. For example, for a 60-inch width, three widths are needed. For a 72-inch-wide measurement, four widths will be used and some will be cut off and wasted.

The cut length will be three times the finished length; so, for example, if the finished length is to be 36 inches, then the cut length will be 108 inches.

Multiply the number of widths by the cut length for total inches; then divide by 36 for the number of yards; finally, round up to the next whole

Table 6-9 Country Curtain Calculation Chart

Rod Size (in.)	Approximate Curtain Size (width x length) (in.)	Widths Required	Curtain, Single Ruffle, & Bow Tie (yds.)	Optional Double (Layered) Ruffle (yds.)	Optional Lace Trim per Ruffle (yds.)
20- 27	90 x 45	2	9	4	20
20- 27	90 x 65	2	12	6	30
20- 27	90 x 96	2	16	8	40
27- 36	135 x 45	3	11	5	25
27- 36	135 x 65	3	15	7	35
27- 36	135 x 96	3	20	9	45
37- 48	180 x 45	4	14	6	30
37- 48	180 x 65	4	18	8	40
37- 48	180 x 96	4	24	10	50
49- 59	225 x 45	5	16	7	35
49- 59	225 x 65	5	21	9	45
49- 59	225 x 96	5	28	11	55
60- 70	270 x 65	6	24	10	50
60- 70	270 x 96	6	32	12	60
71- 80	315 x 65	7	27	11	55
71- 80	315 x 96	7	36	13	65
81- 90	360 x 65	8	30	12	60
81- 90	360 x 96	8	40	14	70
91-100	405 x 65	9	33	13	65
91-100	405 x 96	9	44	15	75

Valance	Approximate Size	Widths Required	Single Ruffle	Optional Double (Layered) Ruffle	Optional Lace Trim per Ruffle
12	45	1	1 1/4	1	5
24	90	2	3 1/2	2	10
36	135	3	5 1/4	3	15
48	180	4	7	4	20

Swag Valance	Approximate Size	Widths Required	Single Ruffle		Optional Lace Trim per Ruffle
20-27	90 x 45	2	6		15

Tiers With Bottom Ruffles	Approximate Size	Widths Required	Single Ruffle	Optional Double (Layered) Ruffle	Optional Lace Trim per Ruffle
20-27	90 x 25	2	4	2	10
20-27	90 x 50	2	5	2	10
28-36	135 x 25	3	6	3	15
28-36	135 x 50	3	7 1/2	3	15
37-48	180 x 25	4	8	4	20
37-48	180 x 50	4	10	4	20

Note: Curtains 4-1 fullness; ruffle 5-1 fullness, 8 inches deep, 4-inch header.

yard. For example, if three widths are needed, each 108 inches long, then total inches is 324; 324 divided by 36 equals 9 yards.

Trimming for the scallops will be approximately 150 percent, or 1 1/2 times the width of the shade. If the shade is 72 inches, multiply 72 by 1.5 for 108 total inches, then divide by 36 for 3 full yards. Round up if the yardage is an additional .3 or more. (For example, if the yardage calculates to 1.3, round up to 2 full yards of trimming.)

Fabrication, or labor to sew, is determined by the number of Austrian "strings"—the tape sewn onto the back that draws the shade into gathers. Consult with the workroom for this charge.

Pouf Shades

Since pouf shades also have scalloped hems, the same considerations for inside versus outside installation prevail as for Austrian shades.

Pouf shades are between 2–1 and 2.5–1 (200 to 250 percent) fullness. Therefore one width of 48-inch-wide fabric will cover 24 inches of board at 200 percent (or 2 times) fullness and approximately 20 inches of board at 250 percent fullness. Round up to the next whole width, and the workroom will determine whether the extra will be trimmed as waste.

The cut length is figured by adding 40 inches to the finished length. Therefore, to find the yardage for a pouf shade finished to 40 inches wide by 60 inches long at 250 percent fullness, you would calculate:

$$2w \text{ (250\% fullness)} \times 100 \text{ (cl)} = 200 \div 36 = 5.5, \text{ or 6 yards}$$

Trimming for scalloped hems for pouf shades is determined in the same way as for Austrian shades: one and one-half the finished width of the board becomes the yardage. Pouf shades are priced either by the string (balloon or pouf tape) or by the foot. Consult the workroom for labor pricing.

Roman Shades

Flat Roman shades use little more than the actual area to be covered. To calculate yardage, first determine whether the shade is to be an inside mount or an outside installation. If it is mounted inside the window frame, deduct ¼ inch on each side for clearance. Outside the frame the shade may be mounted onto the casing or wider and perhaps higher. Add 6 inches total to the finished width for side hems. Then divide by the width of the fabric. For example, if the finished width is 36 inches, add 6 inches for side hems (42 inches). If the fabric width is 48 inches, then a 6-inch strip of fabric will be trimmed off lengthwise. When two widths are required it is a good idea to split one vertically and sew one-half on each side of the other width to avoid a center seam.

The finished length is determined, and then 12 inches are added for tucks and hems. Also, when Roman shades are designed with scalloped or cut-out hems, the length may need to be extended to prevent exposing any window. Multiply the number of widths by the cut length, and then divide by 36 inches.

The width for pleated Roman shades, like that for flat Romans, is the finished measurement plus 6 inches. Cut length is double the finished length, plus 12 inches. For example, if the finished length is 48 inches, the cut length is calculated as 48 times 2, or 96 inches, plus 12 inches, or 108 inches total. Again, multiply the number of widths by the cut length, and divide by 36 for the yardage. Round up to the next whole yard.

Roman shades usually are lined, and the same yardage is needed for lining as for decorative fabric.

Fabrication for Roman shades is priced per square foot. To find the square footage, multiply the finished width by the finished length and divide by 144 inches (the number of inches in a square foot). Then round up to the next whole number. For example, a Roman shade 66 inches wide by 82 inches long is 5,412 square inches; divide by 144 to get 37.58, which is rounded up to 38 square feet. Of course, if the dimensions are even feet, such as 60 inches (5 feet) by 72 inches (6 feet), then 5 times 6 feet equals 30 square feet. Consult the workroom for price-per-square-foot labor to sew (lined and unlined). Also obtain workroom prices on insulated Roman shades.

Flat Fabric Shades

Flat fabric shades generally are of the roll-up variety. Fabric shades fastened to wood rollers require the finished width plus 2 or 3 inches for side hems, and the finished length plus 14 inches (12 for extra length to operate the roller shade and 2 for bottom hems).

Other flat window styles include handkerchief curtains (see fig. 5–11). This treatment will require yardage to the exact width and length of the panel, plus 6 inches for hems and headings in the length and width per panel. Order the same yardage for lining fabric, being careful to add in pattern repeat for the cut length.

CALCULATIONS: FABRIC VALANCES

The main decision with many fabric valances is whether to run the fabric in vertical sections to match the drapery, which requires seams, or to railroad the fabric (run it horizontally). Railroading the valance fabric eliminates seams but increases the chance that the fabric will appear a different color because the warp and weft threads have changed positions—a very real problem.

Valance styles that can be computed in vertical cuts or horizontal railroading include shaped pelmets, shirred valances, and flat or pleated valances. The yardage requirements will be similar. The methods of calculating each way are listed below.

Valances in Vertical Cuts

This method is similar to figuring number of widths for draperies and curtains. The finished width of a valance, however, is figured differently.

To find the finished width, measure the valance rod, including returns. If draperies are installed beneath:

- Measure the rod width.

- Add 1 inch on each side to the rod width to find the rod or board width of the valance. This clearance (2 inches total) will allow access to the rods beneath.

- Add the returns. A valance rod with no treatment beneath will have a return of about 3 inches (the hardware catalog will list the projection, which is covered with the fabric return). A valance over one layer of drapery will have a return of 6 inches on each side, or a total of 12 inches. A valance over two layers of drapery will have a 9-inch return on each side, or 18 inches total. A valance over three layers of drapery will have a return of 12 inches on each side, or 24 inches total (refer to table 6–3). For example, if a drapery rod width is 48 inches, add 1 inch on each side for clearance, then the return depth. If this valance were placed over two layers, the return would be 9 inches on each side. The calculation would read:

$$w + clear \ (clearance) + rt \ (returns) = fw$$
$$48 + 2 + 18 = 68 \ inches \ finished \ width$$

The number of widths will be determined by the style. Refer to table 6–4 for figuring widths by fullness. This will work nicely for shirred as well as for pleated valances. In the case of a flat pelmet with only a few pleats, still figure 200 to 250 percent fullness. For a flat pelmet that will be quilted, add 20 percent to the total yardage.

The valance depth is measured to the deepest point. A measurement also will be needed for the highest point on a scalloped or swagged valance or pelmet. However, the deepest point is the basis for calculating yardage. The hems and headings requirement will vary according to style. In many cases the valance is either completely self-lined or lined with a plain fabric.

When the valance is to be self-lined, double the measurement of the deepest point, then add 2 inches for the seams and at least 1 inch for every rod pocket (for rod clearance on shirred valances). It is best to figure generously in this case. For example, if the depth is 15 inches, multiply that by 2 (double the depth), add 2 inches for seams, and 1 inch extra for each shirred rod pocket. The calculation for each width will be:

$$15 \times 2 = 30 + 2 + 1 = 33 \text{ inches cut length}$$

When the valance is lined with lining fabric, add 4 inches total to the cut length (seams and extra in case of flaws), multiply by the number of widths, divide by 36 for the yardage, round up to the next whole yard, and order the same amount of lining fabric. For a 15-inch depth valance requiring five widths, the calculation would read:

$$\text{facia depth} + \text{seams (4 in.)} = (cl \times w) \div 36 = yd$$
$$15 + 4 = 19 \times 5 = 90 \div 36 = 2.5, \text{ rounded up to 3 yards}$$

Railroaded Valances

Railroading means turning the fabric to run horizontally so that there are no seams (and consequently no cuts or widths). Yardage is computed by taking the finished *horizontal* length (fl), multiplying it by the desired fullness (2, 2.5, or 3), and dividing by 36 for the total yardage.

$$(fl \times fullness) \div 36 = yd$$

Railroading ensures ample fabric for the facia depth (vertical measurement), which usually is between 12 and 24 inches. The standard fabric width is around 48 inches, which will leave enough fabric to self-line the valance, if desired. If a lining fabric is desired or the valance is narrow, any extra fabric typically is cut off and discarded.

Austrian Valances

Yardage and labor to sew Austrian valances are figured the same as for Austrian shades. Every 20 inches of board or valance width will require a 48-inch width of fabric. The cut length is three times the finished length. Trim is one and one-half times the width.

Pouf Valances

One width of 48-inch-wide fabric covers 24 inches of rod at 200 percent fullness and approximately 20 inches of board at 250 percent fullness.

The finished length will be 3 inches longer than the installed length because of the process of "poufing" the fabric. This is done by one of these methods:

- Sewing the decorative and lining fabrics together, then pulling the fabrics apart at the bottom, or poufing the valance, which lifts the finished length about 3 inches.

- Using one fabric with no bottom seam (self-lining) and pulling the fabric apart to pouf. (Tissue paper may be used to achieve the pouf in soft, opaque fabrics.)

- Sewing in a rod pocket at the top and bottom and then installing the rods 3 inches (a general rule) closer together than the finished length of the shade.

This last method also can create a valance attached to a curtain (made with one piece of fabric). This is done with a top rod pocket and ruffle, then a space of around 24 inches, and then another rod pocket, which is brought up under the first rod and installed on a curtain rod a few inches below. The curtain continues on, so that the finished length is approximately 12 inches longer than the installed length. This may save labor costs.

Swags, Festoons, and Cascades

Figure 5-13 illustrates some of the many varieties of swags or festoons. These originally were intended for narrow windows and were used singly (one to a window). However, in many interiors today multiple swags are specified. To determine the number of swags, sketch the window and a proposed arrangement of swags. Odd numbers are used except when a running swag (see fig. 5-13o) is desired. Remember to sketch each swag overlapping the next, or overlapping or being overlapped by a cascade by nearly one-half. This sketch can be rough because it is simply to determine the number of festoons that are most aesthetically pleasing for the space and window dimensions. Then refer to table 6-10 to determine the exact width of each swag.

If there were an ideal size to festoons, it would be 36 by 15 inches, although these dimensions may be too small for certain installations. There are restrictions on sizes. A swag cannot be wider than the width of the fabric because a seam will spoil the appearance of the finished festoon. The exception is when the festoon is railroaded and loosely draped in a swagged manner. Also, depths of more than 24 inches usually are considered ponderous and ill-proportioned.

Table 6-10 Computing Number and Widths of Swags

Selected Number of Swags	Area to be Covered (Fill In)	Divide by	Yields Width of Each Swag
3		2 =	
4		2 ½ =	
5		3 =	
6		3 ½ =	
7		4 =	
8		4 ½ =	
9		5 =	
10		5 ½ =	
11		6 =	

Swags must always be lined. Plain and sheer fabric swags often are self-lined. Printed, expensive, or fragile fabrics that need protection against sun are lined with a cream, white, or matching colored fabric.

Swags or festoons generally are given triple fullness. This means that the cut length is three times the finished depth. For example, a festoon 17 inches deep will require three times 17 inches for the face fabric, calculated as follows:

$$17 \times 3 = 51 \div 36 = 1.4 \text{ yards for the face and } 1.4 \text{ yards lining}$$

Self-lined, the swag would require double 1.4, or 2.8, rounded up to 3 yards. Table 6–11 lists self-lined and facia-only festoon yardage.

Cascades and jabots can be short, long, or any length in between, depending on the desired finished look. A cascade may take the place of side draperies or simply cap the end of a swag arrangement. One-third of the total drapery treatment is a good length for cascades. A standard size is approximately a 14-inch facia width plus returns and a 30- to 36-inch length. Cascades are always self-lined. Table 6–12 lists the yardage required.

Table 6–11 Yardage Chart for Swags (Using 48-inch Plain Fabric)

Width (in.)	30	41–42	42–54	55–65	66–77	78–90
Number of Swags	1	1	2	2	3	3
Facia Depth to 17 inches						
Self-lined	3	3	6	6	9	9
Facia only	1 ½	1 ½	3	3	4 ½	4 ½
(Order same yardage of lining fabric.)						
Facia Depth to 18–21 inches						
Self-lined	4	4	7	7	11	11
Facia only	2	2	3 ½	3 ½	5 ½	5 ½
(Order same yardage of lining fabric.)						
Facia Depth to 22–24 inches						
Self-lined	4	4	8	8	12	12
Facia only	2	2	4	4	6	6
(Order same yardage of lining fabric.)						

Table 6–12 Yardage for Cascades and Jabots

Length (in.)	8- to 12-inch Width (yds.)	12- to 18-inch Width (yds.)
Cascades		
24–36	3	4 ½
36–57	4	5 ½
48–59	5	7 ½
60–69	6	9
70–79	7	10
80–83	7	10 ½
84–96	8	12
Jabots		
To 40	4	

Note: Jabots longer than 40 inches are not recommended.

SPECIFICATIONS

Figures 6–1 through 6–7 show a sampling of purchase order, specification sheets or drapery work orders, and installation work orders. When these forms are not filled out correctly, the designer is liable for any mistakes that result from incorrect information. Mistakes can be costly in every respect, and great care should be taken to double-check figures and ordering information to see that it is accurate. The extra effort to do so at this point could very well save anguish and lost time and profit later on.

Purchase Orders

A purchase order, such as the one shown in figure 6–1, is a simple form that allows the designer to order merchandise, including fabric, hardware, and other items. Information such as the following is supplied to the vendor, or wholesale supply source (manufacturer or distributor):

- Name of designer or firm doing business, address, phone number, person placing the order, and account number with vendor.
- Name of vendor to whom the purchase order is being sent.
- Date of order.
- Date goods are needed (be specific).
- Sidemark (the customer's last name or job number).
- Quantity of goods.
- Name, color, stock number, or description of goods.
- Price per item, and extension of pricing for the total ordered of that item. (Example: $10 per yard; total $70 for 7 yards.)
- Special instructions.
- Signature of person placing order.

When ordering fabric be certain to list the number of cuts and the cut length of each. When a pattern repeat is involved, add the number of complete pattern repeats needed per cut. For example, the designer may specify: "21 yards—if necessary to cut, then 6 cuts, each 2 complete pattern repeats (25 inches × 2 = 50 inches per cut)."

It is a nuisance to spell this out, but it is the best insurance the designer can have against flawed goods or cuts of fabric that are incorrect lengths.

Specifying Work Orders

Before the designer can fill out the work order and sales ticket, the information must all be present and the costs must be added up. Figure 6–2 consists of the most important items that are needed to order fabric and hardware and to specify construction and installation.

Figure 6–3 is a sample price chart that the designer will fill out according to the current prices charged by the workroom and installer. Prices vary from city to city, and even from workroom to workroom, and invariably will continue to rise. The chart should therefore be used to keep the designer abreast of current, applicable pricing.

PURCHASE ORDER

VENDOR: PURCHASE ORDER NO
NAME AND ADDRESS OF TEXTILE MANUFACTURING OR DISTRIBUTING COMPANY   00001

SOLD TO ____ NAME AND ADDRESS OF PURCHASER: _____   SHIP TO ____ SAME AS PURCHASER, OR _____
             INTERIOR DESIGN FIRM OR _____   MAY BE "DROP SHIPPED" _____
             WINDOW TREATMENT COMPANY _____   TO WORKROOM OR CLIENT _____

DATE	DATE REQUIRED	HOW SHIP	TERMS

QUANTITY	PLEASE SUPPLY ITEMS LISTED BELOW	PRICE	UNIT
1			
2			
3			
4			
5			
6			
7			
8			
9			
10			
11			
12			
13			
14			
15			
16			
17			
18			
19			
20			
21			
22			

IMPORTANT
  OUR ORDER NUMBER MUST APPEAR ON ALL INVOICES, PACKAGES, ETC.
  PLEASE NOTIFY US IMMEDIATELY IF YOU ARE UNABLE TO SHIP COMPLETE ORDER BY DATE SPECIFIED.

PLEASE SEND   COPIES OF YOUR INVOICE WITH ORIGINAL BILL OF LADING

PURCHASING AGENT

6-1 Sample purchase order.

Name

Address   City   State

Phone (Residence)   (Work)

Date Windows Measured   Job Sold?   Yes   Call Back

Approximate Date Draperies to be Installed

SPECIFICATIONS FOR:	ROOM	OVERDRAPERY	SHEER	PRIVACY	VALANCE	SHADE
Finished Width (FW)						
Finished Length (FL)						
Left Return (LR)						
Right Return (RR)						
No. of Widths* (W)						
Cut Length (CL)						
Fabric Company						
Fabric Name						
Fabric Color						
Fabric Width						
Trim or Banding						
Fabrication Cost						
Hardware & Cost						
Installation Cost						

	ILLUSTRATIONS AND SPECIAL INSTRUCTIONS:
Subtotal	
Tax	
Total	
Less Deposit	
Balance Due	
Sales Ticket No.	

*Seamless Sheers Priced in Widths. See figure 6-3, Fabrication and Installation Price Chart.

6-2 Fabric treatment specification checklist.

ITEMS TO BE FABRICATED	FABRICATION COSTS
Pinch-pleated draperies per width unlined	
Pinch-pleated draperies per width lined	
Seamless draperies per ___ inches	
Ties for tieback draperies, per pair	
Ties with fringe, per pair	
Ties with banding, per pair	
Ties with ruffles, per pair	
Swags, each	
Cascades, per pair	
Roman shades per square foot	
Austrian, shirred, and box-pleated pouf shades	
Valance per running foot: shirred	
Pleated valances	
Quilted valances	
Speciality (cornices)	
Ruffles per running foot	
Banding per running foot (sew/fuse)	
Fringe to sew/fuse per running foot	
Shirred curtains per width	
ITEMS TO BE INSTALLED	**INSTALLATION COSTS**
Per width rod and drapery	
Per width drapery on existing rod	
Per pair ties	
Per foot or per bracket for shades	
Per foot valances	
Per foot cascades	
Measuring fee	
Return fee to correct problem	
Return fee to remove draperies	
Return fee to rehang draperies	

6-3 Fabrication and installation price chart.

Adding up the Costs

The costs that are totaled to arrive at a sales price for soft window treatments include:

- The total cost of all the yardage (yards multiplied by cost per yard), including lining fabric.
- Labor to sew draperies (number of widths multiplied by cost per width, or, for shades, total square footage price).
- The total cost of yardage trimming (braid, gimp, banding/ruffle).
- Labor to fuse or sew on trimmings (number of feet or yards multiplied by cost per foot or yard).
- Hardware costs (per rod or per set of rods).
- Installation costs (number of widths multiplied by cost per width).

Subtotal these amounts and then add tax to arrive at a total cost. Collect from the client a deposit (50 percent is customary, unless the treatment is financed on a charge account).

Work Orders or Specification Sheets

Figures 6–4 through 6–7 show samples of various work order forms or specification sheets for soft window coverings. The design or decorating firm or workroom/manufacturer may opt for a more simple or complex form, and the installer may work from this form or from a different installation work order (a sample follows).

Forms can be custom-tailored to the needs or desires of the interior design firm or workroom and purchased through a business forms company, which also will give advice and options for size, numbers of duplicates, color of paper, and quantity of the forms. The form used is not a matter of great importance; rather, the important idea here is that the designer thoroughly and correctly fill out a form that is understandable by the workroom. Do not leave any blanks. For example, if you are planning for one return only (on the right side, let's say), then place a zero (0) in the slot for left return. It also is wise to include any sketches, patterns, or templates (on kraft paper) that will help the workroom understand what is being ordered, the correct dimensions, and the overall treatment composition.

SELECTING HARDWARE

Hardware is purchased by the designer or decorator through a distributing company, using a purchase order such as the one in figure 6–1. If the distributing company also manufacturers the draperies or soft treatments, the rods can be delivered with the finished draperies, if specified. These companies provide general hardware catalogs that list various sizes, projections (outside bracket depth), clearances (distance inside the rod to the wall), package quantity and pricing, broken package (single-item) pricing, and color finishes. Prices often are given for both wholesale and retail listings.

When the type of window treatment is selected, the designer will then turn to the hardware catalog and choose the type of rod that is best suited for the installation. A general rule is to use the very best rods the client

6-4 Drapery order and workroom specification sheet.

DRAPERY ORDER AND WORKROOM SPECIFICATION SHEET

NUMBER:

STORE NAME:

SALESPERSON/   **SALESCHECK #:**

DESIGNER: **DATE:**

CUSTOMER'S NAME: **ADDRESS:**   **HOME PHONE:**   **SPECIAL DELIVERY:**

CITY: **WORK PHONE:**   **APPROXIMATE DELIVERY DATE:**

NUMBER	ROOM	FABRIC SOURCE OR COMPANY	FABRIC NAME	FABRIC COLOR	PAIR PANEL SHADE OR VALANCE	ROD BOARD WIDTH	LEFT RETURN	RIGHT RETURN	FINISHED OR PLEATED WIDTH INCL. RETURNS AND OVERLAPS	CLOSE RIGHT OR LEFT OR CENTER	LINED? YES OR NO	LINING FABRIC	LINING COLOR	CUT LENGTH	FINISHED LENGTH	TYPE OF PLEAT	NUMBER OR WIDTHS	TOTAL YARDS	PRICE PER YARD	TOTAL FABRIC COST	ROD COL. AND NO.	ROD PRICE
1.																						
2.																						
3.																						
4.																						
5.																						
6.																						
7.																						
8.																						
9.																						
10.																						

INSTALLATION

ITEM INSTALLED	HOW MANY WIDTHS/ FEET	PRICE PER WIDTH/ FOOT	TOTAL COST
DRAPERIES & RODS			
DRAPERIES ONLY			
VALANCES & SHADES			
TIES & MISC.			

FABRICATION

ITEM SEWN	HOW MANY WIDTHS/ FEET	PRICE PER WIDTH/ FOOT	TOTAL COST
UNLINED DRAPERIES/ CURTAINS			
LINED DRAPERIES/ CURTAINS			
TIES & TRIMS			
SHADES & VALANCES			

SUBTOTALS

FABRIC COSTS, INCL. TRIM	
FABRICATION	
HARDWARE	
INSTALLATION	
SUBTOTAL	
LESS DEPOSIT	
BALANCE DUE UPON COMPLETION	

SPECIAL INSTRUCTIONS AND ILLUSTRATIONS:

APPROVED AND ACCEPTED BY CUSTOMER:

I DO / DO NOT DESIRE INSTALLATION _____ SIGNATURE

236

6-5 Soft treatment specification sheet.

DATE OF ORDER
DATE PROMISED
PAGE _____ OF _____
WORKROOM
FIRM
DESIGNER

CUSTOMER
ADDRESS
CITY _____ ZIP
PHONE (HOME) _____ (WORK)

LOCATION:

LINE	QUANTITY		HEADINGS	FINISHED	FINISHED	WIDTHS PER PAIR OR PANEL	RETURN		HOOK	FABRIC NAME		CUT LENGTH SOLID	REPEAT SIZE	CUT LENGTH PRINT	TOTAL WIDTHS	TOTAL YARDS (FABRIC)	FABRIC
	PAIRS	PANELS	POCKET SIZES	WIDTH	LENGTH		LT/RT	SIZE	SET	WIDTH							
1																	LINING TOTAL YARDS
2																	
3																	TRIM TOTAL YARDS
4																	

DRAPERY FABRIC
| UNIT | COST | TOTAL |

LINING/TRIM
| UNIT | COST | TOTAL |

HARDWARE
| UNIT | COST | TOTAL |

INSTALLATION
| UNIT | COST | TOTAL |

FABRICATION
| UNIT | COST | TOTAL |

SPECIALTY LABOR
Ruffles: ____ yds. @ ____ = $ ____
Ties: ____ yds. @ ____ = $ ____
Banding: ____ yds. @ ____ = $ ____

ACCESSORIES
☐ Pillows
☐ Bedspreads
☐ Dust Ruffles
☐ Pillow Shams
☐ Table Covers

SPECIAL INSTRUCTIONS

DRAPERY ROD
HARDWARE	QUANTITY	DRAPERY ROD
1		
2		
3		
4		

SUMMARY | **COSTS**
FABRIC
LINING
RODS
INSTALLATION
FABRICATION
SPECIALTY
ACCESSORIES
SUBTOTAL
TAX
TOTAL

6-6 *Manufacturers' drapery order form.*

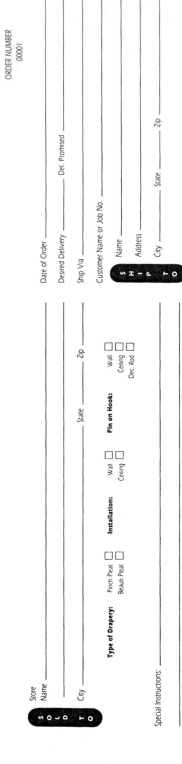

6-7 Custom ruffled-curtain order form.

Custom Orders

Not subject to
cancellation or changes.

Order Number
00001

BILL TO:
FIRM NAME _____

STREET _____

CITY _____ STATE _____

ZIP CODE _____ PHONE _____

SHIP TO:
FIRM NAME _____

STREET _____

CITY _____ STATE _____

ZIP CODE _____ PHONE _____

ACCT.
NO. _____

DEPT. NUMBER		YOUR ORDER NUMBER		ORDER DATE		SHIP VIA:				MARK PACKAGE		

Quantity	Item	Fabric Type	Fabric Color		Ruffle Size	*Total Width	†Total Length	Trim	Special Instructions	Price Per Pair	Extension
			Body	Ruffle							

SPECIAL COMMENTS AND SKETCHES:

*TOTAL WIDTH—STATE TOTAL INCHES PER PAIR
†TOTAL LENGTH INCLUDES FRILL

SALESPERSON _____

239

can afford; often the cost difference is slight between the lowest- and the highest-quality conventional traverse rods.

There are times when existing hardware will be retained at the request of the client. However, a new drapery hung on an old rod is rarely a good choice. The strings or cords that operate the rod can break, and other mechanical failures typically occur shortly after the new treatment is installed. When problems develop the client is, unfortunately, quick to blame the new treatment or the designer. It is best to protect both yourself and the new draperies with new, sturdy rods. If the client insists on using older hardware, then the designer should at least strongly recommend that the rod be restrung (have new cords put into the old rod) by the installer. This will cost money, too, but it is a way of protecting the client's investment in custom window coverings.

Types of Rods

There are basically two types of rods: curtain rods, which have no mechanism for drawing fabric open and closed, and traverse rods, which have either cords or sliding parts that allow the draperies to be operated by a cord or with a wand or to be positioned by hand.

Curtain rods obviously are simpler. They can be divided into two categories: those hidden by the fabric and those that are decorative and meant to be seen.

Figure 6–8 a–i shows a variety of standard metal curtain rods that typically are covered by fabric. The fabric can be shirred onto these rods, or

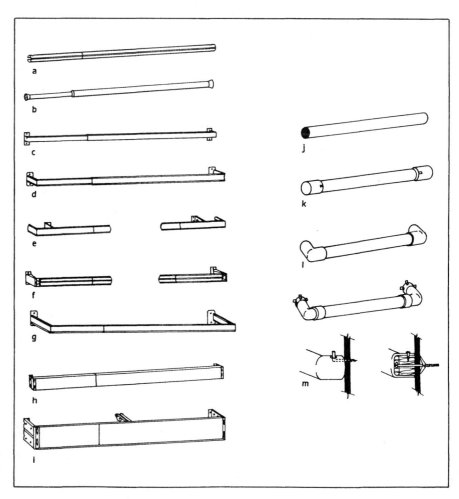

6-8 Curtain rods.

a   Utility rod to be mounted inside a window frame on small brackets.

b   Spring-tension telescoping curtain rod. This needs no brackets and holds with spring-tension pressure on the rubber end pads.

c   Close-set curtain rod with an outside mount.

d   Standard telescoping curtain rod with a 2- to 3-inch projection.

e   Separated curtain rods with adjustable placement brackets for mounting into wood where it is located and extending the curtains beyond the window.

f   Standard separated curtain rods, also available with swinging crane arms for French doors and casement windows.

g   Valance curtain rod with deep projection.

h   Wide telescoping curtain rod, which is set close to the wall.

I   Extra-wide, flat telescoping curtain rod.

J   PVC (polyvinyl chloride) plumbing pipe used for curtain rods, custom-cut to fit the length. The pipe is inexpensive and gives a pleasing, rounded rod pocket.

k   PVC pipe with end caps.

l   PVC pipe with elbows for projections.

m   Three methods of fastening PVC pipe to the wall: with angled brackets, with hook screws, or with wood blocks toggle-bolted on, over which the pipe is placed and anchored from the top with a screw.

drapery pins can be hooked over narrow ones to support stationary drapery panels. Figure 6–8 j–l shows polyvinyl-chloride pipes made for plumbing. These plastic pipes are inexpensive, lightweight, easy to install, and give a nice rounded look to shirred treatments. They are installed, as shown in figure 6–8m, with angle brackets; with hook-screws (the hole must be drilled); or with a wood block affixed with a toggle bolt over which the elbow is fitted and fastened (see also fig. 6–18).

Figure 6–9 shows the three most often used decorative curtain rods: the brass rod, the fluted wood rod, and the plain wood rod. There are two styles of wood brackets as well. Wood rods can be stained, painted, or covered with wallpaper or fabric. Fabric can be shirred onto brass or wood rods, or rings through which hooks are attached can be used to draw pleated draperies. One ring is drawn on each rod in figure 6–9c to illustrate that decorative curtain rods may have rings added to become hand-drawn traverse rods.

Traverse rods are shown in figures 6–10 through 6–12. These rods, too, may be categorized as either structural and decorative. The structural rods (figs. 6–10 and 6–11) typically are covered by top treatments or are left exposed when opened. As such, they are slender and relatively unnoticeable. Figure 6–10 shows three of the commonly used conventional traverse rods: the single traverse, double traverse, and single one-way rod. Components include the *end bracket* (containing the end housing mechanism, which connects the draw cord to the carriers), *center support* (for wider rods), *carriers* (drapery hooks or pins are hooked through these), *master carriers* (overlapping "arms"), *cords,* and *pulley.* These components are available in several quality levels; the lower-priced rods will have "tassel" weighted cords and the higher-quality ones will have tension-pulley cords, as seen in figure 6–10. Because draperies are heavy and receive a lot of use, a stronger, higher-quality rod will prove that long life is cheaper than replacement.

Figure 6–11 shows architectural rodding, which are simplified, sturdy traverse rods with carriers that are not attached to cords but slide on ball bearings and are drawn open and closed with a wand. Figure 6–11a shows a section of track hardware, where panels are attached to rollers and glide to cover the glass with flat, overlapping sheets of fabric. Figure 6–11b shows typical architectural hardware commonly used in nonresidential settings, such as hotels and offices, where the draperies are drawn frequently

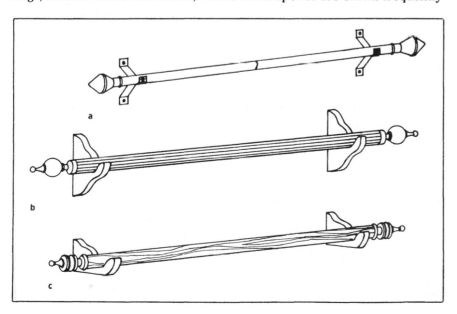

6-9 Round and wood rods.

a Telescoping brass café rod on decorative brackets.

b Fluted wood-pole rod on large brackets with end finials. The finials are selected from a small variety of styles and purchased separately. The solid wood comes in even-foot lengths and is cut to the specified length by the installer.

c Plain wood rod on smaller brackets that allow shallow curtain rods to be placed beneath.

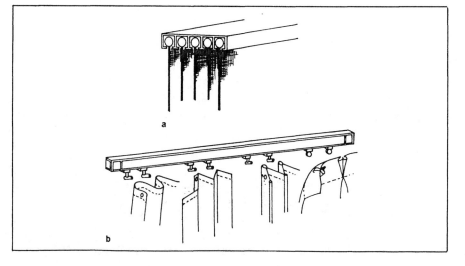

6-10 Traverse rods.

a Conventional single-hung traverse rod. The end brackets support the rod; the end housing contains the cord mechanism. Carriers are sliding plastic holders for drapery hooks; master carriers are the middle overlapping arms. The center support is needed for widths over 30 inches. The enlarged cutaway drawing shows the cord-pulley mechanism anchored to the floor or wall and the proper placement of draperies on the rod. Begin at the middle and work toward the outside so that carriers can be added or taken away as needed.

b Double traverse rod set with double end brackets and center support. This is used for two sets of pleated draperies—a sheer underdrapery and opaque overdrapery, for example.

c A one-way traverse rod with two center supports. Here the master carrier should take the drapery slightly past the glass. Double one-way traverse rods simply need double end brackets and center supports.

6-11 Sliding-panel or track hardware.

a Sliding-panel hardware: fabric panels are hung on sliding tracks and are closed with an attached baton that draws the connected, successive panels. This creates a simple, structural, and handsome look.

b Typical "made-to-measure" (nontelescoping) architectural rodding for contract draperies, with four examples of curtain headings: the roll, or ripple heading; two accordion headings; and the pinch-pleat heading. The rod is slender and unnoticeable; the draperies are not full and take up little stacking space. Draperies may have a cord draw or baton draw and will be made to the exact dimensions specified by the designer.

and where the cords may not stand the use and potential abuse. As can be seen, there is some flexibility in the type of pleat. The roll or accordion heading takes less fabric than pinch-pleat draperies and can stack in a smaller space.

Figure 6–12 shows several of the many styles of decorative rods. Some imitate brass café rods; others look like wood or wrought iron. All have hidden cords, pulleys, and mechanisms that allow them to be operated in the same way as the conventional traverse rod. These are most often used

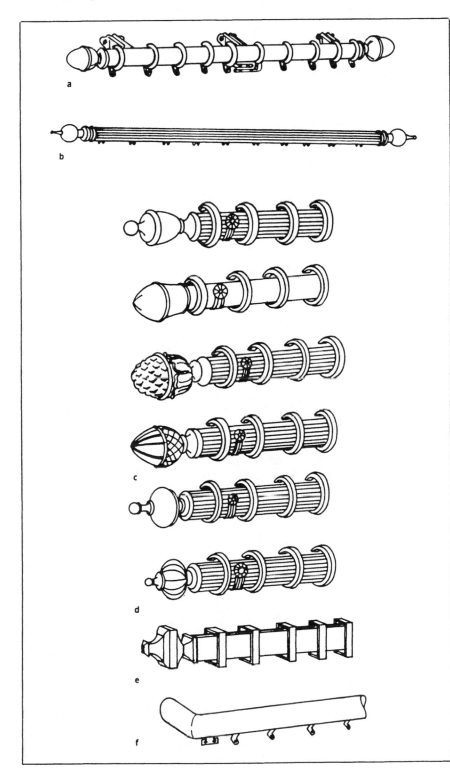

6-12 Decorator rods.

a   Brass decorator traverse rod that is drawn with cord pulleys.

b   Round imitation-wood rod for architectural contract drapery.

c   Metal decorator rods in plain brass or fluted metal. They often come in brass, antique brass, or white antique finishes.

d   Imitation-wood decorator traverse rods.

e   Metal rod, usually black to create a Spanish wrought-iron look.

f   Polished chrome "structural" decorator rod – a sleek, contemporary look. Available with silver, gold or colored finish.

alone because of the type of bracket required. However, double or extension brackets are available that attach a decorative rod over a conventional traverse rod. The advantages of decorative traverse rods are that they can carry out a theme or look in a room, they can take the place of a top treatment, and they are more interesting than plain conventional rods, which some people find unattractive.

The disadvantages include a higher cost than conventional traverse rods and the fact that the style can become dated or inappropriate for a new décor.

Special rodding is available as packaged bay or bow rodding (single or double curtain or traverse rods), or bendable rodding, as seen in figure 6–13. These types of rodding will be listed in the hardware catalog. The installer can advise the designer on the type of special rodding to order for a particular installation.

Special rodding also includes sets of conventional rods that are used for special circumstances, such as bay and bow windows. Figure 6–13 illustrates several kinds of rounded and angled hardware in single or double sets.

6-13 Curtain hardware.

a Sections of "cut-to-measure" curtain rods that can be purchased in lengths, cut, and bent to fit by the installer.

b Made-to-measure sets of curtain rods in special shapes. The designer supplies the manufacturer/distributor with sizes and dimensions. Rods are then custom-made to fit the window.

c Single and double sets of bay and bow made-to-measure rods.

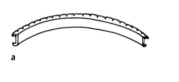

a

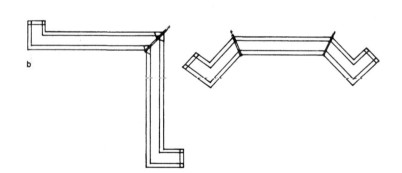

b

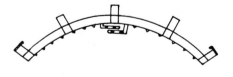

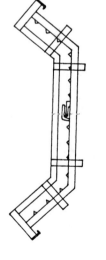
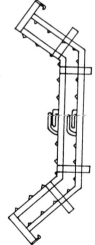

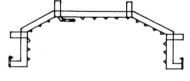
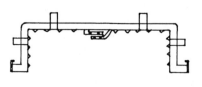

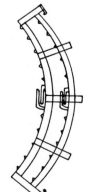

c

INSTALLATION

The quality of installation is as important as the quality of the fabric and fabrication workmanship. An expert installation will yield a truly professional-looking treatment, whereas a poor installation will diminish and perhaps destroy its effect. It is always wise to use professional installers whenever possible. The installer can be of great help to the designer by double-checking measurements before construction of soft treatments and by educating the designer about what is possible and realistic in window coverings.

Tools and accessories used by the installer represent an investment and help the installer to do the job more easily and with greater efficiency. These tools include a tool belt, a drill and various drill bits, a cordless screwdriver, a hammer, a knife, an awl (small pointed tool for making holes), a vise grip, pliers, a rod cutter, a file, a lacing tool, a hot-glue gun, a steam iron, and a step ladder.

A truly professional installer will be courteous to the client and handle the client's furnishings with care and respect. The furniture should be moved away from the window before the treatments are installed, and the installer also should clean up any mess, such as boxes, plastic, and extra parts, on the completion of the job. The installer who does these things will give the client a better opinion of the designer as well.

The Basic Process

It is a boon to the interior designer or decorator to understand the process of installation for several reasons:

- It is helpful when specifying the treatments and correct hardware.

- It aids in communication with the installer for a better finished product.

- It gives the designer greater expertise when solving problems made known by the client.

The installation of both curtain rods and traverse rods begins with measuring for the installation of brackets. This is done by marking the wall with the measurements written on the "ticket" pinned to the top of the draperies. The brackets are installed at the *rod width* or bracket-to-bracket measurement supplied by the designer and at the finished length. Conventional pleated draperies are hung $1/2$ inch above the rod, so that they are $1/2$ inch above the floor. Complete instructions for installing conventional and decorative traverse rods are included in the package.

The curtains or draperies are next hung on the rod. Shirred treatments are slid onto the rod first, and then the rod is hung in place. To install draperies on conventional traverse rods, the procedure is as follows:

- Close the drapery rods so that the master carriers nearly meet in the center.

- Look at the draperies to determine which side has the returns (the fabric that covers the projection or the end bracket). The heading will be wider from the pleat to the end of the drapery on the return side. Draperies should overlap 2 inches on each side of the leading edge (the sides that come together as the draperies are closed). Also, if there are any half-widths (or split widths), they should be sewn on the outside of the panel. (A panel is a single unit of seamed fabric by itself or as half of a pair.)

- Insert the pins at the proper height (fig. 6–14). The best drapery hooks or pins are the standard short, adjustable placement pins seen in the figure, which can be moved up to lower the drapery and down to raise the drapery. This achieves the exact position of the draperies in relation to the rod and the floor. If the floor is uneven, the pins can make a section of the drapery higher or lower. Adjusting the hooks also is important if the draperies shrink after cleaning, so that the drapery will not be too short. Pinch the pin opening together somewhat after inserting it, so that it will not slip out of the carrier hole.

- Start at the master carrier and work toward the outside bracket. Do not skip any carriers for two reasons: (1) The extra carriers will cause bulk and perhaps bind or interfere with the operation of the hardware. (2) There may not be enough carriers at the end of the rod to complete the drapery hanging. If you do run out of carriers, the "end gate" can be opened to add needed carriers or to remove extras.

- Insert the next-to-the-last pin in the corner of the end bracket and the last pin (end of the "return") at the base of the bracket next to the wall (see fig. 6–10a).

- When the panels are hung do not open and close them before you "break the buckram." This means that the buckram, or stiffened heading, *must* be hand creased: forward between the pleats for conventional rods and backward for decorator rods (beneath the rod) to allow the draperies to stack open smoothly (fig. 6–15). If the buckram is not creased before the draperies are opened, it will crumple and "memorize" these crumples. The drapery headings always will look terrible and will never open nicely or stack smoothly. To break the buckram, pinch it between the thumb and forefinger and gently but firmly crease it vertically, being careful to crease it straight.

- Open the draperies very slowly and carefully, watching to see that the headings have memorized your crease. If any part begins to buckle, stop and recrease the fold.

- After the draperies are hung, steam out any wrinkles and gently train the folds by hand into nice, straight (or tied-back diagonal) lines. This is referred to as dressing down the draperies and is important to the finished look of the treatment. Then use some soft cloth, string, or paper strips to tie the draperies in the open position at the bottom, middle, and top beneath the pleats. Leave the draperies in this position until the folds memorize this position—up to three days. This is a finishing touch that is well worth the patience needed to leave the draperies tied up. The bottoms will not flare, and the front of the folds will be smooth and even. Hem tape or string is available to hold the back of the folds in place.

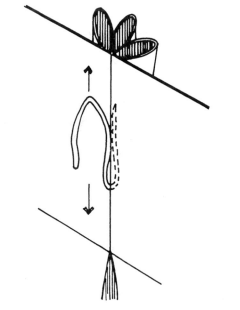

6-14 Standard short drapery hook that can be placed as needed to install, raise, or lower draperies.

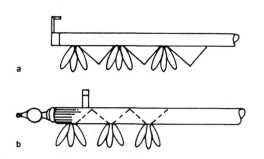

6-15 "Breaking the buckram."

- **a** Breaking the buckram forward for a conventional traverse rod installation. The draperies are hung on the face of the rod.
- **b** Breaking the buckram backward for a decorator rod. The draperies hang beneath the rod, leaving space between the pleats for the folded heading.

Many drapery, valance, and poufed curtain treatments need special hand dressing to achieve a finished and beautiful effect. Expert hand dressing can come only from experience and sensitivity. The installer who can pay particular attention to detail, who can work with the treatment until it looks just right to a critical eye, is indeed a valuable asset to the interior designer.

Installing Decorator Rods

Decorator rods are placed higher than conventional traverse rods because the drapery is hung under the rod. The finished length plus 1/2 inch will be just under the bottom of the rod (see figs. 6–12 and 6–14).

Installing Tieback Draperies

Tieback draperies should be specified to lie flat rather than be fan-folded (see chapter 5) so that when they are hung, they can be hand dressed, or "dressed down," and trained to fall into gently diagonal lines at the desired angle. Special hardware is needed in one of three forms: (1) the tieback hook, (2) the decorative tieback holder that has a long neck or stem to prevent the tie from crushing the drapery, and (3) the concealed tieback holder (fig. 6–16). Decorative and concealed tieback holders can be extended to accommodate a double return of up to about 6 inches. For three layers some crushing of the fabric is inevitable.

Installing Valances and Shades

Fabric shades and valances occasionally are hung on curtain rodding, depending on the style and the heading, if any, that is used. Often valances, pelmets, and shades are hung on a board. There are two basic ways of attaching fabric to a board. First, you can fuse or sew one part of a hook-and-loop fastener onto the fabric's wrong side and staple or glue its companion onto the board (fig. 6–17a). This is a smart way to attach shades and valances, because it is easy to remove the treatment for cleaning. The disadvantage lies in the relative amount of weight that can pull the tape apart. The second way to attach a fabric valance to a valance or mounting board is by stapling or nailing the treatment to the board, either hiding the staples in the side of a pleat or stapling a tail or strip (sewn onto the top of the valance) to the board (fig. 6–17b). This system is less costly than the fastener tape method.

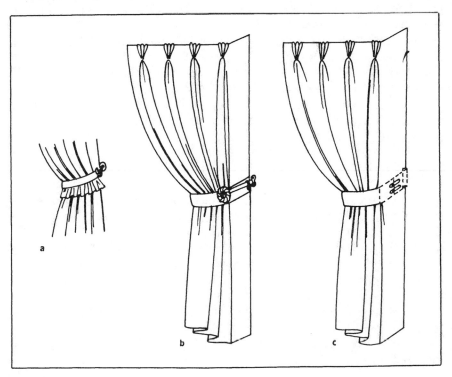

6-16 Tieback holders.

a A standard tieback hook for simple curtains and single-hung installations.

b Extended decorative tieback holder for a double-hung installation (two layers of draperies).

c Concealed tieback holders that slide, or telescope, to the needed depth. This example is for a double-hung installation.

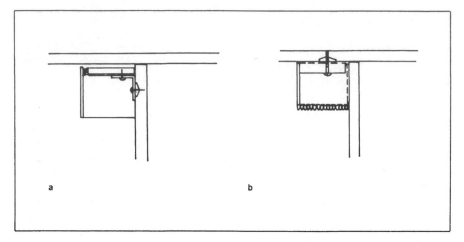

6-17 Installing valances.

a Valance attached to a board with Velcro-type fastening tape for easy removal. The board is anchored to the wall by means of an angle-iron bracket and a toggle bolt.

b Valance stapled over the top of a board, which is then bolted to the ceiling. Alternatively, the top can be stapled to the board and the valance installed as in figure 6-17a.

Rods for matching draperies should be hung on the wall beneath valance boards and not fastened to the board itself, because the board can work loose from the extra weight and strain placed on the wall fasteners. Also, it is difficult to hang draperies and to remove them for cleaning; there is not enough room above the rod. A wall-mounted rod has gravity working for, not against, the installation; the weight behind the fastener pulls downward.

Using Wall Fasteners

Wall fasteners are used to securely install brackets and boards for window treatments (fig. 6–18). The wood screw (fig. 6–18a) and the self-drilling screw (fig. 6–18b) will hold where there is solid wood (within 3½ inches from the window on each side). However, many treatments are measured to certain proportions, and wall anchors will be needed to secure the weight of the treatment. This is particularly true where sheetrock (plasterboard or gypsum board) cannot support the draperies and the treatment cannot be anchored into wood. The three most common types of fasteners are shown in figure 6–18 c–e. These are the toggle bolt, the molly, and the wall anchor, or plug and screw.

The toggle bolt, has a collapsible wing nut that is inserted through a hole drilled wider than the screw threads. The wing then pops out to the open position. As the screw head is twisted, the wing is pulled in tightly against the inside of the wall, preventing the screw from pulling out of the wall. The molly bolt works in a similar way, but the anchor encases the screw as illustrated. The wall anchor, or plug and screw, often is used for masonry wall installations.

Motorized Rods

Motorized or automatic rods are available from all major hardware companies. These devices are relatively simple to install; and although they do add to the cost of treatment, they are a necessity where controls are inaccessible or where the occupant is handicapped in some way. Motorized hardware also can be a boon to energy conservation, with options such as timing devices or temperature-sensing controls. Further, automated hardware is desirable in luxury housing—costly quality-constructed homes with many built-in amenities and convenience devices. In nonresidential installations, such as a board of directors' conference room, automation is desirable not only because it is convenient but also because it bespeaks an image of success and power.

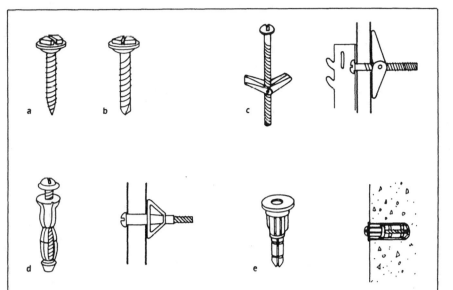

6-18 Fasteners for installing soft window treatments.

a Standard wood screw.

b Self-drilling wood screw. The point is similar to a drill bit.

c Two views of the toggle bolt: the wing collapses to enter the drilled hole for the screw (*left*), and then tightens against the wall to anchor the hardware (*right*).

d The molly bolt encased in a plug that also spreads out to anchor against the wall. This gives security to hardware installed in plasterboard or in other hollow walls between wood building studs.

e Self-drilling screw for wood or metal surfaces. No predrilling is needed.

Stacking the Drapery Layers

No doubt every drapery installer has at some point become frustrated with a work order from a designer or decorator with instructions to install a window treatment that "doesn't work." A common mistake is to specify that the installer hang privacy draperies, sheers, and tieback overdraperies under an existing cornice with a projection clearance (inside measurement) of only 4½ inches. Always keep in mind that the first layer of drapery needs 3½ to 4 inches clearance to allow the installation of an operable traverse rod, and each layer on top will need about 2 more inches clearance in order to traverse. A stationary drapery will need slightly less, so that this set of three layers would require at least 8 inches if the draperies are to fit into the window.

When a special circumstance arises, it is always best to pick up the phone and talk over the proposed window design with your drapery workroom manager or an experienced installer. To sell, order, and deliver a window treatment that cannot be installed will cause more grief and financial loss than the chance was worth. It is much better to be certain than to be sorry.

Chapter 7 HARD WINDOW TREATMENTS

In today's interior design, hard treatments are equally as important as fabric treatments at the window. This was also true in the past; in fact, as we look carefully through the pages of history, we see that many historical or period treatments used shutters, screens, panels, or pull shades—either alone or overlaid with fabric. These hard treatments, also called *hardlines* (because of the general severity, or straightness, of the lines), have lasted throughout the years and proven their worth in terms of beauty, durability, and ease of maintenance.

Hard treatments—blinds, shutters, shades, and screens—are made of metal, wood, plastic, or strong fabric. The working parts are made of metal or plastic, and any cords usually are tough braided nylon. These durable materials are assembled in factories or manufacturing plants and therefore sometimes are called factory-made treatments. Hardlines are made either to standard measurements for stock merchandise or to custom measurements in colors and options selected by the designer or client. Hard treatments take from two hours up to four weeks to manufacture and deliver, and then the installer affixes them at a cost per bracket, per foot, or per unit.

Prices for factory-made hard treatments vary considerably, from very inexpensive to very costly. Inexpensive varieties are available as stock merchandise through department and home-improvement stores. The most common of these stock hard treatments are shutters, pull shades (generally of vinyl), and plastic or metal miniblinds, all discussed later in this chapter. Costly hardlines are custom-ordered through interior designers, decorators, and window treatment specialists. Exact costs depend on the size, shape (angles and circles are very expensive), material, finish, and trimming of the treatment.

Also discussed in this chapter are surface ornamentations (folk paintings, art glass, and stenciling), which, strictly speaking, are neither hard nor soft treatments.

THE BENEFITS OF HARD TREATMENTS

Although all hard treatments have individual benefits as well as disadvantages, a common set of advantages makes them appealing.

Aesthetics

Hard window treatments often are preferred over fabric treatments because of the simple good looks of blinds, shutters, shades, and screens. To some people, nothing can surpass the beauty of the streamlined and subtle wide-louver plantation shutter.

Likewise, the simple miniblind gives a structural, clean effect at the window. Also, the vertical-louver blind has become one of the best-received hard treatments. It gives the vertical effect of draperies in a more simple, structural way, without the fuss and maintenance of fabric treatments. Many hard treatments have a streamlined aesthetic appeal that complements the often busy and complex lifestyle of so many people today. Pleated fabric shades combine simple, sleek lines with the visual softness of pattern and/or texture. The aesthetic appeal of a well-designed hard treatment can certainly last for many years.

Cost

Hardlines generally are less costly than soft window treatments, although some vertical louvers and custom wood treatments, such as wood blinds and shutters, are more expensive than draperies. Miniblinds are perhaps one of the most economical treatments, and the hard treatments available as stock merchandise can be quite inexpensive. The lower cost factor coupled with durability make hard treatments very attractive.

Durability

Generally speaking hard treatments are more durable than soft treatments. Because of the nature of the materials (wood, metal, plastic, tough polyester fabric, and nylon cord), there is little or no fading from the sun, disintegration of materials, or wearing out of parts. The materials often look good and perform well for a long time.

Installation

With the exception of shutters, hard treatments are simple and easy to install, requiring few skills and tools beyond an instruction sheet and a screwdriver. For most hardlines a bracket is installed and then the treatment is slipped into the bracket. The unit can then be easily removed for cleaning or window repair, if needed.

Insulation

Hard treatments vary considerably in their ability to insulate. In order of effectiveness the most insulative hard treatments are the insulated wood shutter (see figs. 1–15 and 1–16), the opaque roller shade, the woven-wood shade (solidly woven with bulky yarn), and the metallized pleated fabric shade. Vertical-louver blinds made of solid vinyl also can be insulative when fully closed. Generally whenever slats, gaps, holes, or other perforations are present in the treatment, the insulative ability is lowered (see also chapter 1).

Maintenance

Maintenance is a positive factor in the selection of hard treatments. Unlike fabric treatments that are regularly laundered or professionally cleaned, hard treatments need little if any professional care; they require only occasional shaking, dusting, or vacuuming. Dirt and grease buildup can be cleaned off with mild detergent and a soft cloth. Where interiors are fitted with miniblinds or vertical blinds, professional "sonic" cleaning methods are now widely available through cleaning companies that remove the blinds and clean them at their place of business (or at the site if the number of blinds is great), then return them looking like new. This service is particularly attractive for larger homes or nonresidential buildings that are filled with blinds, where the task of cleaning them by hand would be overwhelming. Horizontal slats do catch dust whereas vertical louvers shake dust free each time they are operated. Repetitive cleaning of blinds will not harm the material, which is not the case when cleaning fabric. After a few dry cleanings and a few years at the window most fabrics become tender, easily falling into shreds. Moreover, fabric can become permanently stained with moisture or grease. Hard treatments usually are impervious to both these villains.

Plants and Hard Treatments

Many hard treatments, particularly those that are made with slats or louvers, are ideally suited for plants at the window. This is because blinds and louvered shutters diffuse or deflect light so that it is not too intense or direct. In addition, slats or louvers can be adjusted to cut down on the amount of solar gain and to shade plants when necessary. Light can be adjusted to shine on one plant, for example, while another remains in shade. Another advantage is that the flowing, robust lines and shapes of plants contrast beautifully with the clean, straight lines of most hard treatments.

Special Sizes and Shapes

Hard window treatments are well suited for unusual sizes and shapes of windows. Windows that are round, arched, octagonal, triangular, trapezoidal, and pentazoidal can be fitted exactly with custom hard treatments. These treatments may be permanently fixed—such as pleated shades fanfolded into arches or round windows—or possibly operable—such as movable louvered shutters, miniblinds, or vertical louvers.

When specifying special shapes, take all the measurement dimensions, including angles by exact degree, and preferably include a template made by taping kraft paper over the window and tracing the window precisely. Fold the paper and send it to the factory along with the order form. Specially sized and shaped window treatments will be more costly. There is always a surcharge for unusual shapes, sometimes into the hundreds of dollars. Carefully check this before quoting a price to the customer.

Sunlight Control

Hard window treatments such as blinds, shutters, and metallized pleated fabric shades are highly effective in controlling the amount of sunlight, glare, and solar gain. Whereas metallized pleated fabric shades act as "sunglasses" for the window, horizontal miniblinds and standard movable louvered shutters can be tilted up to cast a shadow beneath the shade, allowing some light while diffusing the brightness and ensuring daytime privacy. Vertical blinds likewise control sun quite effectively because of the adjustable position of the vanes or louver slats.

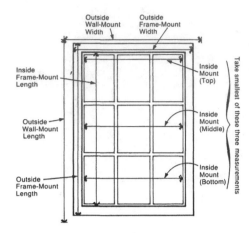

7-1 Measuring for blinds, shutters, shades, and screens. Check for square, even measurements for any inside installation.

Versatility

Versatility is another key factor in the popularity of hard window treatments. A relatively simple and neutral-colored or natural-material blind, shutter, shade, or screen can blend nicely with many styles of furnishings and will possibly last long enough to serve well through several redecoratings. Of course, most hard treatments are available in a variety of contemporary colors that are suitable for more decorative window treatment designs.

MEASURING FOR HARD TREATMENTS

Factory-made hard window treatments are installed in one of two ways: inside the window frame, which is called *inside mount* or *inside installation,* and outside the window frame on the wall or on the ceiling, which is termed *outside mount* or *outside installation.* Figure 7–1 illustrates a simple window and the standard measurements that must be taken for any factory-made hard treatment.

Samples of order forms are found following illustrations of each type of hard treatment in this chapter. On the order form an inside mount should be abbreviated I/M or IM; inside installation should appear as I/I or II, and inside bracket should be listed as I/B or IB. Likewise, outside mount should be O/M or OM, outside installation should be O/I or OI, and outside bracket should be O/B or OB.

Hardlines cannot be altered as easily as draperies, if they can be altered at all. A mismeasurement or error in ordering often is the fault of the designer, who will likely end up "eating" the cost of replacement. Therefore it is extremely important to be careful and exact when measuring, recording, and ordering hard treatments.

Although the measuring guidelines for both inside and outside installations are similar to several of the soft treatment guidelines, they differ in some respects. Measuring guidelines include the following:

- Know which measurements are needed for an inside or an outside installation (see fig. 7–1). Include the floor-to-sill height *or* the desired length of the wand or baton.

- Use a steel retractable tape measure at least 10 feet long that is easy to work and strong enough to stay stiff.

- For widths longer that an arm span, have someone assist in holding the tape at the beginning end. You read the measurement.

- Record every measurement as you take it. Never take two measurements and then try to remember which was which.

- Record *width* first, then *length.* This is standard on all order forms throughout the window treatment industry.

- Record in inches, never in feet, and record every fraction of an inch.

- For inside-mount installations, measure the *width* in three places: near the top, in the center, and at the bottom. The smallest measurement will have to be notated so that the treatment will fit.

- For inside-mount installations, measure the *length* in two places: near each side. Order the shortest measurement.

- Write clearly in a notebook, not on separate sheets of paper that can be lost. Note any promotional sales; special circumstances; or requests for control location, window operation or hardware, angles in windows, or other particulars. Draw sketches or make notes to help you remember.

- Make a template when the window is an unusual shape by taping kraft paper and carefully tracing the opening.

INSTALLATION: INSIDE MOUNT

An inside mount is set inside the window frame. When placing the order for an inside mount, mark the box titled *inside mount* (IM) or *inside bracket* (IB). This will tell the factory which kind of brackets to send with the blind or shade. The factory will take a ½-inch deduction on miniblinds and shades. No deduction will be taken for vertical-louver blinds, shutters, or shoji screens.

The advantages of an inside mount include:

- The treatment takes no wall space and does not project into the room, making it easy to drape over the top, if desired.

- The window frame is exposed, which is a boon where the frame is architecturally interesting or beautiful. The frame may form a finishing touch to the hardline.

- Hardlines often look better when set into the window frame. Since most hardlines have no returns (sides to window), the window opening boxes in the blind, shutter, shade, or screen, giving it a finished appearance.

- In deep-set windows the treatment can be installed close to the glass, in the middle of the frame depth, or toward or flush with the wall. A treatment next to the glass with a deep windowsill can allow plants to be placed on the sill. Never place plants between the treatment and the glass. The heat and cold trapped in the pocket will alternately "cook and freeze" the plants, and they will quickly die.

The disadvantages of an inside mount include:

- A clearance or deduction is taken at the factory to make sure that the treatment will operate without rubbing against the sides of the window frame. This causes a light strike, or a small gap, and perhaps gives less privacy.

- Most windows are not perfectly square due to lack of fine craftsmanship or due to the settling that takes place after a home or building is constructed. Because hard treatments must be manufactured to the smallest measurements, light strikes appear where the window is slightly wider. This may emphasize the irregularity of the dimensions.

- Some treatments, such as shutters, are extremely difficult to install when the window is not perfectly square. In this case the shutters should either be mounted on the outside or prehung—installed into a frame that can be planed (cut to fit) by the carpenter who installs them (see "Shutters" section later in this chapter).

INSTALLATION: OUTSIDE MOUNT

For an outside mount the treatment typically is mounted about 1 ½ inches beyond the frame width and 1 ½ inches above the window and to the sill on the bottom. Generally this treatment covers only the window or part of the window. For example, shutters may cover only the lower half of the window. Miniblinds usually are specified to the size of the window frame.

When placing the order check the appropriate box to receive the proper brackets; no deductions should be taken by the factory.

Advantages of an outside mount include the following:

- There is the possibility of extending the window treatment higher, lower, or wider than the window. This is not recommended for blinds that will expose the wall when they are open; but for many hard treatments, such as shutters, roller shades, and shoji screens, an extended installation can make the window look wider. It can also allow for stacking area when needed.

- The light strike can be diminished or almost eliminated by extending the treatment wider than the window.

- The problem of fitting the treatment to uneven or "out-of-square" windows is eliminated.

- There are fewer measuring and installation complications with an outside mount, because the squareness of the angle will not be as important an issue.

Disadvantages of an outside mount include:

- The treatment may look unfinished or awkward because of the lack of return on most hard treatments.

- It may be more difficult to layer a soft treatment over an outside-mount hard treatment because of the projection depth of the hard-line treatment. However, this is rarely a prohibitive factor.

- An outside mount is a little larger than an inside mount, which could then put the treatment in a higher price category.

HORIZONTAL BLINDS

A blind consists of slats that can be controlled to stack up (or in the case of vertical louvers—stack off) to a small space. These slats also can be tilted for maximum sunlight control and privacy.

Horizontal blinds include Venetian blinds, miniblinds, micro-miniblinds, and wood blinds, each of which will be discussed below.

Horizontal blinds offer many decorating pluses that other treatments lack. Perhaps the main benefit is that blinds let you have the best of both worlds. Two separate cords control the functions: one for tilting the slats and the other for lifting the blinds. The slats can be adjusted to any angle— open, tilted up or down, or fully closed. The light can be directed toward ceiling or floor, permitting both light and privacy to coexist to a degree. When the blinds are tilted upward, they cast a shadow below and direct some light toward the ceiling. Conversely, when tilted downward they cast the shadow on the ceiling, but throw some light on the area below, thus darkening the room more effectively. The lift cord controls the height to which the blind is raised. The user can raise the blinds completely or partially. Slats stack easily and take up a fairly small space at the top.

Venetian Blinds

Venetian blinds (fig. 7–2) are one of the oldest of the hardline treatments. They have been seen in America (made of wood) since the Georgian era and were particularly popular during the 1930 to 1950 Early Modern period. They are made of 2-inch-wide aluminum slats held together by a 1-inch-wide cotton braid "ladder." The original blinds came only in an off-white baked enamel, but today Venetian blinds are available in a variety of colors. The cotton braid can be ordered in a matching or contrasting color or can have a woven pattern. Or the braid can be replaced with nylon cord.

Venetian blinds are handsome and tend to have a masculine appearance. Yet in today's decorating scene, they may look dated, clinical, or even homely. Furthermore, they are dust catchers of the first degree because of the width of the slats, and they are cumbersome to clean because it is difficult to reach behind the cotton braid for dusting.

Miniblinds

Miniblinds, seen in figure 7–3, are a form of Venetian blind. They operate on the same principle, the exception being that the tilt cord is replaced by a wand and that the cumbersome 1-inch-wide cotton braid is replaced by a strong, slender nylon cord that matches the slat color. Of course, the main difference is in the slats themselves, which are 1 inch wide. When fully opened these horizontal slats are nearly invisible. For clients who do not want to obstruct a view but who need privacy at times, they are a good solution. Miniblinds are tremendously popular among urban and suburban dwellers alike and in nonresidential design, as well, for many of the same reasons.

Miniblinds offer all the benefits of Venetian blinds and more. They are handsome, sleek, and compatible with most modern architecture and design, although they blend well with almost any decorative mode. The almost invisible nylon cord is a marked improvement and the tilting wand usually is transparent. Placement of the wand and cord can be specified—one on the left and the other on the right, or both on the same side.

A wide assortment of colors, patterns, and textures is available representing current interior design trends. However, the disadvantage to ordering colors or patterns is three-fold:

1. A definite color can be displeasing from the exterior of the home or building and in comparison to other window treatments.

2. The client may quickly tire of the color or pattern.

3. The client may have trouble making color scheme changes because of it.

The client should be alerted to drawbacks and perhaps directed to a neutral color or a white or off-white blind rather than a brilliant color. Custom blinds can be ordered to have color on the side that faces the room and an off-white on the side that faces the exterior. However, if the slats are directed so that the color side is facing out, then the problem of the exterior view will not be solved.

7-2 Venetian blinds with wide tape.

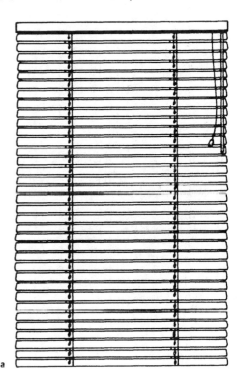

7-3 Miniblinds.

a The classic miniblind.

b Angled miniblinds with open louvers. Angled miniblinds are always a costly treatment.

Miniblinds are one of the least expensive of all the custom hard treatments, and the client can easily replace the blind at whim. Miniblinds also are sold as stock items in department stores in standard sizes. They are usually available in white or off-white and at a fraction of the cost of custom blinds. The material may be either aluminum or very economical vinyl.

Most manufacturers offer decorating flexibility, selling individual blinds in a color sequence where the designer determines how many slats of which colors are used and where they are placed. The effect is striped. Figure 7–4 is a sample order form for striped miniblinds.

Miniblinds generally come with a valance—two slats attached with brackets to cover the headrail. Some companies offer a trim edge that is placed around the perimeter of the blind, boxing it in to define and emphasize the shape. The valance and trim may be the same color or of a contrasting color. Cords, likewise, may be the same color or contrasting. Most people prefer to keep the colors on the blind unified, because a change in color, whether it be in a striped slat arrangement or in contrasting valance or trim, will transform an otherwise background treatment into a decorative feature that may have questionable design integrity.

Miniblinds are fairly effective as solar reflective treatments, with the light colors or whites being the most energy-efficient. They are tremendously durable; there is practically nothing to wear out. If the slats are bent, they can be reshaped into position easily. Some are made of fabric.

The stacking space of miniblinds is a mere one-twentieth of the window space. This enhances their streamlined effect. They are easy to install, simply snapped into the brackets and snapped out for cleaning. They are light and easy to handle. They may be mounted inside or outside the window frame and are an ideal undertreatment.

Like Venetian blinds miniblinds are dust catchers. Unlike Venetian blinds, however, they are relatively easy to clean without being removed from the window. Vacuuming or dusting usually is sufficient. An occasional showering (in the shower or under the garden hose) is all that is needed to clean blinds thoroughly unless a grease buildup had made their surface quite dirty. In this case, a mild soap solution, perhaps with vinegar, will remove the buildup. Sonic cleaning is an excellent way to remove dirt from blinds, especially if a large number of blinds require cleaning.

There is a negative side. Here are some of the factors:

- Miniblinds without overtreatments can look cold and hard.

- Since miniblinds do not absorb sound, they can actually amplify indoor noise.

- Miniblinds are not good winter window insulators. (However, they are better than an untreated window, as they will provide some blockage of heat/cold transfer and will appear warmer than a naked window.)

- Miniblinds cannot fully darken a room. There is a light strike with inside-mount blinds because of the clearance needed to operate them without rubbing the sides as the blind is raised or lowered.

Figure 7–5 is a sample order form for miniblinds and micro-miniblinds, which shows the categories of information that the designer will need to supply to the manufacturer.

7-4 Sample order form for multicolored (striped) blinds. →

USE THIS GUIDE TO CONVERT LENGTH TO NUMBER OF SLATS

Measurements (in inches) from top of head to bottom of bottom rail

INCHES	QUANTITY OF SLATS	INCHES	QUANTITY OF SLATS	INCHES	QUANTITY OF SLATS	INCHES	QUANTITY OF SLATS
12	13	38	47	64	80	90	113
13	14	39	48	65	82	91	114
14	15	40	49	66	83	92	115
15	17	41	50	67	84	93	117
16	18	42	51	68	86	94	118
17	19	43	53	69	87	95	119
18	21	44	54	70	88	96	120
19	22	45	56	71	89	97	122
20	23	46	57	72	90	98	123
21	24	47	58	73	91	99	124
22	26	48	59	74	92	100	126
23	27	49	60	75	93	101	127
24	28	50	62	76	94	102	128
25	30	51	63	77	95	103	130
26	31	52	65	78	97	104	131
27	32	53	66	79	98	105	132
28	34	54	67	80	99	106	134
29	35	55	68	81	101	107	135
30	36	56	70	82	102	108	137
31	37	57	71	83	103	109	138
32	39	58	72	84	105	110	140
33	40	59	74	85	106	111	141
34	41	60	75	86	107	112	142
35	43	61	76	87	109		
36	44	62	78	88	110	Add one slat	
37	46	63	79	89	111	for every additional ¾"	

THE PARTS OF THE BLIND FOR WHICH YOU MUST SPECIFY COLOR

A Head
B Bracket
C Valance
D Ladder
E Cord
F Bottom Rail
G Definition Sides
H Definition Bottom

	Blind No. 1	Blind No. 2	Blind No. 3
	Color Number & Name	**Color Number & Name**	**Color Number & Name**
A Head B Bracket			
C Valance			
D Ladder			
E Cord			
F Bottom Rail			
G Definition Sides			
H Definition Bottom			
	List Number of Slats in This Column ▼	List Number of Slats in This Column ▼	List Number of Slats in This Column ▼
	Total	Total	Total

1. In any striping arrangement, depending on blind length and due to flexibility of the ladders, the quantity of slats in the blind may differ from the Slat Quantity Guide. Please put the symbol + next to slat color or colors where the factory may make adjustments, if necessary.
2. Specify color on room side of Valance, otherwise factory will make color of Valance the same as the top slat in blind. For Tiltone slat, the Valance color will match decor color of top slat unless otherwise specified.
3. Enter the quantity of slats for that blind length as found in the Slat Quantity Guide. The length dimensions include the head and bottom rail. Example: A blind 92" long has 115 slats. The 92" includes the head and bottom rail for which the color must be specified along with the colors for the 115 slats.
4. List the colors by number and name in the order they appear in blind starting at top of blind.
5. The total of slat quantity indicated for each color must add up to the total quantity of slats as in the chart above.
6. If two or more colors are to alternate repeatedly with the same quantity of slats each time that color is repeated, then list at least two complete repeats and add note, "repeat to bottom of blind". However, indicate if the color of the last slat at bottom of blind is important to you as there may be insufficient slats to complete a cycle.
7. To avoid possibility of dye transfer from darker color ladders to lighter color slats, white or compatible color ladders are recommended. Factory will use white ladder and cord if color is not specified.
8. Please note that the Guide gives the total quantity of slats, not a slat's position in the blind.
9. This form from Levelor Lorentzen Inc. (Hoboken, NJ).

7-5 *Sample order form for miniblinds and micro-miniblinds.*

CHARGE TO: _____

SHIP TO: _____

SHIPPING INSTRUCTIONS:

WILL CALL	SHIP VIA	DELIVERY

DATE _____ SIDE MARK _____

P.O. NUMBER _____ ORDERED BY _____ PHONE _____ TAKEN BY _____

	QUANT.	IB/OB	WIDTH	LENGTH	CONTROL TILT	CONTROL LIFT	HOLD DOWN	SILL HEIGHT	COLOR NAME AND NUMBER
A									
B									
C									
D									
E									
F									
G									
H									
I									
J									

SPECIAL INSTRUCTIONS

TERMS: CASH DISCOUNT 2% 10 DAYS; NET 30 DAYS AT SELLER'S OFFICE. A finance charge of 2% per month, 24% per annum on all past due accounts. Purchaser agrees to pay all costs of collection including court costs and a reasonable attorney's fee in case suit or action is commenced to collect all or any part of this account.

ALL CLAIMS FOR SHORTAGES, ERRORS OR DEFECTIVE GOODS MUST BY MADE WITHIN 5 DAYS OF RECEIPT OF GOODS. **ALL ORDERS IN WORK ARE NOT SUBJECT TO CANCELLATION. ALL ORDERS ARE SUBJECT TO FACTORY ACCEPTANCE.**

ORDERED BY: _____

Micro-miniblinds

Micro-miniblinds have ½-inch slats rather than the 1-inch slats of conventional miniblinds. Moreover, they have twice the number of slats and produce a sleeker, finer, more delicate look at the window. The advantages and disadvantages are essentially the same as for miniblinds, except that 1-inch miniblinds are sturdier then micro-miniblinds (fig. 7–6).

Wood Blinds

Horizontal wood blinds (fig. 7–7) offer much the same advantages as metal blinds, such as versatility in controlling the direction of light and amount of privacy. For clients who admire the natural look of wood but who do not want to encumber their view with framed shutters, wood horizontal blinds may be the answer; they produce a solid louvered wall when closed and combine the high-quality, classic look of a louvered treatment with the contemporary look of metal miniblinds.

Wood is a natural insulator against heat and cold. As compared with metal miniblinds, wood blinds rate higher in winter insulation. As a summer shading device, they also are fairly effective, although lighter colors or stains are better at reflecting heat than darker stained or colored shades. In hot climates the sun may bleach out the stain color.

Although expensive, wood blinds will rarely, if ever, need replacing. Required stacking is greater, yet these blinds often are not raised. They are an impressive and handsome treatment; the wide slats offer exceptional light, view, and privacy control. Like other horizontal louvered treatments, wood blinds are dust catchers.

A sample order form for horizontal wood blinds is shown in figure 7–8.

VERTICAL BLINDS

Vertical blinds can be divided into two categories: louvered blinds made of a variety of flat vane, or slat, materials and wood vertical-louver blinds. The latter operate the same way as the former but are distinguished by the weight, bulk, and cost of the wood from the lighter-weight vinyl, plastic, metal, or fabric vanes.

Louvers

Vertical-louver blinds, seen in figures 7–9 and C-22, are made of slats, or vanes, that are approximately 4 inches wide. Since individual vanes are clipped to a headrail with a traverse and tilting mechanism, vertical louvers are well suited for angled windows (fig. 7–9b). The position of pull cords or chains that operate the blinds is specified by the designer. The chain that connects the vanes at the bottom (fig. 7–9c) sometimes is used to keep the blinds in control when they are opened and closed.

Vertical louvers are made from a variety of materials—from polyvinyl chloride to metal to macramé to various polyester fabrics. Vinyl vanes also come with grooves that allow fabric or wallpaper to be slid in place and glued. The vertical louvers can then appear as drapery fabric or as an extension of the wall covering. Plastic vanes can imitate woven woods, grass cloth, burlap, and many other contemporary interior design textures (fig. 7–9d).

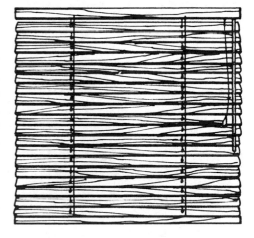

7-6 Micro-miniblinds with ½-inch louvers—a finer, more delicate look.

7-7 Wood blinds—the handsome quality of wood with a clean, contemporary look.

7-8 Sample order form for wood miniblinds.

BILL TO: (DEALER) P.O. NO. — Date _____ 19 __ Pg _____ of _____

SOLD TO SIDE MARK OR (RETAIL CUSTOMER)

( ) SHIP TO   ( ) INSTALL AT

VIA — TERMS

DEALER#   PHONE

PHONE

ROOM OR LOCATION	ITEM NO.	ENTER # IF NOT BELOW	QUANTITY	Installation IB, OB OR DOOR	Area Measured in Inches WIDTH	LENGTH	HOLD DOWN CONDITION	Mark if Special — Control Position TILT	LIFT	SILL HEIGHT IN INCHES	SLAT STAIN TONE NAME & NO.	UNIT PRICE	TOTAL
	1												
	2												
	3												
	4												
	5												
	6												
	7												
	8												
	9												
	0												

SIGNED: (DEALER-DESIGNER-DECORATOR)   DATE   ACCEPTED BY: DATE

☐ REMEASURE   ☐ DIMENSION APPROVED

REMEASURED BY _____ DATE _____

THIS IS A CUSTOM ORDER AND NOT SUBJECT TO CHANGE OR CANCELLATION.

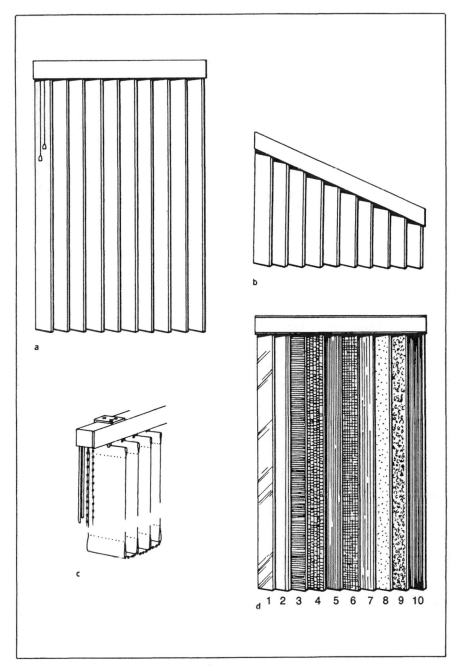

7-9 Vertical louvers.

a Vertical-louver blinds open and close like draperies and may rotate 180 degrees, with a separate cord or chain control.

b Vertical-louver blinds with a diagonal headrail. This is a good solution to angled windows in contemporary interiors.

c Closeup of the headrail without the valance, showing a draw cord and tilt chain. The optional bead chain at the hem keeps the blinds from flapping around when operating.

d A sample of textures available for vanes: (1) reflective metal, (2) vinyl with insert channels, (3-7) textured fabric, (8) perforated vane (admitting pinholes of light), (9) printed fabric or wallpaper insert, (10) colored fabric.

Verticals can be adjusted to any angle and closed to either side of the 180-degree pivot. Tilting the blind controls light and privacy, much as with a miniblind, except that the light cannot be directed upward or downward. However, solid (opaque) vanes offer a greater degree of privacy than do horizontals. Verticals also can be opened much the same as conventional traverse rod draperies. They can be ordered to stack off to the left or to the right or ordered as a split draw. Figure 7–10 is a sample order form for vertical-louver blinds. Table 7–1 lists stackback measurements.

Verticals offer a precise and contemporary look similar to drapery but with the ease of maintenance typical of hardline treatments. Vanes are not dust catchers and will largely "self-clean" by shaking loose dust as they are tilted, opened, or closed. They also may be sonic cleaned or cleaned by vacuuming, dusting, or using a soft cloth and mild detergent.

7-10 Sample order form for vertical-louver blinds.

CHARGE TO _____

TEL. _____

ORDER NO. _____

DEPT. NO _____

SHIP TO _____

TEL. _____

SHIP. INST. _____

SIDEMARK _____

ORDERED BY _____

DATE _____

□ ORIGINAL ORDER
□ CONFIRMING ORDER

IMPORTANT

MEASUREMENTS
OUTSIDE VERTICAL—WILL BE MADE TO EXACT MEASUREMENTS PROVIDED
INSIDE VERTICAL—WILL HAVE FACTORY ALLOWANCES

CAUTION
BLINDS ARE CUSTOM MADE AND NOT RETURNABLE

ALL BLINDS WILL BE MADE WITH ELITE HARDWARE UNLESS OTHERWISE SPECIFIED

ITEM NO.	QUAN-TITY	ROOM LOCATION	WIDTH IN INCHES	LENGTH IN INCHES	TYPE OF MEASURE		TYPE OF BRACKET		TYPE OF HARDWARE				POSITION OF CONTROLS		LOUVER TYPE	LOUVER COLOR	INSERTS		TYPE FOR COLOR	VALANCE TYPE		PRICE
					INSIDE MAKE ALLOW	OUTSIDE CUT ALLOW	CLIPS	WALL BRACKET	1 WAY (FROM CLOSED POSITION) RIGHT TO LEFT	1 WAY LEFT TO RIGHT	SPLIT DRAW	HEAVY DUTY	RIGHT SPLIT DRAW	LEFT DRAW ONLY			YES	NO		INSIDE	OUTSIDE	
1																						
2																						
3																						
4																						
5																						
6																						
7																						
8																						
9																						
10																						

SIGNATURE _____

Table 7-1 Stackback

Two-way Draw Stack Chart		
Window Opening (in.)	Rod Length (in.)	Stackback (in.)
16	24	4
20	29	4 1/2
26	36	5
32	43	5 1/2
38	50	6
43	56	6 1/2
48	63	7 1/2
54	70	8
60	77	8 1/2
66	84	9
72	91	9 1/2
77	98	10 1/2
83	105	11
89	112	11 1/2
95	119	12
97	122	12 1/2
102	128	13
113	140	13 1/2
118	146	14
124	154	15
130	161	15 1/2
136	168	16
141	174	16 1/2
147	181	17
152	187	17 1/2
156	192	18

One-way Draw Stack Chart		
Window Opening (in.)	Rod Length (in.)	Stackback (in.)
29 1/2	38	8 1/2
34	43	9
36 1/2	46	9 1/2
39 1/2	50	10 1/2
45 1/2	57	11 1/2
49 1/2	62	12 1/2
52	65	13
58	72	14
63	78	15
65 1/2	81	15 1/2
71	88	17
77 1/2	95	17 1/2
80	99	19
82	102	20
88 1/2	109	20 1/2
94	116	22
100	123	23
106	130	24
112	137	25
117 1/2	144	26 1/2
126 1/2	154	27 1/2
132	161	29
141	171	30
144	175	31
150 1/2	182	31 1/2
153	185	32
156 1/2	189	32 1/2
156 1/2	192	35 1/2

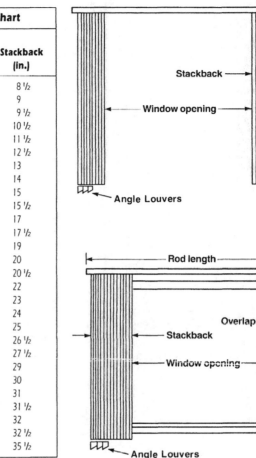

Measure window opening and find measurement on chart. Read across to find rod length you should order. This will allow blind, when opened, to clear window.

Note: To figure exact rod length when window opening falls between measurements listed, refer to least measurement for stackback. Rod length can be figured by doubling stackback and adding to window opening measurement.

Measure window opening. Add, and consider as part of opening, desired *extra width* for overlap beyond window. Find window opening measurement on chart and read across to find rod length you should order.

Note: To figure exact rod length when window opening falls between measurements listed, refer to least measurement for stackback. Rod length can be figured by adding stackback to window opening measurement.

The width of the blind will be manufactured to within 1/8 inch of the size ordered. The factory also will take an allowance for sill clearance, as the blinds open and close horizontally. Inside and outside installation must be indicated. Clips normally are used for inside mounting, and wall brackets are normally used for outside mounting. Heavy-duty hardware can be specified for wide expanses. An "Insert" column on the order form is for specifying laminated fabric inserted into grooved slats. Grooved vanes also are used to hold in customers's own material (C.O.M.) or wallpaper. Strips of custom fabric or wallpaper need to be stiffened first in order to slide into the grooves. The fabric inserts can make the vertical louvers look like draperies and offer less maintenance (plastic vanes protect the fabric from sunlight deterioration, and less cleaning is needed). Wallpaper inserted into the vanes can make the closed blind seem like an extension of the wall. Note that careful cutting and matching is important in patterned fabric or wall coverings.

Vertical louvers reject up to 75 percent of solar-heat gain through windows, depending on the material used for the vanes (see fig. 7–9d). Solid vinyl slats are perhaps the best choice for winter insulation. But bear in

a

b

7-11 Vertical wood blinds.

a Vertical wood blinds may be stained in a variety of colors.

b Vane shapes shown in cross section.

mind that treatments with slats are never highly effective as insulation.

Verticals are relatively durable window treatments. Although there is a variety of materials from which to choose, most will last a very long time and many will pass fire-safety code specifications. Verticals are more costly than miniblinds but less so than shutters.

The disadvantages of vertical-louver blinds include the following:

- Hard materials tend to amplify noise (this is lessened when fabric vanes are used).

- When mounted inside the window frame, the light strike is minimal; but on an outside mount, the light strike is prominent, since there is no return. (The blinds can be stacked off the glass, as with a drapery treatment, but verticals require far less stackoff space—only about one-eighth the window width.)

Wood Blinds

Worthy of separate mention are vertical wood louvers, which offer many of the advantages of wood miniblinds yet with the drapery effect of the vertical-louver system. Wood verticals offer the warmth and beauty of wood and a somewhat higher insulative value (fig. 7–11a). Another difference is the shape of the vane, which can be cut into zigzag, S-shape, torpedo, or flat louvers, as seen in figure 7–11b.

Like all wood treatments, vertical wood blinds cost considerably more than vinyl, metal, or fabric counterparts. They also reflect indoor noise. Some people, however, believe that the beauty of wood verticals offsets these disadvantages.

SHUTTERS

Although shutters are not as popular and affordable as horizontal and vertical blinds, they are perhaps the most enduring and classic of all the hard treatments. What began in ancient Greece as a stone slab mounted onto a pivot (fig. 7–12a) now has taken on many forms. The pivoting shutter can be made of wood or a fabric-covered insulative board. Solid riveted and plank shutters have been used as exterior and interior hinged or sliding window treatments and doors (fig. 7–12 b–c).

The two most refined styles of shutter, used from the time of the Renaissance through today, are the raised-panel shutter and the louvered shutter (movable or nonmovable). These are seen in figure 7–12 d–e. Solid raised panels are also shown in figures C-4 and C-10. Insert shutters (see fig. 4–3) are wood frames filled with materials such as woven wood, pierced wood, bamboo, metal mesh, wood lattice, or shirred fabric. They can give authenticity to an interior, depending on the color of the wood paint or stain and the type of material. Insert shutters are ideal for diffusing light but have limited privacy protection.

Shutters can be given a wood stain or painted and repainted any desired color. However, the paint cannot be stripped off because the shutter frames are glued together, and the stripping process would loosen the glue, causing the shutters to fall apart. The exception here is when antique panel shutters are worth hand stripping and refinishing by a wood-working craftsperson.

Shutters are versatile, used not only for window treatments, but also on full-length door windows, as room dividers, as cabinet fronts, as closet

doors, and as cupboard partitions. Any of these uses can inspire or echo the way the shutter is used at the window. Shutters also can be used as free-standing screens.

Louvered Shutters

Movable louvered shutters are by far the most popular of the shutter styles today. One reason is that they can provide both light and privacy to a desired degree by adjustment of the louvers. Further, individual panels can be adjusted to direct light where it is wanted—on a plant, for example—while shading adjoining areas—near a sensitive fabric or wood furniture piece, for example. Shutters that treat only the lower half of a window are single-hung café shutters. This treatment assures privacy below, where people are seated, and light, view, and ventilation above (fig. 7–13).

Louvers come in different widths—1 inch, 2 inches, 2½ inches, 3 inches, 3½ inches, and even 4 inches. The wider the louver, or blade, the thicker it becomes. Wide shutters can be custom-made of finely grained wood or roughly cut rustic wood. Wide-blade shutters are called plantation shutters (fig. 7–14a). They originally were used in plantation houses to direct much-needed breezes for ventilation while shading the interior from the hot sunshine of the Deep South. Plantation shutters are dramatic and effective

7-12 Conventional shutters.

a Pivoting shutters, which can be made of stone, plain wood, or fabric-covered wood.

b Rustic riveted wood shutters.

c Plank shutters.

d Raised-panel wood shutters, which may be painted. This style is a formal Colonial favorite.

e Movable-louver shutters control light and give privacy.

7-13 Classic single-hung café shutter, which covers the lower half of the window to give light above and privacy below.

7-14 Custom shutters.

a Plantation shutters. The dividing slat in the center gives strength and stability to the blind.
to the blind.

b Control rod positioned off-center for an unusual look.

c Vertical-blade shutters emphasize vertical lines and resist catching dust.

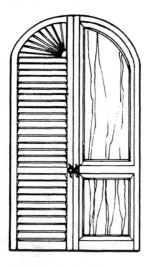

7-15 Arched shutter (left) tops a nonmovable shutter. Its companion is a raised-panel solid-wood shutter with a custom arch at the top (right).

in tall or large-scale interiors, and they are most often used alone. As such they become a part of the architecture in addition to being a handsome window treatment.

Other styles of shutters include the offset placement of the louver-adjuster bar, or control bar (fig. 7–14b), and shutters that have vertical blades or louvers (fig. 7–14c). In vertical-louver shutters, the control bar can be placed at any desired height.

Shutters also nicely cover angled or rounded windows. Figure 7–15 shows a segmental shutter with a fanlight top. Fanlight shutters as well as angled shutters can be made into movable or nonmovable blade units. The companion shutter is a floating-panel shutter, which allows the flat panels to expand and contract with humidity as they float within the frame. The segmental window and arched shutter treatment is typically French (see chapters 2 and 4).

Solid Shutter Panels

Solid shutter panels (see figs. 4–28, 7–12, and 7–15) and nonmovable-louver shutters offer absolute privacy at night when closed over the window.

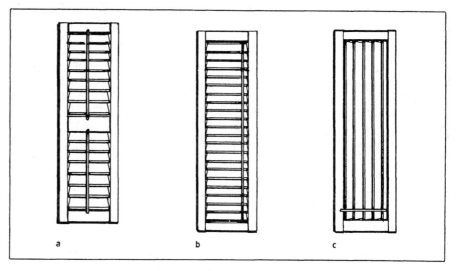

Solid shutters can be highly insulative, if perimeters are sealed and meeting edges are rabbeted (sides cut to interlock). Fixed louvers, accepted for their exterior and interior use, offer the handsome look of solid wood; the flat or raised panels may be stained or painted. They represent a frank, structural use of materials, although the shutters can be carved to authenticate a period; for example geometric designs reflect the Moor-dominated Spanish style. Nonmovable louvers are similar in appearance to movable louvered shutters. They are used more often on the exterior, for decoration, insulation, privacy, or shading.

The shutter is so classic that it will continue to withstand the test of time. Indeed the high cost of shutters need not be a deterring factor when one calculates the estimated number of years of use divided into the total cost. This is termed *life-cycle costing*. Often it turns out that shutters are actually less costly than fabric treatments.

Shutters with horizontal blades are dust catchers and will require some upkeep. Generally shutters are constructed of relatively narrow panels in a series of vertical frames (stiles) and horizontal members (rails). A divider stile in the center of tall shutters give stability to the louvers by anchoring the frame.

The quality of shutters varies considerably, from ready-made to fine-quality custom-made. The cheaper versions can be effective window treatments, whereas custom shutters will require an investment attitude on the part of the client, but one that will almost always lead to a satisfying result.

Exterior shutters are discussed in chapter 1. Figure 7–16 is a sample order form indicating the format and information required of the designer by a shutter manufacturer.

Shutter Installation

Types of shutter installation include single-hung full-length, single-hung café, double hung, and sliding shutters.

A single-hung full-length shutter consists of one set of hinged shutters that fold out from the center or either end and cover the entire window. A single-hung café unit covers only the bottom half of the window (see fig. 7–13).

Double-hung shutters consist of two (or more) sets of shutters installed one above the other, with each set operating separately (see fig. 4–14). Shutters today are either mounted on a hanging strip or prehung in a wood frame and installed inside or on the window frame, or on the wall. Hinged shutters are very difficult to adjust if the window is "out-of-square" and should therefore be mounted outside the window box whenever possible. Because shutters are heavy, a span of four or more panels should be supported by a frame or should rest on the windowsill so that the weight does not pull out the hinges.

Sliding shutters are an excellent choice for sliding glass doors (see fig. 4–27) or on angled attic windows. Shutters that slide may be handled in stacked fashion, as are shoji screens (see figs. 7–30 and 7–31).

Table 7–2 indicates the number of panels that typically are used in each category of widths and the width and length of each individual shutter that would be used in a hinged set. This information is useful to the designer when selecting standard shutters and deciding how many shutter panels should be used at a window.

SHADES

Shades, particularly the roller or pull shade, have been used in interiors for many years. In America the Dutch colonists used a stiffened, sturdy fabric called Holland cloth mounted on a spring-type roller as early as the 1760s.

Roller Shades

The spring mechanism that we use today for roller shades has been available from the early 1900s, and it has been since only the 1950s that vinyl has been typically used as window shade material. Fabric is still widely employed for window shades, especially to coordinate with a larger fabric scheme in the room. The best-quality fabric shades are laminated to a backing by companies that custom-produce shades to the designer's specifications. Another method is to stiffen the fabric with a starch preparation, which can be done professionally or as a do-it-yourself project.

Roller shades, or pull shades, are attached to a wood or plastic roller and operate either on a spring-tension mechanism (which sometimes "springs" and never works again) or on a pulley system operated with a chain. The spring roller stops at intervals, but it is difficult to control ex-

7-16 Sample order for custom shutters.

SOLD TO:

CITY / STATE / ZIP

DECORATOR'S NAME

SALES CHECK NO.   PURCHASE ORDER NO.

ORDER DATE   WORK ORDER NO.

SHIP TO:

ADDRESS   PHONE NO.

CITY / STATE / ZIP

INSTALLER'S NAME

ADDRESS   PHONE NO.

CITY / STATE / ZIP

ITEM	STOCK NUMBER AND NAME	FABRIC FRAME ONLY INSERT NAME AND COLOR (IF ANY)	NUMBER OF WINDOWS		SHUTTER UNIT SIZE IN INCHES		FACTORY TAKE ALLOW-ANCE*	INSIDE OR OUTSIDE HANG	NUMBER OF PANELS		SPECIFY FINISH COLOR NUMBER AND NAME	SPECIFY COLOR OF HARDWARE AND KNOBS				HANGING STRIPS AND SUPPLIED AUTOMATICALLY UNLESS YOU SPECIFY OTHER TYPE INSTALLATION: CHECK BELOW				SPECIAL KNOBS SPECIFY NUMBER AND COLOR	SELLING PRICE
					WIDTH	LENGTH			FOLD LEFT	FOLD RIGHT		BRITE	ANT	CHR	CER KNOB	BUTT	THROW OUT	TRACK			
1				TOP			☐ YES	☐ IN													
				BOT			☐ NO	☐ OUT													
2				TOP			☐ YES	☐ IN													
				BOT			☐ NO	☐ OUT													
3				TOP			☐ YES	☐ IN													
				BOT			☐ NO	☐ OUT													
4				TOP			☐ YES	☐ IN													
				BOT			☐ NO	☐ OUT													
5				TOP			☐ YES	☐ IN													
				BOT			☐ NO	☐ OUT													

(A) * AN ALLOWANCE IS WHEN THE DIMENSIONS OF A SHUTTER UNIT ARE REDUCED A FRACTION OF AN INCH IN THE WIDTH AND LENGTH. THIS REDUCTION INSURES PROPER FIT AND CLEARANCE IN THE WINDOW. IF FACTORY IS TO TAKE THE ALLOWANCE, MARK BOX YES.
IF YOU WISH THE SHUTTER UNIT TO BE MADE THE EXACT SIZE AS YOU MEASURED, MARK THE ALLOWANCE BOX NO. YOU MUST MARK THIS COLUMN YES OR NO.

(B) ALWAYS MEASURE THE WIDTH AND LENGTH OF THE WINDOW IN THREE PLACES AND RECORD THE NARROWEST WIDTH AND THE SHORTEST LENGTH MEASURED ON THE SPECIFICATION SHEET IN INCHES, USE A WOOD OR METAL RULER.

(C) INDICATE NUMBER OF PANELS TO FOLD LEFT OR RIGHT.

SPECIAL INSTRUCTIONS:

FOR INSTALLER'S USE ONLY

Table 7-2 Shutter Panel Size Selection Chart

Length (in.)	Width (in.)						
	26–28 4 panels	30–32 4 panels	34–36 4 panels	38–40 4 panels	39–42 6 panels	46–48 4 panels	46–48 6 panels
18–20	7 x 20	8 x 20	9 x 20	10 x 20	7 x 20	12 x 20	8 x 20
21–24	7 x 24	8 x 24	9 x 24	10 x 24	7 x 24	12 x 24	8 x 24
25–28	7 x 28	8 x 28	9 x 28	10 x 28	7 x 28	12 x 28	8 x 28
29–32	7 x 28	8 x 32	9 x 32	10 x 32	7 x 32	12 x 32	8 x 32
33–36	7 x 36	8 x 36	9 x 36	10 x 36	7 x 32	12 x 32	8 x 32

Note: For widths wider than 48 inches, divide by the standard panel widths—7 inches, 8 inches, 9 inches, 10 inches, or 12 inches—to determine the number of panels. Also, on an inside mount, deduct the hanging strip width (usually 1 inch or ½-inch each side). This should be indicated in the manufacturer's charts.

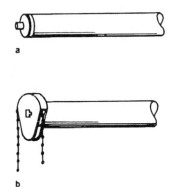

7-17 Shade rollers.

a Spring-tension shade roller.
b Chain-operated pulley shade roller and mechanism.

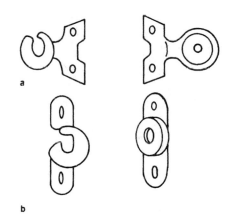

7-18 Mount brackets.

a Outside mount brackets for spring-tension roller.
b Inside mount brackets for spring-tension roller.

actly where, and the shade or shade pull must be operated by hand. Alternatively, the chain-operated pulley can be controlled even at a distance of 3 or 4 feet by pulling the chain, and the shade can be stopped at any height. However, the spring-operated shade is quite economical—perhaps the best bargain for the price in ready-made shades. Pulley shades, comparable to vertical louvers in price, are considerably more expensive (fig. 7–17).

Roller shades must be measured for either an inside or an outside mount, and the designer will need to specify the type because the brackets differ (fig. 7–18). Four dimensions are important to the designer when measuring or specifying custom shades. Illustrated in figure 7–19, these are:

- The *tip-to-tip measurement,* which should be the exact inside window width, less perhaps $\frac{1}{16}$ of an inch for the movement of the flat spring tip.

- The *roller width,* which should be approximately $\frac{1}{2}$ inch smaller than the tip-to-tip measurement.

- The *shade width,* which should be $\frac{1}{4}$ inch narrower than the roller width.

- The *shade length,* which should be the desired length plus 12 inches, so that the shade can be pulled down for the spring action. (Six inches is enough for the pulley shade.)

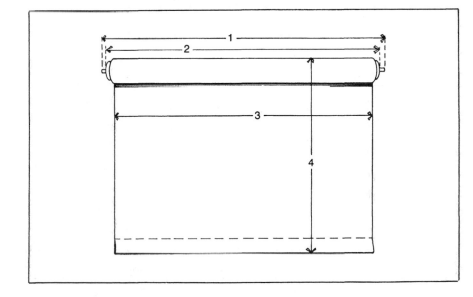

7-19 (*left*) Measuring for a roller shade: tip-to-tip measurement (slightly less than top inside width) or exact measurement for outside brackets (1); Roller width (slightly wider than the shade fabric) (2); Shade width (3); Shade length—desired length plus 12 inches for wrapping around the roller and for pull-release excess (4).

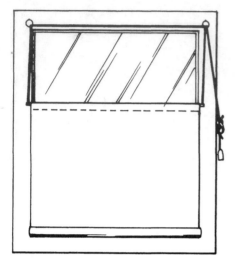

7-20 Roller shade that rolls up from the bottom with cord and pulley.

Shades also can be drawn up from the bottom, as shown in figure 7–20.

Roller shades consist of the shade, also called the skirt, which can be hung in two ways—as a regular roll and a reverse roll. The reverse roll hides the roller: the fabric is on the top and pulls over the front of the roller. The roller also may be covered with a valance and can become decorative (fig. 7–21 a–b). The skirt may have a selection of pulls that protect the shade (fig. 7–21c). Figure 7–22 is a sample order form for roller shades.

Another factory-made roller shade is an insulating shade, which is mounted into a track that seals the window (fig. 7–23). This type of shade can be stopped by hand at any point.

Figure 7–24 shows an accordion shade made of stiffened polyester fabric. Sturdy ribbon is used to draw up this shade, which was a forerunner of the pleated fabric shade.

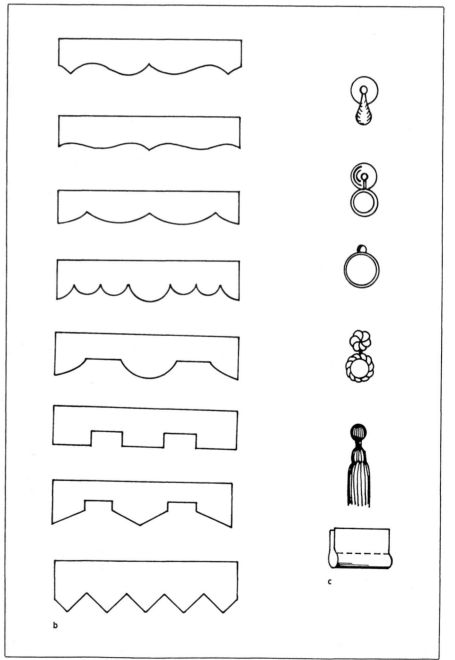

7-21 Pull shades.

a   Pull shade with scalloped valance and skirt edged with fringe.

b   Selection of roller or pull-shade valances.

c   Pull-shade hardware, or pulls.

7-22 Sample order form for custom shades anc shade valances.

ADDRESS _____

CITY/STATE/ZIP _____ PHONE NO. _____

DECORATOR'S NAME _____

SALES CHECK NO _____

ORDER DATE _____

ADDRESS _____

CITY/STATE/ZIP _____ PHONE NO _____

INSTALLER _____

ADDRESS _____

CITY/STATE/ZIP _____ PHONE NO _____

PURCHASE ORDER _____

WORK ORDER NO _____

ITEM	STOCK NUMBER	QUAN-TITY	WIDTH	LENGTH	TYPE INSTALLATION (CHECK ONE)			REPLACE-MENT	SHADE COLOR	HEM STYLE	FRINGE NUMBER	FRINGE COLOR	SHADE PULL NUMBER	ROLL		LAMINATED REG ROLL ONLY		UNIT SELLING PRICE	TOTAL SELLING PRICE
					INSIDE	OUTSIDE	CEILING							REG	R'VSE	MATERIAL	COLOR		
1																			
2																			
3																			
4																			
5																			
6																			
7																			

Valance or Canopy

ITEM	STOCK NUMBER	QUAN-TITY	WIDTH	HEIGHT	COLOR	VALANCE OR CANOPY (CHECK ONE)		HEM STYLE	FRINGE NUMBER	FRINGE COLOR	MATCHING MATCHMAKER VALANCE-CANOPY		UNIT SELLING PRICE	SELLING PRICE
						VALANCE	CANOPY				MATERIAL	COLOR		
1														
2														
3														
4														
5														
6														
7														

Special Instructions: _____

SIGNATURE _____

273

7-23 Insulating shade on a sealed track.

    a   Front view.
    b   Side view.

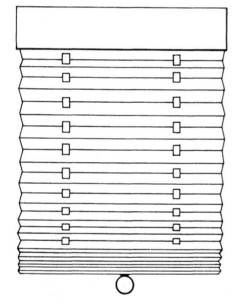

7-24 *(above)* Factory-manufactured accordion shade drawn with a finger pull.

7-25 *(right)* Pleated fabric shades.

    a   Pleated fabric shade.
    b   Micropleated shade with ½-inch folded pleats.
    c   Stacked pleated shade—a sleek hard window treatment.
    d   Pleated shade fitted into a fanlight arched window: a natural choice for this type of installation because it folds easily into a fan.
    e   Angled installation of pleated shade.
    f   Pleated shade in cross section *(top)*, and double-pleated shade with honeycomb construction *(bottom)*.

Pleated Fabric Shades

Pleated fabric shades are perhaps the most popular hard treatment next to miniblinds and vertical-louver blinds. This treatment was first imported from the Netherlands in a limited selection of unattractive colors, which has since been expanded to an amazing array of lovely colors and varied patterns. The fabric is pleated polyester that has been heat set to hold the folds permanently and comes in three varieties: the fabric can be translucent (which cuts glare and gives daytime privacy); metallized (coated with a reflective metal backing to reduce solar gain and keep in winter heat); opaque (to give nighttime privacy), or constructed from a combination of two separate skirts of screening fabric and an opaque fabric fitted onto one headrail. The pleated shade is illustrated in figure 7–25.

The pleated fabric shade offers many advantages. First, there is the clean look of horizontal hardlines yet the softness of fabric. The shades are easily cleaned by dusting and can be sponged off if needed. The colors continually are expanded and changed to meet trends. The stacking height is very slender: 24 inches stacks to $1\frac{3}{4}$ inches, 48 inches stacks to $2\frac{1}{4}$ inches, and 96 inches stacks to $3\frac{1}{4}$ inches. They are sheer, lightweight, and easy to install.

Problems seem to lie in the delicacy of the mechanism, which can sometimes fail, and the fact that standard translucent shades cannot offer nighttime privacy.

Figure 7–26 is a sample order form for pleated fabric shades.

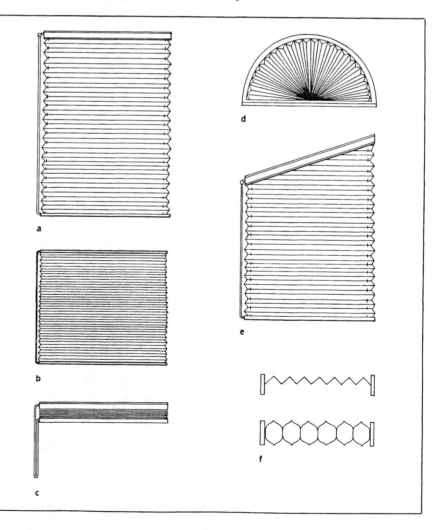

7-26 Sample order form for pleated fabric shades.

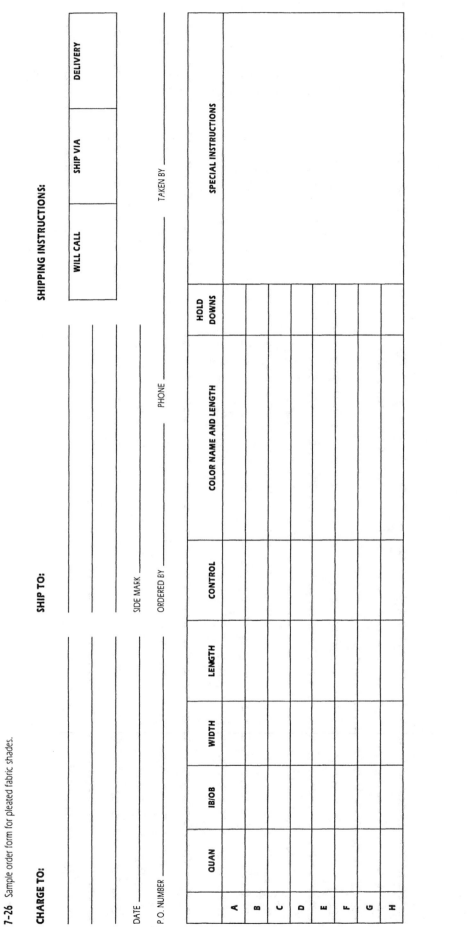

CHARGE TO:

SHIPPING INSTRUCTIONS:

SHIP TO:

	WILL CALL	SHIP VIA	DELIVERY

DATE

SIDE MARK

P.O. NUMBER

PHONE

ORDERED BY

TAKEN BY

	QUAN	IB/OB	WIDTH	LENGTH	CONTROL	COLOR NAME AND LENGTH	HOLD DOWNS	SPECIAL INSTRUCTIONS
A								
B								
C								
D								
E								
F								
G								
H								

SIGNATURE

Woven-Wood Shades

Woven-wood shades have been popular since the mid-1960s, when they were first introduced and accepted in America. The patterns and colors from the 1960s to the early 1980s were somewhat bold and dramatic; now they are subtle and the colors softer and more pleasing, making woven woods a good choice for background treatments, as well as for architecturally supportive and even focal-point treatments.

Woven-wood shades are $1/2$- to 1-inch strips of wood, stained or painted white, that are combined with cotton or rayon yarns in plain or patterned weaves that are available in a variety of colors and textures. Figure 7–27 illustrates the options in woven woods.

Woven woods can be made with varying degrees of warp, or lengthwise, yarn that joins the weft slats together. The greater the quantity or bulk of the yarns used, the greater the degree of privacy, insulation, and cost. Manufacturers change colors and designs periodically, and a variety of color and yarn styles is available, from simple and structural to quite decorative, particularly with shaped skirts and valances trimmed and fringed. Figure 7–28 is a sample woven-wood shade order form.

Woven woods may be mounted inside or outside the window frame, and the stacking distance is about 5 to 10 inches, depending on the length of the shade. These shades may be used alone at the window, as a top treatment, or as a privacy or light-screening shade beneath contemporary textured casement fabrics. Woven woods are good options where several windows need individual treatments in matching sections; they can be topped with one continuous valance. Separate shades are easier to operate than wide shades; those over 6 feet long often involve mechanical difficulties.

Woven-wood shades occasionally have yarns that work loose or unravel at the edges, but these are easy to remove or to reweave. The shades can be dusted or vacuumed, but if they become greasy they pose some problem in cleaning.

Bamboo Shades

For years bamboo shades have been used as sunscreens around patios. In interiors they give a "natural" look that is casual and handsome. Bamboo shades also are called matchstick shades or blinds or bali blinds. Actually, it is erroneous to call them blinds, even though they do have individual slats. They are shades because their slats are woven together and operate as a flat fabric. Made of naturally uneven strips of split bamboo in narrow widths (about $1/2$ inch), the strips are woven with cotton string in a leno (hourglass) weave, about every 5 inches. Attached to two pulleys at the top is a heavier cotton cord that wraps around the shade vertically, rolling the shade up from the bottom. The cord is secured around a two-pronged bracket that holds the shade at the desired height (see fig. 4–2a).

Bamboo shades also are manufactured in even strips and mounted on a spring-tension roller. They usually are found among selections of woven-wood shades that are made of natural wood rather than bamboo (see fig. 4–2b).

Bamboo shades in many sizes are regular stock items in stores and import and mail-order suppliers. Real bamboo shades come only in stock sizes—usually 6 feet long in 3-, 4-, 5-, 6-, or 8-foot widths. Imitation bamboo-slat shades of vinyl are available from many sources in a roll-up style or Roman fold-up style.

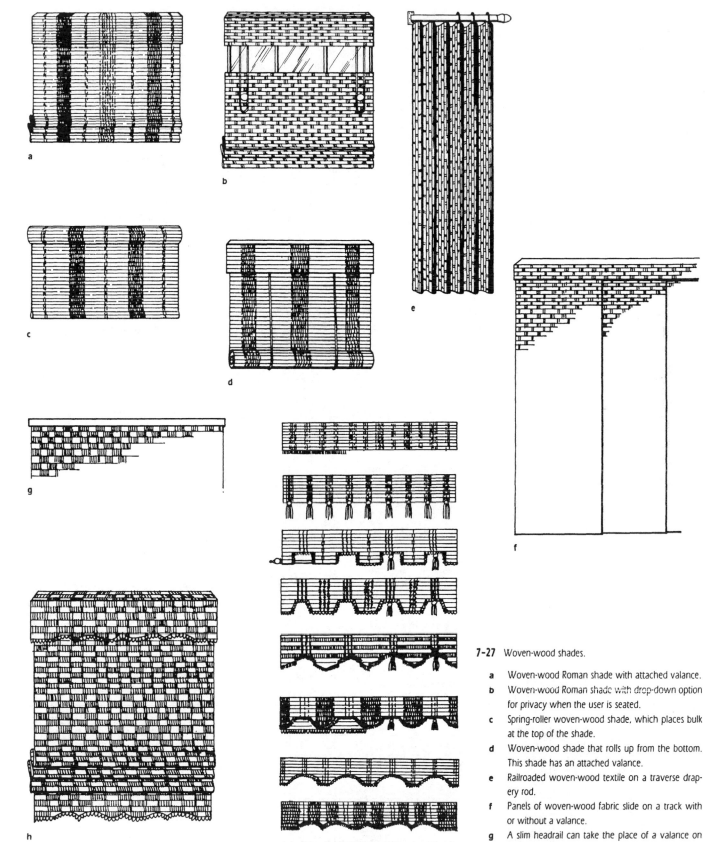

7-27 Woven-wood shades.

a Woven-wood Roman shade with attached valance.

b Woven-wood Roman shade with drop-down option for privacy when the user is seated.

c Spring-roller woven-wood shade, which places bulk at the top of the shade.

d Woven-wood shade that rolls up from the bottom. This shade has an attached valance.

e Railroaded woven-wood textile on a traverse drapery rod.

f Panels of woven-wood fabric slide on a track with or without a valance.

g A slim headrail can take the place of a valance on woven-wood shades.

h Decorative scalloped and fringed woven-wood skirt and valance.

i Selection of valances for woven woods.

7-28 Sample order form for woven-wood shades.

CHARGE TO: _____

SHIP TO: _____

PURCHASE ORDER: _____ DATE: _____ CUSTOMER NO.: _____ SIDE MARK: _____

	QUAN	IB/OB	WIDTH	LENGTH	CONTROL	WOVEN-WOOD NAME AND LENGTH	TRIM	SHADE STYLE
A								
B								
C								
D								
E								
F								
G								
H								

SPECIAL INSTRUCTIONS

_____
SIGNATURE

The cost of bamboo shades is low compared to other hard treatments. Woven-wood bamboo or imitation bamboo shades will be moderate in cost, but definitely will cost more than shades made of real bamboo. These shades often are used alone, since they are appropriate in casual settings. They may also be used as a light-screening undertreatment, but they will not give complete nighttime privacy.

SCREENS

Many varieties of screens are on the market today, and all will fit into one of two general categories—sliding or folding. A sliding screen is one that is set into a track at the top and at the bottom and will stack one panel behind the other. A folding screen is a free-standing or side-hinged unit with two or more panels.

Screens used for window treatments generally are made of wood or a woven material, such as rattan, and the designer can collaborate with a carpenter to build a wide variety of sizes and designs. Further, the surface of custom screens can be decorated with wood stain, paint, wallpaper, fabric, stencilwork, or even folk painting. In this section will be discussed the three types of screens that are manufactured for window treatments— lattice and pierced screens, shoji screens, and solid-panel screens.

Lattice and Pierced Screens

Lattice screens are sliding or folding screens made of wood frames that encase strips of overlapping wood that crisscross at right angles diagonally or vertically (see fig. 4–6). Equal spaces between the strips create a checked or diamond-shaped pattern and serve to filter and diffuse light. Lattice screens are available at many prices, from inexpensive garden lattices sold by home-improvement centers to custom lattices manufactured by quality shutter companies.

Shutter manufacturers that produce lattices may offer options such as double slats that close when one set slides on top of the other for nighttime privacy, or, as seen in figure 4–6c, the lattice screen can be framed and topped with architectural molding or woodwork. Lattice screens also may be backed with shirred or flat fabric, paper, or wall-covering material, which will lend more privacy and further cut down the amount of light coming into the room. Lattice screens are particularly nice in climates with strong, relentless sunshine. The light-diffusing properties coupled with the durability of wood make them very attractive. Slats can be placed close together or as far as 6 inches apart, and the depth of the slat can be $1/4$ inch to 3 inches, overlapping or grooved to fit together.

The problems with lattice screens lie mainly in the fact that nighttime privacy is not ensured and the insulative properties for colder-climate applications are poor.

Pierced Oriental Screens

Many import stores and wholesale design sources carry a variety of woven or pierced oriental screens. Mainly imported from India, pierced screens are ornately carved folding, free-standing units. They can be placed in front of windows to allow pinholes of light to penetrate into the room in an interesting pattern, creating an exotic background. Prices vary according to quality, but they are generally within most budgets. These screens can, of course, be used for other purposes, such as for room dividers.

The pierced screen rates high as a shading device but low as an insulation device. The screens are cumbersome to move and usually are left in one place, blocking the view on a semipermanent basis.

Shoji Screens

Shoji screens and Chinese screens are categorized together because they are constructed in the same manner: a wooden frame and grid or fretwork pattern made of wood strips is glazed with rice, mulberry, or other oriental paper (see fig. 4–4). Japanese shoji screens are popular in many Western interiors and often are used where a high-quality, classic, and slightly exotic look is desired. As shown in figure 4–4, shoji can be simple or complex in design. The workmanship will vary depending on the selection of moderately priced, factory-made screens versus expensive screens created by master craftsmen.

It should be noted that in Japan, several specialized crafts are involved in the making of shoji screens. These specialties include staining or lacquering the wood, making the paper by hand, forming the brass finger-pulls (hardware), fitting together the stiles, tracks, and lattice, and hanging the paper. Each requires a long apprenticeship under experienced masters. Although they may appear simple to some, the crafts involved in making authentic shoji require great attention to detail, and impatience and shortcuts will always yield inferior results. The client who wishes to incorporate authentic, high-quality shoji screens as window treatments will likely have an appreciation for fine design and workmanship, and a budget to accommodate it.

A distinct charm and mystique endures in the shoji screen. It symbolizes the historic Japanese values of dignity, gentility, and serenity. Many Westerners have learned to appreciate these values greatly within the past several decades, through significant oriental influences in architecture and the decorative arts. With a classic combination of materials and a precise organization of rectangles in pleasing proportions, shoji screens provide constant diffused light, which is quite desirable in many settings. They also provide a fair amount of privacy. Sliding shoji screens open and close quietly, maintaining a sense of tranquility.

A study in planes and symmetry, shoji screens may be simple, unadorned, and structural, or complex, decorative, and ornamented. The latticework of the shoji can be custom-designed (by the designer or architect) to suit nearly any decorative taste. The paper may be removed to expose the latticework, which might be incorporated into an architectural theme. The paper also may be replaced with an opaque or translucent cloth for a different effect.

An even more solid appearance can be obtained by replacing the paper and latticework with a wood panel that can be left natural, stained to accentuate the wood grain, or painted with a landscape or oriental design (such as a fruit blossom branch, an orchid pattern, or a design inspired by a fabric or carpet pattern). Or the solid wood can be pierced with a special design. Although far from traditional, even stamped, tooled, or pierced light-gauge sheet metal or macramé can be used in place of or in conjunction with the paper and latticework.

All the screens illustrated in chapter 4 may be used as either sliding partitions (see figs. C-1 and C-2) or as hinged, free-standing, or folding units (fig. 7–29). Folding shoji screens are lightweight, portable, and easily stored—an ideal treatment for people who rent or who move frequently. They are made in the same way as sliding shoji, except that the individual panels are proportionately taller. The "ears" are cut off flush at the top

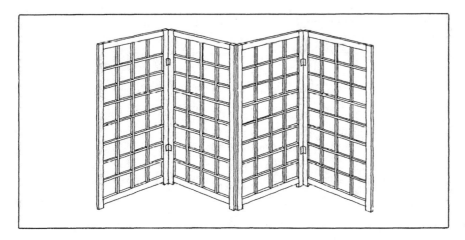

7-29 A free-standing four-panel shoji screen with square grids.

but extend slightly at the bottom to keep the lower rail off the floor and to protect the screen. The panels should be made in even numbers and may be attached with single hinges (that fold one way) or double-action hinges (that fold both ways).

When shoji are used as sliding screens, they are mounted in tracks. The number of shoji panels can be determined by the designer according to the standard sizes offered by manufacturers, or in consultation with a shoji craftsman who builds entire screens for American or Western interior design jobs. While the traditional dimensions of shoji are approximately 3 feet by 6 feet, the size may vary according to needs. Remember that narrower panels make a room look taller, while wider panels make a room look more spacious.

Figure 7–30 illustrates some standard shoji stacking and folding arrangements. It is important to note that there is an overlap in sliding screens that equals the width of the stile, or vertical member of the shoji frame.

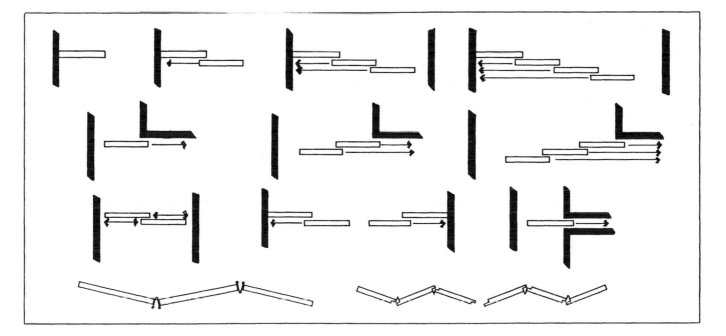

7-30 Standard stacking and folding arrangements for shoji screens. The sliding screens overlap slightly to the width of the vertical frame stile. Small-panel screens have rabbeted stiles that interlock to prevent a light strike between the panels.

As shown, this stile width will need to be added to the width opening when the width of each screen or panel is determined. A simple equation for figuring the width of custom-made screens is as follows:

$$\frac{S + (SW \times OL)}{P} = IPW$$

S = Span distance (width of opening)
SW = Stile width (vertical frame member)
OL = Number of overlaps (see fig. 7–30)
P = Number of panels (use an even number for symmetrical stacking)
IPW = Individual panel width

This formula will be used by the designer who is taking custom measurements and supplying to the craftsman or manufacturer the exact dimensions for making shoji screens for a custom installation. Also, remember that the shoji tracks may be recessed into the floor and ceiling, and this will make the screen longer than the standard floor-to-ceiling measurement. Here it is wise to consult with the installer or craftsperson for precise dimensions for recessing the tracks. Figure 7–31 illustrates a very wide sliding door or picture window arrangement and shows the placement of the track and the stacking shoji pairs on each side of the glass.

Solid Panels

Discussed above is the possibility of building a shoji screen frame and filling it with solid wood or sheet metal rather than with paper. Solid panels at the window can take many forms, and again, there is a great deal of latitude in design. Standard wood, steel, or fiberglass doors can be used as sliding panels at the window, as can sliding or hinged insulating solid-shutter panels. Although solid panels will block all light and view, and may possibly be cumbersome to move and perhaps take up needed wall space,

7-31 Shoji screens at a sliding glass patio door.

a Patio door or picture window flanked by shoji screens.

b Horizontal cross section shows track and stacking location of two shoji screens on each side of the glass.

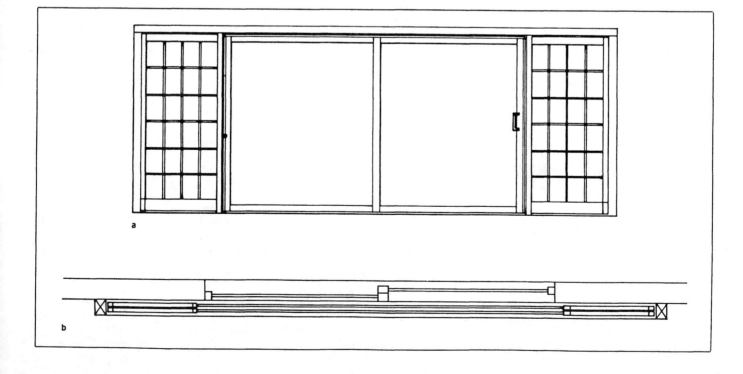

a

b

solid panels have some distinct advantages. For example, solid panels at the window guarantee privacy when closed, darken the room for sleeping or viewing media (such as television, video, movies, and slides), and are good insulators. From the interior design and decoration standpoint, the greatest plus is the possibility of surface ornamentation: decorating the panel with fabric, wall covering, tooling, or painting.

SURFACE ORNAMENTATION

An examination of hard treatments would not be complete without a discussion of the creative possibilities of paint at the window in the form of folk painting and stenciling. These two historic forms of ornamentation have been used as decorative trim around window frames, on roller blinds, and on wood shutters and wood vertical-louver blinds with great success. Often a bit of Old World charm in the right setting can add a finishing touch that can be accomplished in no other way.

Folk Painting

Folk painting is a common art form that originated in Europe and has become quite popular in America with the 1980s revival of "country" art and interior design. One form of folk painting, Norwegian rosemaling, is seen in figure 4–28.

This renewed interest in folk painting is generally based on the many traditional European styles, expanded and adapted to American or Western tastes. While it is true that some bad design or poor-quality artwork exists due to the amateur element inherent in folk painting, there also are some beautifully conceived and executed forms that can enhance window treatments.

Wood treatments are the ideal medium, since folk painting is traditionally and most easily executed on wood. The designer who incorporates folk painting in an interior will likely commission a folk artist to employ certain styles and colors but with an interpretation and skill that belongs only to the artist. Possibly the designer may see a picture in a magazine or book and instruct the artist to duplicate it exactly. This approach, however, may reduce the artistic endeavor to mere copy work.

Classic or recognized forms of folk art include the following categories.

German and Bavarian Folk Art

German and Bavarian folk art uses large-scale bold patterns, flowers, and scrolls (fig. 7–32a). Colors are rich, deep, and vivid—sometimes even intense.

Swiss Folk Art

This is done on a much more delicate scale with a prevalence of hearts and dainty flowers, such as edelweiss. Within this category falls *alpbach,* which is a style that originated in the "back of the Alps." It differs from other European pieces in that the wood is first stained to a mellow patina. Patterns feature birds, scrolls, and such flowers as tulips, carnations, and edelweiss in asymmetrical, lined arrangements.

French Folk Painting

French folk painting has softer colors and features many scrolls, birds, and flowers on a delicate, feminine scale.

English Folk Painting

These pieces have colors that are dulled or neutralized, with gardens, architecture, and historic costume as the basis for their designs.

Russian Folk Painting

These pieces are unique among the European styles. Wood or black backgrounds are painted in light, airy pastels and edged in gold or bronze. The effect is stunning and incredibly rich—at once delicate and dramatic.

Gypsy Folk Painting

Gypsy folk painting has the style and flavor expected of these European nomads. Painting is bright, colorful, and exotic. Lines among the floral arrangements flare out in loose scrolls, giving an exciting, vibrant, and handsome effect.

Scandinavian Folk Painting

Scandinavian backgrounds usually are painted a dark color with designs that vary from light and delicate to bold and vivid. The style that has become best known is called Norwegian rosemaling (flower painting), and it is based on S and C shapes and floral forms (fig. 7–32 b–c). Traditional colored backgrounds are dark teal blue, blue, green, black-green, and black, with contemporary colors: medium blue, teal blue, olive green, off-white, and gold.

7-32 Examples of folk painting.

a German floral pattern, an example of European folk painting that can be used around the window or on a hard window treatment as surface ornamentation.

b Norwegian rosemaling in the Rogaland style showing Rococo scrolls.

c Norwegian rosemaling showing Telemark-style scrolls.

d American folk painting in the Pennsylvania Dutch (Deutsche) style, also called tole work.

American Folk Painting

This style evolved as settlers experienced a cross-influence of pure styles from Europe. Two styles that have survived and been revived from colonial America are Primitive and Pennsylvania Dutch or tole painting. Contemporary folk art includes country, dot, and realistic painting. Each of these styles bears separate mention:

- *Pennsylvania Dutch,* or *tole,* work is primarily German in style with some influence of Netherlands Dutch. Colors are bright and cheerful, sometimes lightened into tints and pastels. Motifs are simple arrangements of hearts, scrolls, dots, and flowers—mainly tulips and carnations (fig. 7–32d).

- *Country* is a style that evolved from Old World landscapes and farm scene paintings of buildings, water mills, animals, fruits, vegetables, and grain. Colors range from vivid to dull and often are antiqued, or splattered with stain to look old and homey. Within this, *dot art* is a form of country painting in which dots make up flowers, leaves, and accents.

- *Realistic* painting has a magical, almost fairy-tale quality, in which scenery or landscapes are almost too beautiful to be true—children are cherubic; floral arrangements are misty and glistening with drops of dew and look so real that they beckon us to share their fragrance and fragile beauty.

Oriental-style Painting

Oriental-style painting is highly artistic and carefully planned. Featured are Japanese nature forms—cherry and plum branches in full blossom, pine branches, songbirds and exotic phoenixes, peacocks, butterflies, bamboo—Mt. Fuji, women in kimonos with elaborate headdresses, waves, and clouds. The forms can be realistic or stylized, but the overall effect is asymmetric and quite stylized. Chinese motifs include architecture and fretwork forms, mountains, garden and water scenes, and men dressed in long silk robes. Orchids, chrysanthemums, peonies, and other exotic flowers are favored. The effect is clean, light, and uncluttered, with little detail. Fusuma screens are interior shoji screens block-printed or hand-painted with Japanese or Chinese motifs.

Stenciling

Stenciling, a charming colonial surface ornamentation, is shown in figures 4–12 and 4–13. Those motifs are typically New England and represent a selection of many that are considered classic and tasteful in provincial settings. Stencils are patterns cut out of thin, flexible materials, such as plastic or waxed paper, on which paint is applied with a round, flat-bristled brush or pad. A variation of stencilwork is air-brush painting, where the paint is blown through a nozzle for a light, airy, unfinished look.

The designer who incorporates stencilwork will hire a stencil artist and commission a job in a custom combination of colors and patterns. The artist may use existing stencils or may create new ones to coordinate with interior furnishings, particularly fabrics, rugs, and wall coverings. Favored Early American stencilwork often is done in a Pennsylvania Dutch style, with hearts, tulips, carnations, birds, vines, and dainty bouquets as favored motifs. Of course, motifs from around the world, as well as contemporary designs, are all good candidates for stencilwork.

Stencilwork is ideal for window shades of fabric or vinyl (use a paint that will adhere to the vinyl); as a trim around the window frame (see fig. 4–13); and on curtains, valances, Roman shades, or other fabric treatments, as well as on shutters, vertical blinds, and panels.

Art Glass

Art glass is a both a window because it is glass and a hard window treatment because it treats the glass with pattern, texture, and color, and obscures view. Many written works examine the origins, history, and evolution of stained, leaded, and beveled glass. It is beyond the scope of this book to delve into this fascinating and complex history, but consult the bibliography at the end for sources that treat the subject in depth.

Art glass turns a lovely piece of original artwork into a spectacular play of light, shadow, and hue that delights the eye, and can cheerfully enhance or dramatically dominate the design of an interior. As the light of day or night changes, so do the intricacies, nuances, and moods of the glass. Many observers find the continual metamorphosis of pattern, texture, color, and light emotionally uplifting, as well as aesthetically pleasing.

Art glass often needs no other window treatment when the pattern obscures a clear view of the interior from outside; similarly, when the view looking out is undesirable, art glass is a good choice. Art glass may be hung in front of or leaned against plain glass—a good alternative when the occupant is not permanently residing in the home or office and wishes to remove the glass easily. From either the inside or the outside, supplemental spotlights can be used to augment the beauty of art glass.

The designer may custom-design art glass or may select from patterns designed by the stained-glass artisan who is commissioned to do the work. Art glass is planned to coordinate with color schemes and the overall design of the interior. Often a design will come from a wonderful patterned fabric, rug, wall covering, or treasured piece of artwork. Other sources for inspiration include glass seen in interior design and craft magazines and in actual installations. The designer will benefit from observing what light does to color combinations and designs during different times of the day.

Art-glass supply sources will be able to provide names of artisans. Word-of-mouth and printed advertising, such as the telephone yellow pages, are other ways to find custom artisans. Art-glass costs are charged on a per-foot basis and will vary according to the geographic area, the artisan's expertise and fame, and the type of glass used. Plain glass will be less expensive than specialty types. These include antique glass, which has random streaks for an "old" look; reamy glass, which also is streaked; bubbled, or seedy, glass, which contains round or elongated air pockets; striated glass, which is etched with lines; sanded glass, which is rolled onto sand for an irregular texture; crown glass; cylinder, or muff, glass; and sheet glass (see chapter 1). Art glass also may be decorated by painting, etching, sand blasting, engraving, and even layering the glass in different colors or encasing it in layers of gold or silver. When encased glass is etched or engraved, the effect is jewel-like and spectacular.

Art glass, particularly beveled glass, also is a stock item. Companies that specialize in stock art glass and imitation art glass (Plexiglas) panels sell only to the trade. Furthermore, art glass can sometimes be salvaged from old buildings, and the authenticity adds to its value. Contact professional salvage companies for information.

The cost of installing the glass is separate from the purchase price. Often art glass is sandwiched between sheets of plain glass to protect it, to make the window more energy-efficient, and to make cleaning easier.

Samples of both historic and contemporary art glass are illustrated in figures 4–18, 4–20, 4–25, 4–31, 4–34, 4–36, 4–37, and 4–39. Chapter 4 describes the periods to which these pieces belong.

Glass Block or Architectural Glass

Architectural glass, shown in figure 4–38, is more than just window glass. Glass block is a structural building element that gives translucence to an interior and is used to compose an interesting arrangement of squares and geometric forms in an often artistic manner. Having made a strong comeback after several years of nonpopularity in modern architecture, it is used as an integral part of a design statement and as a practical means of admitting light without glare and with a measurable amount of privacy. Glass block also is incorporated into curved walls, to emphasize an unusual architectural shape.

Chapter 8   HARD AND SOFT: COMBINING WINDOW TREATMENTS

As discussed throughout this book, many factors go into the selection of just the right window for a particular setting. However, many of the most interesting treatments are not immediate success stories, but rather ones that evolve from a basic window treatment that satisfies some of the requirements for function, energy consciousness, and beauty, into something more than basic. For example, a basic treatment may be a shade or blind that provides privacy and light control and serves as a shading device. A single treatment such as this often is selected with economy in mind. Later, after a period of postoccupancy evaluation, the owner or occupant has had time to live with the treatment and evaluate what further goals, if any, need to be accomplished at the window. The customer may then call back the designer or decorator and request that the treatment be layered with another treatment, perhaps to carry out a decorative theme, to diffuse daylight, or to guard against winter heat loss. Layering treatments is done by adding an undertreatment or an overtreatment, either hard or soft.

The miniblind often is chosen to cover all the windows in a home; the look is sleek and neutral, and light and privacy are easily controlled (see chapter 7). However, the miniblind by itself can look hard and cold, and it does little to carry out decorative schemes. Popular soft treatments for layering over the miniblind include curtains, draperies, top treatments, and custom-made fabric shades. Popular hard treatments that also serve as undertreatments include Venetian blinds, micro-miniblinds, vertical-louver blinds, shutters, roller shades, and pleated fabric shades.

Two, three, and sometimes four layers at the window are not uncommon, and even five layers are feasible. In figure 8–1a, a traditional residential window is draped with separated tiebacks and topped with an upholstered wood cornice or a padded all-fabric pelmet. The treatment is handsome, well proportioned, and architecturally supportive with its relatively clean, straight lines. Beneath the tiebacks, sheers are stacked so that daylight and view are unencumbered and can be frankly enjoyed. The clear glass also may permit sunshine to penetrate through the glass, giving warmth to the interior. The fabric surrounding the window softens the lines and provides comfort.

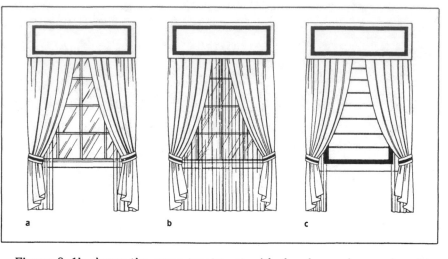

8-1 *Utilizing layered window treatments.*

a *Tieback draperies and sheers drawn open allow sunshine and a clear view outside, making the most of natural light.*

b *Sheers closed to give daytime privacy, to cut solar gain, or to diffuse excessive sunshine. The upholstered cornice can keep built-up heat from coming into the room.*

c *Insulated Roman shade hidden behind the top treatment.*

Figure 8–1b shows the same treatment with the sheers drawn closed to give daytime privacy, diffuse light, and provide some means of shading the interior against direct solar gain in the summertime. The upholstered cornice or padded pelmet can prevent direct solar gain, or heat amplified through the glass, from entering the room through the top of the treatment if the top of the treatment is mounted onto the ceiling or onto a cornice board.

Figure 8–1c again shows the same treatment, this time layered with an insulated Roman shade. The shade gives nighttime privacy and can darken the room for daytime sleep or to eliminate light for viewing movies. The shade also provides insulation against solar gain in the summer and against heat loss in the winter. The banding, seen on the shade, cornice, and ties around the tiebacks, serves to bring the treatment together aesthetically.

SOFT PLUS SOFT

Soft fabric window coverings often are combined for many reasons. Fabric layered with fabric creates an ambience, a softness, and a sophistication that can be achieved only with textiles. Textures that are elegant and sensual—such as textured silk (silk-like polyester), or rayon/acetate combined with an underdrapery sheer—create an aura of richness. When compounded with an appropriate and well-proportioned fabric top treatment, the window can assume grandeur and importance.

Fabric has for centuries made a statement. It says that the homeowner seeks privacy and enclosure and perhaps is providing evidence of status or wealth. Indeed, some fabrics are so expensive (hundreds of dollars a yard) that only the wealthy can afford to be generous with them. However, fabrics exist at every price level; and at every price level the wise selection of textiles can contribute depth and luxury to an interior.

Figures 8–2 and 8–3 show soft-plus-soft treatments that express a restrained formality. Figure 8–2 shows pinch-pleated overdraperies with underdraperies. The overdraperies may be of an opaque fabric that will be drawn to ensure nighttime privacy, to darken the room, or to insulate against outside heat and cold. The overdrapery also may be a sheer or semisheer fabric, such as a novelty weave casement, a lace, or even a plain or printed fabric. If so, then the underdrapery would likely be a privacy drapery that is drawn only at night or for protection against periods of extreme heat or cold. The privacy drapery might be white, off-white, or colored fabric; it also might be constructed from an insulative

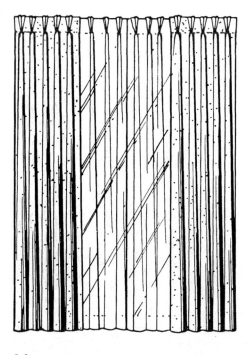

8-2 *Sheer underdrapery with opaque overdrapery is a simple but effective treatment combining more that one layer of fabric. The weight, color, and texture or pattern of the fabric gives individuality to this standard treatment.*

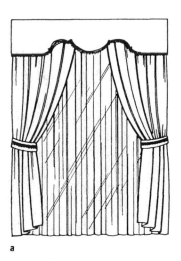

a

b

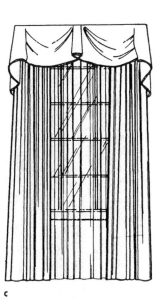

c

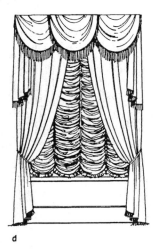

d

e

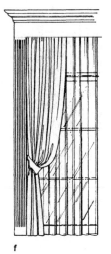

f

g

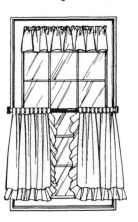

h

8-3   Fabric-on-fabric treatments.

a   Fabric treatment with four layers—upholstered cornice, overdrapery, sheers, and privacy draw drapery. The tiebacks here are separated and act as stationary side panels.

b   An elaborate layered fabric treatment with festooned bell valance, overdraperies, and underdraperies that draw into the bay window.

c   A simpler version of figure 8–3b with side bells extending into cascades; a formal, symmetrical treatment.

d   An Austrian sheer shade edged with a tiny ruffle repeats the generous depth of these formally balanced swags and cascades. Heavy fringe and deep top treatments were hallmarks of the Empire and Victorian periods.

e   Narrow shirring on an Austrian sheer gives theatrical drama to this overlapped shaped pelmet with flaglike cascades.

f   A partial view of an elegant tied-back side panel gracefully held with a shaped tie over sheer underdraperies. Architectural millwork frames the treatment.

g   Bishop's sleeve side-panel curtains flank this pouf shade. The set is topped with a wide shirred valance.

h   Ruffled cottage curtains are threaded onto a café rod with tabs and slid open and closed by hand. Above, a simple shirred valance softens the top of this traditional sash window.

black-out fabric. This treatment is typical of quality hotel rooms and non-residential suites because it softens or deadens interior noise, and because the volume of fabric gives a feeling of security and richness.

Figure 8–3a shows separated tiebacks topped with an upholstered cornice or fabric pelmet. Beneath the tiebacks is a sheer fabric, and beneath the sheer fabric is a privacy drapery. This look is quite formal—nearly always the case when sheer fabrics are combined with satinlike overdraperies and edged with trimming such as gimp, braid, or fringe.

Lavish richness is evident in figure 8–3b. This fabric-on-fabric treatment reveals underdrapery that traverses inside the bay window, with overdrapery and an extended bell valance edged in fine fringe.

A similar three-layer fabric treatment on a narrow window, illustrated in figure 8–3c, has side bells that extend downward into cascades.

Two treatments revived from the American Empire period are shown in figure 8–3 d–e, where generous swags and cascades are edged with deep fringe over the top of sheer Austrian shades, suggesting posh elegance and rich, formal furnishings.

A more restrained formality is evident in figure 8–3f, where a gracefully shaped tie secures the slender side panel installed inside a wooden cornice flanked with a fluted pilaster. Here the fabric window treatments balance the architectural millwork with softness.

Figure 8–3g shows a feminine layered fabric treatment: a balloon fabric shade and tiered bishop's sleeve, or teardrop side-panel, curtains with a shirred valance. Fabric with fabric also can be provincial or countrylike. Figure 8–3h shows a simple café curtain held onto a rod with tabs, with a simple shirred valance.

HARD PLUS SOFT

In the 1970s and 1980s hard treatments enjoyed a surge of popularity at the window. Fabric was swept aside in favor of treatments that needed no trips to the dry cleaner or washing machine, that had materials and components which would never need replacing, and that could provide privacy and light control without unnecessarily occupying stackback wall space when opened. Entire homes were, and still are, outfitted with miniblinds, vertical-louver blinds, pleated shades, and shutters, with more than occasional appearances from woven-wood shades, roller shades, and screens.

However, as time passes and as people live out the first year or two in their new homes, they often realize that something is missing—the softness, pattern or texture, and quiet that only fabric can offer. Yet few are willing to give up the hard window treatment because of all its many advantages. Logically, then, comes the combining of hard and soft window treatments.

Although hard and soft treatments can work nicely together, not every hard treatment is appropriate with every soft treatment, and careful evaluation is the key to creating successful combinations. It is helpful to discuss each hard treatment in terms of the kinds of soft treatment that will combine with it to yield satisfactory results.

Venetian Blinds

Venetian blinds are larger in scale and the historical forerunner of miniblinds. They combine well with heavy draperies that are tied back or hung straight. Period valances also are appropriate over Venetian blinds, as are asymmetrical treatments in opaque or textured sheer fabrics. Some medium- to large-scale patterned and heavily textured fabrics (nubby weaves) will do well, too, and even very slick, satiny fabrics can be attractive over Venetian blinds. Figure 8–4 shows an Empire-inspired drapery over Venetian blinds.

Miniblinds

Perhaps the most versatile of all hard treatments, miniblinds can quite easily be combined with nearly any style of treatment, from the straight lines of plain or slightly textured pinch-pleat draperies (fig. 8–5a) to the fussiness of Priscilla curtains (fig. 8–5b). Miniblinds can be layered over with Roman or pouf shades or can be installed over the top of roller shades for added window insulation. Miniblinds with a soft valance (fig. 8–5c) or with an upholstered cornice or lambrequin that frames the window (fig. 8–5d) also can soften hard lines. Miniblinds, however, look sleek and contemporary, and, although they can be placed under sheers, there will be times when the formality or historic flavor of a room will preclude them.

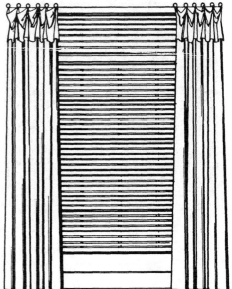

8-4 Venetian blinds, shown here without the wide tape, can make a bold statement. Here they are softened with self-valance draperies with loose pleats attached to café rings.

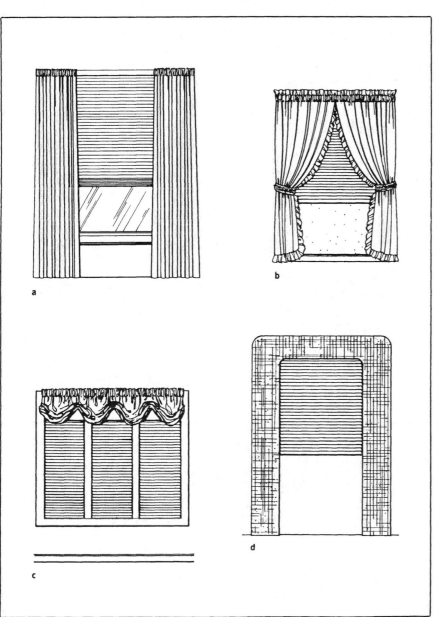

8-5 Miniblind treatments.

a A simple approach to window dressing, shown here as a miniblind with shirred curtains without ruffles.
b A fussier look may likewise be achieved with miniblinds as a privacy undertreatment. This beruffled tieback is a center-meet Priscilla curtain.
c This balloonlike valance provides a graceful counterpoint to the frankly structural lines of the practical miniblind.
d A lambrequin or cantonniere is a three-sided upholstered cornice that extends to the floor, seen here as a frame around a miniblind.

8-6 A soft-fold Roman shade echoes the fine horizontal lines of the accompanying miniblind.

Micro-miniblinds

Micros have a slightly finer, more delicate look and will blend with lightly scaled fabric treatments and furnishings. Choose lightweight fabrics in pleated, shirred, or smocked headings. A soft fabric treatment is often quite compatible with these 1/2-inch-slat blinds. Figure 8–6 shows a soft-fold Roman shade over micro-miniblinds.

Wood Blinds

In America, the wood blind dates to the early Georgian era, when it was often stained a rich cherry or walnut color. It was, essentially, the first Venetian made of wood, complete with wide tape to hold the slats together.

In the 1970s and early 1980s, the wood blind held little interest because it was cumbersome and costly compared with the miniblind. Two factors have brought the wood blind back into favor: the influence of the Territorial Southwest (Santa Fe) style, and the general willingness today to spend more money on window treatments to achieve a desired look. The wood blind combines the streamlined look of miniblinds and the richness of wood. Figure 8–7a shows the Southwest influence in wooden pegs and the softly thrown-over appearance of this informal American Empire–originated festoon. A similar yet more formal variation is seen in figure 8–7b. This treatment hangs best if each festoon and side panel is constructed separately, then fastened together with hook-and-loop tape. Figure 8–7c shows 2-inch-wide wood blinds with the natural wood grain exposed (stained, rather than painted) and a bit of lacy fabric hung in French Empire fashion as an abbreviated version of Napoleon's Malmaisson walls.

8-7 Wood blind treatments

a A loosely swagged fabric atop a wood miniblind creates a casual Southwest look.

b Wider wood blinds painted and used in a more formal treatment with threaded festoons attached to side panels that puddle onto the floor.

c Wide wood blinds stained to reveal the wood grain, with an embroidered valance, simply festooned.

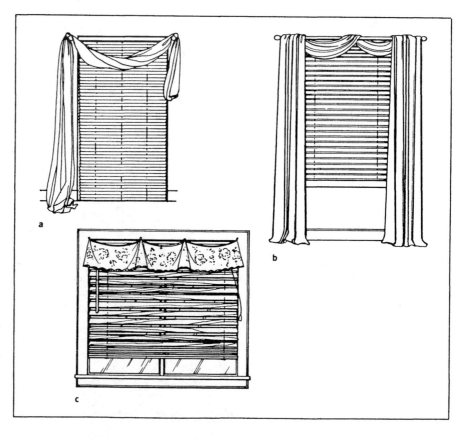

Vertical Louvers

Vertical louvers are the cleanest and most frank of the hardline treatments. The vertical lines imitate draperies, so that overdraperies may look redundant if they also are primarily vertical. The appropriateness of verticals with other soft treatments depends on the types of material used. Vinyl vanes or louvers and certain textures are clearly contemporary and will blend only with casual textured fabrics. On the other hand, some stringlike fabrics combined with formal applications can be effective under formal treatments.

Vertical louvers make dignified and handsome underdraperies without the problems of fabric. They will likely not fade; they will require no trips to the dry cleaners; they will stack out of the way and will present a clean and effective line at the window. Because of the wide variety of textures and levels of translucence, from sheer to opaque, vertical louvers can be as casual or as formal as the fabric overtreatment. Figure 8–8a illustrates a commanding Empire asymmetrical swag and cascade arrangement over vertical louvers, and figure 8–8b shows a less formal combination, with one loosely draped tieback. Certainly more standard treatments, such as evenly matched pairs of tiebacks or symmetrical top treatments, would also do well. These treatments succeed, however, because they counterpoint the strictness of the vertical lines—the first working with and emphasizing the unyielding lines; the second opposing the hard treatment with fluidity.

Shutters

Better than any other hardline, shutters cross the boundaries of time. They are equally at home with traditional as well as modern settings, and the variety of styles makes them quite versatile. Figure 8–9a shows narrow

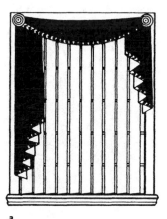
a

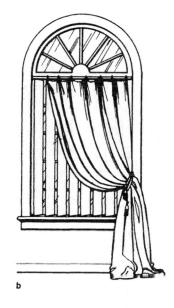
b

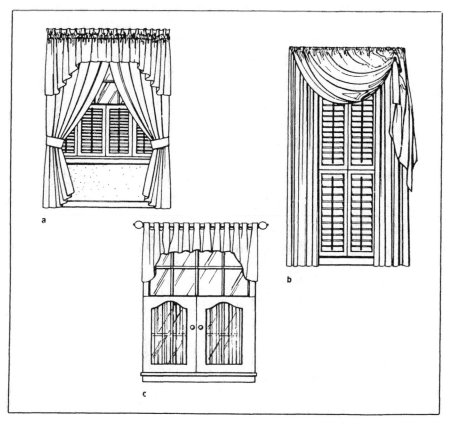

8-8 Vertical-louver treatments.

a Vertical louvers add linear strength beneath an Empire-style swag and asymmetrical cascade.

b A deeply curved tieback form is counterpointed with the vertical louvers as undertreatment. The play of curved and straight lines makes this an intriguing window treatment.

8-9 Shutter treatments.

a Single-hung café shutters provide privacy and yet allow clear light from above, filtered light below. Tieback draperies are topped with a high ruffled and shirred fabric valance, softly falling into cascades on either side.

b Plantation shutters are teamed up with generous side panels and an unusual swagged valance created from an overdrapery panel on a curtain rod.

c Arched insert-shutter frames are filled with sheer fabric. The threaded valance follows the curved lines with a wider arch of its own.

louvers beneath a formal tied-back treatment with a flowing, shirred valance. These shutters are single hung in a café fashion that gives privacy below and admits light above. Figure 8–9b shows wider louvers in a double-hung arrangement with stately side panels and a sumptuous swagged valance.

Rustic wood, or antiqued, shutters have a distinctively country flavor, while shutters painted white or light pastel colors are much more formal. Narrow louvers are considered traditional and combine nicely with tieback draperies or ruffled or tiered curtains. Wide-louvered plantation shutters rarely are used with soft treatments because they are considered a part of the structural architecture, but they may combine with draperies with simple textures and uncomplicated pleats.

Insert shutters with screens or fabric can be combined nicely with fabric, as they serve the purpose of sheer underdraperies or curtains: they diffuse light and provide a privacy screen. Figure 8–9c shows café-insert shutters with a threaded "tab" valance to soften the upper portion of the window. They also are lovely because they offer a variety of materials at the window. The color of the shutter frame and insert material should be harmonious with the drapery or curtain fabric so that the treatment appears as a whole, well-thought-out design and not as an afterthought.

Roller Shades

Roller shades are an ideal undertreatment because they are relatively inexpensive, take up little stacking space (only the size of the roller), and can be mounted next to the glass so that the shade skirt is operated behind the treatment. Opaque vinyl shades can give total privacy to any treatment; the width of the shade should not exceed 6 feet for operational reasons. Ideally, roller shades look and perform best in relatively narrow windows because they are flat (not handsome from the exterior) and because springs can break easily on wide blinds. Figure 8–10 shows a roller shade used with lavish amounts of fabric, straight and tied back. In figure 8–10a the shade appears on top of the sheer underdrapery. Roller shades also are effective combined with café treatments, such as single-hung café shutters (a traditional treatment) or a tiered café curtain. Use roller shades behind sheer or semisheer fabrics, novelty knit or woven casement fabrics, narrow tieback curtains or draperies, and even other hard treatments where privacy and energy efficiency need to be enhanced.

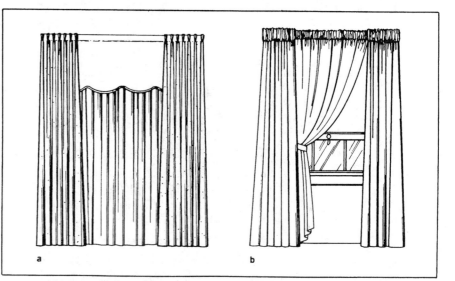

8-10 Roller-shade treatments.

a   This roller shade with scalloped hem is mounted on top of underdraperies, creating a type of inset top treatment as well as a privacy treatment.

b   Side panels and an asymmetrically tied-back undercurtain frame this straight pull shade.

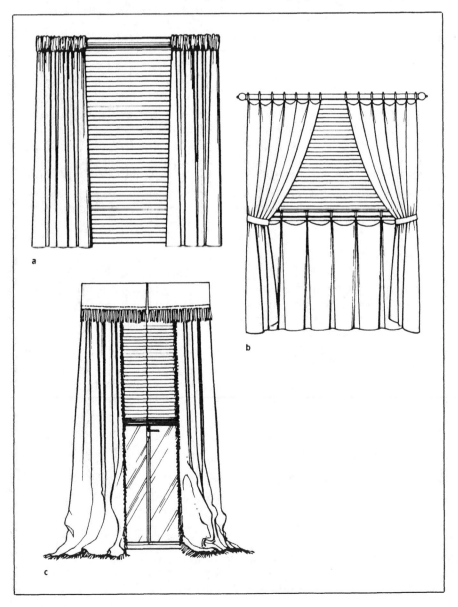

Pleated Fabric Shades

Like roller shades, pleated fabric shades take up very little stacking space. They are more handsome to view under fabric treatments, from both the inside and the outside, but only some of the fabrics are opaque. A good option is to combine pleated fabric shades with curtains in place of sheers, or where a screening treatment is needed but there is no space for another drapery rod (fig. 8–11a). Pleated shades fit neatly into the window opening and can be used above café treatments, dropping to the top, behind, or in front of a tiered curtain (fig. 8–11b). Figure 8–11c shows a formal European pelmet, deeply fringed, and side panels puddled on the floor with a pleated shade beneath.

Woven-Wood Shades

Woven-wood shades can function effectively as undertreatments. When solidly woven they can provide privacy behind draperies or curtains and can increase the energy efficiency of these treatments. Figure 8–12a shows woven woods beneath a one-way pleated drapery on a wood pole rod.

8-11 Pleated fabric shade treatments.

a Pleated fabric shades create a look similar to that of miniblinds and can provide privacy when an opaque fabric is selected. Here the shade is balanced with side curtains shirred onto a wide rod.

b A pleated shade provides sun screening and possible privacy in this tiered café curtain arrangement.

c In this formal treatment, a pleated shade is placed beneath long side panels and a fringed pelmet.

8-12 Woven-wood treatments.

a A woven-wood shade with straight-edge self-valance is companioned with a single side-panel drapery attached with rings to a wood pole rod.

b This woven-wood treatment consists of only a valance above a shirred café curtain.

Woven woods are slightly more bulky and do require more stacking space than horizontal blinds, roller shades, or pleated shades. However, the wood and textured yarn may serve to complement casual décor. More formal fabrics and settings will need careful evaluation to see that the woven-wood material is harmonious. Woven-wood shades are effective when combined with café curtains because they give privacy above, and they can even function as a café treatment when the fabric drapery is opened or when it does not give sufficient privacy. Valances of woven wood also can be used on top of fabric treatments (fig. 8–12b).

Bamboo Shades

Bamboo shades are economical undertreatments that are effective shading devices, giving daytime privacy and a degree of nighttime privacy. They are good choices behind curtains, draperies, and tiebacks (fig. 8–13) or above café treatments where the fabric or use of the fabric is decidedly casual or ethnic. Bamboo shades will lend an air of authenticity to an African, Oriental, and South Seas ambience and will combine well with fabrics that have a similar feel. While it is possible to combine bamboo shades with formal fabrics, that would be an unusual installation. It is safer and wiser to keep bamboo shades with informal fabrics.

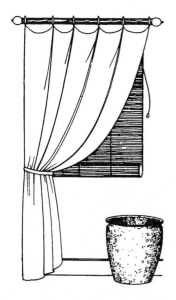

8-13 A roll-up bamboo shade mounted beneath a heavy drapery with little fullness suggests a primitive or ethnic treatment.

Pierced, Lattice, and Shoji Screens

These can be handsome beneath plain or textured fabrics or even behind printed fabrics that have an exotic or oriental pattern (fig. 8–14a). They may be placed at the window and flanked with stationary panels of fabric, topped with only a valance or cornice, or framed with a lambrequin (fig. 8–14b). Some scrutiny is necessary for combining screens with fabric at the window. Screens are structural and frank materials, and fabric might compete with or lessen the lines or the integrity of the screen, which is really meant to be used alone.

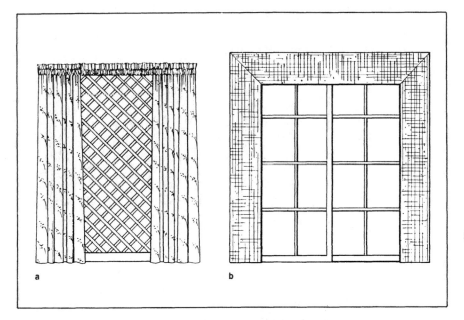

8-14 Lattice screen treatments.

a A custom lattice screen makes an exotic glare-diffusing device behind a patterned curtain.

b Sliding shoji screens framed with a wide lambrequin give importance to this large-scale treatment.

GUIDELINES FOR COMBINING WINDOW TREATMENTS

Combining soft with soft, or hard with soft, window treatments is not difficult if common sense guides the designer's decisions. While no hard-and-fast rules exist, a few guidelines may be helpful in choosing window treatment combinations.

- *Let the architecture and furnishings dictate the level of formality and the appropriateness of the style.* If the home is decorated in a grand Georgian style, then shutters with overdraperies would be a better choice than vertical louvers or bamboo shades. If the home decoration has a distinct oriental flavor, then shoji, lattice, or pierced screens will be nicer than Venetian blinds. Likewise, a formal Georgian drapery-and-shutter combination in an Oriental Modern interior would be ridiculous. Let the window treatment combination support, not detract from or compete with, the established style.

- *Stick to a theme.* Let all the elements of the treatment be compatible. This is done by judging the ambience or style of each treatment and fabric. If the overtreatment is decidedly feminine—for example, of a delicate fabric with many ruffles—then choose a hardline that complements and carries out the theme. At the opposite end of the spectrum, if the theme is to be strong and masculine, then small-scale, delicate patterns and materials should be avoided.

- *Where no definite style exists, choose combinations that will provide a neutral background suitable for a variety of furnishing styles.* Do not establish a "locked-in" decorative style at the window before any furnishings are purchased. Also, consider beginning with a basic hard *or* soft treatment that can be expanded with other, perhaps more decorative components as the interior evolves.

- *Pay close attention to the compatibility of textures.* Satins, damasks, brocades, refined velvets, and silklike textures are compatible with refined (polished wood or painted wood) shutters and screens, pleated shades, micro-miniblinds, and perhaps miniblinds. They also will work with plain or refined-texture roller shades. Nubby-textured fabric knit or woven with bulky complex or novelty yarns will be appropriate with all blinds, plain or coarsely textured roller shades, woven-wood shades, bamboo shades, pleated shades, and natural wood or painted/antiqued shutters and screens.

- *Keep proportion and scale harmonious.* Proportion refers to the size relationship between the individual parts of a window treatment or between more than one treatment. For example, very large-scale patterns may seem ponderous and heavy in comparison to delicate micro-miniblinds, and plantation shutters will overwhelm small-scale printed "country" fabrics. Proportion and scale also have to do with the amount of area covered. If draperies cover an entire wall (each side of the window) and are hung floor-to-ceiling, then a small single-hung café shutter may seem ill-proportioned compared with the quantity of fabric. Sketching the proposed treatment to scale (1 inch equalling 1 foot, for example) will give an idea of the rightness of the proportions.

- *Aim for one pattern at the window.* Be aware of fabric textures that can visually compete with a window treatment fabric that has a definite pattern. Patterns and textures need to be carefully coordinated to create a pleasing unity. Small or subtle patterns can combine nicely at the window if they are coordinated as part of a designed collection or coordinated by the designer. It is wise to keep one pattern clearly dominant, with other patterns as accents, so that competing patterns do not destroy the design integrity of the treatment.

- *Choose colors that are compatible.* This does not mean that if the drapery is beige with tiny red flowers then the miniblind should be bright red. Rather, let the most neutral of the colors in a pattern be the basis for combining hard treatments with fabric; perhaps use the red as a piping accent on the ties and let the blinds, shutters, shades, or screens match or blend with the neutral background. Use discrimination in color choices. Remember, a dull neutral color in a medium value (neither too light nor too dark) will blend best with a variety of furnishings and will be pleasing for longer. Bright, intense, or faddish colors will soon wear out their welcome, as will obvious, brightly patterned fabrics.

- *Avoid lines that compete with other lines or patterns.* If a miniblind is placed over a casement fabric with a strong vertical pattern, the effect will be confusing. The same applies for vertical louvers with a busy or horizontal design. Any time light comes through a window, the lines of hard materials and of fabric patterns and textures will be emphasized. Always hold up samples of both treatments to the window light together, so that you can judge whether a conflict will emerge. Natural light reveals much more in installed treatments than in isolated, flat samples.

- *Make sure each layer is really needed.* Here, evaluate *function.* Determine what purpose each layer will serve, and then weigh it in terms of cost effectiveness, bulk or space occupied around the window, projection into the room, and ornateness versus simplicity as compared to the architecture and furnishings.

- *Plan for at least one layer to close for complete nighttime privacy.*

- *Plan for the controls to be easily accessible.*

Chapter 9   BUSINESS MATTERS: RESIDENTIAL AND NONRESIDENTIAL

Today window treatment is a multibillion-dollar industry, the scope of which entails career opportunities at various levels for individuals motivated in the field.

The term *trade* refers to the professionals who sell window treatments to the public, namely architects, interior designers, and interior decorators. The term *industry* refers to the composite of companies that design, develop, manufacture, or market hard and soft treatments.

THE MANUFACTURER AND THE RETAILER

The window treatment business combines products and skills of both manufacturers and retailers. The acquisition, handling, and effective interaction necessary for maintaining a good client network will be discussed later in this chapter.

The Manufacturer

The manufacturer, distributor, or supplier may specialize in one type of treatment, such as miniblinds, or even a treatment component, such as louver slat material. A fabric company may perform only one aspect of fabric production, such as dyeing and printing (called a horizontal operation), or it may produce fabric from start to finish (called a vertical operation). Fabric is purchased in large quantities by distributors, or jobbers, who buy job, or entire dye lots (also called job lots), of fabric from which they produce sample books. They then sell to the trade or the retail design firm (discussed below). The term *fabric house* refers to a company with a well-known name that sells unique fabrics intended for quality interior design applications, such as window treatments, wall and furniture upholstery, and bed appointments.

Regardless of what type of manufacturing operation, product, or component is involved, the manufacturer depends on its sales representatives, or reps, to deliver samples and sell the company's lines to the trade or retailer.

The trade industry is a highly competitive entity, and, as evidenced by the appendices at the end of this book, there are hundreds of wholesale companies (called sources, distributors, manufacturers, or suppliers, depending on the line of goods they carry or produce) from which to choose. The retailer may have an account (and therefore the ability to purchase goods at wholesale) with many of these companies. However, it is always best to do the majority of one's business with as few companies as possible so that better service can be expected. A multiproduct distributor, for example, can supply many types of window coverings. When the distributor or manufacturer is familiar with a retailer because of a sizable volume of goods ordered on a continual basis, then the sales rep and the staff are willing to work harder for that retailer, supplying samples of window treatments and fabrics at reduced cost, or no cost, and pushing through rush jobs, for example. (See also "Working with the Manufacturer" later in the chapter.)

The Retailer

The retailer takes the form of architect, interior designer, decorator, general contractor, or window treatment salesperson or specialist. This person may work for a large department store chain, for an architectural or interior design firm, for a construction company, or from a home studio. The studio may even be "on wheels" because samples are routinely taken via car or van to the home or site.

The retailer is the person or firm who obtains samples and orders merchandise at wholesale from the manufacturer and sells to the public at retail. The markup, or profit margin, is at the discretion of the professional and is customarily double the wholesale price on fabric and hard window treatments but less on hardware or rods.

The professional retailer has opportunities today in both residential and nonresidential interiors. The consideration and approaches to the sale are somewhat different, and the requirements and procedures vary between these two major divisions of interior design. The similarities and differences are discussed in this chapter. While some window treatment specialists sell successfully in both areas, it is more common, and even recommended, to specialize in either residential *or* nonresidential design or even within an area of contract or nonresidential work.

Yet another professional is the specifier, a person who works independently or for a national or international corporation, such as a hotel chain, company, or business that continually builds or remodels and thus needs sizable quantities of window coverings. The specifier may find a wholesale source for the product specified by the building's architect so that the company purchases it from a retailer; or the specifier may process the order, purchasing directly from the manufacturer for the corporation.

RESIDENTIAL CONCERNS

Residential window treatments include those for detached dwellings, privately owned condominiums or flats, vacation houses or cabins, mobile homes, leisure craft or recreational vehicles—anyplace where the occupant is the owner and lives there part or all of the time. The client is the person who makes the ultimate decisions regarding who will pay for the window treatment, and who will enjoy living with it.

The successful completion of residential work owes a great deal to the relationship between designer and client. Indeed, the importance of this interaction is a primary difference between residential and nonresidential work.

Finding Clients

Those who enter the residential interior field often are overwhelmed with the initial task of finding clients. It takes time to build a real following, and much of the groundwork must be laid before any business can be conducted.

The first thing many successful professionals do is to find out all they can about their targeted market—who the potential clients are, where they live or work, what their income and general education level is, what their tastes or needs are (which, of course, may vary individually), and exactly what their expectations will be.

This information can be uncovered by reading local newspapers and magazines and by visiting other professionals who work in the area—architects who specialize in custom homes, residential general building contractors, real-estate agents, drapery installers, other subcontractors, and even lending institutions where home mortgage loans are secured. The designer should leave a stack of business cards or fliers that introduce the company; list professional services, expertise, background, and years of related experience; and perhaps even include a photograph. Leaving cards and fliers is even more effective if there is a display unit or attractive container to hold them. Fliers also can be distributed door to door or perhaps included in local newspapers. This same information may be used as the basis for Yellow Pages, newspaper, and radio ads, and for the section of the local newspaper that spotlights new businesses.

In new residential developments where there are as yet no window coverings hung, an informal door-to-door technique can be effective. The designer should be brief and never pushy. Asking for an appointment to come back with samples is the goal. Perhaps offering a free consultation (say, a half hour) for interior design and decoration ideas on the first visit will be effective. A coupon for drapery cleaning with the purchase or any free service might also lead to an appointment.

Sponsoring an open house, particularly if light refreshments are served, is a good way to increase public awareness of one's firm. Local newspapers often are happy to write articles about open houses, new or expanding businesses, or changing personnel. Further, a public marketing firm may offer advice, layouts, and advertising services as part of a marketing plan for the business.

Handling Clients

The client or customer of the residential window sales may be a single person or two or more individuals, such as a husband-and-wife team. Further, family members, in-laws, or even friends may become included in the decision-making party.

Because residential clients are obliged to pay for window treatments and to live with their choices, and because nonresidents may be involved, the decision can become an emotional and perhaps drawn-out process. Further, personalities clearly come into play in residential design. There may even be a power struggle between the husband and wife, for example, where both will have strong opinions about different window-covering solutions or about different perceptions of the needs of the interior and its occupants. These are facets of the window treatment business that the professional needs to deal with, preferably, of course, in a professional manner. Handling people well is such an important part of residential sales that success often can be pinpointed to charismatic dealings of the designer with the client, and, of course, the business finesse it takes to stay financially afloat.

Making Good Impressions

When the residential client meets an interior designer, decorator, or window treatment specialist, he or she does some mental sizing up. The first impression usually will open or close the door of opportunity with new clients, so it is important to look and act like a professional who is interested in creating individual, beautiful, and effective window treatments. The following factors contribute to good first impressions:

- *Greeting.* Make your smile genuine and extend a warm and friendly handshake.

- *Credentials.* Carry a briefcase and be handy with a business card to prove that you are a legitimate window treatment professional.

- *Neatness.* Check to be sure that your hair is neatly combed (and clean, of course). Good grooming, from clean skin and teeth to laundered and pressed clothing in good repair, says to the client that you care about your appearance and probably about your job, as well.

- *Conservative dressing.* Choose conservative clothes, manicures, shoes, and accessories, such as jewelry, attachés, and purses. Wild or outlandish colors will probably *not* make a good first impression. Likewise heavy makeup or fingernails of extreme length may be offensive to some people, giving the impression that you are all show and no performance. However, *look* well designed yourself.

- *Appropriate dressing.* If your meeting is to take place in a wealthy part of town, put on your best wool or linen suit. If it is in a new construction area, dress casually and be prepared to tromp across floor joists. You might appear ridiculous, or make the client uncomfortable, if you are overdressed for the situation. "Dress-for-success" experts say that one's clothes should largely be unnoticeable, so that attention is drawn to you, the professional, rather than to what you are wearing. Pay attention to dressing styles and mannerisms in the locale where you work.

- *Personal hygiene.* If you smoke, drink, or eat spicy food, your client should not smell it on your clothes or breath. Use breath mints, if necessary, and a cologne or perfume that is subtle. The nose is perhaps the most sensitive and commanding organ we have. It is not worth offending a client just because you craved a spicy German sausage an hour before your meeting.

- *Complimenting.* Tell the client if you like his or her living room furniture, artwork, or even poodle—anything that will convey that you are interested in his or her home. The client may relax and return the compliment, looking more favorably on you. But be careful. Always be sincere, and do not overdo it. A true professional knows when to stop talking.

- *Graciousness.* Do not criticize another professional's work. He or she may have just left a bid on the same window treatment, and your criticism may make the client defend the competitor. If the client discloses that a competitor has bid on the treatment, then tell the client what you can offer beyond the competitor's services. Perhaps you can propose to photograph the finished work for portfolio or possible publication. Or you might offer a free miniblind duster, or a coupon for a first cleaning at a local, reputable cleaning company. Of course, let the client know of cost-cutting options within your bid if price is the determining factor for winning the bid.

Sizing up the Customer

Part of making a good impression is sizing up the customer so that you can respond in a way that will build understanding and rapport. Psychologists have repeatedly analyzed personalities and have found that, although many distinct traits make each person individual, there tend to be three general personalities: amiable (friendly, trusting, and open); bombastic (aggressive, domineering, and authoritative); and conservative (factual, precise, and productive). Although there are crossover traits, and some people are a combination of all three types, often a client will fit primarily into one category.

If it is discovered that a client is amiable, then personal attention, honesty, and integrity will be paramount in your professional relationship. If the client leans toward being bombastic, then feel free to give him or her respect and admiration but with a firm hand or sense of control over the interaction. Conservative types appreciate to-the-point presentations with facts and figures written down.

Staying in Control

Because selling residential window treatments can be a group experience, a few guidelines are listed here for staying in control, which will make the situation more comfortable for everyone. These include:

- *Recognize a group spokesperson.* The person who actually will live with the treatment, who will pay the bill, or who obviously is the voice should make the final decisions.

- *Choose a proper position.* When working with a husband and wife, position yourself in front of them or sit nearer to the wife; never sit between them. This will avoid putting you in the awkward role of referee or of making you appear to favor or patronize. Address both spouses and treat them with equal respect. If the couple cannot agree, then politely suggest that they work out their conflict and set up a return appointment.

- *Turn objections into advantages.* Use a statement such as, "I am glad you asked that question. I can see that you have thought this aspect through." Then you will have more opportunity to explain the merits of the treatment, justify the cost, or reverse whatever the objection may be.

- *Look for hidden concerns.* Often an objection will be voiced, but there will be a more important concern unspoken. The professional should try to discern whether an objection to the color, for example, is actually insecurity about an entire color scheme or perhaps even about the price.

- *Remain optimistic.* The most important aspect of staying in control is to assume continually that the client *will* buy from you. Whenever 9a negative comment is made, counter it with a positive comment.

- *Learn to recognize body language.* For example, if clients cross their legs, widen their eyes, or sit back or otherwise relax, then you have made your point and the customers are agreeing with you.

These few guidelines can help you to be less frustrated when problems in selling arise and to learn to enjoy the challenges.

Closing the Residential Sale

The designer or decorator often will begin by discussing options and showing samples or by sketching the finished product. Next, he or she will take measurements and compute yardages and prices. Finally, he or she will write the sales receipt and take the order including the customer's signature and, routinely, a deposit of up to half the total cost. In a home with many windows to be treated, this procedure can take up to several hours, and the bid may be collected and compared against a competitor's.

Because there is an inherent risk in spending a great deal of time and then losing the sale, closing the sale (obtaining a signed order and deposit) is crucial to the success of window treatment specialists or interior designers. There are many ways to close the sale, and, although the topic is beyond the scope of this book, the skills involved are worth the effort to learn. Many good books have been written solely on the skills and techniques of salesmanship. Also, sales seminars are sponsored by many different organizations throughout the country, and these can be of great help to the window treatment specialist.

NONRESIDENTIAL CONCERNS

Nonresidential or contract window treatments are those installed in the following areas:

- *Offices:* including law and medical offices and government facilities—in both small and high-rise buildings.

- *Institutions:* including health care, medical, and geriatric facilities; schools; colleges; and universities.

- *Hospitality:* including hotels; motels; restaurants; and leisure and entertainment facilities.

- *Industrial:* including large fabricating, research, technology, and light-industry buildings.

- *Retail:* including department stores, boutiques, and malls. (This area may call more often for exterior treatments, such as logo awnings or rolling shutters.)

- *Model homes and condominiums:* including developments where the client is not the occupant.

The window treatment professional may specify for or sell to clients in all these areas, or, more commonly, may specialize in one area. Many professionals specialize even further, working on only government contracts or high-rise office buildings, for example, because each area has specific needs:

- *Different requirements* (labor or building and fire-safety codes, for example).

- *Different procedures* (paperwork and bidding processes, for example).

- *Different labor requirements* (union versus nonunion).

- *Different pricing structures* based on markup (cost plus a percentage), markdown (retail less a percentage), and quantity (which affects prices).

- *Different types of authority personnel* (the government official or corporation board members, the developer, or the independent owner).

Knowing about and dealing with limited areas of contract window treatments is a good idea because liability has become so great. The person selling the goods has far greater responsibility for ensuring correct specifications, procedures, and installation than ever before, as is testified by the increased number of lawsuits against professionals.

Many nonresidential window treatment professionals whose practice is at least 80 percent nonresidential work are members of the IBD (Institute of Business Designers). This network organization helps the designer to become familiar with the complex requirements in contract design. The address for IBD is 1155 Merchandise Mart, Chicago, IL 60654.

Dealing with Other Professionals

A major difference between residential and nonresidential work is the cast of characters. Residential work involves a small group (and often just one person), but personality management skills are vital. In contract work there is a greater number of players.

For example, sometimes it is difficult to figure out who actually has the authority to purchase. It will vary from situation to situation; only research will determine whether it is the owner or developer, the architect, the interior designer of the entire project, the general contractor, the purchasing agent, or the tenant.

One or more of these persons will be involved in the specification/selection/ordering process, although only one person will be responsible for payment. A sizable part of the contract window-covering business, then, is people-oriented and research-oriented; it involves making contact with responsible parties and working with them toward a goal. In contrast with residential work, however, nonresidential work involves far less in the way of personal preferences, strong emotions, and advice from family and friends; it is usually just a business dealing.

The Owner or Developer

The owner or developer may or may not live in the general vicinity of the project and may or may not be involved with its construction and maintenance, but he or she may still have the final say in selecting the window treatments and paying for them.

The Architect

The architect writes the specification and may sublet construction contracts and supervise the construction of the building to ensure that it satisfies the specifications, safety codes, and goals of the owner or developer.

The Interior Designer of the Entire Project, or Project Manager

This person may not actually purchase the window treatments but may sublet that part of the contract in favor of working with the owner or architect on proxemics and human dimensions; space planning and furnishing layout; and specification of fixtures, furnishings, and finishes.

The Purchasing Agent

The purchasing agent acts for the owner or developer, for the architect, or for the general contractor. This person makes final decisions as to bid awards and may or may not be separate from the persons listed above.

The Tenant

The tenant may be the person involved in selecting window coverings, if they are not included in the building specifications. In this case more flexibility and creativity may be possible for contract window coverings, although codes and minimum specifications may still be a factor in the decision-making process.

Codes and Specifications

Codes are regulations established by national, state, and local government agencies. They are intended to ascertain, as far as possible, the safety of the people who work in or obtain services from public buildings.

Codes must be satisfied before an interior can pass building inspection and be able to open for business. Codes are met through specifications, or written criteria drafted by the architect or interior designer. The contract designer or window treatment professional will obtain a copy of the specifications, or specs, that relate to the interior in order to find a product that will meet all the requirements.

In government work the specifications take the form of an RFP, or Request for Proposals, to which the several bidders respond with itemized information on the product, the price, and the profit margin; the lowest bid usually is awarded the contract. A similar procedure is used by many large corporations or development companies. (See also "Quantities and Costs" below.)

Specifications come to the window treatment specialist as a list of criteria that dictate the following:

- *The type of treatment.* These include draperies, shades, shutters, horizontal or vertical blinds, exterior or interior shading devices, and insulative treatments.

- *The estimated or maximum cost per unit or per job.* This is given as a margin between a high (maximum) and low (minimum) dollar amount. In some cases only the maximum amount, or "ceiling," is given; in other cases no estimated or maximum amount is listed at all. (See also "Quantities and Costs" below.)

- *The minimum qualifications.* These might be fiber or material type, fiber weight or density, and fabric finishes. They even may include a specified color and texture.

- *The durability, stability, and flammability of the product.* These are based on the results of standardized tests used to meet building safety codes and architectural recommendations.

- *The tests and ratings relative to health standards, safety, aesthetic standards, and durability.* The specs may list the name of a certain test as a standard to judge materials in the submitted bid or proposal contract.

Health/Safety

Requirements are generally that materials resist the following:

- *microorganisms,* including mold, mildew, bacteria, and insects that eat or destroy the material

- *static electricity* that can damage sensitive machinery or become a fire hazard

- *fire ignition, flame spread, and smoke and toxicity levels.* Of the many available flammability tests, the best known are the Steiner Tunnel (ASTM) Test, the Chamber Test, and the Methenamine Pill (pellet ignition) Test. (This is a complex topic worthy of further research and study. Textbooks and manufacturers' literature on textiles and fibers are a good source. For more information, see the bibliography at the end of this book.)

Aesthetic Standards

Aesthetic standards that can be assured by test results include:

- *colorfastness,* or resistance to fading from sunlight exposure, cleaning, and atmospheric elements or gas. (The Fade-Ometer measures sunlight fading.)

- *drapability,* or the way a drapery fabric hangs. (A too-soft fabric will hang limply and without body; a too-stiff fabric will flare out and will not fall into pleasing folds. This can be determined by hanging a length of fabric made into a sample drapery for a few hours to several days.)

Durability

Tests for durability measure:

- *inherent strength,* or tenacity
- *flexibility* (elasticity and recovery)
- *dimensional stability* (resistance to sagging or elongation and hiking)
- *abrasion resistance* (unaffected by handling or rubbing)

Product Specifications

The term *specifications* has two meanings: the written requirements of the interior furnishings and components for the purpose of meeting building codes, as listed above, and the written list of features offered by a manufactured window-treatment product. The designer needs to be able to compare the list of requirements with the list of features. In this way a product can be selected for a proposal and price bid that will match the building specifications. The list of features, commonly called product specifications, will give information such as:

- the material used, including fiber, metal, or compound content, along with fiber content of cords, yarn, or trimmings

- the surface texture

- the degree of opacity (translucent to room darkening)

- the type and location of controls (cords or wands)

- the flammability rating (if tested)

- the sunlight susceptibility rating (if tested)

Extended Time Frame

With large projects and with new construction, designers usually work within extensive time frames. Window treatments are planned, bids secured, and contracts awarded even before ground-breaking for the new building begins. From inception to completion, a contract job may take from six weeks to three years. Interior designers and window treatment professionals who specialize in the contract market, therefore, should be people who enjoy long-range projects, doing research, and working with many people. They also need to keep abreast of new building styles and construction techniques, of the latest products and methods that improve the quality of contract window coverings, and of who is who in new construction.

One of the difficulties posed by a long time frame is the uncertainty of when to order the window treatments. If problems delay the completion of the construction or remodeling, the designer may be faced with the task of storing window coverings that have been ordered and delivered but cannot be installed. If the treatments end up in a warehouse, for example, there is the question of who will pay the storage costs and the problem of collecting money for uninstalled treatments so that the wholesale bill can be paid. If the supplier grants an extension of payment, there will be a sizable service or interest charge. Or, if a loan has to be secured to pay bills, the profits can be lost to interest payments. These stipulations must be thoroughly covered in the initial contract, which includes the length of time before completion.

In situations where the tenant has already moved in, the order-to-installation time may be similar to, or even less than, residential time frames (one to six weeks). In some cases rush jobs are requested and are feasible with cooperation from the jobber or manufacturer, if the professional has an account in good standing and regularly places large orders.

Labor Unions and Regulations

Before quoting prices on any contract installation, the window treatment professional must thoroughly investigate the requirements for union labor, including scheduling, that might affect the job. Labor unions often are required for contract installation, yet the appearance of more than one union employee to install window treatments can actually double the cost. The unions also have strict rules as to who can install or work in the interior and who must assist. Union employees are allowed only a certain number of working hours before overtime pay must be charged.

Legal Contracts and Liabilities

The legal issues of contract work can be complex and weighty. Myriad points should be considered by the professional for legal protection against designer liability. A few of these include:

- Know how long it will be before installation is expected. Who will store the window treatments until they are installed if there is a construction or completion delay? Who will pay for storage and interest charges?

- Find out who is responsible if the material proves not to be durable. (The designer may be the liable party unless otherwise legally specified in a contractual agreement.)

- Make sure the installer is able to give quality service, and know the possible legal actions if the quality falls below expectations.

- Know if there is a union involved. Legislation in this area is strong, and union regulations and rules change often. Research this matter carefully to avoid pitfalls. It is better either to be a union member or not go in on union work.

- Be certain which rooms and which windows you are bidding for. Put everything clearly in writing. Make no assumptions as to the number or the size of windows or any other aspect of the job.

- Know exactly who is responsible for payment. Find out whether there are stipulations concerning payment in full and any accrued, although unforeseen, interest charges.

- Find out who is responsible for maintenance and how far your liability goes once the job is completed.

- Obtain written documentation from the manufacturer as to how long the product should last, and obtain any warranty that might be available. Put these in writing, excluding yourself from liability; give one copy to the client and keep one for yourself in the client's file.

See the bibliography for books now on the market that dispense legal and business advice to the designer who takes on contract work.

Maintenance and Longevity

The longevity of a product in a contract setting depends on the reaction to environmental factors, the level of use and wear, and the kind of maintenance. Although dirt on a blind or shade does not affect the life span of the product, it may prematurely damage a fabric treatment. Keeping the treatment clean is important because it will prevent a buildup of airborne impurities, dirt, grease, smoke, or smog. A buildup can make the blind far more difficult to clean. More important, it can make the interior seem dirty to people who look at or through the windows. This has a psychological effect on customers or clients, as well as on working personnel. When an environment is unclean, employees may be given the impression that their work is unimportant, and clients will form a low impression of the business or organization. Keeping both hard and soft treatments clean leads the people who occupy the interior to feel good about where they are and what they are doing.

With this in mind the designer or decorator would be wise to recommend to the client a professional maintenance and cleaning company. Such companies are routinely contracted by businesses and organizations to come in on a regular basis. Another advantage to a maintenance organization is that it frees those who work at the business from trying to clean as they work, which, in most cases, is not possible anyway.

For fabric treatments maintenance involves vacuuming, shaking, and other means of keeping the surface from becoming embedded with layers of soil. Professional dry cleaning should take place only when necessary—the frequency will depend on the cleanliness of the air. Every six months is the maximum; more frequent cleaning will cause the fabric to become tender and to easily rip or fall into shreds. Recommend a dry-cleaning or maintenance company that guarantees no shrinkage.

Until recently, it was difficult to have hard treatments cleaned professionally. With the arrival of sonic-cleaning equipment, however, some maintenance companies will now take down, clean, and then reinstall hardlines, as they do for pleated draperies.

Maintenance also refers to the way the treatment is operated, with respect and care or with abuse. This aspect certainly is beyond the control of the designer, yet he or she should take steps to inform the client of the proper operation, use, and care of the treatment. Information should be in written form, and a copy should be kept by the professional as a protection against future litigation—an unfortunate, but real threat. Again, any written contract should disclaim the designer's responsibility against damage caused by misuse or rough treatment of the window covering.

Materials and Wholesale Sources

Both hard and soft materials used in nonresidential interiors must meet safety codes. Nonresidential materials are, necessarily, less decorative and more functional, durable, and practical than residential materials. Fabrics usually must have been tested for health standards, safety, aesthetic standards, and durability.

Although fewer tests exist for drapery rods and hard window treatment materials, this hardware needs to be strong enough to withstand years of use and potential abuse. Since written information about the durability of these products may not be readily available, the designer usually must rely on the manufacturer's sales representative for recommendations in meeting durability criteria.

The advantage to dealing with only a few companies that have quality products and with whom the professional does repeated business is that the rep will become a member of the professional team, willing and able to give advice on selecting the right product for the installation. The rep can give invaluable help in finding a product to meet specifications, in filling out orders, and in personally seeing through the manufacture and delivery of the goods on time. Where any information exists or can be obtained, the rep is the link between the designer and the manufacturer, and so he or she becomes a very important person in the contract window-covering business.

Manufacturers often have separate departments that handle contract treatments. They may even have a program for ready-made contract draperies that gives the design firm a competitive edge in the bidding process and simplifies cost estimating and ordering. It is important for the contract designer to search the market for sources that offer prompt service, high standards of materials and craftsmanship, and competitive prices. With few exceptions the distributor or manufacturer will be happy to answer questions concerning its products with the hope that the designer will want to select those goods. Do not hesitate to call or inquire about a product that interests you. An inquiry is not an obligation to buy anything; it is merely an opportunity for judging whether to select or reject the product.

Quantities and Costs

The number of contract window coverings can range from as few as six similar treatments to as many as several hundred. The greater the quantity, the lower the price per unit obtained from the manufacturer and passed on to the client. This is crucial because, in cases of government, corporation, or other large projects, the specifications may limit cost or give allotments for a total amount that can be expended on window treatments from the building's construction budget. This limitation forms a basis for bids that are submitted by various window treatment firms.

When the cost per unit is obtained from the manufacturer's representative, the price will then be adjusted to include a markup, such as cost plus 10 percent for large quantities or retail less 20 or 30 percent for smaller jobs. Also, the goods may be sold at wholesale, and a design fee may be charged rather than a profit margin. The variable in markup, selling price, or design fee will be determined by the parameters of each individual job. In other words each job has to be carefully evaluated before a decision is made as to what method will be used and what profit margin will be charged.

Relative Uniformity

Unlike residential installations, where every window may have different measurements and individual rooms often receive custom-designed treatments, contract installations are relatively uniform, using the same treatment at most or all of the windows. The repetition of treatments gives the exterior an orderly appearance—a relative uniformity that bespeaks the professional nature of contract interiors. Further, the measurements often are taken from blueprints, where windows are typically seen in quantities of a standard size. In contract installations all treatments tend to be identical, and the most commonly used varieties are miniblinds, vertical louvers, casement-cloth draperies, and pleated shades.

Research

Research is necessary for writing specifications and to assure the quality of the materials to be used. This is the responsibility of the architect or interior designer, who must perform research to ensure that codes and building regulations are met to the fullest degree. The specs that are followed by the interior designer or window treatment specialist also will require research in order to determine the product that will meet all the stringent qualifications. Also, the designer may be required to produce documentation proving that the product does meet those standards.

Another facet of research is the arrangement and organization of all the details that are involved in orchestrating large quantities of window treatments: ordering and documentation, receiving, storage, delivery, installation, and inspection. All these aspects must be planned in advance and must include considerations of personnel, legal matters, labor unions, and building inspection where applicable.

Closing the Contract Sale

When the window treatment specialist presents solutions and cost estimates to residential clients he or she addresses only a small number of people; the presentation in a contract situation usually involves a larger group, individually or collectively. It is possible that the presentation will be made to just one person, but a series of people may need to be contacted, one after another, and each may require a hearing of the proposal and bid. Or a group, such as a board of directors or a representative party, may collectively view the presentation. The type of presentation will depend on the audience. It may simply be a written bid or estimate, or it may entail trying to please a gathering of representatives with large samples, even sketches and color-sample boards.

Often the designer will find that a decision is not made on the spot. If competitive bids are being sought, then a number of proposals will be gathered and the deciding party will collaborate to determine which firm is awarded the contract. Often the presentation will include cost breakdowns; color-sample boards; charts, graphs, or written information of the possible effects of well-chosen or quality window coverings on employee productivity; and details about energy efficiency, life expectancy, life-cycle costing, health and safety factors, and means of meeting specifications or codes.

The contract presentation needs to be very businesslike and direct. The persons receiving the estimate usually will be quite busy and may resent prolonged discussions or lengthy persuasion techniques. However, techniques of closing the sale can be a great aid to the window treatment professional. Several good books have been written on salesmanship, and they are certainly worth the time to read.

COMMON GROUND: RESIDENTIAL AND NONRESIDENTIAL CONCERNS

Although many differences exist between the business of residential and nonresidential window coverings, there is some common ground. For both residential and contract work, the selection of and the effective working relationship with manufacturers is critical; other factors of common concern are the skills needed to stay in business and to ensure repeat window-covering sales.

Working with the Manufacturer

A productive business relationship between design firm and manufacturer or distributor is based on mutual respect and reliability. It is best to start out with a clear understanding of who is responsible for what.

The responsibilities that fall on the designer or decorator include:

- Correctly taking measurements.

- Accurately filling out the order forms, including any special features, colors, styles, accessories, or trimmings.

- Correctly noting information as to where and how to ship and when to expect delivery.

- Immediately notifying the client in case of problems, and assuming a controlled, mature attitude when working out errors. (Be careful not to accuse or offend the manufacturer.)

- Utilizing lines of communication through the sales rep.

- Promptly paying bills and expressing appreciation where needed.

Responsibilities of the sales representative include:

- Supplying the design or decorating firm with current window-covering samples, literature, and price charts.

- Acting as liaison in case of special needs, such as obtaining samples in large sizes or quantities, providing price quotes and product specifications, pushing through rush jobs, and communicating with the manufacturer in case of flawed, broken, or incorrect merchandise.

- Being accessible when needed.

The design firm should select manufacturers that can provide the following:

- A variety of window-covering products or types of fabric.

- Availability of the product without a delay for back orders.

- Good to excellent delivery time.

- Accuracy in processing orders.

- Free freight or delivery where possible.

- Warranties that indicate quality merchandise and that will be honored by the company.

- Simplicity in the operation of the product so that breakage from consumer use can be minimized.

- Pleasant personnel who are willing to service your firm cheerfully.

Staying in Business

The business of window coverings is potentially a lucrative one. It also can be riddled with problems, errors, and financial loss. Many interior design firms and departments within chain stores that have entered the window-covering field have done well; others have survived but not prospered; and still others have gotten out of the business because of the frustrations that seem to come with it. Indeed, it is not an easy way to make a living, but it can be very satisfying and even enjoyable for those who like to be involved with people, experience a change (the business is rarely dull), and earn the rewards that come from seeing interiors become more practical and beautiful.

Many good books exist that discuss business entrepreneurship, management, and marketing, some of which can be found in the bibliography and may be considered essential reading. Although it is beyond the scope of this book to discuss all elements that make up a successful design or window-covering business, three topics—finances, product, and personnel and service—merit special mention here.

Finances

A new company starting out with wholesale sources is routinely given products on a proforma or C.O.D. basis. Proforma means paying for the product in advance, with the placement of the order. C.O.D. means paying in full on delivery and will include a surcharge for the C.O.D. collector, usually the surface carrier (truck line). When a design firm has proven that it can pay, or when it has other credit accounts with good ratings, it can then request an open account with the wholesaler. This allows goods to be ordered, delivered, and subsequently billed (up to an established credit limit), with the entire bill due within thirty days. Some distributors will offer an additional 2 percent off the bill if it is paid within ten days. Paying an open account billing promptly is a key to financial success, for no company wants to lose business by having an open account canceled due to nonpayment. It is important to maintain open accounts in good standing if the design firm wishes to open new accounts with other wholesale sources. Also, when a window treatment retailer opts to use the money that is collected from clients elsewhere and not pay bills, that company will find itself seriously in debt and facing litigation plus the costs of attorneys' fees for collection.

Therefore, when money is collected from a client, the bills to the wholesaler must be paid first, then sales taxes must be set aside for payment to the state (yearly, semi-annually, or quarterly, depending on the volume of purchases). Whatever is left over is divided among wages or commissions; company overhead (rent, utilities, company expenses); and investment capital for expansion or improvement of the company.

Wages or commissions are the way that sales personnel, designers, or decorators are paid. Some firms will offer a flat salary or wage, paid every two weeks. The problem with a flat salary is that it provides no motivation to sell, and selling is what keeps a window treatments business solvent and thriving. Therefore, most companies will pay employees on a commission-only, salary draw versus commission, or salary plus commission basis.

Commission-only means that the designer or decorator is paid a percentage of the profit or of the gross sale (total before sales tax). The typical percentage of the gross sale is from 6 to 12 percent. If the actual profit on the jobs if 40 percent of the gross amount, then, say, 10 percent of the total is really about 22 percent of the profit. The advantage to commission-only positions is that salespersons will work harder, knowing it is up to them to determine how much they will earn. The owner is also protected against having to pay an employee who does not bring in the sales to cover his or her salary.

Salary draw versus commission means that a salary is ensured to the employee whether or not sales cover it. Beyond the salary, the employee is paid a commission of, perhaps, 6 percent. When sales are tallied, any salary that was drawn or paid to the employee when sales were low is deducted from excess sales. This guarantees a minimum salary while spurring the employee to keep up sales so that draw will not be deducted from commission. Essentially, this is a commission-only arrangement, only with more security for the employee. Customarily, if the designer or decorator cannot sell, then he or she loses the job and it is given to another person with more ambition or enthusiasm for selling.

Salary plus commission is the safest, most appealing offer to the designer, decorator, or window treatment salesperson. This means that the salary is guaranteed, and any sales made are paid at a commission that is added to the salary. Of course, this arrangement is somewhat risky to the employer if the guaranteed wage deters the employee from selling, but it also stands to make the employer more money, particularly if the employee is a good salesperson, because the commission is customarily less than in a commission-only arrangement. An aggressive person can actually make more on a higher commission without any guaranteed wage, although it is a risky way to earn a living.

Product

Certainly another key to success in the window-covering business is having a product that can be relied on for quality, durability, ease of maintenance, reasonable cost, and design appeal. Further, many design firms that are successful have a variety of products from which customers can choose. These firms shop around—comparing features, cost, and service offered by wholesale manufacturers—and select those with the best combination for their market. Typically the design or decorating firm will carry one to several lines of fabric for custom soft treatments and will have a good selection of hard treatments, including horizontal and vertical blinds, shutters, shades, and screens. When the manufacturer offers a discount below wholesale, then the retailer can pass that savings on to the customer as a discount from retail. Knowing that the wholesaler will repair broken or malfunctioning merchandise, and is reasonable when problems arise or miscommunications take place, also is a major inducement for selecting that wholesaler's product; the service the design firm receives is inevitably passed on to the customer.

Personnel and Service

The final key to staying in the window treatment business is the people connection. Ever so often it is the person who deals with the client who really makes the difference in whether the client is sold on the first job and comes back to do repeat business. An insightful professional can ensure success simply by implementing a golden rule: Treat others as you would like to be treated. Although there are unscrupulous people in the retail world, the truly successful window treatment person is one who is completely honest with the client and the wholesaler, who is courteous and friendly, who can take care of problems promptly, and who can treat the customer with care and respect—as if there were no other customers in the world. The ways to communicate this rapport is through:

- a pleasant tone of voice (both in person and on the telephone)
- a spirited level of enthusiasm throughout all conversations and presentations
- a quick and genuine smile (and a happy attitude)
- a sincere handshake or touch, such as a pat on the back or arm, when appropriate
- a personal interest in the client's work or family
- a promptness in returning calls or seeing to problems

The successful window-covering professional treats the wishes and demands of clients with respect, carefully listening and responding to the client's needs.

These attributes—naturally possessed or gleaned through effort and training—will lead to the kind of service that builds a real following. Rules of good service include the following:

- Be on time for appointments; call to say if you will be late, and never "stand up" a client.

- Be honest about delivery dates. If the product will take eight weeks, then tell the client. Do not tell him or her that it will take two weeks and then call to say it will be another six.

- Notify customers immediately of any delays or back orders.

- Schedule installation with consideration for the client's schedule.

- If the installer is held up on another job, let the client know of the delay.

- Inspect the finished product, take care of any problems or discrepancies without delay, and never act inconvenienced when serving the customer in this role (even when it is not pleasant). Rather, show genuine enthusiasm for the merits of the treatment. Remember that often a client is shocked with the change at the window and may take a while to accept the new treatment emotionally. (This may sound silly, but it is almost universally true.) If you can be there at the end of the installation to smooth, assure, and compliment the client on the wise decision and the beauty of the treatment, the client not only will be impressed with your service but also will be grateful and send you referrals or repeat business.

- Send reminder cards to the client about cleaning services, sales on other products, or encouragement to do yet another room.

- Keep customers posted on new products or color lines that you can endorse and sell with confidence. This will likely be appreciated.

- Send billings when the job is complete and the customer is satisfied. Be firm on collecting the full amount; do not let the customer "nit-pick" and try to lower the price once the job is complete. It is only professional to stand firm on the collection of outstanding amounts due on a window treatment. Proper billing is a part of the services that will help the customer to respect the design or decorating firm.

In the window treatment field, repeat business and referral business are important aspects of successful careers, whether part time or full time. Repeat business often is the result of satisfied customers who liked the designer, the product, and the service offered by the firm. The happy customer is almost always willing to refer you to friends and associates and will be glad to accept business cards to give to these people. The window treatment business is stimulating because of the variety of people you meet and work with. The various companies are developing and improving product features at an astounding pace, which is a tribute to the free-enterprise system. Indeed, the field itself is wide open to the aspiring and innovative person. Success is waiting.

SOURCES, TERMINOLOGY, AND REFERENCES

The following appendices, glossaries, and multipart bibliography are designed to aid the reader seeking information, products, and services related to the many specialized branches of the window treatment industry.

Appendices 1 through 11 are listings of wholesale and retail companies that serve various areas of the window and window treatment market. Some companies sell to distributors only; others sell to retailers, interior designers, architects, and workrooms. Some are exclusively retail; others do wholesale business as well; and yet others are exclusively wholesale, although they generally are glad to refer potential customers to their retail representatives and outlets. Companies listed are in no way endorsed by the author or publisher.

Two categories are purposely omitted from these listings: (1) regional and local window manufacturers and (2) independent soft treatment workrooms and window treatment specialists. These omissions are due simply to space considerations: regional and local window manufacturers number in the thousands. Appendix 1 contains a sampling of manufacturers that advertise nationally and may have local representatives; but often local glazing businesses do fine window-manufacturing work, using glass from the same sources. Consult telephone and business directories and newspaper advertising to find these companies, and do not hesitate to ask for references to establish the quality of material, workmanship, and service.

Independent soft treatment workrooms and window treatment specialists are perhaps even greater in number. A window treatment specialist may be a department-store salesperson, may be employed in a large or small interior design firm, or may be an interior designer or decorator working alone—even out of a home or vehicle. Additionally, interior design firms may offer specification and production services for window treatments. Workrooms range from large manufacturing businesses (sometimes incorporating many multi-product distributors) to small independent businesses with only a few employees. Each type has its advantages and disadvantages, and all fill particular needs. To find a reputable retailer or workroom, consult the advertising media and follow through on word-of-mouth references, as with window companies.

The products or services of individual companies are listed in nearly every one of the first eleven appendices. Some companies, however, may have additional offerings. Becoming knowledgeable about window coverings requires continual study. The industry is alive with new products and vibrant with the enthusiasm that helps to sell them. All readers of this book, therefore, have the responsibility to find out what is available and to develop a discriminating eye in the selection of appropriate windows and window treatments.

To this end as well, appendix 12 offers supplemental information on natural and man-made fibers and their comparative properties in interior design usage. And the last appendix, 13, contains valuable information on fabric construction, coloring, and finishing, to help the designer understand the aspects of making decorative fabrics into the quality goods sold today.

Following the appendices, three glossaries provide concise definitions of many of the terms used in this book. They are divided into the areas of general window treatment terminology, business and contract terminology, and names and applications for a variety of fabrics categorized by weight.

Finally, the book concludes with a bibliography for those who wish to learn more about specialized areas of the window treatment industry, from art glass to textiles. All readers are encouraged to explore the body of literature related to this multifaceted and fast-growing field.

Appendix 1   Glass and Greenhouse Manufacturers

Anderson Corporation
P.O. Box 12
Bayport, MN 55003
(Product: Windows for greenhouses/
  solariums)

Brady & Sun Inc.
97 Webster Street
Worcester, MA 01603
(Product: Greenhouses/solariums)

California Glass Bending Corp.
320 E. B Street
Wilmington, CA 90744
(Product: Architectural bent glass)

English Greenhouse
1501 Admiral Wilson Boulevard
Camden, NJ 08109
(Product: Greenhouses/solariums)

Evergreen Systems
P.O. Box 128, Highway 26
Burnet, WI 53922
(Product: Sunrooms/greenhouses)

Florian Greenhouse Inc.
584 32nd Street
Union City, NJ 07087
(Product: Greenhouses/solariums)

Gammans Industries
360 Farmel Industrial Boulevard
P.O. Box 1181
Newman, GA 30264
(Product: Custom and standard glass
  enclosures)

Hurd Millwork Co.
520 S. Whelen Avenue
Medford, WI 54451
(Products: Windows; heat-loss
  reflectives)

Janco Greenhouses
9390 Davis Avenue
Laurel, MD 20707
(Product: Greenhouses)

Kawall Structures, Inc.
37 Union Street
P.O. Box 4105
Manchester, NH 03108
(Product: Greenhouse structures)

Leisure Products Systems
P.O. Box 5853
San Jose, CA 95150
(Product: Greenhouses/solariums)

Lord and Burnham
Box 225
Irvington, NY 10533-0255
(Product: Greenhouses)

Marvin Windows
Warroad, MN 56763
(Product: Windows)

Nana Enterprises
707 Redwood Highway
Mill Valley, CA 94941
(Product: Greenhouses/solariums)

J. A. Nearing
9390 Davis Avenue
Laurel, MD 20707
(Product: Greenhouses/solariums)

Newcroft
P.O. Box 464
Morwell, MA 02061
(Product: Greenhouses/solariums)

Norco Windows, Inc.
P.O. Box 309
Hawkins, WI 54530
(Product: Windows)

O'Keeffe's
75 Williams Avenue
San Francisco, CA 94124
(Product: Greenhouses/solariums)

Peerless Products
2534 Madison Avenue
Kansas City, MO 64108
(Product: Greenhouse windows)

Pella Rolscreen Co.
100 Main Street
Pella, IA 50219
(Product: Windows and sunroom
  windows)

Plasticrafts, Inc.
600 W. Bayawd Street
Denver, CO 80223
(Product: Skylights)

Pozzi
62845 Boyd Acred Road
Bend, OR 97708
(Product: Windows)

PPG Industries Inc.
One Gateway Center
Pittsburgh, PA 15222
(Product: Glass)

Rohm and Haas
Independence Mall West
Philadelphia, PA 19105
(Product: Plexiglas)

Rollamatic Roofs Inc.
1400 Yosemite Avenue
San Francisco, CA 94124
(Product: Automated glass roof)

Roto Frank of America Inc.
Research Park
P.O. Box 599
Chester, CT 06412
(Product: Roto roof windows)

Seasonall Industries
Indiana, PA 15701
(Products: Storm windows; green-
houses)

Solar Structures
P.O. Box 100 SA
Wheeling, IL 60090
(Product: Solar greenhouses)

The Sun Co.
14217 N.E. 200th Street
Woodinville, WA 98072
(Product: Insulative window devices)

**Sunbilt Solar Products by
    Sussinan, Inc.**
109–10 180th Street
Jamaica, NY 11433
(Product: Sunrooms/greenhouses)

Sunroom Designs
Depot & First Street
Youngwood, PA 15697
(Product: Sunrooms)

**Sun System Solar Greenhouses
    Inc.**
75 Austin Boulevard
Commack, NY
(Products: Solar greenhouses/solar-
    iums)

Texas Greenhouse
2701 St. Louis Avenue
Fort Worth, TX 67110
(Product: Greenhouses/solariums)

Unisun
430 Hudson River Road
Waterford, NY 12188
(Product: Solariums)

Velux-America Inc.
P.O. Box 3268
Greenwood, SC 29648
(Product: Roof windows)

Velux-Canada Inc.
16804 Hymus Boulevard
Kirkland, P.Q. Canada H9H3L4
(Product: Roof windows)

Ventarama Skylight Corp.
75 Channel Drive
Port Washington, NY 11050
Also:
140 Cantiague Rock Road
Hicksville, NY 11801
(Product: Ventilating skylights)

Wasco Products Inc.
P.O. Box 351
Sanford, ME 04073
Also:
P.O. Box 734
Ennis, TX 75119
(Product: Sky windows)

Wausau
1415 West Street
Wausau, WI 54401
(Product: Windows for greenhouses)

Appendix 2   Energy-Efficient Treatment Companies

AB Sani-Maskiner
P.O. Box 9042
Jagersrovagen 202
S-200 39 Malmo, Sweden
(Product: Awnings)

Accent Awnings
P.O. Box 777
Chester, PA 19016
(Products: Awnings; rolling shutters;
    skylight shades; insulating shutters)

Aero Drapery
P.O. Box 32606
Charlotte, NC 28232
(Product: Insulating Roman shades)

Al Can Building Products
280 N. Park Avenue
Warren, OH 44482
(Products: Awnings and shutters)

Alpha Productions Inc.
10459 Jefferson Boulevard
Culver City, CA 90232
(Product: Awnings)

American German Industries Inc.
14601 N. Scottsdale Road
Scottsdale, AZ 85260
(Product: Roladen shutters)

**American International Windows
    Systems Inc.**
615 N. Salina Street
Syracuse, NY 13208
(Products: Energy-efficient window
    components; insulative shutters)

American Rolladen Corp.
4126 Blalock
Houston, TX 77080
(Product: Rolling shutters)

Anchor Industries Inc.
1100 Burch Drive
Evansville, IN 47733
(Product: Awnings)

Apex Mills Corp.
P.O. Box 0
Lynnbrook, NY 11563
(Product: Insulative fabric and
    materials)

Appropriate Technology Corp.
7 Technology Drive
Brattleboro, VT 05301
(Products: Insulative window materi-
    als and coverings; insulated fabric
    shades)

Architectural Concepts
P.O. Box 292A Snug Harbor
Duxbury, MA 02332
(Product: Awnings)

Art-Tic Systems Inc.
P.O. Box 338
Silt, CO 81652
(Product: Insulated shades)

The Astrup Company
2937 W. 25th Street
Cleveland, OH 44113
(Products: Retractable awnings and
    accessories)

Automatic Devices Co.
2121 S. 12th Street
Allentown, PA 18103
(Product: Insulated fabric draperies)

Awning and Supply Co. Inc.
203 Commission Boulevard
Lafayette, LA 70508
(Products: Fabric and canvas awn-
    ings; window energy systems;
    thermo-stop blinds)

Awnings Unlimited Inc.
1814 George Avenue
Annapolis, MD 21403
(Products: Awnings; insulating shades)

Awntop Duracote Corp.
350 N. Diamond Street
Ravenna, OH 44266
(Product: Awnings)

Baker Drapery Corp.
1116 Pioneer Parkway
Peoria, IL 61615
(Product: Snap-a-Pleat drapery sys-
    tems)

B & B Manufacturing Inc.
11920 W. Carman Avenue
Milwaukee, WI 53225
(Product: Reflective film)

Baltimore Canvas Products
2861 W. Franklin Street
Baltimore, MD 21223
(Products: Awnings and accessories)

Baumann Inc.
1000 N. Rand Road, Building 114
Wauconda, IL 60084
(Product: Exsotrol blinds, exterior solar controls)

Becher/Schmidt U.S.A.
15 Park Avenue
Westwood, NJ 07675
(Product: Awnings)

Joel Berman Associates Inc.
102 Prince Street
New York, NY 10012
(Product: Mecho shade systems)

John Boyle & Co. Inc.
P.O. Drawer 672
Statesville, NC 28677
(Product: Awnings)

Brulene Inc.
576 Dunbar Road
Kitchener, Ontario
N2M 2X3 Canada
(Products: Blinds and shutters; extrusions and weather stripping)

Canvas Products of Jacksonville Inc.
11320 Distribution Avenue E.
Jacksonville, FL 32224
(Product: Awnings)

Catco Supply Inc.
104–030 180th Street
Jamaica, NY 11433
(Product: Awnings)

Chemstyle Inc.
5801 W. Mount Hope
Lansing, MI 48901
(Product: Insulating sun shade screening)

City Awning
1311 West Street (Rear)
Annapolis, MD 21401
(Products: Awnings; storm windows)

Clear-View Shade Inc.
6124 N. Broadway
Chicago, IL 60660
(Product: Transparent and reflective shades)

Clopay Corp.
101 E. 4th Street
Cincinnati, OH 45202
(Product: Silver Energy Guard window shades)

Conservative Concepts Ltd.
P.O. Box 376
Stratton Mountain, VT 05155
(Product: Warm-In drapery liners)

Creative Energy Products Inc.
1406 Williamson
Madison, WI 53703
(Product: Insulative window treatments)

Creative Windows and Walls
3000 Washtenaw
Ann Arbor, MI 48104
(Product: Insulative window systems and treatments)

C. D. Davidson & Assoc. Inc.
P.O. Box 1293
Pontiac, MI 48057
(Product: Shutter Shields)

Del Mar Window Coverings
7150 Fenwick Lane
Westminster, CA 92683
(Product: Softlight blinds)

Deposition Technology Inc.
8963 Carroll Way
San Diego, CA 92121
(Product: Solar-Gold 80 and Wintergold 80; window film)

Designer Window Systems
4330 Beltwood Parkway South
Dallas, TX 75234
(Products: Insulating panels; window moldings; shades)

Doff Products
405 Cedar Avenue
Minneapolis, MN 55454
(Product: Insulating shades)

The Drapery Lady
P.O. Box 71
Melbourne, FL 32935
(Products: Solar shades; fabric sunshades)

Dunmore Corp.
Newtown Industrial Common
207 Penns Trail
Newtown, PA 18940
(Product: Dun-Ray solar film)

Duracote Corp.
350 N. Diamond Street
Ravenna, OH 44266
(Products: Blackout and reflective shades; washable reflective fabric)

EGE System Sun Control Inc.
1803 132nd Avenue, N.E.
Bellevue, WA 98005
(Product: Awnings and equipment)

Eide Industries Inc.
16215 Piuma Avenue
Cerritos, CA 90701-1528
(Products: Awnings; contract sealing and sewing)

Energy Industries
Solar Shutter Division
2010 N. Redwood Drive, Route 1
Independence, MO 64050
(Product: Translucent insulating In-Sol sliders)

Energy Saver Shades
6715 H. Backlick Road
Springfield, VA 22150
(Product: Energy Saver shades and track system "Wind-stop")

Energy Savings Marketplace Inc.
82 Boston Post Road
Waterford, CT 06385
(Products: Awnings; insulated and quilted fabrics)

Energy Warehouse, Inc.
6523-B E. 46th Street
Tulsa, OK 74145
(Products: Film; variety of shades)

Enpro/Energy Products Distributors
9444 Old Katy Road, Suite 115
Houston, TX 77055
(Products: Film; skylight covers and weather stripping)

Environmental Seal & Security
2601 E. Katella Avenue
Anaheim, CA 92806
(Products: Insulating shades and shutters; movable insulation)

Euroll Inc.
4089 S. Rogers Circle
Boca Raton, FL 33431
(Products: Insulating exterior shutters and motors)

European Energy Savers
2911 W. Fairmont Avenue
Phoenix, AZ 85017
(Products: Alu-Therm windows; Euro Shield rolling shutters)

Fell-Fab International Inc.
P.O. Box 3303, Station C
Hamilton, Ontario
L8H 7L6 Canada
(Product: Awnings; contract sealing and sewing)

Felton Brush Co. Inc.
315 Wilson Street
Manchester, NH 03015
(Products: Weather stripping; edge-sealing systems)

Fibert Industries
Cleanese Corp.
1614 Campbell
Oakland, CA 94607
(Product: Polar Guard fiberfill for thermal window insulation)

Florida Shades Inc.
1000 U.S. Highway 19 South
Palm Harbor, FL 34684
(Product: Energy-efficient shades)

FTR Insulated Shutter Systems
5725 Arapahoe
Boulder, CO 80303
(Product: Wovoak insulating shutters)

H. Gartenmaier
Postfach 1106
Keplerstrasse 4
D-7208 Spaichingen
Federal Republic of Germany
(Product: Manual and automated awnings and blinds)

Gila River Products
6615 W. Boston Street
Chandler, AZ 85224
(Product: Window film)

Glare-Con Inc.
610 Colcord Drive
Oklahoma City, OK 73102
(Product: Skylight systems; blinds, shades, and shutters)

Glen Raven Mills Inc.
1831 N. Park Avenue
Glen Raven, NC 27215
(Product: Awnings)

Gottlieb Binder Bandweberei
Bahnhofstrasse 19
7038 Holzgerligen
Federal Republic of Germany
(Product: Awnings and fasteners)

Graber Industries
7549 Graber Road
Middleton, WI 53562-1096
(Product: Magnetic tape kits for shades)

Guilford Mills Inc.
P.O. Box U-4
Greensboro, NC 27402
(Product: Energy-efficient blinds, shades, and fabrics)

Heli-X-Shade Co.
80 Roebling Street
Brooklyn, NY 11211
(Product: Insulating shades—reflective, greenhouse, skylight, and automated)

Hendee Enterprises Inc.
P.O. Box 460
Bellaire, TX 77401
(Products: Awnings; screens; greenhouse shades)

Home & Castle Architectural Shading Systems
7531 Coldwater Canyon Avenue
North Hollywood, CA 91605
(Products: Insulating shades; greenhouse insulation; motorized systems)

IMPAC S.P.A.
Via Mazzini 3
Carugate (Milan) 20061
Italy
(Product: Awnings and rolling shutters)

Insulating Shade Co. Inc.
P.O. Box 282
Bradford, CT 06405
(Product: Insulating shades)

Insul-Shade
4244 Ridge Lea Road
Amherst, NY 14226
(Product: All-Season vinyl tracking insulated shade systems)

Insul Shutter Inc.
P.O. Box 338
Silt, CO 81652
(Product: Insul shutter)

International Blind Co.
P.O. Box 777
Chester, PA 19016
(Product: Awnings and rolling shutter kits)

International Sun Control Inc.
1438 10th Court
Lake Park, FL 33403
(Product: Roll-A window shades)

International Vertical Systems
8438 N.W. 66th Street
Miami, FL 33166
(Product: Reflective film; vinyl extrusions)

Intex Plastics Corp.
P.O. Box 948
Corinth, MS 38834
(Products: Awnings; canopies and vinyl shades)

Jaksha Energy Systems Inc.
5900 Deerhaven Road
Lincoln, NE 68516
(Products: Greenhouse and movable insulation; insulating shades; motorized rolling shutters)

Joanna
Division of CHF Industries
2141 S. Jefferson Street
Chicago, IL 60616
(Product: Joanna window shades)

Johnson Laminating & Packaging
20631 Annalee Avenue
Carson, CA 90746
(Product: Reflective window film)

Johnson Plastics
10804 Normandale Boulevard
Minneapolis, MN 55437
(Products: Window and shade film; sealing systems and fasteners; greenhouse insulation; weather stripping; interior storm windows)

Kabar Manufacturing Corp.
140 Schmitt Boulevard
Farmingdale, NY 11735
(Product: Sealing equipment)

Kalex Chemical Co.
57-27 49th Street
Maspeth, NY 11378
(Products: Translucent window film; insulating shades)

Keller Products Inc.
41 Union Street
P.O. Box 4105
Manchester, NH 03108
(Product: Track Edge sealing system;
weather stripping)

Kenfair Manufacturing Co.
840 S. Pickett Street
Alexandria, VA 22304
(Product: Insulating fabrics and
shades)

Kingly Sealy Thermos Co.
37 East Street
Winchester, MA 01890
(Products: Astrolon III and VIII; reflective fabrics)

Kirsch
309 N. Prospect Street
Sturgis, MI 49091
(Products: Verosol blinds; wovenwood shades)

Kleen-Tex Industries Inc.
P.O. Box KTI
La Grange, GA 30241
(Products: Awnings; exterior and vinyl shades; greenhouse shades)

Laurco Fabrics Inc.
2331 S. Mead
P.O. Box 16011
Wichita, KS 67216
(Products: Edge-sealing systems; laminated shades; custom draperies)

Levolor Lorentzen Inc.
1 Upper Pond Road
Parsippany, NJ 07054
(Products: Awnings; screens; blinds;
exterior shades)

M. J. Linn Inc.
Samson Aluminum Ltd.
2049 Ninth Avenue
Ronkonkoma, NY 11779
(Product: Energy-efficient blinds)

Madico Inc.
P.O. Box 4023
45 Industrial Parkway
Woburn, MA 01888
(Product: Energy control window film)

The Magnet Store
607 S. Gilbert
Castle Rock, CO 80104
(Products: Zip-grip magnetic strip and
tape; other magnetic devices)

Marchant Industries Inc.
1600 Northside Drive, N.W.
Atlanta, GA 30318
(Product: Awnings; rolling shutters)

Martin Processing Inc.
P.O. Box 5068
Martinsville, VA 24112
(Product: Llumar solar film)

Metalized Products
224 Terminal Drive S.
St. Petersburg, FL 33712
(Product: Sungard solar film)

Metal J. Channel
Hownet Building Products Division
P.O. Box 4515
Lancaster, PA 17604
(Product: Semirigid fiberglass board)

Metzger Brothers
60 Center Street
Rutland, VT 05701
(Product: Awnings)

Meyer Drapery Services Inc.
330 N. Neil Street
Champaign, IL 61820
(Product: Thermal-backed lining fabric)

Midwest Marketing Inc.
P.O. Box 2063
East Peoria, IL 61603
(Products: Window film; interior storm
windows; transparent shades)

**Minute Man Storm Windows/
Minute Man Anchors Inc.**
305 W. Walker Street
East Flat Rock, NC 28726
(Product: Plastic storm window kits)

Sally Munroe Interior Designs
94 Stony Ridge Road
Auburn, MA 04210
(Product: Main Puffins insulated window shutters)

Nanik
7200 W. Stewart Avenue
Wausau, WI 54401
(Product: Interior storm windows)

National Felt Corp.
P.O. Box 150
Easthampton, MA 01027
(Product: Weather stripping)

Nichols-Homeshield Inc.
3755 E. Main Street
St. Charles, IL 60174
(Products: Window hardware; magnetic fasteners; interior storm windows)

One Design Inc.
Mountain Falls Route
Winchester, VA 22601
(Product: Rolldoor)

Orcon Corp.
33430 Western Avenue
Union City, CA 94587
(Products: Fabric awnings; insulative lining; reflective, transparent film
and shades)

Owens-Corning
Fiberglas Tower
Toledo, OH 43659
(Product: Semirigid Fiberglas board)

Patio Blinds
750 N. Batavia Street
Orange, CA 92668
(Product: Blinds)

Pease Industries
Rolling Shutter Division
7100 Dixie Highway
Fairfield, OH 45014
(Product: Pease rolling shutters)

Perkasie Industries Corp.
50 E. Spruce Street
Perkasie, PA 18944
(Product: Plastic storm window kits)

Perma System Sun Control
5675 E. Oakbrook Parkway
Norcross, GA 30093
(Product: Ready-made awnings)

Peterson Products
491 W. Main Street
Avon, MA 02322
(Products: Awnings; canopies; greenhouse shades)

Phifer Western
14408 E. Nelson Avenue
City of Industry, CA 91744
(Product: Solar screens)

Phifer Wire Products Inc.
P.O. Box 1700
Tuscaloosa, AL 35403
(Products: Greenhouse insulation;
screening)

Plaskolite Inc.
P.O. Box 1497
Columbus, OH 43216
(Products: Interior storm windows;
acrylic sheeting for glazing; mov-
able insulation)

Plastic-View Inc.
15468 Cabrito Road
P.O. Box 25
Van Nuys, CA 91408
(Products: Film; transparent and re-
flective shades)

Plum Industries Inc.
P.O. Box 14
Delta, OH 43515
(Products: Insul-Trac hardware; win-
dow dressings; Window Fleece in-
sulating fabric)

Quality Builders Inc.
D/B/A Solar Miser
P.O. Box 1209
Priest River, ID 83856
(Product: Energy audit meters)

Reel Shutters
9517 Chef Menteur Highway
New Orleans, LA 70127
(Product: Rolling shutters)

Riri Inc.
200 Airport Executive Park
Spring Valley, NY 10977
(Products: Awnings and canopies;
components; motorized systems)

Robeco Chemicals Inc.
99 Park Avenue
New York, NY 10016
(Products: Greenhouses; acrylic glazing; film)

Rockland Industries Inc.
1601 Edison Highway
Baltimore, MD 21213
(Products: Movable insulation; insulative shades; Roc-lon products)

Rollac Shutter of Texas Inc.
10800 Blackhawk Boulevard
Houston, TX 77089
(Products: Window treatment controls; insulating shutters and components)

**Roll-A-Way Insulating Security
Shutters**
10601 Oak Street
St. Petersburg, FL 33702-1898
(Products: Window treatment controls; decorative and insulating
shutters)

Roll Shutter Supply Inc.
7722 E. Gray Road
Scottsdale, AZ 85260
(Product: Insulating shutters and components)

Salco Inc.
1420 Major Street
Salt Lake City, UT 84115
(Product: Energy-efficient fabrics and
interior treatments)

Schmitz-Werke GmbH & Co.
Hansetrasse 87
D-4407 Emsdetten
Federal Republic of Germany
(Product: Fabric and aluminum awn-
ings)

Sealmaster Inc.
10431 Lexington Drive
Knoxville, TN 37932
(Products: Energy audit meters; insulating window-sealing systems;
shutters and accessories; interior
storm windows)

Serrande of Italy
P.O. Box 1034
West Sacramento, CA 95691
(Product: Serrande shutters)

Mark Sherwood Solar Products
Division of Kingston Industries
205 Lexington Avenue
New York, NY 10016
(Product: King-Lux reflective alumi-
num sheeting)

Shutter Haus Inc.
1000 Savage Court
Longwood, FL 32750
(Products: Insulating shutters; shades;
motorized systems)

Shutters Inc.
110 E. 5th Street
Hastings, MN 55033
(Product: Movable insulation)

Shutter Source International
211 N.W. Fifth Avenue
Hallandale, FL 33009
(Product: Exterior, insulating, metal,
and rolling shutters and components)

SIMU/U.S. Inc.
624 Douglas Avenue
Suite 1418
Altamonte Springs, FL 32714
(Products: Awnings; blinds; rolling
shutters; motorized systems)

Snyder Manufacturing Co. Ltd.
Box 188
3001 Progress Street
Dover, OH 44622
(Products: Awnings and canopies;
laminated fabrics; services)

The Soft Path
2927 Paseo
Oklahoma City, OK 73103
(Products: Movable greenhouse insulation; insulating shades)

Solar Drape
225 Portage Road
Lewiston, NY 14092
(Product: Solar Drape automatic drapery control systems)

Solar Energy Components Inc.
212 Welsh Pool Road
Lionville, PA 19353
(Product: Thermo-Shades)

Solaroll Shade and Shutter
P.O. Box 428
Pompano Beach, FL 33061
(Product: Solaroll exterior window
blinds)

Solar Plastics Extrusions Inc.
247 Bridgeland Avenue
Toronto, Ontario
M6A 1Y7 Canada
(Product: Solar-sealing components)

Solar Screen
53–11 105th Street
Corona, NY 11368
(Products: Kool Vue solar screens; reflective film; transparent shades)

Solar Useage Now Inc.
P.O. Box 306
Bascom, OH 44809
(Products: SUN catalog products)

Solidyne Inc.
Thermatron Division
60 Spence Street
Bay Shore, NY 11706
(Product: Sealing equipment)

Sol-R-Veil Inc.
635 W. 23rd Street
New York, NY 10011
(Product: Sol-R-Veil interior/exterior
sunshade systems)

Somfy Systems Inc.
2 Sutton Place
Edison, NJ 08817
(Products: Motorized systems for awnings, shutters, shades, skylights;
movable insulation)

Steven Fabrics Co.
1400 Van Buren Street, N.E.
Minneapolis, MN 55413
(Product: Warm Window insulated
Roman shade systems)

**Story Design and Manufacturing
Co. Inc.**
790 W. Chicago Street
Algonquin, IL 60102
(Products: Skylight shades; laminated
shades)

Sun Control Products Inc.
431 Fourth Avenue, S.E.
Rochester, MN 55904
(Product: Energy-efficient shades)

Sunflake
625 Goddard Avenue
Ignacio, CO 81137
(Product: Sunflake windows)

Sun Quilt Corp.
P.O. Box 374
New Port, NH 03773
(Product: Sun Quilt thermal movable
insulation and sun covers)

Suntrak Industries Inc.
225 E. Wisconsin
Nashotah, WI 53058
(Products: Movable insulation; greenhouse, skylight, and motorized
shades and screens)

Tempo Industries Inc.
625 Forest Edge Drive
Vernon Hills, NJ 60061
(Product: Insulated quilted shades;
skylight systems)

Textile Commission
217 Chestnut Street
Philadelphia, PA 19106
(Products: Awnings; hardware and
motorized systems; hook-and-loop
fasteners)

**Thermal Technology Corp. of
Aspen Inc.**
601 Alter Street
P.O. Box 682
Broomfield, CO 80020
(Products: Movable insulation; auto-
mated, screening, greenhouse, and
insulating shades)

Thermal Wall Insulating Shutters
Rd. #1, Box 462-A
Voorheesville, NY 12186
(Product: Insulating shutters)

Thermatron
60 Spence Street
Bay Shore, NY 11706
(Product: Sealing equipment)

Thermo Tech Corp.
410 Pine Street
Burlington VT 05401
(Product: Storm window frame kits)

3M Energy Control Products
3M Center
Building 225-4S
St. Paul, MN 55144
(Products: Window film; Thinsulate R;
insulating fabrics; shade information)

Tietex Corp.
P.O. Box 6218
Spartanburg, SC 29304
(Product: Greenhouse shades)

Titan Seal Corporation
P.O. Box 61
14 Ames Street
Dedham, MA 02026
(Product: Titan Seal magnetic interior
windows and door seals)

United Textile & Supply Co.
1641 N. Allesandro Street
Los Angeles, CA 90026
(Products: Awnings; canopies; hardware motorized systems; greenhouse and skylight shades)

Verosol USA Inc.
215 Beecham Drive
P.O. Box 517
Pittsburgh, PA 15230
(Product: Greenhouse and skylight
shades and systems)

Vicon Energy Systems
275 Circuit Street
Hanover, MA 02339
(Product: Magnetite inside magnetic
insulating windows)

Jim Walter Plastics
4747 Hollins Ferry Road
Baltimore, MD 21227
(Products: Movable insulation; insulative shutters; extrusions)

Wind-N-Sun Shield
P.O. Box 2504
Indian Harbour Beach, FL 32937
(Products: Thermal Drapemates;
drapery-liner panels and shades)

Zenith Insulating Products Inc.
213 East Superior Street
Duluth, MN 55802
(Product: Roman shades)

Zomeworks
P.O. Box 712
Albuquerque, NM 87103
(Product: Greenhouse accessories and
insulation)

Appendix 3   Multiproduct Distributors

Multiproduct distributors may carry some or all of the following: vertical, horizontal, and bamboo blinds; pleated, decorative, vinyl, insulating, and pull shades; woven-wood shades; wood, decorative, and insulative shutters; various insulative window treatments and supplies; decorative and support fabrics; findings, thread, trimmings, and fabric accessory items; workroom services and supplies; contract drapery services; custom fabric shades—Roman, insulating, balloon, and Venetian; valances, cornices, and lambrequins; drapery hardware; and consultation and installation services.

Acme Window Covering Ltd.
3000 Madison Street
Bellwood, IL 60104

Aero Drapery
3525 State Road, 32 W.
P.O. Box 419
Westfield, IN 46074

American Abalene Decorating Service
224 N. 8th Street
Brooklyn, NY 11211

Amjacs Interwest
4645 S. 400 West
Murray, UT 84123

Barker Supply Co. Inc.
819 N. Seventh Avenue
Phoenix, AZ 85007

Beauti-Vue Products Corp.
Bristol Industrial Plaza
Bristol, WI 53104

Belaire Products Inc.
400 Ninth Avenue
New Orleans, LA 70115

Bishop's Inc.
416 N. Craig Street
Pittsburgh, PA 15213

The Blind Factory
96 N. Beverwyck Road
Lake Hiawatha, NJ 07034

Blind Factory Southwest
516 E. Juanita Avenue
Mesa, AZ 85234

A. J. Boyd Industries Inc.
P.O. Box 401
Whitehall Road
Andover, NJ 07821

The C-Mor Company
7 Jewell Street
Garfield, NJ 07026

Condell Designs
16651 14 Mile Road
Fraser, MI 48026

Consolidated Textile Company
450 N. Wells Street
Chicago, IL 60610

Decorama Desley Cortley
303 Fifth Avenue
New York, NY 10016

Del Mar Window Coverings
7150 Fenwick Lane
Westminster, CA 92683

Diversified Drapery Products
5929 Kester Avenue
Van Nuys, CA 91411

Döfix-Döhlemann GmbH
Tobelwassenweg 25
7315 Weilheim Teck
Federal Republic of Germany

Fabricut/Trend of the Times
9303 E. 46th Street
Tulsa, OK 74145

Frank's Window Fashions
979 Third Avenue, Room 1401
New York, NY 10022

Glamour Line
149 Bowes Road
Concord, Ontario
L4K 1H3 Canada

Graber Industries
7549 Graber Road
Middleton, WI 53562-1096

Hanmars Potpourri
Windows Plus
979 Third Avenue, Suite 1427
New York, NY 10022

Interior Concepts Inc.
3839 W. Devon
Chicago, IL 60659

Iozza Industries Ltd.
240 Humberline Drive
Rexdale, Ontario
M9W 5X1 Canada

Joanna
Division of CHF Industries
2141 S. Jefferson Street
Chicago, IL 60616
Salt Lake City, UT 84110

Kirsch
309 N. Prospect Street
Sturgis, MI 49091

London Textiles Inc.
P.O. Box 690634
Tulsa, OK 74169

Lozano Fisher Inc.
979 Third Avenue
New York, NY 10022

Meyer Drapery Service Inc.
330 N. Neil Street
Champaign, IL 61820

S. Morantz Inc.
4056 Chestnut Street
Philadelphia, PA 19104

Newell Window Furnishings Co.
916 S. Arcade Avenue
Freeport, IL 61032

Norman's of Salisbury
P.O. Drawer 799
Salisbury, NC 28144

Profile Corp.
1440 S.W. 28th Avenue
Pompano Beach, FL 33069

Romax Associates Ltd.
47 Glen Cove Road
Greenvale, NY 11548

Roper
9325 Snowden River Parkway
Columbia, MD 21046

Royal Crest Inc.
14851 W. 11 Mile Road
Oak Park, MI 48237

Salco Inc.
1420 Major Street
Salt Lake City, UT 84115

David Sloan Creations Inc.
Building B-4W
Airport Industrial Office Park
Valley Stream, NY 11581

Sol-R-Veil Inc.
635 W. 23rd Street
New York, NY 10011

Terry Fabrics Inc.
74 Coit Street
Irvington, NJ 07111

Tropicraft Inc.
P.O. Box 42010
San Francisco, CA 94142

Webb Designs Inc.
P.O. Box 1405
El Cajon, CA 92022-1405

Window Coverings Inc.
P.O. Box 14160
2010 S.E. 8th Street
Portland, OR 97214

Window Fascination
8002 Third Avenue
Brooklyn, NY 11209

Win-Glow Window Coverings
2390 Zanker Road
San Jose, CA 95131

Wisconsin Drapery Supply
24110 Blue Mound Road
Waukesha, WI 53118

Appendix 4 Mail-Order Curtains and Draperies: Wholesale and Retail

WHOLESALE: READY-MADE CURTAINS AND DRAPERIES

ASI Drapery Apt. Specialists
5221 W. Jefferson Boulevard
Los Angeles, CA 90016

Associated Drapery & Textiles
Field Station Box 4701
St. Louis, MO 63108

Baron Draperies Inc.
7449 Woodley Avenue
Van Nuys, CA 91406

Burlington House Draperies
1345 Avenue of the Americas
New York, NY 10105

Cadillac Curtain Co.
295 Fifth Avenue
Room 1203
New York, NY 10016

Cameo Curtains Inc.
261 Fifth Avenue
New York, NY 10016

Contemporary Classics
295 Fifth Avenue
New York, NY 10016

Creative Textiles
4150-A Florin Perkins Road
Sacramento, CA 95826

Crest Manufacturing Inc.
2906 Nottingham
Missouri City, TX 77459

Croscill Inc.
261 Fifth Avenue
New York, NY 10016

The Curtron Curtain Inc.
261 Fifth Avenue
New York, NY 10016

D'Art Fabrics Inc.
7171 N.W. Twelfth Avenue
Miami, FL 33150

Decrotex Inc.
87–46 123rd Street
Richmond Hill, NY 11418

Mark Evan Products Inc.
261 Fifth Avenue
New York, NY 10016

Everlon Inc.
295 Fifth Avenue
New York, NY 10016

Fashion Craft
P.O. Box 1209
Henryetta, OK 74437

GEA Designs
2806 S. Main Street
Los Angeles, CA 90007

Greenwood Mills Marketing Co.
111 W. 40th Street
New York, NY 10018

Louis Hand
Division of Aberdeen Manufacturing
Corp.
16 E. 34th Street
New York, NY 10016

Home Curtain Corp.
295 Fifth Avenue
New York, NY 10016

Home-Tex Fashions Inc.
5215 Lakeland Avenue N.
Minneapolis, MN 55429

Louis Hornick & Co. Inc.
261 Fifth Avenue
New York, NY 10016

Max H. Kahn Corp.
261 Fifth Avenue
New York, NY 10016

S. Lichtenberg & Co.
261 Fifth Avenue
New York, NY 10016

Lorraine Linens
1 E. 33rd Street
New York, NY 11566

Metro Blind & Shade
5206 Airport Freeway
Ft. Worth, TX 76117

Midwest Fabricating Inc.
25611 Coolidge
Oak Park, MI 48237

Midwest Window Art
703 N. 13th Street
St. Louis, MO 63103

Milford Stitching Co. Inc.
639 S. Marshall Street
Milford, DE 19963

S. Morantz Inc.
4056 Chestnut Street
Philadelphia, PA 19104

National Curtain Corp.
261 Fifth Avenue
Room 906
New York, NY 10016

Oxford Drapery Co.
261 Fifth Avenue
New York, NY 10016

Phase III Creative Concepts
2210 Wilshire Boulevard, Suite 264
Santa Monica, CA 90403

Quaker Lace Co.
24 W. 40th Street
New York, NY 10018

Ready Ruffles
6721 Market Street, Dept. C–L3
Wilmington, NC 28405

Regent Curtain Corp.
261 Fifth Avenue
New York, NY 10016

Reliable Fabrics
1691 Revere Beach Parkway
Everett, MA 02149

Rennie-Sunshine Home Fashions
295 Fifth Avenue
New York, NY 10016

Richloom Fabrics Corp.
261 Fifth Avenue
12th Floor
New York, NY 10016

Shadow Interiors
State Road 5 North
P.O. Box 277
Shipshewana, IN 46565

Styleline
Division of Daston Inc.
Highway 14 N.
Walworth, WI 53184

T.D.I. Drapery Importing Co.
20 W. 33rd Street
New York, NY 10001

Val-Able Industries
777 Alness Street
Downsview, Ontario
M3J 2H8 Canada

Wesco Fabrics Inc.
4001 Forest Street
Denver, CO 80216

RETAIL

Laura Ashley
979 Third Avenue
New York, NY 10022
(Products: Balloon shades; fabrics; wallpaper; paint; home furnishings; accessories)

Caroline Country Ruffles
P.O. Box 632
Dallas, NC 28034
(Products: Curtains; bedspreads)

Colonial Maid Curtains
Dept. AAS-BV
Mamaroneck, NY 10543
(Products: Curtains, bedspreads, dust ruffles—Colonial reproductions)

Conran's Mail Order Catalog Dept.
145 Huguenot Street
New Rochelle, NY 10801
(Products: Blinds, shades, kits)

Country Curtains
Dept. #4978
Red Lion Inn
Stockbridge, MA 01262
(Products: Curtains, spreads, table covers)

Curtain Corner
Dept. CL10
1119 W. St. George Avenue
Linden, NJ 07036
(Product: Ready-made curtains)

Kountry Rufflers
Buckeye Drive
Wilmington, NC 28405
(Product: Ruffled curtains; handmade ruffles and accessories)

New England Ltd.
P.O. Box 3619
Newport, RI 02840
(Products: Window dressings and accessories)

Norman's of Salisbury
P.O. Drawer 799
Salisbury, NC 28144
(Product: Casual and formal ready-made curtains)

Old Colony Curtains
Box 759
Westfield, NJ 07090
(Product: Ready-made curtains)

Paramount Shade and Drapery
979 Third Avenue
New York, NY 10022
(Product: Ready-made curtains)

Persnickety
P.O. Box 289
117-B Harry F. Byrd Highway
Sterling, VA 22170
(Product: Curtains; bedding; wallpaper)

Rue de France
78 Thames Street
Newport, RI 02840
(Product: French-lace country curtains)

Sears Roebuck and Co.
2650 E. Olympic Boulevard
Los Angeles, CA 90051
(Products: Ready-made curtains; draperies; hardware; blinds and shades)

Solar Drape
3115 S. La Cienega Boulevard
Los Angeles, CA 90016
(Product: Ready-made curtains)

Spiegel Catalog Division
P.O. Box 6340
Chicago, IL 60680
(Products: Ready-made curtains; draperies; hardware; blinds and shades)

Appendix 5 Fabric Companies

AB Kinnasand
Box 66
S-511 01 Kinna
Sweden
(Product: Scandinavian drapery and coordinated wall coverings)

Academy Handprints Ltd.
14–16 Irving Place
Woodmere, NY 11598
(Product: Designer fabrics)

ADO Corp.
P.O. Box 3447
Spartanburg, SC 29304
(Product: Quality-guaranteed drapery fabric)

Ametex/Robert Allen Contract Fabrics
261 Fifth Avenue
New York, NY 10016
(Products: Drapery; upholstery; bedspreads; wall-covering fabrics; flame-retardant contract fabrics)

Apex Mills Corp.
P.O. Box 0
Lynnbrook, NY 11563
(Product: Insulative fabrics)

Apogee Fabrics Inc.
979 Third Avenue
New York, NY 10022
(Product: Custom-embroidered quilting and fabrics)

Arc-Com Fabrics Inc.
33 Ramland South
Orangeburg, NY 10962
(Product: Commercial designer upholstery and wall coverings)

Architex International
625 W. Jackson Boulevard
Chicago, IL 60606
(Products: Drapery; upholstery fabric; wall coverings)

Ardison Fabric Mills Inc.
210 E. 58th Street
New York, NY 10022
(Products: Drapery; upholstery; wall coverings)

Laura Ashley Decorator Collection
979 Third Avenue
New York, NY 10022
(Products: Fabrics for draperies and upholstery; wall coverings and wallpaper; trimmings)

Atlanta Architectural Textiles Inc.
P.O. Drawer 52106
Atlanta, GA 30324
(Product: Contract fabrics)

Atrium Industries
18953 N.E. Third Court
North Miami Beach, FL 33179
(Products: Fabric and wall coverings; window-covering fabrics)

Baker, Knapp & Tubbs
917 Merchandise Mart
Chicago, IL 60654
(Product: Exclusive contract and residential textiles)

Bally Ribbon Mills
23 N. 7th Street
Bally, PA 19503
(Products: Woven tapes; webbing; fabric)

Bammental Wallcoverings
1751 N. Central Park Avenue
Chicago, IL 60647
(Product: Coordinated fabrics and wall coverings)

Charles Barone Inc.
9505 W. Jefferson Boulevard
Culver City, CA 90232
(Products: Wallpapers; correlated fabrics)

Bayberry Europa
979 Third Avenue
New York, NY 10022
(Product: Italian handprinted and glazed fabric—custom available)

Bayberry Inc.
3600 N.E. Second Avenue
Miami, FL 33137
(Products: Designer fabrics; coordinated wall coverings)

Bayeux Fabrics Inc.
132 Beaver Brook Road
Lincoln Park, NJ 07035
(Product: Knit fabrics)

Beacon Looms Inc.
295 Fifth Avenue
New York, NY 10016
(Products: Fabrics; draperies)

Bedspreads by Thomas
5820 Washington Avenue
Houston, TX 77007
(Products: Fabrics, quilting sevice)

Belgian Linen Association
280 Madison Avenue
New York, NY 10016
(Products: Upholstery; wall coverings;
    drapery fabric; residential and con-
    tract linens)

Bently Mills Inc.
P.O. Box 527
La Puente, CA 91747
(Products: Contract fabrics; coordinat-
    ing carpets)

Bergamo Fabrics Inc.
37–20 34th Street
Long Island City, NY 11101
(Product: Fine textiles)

B. Berger Co.
23533 Mercantile Road
Cleveland, OH 44101
(Product: Decorator fabrics)

B. I. Company
1225 N. Pine Lake Drive
Tampa, FL 33612
(Product: custom vinyl shower and
    cubicle curtains)

Bloomcraft Fabrics
381 Park Avenue S.
New York, NY 10016
(Products: Fabrics; ensembles)

André Bon
979 Third Avenue
New York, NY 10022
(Products: Fine French fabrics; wall
    coverings and trimmings)

Boussac of France
979 Third Avenue
New York, NY 10022
(Products: Fabrics; wall coverings; up-
    holstery)

Louis W. Bowen
200 Garden City Plaza
Garden City, NY 11530
(Products: Wall coverings; coordi-
    nated fabrics)

D. S. Brown Co.
Pacific Design Center #272
8687 Melrose Avenue
Los Angeles, CA 90069
(Product: Quality woven fabrics)

Bruin Plastics Company
P.O. Box 175
Glendale, RI 02826
(Products: Vinyl, flame-resistant, re-
    flective, and metallized fabrics)

Brunschwig & Fils
979 Third Avenue
New York, NY 10022
(Products: Wallpaper; upholstery and
    drapery fabric)

Burlington
1-800-345-6348
(Product: Fireproof contract fabrics)

California Drop Cloths Inc.
712 Grandview Street
Los Angeles, CA 90057
(Products: Fabrics; wall coverings—
    including hand-painted designs)

**California Webbing Industries
Inc.**
5065 Pacific Boulevard
P.O. Box 58165
Los Angeles, CA 90058
(Product: Webbing)

Alan Campbell Inc.
979 Third Avenue
New York, NY 10022
(Product: Designer fabrics)

Manuel Canovas Inc.
979 Third Avenue
New York, NY 10022
(Products: Fabrics; wall coverings)

Carefree Wallcoverings
23645 Mercantile Road
Cleveland, OH 44122
(Products: Wall coverings; coordi-
    nated fabrics)

Carleton V Ltd.
979 Third Avenue
New York, NY 10022
(Products: Wallpaper; cotton fabrics)

Wayne Carlson Wallpapers
473 E. Channel Road
Benicia, CA 94510
(Products: Coordinated fabrics and
    wall coverings)

Carousel Designs
P.O. Box 370-943
369 N.E. 59th Street
Miami, FL 33137
(Products: Wall coverings; fabrics—
    contemporary designs)

L. E. Carpenter and Co.
101 Henry Adams Street
San Francisco, CA 94103
(Products: Fabrics; wall coverings)

Ronald Charles Associates Inc.
3900 N. Miami Avenue
Miami, FL 33137
(Products: Fabrics; wall coverings—
    custom available)

Charleston Corp.
824 S. Freeway
Fort Worth, TX 76104
(Product: Specialize in cotton fabrics)

Charterhouse Designs Ltd.
979 Third Avenue
New York, NY 10022
(Product: Correlated wall coverings
    and fabrics)

China Seas Inc.
21 E. 4th Street
New York, NY 10003
(Product: Fabrics, including batiks,
    screenprints, damask, and ultra-
    suede)

Clarence House
211 E. 58th Street
New York, NY 10022
(Products: Upholstery; drapery fab-
    rics)

Cyrus Clark Co. Inc.
267 Fifth Avenue
New York, NY 10016
(Products: Decorative and drapery
    fabric)

**Cohama Specifier Contract
    Fabrics**
1407 Broadway
New York, NY 10018
(Products: Casements; draperies; cor-
    related quilted fabrics and wall cov-
    erings—contract fabrics)

Collins & Aikman Corp.
311 Smith Industrial Boulevard
Dalton, GA 30720
(Product: Wall coverings and coordinating fabrics; residential and contract textiles)

Commercial Drapery Contractors
1981 Moreland Parkway
Annapolis, MD 21401
(Products: Contract draperies; fabric)

Commins of California, Inc.
5401 Telegraph Road
Los Angeles, CA 90040
(Products: Decorative fabrics)

Connaissance
Available at John Edward Hughes
200 Dallas Design
1025 N. Stemons Freeway
Dallas, TX 77054
(Products: Fabrics; wall coverings)

Coral of Chicago
2001 S. Calumet Avenue
Chicago, IL 60616
(Products: Casements; flame-resistant [verel modacrylic] drapery and contract fabrics)

Corraggio Designs Inc.
1271 120th Street
Bellevue, WA 98005
(Product: Wide-width seamless casements and drapery fabrics)

Cowtan & Tout
979 Third Avenue
New York, NY 10022
(Products: Wall coverings; fine chintzes; handblocked wallpapers)

Craig Fabrics
979 Third Avenue
New York, NY 10022
(Products: Contemporary designer fabrics; residential and contract fabrics)

Culbert International Inc.
5120 Woodway, Suite 203 S.
Houston, TX 77056
(Product: Fine imported fabrics)

Rose Cumming
232 E. 59th Street
New York, NY 10022
(Products: Fabrics; antiques; decorations)

Darr Fabrics Inc.
7171 N.W. Twelfth Avenue
Miami, FL 33150
(Product: Variety of interiors fabrics)

David and Dash
2445 N. Miami Avenue
Miami, FL 33137
(Product: Fabrics and wall coverings for all interior uses)

Dazian's Inc.
165 S. Robertson Boulevard
Beverly Hills, CA 90211
(Products: Drapery; cubicle and bedspread flame-resistant fabrics)

Decorative Aides Co. Inc.
317 St. Paul's Avenue
Jersey City, NJ 07306
(Products: Macramé; string textiles and trim)

Decorators' Walk
245 Newton Road
Plainview, NY 11803
(Product: Variety of fabrics)

Decrotex Inc.
87–46 123rd Street
Richmond Hill, NY 11418
(Product: Fine European seamless drapery fabrics)

Deschemaker Inc.
979 Third Avenue
New York, NY 10022
(Product: Designer textiles)

Design Printery Inc.
211 Mt. Prospect Avenue
Clifton, NJ 07015
(Product: Designer fabrics)

Designtex Fabrics
56–08 37th Avenue
Woodside, NY 11377
(Product: High-quality contract upholstery)

A. L. Diament and Co.
979 Third Avenue
New York, NY 10022
(Products: Wall covering and matching fabrics)

DiversiTech General
Coated Fabrics Division
P.O. Box 875
Toledo, OH 43696-0875
(Product: Contract upholstery)

Donghia Furniture and Textiles
485 Broadway
New York, NY 10013
(Product: Contract and residential high-quality textiles)

Drapery Corp. of America
40–42 Home Place
Lodi, NJ 07644
(Product: Flame-resistant contract fabrics and draperies)

Duracote Corp.
350 N. Diamond Street
Ravenna, OH 44266
(Product: Reflective and vinyl fabric)

Duro, AB Durotapet
Box 907
32 Gavle
Sweden
(Product: Light Swedish print drapery fabrics)

Econ-O-Fabrics Inc.
1775 Fifth Avenue
Bayshore, NY 11706
(Product: Variety of fabrics)

Eisenhart Wallcoverings Co.
P.O. Box 464
Hanover, PA 17331
(Products: Fabrics; wall coverings)

Erwin-Lambeth Inc.
201 E. Holly Hill Road
Thomasville, NC 27360
(Product: Fabric for drapery and upholstery)

Essex Fabrics
950 Vallejo Street
Denver, CO 80204
(Product: Fabric for drapery and upholstery)

Eurotex Inc.
165 W. Ontario Street
Philadelphia, PA 19140
(Products: Wall coverings; rugs; broadloom fabrics; wools; synthetics)

Everlon Inc.
295 Fifth Avenue
New York, NY 10016
(Products: Macramé fabric; drapery fabric; trimmings)

Fabricut/Trend of the Times
9303 E. 46th Street
Tulsa, OK 74145
(Product: Variety of fabrics)

Facile Technologies Inc.
185 Sixth Avenue
Paterson, NJ 07524
(Products: Insulative, metallized, laminated, reflective, and vinyl fabrics)

Farmhouse Studio Fabric
2215 E. 350th N.
LaPorte, IN 46350
(Products: Original silkscreen textiles and wall coverings)

First Editions Wallcoverings
979 Third Avenue
New York, NY 10022
(Products: Wall coverings; fabrics)

L. F. Fogt Aktieselskab
Radhus plads 77 DK-1504
Copenhagen V, Denmark
(Product: Upholstery—featuring Irontex)

Fonthill Ltd.
979 Third Avenue
New York, NY 10022
(Product: Decorative fabrics)

Fox-Wells & Co. Inc.
Contract Division
58 W. 40th Street
New York, NY 10018
(Products: Variety of fabrics; insulative and contract draperies)

Frankel Associates Inc.
1122 Broadway
New York, NY 10010
(Products: Fabrics; wall coverings—contract and residential)

Futura Fabrics Inc.
4307 Delemere Court
Royal Oak, MI 48073
(Products: Seamless wide-width drapery fabrics; exclusive imports)

Gardisette USA Inc.
P.O. Box 2586
Anderson, SC 29622
(Product: Drapery fabric)

Bea Gebaide Inc.
3850 N.E. Miami Court
Miami, FL 33137
(Products: Fabric; wall coverings; correlated fabrics; trimmings; custom printing and weaving)

George M. Fabric Co.
111 W. 21st Street
Los Angeles, CA 90007
(Product: Variety of fabrics)

Gilford Inc.
250 Park Avenue South
New York, NY 10003
(Products: Wall coverings; coordinated fabrics)

Givenchy (Collins & Aikman Co.)
23645 Mercantile Road
Cleveland, OH 44122
(Products: Wall coverings; fabrics)

Glant Fabrics
P.O. Box C-3637
Seattle, WA 98124
(Product: Fabrics, including silks and Italian fabrics—residential and contract)

Glen Raven Mills Inc.
1831 N. Park Avenue
Glen Raven, NC 27215
(Product: Fabrics)

Yves Gonnet
1440 Broadway
New York, NY 10018
(Product: Fine selection of designer fabrics)

B. F. Goodrich Company
Fabricated Polymers Division
500 S. Main Street
Akron, OH 44318
(Products: Fabric; wall coverings)

Charles R. Gracie & Sons Inc.
979 Third Avenue
New York, NY 10022
(Products: Wall coverings; fabrics)

Greff Fabrics Inc.
200 Garden City Plaza
Garden City, NY 11530
(Products: Wall coverings; fabrics—high-quality commercial and residential)

Groundworks Inc.
79 Fifth Avenue
New York, NY 10003
(Product: Fabrics—contemporary prints)

Guadalupe Hand Print Fabrics
P.O. Box 877
Boerne, TX 78006
(Product: Hand-printed fabrics with Western backgrounds)

Gucci
685 Fifth Avenue
New York, NY 10022
(Product: International designer prints)

Gudbrandsdalens Uldvarefabrik A.S.
Herbert J. Stein
141 E. 56th Street
New York, NY 10022
(Product: Scandinavian sturdy upholstery)

Guilford Mills Inc.
P.O. Box U-4
Greensboro, NC 27402
(Product: Insulative lining, metallized fabrics)

Hamilton Web
24 W. 40th Street
New York, NY 10018
(Products: Drapery fabric; trimmings)

Harrington Textiles Inc.
499 E. Walnut Street
North Wales, PA 19454
(Product: Contract and residential fabrics)

S. Harris
9303 E. 46th Street
Tulsa, OK 74145
(Product: Drapery and wall-covering fabrics for contract and residential use)

Heritage Imports Inc.
P.O. Box 328
Pella, IA 50219
(Product: Imported European lace)

Hasi Hester
Pacific Design Center #B-650
8687 Melrose Avenue
Los Angeles, CA 90069
(Products: Coordinated wall coverings
and fabrics)

S. M. Hexter Co.
2800 Superior Avenue
Cleveland, OH 44114
(Product: Contemporary fabrics)

Hinson and Co.
27–35 Jackson Avenue
Long Island City, NY 11101
(Products: Wallpapers; fabrics)

**Home and Castle Architectural
Shading Systems**
7531 Coldwater Canyon Avenue
N. Hollywood, CA 91605
(Product: Insulative, flame-resistant
fabrics—contract)

Home Curtain Corp.
295 Fifth Avenue
New York, NY 10016
(Product: Drapery fabric)

Homestead Fabrics Inc.
135 W. 41st Street
New York, NY 10036
(Product: Flame-resistant fabrics for
commercial and residential use)

Home-Tex Fashions Inc.
5215 Lakeland Avenue N.
Minneapolis, MN 55429
(Product: Imported and decorative
drapery fabric)

The Huntington House Collection
10 New England Executive Park
Burlington, MA 01803
(Products: Fabrics; wall coverings)

Imperial Wallcoverings
Division Collins & Aikman
23645 Mercantile Road
Beechwood, OH 44122
(Products: Wall coverings; coordi-
nated fabrics)

Importex
1201 Story Avenue
Louisville, KY 40206
(Products: Wall coverings; fabrics—
exotic fibers included)

Industrial Textile Corp.
3317 Exposition Place
Los Angeles, CA 90018
(Product: Awnings—exterior, flame-
resistant, laminated and woven fabric)

International Fabrics Inc.
1011 Porter Street
P.O. Box 1448
High Point, NC 27260
(Product: Contract fabrics)

International Seamless Fabrics
249 S. Los Angeles Street, 2nd Floor
Los Angeles, CA 90012
(Product: Domestic and imported fabrics)

Intex Plastics Corp.
1255 Lynnfield Road
Suite 257
Memphis, TN 38119
(Product: Laminated and vinyl fabrics)

International Textile Corporation
205 Lexington Avenue
New York, NY 10016
(Product: Imported fabrics, including
Oy Tampella Ab textiles from Fin-
land)

Italian Embassy
Commercial Office
1601 Fuller Street, N.W.
Washington, D.C.
(Request *Textalia Casa:* directory for
Italy's finest home textiles—uphol-
stery, drapery, linens, and trim-
mings)

Jeremiah Prints Ltd.
300 E. 59th Street
New York, NY 10022
(Products: Fabric; wall coverings)

Joanna
Division of CHF Industries
2141 S. Jefferson Street
Chicago, IL 60616
(Product: Decorative, flame-resistant
laminated, metallized, reflective,
sheer, and vinyl fabrics)

Judscott Handprints Ltd.
2269 Saw Mill River Road
Elmsford, NY 10523
(Products: Fabric; wall coverings—
custom work)

Kalex Chemical Co.
57–27 49th Street
Maspeth, NY 11378
(Product: Vinyl fabric)

Kassel Corporation
16 Arrow Road
Ramsey, NJ 07446
(Products: Wall coverings; fabrics)

Kas-Tex Corp.
5899 Downey Road
Vernon, CA 90058
(Product: Variety of fabrics)

Katzenbach & Warren Inc.
950 Third Avenue
New York, NY 10022
(Products: Matching fabrics and wall
coverings)

Kenfair Manufacturing Co.
840 S. Pickett Street
Alexandria, VA 22304
(Product: Blackout and laminated fabrics)

Kenmill Home Furnishings
Division of Richloom Inc.
261 Fifth Avenue, 12th Floor
New York, NY 10016
(Product: Broad range of fabrics and
patterns for home and contract installations)

The Kenyon Piece Dyeworks Inc.
100 Main Street
Kenyon, RI 02836
(Products: Fabric finishing; fiberfill;
flame-resistant, metallized, and reflective fabrics)

Kiesling-Hess
300 W. Bristol Street
Philadelphia, PA 19140
(Product: Fine finishing of decorative
fabrics)

The Kipp Collection
9012 Melrose Avenue
West Hollywood, CA 90069
(Product: Fabrics, including Ross
hand-painted fabric and silk suit-
ing upholstery)

Kirk-Brummel Associates
979 Third Avenue
New York, NY 10022
(Products: Wall coverings; fabrics—
exotic prints and textures)

Kleen-Tex Industries Inc.
P.O. Box KTl
La Grange, GA 30241
(Product: Vinyl fabrics)

Knoll Textiles
Division of Knoll International
655 Madison Avenue
New York, NY 10021
(Products: Contract wall, upholstery,
and drapery fabrics)

Kravet Fabrics Inc.
225 Central Avenue South
Bethpage, NY 11714
(Product: Variety of prints and textures)

Boris Kroll Fabrics Inc.
66 Gray Street
Paterson, NJ 07501
(Products: Jacquard weaves; hand-
screened custom-designed and
dyed contract textiles)

**Kroupana (carried by Wolverine
Leathers)**
123 N. Main Street
Rockford, MI 49351
(Product: Stain-resistant pigskin suede

The Lackawanna Leather Co.
P.O. Box 939
Conover, NC 23613
(Product: Leather)

Lamotite Inc.
2909 E. 79th Street
Cleveland, OH 44104
(Products: Drapery lining; insulating
lining and materials; laminating
services)

Lazarus Contract
9303 E. 46th Street
Tulsa, OK 74145-4895
(Products: Contract fabrics and wall
coverings; residential fabrics)

Jack Lenor Larsen, Inc.
41 E. 11th Street
New York, NY 10003
(Products: Fabrics for upholstery,
drapery, and wall coverings)

Leathercraft Inc.
P.O. Box 639
Conover, NC 28613
(Product: Leather)

Lee Jofa Inc.
800 Central Boulevard
Carlstadt, NJ 07072
(Products: Fabrics; wall coverings)

Liberty Fabrics of New York Inc.
2 Park Avenue
New York, NY 10016
(Products: Decorative and flame-
resistant fabrics and draperies)

Liberty of London Inc.
108 W. 39th Street
New York, NY 10018
(Product: Fabrics)

**M. J. Linn Inc./Samson Aluminum
Ltd.**
2049 Ninth Avenue
Ronkonkoma, NY 11779
(Product: Decorative fabrics)

Louver Magic Inc.
99-A Bell Street
West Babylon, NY 11704
(Product: Decorative, contract, insulative fabrics)

Maharam/Vertical Surfaces
P.O. Box 6900
45 Rasons Court
Hauppauge, NY 11788
(Product: Contract textiles)

Manuscreens
Division of J. Josephson Inc.
20 Horizon Boulevard
South Hackensack, NJ 07606
(Product: Silk-screened companion
fabrics and wall coverings)

Marianne Fabrics Inc.
I-85 at New Cut Road
Spartanburg, SC 29301
(Product: Seamless fabrics)

Marignan
979 Third Avenue
New York, NY 10022
(Products: Designer prints; French
fabrics)

Marimekko Inc.
One Dock Street
Stamford, CT 06902
(Product: Contemporary Scandina-
vian designs)

Marvin Fabrics Co. Inc.
261 Fifth Avenue
New York, NY 10016
(Product: Fabrics)

Modern Textile Fabrics Inc.
708 Broadway
New York, NY 10003
(Products: Macramé; contract, flame-
resistant fabrics)

Naco Fabrics
145 Plant Avenue
Hauppauge, NY 11788
(Product: Contract and residential
quality fabrics)

National Felt Corp.
P.O. Box 150
Easthampton, MA 01027
(Products: Blackout, insulative lining;
nonwoven, reflective support fab-
rics; pleatable fabrics)

Naugahyde-Uniroyal
515 E. Dyer Road
Santa Ana, CA 92707
(Product: Vinyl-coated fabrics)

Newcastle Fabrics
80 Wythe Avenue
Brooklyn, NY 11211
(Product: Decorative, contract win-
dow-shade sunscreen fabric)

Odenheimer & Baker Fabrics
2260 Townsgate Road
Westlake Village, CA 91361
(Product: Variety of fine decorative
fabrics—residential and contract)

OJVM Wallcoverings
4B Marlboro Industrial Park
P.O. Drawer O
Marlboro, NJ 07746
(Products: Contract wall covering and
fabric)

O'Krent Fabrics Inc.
P.O. Box 12009
San Antonio, TX 78212
(Product: Designer fabrics)

Old Deerfield Inc.
134 Sand Park Road
Cedar Grove, NJ 07009
(Products: Cotton prints; wall coverings with coordinated fabric)

Old World Weavers
979 Third Avenue
New York, NY 10022
(Products: Fabrics; trimmings)

Orcon Corp.
33430 Western Avenue
Union City, CA 94587
(Product: Insulative lining)

Ouimet Corp.
230 Elliot Street
Brockton, MA 02403
(Product: Vinyl, laminated fabrics)

Panoramic Shades
221 Rayette Road
Concord, Ontario
L4K 2G1 Canada
(Product: Imported fabrics)

Paramount Fabrics Inc.
4556 Tennyson Street
Denver, CO 80212
(Products: Decorative and flame-resistant fabrics)

Parker Knoll Textiles Ltd.
P.O. Box 30
West End Road
High Wycombe, Bucks HP 112QD
England
(Product: Designer fabrics)

Pedlar & Co. Imports Inc.
2611 Fairmount Street
Dallas, TX 75201
(Product: Trimmings for drapery, upholstery, and wall coverings)

Phifer Wire Products Inc.
P.O. Box 1700
Tuscaloosa, AL 35403
(Products: Drapery lining fabrics; exterior, flame-resistant woven fabrics)

Pindler & Pindler Inc.
2580 Sante Fe Avenue
Redondo Beach, CA 90278
(Products: Wallpaper; fabrics)

Polylok Corp.
31 West 54th Street
New York, NY 10019
(Product: Contract, decorative, flame-resistant fabrics)

Quadrille Wallpapers & Fabrics Inc.
979 Third Avenue
New York, NY 10022
(Products: Wallpaper; fabrics—cotton and chintz prints)

Quaker Fabric Corp.
205 Lexington Avenue
New York, NY 10016
(Product: Historic American fabrics)

Raintree Designs
979 Third Avenue
New York, NY 10022
(Products: Wall coverings; fabrics including custom designs)

Rancocos Fabrics Inc.
979 Third Avenue
New York, NY 10022
(Product: Residential and commercial wall and upholstery woolen fabrics)

R. J. Randolph Inc.
916½ N. La Cienega
Los Angeles, CA 90069
(Product: Hand-painted customized fabrics)

Randolph & Hein
1 Arkansas Street
San Francisco, CA 94107
(Product: Designer fabrics)

Richloom Fabrics Corp.
261 Fifth Avenue, 12th Floor
New York, NY 10016
(Product: Decorative and contract fabric)

Robeco Chemicals Inc.
99 Park Avenue
New York, NY 10016
(Product: Flame-resistant and vinyl fabric)

Rockland Industries Inc.
1601 Edison Highway
Baltimore, MD 21213
(Product: Drapery lining—residential and contract)

Rodolph Inc.
999 W. Spain Street
P.O. Box 1249
Sonoma, CA 95476
(Product: Fine designer textiles)

Sheri Roese Inc.
14601 S. Main Street, #101
Gardena, CA 90248
(Product: Hand-painted silks)

Maya Romanoff Corp.
1730 W. Greenleaf
Chicago, IL 60626
(Products: Custom and stock hand-dyed fabrics and wall coverings)

Ben Rose Inc.
6828 N. Clark Street
Chicago, IL 60626
(Product: Hand-screened prints, casements, contract fabrics)

Rosecore Carpet Co. Inc.
979 Third Avenue
New York, NY 10022
(Products: Companion designs; wool carpets; coordinating fabrics and wall coverings)

Arthur Sanderson & Sons
979 Third Avenue
New York, NY 10022
(Products: Fabrics; wall coverings)

S & S Fabrics
1367 N. Miami Avenue
Miami, FL 33136
(Products: Contract and residential fabrics; drapery services)

Sarda Hermanos
Calle Mallorca, 237
Barcelona 8
Spain
(Product: Fine lace)

Sateens Inc.
5620 Kennedy Boulevard
West New York, NJ 07093
(Product: Decorative and imported fabrics and draperies)

Scalamandre Inc.
37–24 24th Street
Long Island City, NY 11101
(Product: Contract and residential wall coverings, upholstery, drapery, and trimmings)

Scancelli
190–212 Van Winkle Street
P.O. Box 416
East Rutherford, NJ 07073
(Product: Coordinated wall coverings and fabrics)

Schmitz-Werke GmbH & Co.
Hansetrasse 87
D-4407 Emsdetten
Federal Republic of Germany
(Products: Drapery; blackout fabrics)

F. Schumacher & Co.
79 Madison Avenue
New York, NY 10016
(Product: Wall coverings and fabrics—
   residential and contract)

J. Robert Scott & Associates
8727 Melrose Avenue
Los Angeles, CA 90069
(Product: Correlated fabrics and wall
   coverings)

Scroll Fabrics Inc.
4500 Highlands Parkway
Smyrna, GA 30080
(Product: Fabrics; quilting service)

Seabrook Wallcoverings Inc.
1325 Farmville Road
Memphis, TN 38122
(Product: Variety of fabrics)

Seacove Handprints Inc.
13580 Wright Circle
Tampa, FL 33624
(Product: Coordinated wall coverings
   and fabrics)

Sidlaw of Scotland
3260 Powers Ferry Road
Marrietta, GA 30067
(Product: Textile wall coverings)

Sirmos Etalage
979 Third Avenue
New York, NY 10022
(Product: Fabrics for drapery and upholstery)

The Soft Path
2927 Paseo
Oklahoma City, OK 73103
(Product: Insulative fabrics)

Sommer Wallcoverings
965 Jefferson Avenue
Union, NJ 07083
(Product: French fabrics and wall coverings)

Spring Mills
Retail & Specialty Fabrics Division
104 W. 40th Street
New York, NY 10018
(Products: Ultrasuede, textiles)

Stauffer Chemical Co.
Fabricated Products Division
Livingstone Avenue
Dobbs Ferry, NY 10522
(Product: Vertical blinds; fabrics and
   coil stock; flame-resistant fabrics)

Stead Textile Co. Inc.
1334 State Street
Chicago Heights, IL 60411
(Product: Decorative, finished, flame-
   resistant, imported, quilted, lining,
   sheer and woven fabrics)

Clifford Stephens
101 N. Fairfax Avenue
Los Angeles, CA 90046
(Products: Wall coverings; fabrics including French bed, bath, and table
   linens)

Steven Fabrics Co.
1400 Van Buren Street N.E.
Minneapolis, MN 55413
(Products: Drapery and lining fabrics)

Stratford Hall Inc.
459 S. Calhoun Street
Ft. Worth, TX 76104
(Product: Contract and residential fabric)

Stroheim & Romann Inc.
10 W. 20th Street
New York, NY 10011
(Product: Fabrics for upholstery, drapery, and wall coverings)

Superior Shade & Blind Co. Inc.
1541 N. Powerline Road
Pompano Beach, FL 33069
(Product: Decorative, contract, imported, and woven fabrics)

Sureway Trading Enterprises
111 Peter Street, Suite 212
Toronto, Ontario
M5V 2H1 Canada
(Product: Contract, macramé, flame-
   resistant, imported fabrics)

T. D. I. Drapery Importing Co.
20 W. 33rd Street
New York, NY 10001
(Product: Decorative, finished, imported, seamless, sheer, macramé,
   and woven fabrics)

Telos 90
979 Third Avenue
New York, NY 10022
U.S. Importer:
Hillman Co. Inc.
1694 Maxwell
Troy, MI 48084
(Product: Modular sliding fabric pan-
   els)

Textiles Unlimited
P.O. Box 345
Stratford, CT 06497
(Product: New York decorative fabric
   source)

Textures and Co.
P.O. Box 271143
Houston, TX 77277
(Product: Interiors textiles)

Thermovane Inc.
125 Getty Avenue
Clifton, NJ 07011
(Products: Vertical blind fabric; contract, decorative, flame-resistant,
   insulative, reflective, sheer and
   woven fabrics)

Richard E. Thibaut Inc.
706 S. 21st Street
Irvington, NJ 07111
(Product: Contract and residential wall
   coverings; companion fabrics)

Jim Thompson Thai Silk/Rodolph
561 Broadway
P.O. Box 1249
Sonoma, CA 95476
(Product: Residential textiles)

Threadtex
411 Fifth Avenue
New York, NY 10016
(Exclusive worldwide agents of the
   Sea Island Cotton Growers Associ-
   ation Ltd.)

Thybony Wallcoverings
2435 W. Belmont Avenue
Chicago, IL 60618
(Product: Coordinated wall coverings
   and fabrics)

Tietex Corp.
P.O. Box 6218
Spartanburg, SC 29304
(Product: Decorative, flame-resistant,
   and reflective fabrics)

Tiffany Prints
A. Collins & Aikman Co.
23645 Mercantile Road
Cleveland, OH 44122
(Product: Fabrics and wall coverings)

Tioga Mill Outlet
200 S. Hartman Street
York, PA 17403
(Product: Shop-by-mail discount fabrics)

Titan Seal
Division of Ludlow Corp.
P.O. Box 1566
4031 Ross Clark Circle, N.W.
Dothan, AL 36302
(Product: Contract, decorative, exterior, fiberfill, finished, insulative, reflective, vinyl, woven and screening fabrics)

Tomsaco Fabrics Inc.
5620 Kennedy Boulevard
West New York, NJ 07093
(Product: Decorative imported fabric)

Tressard Fabrics Inc.
979 Third Avenue
New York, NY 10022
(Product: Designer fabrics and wall coverings)

Tri-Mark Tulip
1006 Arch Street
Philadelphia, PA 19107
(Product: Contract fabrics)

Twitchell
P.O. Box 1566
Dothan, AL 36302
(Product: Decorative and flame-resistant fabric)

Unika Vaev
305 E. 63rd Street
New York, NY 10021
(Product: Natural-fiber textiles)

United Textile and Supply Co. Inc.
1641 N. Allesandro Street
Los Angeles, CA 90026
(Products: Exterior, flame-resistant, imported fabrics; exterior cordage)

Jack Valentine Inc.
104 E. 25th Street
New York, NY 10010
(Product: Decorative fabrics—tropical, floral, and exotic prints)

Valley Forge Fabrics Inc.
7 W. 22nd Street
New York, NY 10010
(Products: Flame-resistant fabrics)

Val. Mehler Aktiengesellschaft
Edelzeller Strasse 44
D-6400
Federal Republic of Germany
(Product: Exterior awning, finished, laminated, and woven fabrics)

Albert Van Luit
200 Garden City Plaza
Garden City, NY 11530
(Products: Wall coverings; fabric coordinates)

Variations
168 Northeast 40th Street
Miami, FL 33137
(Product: Designer fabrics)

Varinit Corp.
Box 6602
Greenville, SC 29606
(Product: Contract, flame-resistant, insulative, lining, and sheer fabrics)

Vermillion
1933 S. Broadway
Suite 226–228
Los Angeles, CA 90007
(Product: Modern, contemporary, and exotic fabrics)

T. J. Vestor
U.S. Distributors:
Cali-secca Inc.
8648 Sunset Boulevard
Los Angeles, CA
(Product: Fine Italian fabrics; toweling and bedding)

Wall Pride Inc.
7050 Valjean Avenue
Van Nuys, CA 91406
(Products: Upholstery; wall coverings)

Warner Co.
108 S. Des Plaines Street
Chicago, IL 60606
(Product: Wall coverings; fabrics)

Waverly Fabrics
Division of F. Schumacher & Co.
79 Madison Avenue
New York, NY 10016
(Product: Historical and contemporary fabrics and wallpapers)

Helen Webber Designs Ltd.
74 Digital Drive, Studio 8
Novato, CA 94949
(Product: Wall coverings; tapestries)

Wesco
4001 Forest
Denver, CO 80216
(Product: Designer fabrics including exclusive European designs)

Westgate
1000 Fountain Parkway
Grand Prairie, TX 75050
(Product: Broad selection of residential and contract fabrics)

West Point Pepperell
P.O. Box 58440
Dallas, TX 75258
(Product: Awning and canopy fabric)

Window Fashion Fabricators Inc.
1334 State Street
Chicago Heights, IL 60411
(Product: Decorative, finished, imported sheer and woven fabrics)

Window Modes/Modern Window
979 Third Avenue
New York, NY 10022
(Products: Hand-woven string vertical louvers; string draperies)

Winfield Design Associates Inc.
2690 Harrison Street
San Francisco, CA 94110
(Products: Wall coverings; coordinated fabrics)

Woodson Wallpapers Co.
200 Lexington Avenue
New York, NY 10016
(Products: Fabrics; wall coverings)

World Wide Importing Ltd.
240 Humberline Drive
Rexdale, Ontario
M9W 5X1 Canada
(Products: Draperies; vertical blinds; fabrics; laminated shades)

Zumsteg
979 Third Avenue
New York, NY 10022
(Products: Wall coverings and high-quality decorative fabrics—including European-designed fabrics)

Appendix 6 Workroom Supplies and Equipment

Adler America Inc.
4661 Hammermill Road
Tucker, GA 30084
(Products: Sewing equipment)

Ambassador Industries Inc.
2754 W. Temple Street
Los Angeles, CA 90026
(Products: Workroom supplies)

Ametek Inc.
P.O. Box 339
Odenton, MD 21113
(Product: Monofilament thread)

Baker Drapery Corp.
1116 Pioneer Parkway
Peoria, IL 61615
(Product: Snap-a-Pleat pleating system)

Brother International Corp.
8 Corporate Place
Piscataway, NJ 08854
(Products: Drapery workroom equipment; blind- and shade-manufacturing equipment)

Bruin Plastics Company Inc.
P.O. Box 175
Glendale, RI 02826
(Product: Oui-Lok hook-and-loop fasteners)

Al Burkhardt Custom Shade Co.
1152 Second Avenue
New York, NY 10021
(Fabric shades service)

Condell Designs
16651 14 Mile Road
Fraser, MI 48206
(Products: Workroom notions and supplies)

CONSEW—Consolidated Sewing Machine
56–65 Rust Street
Maspeth, NY 11378
(Products: Cutting, sewing, quilting, shade, and blind equipment)

Conso Products Co.
295 Fifth Avenue, Suite 1618
New York, NY 10016
(Products: Drapery pleating systems; trimmings; workroom thread; notions and supplies)

Creative Engineering and Manufacturing Corp.
5719 W. Highway 22
Crestwood, KY 40014
(Products: Workroom equipment and supplies; consultation; contract drapery service)

Decorative Aides Co. Inc.
317 St. Paul's Avenue
Jersey City, NJ 07306
(Product: Pressure-sensitive tape)

Drapemaker Industries
1401 Ouest Legendre
Montreal, Quebec
H4N 2B9 Canada
(Product: Pleating tapes)

Eastern Sewing & Shoe Machinery Corp.
134–136 W. 25th Street
New York, NY 10118
(Products: Cutting, sewing, and quilting equipment)

Eastman Machine Co.
779 Washington Street
Buffalo, NY 14203
(Products: Cutting equipment)

Emerling & Co.
574 Weddell Drive, #9
Sunnyvale, CA 94089
(Products: CALHOOK sample management products; fabric estimators)

Eton Systems Inc.
4000 McGinnis Ferry Road
Alpharetta, GA 30201
(Products: Sewing equipment)

EWC—Eastern Woolen Co.
230 E. 5th Street
St. Paul, MN 55101
(Products: Cutting, sewing, steam, and sealing workroom equipment)

Fasnap Corp.
23765 C.R. 6
Elkhart, IN 46515
(Product: Hook-and-loop and snap fasteners)

Hanmars Potpourri Windows Plus
979 Third Avenue
New York, NY 10022
(Product: Fabric shades service)

The Heminway & Bartlett Manufacturing Co.
67 Mason Street
Greenwich, CT 06830
(Products: Findings; hook-and-loop
    fasteners; thread)

Hoffman Brothers
5290 N. Pearl Street
Rosemont, IL 60018
(Products: Cutting, sewing, and quilt-
    ing equipment)

Home & Castle Architectural Shading Systems
7531 Coldwater Canyon Avenue
North Hollywood, CA 91605
(Products: Workroom supplies; shade
    fabricating)

House of Rods Inc.
262 Dove Drive
New Pt. Richey, FL 33552
(Product: Workroom supplies and
    findings)

Interior Textiles
Columbia Communications Inc.
370 Lexington Avenue
New York, NY 10017
(Product: Curtain, drapery, slipcover,
    and accessory yardage charts)

Jacobson Plastics Inc.
1375 Gladys Avenue
Long Beach, CA 90804
(Products: Workroom supplies)

Jado Sewing Machine Co.
40–08 22nd Street
Long Island City, NY 11101
(Products: Automated sewing equip-
    ment)

Johnson Plastics
10804 Normandale Boulevard
Minneapolis, MN 55437
(Products: Workroom supplies)

Juki America Inc.
421 N. Midland Avenue
Saddle Brook, NJ 07662
(Products: Quilting and sewing work-
    room equipment)

McMurray Co.
702 N. Mariposa Street
Burbank, CA 91506
(Products: Workroom supplies and
    services)

The Magnet Store
607 S. Gilbert
Castle Rock, CO 80104
(Products: Magnetic window-covering
    supplies)

Maxant Master Inc.
404 Atlantic Avenue
Oceanside, NY 11572
(Products: Cutting and sewing equip-
    ment)

The Measuregraph Co.
4600 Waldo Industrial Drive
High Ridge, MO 63049
(Products: Workroom equipment)

Modern Mono Inc.
P.O. Box 1245
Waynesboro, VA 22980
(Product: Nylon monofilament sewing
    threads)

S. Morantz Inc.
4056 Chestnut Street
Philadelphia, PA 19104
(Products: Workroom equipment and
    supplies)

Morgan Manufacturing & Engineering Co.
1611 Fabricon Boulevard
Jeffersonville, IN 47130
(Products: Drapery workroom equip-
    ment)

National Felt Co.
P.O. Box 150
Easthampton, MA 01027
(Product: Drapery headings)

Nu Modes
181 Chrystie Street
New York, NY 10002
(Product: Fabric shades)

OB/MASCO Drapery Hardware
1435 Folsom Street
San Francisco, CA 94103
(Products: Workroom supplies)

Ouimet Corporation
230 Elliot Street
Brockton, MA 02430
(Products: Hook-and-loop fasteners;
    plastic extrusions)

Pfaff-Pegasus of USA Inc.
3875 Green Industrial Way
Atlanta, GA 30341
(Products: Sewing equipment)

Quiltcraft Industries Inc.
1933 Levee Street
Dallas, TX 75207
(Product: Quilting service)

Robinson Thread Co. Inc.
19 McKeon Road
Worcester, MA 01613
(Products: Findings and thread)

Roman Shades by Ray
612 S. La Brea Avenue
Los Angeles, CA 90036
(Product: Fabric shades service)

Sonics & Materials Inc.
Kenosia Avenue
Danbury, CT 06810
(Product: Pinsonic sewing equipment)

Speed-O-Pin Machine Manufacturing Co.
1375 Gladys Avenue
Long Beach, CA 90804
(Products: Workroom supplies; pleat-
    ing tape; pinning equipment)

Sprayway Inc.
484 Vista Avenue
Addison, IL 60101
(Products: Aerosol workroom prod-
    ucts)

Textol Systems Inc.
435 Meadow Lane
Carlstadt, NJ 07072
(Products: Shade tape and rings; rip-
    ple nylon snap tape)

Thomas & McNeal Inc.
1902 S. Harrison Street
Ft. Wayne, IN 46804
(Products: Workroom supplies)

Tuggles Associates Ltd.
544 Southlake
Richmond, VA 23236
(Products: Drapery fabric; lining and
    workroom services)

United Textile & Supply Co.
1641 N. Allesandro Street
Los Angeles, CA 90026
(Products: Findings; thread hook-and-
loop fasteners)

U.S. Blind Stitch Machine Corp.
79 Express Street
Plainview, NY 11803
(Products: Sewing equipment)

Velcro U.S.A. Inc.
406 Brown Avenue
Manchester, NH 03108
(Product: Hook-and-loop fasteners)

Wellington-Puritan Inc.
P.O. Box 224
Madison, GA 30650
(Product: Cordage)

Window Works
912 Excelsior Avenue
Hopkins, MN 55343
(Products: Workroom supplies; shade
hardware; Roman shades)

Wolf Machine Co.
5570 Creek Road
Cincinnati, OH 45331
(Products: Cutting and workroom
equipment)

Appendix 7   Drapery Hardware and Installation Aids

Matthew Adam Inc.
2074 Congressional Drive
St. Louis, MO 63141
(Products: Installation supplies)

Ambassador Industries Inc.
2754 W. Temple Street
Los Angeles, CA 90026
(Product: Drapery hardware)

Automated Drapery Controls
2800 Neilson Way
Santa Monica, CA 90405
(Product: Drapery controls)

Baker Drapery Corp.
1116 W. Pioneer Parkway
Peoria, IL 61615
(Product: Snap-a-Pleat drapery system)

Beauti Pleat Inc.
6631 Mayfair
Houston, TX 77087
(Product: Beauti Pleat hardware system)

Eli Custom Window Treatment Ltd.
45–20 38th Street
Long Island City, NY 11101
(Products: Motorized equipment)

Fiber-Seal International Co.
11714 Forest Central Drive
Dallas, TX 75243
(Professional fabric care and maintenance)

Allen Field Co. Inc.
10 E. 22nd Street
New York, NY 10010
(Products: Blinds; shades; components)

Friedman/Gellman
19 Engineers Lane
Farmingdale, NY 11735
(Products: Drapery workroom equipment)

Garfield Industries
P.O. Box 5265
Shreveport, LA 71105
(Product: Adjustable brackets)

H. Gartenmaier
Keplerstrasse 4
D-7208 Spaichingen
Federal Republic of Germany
(Product: Motorized systems for blinds, draperies, and shades)

Glare-Con Inc.
610 Colcord Drive
Oklahoma City, OK 73102
(Product: Motors and motorized systems)

Graber Industries
7549 Graber Road
Middleton, WI 53562-1096
(Product: Drapery hardware)

Guilford Mills Inc.
P.O. Box U-4
Greensboro, NC 27402
(Products: Blinds; shades)

Home & Castle Architectural Shading Systems
7531 Coldwater Canyon Avenue
North Hollywood, CA 91605
(Product: Motors and motorized systems)

House of Rods Inc.
262 Dove Drive
New Pt. Richey, FL 33552
(Product: Drapery hardware and installation equipment)

S. Kaplan Sewing Machine Co. Inc.
107 W. 25th Street
New York, NY 10001
(Products: Cutting, sewing, and slitting equipment)

Kenney Window Fashions
1000 Jefferson Boulevard
Warwick, RI 02886
(Products: Drapery hardware; motors and motorized systems)

Kirsch
309 N. Prospect Street
Sturgis, MI 49091
(Product: Drapery hardware)

L. E. G. Motorized Systems
20258 N.E. 15th Court
North Miami, FL 33179
(Product: Motorized drapery systems)

McMurray Co.
702 N. Mariposa Street
Burbank, CA 91506
(Product: Drapery hardware and installation supplies)

The Magnet Store
607 South Gilbert
Castle Rock, CO 80104
(Product: Magnetic window coverings)

Mann Drapery Manufacturing Inc
5935 Kester Avenue
Van Nuys, CA 91411
(Product: Drapery hardware and workrooms)

Mark Window Products
2625 Rouselle Street
Santa Ana, CA 92707
(Product: Drapery hardware)

OB/MASCO Drapery Hardware
1435 Folsom Street
San Francisco, CA 94103
(Products: Drapery hardware; aluminum extrusions; motors and motorized systems for draperies)

Paramount Fabrics Inc.
4556 Tennyson Street
Denver, CO 80212
(Product: Drapery hardware)

Plastic Products Inc.
Luxout Products Division
P.O. Box 1118
Richmond, VA 23208
(Product: Motors and motorized systems)

Roper Eastern
9325 Snowden River Parkway
Columbia, MD 21046
(Product: Drapery hardware)

R. H. Rowley Company
615 Meeks Road R-8
Gastonia, NC 28054
(Product: Window-treatment installation supplies)

Shades Unlimited
3400 N. Powerline Road
Pompano Beach, FL 33069
(Product: Drapery hardware)

SM Automatic
10301 Jefferson Boulevard
Culver City, CA 90232
(Products: Drapery hardware and controls; motors and motorized systems for blinds, draperies, and shades)

Solar Drape
225 Portage Road
Lewiston, NY 14092
(Product: Automated drapery controls)

South Bound Millworks
P.O. Box 349
Sandwich, MA 02563
(Product: Rods and brackets)

Speed-O-Pin Machine Manufacturing Co.
1375 Gladys Avenue
Long Beach, CA 90804
(Products: Drapery hardware; Jet Pinner)

Spring Crest Co.
505 W. Lambert Road
Brea, CA 92621
(Product: Spring Crest drapery systems)

Appendix 8   Blind, Shade, and Shutter Manufacturers

AB Sani-Maskiner
P.O. Box 9042
Jagersrovagen 202
S-200 39 Malmo
Sweden
(Products: Hard treatments; manufacturing supplies and equipment)

A. C. Shutters
P.O. Box 6716
Cleveland, OH 44101
(Product: Energy-efficient shutters—exterior, insulating, greenhouse, rolling)

Adjustatrak Inc.
6714 White Drive
West Palm Beach, FL 33407
(Products: Vertical blinds; hardware)

Adler America Inc.
4661 Hammermill Road
Tucker, GA 30084
(Products: Blind and shade equipment)

Ambassador Industries Inc.
2754 Temple Street
Los Angeles, CA 90026
(Products: Blinds and components)

American Home Furnishings
9743 E. 54th Street
Tulsa, OK 74145
(Product: Narrow-Vue verticals)

Annex Manufacturing Inc.
3915 Bonnieview Road
Dallas, TX 75216
(Product: Blinds)

Arrow Adhesives
4671 E. 11th Avenue
Hialeah, FL 33013
(Products: Vertical blind components and adhesives)

Awning and Supply Co. Inc.
203 Commission Boulevard
Lafayette, LA 70508
(Product: Exterior window treatments)

Bali Blinds
Marathon Carey-McFall
Loyalsock Avenue
Montoursville, PA 17754
(Product: Horizontal miniblinds)

B & B Manufacturing
11920 W. Carmen Avenue
Milwaukee, WI 53225
(Product: Blind and shade manufacturing equipment and adhesive)

Belding Corticelli Thread Co.
1430 Broadway
New York, NY 10018
(Product: Stock blinds)

Beltek Industries Inc.
3555 E. Cremazie, Suite 215
Montreal, Quebec
H1Z 2J3 Canada
(Products: Blinds; components and hardware)

The Blind Factory
96 N. Beverwyck Road
Lake Hiawatha, NJ 07034
(Products: Blinds; shades)

Blind Factory Southwest
516 E. Juanita Avenue
Mesa, AZ 85234
(Products: Blinds; shades)

The Blind Maker
2013 Centimeter Circle
Austin, TX 78758
(Product: Blinds)

Blind Shine Company
3629 MacArthur Boulevard
Santa Ana, CA 92704
(Product: Blind-cleaning products)

A. J. Boyd Industries Inc.
P.O. Box 401
Whitehall Road
Andover, NJ 07821
(Product: Blinds and components)

Breneman Inc.
1133 Sycamore Street
Cincinnati, OH 45210
(Product: Woven-wood shades)

Broward Window Shade Co. Inc.
1980 Stirling Road
Dania, FL 33004
(Products: Shades; blinds)

Builders Maintenance Services Inc.
25611 Coolidge Highway
Oak Park, MI 48237
(Product: Blind-cleaning equipment)

C & M Shade Corp.
50 Lewis Street
South Hackensack, NJ 07606
(Products: Shades; blinds)

Carnegie Fabrics Inc.
110 N. Centre Avenue
Rockville Centre, NY 11570
(Product: Fabric verticals)

Clopay Corp.
101 E. 4th Street
Cincinnati, OH 45202
(Product: Woven shades)

The C-Mor Company
7 Jewell Street
Garfield, NJ 07026
(Product: Bead chain-operated shades)

Conrad Imports Inc.
575 10th Street
San Francisco, CA 94103
(Product: Shades)

Conso Products Co.
295 Fifth Avenue, Suite 1618
New York, NY 10016
(Product: Fabric and macramé vertical blinds)

Coral of Chicago
2001 South Calumet Avenue
Chicago, IL 60616
(Product: Vertical blinds)

Cortina Shade Manufacturing Inc.
112 Greylock Avenue
Belleville, NJ 07109
(Product: Wood blinds)

**Custom Bilt Products Company
Inc.**
6524 Ellis Avenue S.
Seattle, WA 98108
(Products: Blinds; shades; shutters)

Decorative Aides Co. Inc.
317 St. Paul's Avenue
Jersey City, NJ 07306
(Product: Vertical blind fabrics)

Del Mar Window Coverings
7150 Fenwick Lane
Westminster, CA 92683
(Products: Woven wood shades;
blinds; shades)

Designer Vertical Blind
27209 West Warren
Dearborn Heights, MI 48127
(Product: Vertical blinds)

Designs in Blinds Inc.
830 N.W. 57th Court
Ft. Lauderdale, FL 33309
(Products: Blinds; shades)

Dixie Verticals
Division of Hunter Douglas
3363 N.W. 54th Street
Miami, FL 33166
(Products: Vertical blinds; fabrics)

John Dixon Inc.
23500 Mercantile Road
Beechwood, OH 44122
(Product: Vertical blinds)

Doff Products
405 Cedar Avenue
Minneapolis, MN 55454
(Products: Shade- and blind-
manufacturing equipment; materials and supplies)

Drapery Depot
2432 Erringer
Simi Valley, CA 93065
(Product: Blind-cleaning equipment)

Duratex Inc.
6728 Federal Boulevard
Denver, CO 80221
(Products: Blinds; shades; shutters)

**Eastern Sewing and Shoe
Machinery Corp.**
134–136 W. 25th Street
New York, NY 10118
(Products: Shade, blind, and sealing
equipment)

**Eli Custom Window Treatments
Ltd.**
45-20 38th Street
Long Island City, NY 11101
(Products: Blinds; shades)

**Elite Vertical and Horizontal
Blinds Manufacturing Co. Ltd.**
90 Wildcat Road
Downsview, Ontario
M3J 2V4 Canada
(Product: Blinds and supplies)

Elkhart Door Inc. (E.D.I.)
P.O. Box 2177
1515 Leininger Avenue
Elkhart, IN 46515
(Product: Woven-wood roll goods)

Essex Shade Co.
625 Ramsey Avenue
Hillside, NJ 07205
(Products: Blinds; shades)

Evashin Wood U.S. Co.
270 S. Milpitas Boulevard
Milpitas, CA 95035
(Product: Woven-wood roll goods)

Faber Industries Ltd.
225 Industrial Drive
Fredericksburg, VA 22401
(Products: Blind- and shade-
manufacturing equipment)

Flexalum Decor Blinds
Hunter Douglas Inc.
2 Park Way & Route 17 S.
Upper Saddle River, NJ 07458
(Products: Miniblinds; vertical lou-
vers)

Florida Shades Inc.
1000 U.S. Highway 19 S.
Palm Harbor, FL 34684
(Products: Shades; blinds)

Gali Manufacturing Corp.
215 W. 21st Street
Hialeah, FL 33010
(Products: Blinds; components; fabric)

G & L Shades Inc.
2350 Harris Way
San Jose, CA 95131
(Products: Blinds; shades)

Garci Plastic Industries
1730 W. 38th Place
Hialeah, FL 33012
(Product: Vinyl blinds and components)

H. Gartenmaier
Postfach 1106
Keplerstrasse 4
D-7208 Spaichingen
Federal Republic of Germany
(Product: Manual and automated
blinds and awnings)

GEMCO Inc.
920 Essex Street
Brooklyn, NY 11208
(Product: Vertical blinds)

General Clutch Corp.
425 Fairfield Avenue
Stamford, CT 06902
(Product: Blind and shade components)

Glare-Con Inc.
610 Colcord Drive
Oklahoma City, OK 73102
(Products: Shades; blinds; shutters)

Graber Industries
7549 Graber Road
Middleton, WI 53562-1096
(Product: Blinds; shades)

Hamilton Web
24 W. 40th Street
New York, NY 10018
(Products: Blinds; webbing)

Heeshade
195 Nantucket Boulevard
Scarborough, Ontario
M1P 2P3 Canada
(Products: Blinds; shades)

Paul Heinley Shutters
Division of Lenyo Corp.
3350 Hayden Avenue
Culver City, CA 90232
(Products: Shutters; shoji screens; louvers; dividers)

Heli-X-Shade Co.
80 Roebling Street
Brooklyn, NY 11211
(Products: Manual and motorized
shading systems; shades)

Historic Windows
Box 1172
Harrisonburg, VA 22801
(Product: Authentic Early American
hardwood shutters)

Hoffman Brothers
5290 N. Pearl Street
Rosemont, IL 60018
(Products: Blind- and shade-
manufacturing equipment)

Holland Shade
21-07 Borden Avenue
Long Island City, NY 11101
(Products: Custom shutters; shades;
miniblinds; Venetian blinds)

House of Rods
262 Dove Drive
New Pt. Richey, FL 33552
(Products: Blind-cleaning equipment)

**Hunter Douglas North American
Operations**
2 Park Way & Route 17 S.
Upper Saddle River, NJ 07458
(Products: Blinds; shades)

International Blind Co.
P.O. Box 777
Chester, PA 19016
(Products: Awnings; blinds; rolling
shutters)

International Vertical Systems
8438 N.W. 66th Street
Miami, FL 33166
(Product: Blinds)

Jacobson Plastics Inc.
1375 Gladys Avenue
Long Beach, CA 90804
(Products: Blinds; blind- and shade-
cleaning equipment; shade and
shutter hardware and components)

Jag Corp.
7020 E. 38th Street
Tulsa, OK 74145
(Product: Blinds)

Jencraft Corp.
1 Taft Road
Totowa, NJ 07512
(Products: Blinds; bamboo and
matchstick shades; pleated and
pull shades; woven-wood shades;
shutters)

J. K. Enterprises
1375 Gladys Avenue
Long Beach, CA 90804
(Products: Blind- and shutter-cleaning
equipment)

Joanna
Division of CHF Industries
2141 S. Jefferson Street
Chicago, IL 60616
(Products: Blinds; shades; hardware)

Juki America Inc.
421 N. Midland Avenue
Saddle Brook, NJ 07662
(Products: Blind- and shade-
manufacturing equipment)

Kaleidoscope Industries Inc.
1265 Grand Oak Drive
Howell, MI 48843
(Product: Vertical and horizontal
blinds)

Kalex Chemical Co.
57-27 49th Street
Maspeth, NY 11378
(Product: Vinyl shades)

Kenney Window Fashions
1000 Jefferson Boulevard
Warwick, RI 02886
(Products: Venetian blinds; wood
blinds; woven-wood shades; vinyl
and pleated shades)

Kirsch
309 N. Prospect Street
Sturgis, MI 49091
(Products: Blinds and components;
decorative, pleated, and woven-
wood shades)

Julius Koch USA Inc.
387 Church Street
P.O. Box A-995
New Bedford, MA 02741
(Products: Blinds; components; fabric)

Lafayette Venetian Blinds Inc.
820 Roberts Street
P.O. Box 646
Lafayette, IN 47902
(Product: Venetian blinds)

Laurel Manufacturing Co. Inc.
64-15 Grand Avenue
Maspeth, NY 11378
(Product: Blinds)

L. E. G. Motorized Systems
20258 N.E. 15th Court
North Miami, FL 33179
(Products: Blinds and components;
motors and motorized systems)

Levolor Lorentzen Inc.
1 Upper Pond Road
Parsippany, NJ 07054
(Products: Blinds and components;
   woven-metal shades)

Lifetime Vertical Corp.
140 Admiral Street
P.O. Box 9359
Bridgeport, CT 06601-9359
(Products: Hard treatment compo-
   nents and cleaners)

Lightworks
3345 Hunting Park Avenue
Philadelphia, PA 19132
(Product: Litepanel lighting systems
   for windows, dividers, and so on)

London Textiles
P.O. Box 690634
Tulsa, OK 74169
(Product: Vertical blinds)

Louverdrape Inc.
1100 Colorado Avenue
Santa Monica, CA 90401
(Product: Vertical blinds)

Louver Magic Inc.
99-A Bell Street
West Babylon, NY 11704
(Products: Blinds; hardware; motorized systems)

Macramates Inc.
2005 N.W. 62nd Street
Ft. Lauderdale, FL 33309
(Product: Macramé window treatments)

Maen Line Fabrics Inc.
219 Chestnut Street
Philadelphia, PA 19106
(Product: Decorator fabrics)

M & B
1818 S. Oak Street
Los Angeles, CA 90015
(Products: Wood blinds; miniblinds;
   vertical blinds)

Mann Drapery Manufacturing Inc.
5935 Kester Avenue
Van Nuys, CA 91411
(Product: Vertical blinds)

Marathon Carey-McFall Company
Route 405
P.O. Box 500
Montgomery, PA 17754
(Product: Bali blinds)

Marchant Industries Inc.
1600 Northside Drive, N.W.
Atlanta, GA 30318
(Product: Blinds—contract installations)

Mark Window Products
2625 Rouselle Street
Santa Ana, CA 92707
(Product: Blinds)

Mastercraft Industries Inc.
120 W. Allen Street
Rice Lake, WI 54868
(Product: Shutters)

Modern Window Corp.
200 Lexington Avenue
New York, NY 10016
(Products: Custom-woven shades; vertical blinds)

Montage Inc.
8815 Herrick Road
Twinsburg, OH 44087
(Products: Vertical blinds; blind and
   shade components)

Nanik
7200 Stewart Avenue
Wausau, WI 54401
(Product: Vertical and horizontal
   blinds—metal and wood)

National Felt Corporation
P.O. Box 150
Easthampton, MA 01027
(Product: Vertical fabric blinds)

Newcastle Fabrics
80 Wythe Avenue
Brooklyn, NY 11211
(Product: Vertical fabric blinds)

Newell Window Furnishings Co.
916 S. Arcade Avenue
Freeport, IL 61032
(Product: Vertical blinds)

OB/MASCO Drapery Hardware
1435 Folsom Street
San Francisco, CA 94103
(Product: Variety of hardline treatments)

Ohline Corp.
1930 W. 139th Street
Gardena, CA 90249
(Products: Louvered, inert, rigid, and
   decorative wood shutters; blinds)

Olfa Products Corp.
P.O. Box 747
Plattsburgh, NY 12901
(Products: Cutting- and film-
   installation equipment)

Panoramic Shades
221 Rayette Road
Concord, Ontario
L4K 2G1 Canada
(Products: Vertical blinds; component
   parts for manufacturing blinds)

Patio Blinds of California
750 N. Batavia Street
Orange, CA 92668
(Products: Exterior and interior blinds
   and shades)

Pease Industries Inc.
Rolling Shutter Division
7100 Dixie Highway
Fairfield, OH 45014
(Products: Rolling shutters; motors
   and motorized equipment and
   components)

Perma System Sun Control
5675 E. Oakbrook Parkway
Norcross, GA 30093
(Products: Awnings and canopies;
   hardware; sun/wind sensor controls)

Pinecrest Inc.
2118 Blaisdell Avenue
Minneapolis, MN 55404
(Products: Shutters; sunshades)

Roper Eastern
9325 Snowden River Parkway
Columbia, MD 21046
(Products: Blinds and components;
   pleated blinds)

Royal Crest Inc.
14851 W. 11 Mile Road
Oak Park, MI 48237
(Products: Woven-wood shades;
   blinds)

Shades II
5191 Oceanus Drive
Huntington Beach, CA 92649
(Product: Carved-wood blinds)

Shades Unlimited
3400 N. Powerline Road
Pompano Beach, FL 33069
(Products: Blinds; shades)

Shutter Mart
1022 Morena Boulevard
San Diego, CA 92110
(Product: Custom shutters)

Shutters/East Inc.
P.O. Box 4500034
Atlanta, GA 30345
(Product: Custom shutters)

Shutters Inc.
110 E. 5th Street
Hastings, MN 55033
(Product: Insulated shutters)

Silverado Service Co.
2130 Pickett Road
Calistoga, CA 94515
(Products: Woven-wood roll goods;
   shade hardware)

David Sloan Creations Inc.
Airport Industrial Office Park
Building B-4W
Valley Stream, NY 11581
(Product: Vertical blinds)

SM Automatic
10301 Jefferson Boulevard
Culver City, CA 90232
(Product: Automated window-
   treatment hardware)

Sonic Systems Sales Inc.
P.O. Box 712
Portsmouth, VA 23705
(Product: Blind-cleaning equipment)

Spectrum Fabricators Inc.
237 South Avenue
Garwood, NJ 07027
(Products: Venetian and wood blinds;
   vertical blinds)

Spring Crest Co.
505 W. Lambert Road
Brea, CA 92621
(Product: Blinds—vertical and horizontal)

Stanfield Shutter
3214 S. 300th West
Salt Lake City, UT 84115
(Product: Shutters)

Stemtec Systems Ltd.
Unit 33-601 Bocoman Avenue
Winnipeg, Manitoba
R2K 1P7 Canada
(Product: Track hardware; blind-
   cleaning equipment)

Sunshine Drapery Co
11660 Page Service Drive
St. Louis, MO 63146
(Products: Blinds; shades)

Suntec Wholesale
2410 Tarpley Drive, #304
Carrollton, TX 75006
(Products: Vertical blinds; blind- and
   shade-manufacturing equipment
   and hardware)

**Superior Window Covering
   Products Ltd.**
235 West Seventh Avenue
Vancouver, British Columbia
V5Y 1L9 Canada
(Products: Venetian blinds; mini-
   blinds; vertical blinds; metallizing
   services)

Super-Weave Inc.
707 Race Street
Cincinnati, OH 45202
(Product: Vertical blind fabric)

Sureway Trading Enterprises
111 Peter Street, Suite 212
Toronto, Ontario
M5V 2H1 Canada
(Product: Vertical blinds)

Harold Tallent Enterprises
226 N. Second Street
Upland, CA 91786
(Product: Blind Shine Dusters)

Temperflex Metals Corp.
6401 Virginia Manor Road
Beltsville, MD 20705
(Products: Horizontal and vertical
   blind components)

Tempo Industries Inc.
625 Forest Edge Drive
Vernon Hills, IL 60061
(Products: Vertical and horizontal
   blinds; woven-wood shades;
   pleated shades; wood blinds)

Tentina Window Fashions
1186 Route 109
P.O. Box 615
Lindenhurst, NY 11757
(Products: Blinds; shades)

Texton Inc.
114 Kirby
Garland, TX 75042
(Products: Blinds, shades)

Thermal Wall Insulating Shutters
Road #1, Box 462-A
Voorheesville, NY 12186
(Product: Custom and decorative
   shutters)

Thermo Plastics Corp.
4104 Hahn Boulevard
Ft. Worth, TX 76117
(Product: Plastic, vinyl extrusions)

Thermovane Inc.
125 Getty Avenue
Clifton, NY 07011
(Products: Vertical blind fabric; macramé)

Tietex Corp.
P.O. Box 6218
Spartanburg, SC 29304
(Product: Vertical blinds)

United Vertical Blind Corp.
3740 San Gabriel River Parkway
Pico Rivera, CA 90660
(Products: Vertical blinds; coil stock;
   fabric; components; contract installation)

Urkov Manufacturing
231 S. Green Street
Chicago, IL 60607
(Product: Blinds)

Velux-America Inc.
74 Cummings Park
Woburn, MA 01801
(Product: Blinds)

Verosol USA Inc.
215 Beecham Drive
P.O. Box 517
Pittsburgh, PA 15230
(Products: Pleated shades; hardware)

Vertisun Vertical Blinds Inc.
7321 N.W. 61st Street
Miami, FL 33166
(Products: Vertical blinds; hardware;
   cloth shades)

Warren Shade Co.
2905 E. Hennepin Avenue
Minneapolis, MN 55413
(Products: Wood-slat roll-up shades;
   wood fabric folding doors)

Weavemaster Corp.
1186 Route 109
Lindenhurst, NY 11757
(Product: Woven-wood roll goods)

Wing Industries
11999 Plano Road
Dallas, TX 75243
(Product: Wood exterior and interior
   shutters—stock and custom)

Woollyco
P.O. Box 369
Pembina, ND 58271
(Product: Wool hard-treatment dust-
   ers)

World Wide Importing Ltd.
240 Humberline Drive
Rexdale, Ontario
M9W 5X1 Canada
(Products: Vertical blind components
   and fabric; decorative and laminated shades)

Woven Wood Designs
100 Industrial Park
Marianna, FL 32446
(Product: Woven-wood roll goods)

Wrisco Industries
355 Hiatt Drive
Palm Beach Gardens, FL 33418
(Products: Blind-manufacturing equipment and supplies)

Appendix 9   Shoji Screen Manufacturers and Suppliers

Conrad Imports Inc.
575 10th Street
San Francisco, CA 94103
(Product: Fabric for shoji screens)

Design Shoji
841B Kaynyne Street
Redwood City, CA 94063
(Product: Custom shoji screens,
  residential and nonresidential)

Paul Heinley Shutters
Division of Lenyo Corp.
3550 Hayden Avenue
Culver City, CA 90232
(Product: Shoji screen shutters, pan-
  els, and doors)

Miya Shoji and Interiors
107 W. 17th Street
New York, NY 10011
(Product: Shoji screens)

Ohline Corp.
1930 W. 139th Street
Gardena, CA 90249
(Product: Shutters; wood shoji screens)

Pinecrest Inc.
2118 Blaisdell Avenue
Minneapolis, MN 55404
(Product: Shoji screens)

Shoji Workshop
21–10 31st Avenue
Astoria, NY 11106
(Product: Shoji screens)

**Woodline—The Japanese
  Woodworker**
1731 Clement Avenue
Alameda, CA 94501
(Product: Shoji-making tools)

Appendix 10 Surface Ornamentation

Adele Bishop Inc.
P.O. Box 3349
Kinston, NC 28501
(Products: Stencils; mail order)

Gail Grisi Stenciling Inc.
P.O. Box 1263, Dept. CH
Haddonfield, NJ 08033
(Product: Precut plastic stencils)

Stencil House of New Hampshire
P.O. Box 109, Dept. CM
Hookset, NH 03106
(Product: Stencil supplies)

Appendix 11   Art-Glass Manufacturers

Anderson Art Glass
105 N. Union Street, Studio 316
Alexandria, VA 22314
(Product: Art glass)

Architectural Glass Design
P.O. Box 2572
San Anselmo, CA 94960
(Product: Architectural art glass)

Architectural Glass Designs
87 Clinton Avenue N.
Rochester, NY 14604
(Product: Architectural art glass)

Beauvilla Glass Designs
5237 Sepulveda Boulevard
Culver City, CA 90230
(Product: Art glass)

S. A. Bendheim
122 Hudson Street
New York, NY 10013
(Product: Art glass)

Beveled Glass Designs
9216 DeSoto Avenue
Chatsworth, CA 91311
(Product: Beveled art glass)

Beveled Glass Designs
3185 N. Shadeland Avenue
Indianapolis, IN 46226
(Product: Beveled art glass)

Beveled Glass Industries
6006 W. Washington Boulevard
Culver City, CA 90232
(Product: Beveled art glass)

Cherry Creek Enterprises
937 Santa Fe Drive
Denver, CO 80204
(Product: Art glass)

Chrysalis Studios
15211 N.E. 90th Street
Redmond, WA 98052
(Product: Art glass)

Classic Crystal
50 Drumlin Circle Units
Concord, Ontario
L4K 3G1 Canada
(Product: Art glass)

Custom Glass and Mirror
4845 Exposition Boulevard
Los Angeles, CA 90016
(Product: Art glass)

Elegant Entries
65 Water Street
Worcester, MA 01604
(Product: Entry glass and doors)

Fabricated Glass Specialties
318 Rapp Road
P.O. Box 335
Talent, OR 97540
(Product: Art glass)

Franklin Art Glass Studios
222 E. Sycamore Street
Columbus, OH 43206
(Product: Art glass)

Galaxy Glass
P.O. Box 401
Pine Brook, NJ 07058
(Product: Art glass)

Gayoso Glassworks International
878 S. Cooper
Memphis, TN 38104
(Product: Art glass)

Gaytee Stained Glass
2744 Lyndale Avenue S.
Minneapolis, MN 55408
(Product: Stained glass)

Glass Art Collaborative
31 Norfold Road
Arlington, MA 02174
(Product: Art glass)

Golden Age Glassworks
339 Bellvale Road
Warwick, NY 10990
(Product: Art glass)

Jestes Art Design
3020 Bridgeway, #187
Sausalito, CA 94965
(Product: Art glass)

MBC Glass Studio
Stone Schoolhouse Road
R.D. 1, Box 289 A
Bloomingburg, NY 12721
(Product: Art glass)

Oakbrook Esser Studios
129 E. Wisconsin Avenue
Oconomowoc, WI 53066
(Product: Art glass)

O'Neil Studios
2326 S.E. Troutdale Road
Troutdale, OR 97233
(Product: Art glass)

Peachtree Doors
P.O. Box 5700
Norcross, GA 30091
(Product: Doors with art glass)

Pease Ever-Strait Doors
Fairfield, OH 45023
(Product: Doors with insulated leaded-
    glass panels)

Phillips Stained Glass
2310 Superior Avenue
Cleveland, OH 44114–4225
(Product: Art glass)

Pinecrest
2118 Blaisdell Avenue
Minneapolis, MN 55404
(Product: Carved and beveled glass)

Pittsburgh Corning
800 Presque Isle Drive
Pittsburgh, PA 15239
(Product: Art glass)

PPG Industries
One PPG Place
Pittsburgh, PA 15272
(Product: Art glass)

Reflection Studios
1418 62nd Street
Emeryville, CA 94608
(Product: Art glass)

Rowe Studio Stained Glass
4768 S.W. 72nd Avenue
Miami, FL 33155
(Product: Art glass)

Stained Glass Overlay
151 Kalmus Drive, J-4
Costa Mesa, CA 92626
(Product: Stained-glass overlay)

Westchester Art Glass Studios
792 N. Bedford Road
Mount Kisco, NY 10549
(Product: Art glass)

Appendix 12   Fabric Fibers and Textures

Fibers differ in their textures, dye affinities, uses, durability, and care demands. Moreover, dyes, finishes, and texturing processes add variety to a fiber's appearance. There is a set of fairly reliable characteristics for each fiber that renders it a wise or an inappropriate choice for window treatments.

Fibers can be divided into two categories: natural and man-made. Further distinctions are made within each category: natural fibers include cellulosic fibers (those derived from plant sources—for example, cotton and linen) and proteins (those derived from animal sources—for example, wool and silk). Man-made fibers include cellulosics and synthetics.

Some fibers, such as cotton, linen, jute, silk, wool, rayon, acetate, acrylic, modacrylic, nylon, polyester, olefin, saran, fiberglass, and vinyl, are commonly used as components of drapery fabrics. Others are used only occasionally or in blends. To aid in selection a brief analysis of the commonly used fibers is outlined here.

NATURAL FIBERS

Natural fibers are very important to today's window coverings. Cotton, often called "the decorator fiber," is used for prints and solid fabrics. Linen gives crispness and a natural texture so appealing that many fibers and blends imitate the slubbed linen look. Wool adds bulk and character and is seen in high-end textiles and blends. Silk has always been revered as the "queen of fibers," a title earned because of its luxurious drapability.

Cotton

Cotton comes from the soft white filaments that surround the seed pod of a shrublike member of the mallow plant family. Its history dates back as far as India and Egypt in 5000 B.C., yet it has been one of the most important fibers in interior design in all periods.

Positive Characteristics:

- extraordinarily versatile
- highly absorbant

- easily dyed
- soft and cool to the touch
- fuzz, pill, and shed resistant
- abrasion resistant
- readily cleaned
- can be mercerized to increase smoothness, consistency of fiber, and dye affinity

Negative Characteristics:

- inelastic
- flammable
- unresilient
- wrinkles easily
- shrinks when wet
- fades from the sun
- loses body and luster when wet cleaned

Blends:

- polyester: minimizes wrinkling
- rayon and acetate: add luster
- linen: adds crispness and courseness
- union cloth (half linen, half cotton): minimizes wrinkling in cotton and stiffness in linen, uniting the desirable characteristics of both fibers (cotton's softness and absorbency, and linen's crispness)
- wool: adds resiliency, abrasion resistance, and longevity

Uses:

Ideal for draperies, cotton takes textures and prints in dozens of light- to medium-weight fabrics. Other uses include slipcovers, pillows, sheets, wall coverings, upholstery, area rugs, fringes, and toweling.

Cleaning and Care:

Cotton washes well but shrinks in very hot water or in the clothes dryer; washing also removes finishes. It is dry cleanable and needs ironing.

Jute

One of the most useful of the bast fibers (see next section), jute is commercially next to linen in importance. It is obtained from the fibrous skin between the stalk of two tall annual plants indigenous to India: *Corchorus capsularis* and *Corchorus olitorius.*

Positive Characteristics:

- readily available
- inexpensive

- serviceable
- moderately strong
- available in a wide range of textures, from abrasive to silky
- requires little upkeep
- dry cleanable
- lasts indefinitely
- neutral in color
- has a soft luster
- easily dyes
- special finishes can make it resistant to fire, water, corrosion, and rot

Negative Characteristics:

- stiff
- unresilient
- fades to its natural tan color, especially in sunlight
- lacks abrasion resistance
- rots when kept moist
- deteriorates in strength
- lacks durability
- sensitive to chemical and photochemical attack
- has a characteristically musty smell

Blends:

Cotton, linen, wool, silk, rayon, acetate, nylon.

Uses:

Jute is sometimes used as drapery buckram (for narrow heading interfacing); in drapery blends, in small quantities; and in carpet backing, furniture webbing, gunnysacks, twine, and bindings.

Cleaning and Care:

Jute may be hand washed or dry cleaned. In the former case, it must be dried thoroughly, and kept dry to avoid rotting.

Linen

The most ancient fiber, linen is the best-known member of the bast family (fibers derived from the woody stems or leaves of plants). To obtain linen, stems of the flax plant are soaked in a process called retting (literally, "rotting"), which softens the stems and facilitates the removal of the outer layers. The inner fibers are then subjected to many processes and finishes to produce the various quality levels of linen: tow linen is the coarse, very short length; demi-line is the smoother, medium-size length; and line linen is the longest, smoothest, and most lustrous length.

Ramie, or China Grass, also known as grass linen, is the next best-known bast fiber. Strong and lustrous, it is thought to be the "fine linen" referred to in the Bible.

Positive Characteristics:

- crisp and cool
- strong and durable
- highly absorbent
- dimensionally stable
- pill resistant
- has a soft luster
- alkali resistant
- allergy-free
- resists sun deterioration
- holds color well
- retains a crisp, new appearance
- available in a wide range of prices

Negative Characteristics:

- inflexible
- unresilient
- flammable
- creases permanently; wrinkles are hard to remove
- may shrink
- becomes brittle in low-humidity areas

Blends:

- cotton: adds softness, flexibility
- rayon: increases luster

Note: Pure tow linen tends to be too stiff for drapery folds, but that stiffness adds body and crispness to linen blends.

Uses:

In interior design linen is primarily used for draperies, wall coverings, lampshades, slipcovers, upholstery, table linens, and toweling.

Cleaning and Care:

Linen may be washed and bleached, but runs the risk of fading or shrinking. Alternatively, it may be dry cleaned. Stored table linens should be rolled rather than folded, as the fibers can bend permanently and eventually weaken and break.

Silk

According to Chinese legend, silk was discovered approximately in 2690 B.C. by an empress who was the first to unreel the continuous monofilament thread from the cocoon of a silkworm (caterpillar). The process of producing cultivated silk is known as sericulture and is a meticulous, painstaking activity. Today silk is produced in China, Japan, Korea, Taiwan, India, and, to a lesser extent, Italy, France, and England. For centuries it has been woven into fabrics of elegance and prestige. Textures range from the course and natural appearance of wild silk to the refined and exquisite appearance of cultivated, or reeled, silk.

Positive Characteristics:

- extraordinary luster
- naturally beautiful
- cool and dry to the touch
- strong when unexposed to sunlight
- moth resistant
- pill resistant
- flame retardant
- preshrinkable
- takes dye beautifully
- ages gracefully when protected
- lightweight
- drapes beautifully

Negative Characteristics:

- expensive
- susceptible to abrasion
- deteriorates with continuous sunlight exposure or strong light of any kind
- disintegrates in strong bleaches and cleaning acids
- susceptible to beetle damage
- subject to mildew and rot in hot climates
- wrinkles easily (although some feel this adds to its beauty)
- susceptible to perspiration damage
- may yellow with age

Blends:

Silk often is used alone, as it ages gracefully but sometimes prematurely and in blends may wear faster than other fibers. However, some fibers add strength and longevity to silk, while in draperies silk provides luster and drapability to blends. Common blends include linen, cotton, rayon, acetate, and small proportions of other man-made fibers. Silk often is used as embroidery thread in brocade drapery and upholstery fabric.

Uses:

Silk has be used for centuries as drapery whenever it was obtainable and could be afforded. It also is employed for upholstery, wall-covering yardage, wall hangings, accent fabric, bed linens, quality trimmings, fine oriental-rug pile, and accents in wool rugs.

Cleaning and Care:

Silk should be dry cleaned. It may be hand washed in moderate temperatures, but it will wrinkle. It should not be bleached and must not be exposed to the sun for prolonged periods. Silk draperies should always be lined to avoid sun damage.

Wool

The product of the fleece of domesticated sheep, this protein fiber is primarily made up of an epidermal layer, which consists of overlapping scales. The cortex is the inner shaft of the fiber, with the medulla, a microscopic layer, at the center.

Horsehair is classified as a wool variation, although it is a monofilament thread. Goat hair also is loosely called wool.

Positive Characteristics:

- exceptionally resilient
- versatile
- wrinkle resistant
- flame resistant
- retains shape and body unless subjected to heat, water, and agitation
- resists abrasion
- resistant to soil, water, and grease
- an excellent insulator
- accepts dyes
- absorbs up to 20 percent of its weight in moisture without feeling damp
- nonstatic
- blends well with other fibers
- cleans nicely
- available in a wide range of textures, from soft to wiry

Negative Characteristics:

- expensive
- shrinks when exposed to hot, wet cleaning methods
- susceptible to moth damage (this may be treated chemically)
- triggers allergic reactions in some people

- emits a distinctive animal smell when damp

- may shed, fuzz, and pill

Blends:

Wool is often used alone, but is also frequently blended with acrylic, polyester, and nylon for reasons of economy and strength.

Cleaning and Care:

Wool may be dry cleaned, hand washed in cold water, or spot cleaned. It should not be agitated when washed. Cover the fabric with a damp cloth when ironing, and use moderate heat.

MAN-MADE FABRICS

Man-made fibers begin as chemicals and are extruded from a liquid state The ingredients used to form the liquid may be regenerated cellulosic materials, such as in the production of rayon or acetate; they may be based on coal and petroleum products; or they may be of purely chemical derivation. To form the threads, the solution is forced, or *extruded*, through a spinnerette, a device that resembles a shower head with minute holes (fig. A-1). The tremendous variety of textures in yarns and threads is achieved by the shape of the hole, the blend, and the yarn-texturing processes.

Man-made fibers are immensely valuable as window treatment coverings. In particular, modacrylic is inherently flame resistant and meets nonresidential fire and safety codes; polyester successfully imitates silk fabrics and is economical and serviceable for sheers, laces, and casements. The advances in man-made fibers continually make them better products for the consumer and more dependable for the professional who specifies and sells soft window coverings.

Each chemical company markets its generic fibers under a trademark or trade name. It is important to be familiar with these names, since the generic fiber is not identified. The following generic-fiber overview includes major brand names and their producers.

Acetate

Sometimes called artificial silk or poor man's silk, acetate is derived from a chemically compounded cellulose. It was first produced by the Dreyfus brothers of Switzerland, who perfected the acetate dope, or liquid, as a varnish for airplane wings in England during World War I. After the war they developed the process for making acetate fibers. U.S. production, begun in 1929, was officially recognized by the FTC in 1952.

Positive Characteristics:

- lustrous sheen and luxurious feel

- good body

- excellent draping qualities

- holds color well

- dimensionally stable

- wrinkle resistant

- low in static electricity

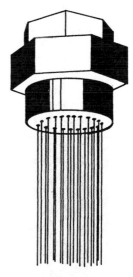

A-1 The spinnerette. Liquid or viscose man-made solutions are forced through the holes and then solidified into monofilaments.

- quick drying
- moth and mildew resistant
- moderate in cost

Negative Characteristics:

- heat sensitive (cannot be heat set)
- highly flammable
- susceptible to sunlight deterioration
- lacks abrasion resistance
- lacks elasticity and resilience
- weak
- dry cleaning usually required
- water-spots
- tends to pill
- has only fair absorbency
- adversely affected by organic solvents such as acetone

Blends:

Rayon, cotton, nylon, wool.

Uses:

Acetate is most frequently used in bedspreads, shower curtains, and lining fabrics. It is used for drapery and upholstery fabrics in blends.

Cleaning and Care:

It is best to dry clean acetate, though some acetates are treated to be washable. Iron at moderate temperature.

Acrylic

Acrylic is a synthetic long-chain polymer made primarily of acrylonitrile, a liquid derivative of natural gas and air. Other ingredients are coal, petroleum, and limestone. Acrylonitrile was first made in 1893 in Germany. In 1944 the DuPont corporation in America developed an acrylic fiber for use during World War II. After the war, research continued, and in 1950 commercial production of this fiber commenced.

Positive Characteristics:

- soft
- warm
- lightweight
- resilient
- resistant to abrasion, sunlight, weathering, moth damage, and mildew
- dyes easily

- washable and quick drying
- generates little static
- nonallergenic
- closely resembles wool
- moderate in cost

Negative Characteristics:

- limp
- tends to crush
- pills
- shrinks
- cannot readily be made flame retardant
- lacks the durability of nylon, polyester, and olefins
- oil-borne matter clings

Trade Names:

- *American Cyanimid:* Creslan
- *Bauer:* Drayton
- *Dow Badishe:* Leacril, Bi-loft, Zefran, Zefstate, Zefchrome
- *DuPont:* Orlon
- *Hoechst:* Dolan
- *Monsanto:* Chemstand, Acrilan

Blends:

- wool: blends with acrylic to lower cost
- cotton: adds strength and absorbency
- nylon: adds firmness
- silk: adds strength and eases care of silk fabric

Uses:

Drapery, curtains, upholstery, carpeting, blankets.

Cleaning and Care:

Acrylic is washable and needs little ironing (use a low setting). Fabric softener reduces static electricity. May be spot cleaned and must be dry cleaned when blended with fibers that cannot be washed.

Modacrylic

Modacrylic is a modified acrylic fiber composed of a copolymer of acrylonitrile and other chemicals, such as vinyl chloride. Union Carbide began producing this material in 1949.

Early modacrylics primarily were used as a minor-percentage fibers in blends with many other fibers, in novelty-weave casement fibers, and for fake fur. Today modacrylic has been developed into a highly desirable drapery fabric that stands on its own. It is inherently flame resistant and often used for draperies in nonresidential settings because it meets stringent fire safety codes.

Positive Characteristics:

- soft

- washable

- shrink resistant

- wrinkle resistant

- highly flame resistant

- resistant to bleach, sunlight, moths, mildew, stains

- drip dries

- holds color well

- drapes well

- bulky

- nonabsorbent

Negative Characteristics:

- lacks abrasion resistance

- requires dry cleaning

- pills

- clings

- collects static electricity

- melts easily

- bulky and dense

- light resistance varies

Blends:

Modacrylic adds softness and bulk or loftiness to cotton, linen, wool, rayon, acetate, nylon, polyester, olefins, and saran.

Uses:

Modacrylic is used in blends for drapery (especially the more bulky casement fabrics) and for upholstery and fake furs. Its flame resistance makes it ideal for contract settings with strict fire codes.

Cleaning and Care:

Modacrylics may be washed or dry cleaned (except for fake furs, which must be dry cleaned). Mild alkaline soaps should be used. As noted above, this fiber is bleach resistant.

Nylon

Nylon is a long-chain polymer fiber derived from petroleum, natural gas (carbon), air (nitrogen and oxygen), and water. The fiber-forming substances—polymides—are dry spun and stretched after cooling. DuPont first introduced nylon in 1939 with its Nylon 6.6, used for women's hosiery. It met with instant acclaim and was for many years called the miracle fiber.

Positive Characteristics:

- exceptionally strong (has the greatest tensile strength of all synthetics)
- high abrasion resistance
- durable
- dyes readily
- washable and dry cleanable
- resists absorption of airborne dirt and oil
- versatile
- repels mildew and moths
- can be heat set—pleats, creases, and embossed patterns last the lifetime of the fabric
- melts before burning
- may be flameproofed for commercial installation
- accepts antistatic treatments
- moderate in cost

Negative Characteristics:

- course texture
- high sheen
- sometimes has garish color
- collects dirt and oil-borne stains on flat surfaces
- sheds, fuzzes, and pills
- sun-fades and disintegrates
- wrinkles permanently
- if not treated, collects static electricity

Note: Problems of garish color, static electricity, high sheen, and coarse texture are being overcome through yarn-texturing processes, finishes, and treatments. Fourth-generation nylons are treated for soil repellency.

Blends:

Nylon is commonly used alone, though it is blended sometimes with cotton, wool, linen, jute, silk, rayon, acetate, polyester, saran, and in small amounts with any of the man-made fibers. Care must be taken in construction that nylon threads do not abrade or cut other fiber yarns.

Uses:

Because of its sensitivity to sunlight, nylon is used in draperies only in blends. It is also used in carpeting, upholstery, wall coverings, and bedspreads.

Cleaning and Care:

Nylon washes well, dries quickly, and requires little ironing, at low heat. It may also be dry cleaned and spot cleaned.

Olefin

Deriving its name from the Latin *oleum*, meaning oil, olefin is made from petroleum products, particularly propylene and ethylene gasses, products of crude-oil cracking. Olefin is a paraffin and has a waxlike quality.

The first olefin was developed in 1873, but because of technical difficulties in polymerization, olefins were not spun into filaments until the 1950s, and then only for small-volume applications. By the late 1970s olefin textile fibers had become indispensable to many facets of design and industry.

Positive Characteristics:

- lightweight
- resilient
- stain resistant
- strong when wet and dry
- washable
- inexpensive
- resists wrinkles, mildew, aging, abrasion, and moths

Negative Characteristics:

- melts easily
- pills
- dyes with difficulty
- collects static electricity
- has plastic feel
- sensitive to sunlight

Blends:

Wool, cotton, rayon, and other synthetics may be blended with olefin in upholstery-weight textiles. As a carpet fiber it is most frequently used alone.

Uses:

Olefin is used for drapery and casement fabrics in blends, and for upholstery, carpets, carpet squares, carpet secondary backing, webbing, and blankets in blends or alone.

Cleaning and Care:

Olefin is washable in warm or cold water, but it is often used in blends that require dry cleaning. It may be spot cleaned. It should be line dried, and ironed at very low heat. Outdoor carpeting may be hosed off.

Polyester

Made of coal, air, water, and petroleum, polyester is a complex ester that forms a long-chain synthetic polymer. In 1930 Dr. Wallace Carothers began experiments that eventually produced polyesters, but he discontinued his research in favor of nylon. British chemists eventually developed a polyester fiber. In 1946 DuPont purchased the exclusive right to produce polyester in the United States; by 1977 there were twenty-three producers.

Positive Characteristics:

- dimensionally stable

- has permanent body

- resists light deterioration, wrinkling, abrasion, shrinking, stretching

- nonallergenic

- may be woven, knit, or tufted

- may be texturized into softer yarns

- strength (polyester is known as "the workhorse fiber"; it is as strong wet as it is dry)

- may be heat set for pleats and creases

- dyes well

- flame-, mildew-, moth-, and insect-proof

- drapes beautifully

Negative Characteristics:

- pills

- oil-borne stains cling (although fabric is often treated with a soil-repellent finish)

- collects static electricity

- crushes more easily than nylon

Blends:

Cotton, wool, acrylic, rayon, acetate, and small amounts of other synthetics.

Uses:

Polyester is used in draperies, casements, sheers, laces, and knit window-covering fabrics manufactured up to 118 inches wide. Its nonwindow applications include upholstery, carpeting, bed linen, and quilt batting.

Cleaning and Care:

Polyester is washable and should be drip dried. It is also dry cleanable, although sheers are often better washed by hand or on a gentle-agitation machine setting than dry cleaned; stains may set in at high cleaning temperatures. (Note that polyester may pick up odors in washing.) It requires little ironing, at moderate heat.

Rayon

Produced from regenerated cellulose nitrate, rayon, the first of the man-made fibers, was invented in 1884 by Count Hilaire de Chardonnet, who built the first rayon factory with a patent to produce artificial silk. In 1925 the U.S. Federal Trade Commission (FTC) permitted the use of the term *rayon* for any fiber produced chemically from cellulose. In 1952 the FTC ruled that there would be two cellulose fiber categories—rayon and acetate.

Positive Characteristics:

- lustrous silklike texture
- capable of being made into cotton-, wool-, or linenlike fabrics
- soft hand, pleasing to eye and touch
- highly absorbent
- can withstand high temperatures for pressing
- dry cleans nicely
- drapes gracefully
- dimensionally versatile
- economical
- available in a wide variety of types and textures

Blends:

Acetate (approximately 60 percent rayon and 40 percent acetate forms a common blend in drapery fabrics and silklike upholsteries), silk, wool, polyester, nylon.

Uses:

Drapery, fringes, upholstery, bedspreads, wall fabrics, lampshades, throw rugs.

Cleaning and Care:

Rayons should be dry cleaned, especially viscose and cuprammonium. They also may be wet cleaned, but may shrink when washed. Iron with moderate heat.

Saran

A copolymer, saran is a plastic vinyl fiber of vinylidene chloride, developed by Dow Chemical in 1940.

Positive Characteristics:

- absorbs little moisture; dries quickly
- tough and durable
- colorfast
- weather, flame, soil, abrasion, crease, and light resistant

Negative Characteristics:

- stiff

- melts easily
- plastic in appearance
- difficult to dye
- expensive

Blends:

Rayon, modacrylic, and various other man-made fibers in smaller percentages.

Uses:

Saran is used in blends for drapery casements. Nonwindow uses include furniture webbing, screens, seat covers, rugs, and indoor and outdoor furniture upholstery.

Cleaning and Care:

Washable at cool temperatures. May shrink and deteriorate at moderate to hot temperatures.

Vinyl

Vinyl is a liquid solution made of a vinyl alcohol, usually hydrochloric or polyvinyl chloride (PVC). It usually is not extruded or spun into fiber form but extruded as a film or coated textile that is flowed onto a knit, woven, or nonwoven fabric.

Positive Characteristics:

- durable
- abrasion resistant
- soil resistant
- stain resistant
- may imitate leather
- may be made in any color or luster
- easy to clean
- moderate in price
- serves as moisture barrier; highly insulative

Negative Characteristics:

- uncomfortable (does not breathe)
- low-end vinyls lack durability
- may crack and split

Blends:

Vinyl is most often extruded as a smooth or textured sheet or textile film and is not blended. However, it is sometimes used as a slit-film flat monofilament yarn with other fibers in casement draperies.

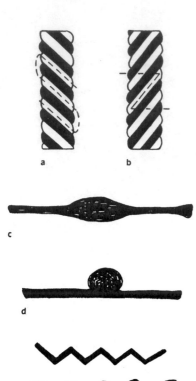

A-2   Common yarn twists.

a   S-twist.

b   Z-twist.

c   Slub yarn, with enlarged slub area in the center.

d   Nub yarn, with clots, or nubs, that may add textural interest or be picked out as a fabric flaw.

e   Crimped monofilaments or textured filaments.

f   Complex, or novelty, yarn.

Uses:

Window shades, upholstery, wall coverings, shower curtains, and, infrequently, draperies.

Care and Cleaning:

Vinyl should be sponge cleaned with warm, sudsy water. Ballpoint ink may be dissolved with hair spray and wiped off. In fabric blends it is best to avoid heat cleaning methods because the fiber may melt.

YARNS AND FABRIC TEXTURES: CREATING VARIETY

Yarns may be texturized to yield variety in the finished fabric. While hand-spun natural fibers possess uneven qualities that often add to their natural beauty and appeal, man-made fibers often are extruded as round, even filaments. To attain some of the beauty and interest inherent in natural fibers, man-made fibers now imitate them as well as possess fascinating textures of their own. This variety is accomplished in a number of ways. The spinnerette holes may not be round, but trilobal, hexagonal, dog-bone shaped, kidney shaped, or dozens of other forms. These shapes not only give some variety to the yarn profile but also change some of the fiber's inherent characteristics, such as reducing sheen.

Since all man-made fibers are extruded, the monofilaments may be crimped (kinked) or heat set into a variety of filament configurations. These yarns will be bulkier and loftier. Further, filaments may be grouped into bundles—called multifilament; crimped; cut into short staple lengths imitative of natural cotton, linen, and wool; and then spun into yarn.

Yarns may be formed of extruded films, slit into split, slit, or tape yarns, as with PVC vinyl or saran. Yarns may either be single or grouped into two- or more ply (single) yarns, and ply yarns may be grouped further into cable, or cord, yarn.

The direction of the twist—S, or right-hand; Z, or left-hand (fig. A-2)—and the amount of tension—slack, tight, or crepe (very tight)—also add variety. Some yarns are not spun at all but are woven as texturized multifilament floss.

Yarns may be complex, or novelty, that is, composed of a core and a fancy thread looped around the core and held with a fine or colorless monofilament binder thread. Examples are bouclé and ratiné yarns. Or yarns may be abraded or woven in strips to form fuzzy chenille yarns. These and many other contemporary techniques of producing yarn add interest and variety to fabrics that cover our windows and enrich our interiors.

Appendix 13 Fabric Construction, Coloring, and Finishing

WEAVE CONSTRUCTION

Although an increasing number of fabrics on the market today are knitted, most fabrics are woven. The complexity of a weave is one factor in its cost. Other factors, including the type and tightness, or sturdiness, of the weave affect its durability.

Weaves are divided into several basic categories. Discussed below, these are the plain weave, the twill weave, the satin weave, the Jacquard weave, and the pile weave. Needle constructions include knit fabrics, malimo, arnache, laces, quilting, and tufting.

An important part of the price and appeal of an interior design fabric is the coloring and finishing process, several of which also are presented here.

Plain Weave

Plain weaves involve the regular interlacing of one warp to one weft thread—over one, under one. They also are called balanced, tabby, taffeta, and regular weaves (fig. A-3). Plain weave and its variations account for over half of all the decorative fabric base constructions.

Rib weave is an unbalanced plain weave; it is also called crammed weave or cord weave. Rib weaves use more warp than weft threads or more weft than warp threads, that is, one set of threads larger and bulkier than the other. (One set may be fine and the other extra-fine).

Basket weave is a balanced plain weave in multiple thread sets—two on two, three on three, four on four, and so on (fig. A-4). An unbalanced basket weave has more threads grouped in one direction. The most frequently used variety is the Oxford weave, which has two fine warp to one heavier filling thread (fig. A-5).

Crepe weave (also known as momie weave or granite weave) uses irregular spacing, floats, and, occasionally, combinations of weaves so that no weave shows on the surface, only a pebbly textured face.

Dobby weave is made by adding a dobby attachment to an automated plain-harness loom, which varies the interlacing to produce small geometric designs and ribbed fabrics.

Leno weave has pairs of warp threads twisted hourglass fashion where the weft threads interlace. Every warp end may be part of a pair, forming *complete leno* (fig. A-6). Leno pairs may be spaced warp, forming open-construction leno. Leno weave may be an occasional variation in a plain weave.

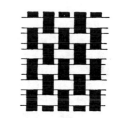

A-3 Plain weave.

A-4 Balanced basket weave: two over two.

A-5 Unbalanced basket weave, called Oxford weave.

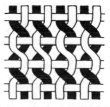

A-6 Leno or doup weave, a variation of the plain weave with hourglass interlacings.

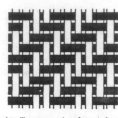

A-7 Balanced twill: warp and weft each float over two and under two.

A-8 Unbalanced twill: warp and weft float over two and under one.

A-9 Satin weave: warp floats over seven and under one.

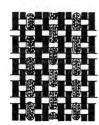

A-10 Pile weave. The third element is woven in, cut, and brushed up to form a pile.

Twill Weave

The base for several fabrics, including many varieties and textures of tweeds (fig. A-7), twill is a sturdy weave that can be tight or loose; its distinguishing characteristic is diagonal wales (ribs) formed by floating a weft yarn over two or more warp yarns, or vice versa. The diagonal wales may have a steep or shallow pitch.

Novelty twills are those that reverse the weave in a regular or irregular order (fig. A-8). Some well-known examples include herringbone, or chevron; houndstooth; and twill-weave tweeds.

Satin Weave

Satin weave is produced by floating warp yarns or threads over four to eight weft threads, then under one (fig. A-9). The one weft thread that holds the warp thread in place is called a *weft tie down*. The long floats, particularly in lustrous filament threads, create a smooth, shiny surface. Satin weaves do not show diagonal lines and may be subject to snags in bulkier weaves, since so much thread floats on the surface.

In *Sateen, satine, horizontal,* or *weft-faced* satin, the weft threads float over four or more warp threads for a look similar to warp-faced satin. This fabric often is made of cotton yarns and printed into decorative textiles.

Jacquard Weave

In Jacquard weaves, two or more sets of threads (warp or weft) are used to produce complex, large-scale patterns on a Jacquard attachment. The loom is a complex machine that can take months to set up but is capable of weaving large volumes of patterned fabric in short lengths of time. Background weaves may be plain, ribbed, twill, satin, or a combination of these. Fabrics include damask, brocade, brocatelle, lampas, matelassé, and figured velvets.

Pile Weave

Pile weaves are accomplished in three ways: (1) By weaving an extra warp or filling yarn into the basecloth as a warp or weft float. The extra yarn is cut with circular knives, then brushed up to form a nap. (2) By looping extra warp or filling threads around fine round wires that are later removed. (3) By face-to-face weaving, where two sets of warps and wefts are placed on top of one another and interlaced with the supplemental warp before being sheared by an automated knife to separate the two pile fabrics. The third method is the fastest and most economical (fig. A-10).

NEEDLE-AND-YARN CONSTRUCTION

Needle-and-yarn construction may never totally replace woven fabrics at the window, but it has become popular in recent years because of its many advantages. Warp knits and laces are excellent for semisheer and casement cloth weights, and quilted fabrics are highly efficient for energy conservation at the window. Needle-and-yarn fabrics are readily available in a wide selection of colors, textures, patterns, and price structures. They frequently are available in widths up to 118 inches, which can eliminate seams and drapery-construction labor. Many knits and laces are of polyester fiber, which is used for fabrics that drape beautifully and are remarkably durable and easy to maintain.

Knits

Knit fabrics are economical and can be rapidly produced because of the multiple needles that work together to form the cloth.

Arnache and Maliwatt

These techniques involve a nonwoven batting web instead of warp and weft yarns. The needles stitch-bond the bat to another fabric. Malipol machines produce pile fabrics punched into a scrim.

Lace

Lace fabrics are made on the following needle-constructed machines: Leavers, Raschel, Schiffli, Bobbinet, and Nottingham. Today's laces often are made in extra-wide widths and in both traditional and contemporary patterns of easy-care fabrics. Lace is making a strong impact on the window-covering market in the area of casement fabrics, which give daytime privacy and reduce glare.

Malimo

Like Raschel knits, malimo fabrics are needle-constructed, except that the weft is "laid" in bands often twelve inches or wider. The vertical knitting is rapidly accomplished with yarn or clear nylon monofilament in a chain stitch. The vertical chain stitch may be supplemented with Jacquard patterns knitted in with colored yarns to form bold geometric patterns. Designs also may be etch- or burn-out-printed (see glossary 3).

Quilting

Quilting is the layering and stitching together of two or more fabrics. Traditionally the decorative face fabric is layered with a wool, cotton, or polyester batting and then backed with a muslin lining and held with tiny stitches by hand or quilting machines. Quilting is most frequently used for adding pattern to plain fabrics or outlining printed designs. It also adds visual comfort and richness, body and bulk, insulation against sound and temperature extremes, and often, durability and dimensional stability.

Insulative fabrics often are produced by sonic sewing or fuse-bond quilting. The fabrics to be quilted are passed between a large metal roller with raised design and an ultrasonic head that releases sonic vibrations that melt the pattern into the fabric. The process takes less than one-third the time of machine quilting, but all the fabrics involved must be thermoplastic. There is less flexibility in fuse-bonding designs than in hand or machine quilting.

Raschel

Raschel, or Rachel, knits can be recognized by the chain of knit stitches running vertically, often with weft threads "laid" and knit into the structure. For window coverings they typically are open or lacy in construction. Stable and handsome, Raschel knits are applicable in both residential and contract settings.

Tufting

Tufting is a process of inserting loops into a woven or nonwoven basecloth that is back coated with latex to hold the tufts in place. The cut or uncut loops form a pile. Velvet and velour fabrics may be constructed by this method.

COLORING

Coloring is an expensive part of decorative textiles that can account for up to half of the wholesale cost of producing the cloth. Coloring is accomplished by dyeing and by printing.

Dyes or dyestuffs are natural and chemical substances combined with a solvent (often water) to form a dye liquor, or dyebath, which colors the fabric in the solution, stock, yarn, or piece-goods stage and in the printing processes. Dyes from natural sources were used exclusively until the late 1800s, when experiments proved dyes could be obtained from coal-tar derivatives and related compounds. Today chemically derived dyestuffs are matched to the chemical structure of the fabric to ensure maximum colorfastness. A fiber that readily accepts a certain chemical dye is said to have an affinity for that dye.

A pigment is an insoluable coloring matter that must be held on the surface of the fabric with binders. Pigments also may be combined with man-made fiber solutions before extrusion. Pigments are inexpensive, easily matched, and impervious to sun fading, but they may wash or wear off and can look painted on. They usually are opaque but may be thinned down to transluscence.

Dyeing Methods

Piece dyeing is the dyeing of fabrics woven into lengths, or pieces, that range from 100 to 200 yards.

Solution or dope dyeing is the addition of dyestuffs or pigments to the viscose solution, or dope. This technique locks color into the extruded filament, making it resistant to sun fading. Since it is economical only in large fiber runs, the manufacturer runs the risk of producing a color that may not be in style by the time it reaches the market.

Stock or fiber dyeing is the dyeing of natural fibers before they are spun, producing even color.

Yarn dyeing is the dyeing of skeins, or hanks, to be used in colored woven, patterned cloth.

Printing Methods

Hand-printing processes include batik (in which wax is applied to fabric before dyeing and removed after dyeing, revealing patterns where the dye has been resisted); tie-dye (in which folded and tied cloth is submerged in liquid, resisting the dye where folds are thick and yarns are tied); ikat (the complex printing of warp yarns before weaving); hand painting; stencilwork; and silk screening (a stencil process using a strong, fine silk or synthetic sheer fabric attached to a wood frame. The screen is positioned, and dye or pigment is squeegeed through the screen where the design has not been opaqued).

Semi-automated and rotary-screen printing are two of the most frequently used methods of printing decorative interior textiles. Semi-automated screens are mechanically lowered, and two workers squeegee the dye onto the fabric through the screen. The screen is raised and the fabric is moved along a conveyor belt. Rotary-screen printing makes a drum of the design screen, and the color is forced onto fabric that moves along a conveyor belt. It is a rapid printing process, as rotary screens of different colors can be placed sequentially. This is one of the most common techniques for printing fabric.

Finally, *roller printing* is accomplished with engraved copper rollers that print a design onto a fabric as it passes a large cast-iron cylinder. The printed fabric is backed with a cloth to absorb excess dye and a rubberized blanket to provide a good surface for a clear print. One copper roller for each color is used, up to sixteen per machine. Printing is accurate, precise, and rapid, but machinery and operation costs are high.

Coloring Terminology

Atmospheric, fume, or gas fading. Condition whereby the color of fabric is changed over time. There is usually no guarantee against this condition by the manufacturer.

Bars, barres, bar marks, or color bars. Faults in a dyed fabric where selvage-to-selvage bands appear in a slightly different color, caused by tension or filling yarn variations.

Bleeding. Dye migration from one area to another during dyeing, printing, or finishing processes, or later, during cleaning.

Blotches. Large areas of background color in designs that have been printed rather than dyed. The design usually overprints or overengraves (overlaps) the blotch so that no unprinted white area will be seen.

Colorfastness. The ability of a fabric to resist fading from sunlight, artifical light, atmospheric gases, wear, cleaning, or perspiration.

Color flags. The small swatches sewn onto a larger folded or hanging sample of a decorative fabric.

Color line. The number of colorways available in a particular design—three to ten in a print fabric and up to twenty in a plain or textured fabric.

Colorway. The particular color or set of colors in a fabric pattern. The fabric may be printed, for example, in blues, in reds, in greens, and in yellows. These choices constitute the color line.

Coverage. The percentage of fabric colored, as opposed to bleached or uncolored gray goods. Coverage ranges from 10 percent to 150 percent (over 100 percent is accounted for in overlays, fall-ons, or overprinting).

Crocking. The rubbing off of color from a fabric. Dry crocking is rubbing off of color by abrasion. Wet crocking takes place when the fabric is damp, from perspiration, for example.

Dye affinity. Ready acceptance of a certain dye by a fiber. Because each fiber has a different chemical composition, each accepts dyes differently.

Dye lots. Complete dye runs in the same dye bath. Colors may vary slightly between dye lots.

Frosting. Occurs when one fiber loses color before another in a union-dyed cloth, so that the fabric looks faded.

Half-tones. Gradual changes in color or value in a pattern done on a roller print or transfer print machine. Also called *ombré printing.*

Match. The precise repetition of dyestuff color from one fabric to another. The same pattern ordered twice may vary in color from different dye lots. To ensure a match the dyelot number must be specified or a swatch of fabric sent to the distributor with instructions to match the color from inventory.

Metamerism. The changing of a hue under different lighting conditions.

Overlays. The areas of a design that overlap. Printed twice and hence usually darker, they also are called *fall-ons.*

Pattern repeat. A whole pattern, including any plain background areas. Repeats are measured from the top of one pattern to the top of the next, or from the middle to the middle.

Penetration. The depth the dye reaches in printed fabrics. Shallow penetration may rub off, leaving abraded unprinted areas, or it may fade quickly.

Pigment. An insoluble coloring matter held onto the fabric surface with binders or mixed with the viscose solution for colorfast extruded color.

Registration. The exact alignment of the colors in patterned screen and roller printing. *Off-registration,* or *off-register, printing* is a technique that causes a fabric to "grin" (show areas of light background). Registration is also called *fit* or *alignment.*

Selvage legend. A printed color key showing small blocks of colors used in the colorway, plus the name of the fabric-converter company.

Shade. Technically means not a different color (as it is sometimes used) but a variation of value within a color. Fabrics that do not match because of shade differences in dye lots are called *off-shade.*

Shading. The color-value change in a fabric's weft or warp direction. A vertical shading fault in drapery fabric means the fabric will be off-shade at the seams and appear unacceptably striped or streaked.

Standard. The dye formula used for a dye run or dye lot. Dye lot difference due to unavoidable chemical composition variations in the dye and fabrics used means the standard, or master, is not always reached.

Strike-off. A sample of a fabric run; one or more pattern repeats used to check the color, pattern, and finish of the cloth. When approved it becomes part of the master for the dye lot. Strike-offs always are done for custom printing as well, to be approved by the designer and the client before the entire length is printed. Also called a *hand strike.*

FABRIC FINISHING

Decorative interior fabrics are treated with an average of six different finishes. Finishing may take place before or after the fabric is dyed or printed. Finishes are given to fabrics for several reasons: as a preparation for other finishes or coloring; to provide special effects such as improved hand and comfort, durability, and resistance to deterioration, soil, fire, and fading; and to increase beauty through enhanced design.

Many standard or functional finishes are done without visible indication. Others are indicated by trade name on the fabric hangtag or specification listing. Fabrics selected for a use that dictates a certain finish, such as flame retardance, can be treated by a fabric-finishing company or by ordering the finish from the converter (the company that colors and prints the fabric). Some finishes, such as soil repellency, can be applied by a workroom or installer. *Durable finishes* are more or less permanent, even with repeated laundering or dry cleaning. *Semidurable finishes* will hold up for a limited number of cleanings. *Nondurable finishes* are removed within the first five cleanings.

Glossary 1   Window Treatment Terms

ACCORDION PLEAT. Large single pleats that snap onto channel slides and often are used in contract draperies. Also, a method of fan folding finished pleated draperies that helps the fabric to memorize the fold lines before installation.

ARCHITECTURAL RODDING. Heavy-duty traverse or sleek channels for contract draperies.

ART DECO. A historic design period within the Modern period, dating from 1909 to 1939.

ART GLASS. Etched, stained, and beveled glass that is used for hard window treatments.

ART NOUVEAU. A Victorian-era (1890 to 1910) design movement whose motifs were based on flowing plant forms.

ASYMMETRICAL BALANCE. Design scheme in which each side of a central point is different, yet the entire treatment has a point of balance, or equilibrium. Draperies tied back to only one side is an example of asymmetrical balance at the window.

AUSTRIAN SHADE (AUSTRIAN POUF OR AUSTRIAN VALANCE). A poufed fabric shade with permanently shirred scallops that draw up from the bottom.

AUTOMATED EXTERIOR ROLLING SHUTTERS. Metal slats that mechanically roll down over the exterior of the glass as a shading device, an insulative treatment, and a privacy treatment.

AWNING WINDOW. A type of window that is hinged on the top and swings out.

BALANCE. A state of equilibrium or rightness; the two basic types are symmetrical, or formal, (mirror image) balance and asymmetrical, or informal, (optically different) balance.

BALI BLIND. See *Bamboo shade.*

BALLOON SHADE. Another name for a poufed or cloud shade, scalloped on the bottom, that draws up in soft, billowy folds.

BALLOON TIEBACKS. Curtains that pouf as they are tied back.

BAMBOO SHADE. Woven slats of split bamboo that make a light-diffusing natural shade which usually is drawn up by hand with a cord. Also called *bali blind*.

BANDING. Strips of fabric folded under on each side and then top-stitched or fused onto the face of a fabric window treatment.

BAROQUE. A period of ornate interior design and decoration in France from 1643 to 1730 and in England from 1660 to 1714.

BASEMENT WINDOWS. Windows that are hinged on the bottom and swing inward.

BATON. A clear plastic wand that is used to draw pleated draperies on carriers in nontraverse architectural rodding. Also used to control tilt in miniblinds.

BAY WINDOW. A window unit that consists of three or more windows that project out with deep angles.

BELL VALANCE. A pleated or shirred valance with a hemline that simulates a series of bell shapes.

BISHOP'S SLEEVE CURTAINS. Tieback curtains that are poufed up, or bloused, two or more times.

BLACKOUT DRAPERY OR SHADE. A heavy, opaque fabric shade that can darken a room; also called *room-darkening drapery/shade*.

BLIND. A horizontal-slatted hard treatment, such as a miniblind, or a vertical vane, such as a vertical-louver blind. Also, English term for *pouf shade*.

BOW WINDOW. A projecting angled window that forms a semicircle.

BOX PLEAT. A flat pleat that has a fold of fabric laid behind the heading.

BRACKET-TO-BRACKET MEASUREMENT. The measurement that determines the placement of brackets that support traverse rods; also called *rod width*.

BROAD GLASS. Old-style glass made by blowing a glass bubble, reheating it, cutting off both ends, slitting it down the middle, and "ironing" it flat. It is curiously wavy.

BUCKRAM. The stiffened narrow fabric that is used for interfacing for drapery pleats; also called *crinoline*.

BULL'S-EYE WINDOW. A round window glazed with flat or convex glass.

BUTTERFLY PLEAT. A two-finger pleat that is bar tacked at the bottom and flares out at the top.

CAFÉ CURTAIN. A curtain that covers only the bottom half of a window.

CANOPY. A projecting valance over a roller shade or headboard.

CANTONNIERE. An upholstered cornice whose sides extend to the floor; also called a *lambrequin*.

CAPE COD CURTAIN. A café curtain that has a ruffle around the sides and bottom; also called a *ruffle-round curtain*.

CARRIERS. Plastic sliding pieces in traverse rods with a hole for inserting the drapery hook.

CARTRIDGE PLEAT. Rounded tubular pleat stiffened with buckram and stuffed with a material such as polyester fiberfill to hold the shape.

CASEMENT. A loosely woven or knit contemporary drapery fabric.

CASEMENT WINDOW. A side-hinged window that swings outward.

CATHEDRAL WINDOW. An angled window that points upward.

CENTER-DRAW. A pair of draperies that open from a center point and are installed on a traverse rod.

CLERESTORY WINDOW. Strips of window set high in the wall for ventilation and light but not for view.

CLOUD SHADE. See *Pouf shade.*

COLONIAL. A period of design in America that was popular primarily before the Revolutionary War. Its generally recognized dates are 1608 to 1790.

COLORFASTNESS. The ability of a fabric to resist fading.

C.O.M. An abbreviation for "customer's own material."

CONDUCTION. The direct transfer of heat through a solid material, such as glass or metal.

CONVECTION. The transfer of heat toward colder areas through air circulation.

CONVENTIONAL TRAVERSE ROD. A cord-and-pulley-operated drapery rod, usually white- or brown-colored.

CORBEL BAY. A bay window on the second floor of a building.

CORD. A cotton or synthetic cable yarn that is used to hold together blinds and shades and to draw traverse draperies, blinds, and shades.

CORNICE. A top treatment constructed of wood. When covered with fabric, it becomes an *upholstered cornice.*

COTTAGE CURTAINS. A general term for all curtains that are casual and would be appropriate as informal treatments. These include *café, Cape Cod,* and *Priscilla curtains.*

COUNTRY CURTAINS. A type of cottage curtain that has ruffled valance, sides, bottom, and ties and is shirred up to five times fullness. Usually of plain or small-scale printed fabric.

COVERAGE. The quantity or fullness of fabric used at the window.

CRINOLINE. Another word for *buckram,* the narrow stiffened interfacing for pleats.

CROWN GLASS. A brilliant type of glass made from hand-blown discs, or crowns, about a meter in diameter.

CROWN MOLDING CORNICE. A wide cornice molding that projects into the room to cover the heading (pleats) of a drapery.

CURTAINS. Fabric shirred or gathered onto a rod. It may be scalloped or pleated if it covers only the lower portion of the glass.

CUSTOM GLAZING. Window glass made and installed in unusual sizes or shapes.

CUT LENGTH. The length of fabric for soft treatments that includes the extra amount needed for hems and headings.

CUTS. The number of widths needed to construct soft treatments.

DEAD-HUNG DRAPERY. Inoperable stationary drapery, usually side panels.

DECORATOR RODS. Decorative large-scale hardware meant to be seen. Usually made of brass, chrome, wood, or antique white or black wrought iron.

DIAPHANOUS SHEERS. Transparent or translucent finely woven drapery or curtains used for daytime privacy to diffuse glare; also known historically as glass curtains.

DIMENSIONAL STABILITY. The ability of a fabric to stay stable without sagging or hiking up.

DORMER WINDOW. A window projecting through the roof.

DOUBLE-FOLD ROMAN SHADE. *See Pleated Roman shade.*

DOUBLE-HUNG DRAPERY. A window treatment consisting of an overdrapery and an underdrapery.

DOUBLE-HUNG SHUTTERS. A layer of shutters above and below a central point.

DOUBLE-HUNG WINDOW. A sash window where both top and bottom sashes slide up and down.

DRAPABILITY. The capacity of a fabric to fall attractively into folds.

DRAPERY (DRAPERIES). Pleated fabric meant to be drawn open and closed.

DRAW DRAPERY. A pleated fabric panel that can be opened and closed on a traverse rod.

DROP-DOWN ROLLER SHADE. Another name for *roller shade.* The roller is at the top of the window.

DYE LOTS. A color run of fabric that may vary slightly from one run or dye batch to the next.

ELEMENTS OF DESIGN. Space, light, color, texture, pattern, ornament, form, and shape.

EMPHASIS. A point of sustained interest, often called a *focal point*; an area in a room that is visually important. A principle of design.

EMPIRE. A historic period in France from 1804 to 1820 and in America from 1820 to 1860.

END BRACKET. The brackets at the end of a traverse rod that support it.

END PLEAT. The last pleat in a drapery that is hooked into the end bracket.

ENERGY CONSERVATION (ENERGY EFFICIENCY). In the context of this book, treating the window with coverings that keep out summer heat and winter cold, thus reducing the amount of mechanically heated or cooled air needed in an environment.

ENGLISH SASH WINDOW. Typically, several rectangular panes of glass set into a sliding frame; also called *Renaissance sash* or *sash window.*

FABRIC CONSTRUCTION. Weaving or knitting yarn, or extruding solution to form fabric.

FABRIC FINISHES. Chemical or mechanical treatments that make a fabric more durable, decorative, or serviceable.

FABRIC SHADES. Any shade made of fabric; includes Roman, Austrian, pouf, or pleated varieties.

FABRIC SLIDING PANELS. Flat overlapping panels of fabric installed on a track rod and drawn with a wand or baton.

FACTORY-MADE TREATMENTS. Hard window treatments—blinds, shutters, shades, or screens; standard items that are ordered from a factory or manufacturer to fit custom specifications.

FAN FOLDING. The folding of pleated draperies into a narrow band in order to set the folds and help the material drape attractively. Fan folding also eliminates unnecessary wrinkling.

FEDERAL PERIOD. The American term for the Neoclassic period, dating from 1790 to 1820.

FENESTRATION. Term for a glazed or unglazed opening in a building.

FESTOON. Another term for a *swag*—a curved, draped valance or scalloped top treatment.

FESTOON SHADE OR BLIND. A decorative swagged or scalloped shade that is softly poufed; also called a *Parisian shade.*

FINISHED LENGTH. The exact vertical measurement of a fabric treatment.

FINISHED WIDTH. The exact horizontal measurement of a fabric treatment. For draperies this also includes overlaps and returns.

FIXED GLASS. Windows that are nonoperable.

FLAT-PANEL SHADES. Simple flat lengths of fabric used for a shade.

FLOAT GLASS. A continuous ribbon of molten glass that moves from the furnace along the surface of molten metal without touching any hard surface. It is brilliant, transparent, and nearly free of flaws. The process by which most glazing is made today.

FOCAL POINT. A center of interest or emphasis. A design principle.

FOLK PAINTING. Floral, scenic painting—such as Norwegian rosemaling and Pennsylvania Dutch tole painting—usually done on wood; a means of decorating hard window treatments.

FRENCH CASEMENT DOOR. Hinged swinging doors with rectangular panes of glass, typically two panes wide, divided by wood grids.

FRENCH DOOR DRAW. One-way traverse rods mounted onto a door or casement window to swing along when it is opened; also called *swinging draw drapery.*

FRENCH PLEAT. A single pleat folded into three or more fingers and bar tacked in place at the bottom of the pleat. The same as a pinch pleat, but the fingers of the fold are not pressed.

FRETWORK. Designs made of interlocking lattice pieces, typically oriental.

FRINGE. Trim for edges of drapery treatments made of narrow braid with attached loops, tassels, or cut threads.

FULLNESS. The amount of fabric shirred or pleated into a treatment, from two times (200 percent) fullness to five times (500 percent) fullness.

FUSING TAPE. Tape of varying widths that has a coating of glue which melts and fuses or bonds two fabrics together when pressed with a hot iron.

FUSUMA. Interior painted or block-printed sliding shoji screen partitions, which originated in the Japanese home.

GENEROUS COVERAGE. A full amount of fabric in a treatment, more than 250 percent, or 2½ times, fullness.

GEORGIAN PERIOD. A historic design period dating from 1700 to 1790 and divided in America into Early and Late Georgian.

GIMP. Cord or narrow braid used as trimming.

GLARE. Strong directional light that causes eyestrain and fatigue and is sometimes accompanied by heat buildup.

GLARE CONTROL. Exterior or interior window treatments that diffuse or screen a strong directional light source.

GLAZIER. One who sets glass in place professionally.

GLAZING. The setting of glass windows into an open fenestration.

GOLDEN MEAN. The pleasing line of division that falls somewhere between one-half and one-third or approximately .618 of the way down from the top or up from the bottom of a treatment. A guideline for the placement of tieback draperies and curtains.

GOLDEN SECTION. A poportion in the ratio of 2:3:5:8:13:21 and so on that guides pleasing size or shape relationships.

GREENHOUSE WINDOW. A standard-size window that projects out at a 90-degree angle, with glass sides and top and with two shelves for plants.

GRILLE. Metal mesh used as screen or shutter inserts. Black mesh cuts heat and glare, which is particularly helpful in hot, arid or humid regions.

GROUP PLEAT. Sets of pleats, usually three per set, with space between each set.

HANDKERCHIEF-PANEL CURTAIN/SHADE. A flat panel or shade pair that is lined, with a corner turned back to expose a triangle of glass.

HARDLINES (HARD TREATMENTS). Factory-made treatments such as blinds, shutters, shades, and screens.

HARMONY. The principle of unity and variety in design, which contributes to the cohesiveness of the interior design plan or theme.

HEAD (HEADRAIL). Top casing across the frame of a shutter.

HEAT LOSS. The transfer of heat to cold, particularly heated air transferred from inside to outside through uninsulated windows.

HEM. The side or bottom of a fabric treatment that is turned under twice and stitched in place.

HOLDBACK. Metal rods with decorative medallions for holding back drapery tiebacks.

HOLLAND SHADE (HOLLAND CLOTH). The original heavy fabric used for roller shades.

HOPPER WINDOW. A top-hinged window that swings inward.

INSERT. A material that is slid into grooves in a shutter frame or vertical-louver vane.

INSIDE BRACKET (I.B.) [INSIDE INSTALLATION OR INSIDE MOUNT (I.M.)]. The placement of a treatment inside the window frame.

INSTALLATION. The process of securing any window treatment, setting it in place with nails or screws.

INSULATIVE VALUE TREATMENT. A window covering that discourages heat/cold transfer at the window, insulating the glass.

INTERLINING. A third layer of stiffened fabric or fluffy batting that serves to deter light penetration or heat/cold transfer through window treatment fabric.

INVERTED BOX PLEAT. A flattened single pleat where the folds are tacked to the face of the drapery.

JABOT. A folded fabric that cascades down to a point and is used between swags or festoons; a formal framing treatment.

JALOUSIE WINDOW. A series of horizontal louvers that open with a crank, providing good ventilation.

KEY FRET OR CUT OUT. A geometric design of rectangles that can be used for valance shapes on cornices, pelmets, woven-wood shades, and roller-shade valances.

KEYSTONE ARCH. A rounded Roman arch that originally had a splayed or angled stone at the top symbolizing the shaped stones that made the arch possible. The keystone today usually is part of a decorative wood molding.

KNIFE PLEAT. A very slender single pleat used in contract settings where straight, sparse draperies are specified.

LAMBREQUIN. An upholstered wood cornice with sides that extend to the floor.

LATTICE SCREENS. Slats of interlacing wood that form a square or diamond-shaped pattern set into a frame.

LENGTH. The vertical measurement of a window treatment and the horizontal measurement of a drapery or curtain rod.

LIGHT STRIKE. The gap on the side or in the center of a window treatment through which light penetrates in a thin shaft.

LINED DRAPERIES. Draperies with a lining fabric sewn onto the back to protect them from sunlight damage, to add insulative value, or to make them hang more attractively.

LINING. A solid-white, off-white, or colored fabric sewn onto the back of a window treatment fabric to protect it. (See *Lined draperies.)* In some cases the lining fabric is the same as the face fabric or consists of a complementary decorative patterned fabric.

LOUVERED SHUTTERS. Wood frames filled with slats of wood that can be movable or nonmovable.

LOUVERS. Horizontal or vertical slats made of wood, metal, or plastic and used in shutters or blinds.

MICRO-MINIBLINDS. Horizontal blinds with $1/2$-inch metal slats that provide a delicate look.

MINIBLINDS. Horizontal blinds with 1-inch metal or plastic slats held together with nylon cord. Have both lift and tilt control.

MODERN PERIOD. The historic design period that dates from 1900.

MOLLY BOLT. A wall anchor plug and screw with elbows that flare out when screwed in. Necessary for installing heavy draperies on hollow walls where wood-framing members are absent.

MOTORIZED RODS. Electrical units that can be attached to drapery hardware that allow opening and closing of the draperies with a switch, by remote control, or with automatic timers or sensors. Motorized controls also are available for blinds, shades, and some shutters.

NEOCLASSIC PERIOD. A historic period of architecture and interior design dating in France from 1760 to 1789, in England from 1770 to 1820, and in America (the Federal Period) from 1790 to 1820.

OFF-CENTER. A window that is not centered on the wall, necessitating that a pair of draperies extending wall to wall be made of different sizes, to meet in the center of the glass when closed.

ONE-WAY DRAW. Draperies or vertical louvers that are installed to stack off only in one direction, closing from left to right or from right to left.

OPACITY. The degree to which solid material obstructs light or view.

ORIEL BAY. A second-story bay window that extends down to the first floor.

ORIENTATION. The direction—north, south, east, or west—a window faces.

ORNAMENT. Embellishment or decoration added to the window treatment.

OUTSIDE BRACKET (O.B.) [OUTSIDE INSTALLATION (O.I.) OR OUTSIDE MOUNT (O.M.)] Interchangeable terms meaning the installation of a factory-made hard treatment (blind, shade, shutter, or screen) on the frame or the wall surrounding the window.

OVERDRAPERY. A drapery fabric installed over another layer of drapery.

OVERHANG. An architectural jetty, or second-story projection, that extends more than one foot beyond the first floor; a shading device.

OVERLAP. Where two leading edges of drapery meet and go past each other 2 inches to discourage a *light strike*.

PANEL. A single solid-wood piece or upholstered sliding partition; also, a drapery length made of one or more widths of fabric that travels in one direction on the rod. A panel may be a one-way drapery draw or half of a pair.

PARISIAN SHADE. A scalloped pouf shade with a gathered or pleated heading and optional ruffled hem; also called a *festoon shade* or *blind*.

PASSEMENTERIE. A category of trimmings that includes braid, gimp, fringe, tassels, and small glass beads.

PATIO DOOR. A sliding or swinging glass door that opens onto a patio area.

PELMET. A stiffened, shaped, and flat fabric valance; also can refer to a shaped upholstered wood cornice.

PENCIL PLEAT. A series of thin folds (each about the width of a pencil) gathered with tape that contains drawstrings.

PENTAZOIDAL WINDOW. An angled window with five sides.

PERIOD WINDOW TREATMENT. A general term for any window covering that can be documented to a historic period of interior design and decoration.

PIERCED SCREEN. A heavily carved screen from the Orient, with holes cut through to allow light to penetrate.

PINCH PLEAT. A single pleat folded and pressed into three fingers and bar tacked at the base to hold the fingers in place.

PIPING. Cotton cording covered with decorative fabric and sewn onto fabric treatments as a trimming; also called welting.

PIVOTING SHUTTERS. A large wood or stone slab that swings on a central pin or dowel set into a hole in the frame.

PLANK SHUTTERS. Vertical strips of wood joined with crosswise planks to form rustic, provincial-looking shutters.

PLANTATION SHUTTERS. Movable wood louvered shutters with very wide blades—3, 3½, or 4 inches wide each. Originally used to direct breezes and as a shading device on southern plantations in America.

PLATE GLASS. Large sheets of glass made by pouring molten glass onto a table and ironing it smooth. Very popular in France from the seventeenth century to the nineteenth century.

PLEAT. A section of fabric sewn together to create fullness. Types include accordion, box and inverted box, cartridge, end, French or pinch, group, knife, plain top, pencil, single, special fold, spring rod, and a variety of *pleater tape* styles.

PLEATED FABRIC SHADE. A factory-made treatment of heat-set polyester fabric that can have a metallized backing to reflect heat to the outside as a shading device or direct heat into the room.

PLEATED ROMAN SHADE. A Roman shade that hangs in horizontally stitched and tailored-looking folds when closed or lowered, to give more fabric fullness to the typically flat shade.

PLEATER TAPE. Strips of woven fabric with drawstrings that are pulled to gather the drapery heading into various pleated configurations.

PORTIERE CURTAINS. Straight or tieback curtains that frame a doorway and serve as a privacy partition.

POUF SHADE (POUF VALANCE). A soft-looking fabric shade or valance with a puffy scalloped hem. Pouf shades draw up vertically from the bottom and have a variety of headings; also called *Parisian, balloon,* or *cloud shades.*

PRINCIPLES OF DESIGN. The theory of design—proportion and scale, balance, rhythm, emphasis, and harmony—that is brought into existence through manipulation of the *elements of design.*

PRISCILLA CURTAINS. Sheer, semisheer, or opaque curtains that have a ruffled valance and ruffled side and bottom hems and ties. They may center-meet or crisscross.

PROJECTING BAY WINDOW. A bay window that has straight sides that meet the building at a 90-degree angle. The sides may be of glass or a solid building material.

PROPORTION. The relationship of parts to a whole as the sizes and shapes are compared. Pleasing proportion is a principle of design accomplished in beautiful interiors.

RADIATION. The transfer of solar heat through space.

RAISED-PANEL SHUTTERS. Historic formal shutters with central panels raised by a recessed molding. Similar to historic raised-panel doors.

RENAISSANCE PERIOD. The rebirth or reawakening of classical art, literature, science, and architecture. Dated from 1400 to 1600 in Italy, 1589 to 1643 in France, and 1558 to 1649 in England (the English Renaissance overlapped the Late Medieval period and developed at a slower pace than in the southern European countries).

RETURN. The flat portion of a drapery heading that wraps around the *end-bracket* projection from the last pleat to the wall.

RHYTHM. A principle of design in which the elements of an interior are united in a connected or cadenced manner. Types of rhythm include transition, gradation, repetition, and opposition.

ROCOCO PERIOD. A French historic period of asymmetrical, curved, decorative ornamentation in interior design, dating from 1730 to 1760.

ROD POCKET. A spaced or hollow seam sewn in the top or bottom of fabric to slide in a rod or dowel in a shirred or gathered fashion or as a flat treatment.

ROD WIDTH. The measurement from the end of one bracket to the end of the other; includes the window width and stackback.

ROLLER SHADE. A flat vinyl or cloth fabric attached to a large wood or metal dowel, with a roller-spring or ball-bearing operable mechanism that raises and lowers the shade.

ROMAN SHADE. A flat custom fabric shade that folds up accordion-style from the bottom. Variations include pleated or double-pick-up Roman shades and soft-fold Roman shades.

ROOM-DARKENING SHADE/DRAPERY. A shade or drapery made of heavy opaque material that blocks light when closed. Also called *blackout shade/drapery.*

RUCHING. Gathering or pleating fabric in a narrow area—such as in welting or piping, ties for tiebacks, or other trimming.

RUFFLE-ROUND CURTAINS. Cottage curtain panels, also called *Cape Cod curtains,* with a continuous ruffle around the sides and bottom and shirred or gathered onto a rod; may be café curtains, tiebacks, and valances.

RUFFLES. A strip of fabric gathered and sewn onto soft window treatments as trimming.

R-VALUE. The rating of a window treatment, wall, or ceiling in its capacity to resist the flow of incoming or outgoing heat.

SASH. The wood frame of a window or door that holds the glass in both sliding and swinging windows.

SASH CURTAIN. A semisheer fabric gathered or shirred onto a rod, both top and bottom, and hung on the sash.

SASH WINDOW. A vertically sliding window. A single-hung sash window has an operable bottom sash; both lower and upper sashes can slide up and down in a double-hung sash window.

SCALE. The relative size of furnishings, patterns, and window coverings. Scale is classified as grand (very large); large, or heavy; medium; and small, or light. An element of design.

SCALLOPS. A series of projected semicircles repeated across the hem of a valance or shade skirt.

SCANT COVERAGE. Skimpy use of fabric at the window to create a flatter, pared-down look.

SHADE. Vinyl or cloth fabric that covers the glass and folds or rolls off the glass to the bottom or, more commonly, to the top. Types include roller shades, custom fabric Roman and pouf shades, and woven-wood shades.

SHADING DEVICE. Any means, interior or exterior, of keeping direct sunlight from penetrating to the interior.

SHAPED VALANCE. A fabric top treatment that has a curved or angled top and/or bottom.

SHEER. A transparent or translucent lightweight fabric used as a glass curtain or as an underdrapery or overdrapery.

SHEET GLASS. Large plates or sheets of glass used for glazing, made by drawing or casting. Used throughout this century for most windows until the development of *float glass.*

SHIRRING (SHIRRED TREATMENT). Gathered-fabric treatment accomplished by sliding a curtain rod or dowel through a rod pocket. The rod is smaller than the fabric width. The wider the fabric in comparison to the rod, the greater the fullness will be.

SHOJI SCREEN. Oriental paper affixed to wood frames with a wood grid to form translucent sliding or stationary panels.

SHUTTERS. Side-hinged folding wood panels that can have louvers or solid or insert panels in the center of the frame.

SILL HEIGHT. The measurement from the floor to the windowsill, used for factory-made treatments when determining the length of the controls.

SILL LENGTH. The measurement of draperies or curtains constructed to end at the windowsill.

SINGLE-HUNG SHUTTER. One set of shutters that covers either the entire window or only the bottom half (café shutters).

SINGLE-HUNG WINDOW. A sash window in which only the bottom sash is operable.

SINGLE PLEAT. Folds of fabric brought forward and seamed; also, one complete pleat of any variety.

SKIRT. The body of a shade as compared to its valance, if there is one.

SKYLIGHTS. Windows of glass or plastic set into the ceiling.

SLATS. A series of wood, plastic, or metal blades, called *louvers* in shutters; *louvers* in horizontal blinds; and *vanes* in vertical blinds.

SLIDING PATIO DOORS. Glass doors that slide to open.

SLIDING WINDOWS. Windows that slide over the top of each other to open; typically made of metal.

SOFT-FOLD ROMAN SHADE. An accordion-folded shade with soft, round, horizontal folds that are somewhat puffy.

SOLAR GAIN. Heat from the sun that enters the interior through glass windows.

SOLARIUM GREENHOUSE WINDOWS. Vertical, angular, or curved-glass walls and ceilings that are intended to augment solar gain; also a source of considerable heat loss.

SOLAR SCREENS. Fine plastic mesh set in metal frames that act as a shading device on the outside of the window. Similar to insect screens but dark in color.

SOUND ABSORPTION. The ability of a window treatment to eliminate or muffle undesirable sound.

SPANISH ARCH. A rounded arch or series of arches reminiscent of Spanish architecture.

SPECIAL FOLD PLEATS. Another name for *accordion pleats.*

SPECIAL RODDING. Hardware for draperies or curtains that can be cut to measure or bent to fit special shapes of windows or types of installations.

SPECIFICATION SHEETS. The work order form that indicates all the necessary information for the construction of custom-made soft window treatments.

SPRING ROLLER. A roller shade affixed to a metal or wood dowel with a spring mechanism.

STACKING (STACKBACK OR STACKOFF). The wall area on either side or at the top of a window where a window treatment will fit when opened.

STANDARD GLAZING. Stock or standard sizes of windows offered by a window company.

STATIONARY OVERDRAPERY. A drapery that is not operable.

STENCILING. Surface ornamentation accomplished by brushing paint over a cut-out pattern, or stencil. Used on the wall around window frames, on curtain or shade fabric, or on wood window treatments.

STILE. The vertical side portions of wood shutters.

SUPPORT FABRICS. Lining and interlining.

SWAG. A semicircular draped fabric top treatment; also called a *festoon.*

SYMMETRICAL BALANCE. Mirror-image balance, such as a pair of tieback draperies or two pair of identical draperies or shades on each side of a central point, for example, a fireplace.

TAMBOUR CURTAINS. Embroidered semisheer or lightweight curtains; originally a folk craft from Scandinavia.

TASSEL. A group of colored threads bound together at the top and hung as a pendant ornament on draperies, valances, or ties.

TASSEL AND SLIDE. Cord tie for tieback draperies, with a large tassel on one end that hangs down as a pendant ornament.

TEARDROP CURTAINS. Curtains poufed and tied back more than once as stationary side panels; also called *bishop's sleeve curtains.*

TIE. A narrow, straight, or shaped strip of fabric that may be trimmed with passementerie, ruffles, or banding and is wrapped around a curtain or drapery panel to secure it to the wall and form a tieback.

TIEBACK. A curtain or drapery that is draped to one side and secured with a tie or metal holdback.

TIEBACK CORD. Braided cord used in place of a fabric tie.

TIER. A layer of fabric—usually a curtain panel—that is overlapped vertically by another layer of fabric.

TIP-TO-TIP MEASUREMENT. The measurement from the end of a roller shade pin to the other end.

TOGGLE BOLT. A wall anchor or fastener that forms elbows inside the wall to anchor a drapery rod permanently in a hollow wall; similar to a *molly bolt*.

TRACK HARDWARE. Slotted metal rods that have sliding carriers to hold drapery hooks but have no cords or pulley systems. The draperies or curtains must be drawn by hand or with a cord or baton (plastic wand).

TRAPEZOIDAL WINDOWS. A four-sided angular window.

TRAVERSE ROD OR HARDWARE. A rod that houses plastic carriers into which drapery pins are hooked and connected with ball bearings, pulleys, and cords, so that a pair of curtains draws open simultaneously when the cord at the end of the rod is pulled.

TRIM (TRIMMING). A general term that encompasses passementerie, fabric banding, welting, and ruffles.

TUBULAR PLEAT. A narrow, round, hollow pleat stiffened with buckram.

UNLINED DRAPERIES. Draperies made of a single layer of fabric without any lining or support fabrics.

UPHOLSTERED CORNICE. A wood cornice padded and covered with decorative fabric.

VALANCE. A fabric top treatment. Types include swags and cascades, pelmets and shirred and pleated valances.

VENETIAN BLINDS. Horizontal louvered blinds made of metal slats 2 inches wide and held together with cord or braid; they have both tilt and lift controls.

VERTICAL LOUVERS. Slats or vanes typically 4 inches wide made of plastic, metal, or fabric and mounted onto a headrail with both tilt and draw controls.

VICTORIAN. An era of revival and combination elements and furnishings that paralleled the Industrial Revolution, dating in England from 1837 to 1910 and in America from 1840 to 1920.

WALL FASTENERS. Molly bolts or toggle bolts—a combination of screws and anchors to secure window treatments in hollow walls.

WIDTH. The horizontal measurement of a window treatment.

WINDOW WIDTH. The horizontal measurement of the glass area only.

WOOD BLINDS. Wood miniblinds or vertical-louver blinds.

WORK ORDER. A sheet that contains information for manufacturing hard treatments, constructing soft treatments, or installing window coverings.

WOVEN WOOD. Fabric made of narrow slats of natural or painted wood woven together with yarn. The fabric is made into Roman or roller shades, valances, draperies, or insert shutters.

Glossary 2   Business and Contract Terms

AESTHETIC STANDARDS. Organized professional testing or evaluation of textiles for colorfastness and drapability.

ARCHITECT. The professional who designs the building and often oversees its construction. The architect writes nonresidential specifications to meet building codes.

ASTM. A designation for the Steiner Tunnel Test, a stringent flammability test for textiles.

C.B.D. (CASH BEFORE DELIVERY). When goods are paid for before they are shipped to the interior designer or decorator; also known as *proforma*.

C.F.A. (CUTTING FOR APPROVAL). Requesting a sample of fabric in stock to check dye-lot color correctness or match. When the fabric is approved, the sample is sent back with instructions to match the yardage to that sample. Distributors may have more than one dye lot in the warehouse at any given time.

C.O.D. (CASH ON DELIVERY). A financial arrangement where goods are shipped to the designer, and the delivery person collects the bill plus delivery charges and a C.O.D. charge as well.

CODES. Local or state rules and regulations that establish quality and safety parameters for furnishings installed in public spaces. Fabrics, for example, must meet certain standards for resistance to flammability, abrasion, colorfastness, and stability.

COLORFASTNESS. The ability of a fabric to resist fading. Tests for colorfastness can be conducted with results that can stand as a type of liability assurance in meeting specifications for longevity; particularly valuable in contract installations where many windows are draped in the same fabric.

CONTRACT. A legally binding written agreement between the interior designer or decorator and the client that outlines goods and services to be rendered, time deadlines, and responsibilities.

CONTRACT DESIGN WORK. Designates nonresidential interior design and encompasses offices, institutions, hospitality situations, industrial situations, and retail and model homes—anywhere except private residences. The term is somewhat misleading, since contracts are customarily drawn up in residential design as well.

COST-PLUS. An arrangement often used in nonresidential, or contract, design, where the designer sells goods to the client at wholesale or net price plus a percentage, usually 5 to 20 percent. The quantity of goods sold makes up for the small profit.

DAYLIGHTING. Partially lighting the interior with natural light through window fenestrations in nonresidential buildings.

DESIGN CENTERS. Huge buildings that house showrooms and cater to the trade—professional architects, interior designers, and decorators—which are located in major metropolitan areas.

DISTRIBUTOR. The wholesale company that sells fabric orders, drapery hardware, and factory-made treatments to the designer or decorator, who then resells them to the client. Fabric distributors also are called *jobbers*.

ENERGY CONSERVATION. Nonresidential window treatments may be required to do one or more of the following: allow year-round daylighting; encourage winter solar-heat gain; provide insulation; provide airtightness in summer and winter when mechanical cooling/heating devices are in operation; refract or absorb summer heat; and allow ventilation during moderate temperature seasons. Energy conservation comprises any and all of these functions.

EXTENDED TIME FRAME. A differentiating factor in nonresidential design, where a contract selling window coverings may not be completed for six months to three years while the building is being planned and constructed.

FABRIC DESIGNATOR. A system of determining fabric construction and color used in specifications: (I) open weave; (II) semiopen weave; (III) closed weave; (D) dark; (M) medium; (L) light. Example: IL = open weave, light-colored fabric.

FABRIC GRADE. A system of determining the cost of a fabric. A-grade fabrics are all one price and the least costly; B-, C-, and D-grade fabrics are increasingly expensive. Often used for fabrics offered by furniture manufacturers.

FABRIC HOUSE. A jobber of national fame or significance whose headquarters usually are in New York City.

FADE-O-METER. A device for measuring the amount of fading or the degree of colorfastness that results after a fabric has undergone prolonged exposure to light.

FENESTRATION DATA OR VALUES. The compilation of data or observation of *U-values*, energy conservation, shading coefficients, solar optics, and visible criteria or properties.

THE 5–10 CODE. A numerical code to conceal a net price. Fabrics and furnishings will have two numbers. Subtract five from the first number, ten from the second number, and then add the two to find the wholesale cost per item or per yard.

FLEXIBILITY. A criterion for fabric durability consisting of elasticity (ability to stretch) and recovery (ability to return to its original shape).

HEALTH/SAFETY REQUIREMENTS. An area where testing can be done to meet codes or specifications consisting of resistance to microorganisms, static electricity, fire ignition, flame spread, and smoke and toxicity (poisonous gas) levels.

HORIZONTAL OPERATION. A fabric-manufacturing enterprise that completes one or only a few of the many steps necessary in the production of finished textiles.

INSTITUTION WORK. Selling interior design products to health-care, medical, and geriatric facilities; schools, colleges, and universities.

INTERIOR ARCHITECT. An interior designer who also is trained as an architect and who understands structural building elements. The interior architect is qualified to perform all design work relating to interior architecture.

INVESTMENT CAPITAL. Money needed to initiate and sustain a new business venture.

INVOICE. An itemized billing for goods sold by the manufacturer to the interior designer or decorator.

JOBBER. A wholesaler that buys job, or dye lots of fabric; cuts and distributes samples to architects, interior designers, and decorators; and sells cut orders to the trade.

LEGAL CONTRACT. See *Contract.*

LIABILITY. The legal and/or financial responsibility for performance, durability, or safety of furnishing items that falls on the architect, interior designer, or decorator who specified, selected, or sold the goods.

LIFE CYCLE. The number of years an item of furnishing actually lasts or is expected to last; also called life span. On the average pull shades last three to five years, draperies last five to eight years, and blinds last eight to twelve years.

LIFE-CYCLE COSTING. The cost of a product (including material, fabrication, and installation) plus the cost of maintenance, divided by the years of expected service life. The total will yield the cost per year of the product, information useful for some businesses or corporations that have yearly budgets which include cost of furnishings.

LIST PRICE. The retail or marked-up price of fabric, hardware, or hard window treatments.

MAINTENANCE. The care and cleaning of window treatments.

MALFUNCTIONING MERCHANDISE. Defects in operation, such as problems with controls that do not work properly, for which the designer may be liable or financially responsible.

MARKUP. The amount or percentage added to a net or wholesale price to arrive at a list price for a fabric or window-covering product.

MERCHANDISE. Window products sold to the client.

MICROORGANISMS. Mold, mildew, or bacteria that eat or otherwise destroy a fabric.

MODEL HOME WORK. Selling window treatments to developments that furnish model homes or model condominiums where the client is not the occupant or user.

MULTIPRODUCT DISTRIBUTOR. A company that supplies the interior designer with both hard and soft window treatments and accessory items.

NET PRICE. The wholesale, dealer, or designer/decorator cost for merchandise.

NOISE CONTROL. The ability of a window covering, particularly a fabric one, to muffle the noise level in an interior. It is determined by the weight or construction of the fabric and by the fullness of coverage at the window.

NONFLAMMABLE. Designation for fabrics and materials that do not burn. These include asbestos and fiberglass.

NONRESIDENTIAL (CONTRACT) DESIGN. Encompasses offices, institutions, hospitality situations, industrial situations, and retail and model homes.

OCCUPANT. A person who resides in a finished nonresidential or residential space; also called the *user.*

OFFICE WORK. Window treatment work specified and sold for law and medical offices, government facilities, small business firms, and high-rise offices.

OPEN ACCOUNT. A credit arrangement between the designer and the supplier or manufacturer, where goods are ordered and delivered; an invoice is sent, usually within ten days; and the balance is due in full within thirty days. May include an additional discount if paid within ten days of billing.

PERFORMANCE CRITERIA. Established categories of product and fabric/material performance that may be evaluated by independent testing laboratories. These categories include health and safety, durability, and aesthetics.

PLEATING SYSTEMS. Commonly used architectural tracks with pinch pleats, accordion pleats, single pleats, or roll pleats. The last three pleat types use heading tapes that snap onto the carriers.

PRODUCT. Any window treatment item that is installed in the interior; it can mean fabric, hardware, or hard window treatments.

PROFORMA. A form of arrangement for buying goods at wholesale, where the designer does not have open-account status, and payment is required before the manufacturer or distributor will ship. It is the same as *C.B.D.* (cash before delivery).

PURCHASING AGENT. A person in nonresidential work who has authority to order or purchase merchandise for the building, job, or development project.

REPRESENTATIVE (REP). A person who travels to all the design firms within a geographical territory to distribute samples, literature, and pricing information on the products and to help the designer or decorator in selecting or specifying correct merchandise, in solving problems, or in obtaining better, faster service.

REQUEST FOR PROPOSAL (RFP). A form distributed to designers who bid on government window coverings or other contracts where money will be disbursed. The RFP requires a complete itemization and breakdown of costs in advance; then one of the lower bids is routinely selected and awarded the bid or contract.

RESALE NUMBER. A tool used by individual states for collecting sales tax. It entitles the firm, or holder, to buy goods at wholesale, then resell them to the public. The holder is required by law to charge and collect sales tax on all items resold, then file periodic sales tax return forms and the collected money to the state.

RESEARCH. The process of obtaining written product information necessary to meet the codes or specifications for a nonresidential interior design installation.

RESIDENTIAL DESIGN WORK. Interior design and decoration, including window treatments, that are sold to the person or persons who will be living in the home. It may encompass more decorative or creative custom-made window treatments than nonresidential work.

RETAIL DESIGN. Selling window treatments to department stores, boutiques, or shopping malls. This type of work often entails exterior treatments, such as logo awnings or rolling shutters.

SHADING COEFFICIENT. A rating determined by testing fabrics for solar optical properties: (1) sunlight transmittance, (2) solar (sunlight) reflection, and (3) solar (heat) absorption. Lower ratings are more efficient for shading (.40 to .60) and are tested with plain and heat-absorbing window glass.

SHOWROOM. A fabric, furniture, carpeting, or accessory company's place of business, where designers order merchandise. An open showroom allows a client to enter but the client usually will not be allowed to purchase goods; a closed showroom allows only architects, interior designers, and decorators to enter and do business.

SOLAR OPTICS. The fabric properties in the three categories listed under *Shading Coefficient.*

SPECIALIZATION. The trend among some window treatment professionals or interior designers to deal in only one area of nonresidential interiors or even a subarea.

SPECIFIER. A person who selects interior furnishings for an interior design project and awards the contracts to provide those items.

STABILITY/DIMENSIONAL STABILITY. A fabric's resistance to sagging or elongation and hiking.

STANDARDIZED TESTS. Tests performed and subsequent ratings produced by independent laboratories to determine aspects of health safety, aesthetic standards, and durability of products used in interiors.

STATIC ELECTRICITY. Stationary electrical charges, such as those produced by friction: potentially destructive to sensitive machinery, a possible fire hazard, and a source of discomfort and irritation to the user.

SUPPLIER. Another term for manufacturer or *distributor.*

TENANT. The person or persons who occupy an office and who often will select and pay for their own window treatments; also called tenant design.

TOXICITY. The poisonous gasses released when items burn. Plastics emit the most toxic fumes of all interior materials.

THE TRADE. The interior design profession. Window coverings "sold to the trade" are purchased from manufacturers by architects, interior designers, or decorators who then resell the goods at a markup to the client.

USER. A term for the person who will occupy a completed interior.

U-VALUE. A rating used in nonresidential testing results based on BTUs (British Thermal Units) of heat transferred each hour per square foot of glass. The heat flow may be winter interior heat loss to the outside or excessive solar heat gain in the summer. Lower ratings are more efficient: .65 to .30 is considered good.

VERTICAL OPERATION. A large or conglomerate manufacturer that produces decorative textiles from the raw goods or fiber state to the finished product, including dozens of manufacturing steps.

VISIBLE PROPERTIES OR CRITERIA. The control of glare and the degree of opacity, which may enhance or interfere with vision through the fenestration.

Glossary 3 Decorative and Support Fabric Terms

This glossary is a selection of the most commonly used window-covering fabrics, arranged alphabetically under each of five categories—transparent sheer fabrics, semisheer and casement fabrics, lightweight opaque fabrics, medium-weight fabrics, and heavyweight fabrics—with an explanation of the applications for each category.

TRANSPARENT SHEER FABRICS

Transparent sheers are thin fabrics placed next to glass to diffuse glare and screen daylight. In the daytime these fabrics—which are woven of very fine threads—afford privacy, blocking a view into the building. In the evening, however, their transparency allows a clear view *from the outside in*, toward the light.

Transparent sheer fabrics are decidedly formal and often are used to great effect in more elaborate rooms. They serve as both curtains and underdrapery sheers (gathered and pleated), and sometimes are used for Parisian or Austrian fabric shades and for sheer swags. Sheer fabrics occasionally are used as bed hangings or curtains. Common examples include the following:

CHIFFON. A softly finished, very transparent sheer. Other fabrics given a soft finish are prefixed with the word *chiffon*, such as chiffon velvet.

CREPE CHIFFON. A diaphanous sheer of fine threads that are tightly twisted into crepe threads. The finish is soft yet slightly pebbly.

GAUZE. Similar to marquisette and scrim, a leno or doup weave of very fine hourglass-twisted and interlaced threads. It is a coarser sheer and comes in various thread-fineness levels—from mosquito netting to cheesecloth.

GEORGETTE. A sheer fabric of slightly creped yarns with a lustrous hard finish.

GRENADINE/MARQUISETTE. A fine, lightweight sheer of tiny threads that are woven in a leno or doup weave. Marquisette is slightly heavier than grenadine and may be woven or flocked with dots or figures.

NET. An open-weave sheer textile in various weights that is made by knotting or looping a continuous filament thread. May have square, hexagonal, or other sizes and shapes to the mesh, and may incorporate novelty threads or embroidery.

NINON. A gossamer or moirelike sheer produced by grouping very fine warp threads in pairs that are tightly woven. The finish is crisp yet not stiff. Sometimes called *French voile, French tregal,* or *triple voile.*

ORGANDY. A very thin, sheer muslin, originally of cotton, that is chemically treated to provide a crisp, wiry, durable finish. White, colored, or printed, it works well for ruffled sheer installations where crispness and transparency are needed. *Semi-organdy* is a semisheer organdy that gives partial transparency.

SHEER. A term that includes many types of diaphanous fabrics.

SWISS. A thin plain-weave fabric with a crisp finish that is ideal for informal curtains. Swiss flocked or embroidered with small dots or figures is called *dotted swiss.*

TARLATAN. A transparent open-weave (originally cotton) muslin that is given a stiff or glazed nondurable (dry-clean-only) finish. White or colored, it is used for curtains and some linings.

TISSUE. Sheers, semisheers, and lightweight fabrics that are produced in their thinnest or lightest form and used for curtains or sheer draperies.

VOILE. A plain balanced weave of single or ply crepe yarns given a soft or (more frequently) crisp, hard finish. May have piqué cords, nubbed yarns, or stripes woven into the fabric. Often has a fine, sandpaperlike feel.

SEMISHEER AND CASEMENT FABRICS

Semisheer and casement fabrics generally are less formal than transparent sheer fabrics. They have a variety of yarns that produce the semisheer or novelty effect. These fabrics often are used alone at the window to diffuse strong light and to give an interesting pattern as well as daytime privacy. When used in offices and other contract settings that are occupied only during the day, they are usually of a variety that does not offer nighttime privacy. Such fabrics may be used as an underdrapery companioned with heavier, opaque overdrapery, or as an overdrapery with a fabric undertreatment or a hardline treatment to ensure nighttime privacy. They also may be used as bed hangings and dividing panels.

ARNACHE/MALIWATT. Fabrics produced on machines that needle-punch, or stitch-bond, nonwoven batting rather than weaving it. A rapid, needle-constructed technique for semi opaque casement draperies and insulated linings.

BATISTE. A fine, balanced plain-weave cloth of carded and combed cotton or imitation yarns. The yarns may be slightly irregular, and the fabric may be bleached, dyed, printed, flocked, or embroidered. Its texture may range from very fine to fairly coarse.

BOUCLÉ MARQUISETTE. A netlike leno sheer with weft threads of novelty bouclé yarn (looped or curled). Texture is pebbly or knotted.

BURN-OUT SHEER (ETCH PRINTING). A casement-weight fabric finished by etching or chemically removing part of the yarns (usually the cotton in a cotton/polyester blend) in a pattern or eyelet dot.

CASEMENT. A general term for casual-, open-, semi-open, or semi-opaque-weave fabrics meant to be used alone at the window. May be a loose or tight, woven or knitted construction in contemporary colors and novelty yarns and weave variations.

CHEESECLOTH GAUZE. An open, plain, loose weave used for very casual curtain installations. Heavier than plain gauze.

DIMITY. A plain-weave cotton semisheer with ribs of plied warp threads spaced lengthwise to create a dainty corded effect. Weft cords may be added to create a check.

DOTTED SWISS. A crisply finished sheer fabric with embroidered or flocked dots, figures, or tiny floral patterns.

EYELET. A semisheer or lightweight opaque cloth with etch-printed holes surrounded by machine-embroidered designs. Usually white or pastel-colored, it often comes with a coordinated scalloped border to be used for trimming.

LACE. A broad term for hand- or machine-made open-construction patterned fabric. Lace used for curtains and draperies usually includes the following machine-made types: Bobbinet, Leavers, Nottingham, Raschel (Rachel), and Schiffli embroidery. The patterns may range from traditional floral to modern abstract.

LAWN. A fine fabric that forms the basecloth for batiste and organdy and may be sheer or semisheer. Usually is printed, although it comes in white and in solid colors. Crease resistant and has good body.

LENO. A variation of the plain weave, where pairs of warp yarns are hourglass-twisted as they are interlaced with the weft, or filling, threads. May be a light- to medium-weight open-weave casement fabric in neutral or contrasting colored yarns. More coarse fabrics will have slub or roving (uneven, slightly twisted) yarns.

MACRAMÉ. A technique of tying knots by hand to create an open, lacy textile. The weight and texture of macramé depend on the type of yarn used.

MALIMO. A needle-constructed casement fabric in which groups of weft yarns are laid across warp yarns in a straight or patterned design, then top stitched with a clear monofilament knit chain stitch. May incorporate the Jacquard attachment for large, geometric patterns.

MESH. A general term for any open-weave or knit textile with a netlike construction. Refers to textiles heavier and less transparent than net.

NET. An open, needle-constructed fabric with angular patterns. Forms the basecloth for some embroidered laces.

SEMI-ORGANDY. A crisp semisheer muslin fabric with a durable finish. May be neutral, dyed, or printed.

RASCHEL (RACHEL KNIT). A vertical or warp-knit needle-constructed technique that produces dimensionally stable casement cloth or open, lacy patterns rapidly and inexpensively.

LIGHTWEIGHT OPAQUE FABRICS

Lightweight opaque fabrics are relatively thin textiles that are quite useful for window coverings. They are flexible and have a fair amount of body, drape attractively unless finished too soft, and have a pleasing hand as a whole. They do not have a great deal of strength or durability because of their thinness and may benefit from being lined. Lightweight fabrics are used for curtains, overdrapery, underdrapery, fabric shades, and soft or reinforced top treatments. They also are useful for accessory items and bed linens and hangings.

ANTIQUE SATIN. A sateen or horizontal satin weave with a face predominately of rayon and a back predominately of acetate (typically 60 percent rayon/40 percent acetate). The horizontal threads are slub yarns, imitating shantung silk. Perhaps the most common of the formal overdrapery fabrics in use today. Can be dressed up or down, made into simple or elaborate treatments, and trimmed with fringe or braid. Comes in a multitude of colors and a variety of textures, from fairly smooth to heavily slubbed. Useful for top treatments (although railroading can be a problem, as warp and weft threads are frequently different colors).

BATIK. A hand-printed textile most often produced in the islands of the South Pacific and in Africa. The cotton cloth is printed with wax and then dyed. The wax resists the dye and the color penetrates wherever the wax is not applied. The wax is removed and reapplied in different places for a multicolored effect.

BROADCLOTH. A cotton fabric with a very fine crosswise cord that is similar to muslin in a plain, solid color. Also, a worsted wool or blend twill that is felted and napped (medium- to heavyweight).

BUCKRAM (CRINOLINE). A loosely woven or nonwoven fabric that has been sized and stiffened to become the interfacing for headings and top treatments. Manufactured up to 48 inches wide, it is typically used in smaller widths, 4 inches being the most common.

CALICO. Cotton or cotton/polyester percale or muslin printed with small floral patterns. Often called *country calico* because of its quaint, provincial designs.

CAMBRIC. Plain-weave cotton or linen that may be finished soft and dull, or stiff and lustrous. For draperies it is a basecloth for printed patterns. Also called *handkerchief linen.*

CHALLIS (CHALLIE). Plain-weave fabric made of cotton, wool, or rayon and given a very soft finish. Tends to hang limply and is most often printed.

CHAMBRAY. Similar to cambric, typically a cotton or linen constructed from colored warp threads and white filling threads in a plain or Oxford weave.

CHINO. A sturdy yet soft fabric, often in khaki or earth-toned colors, constructed with a twill weave.

CREPE DE CHINE. A very lightweight, lustrous plain-weave crepe fabric. Originally of silk, it is also available in rayon or polyester.

EPONGE. A loosely constructed plain-weave fabric containing lofty, highly textured yarns that give a spongy appearance.

EYELET. A decorative effect of burned-out or etched holes surrounded by surface (Schiffli) embroidery on fabrics such as broadcloth, dimity, organdy, and piqué.

FAILLE. The basecloth for moire, a dense, plain weave with flat crosswise ribs. When lightweight it is sometimes used for linings. Moire is a heavier version of faille.

GINGHAM. A plain-weave, yarn-dyed check fabric. Checks range in size from minute to 2-inch squares, depending on the pattern, and form a sequence in which white and colored checks alternate. A casual, multi-use textile.

INDIAN HEAD. A trade name for a sturdy cotton fabric that is preshrunk and colorfast. Has a porous surface and fairly thick yarns.

INDIA PRINT. A lightweight cotton from India printed with small floral, ethnic, or geometric patterns.

LAPPET. A plain-weave variation into which supplemental threads are woven, then trimmed to become a type of discontinuous embroidery. Fabrics are sometimes similar to muslin and fairly natural in color.

MADRAS. Cotton cloth finely woven with stripes, plaids, checks, or occasionally dobby or Jacquard fabrics.

MILANESE. A knit fabric with fine diagonal ribs that is used for curtains. Somewhat similar to tricot.

MUSLIN. A plain-weave cotton or cotton/polyester cloth that forms the base-cloth for many fabrics, including chintz and lawn. May be obtained unbleached, bleached, in plain colors, or printed; patterns may be woven in or embroidered. Commonly used as a lower-count bed sheet fabric.

MYLAR. Trade name for extruded film used as a base for reflective wall coverings. Also slit into tape or split yarns and woven into textiles for novelty effects.

NAINSOOK. A very fine plain-weave, mercerized cotton. Lustrous and sometimes calendered to a high-gloss finish.

NUN'S VEILING. A thin, fine, plain-weave wool that is soft yet firm.

OXFORD CLOTH. A plain-weave variation in which two warp yarns are carried as one. Weights vary from finely woven men's shirting to coarse union (cotton/linen) cloth. Comes in solid colors or is printed.

PAISLEY. A pattern motif printed on or woven into cotton, linen, wool, synthetic, or blend fabrics ranging from light to medium weight. The pattern is a curved teardrop or pear shape that originated in India. Many colors are available, although red is traditionally dominant. Uses vary with weight and type of weave.

PERCALE. A cotton or cotton/polyester plain-weave fabric similar to muslin but with finer threads and higher yarn count. White, solid colored, or printed, it is used for sheets and lightweight draperies and curtains.

PERCALINE. A percale fabric glazed or finished with a moire (watermark) calendering.

PLAID. A printed or woven textile in which squares and rectangles are formed with contrasting colors. Scale of pattern and weight of fabric are variable, depending on the yarn and weave. The best-known variety is the *tartan plaid*, which represents Scottish clans.

PLISSÉ. A fabric with a puckered surface that is chemically produced as an aesthetic finish. It is opaque in most cases, although transparent sheers may be treated with a plissé finish. The finish is durable if cared for properly.

POLISHED COTTON. A plain- or sateen-weave fabric with highly mercerized, glossy yarns. Has a soft finish yet has excellent body and draping qualities. Glazed polished cottons resemble chintz. May be a cotton blend.

SATEEN. A horizontal satin fabric in which long, fine, smooth weft yarns float over four to eight warp threads and then tie down under one. May be plain, printed, or have a woven pattern. Weights range from light to medium; lighter weights often are used for linings.

SATIN. A weave in which warp threads float over four to eight weft threads and then are tied down under one. The random interlacing produces a smooth, lustrous surface. Applications depend on the fiber and type of yarn used; very fine silk, rayon, and acetate yarns yield formal, smooth satins. Also may be a base weave for such Jacquard fabrics as damask and brocade.

SEERSUCKER. A casual, lightweight fabric with permanent woven-in puckers produced by a variation in warp tension. Puckers range from very small to pronounced. Often seersuckers also contain woven patterns or plaid designs.

SHANTUNG. Originally a silk fabric, this lustrous, drapable textile is now constructed of fibers that imitate silk, such as rayon, polyester, or nylon. Has horizontal slub yarns that are meant to be irregular. *Antique satin* and *antique taffeta* are shantung imitations.

SHEETING. Percale or muslin fabrics sized and finished for bed sheets but also used as window treatment fabrics.

SINGLE DAMASK. A lower-quality damask with a low thread count. Patterns often carry floats across the back of the fabric. Lustrous and formal-looking, this is an inexpensive drapery textile.

TAFFETA. Another name for plain weave. Taffeta fabric may have fine, round, crosswise ribs. Can be crisply woven from acetate fibers, often into a plaid design. May be plain or patterned. May be finished into *moire taffeta* (in which ribs are calendered into the watermark), or into *paper taffeta* (lacquer-finished into a crisp stiffness). *Antique taffeta* has slub filler yarns and a near reversible look that imitates fine shantung.

TRICOT. A thin warp-knit fabric with elastic crosswise ribs on the back and inelastic vertical ribs on the surface. Very soft, usually of nylon; infrequently used for draperies because of lack of body. Useful for custom sheeting and for lingerie.

MEDIUM-WEIGHT FABRICS

Medium-weight fabrics generally are stronger and more sturdy than lightweight fabrics. Some drape attractively, and some may be stiff and cumbersome at the window. Several decorative and support fabrics fall into both the light- and medium-weight categories; others are considered either medium- or heavyweight, depending on the fiber used, the type and thickness of the yarn, and the intended purpose. Medium-weight fabrics are commonly used for overdrapery, top treatments, and window shades.

ARMURE. Sturdy multipurpose fabric of small geometric dobby patterns woven (self-colored) onto a rep (ribbed) background; not reversible.

BARK CLOTH. Authentic bark cloth is tapa cloth, pounded from the bark of trees, and produced in Polynesia. *Bark cloth* also means a rough-surface fabric woven with textured yarns. Frequently of cotton or blended fibers, it may be printed, usually with large, unsophisticated floral sprays, or dyed one color. Suitable for overdrapery.

BIRD'S EYE. A fabric patterned all over with diamonds containing a dot in the center. The name derives from the resemblance of the woven dobby pattern to a bird's eye. Also may be woven in one color. Very absorbent.

BROCADE. A Jacquard-woven fabric with a design that looks embroidered. Floating threads on the reverse of the fabric indicate a third set of yarns that creates the figured pattern. Traditionally a formal fabric, today brocade occasionally is woven into casual patterns. Quality brocades are used for draperies and upholstery.

BROCATELLE. A Jacquard fabric similar to brocade that is woven with two sets of warps and wefts to produce a slightly puffed surface. Fine brocatelles are very tightly woven and beautiful and formal traditional fabrics.

BUTCHER LINEN. A versatile unprinted fabric of neutral colors in a plain weave. Originally woven from linen, today this is often made from synthetic fibers or blends that imitate slubby tow linen.

CHEVRON (HERRINGBONE). A reverse or novelty-twill-weave fabric with a zigzag pattern named after the spinal structure of the herring fish. Usually of medium weight, but may vary according to the fiber and the weight and bulk of the yarn. Versatile. Usually comes in neutralized colors.

CREPE. A fabric woven in a plain, satin, or sateen weave of crepe yarns that are so tightly twisted that the surface of the fabric becomes pebbly. Other, ribbed crepes include *Canton crepe* (which is medium-weight, lustrous, and soft, with crosswise ribs), *faille crepe* (which has fine ribs of plied crepe yarn), and *crepon crepe* (which has thick lengthwise ribs). See also *Granite Cloth*.

CRETONNE. Plain-weave cotton fabric that is coarser than chintz and unglazed. Often printed with floral and geometric designs similar to chintz. Fine for draperies, shades, and furnishings. Sometimes called *cotton print*, or *country furnishing fabric*.

DAMASK. A Jacquard fabric with one set each of warp and weft threads. Patterns have traditionally been copies of Italian Renaissance floral designs. The design is slightly raised and is reversed on the back, even if the fabric is not meant to be reversible. Lower-quality damasks may have floating threads on the reverse; higher-quality damasks are tightly woven. Damask is made of many fibers, such as silk; rayon/acetate; and long-staple combed cotton, which can be woven into exquisite fabrics.

DOBBY. A fabric with small woven designs in one or more colors. Small-pattern repeats are possible on a regular floor loom with a dobby attachment. Use and weight depends on the fiber and type of yarn.

DOUBLE KNIT. A fabric knit with double needles that produce a double knit stitch on a double frame. May be patterned on each side and may have ribs. Stretches and is dense and stable.

DENIM. A sturdy twill-weave cotton, often in navy blue, called *jeans fabric*. Also available in other colors. Casual. Multipurpose.

DRILL. A twill-weave cotton cloth similar to denim—usually in a white or neutral color—that forms the basecloth for ticking and khaki.

DUCK. A versatile cotton, blend, or synthetic-fiber cloth of Oxford weave. May be plain or have woven or printed stripes. Also called *sailcloth or sail duck*; heavier yarns yield the more sturdy *awning duck*.

FAILLE. A lustrous ribbed fabric in a plain weave of silk, rayon, acetate, or blends. Medium-weight faille is calendered or pressed with a watermark pattern to create moire.

FILM. An extruded sheet of synthetic polymer, often vinyl, produced in solid white or colors or with printed patterns. Shower and bathroom curtains sometimes are made of this material.

FLANNEL. A wool, wool-blend, or wool-imitation fiber textile of plain or twill weave. The surface is napped to produce a soft, warm hand. Many types of flannel are produced, including *cotton flannel,* or *Flannelette* (which is of lighter weight, napped on one side, and printed in small patterns); *French flannel* (a dense, finely woven twill, napped on one side, produced in plain colors); *suede flannel* (which is napped on both sides, sheared, and pressed); and *Melton flannel* (a dense twill or satin weave, felted or shrunk, and napped).

GABARDINE. A steep twill woven of wool or synthetic fibers with more warp than filling threads. Surface is smooth and tightly woven. Comes in plain colors. Multipurpose.

GRANITE CLOTH (MUMMY OR MOMIE CLOTH). A drapery fabric with fine crepe warp yarns in a plain weave. Originally of linen, may also be of cotton, wool, silk, or rayon.

HOMESPUN. A plain, somewhat loosely woven fabric of bulky yarns that appear to be hand spun. Used for casual draperies and curtains.

HOPSACKING. A casual drapery fabric that imitates the rough, primitive look of jute or hemp sacks, which were originally used to store hops.

HUCKABACK. Small, raised geometric figures in cotton, linen, a blend, or a synthetic. Absorbent. First used as toweling; now also employed for draperies and accessories.

INTERFACING. A nonwoven or plain-weave fabric that is sized and stiffened to give body to shades and top treatments. May also have an iron-on sticky backing. Comes in various weights.

JACQUARD. The name of the loom that produces large and intricate woven patterns in one or several colors. Medium-weight Jacquard fabrics include *brocade, brocatelle, damask,* and *lampas.*

JASPÉ (STRIÉ OR OMBRÉ). A finely striped woven fabric produced by a subtle dye variation in the warp threads. May be a plain, satin, or sateen weave. Looks formal when the yarns are smooth and lustrous. Imitated by roller or screen printing as *shadow print.*

KHAKI. A plain-weave or twill-weave multipurpose fabric dyed in solid "earthy" greenish or pinkish browns or beiges.

LAMÉ. Any fabric woven exclusively or highlighted with gold- or silver-colored threads. Colored threads that are sealed in a clear extruded film are highly cleanable and will not tarnish as authentic metal threads do.

LAMPAS. A Jacquard fabric with a finely ribbed background and raised figures woven with the warp threads and contrasted with "dashes" of colored weft threads that complement the pattern. A formal fabric of varying quality.

MILIUM. Trade name for a triple-layered lining fabric. Two outside layers sandwich an inner layer of aluminized heat-reflectant fabric. Used as lining and interlining. Energy-efficient.

MOIRE. A formal, ribbed fabric in plain colors with a permanent calendered finish that embosses a watermark design in uneven concentric circles. Multipurpose; may form the basecloth for brocaded fabrics. Can be of cotton, silk, rayon, and/or acetate.

OMBRÉ. See *Jaspé*.

OSNABURG. A coarse, medium-weight cotton plain-weave that is undyed. Contains tiny bits of cotton hulls and waste. Used for curtains.

OXFORD CLOTH. Plain-weave variation that carries two finer warp threads as one, interlaced with a heavier weft thread. May be plain or printed. Predominately a multipurpose cotton or union cloth.

PAISLEY. A light- to medium-weight fabric, depending on weave, fiber, and yarn. Printed or woven with the paisley design, a pear or teardrop shape.

PIQUÉ. A plain-weave fabric with a lengthwise spaced rib or cord of heavier or plied yarns. An example is *Bedford cord*. May also incorporate other heavy yarns to yield such fabrics as *bird's eye; goose eye* (a heavier, larger version of bird's eye); and *waffle cloth piqué* (which has small to large squares in a three-dimensional arrangement).

PLAID. A woven or printed crossbar design in which horizontal and vertical bands of color create squares and rectangles; may be of light, medium, or heavy weight.

POPLIN. A multipurpose cotton, synthetic, or blend fabric in a plain weave with raised, round weft cords formed with large filling threads. Often printed with decorative designs.

SAILCLOTH. A lightweight Oxford-weave cotton canvas that is essentially the same as duck. Heavily treated with water repellent, it is used for boat sails. Multipurpose. Available plain, striped, or occasionally printed.

SERGE. A sturdy, tight, right-hand twill with a hard, clear finish and pronounced diagonal ribs both front and back. *French serge* has fine, soft yarns, and *storm serge* has coarse yarns woven into a stiff fabric.

STRIÉ. See *Jaspé*.

TICKING. A strong fabric similar to duck, with narrow herringbone stripes woven in navy blue (or brown, black, or red) on a white or cream warp. Originally used for mattress covers, it now offers a country or provincial look to drapery, walls, upholstery, and other areas. May also be plain weave.

TOILE. A tightly woven cotton or linen plain-weave fabric featuring a natural cream background printed with a pattern in one color (traditionally red, dark blue, olive green, brown, or black). Types include *Toile de Jouy*, French eighteenth-century patterns first roller-printed with provincial scenes; *Federal toile*, incorporating American Federal buildings, eagles, and related motifs; and *French toile*, featuring contemporary patterns such as shells and flowers.

TRICOTINE. Similar to steeply twilled gabardine with a hard, clear finish, tricotine is a sturdy fabric with a double-twill diagonal wale. Originally of wool, it now is made with synthetic wool-like fibers.

UNION CLOTH. A coarse, durable plain-weave fabric of approximately 50 percent cotton and 50 percent linen. May be dyed or printed in large, unrefined patterns. Used for draperies, slipcovers, and some upholstery.

HEAVYWEIGHT FABRICS

Heavyweight fabrics range from those slightly heavier than medium-weight fabrics to very heavy, stiff textiles. Not all of these fabrics will have equal application at the window; within a single decorative fabric construction there may be various weights and drapability levels. Heavyweight fabrics may work well as overdrapery that may not need lining unless it is necessary to protect the color or fiber. Many are appropriate for flat fabric installations, such as awnings or fabric shades.

AWNING CLOTH. A heavy version of sailcloth, this is an Oxford or twill weave that is heavily treated to resist moisture and sunlight/environmental deterioration. Used for exterior and interior awnings. Usually cotton.

BENGALINE. A tightly woven ribbed textile of large filling threads covered with very fine warp threads, giving the fabric a refined, smooth, corded appearance. When cut or woven into narrow widths, bengaline becomes *gros-grain* ribbon.

BOUCLÉ. A sturdy upholstery fabric in a plain or sateen weave with heavy use of tightly curled novelty yarns, also called bouclé. Heaviest weights are similar to frieze; lighter weights are suitable for draperies and resemble heavily slubbed antique satin.

CANVAS. A tightly woven cotton fabric in several weights, from pliable to very heavy and stiff. Canvas may be plain, Oxford, or twill weave and solid or woven with stripes to imitate or become *awning cloth.* This is an indoor/outdoor upholstery fabric and can be used as an inexpensive window treatment textile.

CHENILLE. Any fabric woven with fuzzy chenille yarns. The effect usually is close to velour, although fabrics incorporating only occasional chenille yarns may look smoother.

CHEVRON (HERRINGBONE). A sturdy twill-weave fabric suitable for walls and upholstery as well as for heavy drapery. The reverse zigzag twill also is woven into medium-weight fabrics.

CORDUROY. A pile fabric (usually cotton or nylon) woven into round lengthwise cords, cut open, and napped or brushed up to form the wales. Fabric with very small wales is called *pinwale corduroy;* fabric with fat cords is known as *wide-wale corduroy.* Finer corduroy fabrics do well as heavy window coverings. Wide wales may be awkward to handle and to drape.

CREWEL EMBROIDERY. A basket-weave cotton, linen, or wool background cloth in a natural beige that is densely embroidered with woolen or worsted yarn in a crewel or chain stitch. Designs are taken from East Indian Tree of Life motifs in which the flowers, fruits, and leaves are all different, symbolic of the many varieties of life-giving flora found in the Eastern oasis. Many designs also resemble English garden foliage.

DOUBLE CLOTH (TRUE DOUBLE CLOTH). See *Matelassé.*

FELT. A woven or nonwoven wool fabric that is shrunk through exposure to heat, moisture, and agitation. Comes in a variety of weights—from *craft felt,* to sturdy, napped *upholstery felt.* Colors often are dark or bright.

FLAMESTITCH. An irregular chevron pattern representing the leaping flames of fire. Scale may be large, medium, or small. Fabric may be printed or woven with a twill, Jacquard, or pile weave.

FLANNEL. A cotton or wool fabric that is woven in a plain or twill weave, then napped on one or both sides. *See also under* "Medium-Weight Fabrics."

FRIEZE (FRIEZETTE). A pile-weave fabric of rounded loops of nylon or wool yarns. May be woven in a Jacquard pattern or in simple, straight rows. Extremely durable upholstery textiles. Friezette loops are arranged in straight rows, often of a variegated or mottled yarn color, and resemble needlepoint.

FRINGE. A trimming consisting of a narrow braid and small tassels. Available in a variety and combination of colors. Casual fringe usually is made from cotton, formal fringe from rayon or silk.

GIMP. A narrow trimming braid in a variety of colors and patterns. Covers upholstery tacks on formal furniture and is useful for hiding staples or stitches in top treatments and as a slim drapery trimming.

GROSGRAIN. Narrow widths of ribbed woven fabric. See also *Bengaline.*

HOLLAND CLOTH (SHADE CLOTH). A plain-weave, low-count muslin that is starched, glazed, and sometimes opaqued with an oil treatment. A serviceable window shade fabric, occasionally used for drapery.

INTARSIA. A heavy knit fabric featuring geometric patterns on a solid-color background. Available in a variety of knit stitches. Reversible.

INTERLINING. A heavy, stiffened woven or nonwoven lining cloth that gives body to a treatment. Interlining may also be of a polyester, cotton, or wool batting to muffle noise and provide insulation.

JACQUARD. A patterned fabric woven on the Jacquard loom. Heavyweight Jacquards include flamestitch, frieze, matelassé, needlepoint, tapestry, and figured velvets.

MATELASSÉ (DOUBLE CLOTH). A medium-weight to very heavyweight fabric consisting of two sets of warps and wefts simultaneously woven into separate fabrics, then woven together with the pattern. The background is somewhat puffy, and the design is woven tightly, producing a quilted effect. *True double cloth* fabrics are held together with a fifth set of threads used as a binder that can be clipped to reveal two independent fabrics.

MOHAIR. A strong, resilient upholstery velvet made of the hair of the angora goat. Comes in plain colors.

NEEDLEPOINT. A hand-made looped cross-stitch sometimes imitated in a Jacquard-pile textile of tightly looped stitches. Patternless needlepoint is sometimes called *frieze.* Needlepoint containing large loops is called *grospoint; petit point* is made of tiny stitches.

OATMEAL CLOTH. A medium- to heavyweight linen or linenlike fabric woven with a crinkled, or pebbled, surface similar to the look of oatmeal paper. Strong, durable, and washable.

OTTOMAN. Slightly heavier and coarser than bengaline, a plain weave with heavy weft ribs made of large, round filling yarns and covered entirely with fine warp threads. Ribs may be of alternating sizes.

PILE FABRIC. A textile with a supplemental warp or weft that gives a third dimension to the fabric. Heavyweight pile fabrics include corduroy, frieze, mohair, terrycloth, and velvet.

PLAID. A heavy version of yarn-dyed woven textiles that form crossbar patterns in square or rectangular shapes. Some tweeds have plaid designs.

QUILTED FABRIC. A textile whose weight depends on the number of layers that are stitched together. Usually consists of a decorative face fabric, an interlining or batting, possibly an energy-conservation fabric layer, and a lining cloth. Stitches may be accomplished by hand, by programmed machine, by hand-guided machine quilting, or even by pinsonic quilting, where the stitches are formed by melting pinpoints of fabric together ultrasonically.

RATINÉ. Any fabric woven heavily with ratiné yarns, which are novelty yarns of a kinked and curled thread woven back and forth in rick-rack fashion across a core thread and held with a binder thread. The surface of ratiné fabric is bumpy and textured.

REP (REPP OR FRENCH REPP). A sturdy corded fabric similar to bengaline but not lustrous. It often is of wool and has an understated horizontal or weft rib woven with large filling yarns and fine warp yarns.

SAILCLOTH. A sturdy medium- or heavyweight Oxford weave fabric made of cotton or blends, then finished to be water repellent.

SUEDE CLOTH. A knit or woven pile fabric that is napped then pressed to appear as a cloth of authentic suede (brushed pigskin). Ultrasuede is a trade name for a polyester suede cloth.

TAPESTRY. A hand-woven variation of the plain weave in which yarns are woven in to create a design. Also a Jacquard fabric of several warps and wefts tightly woven to create scenic panels (often historic) or floral designs. Usually contains dark, somber colors, and is most often made of cotton.

TERRY CLOTH. A cotton pile of loosely twisted loops that may be trimmed into a velour with a velvety texture. Used for toweling or very casual curtains.

TWEED. A plain or twill-weave fabric, originally of wool but today also made of nylon. The weave may be a combination, and colored yarns may add variety to the surface. The yarns may be wiry and tightly spun, or bulky and heavy.

VELOUR. Any pile fabric woven with a velvetlike surface. Many fibers are used, and the fabric may be knit, stretch knit, or woven. The yarns may be plied and plain or novelty, for example, chenille.

VELVET. A pile fabric with many variations. May be woven over round wires, knit, flocked, or woven face to face then cut apart. Velvet is most often made from silk, cotton, linen, nylon, or rayon. Some types include: *antique velvet,* woven to look old with colored streaks and some pressing or calendering; *chiffon velvet,* a luxurious, lightweight velvet often given a very soft finish; *crushed velvet,* a deep pile or plush velvet with a sparse weave, sometimes weakly constructed, that is drawn through a narrow tube and crushed under heat and pressure; *cut, beaded, or sculptured velvet,* woven on a Jacquard loom with floral designs and plain backgrounds; *flocked velvet,* created with electrostatically charged fibers that adhere to a woven or knit background and usually printed with bright, garish patterns; *moquette velvet,* which features Jacquard patterns formed from cut and uncut loops on a plain background; *panne velvet,* in which the pile is pressed down in one direction; *plush velvet,* with a deep, sometimes sparse, and crushed pile; *ribbed velvet,* which is woven in rows, then pressed down, like panne; and *velveteen,* a short-pile cotton velvet that may be printed.

VINYL (ARTIFICIAL LEATHER). An extruded fabric flowed onto a woven, nonwoven, or knit basecloth or extruded in sheets for plastic pull shades. Comes in many weights and thicknesses—from translucent to opaque.

WAFFLE PIQUÉ. A three-dimensional woven pattern of squares and hexagons. Sturdy and heavy, with many applications, from upholstery to heavy drapery.

Bibliography

ART GLASS

Armitage, Edward Liddall. *Stained Glass: History, Technology and Practice.* Newton, Mass.: Brandord, 1959.

Arnold, Hugh. *Stained Glass of the Middle Ages in England and France.* New York: Macmillan, 1956.

Baker, John. *English Stained Glass.* New York: Abrams, 1960.

Brady, Darlene A., and William Serban, eds. *Stained Glass: A Guide to Information Sources.* Detroit: Gale, 1980.

Buckley, William Frank, Jr. *Stained Glass.* Garden City, N.Y.: Doubleday, 1978.

Day, Lewis F. *Windows: A Book About Stained and Painted Glass.* London: Batsford, 1897.

Duval, Jean-Jacques. *Working with Stained Glass: Fundamental Techniques and Applications.* New York: Crowell, 1972.

Klein, Dan. *All Color Book of Art Deco.* London: Octopus, Books, 1974.

Koek, Karin E., and Susan Boyles Martin, eds. *Encyclopedia of Associations. Vol. 1: National Organizations of the U.S.* Detroit: Gale, 1988.

Lee, Lawrence. *Stained Glass.* New York: Oxford University Press, 1967.

Peyteins, Patrick. *The Technique of Stained Glass.* New York: Watson-Guptill, 1967.

Sauzay, A. *Wonders of Glass Making.* New York: Scribner, Armstrong, 1872.

Sewter, A. Charles. *The Stained Glass of William Morris and His Circle.* New Haven, Conn.: Yale University Press, 1974.

Sowers, Robert. *Stained Glass: An Architectural Art.* New York: Universe Books, 1965.

Warren, Geoffrey. *All Color Book of Art Nouveau.* London: Octopus Books, 1972.

ENERGY-EFFICIENT TREATMENTS

Bylin, Joan. *Women's Energy Tool Kit: Home Heating, Cooling and Weatherization.* New York: Consumer Action Now, 1980.

Frey, Iris Ihde. *Staple It!: Easy Do-it Decorating.* New York: Crown, 1979.

Langdon, William K. *Movable Insulation: A Guide to Reducing Heating and Cooling Losses Through the Windows in Your Home.* Emmaus, Pa.: Rodale Press, 1980.

Tapscott, Diane Patricia, et al. *A Sunset Book: Curtains, Draperies and Shades.* Menlo Park, Calif.: Lane, 1979.

Windley, Leona. *Energy Efficient Interior Window Treatments.* Logan, Utah: Cooperative Extension Service, Utah State University, 1982.

FOLK PAINTING

Ellingsgard, Nils. *Norsk Rosemaling.* Samlaget, Oslo: Det Norske, 1981.

Foster, Scottie. *Scottie's Bauernmalerei, Bavarian Folk Art, Book 1* and *Book 2.* Springfield, Va.: Scottie's Bavarian Folk Art, n.d.

Hall, Susan Jill. *Primarily Primitives.* San Bernadino, Calif.: Susan Jill Hall, n.d.

Howard, Joyce. *Basics in Folk Art and Tole, Book 1.* Tulsa: Priscilla Hauser, 1979.

Jansen, JoSonja. *Rosemaling Primer.* Vols. 1 and 2 of *The Basics of Folk Painting.* Eureka, Calif.: JoSonja, n.d.

Johnson, Joan. *True Series Tole Painting Books.* Shawnee Mission, Kan.: Joan Patterns, n.d.

Miller, Margaret M., and Sigmund Aaseth. *Norwegian Rosemaling: Decorative Painting on Wood.* New York: Scribner's, 1973.

Richardson, Annie. *Tole Red Two.* Pheonix: Folk Heart Publishing, n.d.

Salinger, Margaretta. *The Flower Piece in European Painting.* New York: Harper, 1949.

Schatz, Claudine. *Rosemaling Roses.* Vols. 1 and 2 of *Hallingdal Rosemaling.* Pea Ridge, Ariz: Claudine's House, 1984.

Smith, Milly. *Primitives Plus, Book 1.* Portland: Dora Lea Hilton, n.d.

Stewart, Janice. *The Folk Arts of Norway.* New York: Dover, 1972.

Thode, Vi. *Rosemaling Instructions: Lesson Book.* Salt Lake City: Zim's, 1978.

———. *Rosemaling.* Salt Lake City: Zim's, 1979.

———. *Rogaland and Telemark Style Rosemaling.* Salt Lake City: Zim's, 1982.

Wasson, Trudy Sondrol. *Authentic Norwegian Rosemaling: Rogaland Style.* Vol. 1. Oelwein, Iowa: T. S. Wasson, 1984.

Wehking, Margaret. *Tole You So,* vol. 1; *Tole You So Again,* vols. 2 and 3. Florissant, Col.: Village Tole Shop, 1981, 1983.

Zuidema, Jacques. *Dutch Floral Painting: Assendelfter Style.* Philadelphia: Priscilla's, n.d.

INTERIOR DESIGN

Allen, Phyllis, and Miriam Stimpson. *Beginnings of Interior Environment.* New York: Macmillan, 1990.

Anderson, Donald M. *Elements of Design.* New York: Holt, Rinehart, and Winston, 1961.

The Architecture of Skidmore, Owings & Merrill, 1950–1962. New York: Praeger, 1963.

Ashley, Laura. *The Laura Ashley Book of Home Decorating.* London: Octopus Books, 1985.

Ball, Victoria Kloss. *The Art of Interior Design.* New York: Wiley, 1982.

Banham, Reyner. *The Architecture of the Well-Tempered Environment.* London: The Architectural Press, 1969; Chicago: University of Chicago Press, 1969.

Battersby, Martin. *The Decorative Thirties.* New York: Walker, 1971.

Benevolo, Leonardo. *History of Modern Architecture.* Cambridge, Mass.: MIT Press, 1971.

Birren, Faber. *Color for Interiors: Historical and Modern.* New York: Whitney Library of Design, n.d.

Bradford, Barbara Taylor. *Easy Steps to Successful Decorating*. New York: Simon and Schuster, 1971.

Conran, Terrence. *The New House Book*. New York: Random House, 1985.

Cook, Olive. *The English Country House: An Art and a Way of Life*. London: Thames and Hudson, 1974.

Daniels, Eugene, FIBD. "Dialogue with Designers," *Draperies and Window Coverings 1,* no. 19 (March 1984).

Design in America: The Cranbrook Vision, 1925–1950. New York: Abrams, 1983.

Draper, Dorothy. *Decorating Is Fun!* New York: Art and Decoration Book Society, 1939.

Dye, Daniel Sheets. *Chinese Lattice Designs*. New York: Dover, n.d.

Evans, Helen Marie, and Carla Davis Dumesnil. *An Invitation to Design*. New York: Macmillan, 1982.

Faulkner, Ray, LuAnn Nisson, and Sarah Faulkner. *Inside Today's Home*. New York: Holt, Rinehart, and Winston, 1986.

Fisher, Richard B. *Syrie Maugham*. London: Duckworth, 1978.

Gakyu, Shobo, ed. *Japanese Interiors*. San Francisco: Japan Publications Trading Center, 1970.

Giedion, Sigfried, ed. *A Decade of Contemporary Architecture*. New York: Wittenborn, 1954.

Girouard, Mark. *Life in the English Country House*. Baltimore: Penguin Books, 1980.

Grillo, Paul. *Form, Function and Design*. New York: Dover, 1975.

Harling, Robert, *The Greatest Houses and Finest Rooms of England*. New York: Viking Press, 1969.

Hicks, David. *On Living—With Taste*. London: Lislie Frewin, 1968.

——. *Living with Design*. London: William Morrow, 1979.

Hiesinger, Kathryn B., and George H. Marcus, eds. *Design Since 1945*. Philadelphia: The Philadelphia Museum of Art, 1983.

Hillier, Bevis. *The Decorative Art of the Forties and Fifties Austerity Binge*. New York: Potter, 1975.

Hitchcock, Henry-Russell, and Philip Johnson. *The International Style: Architecture Since 1922*. New York: Norton, 1966.

Hoffman, Emmanuel. *Fairchild's Dictionary of Home Furnishings*. New York: Fairchild, 1975.

Hussey, Christopher, *English Country Houses: Early Georgian 1715–1760*. London: Country Life, 1955.

——. *English Country Houses: Mid Georgian 1760–1800*. London: Country Life, 1956.

——. *English Country Houses: Late Georgian 1800–1840*. London: Country Life, 1958.

Jacobus, John M., Jr. "Architecture, American Style: 1920–45." In *American Art*. New York: Prentice Hall, 1979.

Johnson, Philip C. *Mies van der Rohe*. New York: The Museum of Modern Art, 1978.

Kaufmann, Edgar, Jr. "Interior Design: Architecture or Decorating?" *Progressive Architecture* (October 1962): 141–44.

Kent, Kathryn. *The Good Housekeeping Complete Guide to Traditional American Decorating*. New York: Hearst Books, 1982.

The Kirsch Company. *Window Treatments Through the Ages*. Sturgis, Mich.: The Kirsch Company, 1976.

McCoy, Esther. *The Second Generation*. Layton, Utah: Gibbs M. Smith, 1984.

Magnusson, Magnus. *Treasures of Scotland*. London: Weidenfeld and Nicolson, 1981.

Mang, Karl. *History of Modern Furniture*. New York: Abrams, 1979.

Moller, Sven Erik, et al. *Danish Design*. Copenhagen: Detdanske Slskab, 1974.

Renner, Paul. *Color Order and Harmony*. New York: Van Nostrand, 1965.

Robsjohn-Gibbings, T. H. *Goodbye, Mr. Chippendale*. New York: Knopf, 1944.

St. Marie, Satenig. *Homes Are for People*. New York: Wiley, 1973.

Stepat-Devan, Dorothy, et al. *Introduction to Interior Design*. New York: Macmillan, 1980.

Tate, Allen. *The Making of Interiors*. New York: Harper and Row, 1985.

Tate, Allen, and C. Ray Smith. *Interior Design in the 20th Century*. New York: Harper and Row, 1986.

Thornton, Peter. *Authentic Decor: The Domestic Interior 1620–1800*. New York: Viking, 1984.

Weale, Mary Jo, et al. *Environmental Interiors*. New York: Macmillan, 1982.

Whiton, Sherrill. *Interior Design and Decoration*. New York: Lippincott, 1974.

PERIODICALS

Architectural Digest. Paige Rense, editor-in-chief. P.O. Box 2415, Boulder, CO 80322.

Designers West. Walton E. Brown, publisher; Carol Soucek King, editor-in-chief. Art Alliance Corporation, 8564 Melrose Avenue, Los Angeles, CA 90069.

Design from Scandinavia. World Pictures, P.O. Box 405, Racine, WI.

Draperies and Window Coverings. P.O. Box 13079, North Palm Beach, FL 33408.

House and Garden. P.O. Box 5202, Boulder, CO 80322.

House Beautiful. P.O. Box 10083, Des Moines, IA 50350.

Interior Design. P.O. Box 1970, Marion, OH 43305.

Interior Designs Buyer's Guide. Cara S. David, editor. 850 Third Avenue, New York, NY 10022.

Interior Textiles. Marc R. Dick, editor. 370 Lexington Avenue, New York, NY 10017.

Metropolitan Home. Dorothy Kalins, editor. 1616 Locust Street, Des Moines, IA 50336.

Window Fashions. Gayle Gutsche, editor. 372 St. Peters Street, Suite 310, St. Paul, MN 55102.

RESIDENTIAL AND NONRESIDENTIAL BUSINESS

Dalton, Gene W., and Paul H. Thompson: *Novations: Strategies for Career Management*. Glenview, Ill.: Scott Foresman, 1984.

Epstein, Lee. *Legal Forms for the Designer*. New York: Contract Books, 1969.

Goslett, Dorothy. *The Professional Practice of Design*. London: Batsford, 1971.

Knackstedt, Mary V. *Interior Design for Profit*. New York: Kobro, 1980.

——. *Profitable Career Options for Designers*. New York: Kobro, 1985.

Loebelson, Andrew. *How to Profit in Contract Design*. New York: Interior Design Books, 1983.

Marchant, Elisabeth. "Selling the Contract Market, Parts I and II." Lecture at World of Window Coverings Convention. Produced by Winco Associates, North Palm Beach, Florida, 1985.

Morgan, Jim. *Marketing for the Small Design Firm*. New York: Whitney Library of Design, 1984.

Porter, Michael. *Competitive Strategy*. New York: Free Press, 1980.

Reznikoff, S. C. *Specifications for Commercial Interiors: Professional Liabilities, Regulations, and Performance Criteria.* New York: Whitney Library of Design, 1981.

Siegel, Harry. *A Guide to Business Principles and Practices for Interior Designers.* New York: Whitney Library of Design, 1982.

Stasiowski, Frank. *Negotiating Higher Design Fees.* New York: Whitney Library of Design, 1985.

Turner, William. *How to Work with an Interior Designer.* New York: Whitney Library of Design, 1981.

Van Caspel, Venita. *The Power of Money.* Reston, Va.: Reston Publishing, 1983.

SHOJI SCREENS

Dye, Daniel Sheets. *Chinese Lattice Designs.* New York: Dover, 1974.

Ecke, Gustav. *Chinese Domestic Furniture.* Rutland, Vt.: Tuttle, 1962.

Garret Wade Company. *1984 Woodworking Tools.* New York: Garret Wade, 1984.

Goto, Shigeri. *Ukiyoe, Taiket.* Tokyo: Sheisha, 1975.

Itoh, Teiji. *The Elegant Japanese House: Traditional Sukiya Architecture.* New York: Walker/Weatherhill, 1969.

———. *The Classic Tradition in Japanese Architecture: Modern Versions of the Sukiya Style.* New York: Weatherhill/Tankosha, 1972.

———. *Traditional Domestic Architecture of Japan.* Tokyo: Weatherhill/Heibonsha, 1972.

Mitz, Rick. *The Apartment Book.* New York: Harmony Books, 1979.

Morse, Edward S. *Japanese Homes and Their Surroundings.* New York: Dover, 1961.

Murawe, Miyeko. *Byobu: Japanese Screens in New York Collections.* New York: Asia Society, 1971.

Naito, Akira. *Katsura: A Princely Retreat.* Tokyo: Kodansha International, 1977.

Nakamura, Katsuya. *Alcove, Ceiling, and Garden.* Tokyo: Johan Shoin, 1966.

Nakashima, George. *The Soul of a Tree: A Woodworker's Reflections.* Tokyo: Kodansha International, 1981.

Odate, Toshio. "Japanese Sliding Doors," *Fine Woodworking,* no. 34 (May–June 1982): 50–58.

Pessoland, Ron. "Filigree Revitalized by Scroll Sawing with a Sabre Saw." *Fine Woodworking,* no. 40 (May–June, 1983): 86–90.

Seiki, Kiyoshi, and Masanobu Kudo. *A Japanese Touch for Your Home.* Tokyo: Kodansha International, 1983.

SOFT WINDOW TREATMENTS

Bostrum, Ethel, and Harry Marinsky. *How to Make Draperies and Slipcovers Including Bedspreads, Curtains, Lampshades and Their Use in Home Decorations.* New York: Gramercy, 1951.

Butler, Margaret G., and Beryl S. Graves. *Fashions for the Home.* New York: Drake, 1972.

Bylin, Joan. *Women's Energy Tool Kit: Home Heating, Cooling, and Weatherization.* New York: Consumer Action Now, 1980.

Candee, Helen Churchill. *Weaves and Draperies.* New York: Frederick A. Stokes, 1930.

Carbone, Linda. Dictionary of Sewing Terminology. New York: Arco Publishing, 1977.

DuBois, M. J. *Curtains and Draperies: A Survey of the Classic Periods.* New York: Viking Press, 1967.

Eames, Alexandra. *Windows and Walls: Designs, Patterns, Projects.* Birmingham, England: Oxmoor House, 1980.

Fishburn, Angela. *Curtains and Window Treatments.* New York: Van Nostrand Reinhold, 1982.

Griggs, LaMar, and Bobbie Tawater. *The Designer's Guide to Window Coverings,* Fort Worth: G-T Designs, 1986.

Hall, Helen. *Simplified Home Sewing.* New York: Prentice Hall, 1943.

Hardy, Kay. *Beauty Treatments for the Home: The Smart Way to Make Draperies, Slipcovers, Lamp Shades, Accessories.* New York: Funk and Wagnalls, 1945.

Helsel, Margery Borradaile. *The Interior Designer's Drapery Sketchfile.* New York: Viking Press, 1969.

The Kirsch Company. *Window Treatments Through the Ages.* Sturgis, Mich: The Kirsch Company, 1976.

——. *Windows Beautiful,* Vol. VI. Sturgis, Mich.: The Kirsch Company, 1977.

——. *A Sketchbook of Suggestions for Exceptional Windows.* Sturgis, Mich.: The Kirsch Company, 1978.

Kirsch/Cooper Industries. *Window Shopping with Kirsch.* Sturgis, Mich.: Kirsch/Cooper Industries, 1983.

Lederer, Delores P. *Custom Draperies: The "Perfectionist's" How-to: Book I.* Hillsboro, Ore.: Lederer Enterprises, 1982.

Ley, Sandra. *America's Sewing Book.* New York: Scribner's, 1972.

Lindahl, Judy. *Decorating with Fabric: Hundreds of Exciting and Creative Fabric Ideas for Decorating Your Home Quickly and Inexpensively.* New York: Butterick Publishing, 1977.

——. *Decorating with Fabric: An Idea Book,* 1980; *Energy Saving Decorating,* 1981; *The Shade Book: How to Make Roller, Roman, Balloon and Austrian Shades,* 1978. Order from Judy Lindahl, 3211 N.E. Siskiyou, Portland, OR 97212.

LouverDrape. *Vertical Imagination.* Santa Monica, Calif.: LouverDrape, n.d.

McMillan, Helen M., and Judith S. Kline. *Planning Your Sewing Needs.* Clemson, S.C.: Clemson University Press, 1974.

Meredith Corporation. *Better Homes and Gardens: Sewing for Your Home.* Des Moines, Ia.: Meredith Corporation, 1974.

Meyer, Judy A. *Sewing Dictionary.* South Brunswick: A. S. Barns, 1980.

Mitchell, Winifred M. *Soft Furnishing in the Home: For the Housewife, Teacher and Student.* London: Batsford, 1961.

Neal, Mary. *Custom Draperies in Interior Design.* New York: Elsevier, 1982.

Noto, V. C., and B. N. Rosenberg. *How the Professional Sells Custom Draperies and Window Coverings.* Pittsburgh: Professional Drapery Institute, 1985.

Phillips, Barty, and Eleanor Van Zundt. *How to Decorate Your Home Without Going Broke.* Garden City, N.Y.: Doubleday, 1975.

Picken, Mary Brooks. *Sewing for the Home: How to Make Fabric Furnishings in a Professional Way.* New York: Harper and Brothers, 1941.

Reader's Digest Complete Guide to Sewing. Pleasantville, N.Y.: Reader's Digest, 1976.

Roday, Jane. *No-Sew Decorating.* New York: Scribner's, 1972.

Screibner, Joanne. *Sewing to Decorate Your Home.* Garden City, N.Y.: Doubleday, 1979.

Sewing and Window Hanging Instructions for Ruffled Curtains. Wilmington, N.C.: Z's Country Ruffling, n.d.

Sewing Instructions for Roc-Lon ® Warm Window ™ Insulated Roman Shade System. Baltimore: Rockland Industries, n.d.

Sherman, Michael P. "The Effects of Interior Drapery on Heat Transmission," *Journal of Interior Design Education and Research* 9, no. 1 (spring 1983).

Stephenson, John W. *Drapery Cutting and Making: A Practical Handbook for Drapery Workers, Upholsterers, and Interior Decorators.* New York: Clifford and Lawton, 1962.

Talbot, Constance. *The Complete Book of Sewing, Dress Making and Sewing for the Home Made Easy.* Garden City, N.Y.: Garden City Publishing, 1943.

Tapscott, Diane Patricia, et al. *A Sunset Book: Curtains, Draperies, and Shades.* Menlo Park, Calif.: Lane, 1979.

Varney, Charleton. *Charleton Varney Decorates Windows.* Des Moines: Creative Home Library in Association with Better Homes and Gardens, Meredith Corporation, 1975.

Wamsutta Mills. *Home Decorating Guide.* New York: Wamsutta Mills, n.d.

Wesco Fabrics Inc. *Decorative Fabrics and Window Coverings Handbook.* Denver: Wesco Fabrics, 1987.

What's New in Insulating Window Fashions. Baltimore: Rockland Industries, 1984.

Windley, Leona. *Energy Efficient Interior Treatments.* Logan, Ut.: Cooperative Extension Service, Utah State University, 1982.

STAINED GLASS

Stained Glass Association of America (SGAA)

For studios, artists, designers, and craft suppliers involved in the promotion of stained, leaded, or faceted windows; associate members are students of the art. Objective is to advance an awareness and appreciation of the craft and to encourage the development of innovative techniques and artistic expression. Assembles exhibits of native stained glass, sponsors a three-year apprentice program, and collects and disseminates documentary information on the stained-glass trade in America. Also sponsors lectures, symposiums, conventions, and exhibitions in cooperation with related organizations and holds competitions, compiles statistics, and offers placement service.

Publications: Kaleidoscope (quarterly); *Stained Glass* (quarterly).

Address: 1125 Wilmington Avenue, St. Louis, MO 63111 (314) 353-5218. Executive Secretary: Naomi M. Mundy.

Periodicals

American Craft. Membership Department, American Craft Council, P.O. Box 561, Martinsville, NJ 08836. (bimonthly).

Creative Crafts. Circulation Manager, Creative Crafts, P.O. Box 700, Newton, NJ (bimonthly).

Kaleidoscope. Available through membership in the Stained Glass Association of America, 1125 Wilmington Avenue, St. Louis MO 63111 (quarterly).

Stained Glass. 21 Tudor Lane, Scarsdale, NY 10583 (914) 725-2361 (quarterly). Has lists of craft suppliers and members.

STENCILING

Appleton, LeRoy. *American Indian Design and Decoration.* New York: Dover, n.d.

Audsley, W., and G. Audsley. *Designs and Patterns from Historic Ornament.* New York: Dover, n.d.

Beardsley, Aubrey. *The Early Work of Aubrey Beardsley.* New York: Dover, n.d.

———. The Later Work of Aubrey Beardsley. New York: Dover, n.d.

Boas, Franz. *Primitive Art.* New York: Dover, n.d.

Chapman, Suzanne E. *Early American Design Motifs.* New York: Dover, 1974.

Fobel, Jim, and Jim Boleach. *The Stencil Book.* New York. Van Nostrand Reinhold, 1983.

Fry, Charles Rahn. *Art Deco Designs in Color.* New York: Dover, 1975.

George Bruce's Son and Co. *Victorian Frames, Borders, and Cuts.* (1882 type catalog.) New York: Dover, 1975.

Grillion, Edmond V., Jr., ed. *Victorian Stencils.* New York: Dover, n.d.

Griesbach, C. B. *Historic Ornament: A Pictorial Archive.* New York: Dover, 1975.

Hawley, Willis M. *Chinese Folk Design.* New York: Dover, n.d.

Laliberté, Norman, and Alex Megelon. *The Art of Stencil: History and Modern Uses.* New York: Van Nostrand Reinhold, 1971.

Loeb, Marcia. *Art Deco Designs and Motifs.* New York: Dover, n.d.

Matsuya Piece-Goods Store. *Japanese Design Motifs: 4,260 Illustrations of Japanese Crests.* New York: Dover, 1972.

Menten, Theodore. *Art Nouveau and Early Art Deco Type and Design.* New York: Dover, n.d.

Meyer, Franz S. *Handbook of Ornament.* New York: Dover, n.d.

Mickel, Adelaide. *Stenciling.* Peoria: The Manual Arts Press, n.d.

Midkiff, Pat. *The Complete Book of Stenciling.* New York: Drake Publishers, 1978.

Mirow, Gregory. *A Treasury of Design for Artists and Craftsmen.* New York: Dover, n.d.

Rubi, Christian. *Cut Paper Silhouettes and Stencils: An Instruction Book.* Van Nostrand Reinhold, 1971

Vanderwalker, Fred Norman. *New Stencils and Their Use.* Chicago: F. J. Drake, n.d.

TEXTILES

American Home Economics Association. *Textile Handbook.* Washington, D.C.: American Home Economics Association, 1974.

The Belgium Linen Association. *Belgium Linen.* New York: The Belgium Linen Association, n.d.

Celanese Fibers Marketing Company. "Facts About Man-Made Fibers." New York: Celanese Fibers Marketing Company, n.d.

Clouzot, H., and F. Morris. *Painted and Printed Fabrics.* New York: Metropolitan Museum of Art, 1927.

Corbman, Bernard P. *Textiles: Fiber to Fabric.* New York: McGraw-Hill, 1975.

Cotton Council. *The Story of Cotton.* Knoxville: Cotton Council, n.d.

Cowan, Mary L., and Martha E. Jungerman. *Introduction to Textiles.* New York: Appleton-Century-Croft, 1969.

Crosicki, Z. *Watson's Textile Design and Color: Elementary Weaves and Figure Fabrics.* Woburn, Mass.: Butterworth, 1979.

Fairchild Publications. *Fairchild's Dictionary of Textiles.* New York: Fairchild Publications, 1979.

Farnfield, C. A., and P. J. Avery. *Textile Terms and Definitions.* New York: State Mutual Book and Periodical Service, 1975.

Hall, A. J. *The Standard Handbook of Textiles*. Woburn, Mass.: Butterworth, 1980.

Hardingham, Martin. *Illustrated Dictionary of Fabrics*. London: Macmillan, 1978.

Hollen, Norma, and Jane Saddler. *Textiles*. New York: Macmillan, 1979.

Italian Trade Center. *Texitalia Casa*. New York: Italian Trade Center, n.d.

Jackman, Dianne R., and Mary K. Dixon. *The Guide to Textiles for Interior Designers*. Winnipeg, Canada: Peguis, 1983.

Joseph, Marjory L. *Essentials of Textiles*. New York: Fairchild, 1971.

Klapper, Marvin. *Fabric Almanac*. New York: Fairchild, 1971.

LaBarthe, J. *Elements of Textiles*. New York: Macmillan, 1975.

Lang, D. *Decorating with Fabric*. New York: Crown, 1986.

Larsen, Jack Lenor, and Jeanne Weeks. *Fabrics for Interiors: A Guide for Architects, Designers and Consumers*. New York: Van Nostrand Reinhold, 1975.

Lewis, Ernst. *Encyclopedia of Textiles*. New York: Macmillan, 1953.

Lewis, Ethel. *The Romance of Textiles*. New York: Macmillan, 1953.

Lyle, Dorothy Siegert. *Modern Textiles*. 2d ed. New York: Macmillan, 1982.

Maciver, Percieval. *The Chintz Book*. London: Heinemann, 1925.

Man-Made Fiber Producers Association. *Man-Made Fibers Fact Book*. Washington, D.C.: Man-Made Fiber Producers Association, n.d.

Murphy, Dennis Grant. *The Materials of Interior Design*. Burbank: Stratford House, n.d.

——. *Fabric Estimator for Draperies and Upholstered Furniture*. Burbank: Stratford House, n.d.

Prentice Hall, Inc. *American Fabrics Encyclopedia of Textiles*. Englewood Cliffs, N.J.: Prentice Hall, 1980.

Thorpe, Azalea Stuart, and Jack Lenor Larsen. *Elements of Weaving*. New York: Doubleday, 1967.

Tortora, Phyllis G. *Understanding Textiles*. New York: Macmillan, 1982.

Wiebel, Adele Coulin. *Two Thousand Years of Textiles*. New York: Pantheon, 1952.

John Wiley & Sons, Inc. *Performance of Textiles*. New York: Wiley, 1977.

Wilson, K. *A History of Textiles*. Boulder, Colo.: Westview Press, 1979.

INDEX